Teacher Edition

SCIENCE

FUSION

fusion [FYOO • zhuhn] a combination of two or more things that releases energy

HOLT McDOUGAL

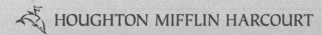

HOUGHTON MIFFLIN HARCOURT

Professional Development

Houghton Mifflin Harcourt and NSTA, the National Science Teacher's Association, have partnered to provide customized professional and development resources for teachers using *ScienceFusion*.

The Professional Development Resources in the NSTA Learning Center include:

—do-it-yourself resources, where you can study at your own pace.

—live and archived online seminars.

—journal articles, many of which include lesson plans.

—fee-based eBooks, eBook chapters, online short courses, symposia, and conferences.

Access to the NSTA Learning Center is provided in the *ScienceFusion* Online Resources.

Acknowledgments for Covers

Iceberg (bg) ©Hans Reinhard/Corbis; *viscous lava* (l) ©Bruce Omori/epa/Corbis; *Mars Rover* (cl) ©Mark Garlick/Photo Researchers, Inc.; *mushroom rock* (cr) ©John Elk III/Alamy; *anemometer* (r) ©Ryan McGinnis/Flickr/Getty Images.

Interior, digital screens: *giraffes* ©Corbis.

Printed in the U.S.A.

ISBN 978-0-547-59388-3

4 5 6 7 8 9 10 2266 20 19 18 17 16 15 14

4500457682   C D E F G

Contents in Brief

About the Program

Teaching Tools

Units at a Glance

Resources

Consulting Authors

Michael A. DiSpezio

Global Educator
North Falmouth, Massachusetts

Michael DiSpezio is a renaissance educator who moved from the research laboratory of a Nobel Prize winner to the K–12 science classroom. He has authored or coauthored numerous textbooks and written more than 25 trade books. For nearly a decade, he worked with the JASON Project under the auspices of the National Geographic Society, where he designed curriculum, wrote lessons, and hosted dozens of studio and location broadcasts.

Over the past two decades, he has developed supplementary material for organizations and shows that include PBS's *Scientific American Frontiers*, *Discover* magazine, and the Discovery Channel. He has extended his reach outside the United States and into topics of crucial importance today. To all his projects, he brings his extensive background in science and his expertise in classroom teaching at the elementary, middle, and high school levels.

Marjorie Frank

Science Writer and
Content-Area Reading Specialist
Brooklyn, New York

An educator and linguist by training, a writer and poet by nature, Marjorie Frank has authored and designed a generation of instructional materials in all subject areas, including past HMH Science programs. Her other credits include authoring science issues of an award-winning children's magazine; writing game-based digital assessments in math, reading, and language arts; and serving as instructional designer and coauthor of pioneering school-to-work software

for Classroom Inc., a nonprofit organization dedicated to improving reading and math skills for middle and high school learners. She wrote lyrics and music for *SCIENCE SONGS*, which was an American Library Association nominee for notable recording. In addition, she has served on the adjunct faculty of Hunter, Manhattan, and Brooklyn Colleges, teaching courses in science methods, literacy, and writing.

Michael R. Heithaus

Director, School of Environment and Society
Associate Professor, Department of Biological Sciences
Florida International University
North Miami, Florida

Mike Heithaus joined the Florida International University Biology Department in 2003. He has served as Director of the Marine Sciences Program and is now Director of the School of Environment and Society, which brings together the natural and social sciences and humanities to develop solutions to today's environmental challenges. While earning his doctorate, he began the research that grew into the Shark Bay Ecosystem Project in Western Australia, with which he still works. Back in the United States, he served as a Research Fellow with National Geographic, using remote imaging in his research and hosting a 13-part *Crittercam* television series on the National Geographic Channel. His current research centers on predator-prey interactions among vertebrates, such as tiger sharks, dolphins, dugongs, sea turtles, and cormorants.

Donna M. Ogle

Professor of Reading and Language
National-Louis University
Chicago, Illinois

Creator of the well-known KWL strategy, Donna Ogle has directed many staff development projects translating theory and research into school practice in middle and secondary schools throughout the United States. She is a past president of the International Reading Association and has served as a consultant on literacy projects worldwide. Her extensive international experience includes coordinating the Reading and Writing for Critical Thinking Project in Eastern Europe, developing an integrated curriculum for a USAID Afghan Education Project, and speaking and consulting on projects in several Latin American countries and in Asia. Her books include *Coming Together as Readers; Reading Comprehension: Strategies for Independent Learners; All Children Read;* and *Literacy for a Democratic Society.*

Program Reviewers

Content Reviewers

Paul D. Asimow, PhD
*Professor of Geology
and Geochemistry*
Division of Geological and Planetary Sciences
California Institute of Technology
Pasadena, CA

Laura K. Baumgartner, PhD
Postdoctoral Researcher
Molecular, Cellular, and Developmental Biology
University of Colorado
Boulder, CO

Eileen Cashman, PhD
Professor
Department of Environmental Resources Engineering
Humboldt State University
Arcata, CA

Hilary Clement Olson, PhD
Research Scientist Associate V
Institute for Geophysics, Jackson School of
Geosciences
The University of Texas at Austin
Austin, TX

Joe W. Crim, PhD
Professor Emeritus
Department of Cellular Biology
The University of Georgia
Athens, GA

Elizabeth A. De Stasio, PhD
*Raymond H. Herzog Professor
of Science*
Professor of Biology
Department of Biology
Lawrence University
Appleton, WI

Dan Franck, PhD
Botany Education Consultant
Chatham, NY

Julia R. Greer, PhD
*Assistant Professor of Materials Science and
Mechanics*
Division of Engineering and Applied Science
California Institute of Technology
Pasadena, CA

John E. Hoover, PhD
Professor
Department of Biology
Millersville University
Millersville, PA

William H. Ingham, PhD
Professor (Emeritus)
Department of Physics and Astronomy
James Madison University
Harrisonburg, VA

Charles W. Johnson, PhD
*Chairman, Division of Natural Sciences,
Mathematics, and Physical Education*
Associate Professor of Physics
South Georgia College
Douglas, GA

Tatiana A. Krivosheev, PhD
Associate Professor of Physics
Department of Natural Sciences
Clayton State University
Morrow, GA

Joseph A. McClure, PhD
Associate Professor Emeritus
Department of Physics
Georgetown University
Washington, DC

Mark Moldwin, PhD
Professor of Space Sciences
Atmospheric, Oceanic, and Space Sciences
University of Michigan
Ann Arbor, MI

Russell Patrick, PhD
Professor of Physics
Department of Biology, Chemistry, and Physics
Southern Polytechnic State University
Marietta, GA

Patricia M. Pauley, PhD
Meteorologist, Data Assimilation Group
Naval Research Laboratory
Monterey, CA

Stephen F. Pavkovic, PhD
Professor Emeritus
Department of Chemistry
Loyola University of Chicago
Chicago, IL

L. Jeanne Perry, PhD
Director (Retired)
Protein Expression Technology Center
Institute for Genomics and Proteomics
University of California, Los Angeles
Los Angeles, CA

Kenneth H. Rubin, PhD
Professor
Department of Geology and Geophysics
University of Hawaii
Honolulu, HI

Brandon E. Schwab, PhD
Associate Professor
Department of Geology
Humboldt State University
Arcata, CA

Marllin L. Simon, Ph.D.
Associate Professor
Department of Physics
Auburn University
Auburn, AL

Larry Stookey, PE
Upper Iowa University
Wausau, WI

Kim Withers, PhD
Associate Research Scientist
Center for Coastal Studies
Texas A&M University-Corpus Christi
Corpus Christi, TX

Matthew A. Wood, PhD
Professor
Department of Physics & Space Sciences
Florida Institute of Technology
Melbourne, FL

Adam D. Woods, PhD
Associate Professor
Department of Geological Sciences
California State University, Fullerton
Fullerton, CA

Natalie Zayas, MS, EdD
Lecturer
Division of Science and Environmental Policy
California State University, Monterey Bay
Seaside, CA

Teacher Reviewers

Ann Barrette, MST
Whitman Middle School
Wauwatosa, WI

Barbara Brege
Crestwood Middle School
Kentwood, MI

Katherine Eaton Campbell, M Ed
Chicago Public Schools-Area 2 Office
Chicago, IL

Karen Cavalluzzi, M Ed, NBCT
Sunny Vale Middle School
Blue Springs, MO

Katie Demorest, MA Ed Tech
Marshall Middle School
Marshall, MI

Jennifer Eddy, M Ed
Lindale Middle School
Linthicum, MD

Tully Fenner
George Fox Middle School
Pasadena, MD

Dave Grabski, MS Ed
PJ Jacobs Junior High School
Stevens Point, WI

Amelia C. Holm, M Ed
McKinley Middle School
Kenosha, WI

Ben Hondorp
Creekside Middle School
Zeeland, MI

George E. Hunkele, M Ed
Harborside Middle School
Milford, CT

Jude Kesl
Science Teaching Specialist 6–8
Milwaukee Public Schools
Milwaukee, WI

Joe Kubasta, M Ed
Rockwood Valley Middle School
St. Louis, MO

Mary Larsen
Science Instructional Coach
Helena Public Schools
Helena, MT

Angie Larson
Bernard Campbell Middle School
Lee's Summit, MO

Christy Leier
Horizon Middle School
Moorhead, MN

Helen Mihm, NBCT
Crofton Middle School
Crofton, MDL

Jeff Moravec, Sr., MS Ed
Teaching Specialist
Milwaukee Public Schools
Milwaukee, WI

Nancy Kawecki Nega, MST, NBCT, PAESMT
Churchville Middle School
Elmhurst, IL

Mark E. Poggensee, MS Ed
Elkhorn Middle School
Elkhorn, WI

Sherry Rich
Bernard Campbell Middle School
Lee's Summit, MO

Mike Szydlowski, M Ed
Science Coordinator
Columbia Public Schools
Columbia, MO

Nichole Trzasko, M Ed
Clarkston Junior High School
Clarkston, MI

Heather Wares, M Ed
Traverse City West Middle School
Traverse City, MI

Power up with

SCIENCE FUSiON

Print

The **Write-in Student Edition** teaches science content through constant **interaction** with the text.

Labs and Activities

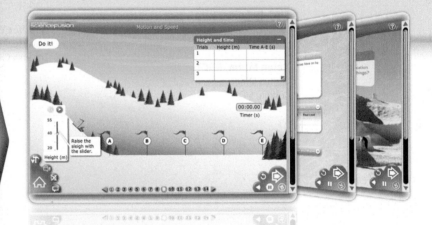

Motion, Forces, and Energy

Lab Manual

Digital

The parallel **Digital Curriculum** provides **e-learning digital lessons and virtual labs** for every print lesson of the program.

Energize your students through a multimodal blend of Print, Inquiry, and Digital experiences.

The Hands-on Labs and Virtual Labs

provide meaningful and exciting inquiry experiences.

Unit Assessment

Formative Assessment

Strategies RTI
Throughout TE

Lesson Reviews SE

Unit PreTest

Summative Assessment

Alternative Assessment
(1 per lesson) RTI

Lesson Quizzes

Unit Tests A and B

Unit Review RTI
(with answer remediation)

Practice Tests
(end of module)

Project-Based Assessment

See the Assessment Guide for quizzes and tests.

Go Online to edit and create quizzes and tests.

See RTI teacher support materials.

Print

The **Write-in Student Edition** teaches science content through constant **interaction** with the text.

Write-in Student Edition

360° of Inquiry

The *ScienceFusion* write-in student edition promotes a student-centered approach for

- learning and applying inquiry skills in the student edition
- building STEM and 21st Century skills
- keeping digital natives engaged and interactive

Research shows that an interactive text teaches students how to relate to content in a personal, meaningful way. They learn how to be attentive, energetic readers who reach a deep level of comprehension.

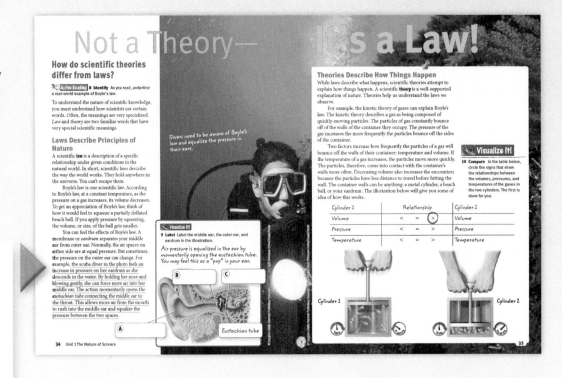

Big Ideas & Essential Questions

Each unit is designed to focus on a Big Idea and supporting lesson-level Essential Questions.

Connect Essential Questions

At the close of every unit, students build enduring understandings through synthesizing connections between different Essential Questions.

Active Reading

Annotation prompts and questions throughout the text teach students how to analyze and interact with content.

S.T.E.M.

STEM activities in every unit ask students to apply engineering and technology solutions in scenario-based learning situations.

Think Outside the Book

Students may wish to keep a Science Notebook to record illustrations and written work assignments. Blank pages at the end of each unit can also be used for this purpose.

Visualize It!

As concepts become more abstract, Visualize It! provides additional support for conceptual understanding.

Labs and Activities

The **Hands-on Labs** and **Virtual Labs** provide meaningful and exciting inquiry experiences.

360° of Inquiry

Labs and Activities

S.T.E.M. Engineering & Technology

STEM activities in every unit focus on

- **engineering and technology**
- **developing critical thinking and problem solving skills**
- **building inquiry, STEM, and 21st Century skills**

Scenario-Based STEM Activity

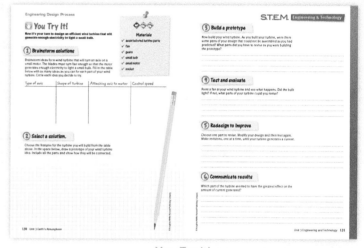

You Try It!

Hands-On and Virtual

Three levels—directed, guided, and independent—of labs and activities plus lesson level Virtual Labs give students wall-to-wall options for exploring science concepts and building inquiry skills.

Hands-On Labs and Activities

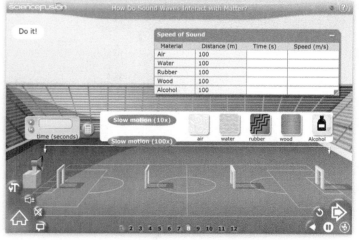

Virtual Lab

The parallel-to-print **Digital Curriculum** provides

e-learning digital lessons and virtual labs

for every print lesson of the program.

360° of Inquiry

Digital Lessons and Virtual Labs

Digital Lessons and Virtual Labs provide an e-Learning environment of interactivity, videos, simulations, animations, and assessment designed for the way digital natives learn. An online Student Edition provides students anytime access to their student book.

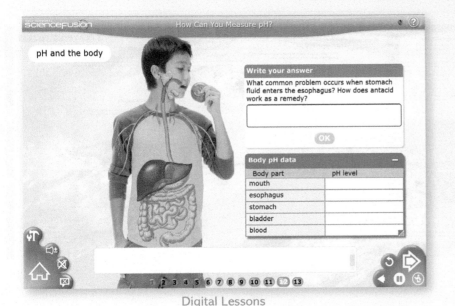

How Can You Measure pH?

pH and the body

Write your answer

What common problem occurs when stomach fluid enters the esophagus? How does antacid work as a remedy?

OK

Body pH data

Body part	pH level
mouth	
esophagus	
stomach	
bladder	
blood	

Digital Lessons

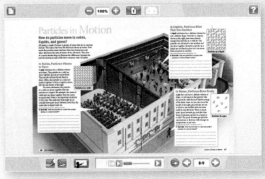

Particles in Motion

Online Student Edition

Video-Based Projects

What Factors Affect the Rate of a >

Do it!

time (min:sec)

CO2 volume (ml)

Time (min:sec)	Whole tablet	Quartered tablet	Crushed tablet
00:00			
00:15			
00:30			
00:45			
01:00			

Virtual Labs

Also available online:
- NSTA *SciLinks*
- Digital Lesson Progress Sheets
- Video-Based Projects
- Virtual Lab Datasheets
- People in Science Gallery
- Media Gallery
- Extra Support for Vocabulary and Concepts
- Leveled Readers

All paths lead to a full suite of print and online
Assessment Options right at your fingertips.

Classroom Management
Integrated Assessment Options

The *ScienceFusion* assessment options give you maximum flexibility in assessing
what your students know and what they can do. Both the print and digital paths
include formative and summative assessment. See the **Assessment Guide** for a
comprehensive overview of your assessment options.

Teacher Online Management Center

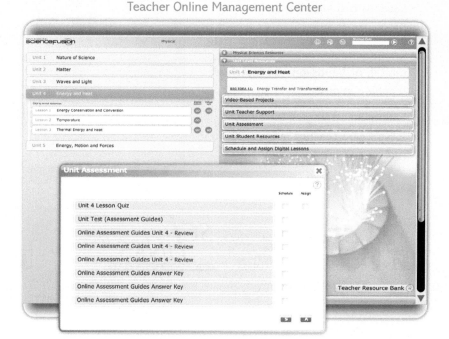

Print Assessment

The print **Assessment Guide** includes

- **Lesson Quizzes**
- **Unit Tests**
- **Unit Performance Assessments**

Online Assessment

The **Digital Assessment** includes

- **assignable leveled assessments for individuals**
- **customizable lesson quizzes and unit tests**
- **individual and whole class reporting**

Customizing Assessment for Your Classroom

Editable quizzes and tests are available in ExamView and online at ⊙ **thinkcentral.com.** You can customize
a quiz or test by adding or deleting items, revising difficulty levels, changing formats, revising sequence, and
editing items. Students can also take quizzes and tests directly online.

Choose Your Options

with two powerful teaching tools— a comprehensive **Teacher Edition** and the **Teacher Online Management Center.**

Classroom Management Teacher Edition

Lesson level teaching support, includes activities, probing questions, misconception alerts, differentiated instruction, and interpreting visuals.

- Lessons organized around a 5E lesson format

- Comprehensive support—print, digital, or hands-on—to match all teaching styles.

- Extension strategies for every lesson give teacher more tools to review and reinforce.

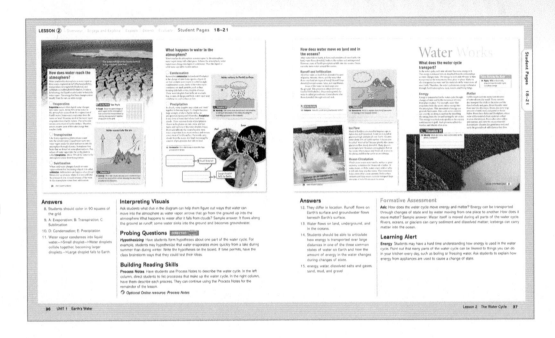

 **National Science Teachers Association**    **SciLINKS. THE WORLD'S A CLICK AWAY**

- Easy access to NSTA's e-professional development center, *The Learning Center*

- SciLinks provide students and teachers content-specific online support.

 Response to Intervention

Response to Intervention is a process for identifying and supporting students who are not making expected progress toward essential learning goals.

 Professional Development

Unit and lesson level professional development focuses on supporting teachers and building educator capacity in key areas of academic achievement.

 **21st Century SKILLS**

Additional support for STEM activities focuses on 21st century skills and helping students master the multi-dimensional abilities required of them in the 21st century.

Probing Questions **(Inquiry)**

Lesson level questions and suggestions provide teachers with options for getting students to think more deeply and critically about a science concept.

Learning Alert  **MISCONCEPTION**

The Learning Alert section previews Inquiry Activities and Lessons to gather and manage the materials needed for each lesson.

Classroom Management
Online teaching and planning

ScienceFusion is a comprehensive, multimodal science program that provides all the digital tools teachers need to engage students in inquiry-based learning. *The Teacher Online Management Center,* at ⊙ thinkcentral.com, is designed to make it easier for teachers to access program resources to plan, teach, assess, and track.

▶ Program resources can be easily previewed in PDF format and downloaded for editing.

▶ Assign and schedule resources online, and they will appear in your students' inboxes.

▶ All quizzes and tests can be taken and automatically scored online.

▶ Easily monitor and track student progress.

Teaching with Technology Made Easy

ScienceFusion's 3,000+ animations, simulations, videos, & interactivities are organized to provide

▶ flexible options for delivering exciting and engaging digital lessons

▶ Teacher Resource Questions, for every lesson, to ensure that the important information is learned

▶ multimodal learning options that connect online learning to concepts learned from reading, writing, and hands-on inquiry

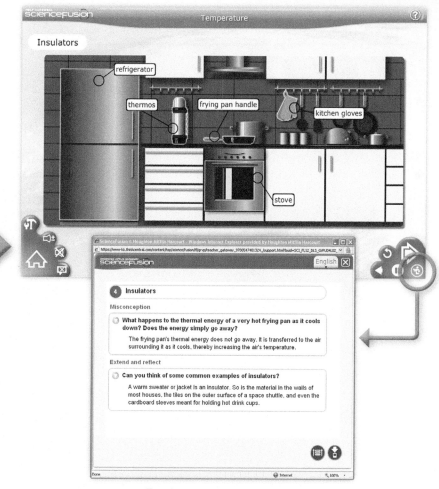

Teacher Resource Questions

Student Edition Contents

These rafters are on a wild ride downriver! They are using the river currents that form as water flows from higher elevations to lower elevations.

Assignments:

_____

_____

_____

_____

_____

_____

_____

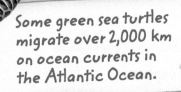

Some green sea turtles migrate over 2,000 km on ocean currents in the Atlantic Ocean.

Surfers love riding ocean waves before they break near shore. The taller the wave, the faster a surfer can travel.

Student Edition Contents

What happens when solar wind particles reach the upper atmosphere over the Arctic? The aurora borealis!

Assignments:

Although humans don't have thick fur or the ability to survive without drinking water for months, we have found other ways to live in extreme climates.

Program Scope and Sequence

ScienceFusion is organized by five major strands of science. Each strand includes Big Ideas that flow throughout all grade levels and build in rigor as students move to higher grades.

ScienceFusion Grade Levels and Units

	GRADE K	GRADE 1	GRADE 2	GRADE 3
Nature of Science	**Unit 1** Doing Science	**Unit 1** How Scientists Work	**Unit 1** Work Like a Scientist	**Unit 1** Investigating Questions
STEM		**Unit 2** Technology All Around Us	**Unit 2** Technology and Our World	**Unit 2** The Engineering Process
Life Science	**Unit 2** Animals **Unit 3** Plants **Unit 4** Habitats	**Unit 3** Animals **Unit 4** Plants **Unit 5** Environments	**Unit 3** All About Animals **Unit 4** All About Plants **Unit 5** Environments for Living Things	**Unit 3** Plants and Animals **Unit 4** Ecosystems and Interactions

GRADE 4	GRADE 5	GRADES 6-8

Unit 1 Studying Science	**Unit 1** How Scientists Work	**Module K** Introduction to Science and Technology
		   Unit 1 The Nature of Science
		   Unit 2 Measurement and Data

Unit 2 The Engineering Process	**Unit 2** The Engineering Process	**Module K** Introduction to Science and Technology **Unit 3** Engineering, Technology, and Society

Unit 3 Plants and Animals
Unit 4 Energy and Ecosystems
	Unit 3 Cells to Body Systems
	Unit 4 Living Things Grow and Reproduce
	Unit 5 Ecosystems
	Unit 6 Energy and Ecosystems
		Module A Cells and Heredity
		   Unit 1 Cells
		   Unit 2 Reproduction and Heredity
		Module B The Diversity of Living Things
		   Unit 1 Life over Time
		   Unit 2 Earth's Organisms
		Module C The Human Body
		   Unit 1 Human Body Systems
		   Unit 2 Human Health
		Module D Ecology and the Environment
		   Unit 1 Interactions of Living Things
		   Unit 2 Earth's Biomes and Ecosystems
		   Unit 3 Earth's Resources
		   Unit 4 Human Impact on the Environment

ScienceFusion Grade Levels and Units

	GRADE K	GRADE 1	GRADE 2	GRADE 3
Earth Science	**Unit 5** Day and Night **Unit 6** Earth's Resources **Unit 7** Weather and the Seasons	**Unit 6** Earth's Resources **Unit 7** Weather and Seasons **Unit 8** Objects in the Sky	**Unit 6** Earth and Its Resources **Unit 7** All About Weather **Unit 8** The Solar System	**Unit 5** Changes to Earth's Surface **Unit 6** People and Resources **Unit 7** Water and Weather **Unit 8** Earth and Its Moon
Physical Science	**Unit 8** Matter **Unit 9** Energy **Unit 10** Motion	**Unit 9** All About Matter **Unit 10** Forces and Energy	**Unit 9** Changes in Matter **Unit 10** Energy and Magnets	**Unit 9** Matter **Unit 10** Simple and Compound Machines

GRADE 4	GRADE 5	GRADES 6-8
Unit 5 Weather	**Unit 7** Natural Resources	**Module E** The Dynamic Earth
Unit 6 Earth and Space	**Unit 8** Changes to Earth's Surface	**Unit 1** Earth's Surface
	Unit 9 The Rock Cycle	**Unit 2** Earth's History
	Unit 10 Fossils	**Unit 3** Minerals and Rocks
	Unit 11 Earth's Oceans	**Unit 4** The Restless Earth
	Unit 12 The Solar System and the Universe	**Module F** Earth's Water and Atmosphere
		Unit 1 Earth's Water
		Unit 2 Oceanography
		Unit 3 Earth's Atmosphere
		Unit 4 Weather and Climate
		Module G Space Science
		Unit 1 The Universe
		Unit 2 The Solar System
		Unit 3 The Earth-Moon-Sun System
		Unit 4 Exploring Space
Unit 7 Properties of Matter	**Unit 13** Matter	**Module H** Matter and Energy
Unit 8 Changes in Matter	**Unit 14** Light and Sound	**Unit 1** Matter
Unit 9 Energy	**Unit 15** Forces and Motion	**Unit 2** Energy
Unit 10 Electricity		**Unit 3** Atoms and the Periodic Table
Unit 11 Motion		**Unit 4** Interactions of Matter
		Unit 5 Solutions, Acids, and Bases
		Module I Motion, Forces, and Energy
		Unit 1 Motion and Forces
		Unit 2 Work, Energy, and Machines
		Unit 3 Electricity and Magnetism
		Module J Sound and Light
		Unit 1 Introduction to Waves
		Unit 2 Sound
		Unit 3 Light

ScienceFusion
Video-Based Projects

⊙ **Available in Online Resources**

This video series, hosted by program authors Michael Heithaus and Michael DiSpezio, develops science learning through real-world science and engineering challenges.

Ecology

Leave your lab coat at home! Not all science research takes place in a lab. Host Michael Heithaus takes you around the globe to see ecology field research, including tagging sharks and tracking sea turtles. Students research, graph, and analyze results to complete the project worksheets.

Module	Video Title
A	Photosynthesis
B	Expedition Evolution Animal Behavior
D	A Trip Down Shark River The Producers of Florida Bay
E	Transforming Earth
I	Animals in Motion
J	Animals and Sound
K	Invaders in the Everglades Data from Space

S.T.E.M. Science, Technology, Engineering, and Math

Host Michael DiSpezio poses a series of design problems that challenge students' ingenuity. Each video follows the engineering process. Worksheets guide students through the process and help them document their results.

Module	Video Title
A	An Inside View**
C	Prosthetics Robotic Assist**
D	Got Water?
E	Seismic Monitoring
F	When the Wind Blows Tornado Warning
G	Soft Landing
H	Just Add Heat
I	Take the Long Way

** In partnership with Children's Hospital Of Boston

Enduring Understandings

Big Ideas, Essential Questions

It goes without saying that a primary goal for your students is to develop understandings of science concepts that endure well past the next test. The question is, what is the best way to achieve that goal?

Research and learning experts suggest that students learn most effectively through a constructivist approach in which they build concepts through active involvement in their own learning. While constructivism may lead to superior learning on a lesson-by-lesson basis, the approach does not address how to organize lessons into a program of instruction. Schema theory, from cognitive science, suggests that knowledge is organized into units and that information is stored in these units, much as files are stored in a digital or paper folder. Informed by our understanding of schema theory, we set about organizing *ScienceFusion*. We began by identifying the Big Ideas of science.

by Marjorie Frank

Big Ideas are generalizations—broad, powerful concepts that connect facts and events that may otherwise seem unrelated. Big Ideas are implicit understandings that help the world make sense. Big Ideas define the "folders," or units, of *ScienceFusion*. Each is a statement that articulates the overarching teaching and learning goals of a unit.

Essential Questions define the "files," or information, in a unit. Each Essential Question identifies the conceptual focus of a lesson that contributes to your students' growing understanding of the associated Big Idea. As such, Essential Questions give your students a sense of direction and purpose.

With *ScienceFusion*, our goal is to provide you with a tool that helps you help your students develop Enduring Understandings in science. Our strategy for achieving that goal has been to provide lesson plans with 5E-based learning experiences organized in a framework informed by schema theory.

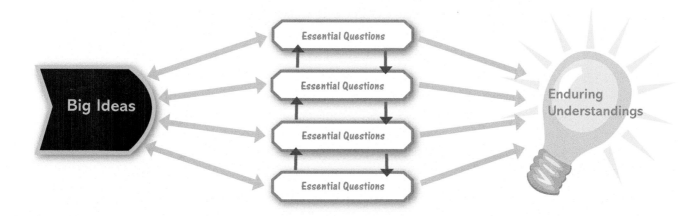

21st Century Skills/STEM

Skills Redefined

Our world has changed. Globalization and the digital revolution have redefined the skill set that is essential for student success in the classroom and beyond. Known collectively as 21st Century Skills, these areas of competence and aptitude go beyond the three Rs of reading, writing, and arithmetic. 21st Century Skills incorporate a battery of high-level thinking skills and technological capabilities.

by Michael A. DiSpezio

21st Century SKILLS — A Sample List

Learning and Innovation Skills

- Creativity and Innovation
- Critical Thinking and Problem Solving
- Communication and Collaboration

Information, Media, and Technology Skills

- Information Literacy
- Media Literacy
- ICT (Information, Communications, and Technology) Literacy

Life and Career Skills

- Flexibility and Adaptability
- Initiative and Self-Direction
- Productivity and Accountability
- Leadership and Responsibility

S.T.E.M.

Curriculum that integrates Science, Technology, Engineering, and Mathematics

21st Century Skills are best taught in the context of the core subject areas. Science makes an ideal subject for integrating these important skills because it involves many skills, including inquiry, collaboration, and problem solving. An even deeper level of incorporating these skills can be found with Science, Technology, Engineering, and Mathematics (STEM) lessons and activities. Hands-on STEM lessons that provide students with engineering design challenges are ideal for developing Learning and Innovation Skills. Students develop creativity and innovation as they engineer novel solutions to posed problems. They communicate and collaborate as they engage higher-level thinking skills to help shape their inquiry experience. Students assume ownership of the learning. From this emerges increased self-motivation and personal accountability.

With STEM lessons and activities, related disciplines are seamlessly integrated into a rich experience that becomes far more than the sum of its parts. Students explore real-world scenarios using their understanding of core science concepts, ability for higher level analysis, technological know-how, and communication skills essential for collaboration. From this experience, the learner constructs not only a response to the STEM challenge, but the elements of 21st Century Skills.

ScienceFusion provides deep science content and STEM lessons, activities, and Video-Based Projects that incorporate and develop 21st Century Skills. This provides an effective learning landscape that will prepare students for success in the workplace—and in life.

Differentiated Instruction

Reaching All Learners

Your students learn in different ways, at different speeds, and through different means. Channeling the energy and richness of that diversity is part of the beauty of teaching. A classroom atmosphere that encourages academic risk-taking encourages learning. This is especially true in science, where learning involves making predictions (which could turn out to be inaccurate), offering explanations (which could turn out to be incomplete), and doing things (which could result in observable mistakes).

by Marjorie Frank

Like most people, students are more likely to take risks in a low-stress environment. Science, with its emphasis on exploring through hands-on activities and interactive reading, provides a natural vehicle for low-stress learning. Low stress, however, may mean different things to different people. For students with learning challenges, low stress may mean being encouraged to respond at the level they are able. Another factor in meeting the needs of diverse students is the instructional tools. Are they flexible? Inviting? *ScienceFusion* addresses the needs of diverse students at every step in the instructional process.

As You Plan

Select from these resources to meet individual needs.

- For each unit, the Differentiated Instruction page in the Teacher Edition identifies program resources specifically geared to diverse learners.

- Leveled activities in the Lesson Planning pages of the Teacher Edition provide additional learning opportunities for students with beginning, intermediate, or advanced proficiency.

- A bibliography contains notable trade books with in-depth information on content. Many of the books are recommendations of the National Science Teachers Association and the Children's Book Council.

- Online Resources: Alternative Assessment worksheets for each lesson provide varied strategies for learning content.

- Online Resources: Digital lessons, virtual labs, and video-based projects appeal to all students, especially struggling readers and visual learners.

- Student Edition with Audio is online as PDF files with audio readings for use with students who have vision impairments or learning difficulties.

- Student Edition reading strategies focus on vocabulary, concept development, and inquiry skills.

As You Teach

Take advantage of these point-of-use features.

- A mix of Directed Inquiry and Independent Inquiry prompts suitable for different kinds of learners

- Short-cut codes to specific interactive digital lessons

Take It Home

As you reach out to families, look for these school-home connections.

- Take It Home activities found at the beginning of many units in the Student Edition

- Additional Take It Home worksheets are available in the Online Resources

- School-Home Connection Letters for every unit, available online as files you can download and print as-is or customize

The 5E Model and Levels of Inquiry

How do students best learn science? Extensive research and data show that the most effective learning emerges from situations in which one builds understanding based upon personal experiences. Learning is not transmitted from instructor to passive receiver; instead, understanding is constructed through the experience.

by Michael A. DiSpezio

The 5E Model for Effective Science Lessons

In the 1960s, Robert Karplus and his colleagues developed a three-step instructional model that became known as the Learning Cycle. This model was expanded into what is today referred to as the 5E Model. To emulate the elements of how an actual scientist works, this model is broken down into five components for an effective lesson: Engage, Explore, Explain, Extend (or Elaborate), and Evaluate.

Engage—The engagement sets the scene for learning. It is a warm-up during which students are introduced to the learning experience. Prior knowledge is assessed and its analysis used to develop an effective plan to meet stated objectives. Typically, an essential question is then posed; the question leads the now motivated and engaged students into the exploration.

Explore—This is the stage where the students become actively involved in hands-on process. They communicate and collaborate to develop a strategy that addresses the posed problem. Emphasis is placed on inquiry and hands-on investigation. The hands-on experience may be highly prescribed or open-ended in nature.

Explain—Students answer the initial question by using their findings and information they may be reading about, discussing with classmates, or experiencing through digital media. Their experience and understanding of concepts, processes, and hands-on skills is strengthened at this point. New vocabulary may be introduced.

Extend (or Elaborate)—The explanation is now extended to other situations, questions, or problems. During this stage the learner more closely examines findings in terms of context and transferable application. In short, extension reveals the application and implication of the internalized explanation. Extension may involve connections to other curriculum areas.

Evaluate—Although evaluation is an ongoing process, this is the stage in which a final assessment is most often performed. The instructor evaluates lesson effectiveness by using a variety of formal and informal assessment tools to measure student performance.

The 5E lesson format is used in all the *ScienceFusion* Teacher Edition lessons.

Levels of Inquiry

It wasn't that long ago that science was taught mostly through demonstration and lecture. Today, however, most instructional strategies integrate an inquiry-based approach to learning science. This methodology is founded in higher-level thinking and facilitates the students' construction of understanding from experience. When offered opportunities to ask questions, design investigations, collect and analyze data, and communicate their findings, each student assumes the role of an active participant in shaping his or her own learning process.

The degree to which any activity engages the inquiry process is variable, from highly prescribed steps to a completely learner-generated design. Researchers have established three distinct levels of inquiry: directed (or structured) inquiry, guided inquiry, and independent (or open) inquiry. These levels are distinguished by the amount of guidance offered by the instructor.

DIRECTED inquiry

In this level of inquiry, the instructor poses a question or suggests an investigation, and students follow a prescribed set of instructions. The outcome may be unknown to the students, but it is known to the instructor. Students follow the structured outline to uncover an outcome that supports the construction of lesson concepts.

GUIDED inquiry

As in Directed Inquiry, the instructor poses to the students a question to investigate. While students are conducting the investigation, the instruction focuses on developing one or more inquiry skills. Focus may also be provided for students to learn to use methods or tools of science. In *ScienceFusion*, the Teacher Edition provides scaffolding for developing inquiry skills, science methods, or tools. Student pages accompany these lessons and provide prompts for writing hypotheses, recording data, and drawing conclusions.

INDEPENDENT inquiry

This is the most complex level of inquiry experience. A prompt is provided, but students must design their own investigation in response to the prompt. In some cases, students will write their own questions and then plan and perform scientific investigations that will answer those questions. This level of inquiry is often used for science fair projects. Independent Inquiry does not necessarily mean individual inquiry. Investigations can be conducted by individual students or by pairs or teams of students.

Response to Intervention

In a traditional model, assessment marks the end of an instructional cycle. Students work through a unit, take a test, and move on, regardless of their performance. However, current research suggests that assessment should be part of the instructional cycle, that it should be ongoing, and that it should be used to identify students needing intervention. This may sound like a tall order—who wants to give tests all the time?—but it may not be as difficult as it seems. In some ways, you are probably doing it already.

by Marjorie Frank

Assessment

Every student interaction has the potential to be an assessment. It all depends on how you perceive and use the interaction.

- Suppose you ask a question. You can just listen to your student's response, or you can assess it. Does the response indicate comprehension of the concept? If not, intervention may be needed.

- Suppose a student offers an explanation of a phenomenon depicted in a photo. You can assess the explanation. Does it show accurate factual knowledge? Does it reveal a misconception? If so, intervention may be needed.

- Suppose a student draws a diagram to illustrate a concept. You can assess the diagram. Is it accurate? If not, intervention may be needed.

As the examples indicate, assessing students' understandings can—and should—be an integral part of the instructional cycle and be used to make decisions about the next steps of instruction. For students making good progress, next steps might be exploring a related concept, a new lesson, or an additional challenge. For students who are not making adequate progress, intervention may be needed.

Assessment and intervention are tightly linked. Assessment leads to intervention—fresh approaches, different groupings, new materials—which, in turn, leads to assessment. Response to Intervention (RTI) gives shape and substance to this linkage.

RTI Response to Intervention

Response to Intervention is a process for identifying and supporting students who are not making expected progress toward essential learning goals.

RTI is a three-tiered approach based on an ongoing cycle of superior instruction, frequent monitoring of students' learning (assessments), and appropriate interventions. Students who are found not to be making expected progress in one Tier move to the next higher Tier, where they receive more intense instruction.

- **Tier I:** Students receive whole-class, core instruction.
- **Tier II:** Students work in small groups that supplement and reinforce core instruction.
- **Tier III:** Students receive individualized instruction.

How RTI and *ScienceFusion* Work

ScienceFusion provides many opportunities to assess students' understanding and many components appropriate for students in all Tiers.

TIER III Intensive Intervention

Individualized instruction, with options for auditory, visual, and second language learners. Special education is a possibility.

Differentiated Instruction Strategies

Online Student Edition

ScienceFusion Components

Online Student Edition lessons with audio recordings

Differentiated Instruction strategies in the Teacher Edition for every lesson

Appropriate for:
- Auditory learners

Appropriate for:
- Struggling readers
- Second-language learners

Students achieving at a lower level than their peers in Tier II

TIER II Strategic Intervention

Small Group Instruction in addition to core instruction

Leveled TE Activities

Alternative Assessment Worksheets

ScienceFusion Components

Leveled activities in the Lesson Planning pages of the Teacher Edition

Alternative Assessment Worksheets

Appropriate for:
- Struggling readers
- Visual learners
- Second-language learners
- Screening tools to assess students' responses to Tier II instruction

Students achieving at a lower level than their peers in Tier I

TIER I Core Classroom Instruction

With the help of extensive point-of-use strategies that support superior teaching, students receive whole-class instruction and engage productively in small-group work as appropriate.

Teacher Edition

Student Edition

Assessment Guide

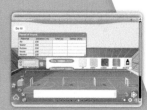

Digital Curriculum

ScienceFusion Components

Student Edition

Differentiated Instruction strategies in the TE for every lesson

Teacher Edition

Assessment Guide

Online Digital Curriculum

Appropriate for:
- Screening tools to assess students' responses to Tier I instruction
- Tier I intervention for students unable to complete the activity independently

Active Reading

Reading is a complex process in which readers use their knowledge and experience to make meaning from text. Though rarely accompanied by obvious large-muscle movement, reading is very much an active endeavor.

by Marjorie Frank

Think back to your days as a college student when you pored over your textbooks to prepare for class or for an exam—or, more recently, concentrated on an article or book with information you wanted to remember.

▶ You probably paid close attention to the text.

▶ Perhaps you paused to ask yourself questions.

▶ You might have broken off temporarily to look up an important, but unfamiliar, word.

▶ You may have stopped to reread a challenging passage or to "catch up" if your mind wandered for a moment.

If you owned the reading material, you also may have used a pencil or marker to interact with the text right there on the page (or in a digital file).

In short, you were having a conversation with yourself about the text. You were engaged. You were thinking critically.

These are the characteristics of active readers. This is precisely the kind of reader you want your students to be, because research suggests that active reading enables readers to understand and remember more information.

Active Reading involves interacting with text cognitively, metacognitively, and quite literally. You can actually see active readers at work. They are not sitting quietly as they read; they're underlining, marking, boxing, bracketing, drawing arrows, numbering, and writing comments. Here is what they may be noting:

▶ key terms and main ideas

▶ connections between ideas

▶ questions they have, opinions, agreements, and disagreements

▶ important facts and details

▶ sequences of events

▶ words, such as *because, before,* and *but,* that signal connections between ideas

▶ problems/solutions

▶ definitions and examples

▶ characteristics

The very process of interacting actively with text helps keep readers focused, thinking, comprehending, and remembering. But interacting in this way means readers are marking up the text. This is exactly why *ScienceFusion* Student Editions are consumable. They are meant to be marked up.

Active Reading and *ScienceFusion*

ScienceFusion includes Active Reading prompts throughout the Student Editions. The prompts appear as part of the lesson opener and on most two-page spreads.

Students are often given an Active Reading prompt before reading a section or paragraph. These prompts ask students to underline certain words or number the steps in a process. Marking the text in this way is called *annotating*, and the students' marks are called *annotations*. Annotating the text can help students identify important concepts while reading. Other ways of annotating the text include placing an asterisk by vocabulary terms, marking unfamiliar or confusing terms and information with a question mark, and underlining main ideas. Students can even invent their own systems for annotating the text. An example of an annotation prompt is shown at right.

> **Active Reading** **5 Identify** As you read, underline sources of energy for living things.

In addition, there are Active Reading questions throughout each lesson. These questions have write-on lines accompanying them, so students can answer right on the page. Students will be asked to **describe** what they've just read about, **apply** concepts, **compare** concepts, **summarize** processes, and **identify cause-and-effect** relationships. By answering these Active Reading questions while reading the text, students will be strengthening those and other critical thinking skills that are used so often in science.

> **Active Reading** **16 Compare** What is the difference between the pulmonary and systemic circulations?

Students' Responses to Active Reading Prompts

Active Reading has benefits for you as well as for your students. You can use students' responses to Active Reading prompts and the other interactive prompts in *ScienceFusion* as ongoing assessments. A quick review of students' responses provides a great deal of information about their learning.

- ▶ Are students comprehending the text?
- ▶ How deeply do they understand the concepts developed?
- ▶ Did they get the main idea? the cause? the order in which things happen?
- ▶ Which part of a lesson needs more attention? for whom?

Answers to these questions are available in students' responses to Active Learning prompts throughout a lesson—long before you might see poor results on an end-of-lesson or end-of-unit assessment. If you are following Response to Intervention (RTI) protocols, these frequent and regular assessments, no matter how informal, are integral parts of an effective intervention program.

The Active Reading prompts in *ScienceFusion* help make everyone a winner.

Project-Based Learning

For a list of the *ScienceFusion* Video-Based Projects, see page xxiv.

by
Michael R. Heithaus

When asked why I decided to become a biologist, the answer is pretty simple. I was inspired by spending almost every day outdoors, exploring under every rock, getting muddy in creeks and streams, and fishing in farm ponds, rivers, and—when I was really lucky—the oceans. Combine that with the spectacular stories of amazing animals and adventure that I saw on TV and I was hooked. As I've progressed in my career as a biologist, that same excitement and curiosity that I had as a ten-year-old looking for a salamander is still driving me.

But today's kids live in a very different world. Cable and satellite TV, Twitter, MP3 players, cell phones, and video games all compete with the outdoors for kids' time and attention. Education budget cuts, legal issues, and the pressures of standardized testing have also limited the opportunities for students to explore outdoors with their teachers.

How do we overcome these challenges so as to inspire kids' curiosity, help them connect with the natural world, and get them to engage in science and math? This is a critical issue. Not only do we need to ensure our national competitiveness and the conservation of our natural resources by training the next generation of scientists, we also need to ensure that every kid grows up to understand how scientists work and why their work is important.

To overcome these challenges, there is no question that we need to grab students' attention and get them to actively engage in the learning process. Research shows that students who are active and engaged participants in their learning have greater gains in concept and skills development than students who are passive in the classroom.

Project-based learning is one way to engage students. And when the stimulus for the project is exciting video content, engaged and active learning is almost guaranteed. Nothing captures a student's attention faster than exciting video. I have noticed that when my university students have video to accompany a lesson, they learn and retain the material better. It's no different for younger students! Videos need to do more than just "talk at" students to have a real impact. Videos need to engage students and require participation.

Teachers and students who use *ScienceFusion* video-based projects have noticed the following:

- The videos use captivating imagery, dynamic scientists, and cool stories to inspire kids to be curious about the world around them.
- Students connect to the projects by having the videos present interesting problems for them to solve.
- The videos engage students with projects woven into the story of the video so students are doing the work of real scientists!

The start-to-finish nature of the video projects, where students do background research and develop their own hypotheses, should lead to students' personal investment in solving the challenges that are presented. By seeing real scientists who are excellent role models gather data that they have to graph and interpret, students will not only learn the science standards being addressed, they will see that they can apply the scientific method to their lives. One day, they too could be a scientist!

Based on my experiences teaching in the university classroom, leading field trips for middle school students, and taking the first project-based videos into the classroom, project-based learning has considerable benefits. The video-based projects generate enthusiasm and curiosity. They also help students develop a deeper understanding of science content as well as how to go about a scientific investigation. If we inspire students to ask questions and seek answers for themselves, we will go a long way toward closing achievement gaps in science and math and facilitate the development of the next generation of scientists and scientifically literate citizens.

Developing Visual Literacy

Science teachers can build the bridges between students' general literacy and their scientific literacy by focusing attention on the particular kinds of reading strategies students need to be successful. One such strategy is that of knowing how to read and interpret the various visual displays used in science.

by Donna M. Ogle

Many young readers receive little instruction in reading charts, tables, diagrams, photographs, or illustrations in their language arts/reading classes. Science is where these skills can and must be developed. Science provides a meaningful context where students can learn to read visually presented forms of information and to create their own visual representations. Research studies have shown that students take longer to read science materials containing combinations of visual displays and narrative texts than they do to read narrative text alone. The process of reading the combination materials is slower and more difficult because the reader must relate the visual displays to the narrative text and build a meaning that is based on information from both.

We also know that students benefit when teachers take time to explain how each visual form is constructed and to guide students in the thinking needed to make sense of these forms. Even the seemingly simple act of interpreting a photograph needs to be taught to most students. Here are some ways to help students develop the ability to think more critically about what they view:

▶ Model for students how to look carefully at a photograph and list what they notice.

▶ Divide the photograph into quadrants and have students think more deeply about what the photographer has used as the focus of the image and what context is provided.

▶ Have students use language such as *zoom, close-up, foreground, background*, or *panorama views* to describe photographs.

The ability to interpret a photograph is clearly a part of the scientific skill of engaging in careful observation. This skill helps students when they are using print materials, observing nature, and making their own photographs of aspects of their experiments.

Attention to the other forms of visual displays frequently used in science is also important to students' learning of scientific concepts and processes. For example, students in grades 4 through 8 need to learn to interpret and then construct each of the types of graphs, from circle graphs and bar graphs to more complex line graphs.

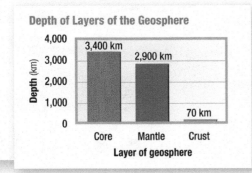

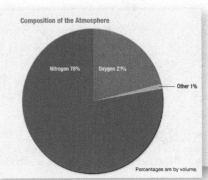

Students also need to be able to read diagrams and flow charts. Yet, in a recent study asking students to think aloud and point to how they visually scan tables and diagrams, we learned how inadequate many students were as readers of these visual forms. Because so much of the scientific information students will encounter is summarized in these visual formats, it is essential that students learn to interpret and construct visual displays.

A second aspect of interpreting visual displays is connecting the information in the visual formats with the narrative text information. Some students misinterpret what they see in visuals when even a few words differ between the text and the illustration. For example, in the excerpt below from a middle school Student Edition, the text says, "the arm of a human, the front leg of a cat, and the wing of a bat do not look alike . . . but they are similar in structure. "

The diagram labels (lower right) showing the bat wing and the cat's leg use *front limb*, not *wing* or *leg*. For students who struggle with English, the differing terms may cause confusion unless teachers show students how to use clues from later in the paragraph, where limb and wing/arm are connected, and how to connect this information to the two drawings. In some cases teachers have students draw lines showing where visual displays connect with the more extensive narrative text content. Developing students' awareness of how visual and narrative information support each other and yet provide different forms in which information can be shared is an important step in building scientific literacy.

Reading science requires students to use specific reading strategies. The more carefully science teachers across grade levels assess what students already know about reading scientific materials, the more easily they can focus instruction to build the scaffolds students need to gain independence and confidence in their reading and learning of science. Time spent explaining, modeling, and guiding students will yield the rewards of heightened student enjoyment, confidence, and engagement in the exciting world of scientific inquiry.

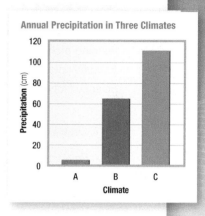

Annual Precipitation in Three Climates

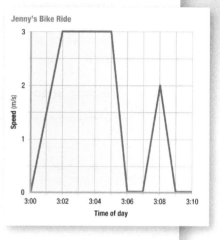

Jenny's Bike Ride

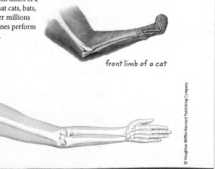

Common Structures

Scientists have found that related organisms share structural traits. Structures reduced in size or function may have been complete and functional in the organism's ancestor. For example, snakes have traces of leglike structures that are not used for movement. These unused structures are evidence that snakes share a common ancestor with animals like lizards and dogs.

Scientists also consider similar structures with different functions. The arm of a human, the front leg of a cat, and the wing of a bat do not look alike and are not used in the same way. But as you can see, they are similar in structure. The bones of a human arm are similar in structure to the bones in the front limbs of a cat and a bat. These similarities suggest that cats, bats, and humans had a common ancestor. Over millions of years, changes occurred. Now, these bones perform different functions in each type of animal.

front limb of a bat

front limb of a cat

Visualize It!

10 Relate Do you see any similarities between the bones of the bat and cat limbs and the bones of the human arm? If so, use the colors of the bat and cat bones to color similar bones in the human arm. If you don't have colored pencils, label the bones with the correct color names.

© Houghton Mifflin Harcourt Publishing Company

Science Notebooking

Science Notebooks are powerful classroom tools. They lead your students deep into the learning process, and they provide you with a window into that process as well as a means to communicate about it. Most middle-school students will have had some experience using a Science Notebook during their elementary years.

Notebook ▶ Why Use a Science Notebook?

A Science Notebook contains the writer's ideas, observations, and perceptions of events and endeavors. A Science Notebook also contains ideas and observations of scientific processes, data, conclusions, conjectures, and generalizations.

Inquiry Skills A Science Notebook is especially important when students do inquiry-based activities. It offers students a single place to record their observations, consider possibilities, and organize their thoughts. As such, it is a learner's version of the logs that professional scientists keep.

In their Science Notebooks, students can

▶ sketch their ideas and observations from experiments and field trips

▶ make predictions about what will happen in an experiment

▶ reflect on their work and the meaning they derived from experiments

▶ make inferences based on the data they have gathered

▶ propose additional experiments to test new hypotheses

▶ pose new questions based on the results of an activity or experiment

Process Skills A Science Notebook is an excellent extension of the textbook, allowing students to further practice and hone process skills. Students will not only apply these skills in relation to the specific science content they are learning, they will be gaining a deeper insight into scientific habits of mind.

In their Science Notebooks, students can

▶ record and analyze data

▶ create graphs and charts

▶ infer outcomes

▶ draw conclusions

▶ collect data from multiple experimental trials

▶ develop 21st Century organizational skills

A student's Science Notebook entry for a *ScienceFusion* Quick Lab

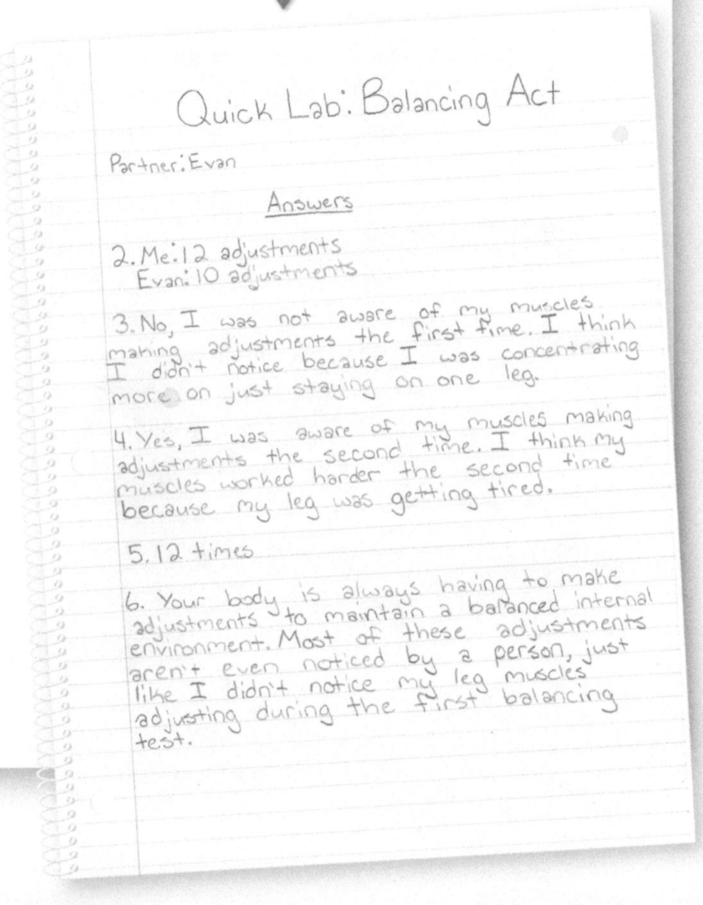

▼

Quick Lab: Balancing Act

Partner: Evan

Answers

2. Me: 12 adjustments
   Evan: 10 adjustments

3. No, I was not aware of my muscles making adjustments the first time. I think I didn't notice because I was concentrating more on just staying on one leg.

4. Yes, I was aware of my muscles making adjustments the second time. I think my muscles worked harder the second time because my leg was getting tired.

5. 12 times

6. Your body is always having to make adjustments to maintain a balanced internal environment. Most of these adjustments aren't even noticed by a person, just like I didn't notice my leg muscles adjusting during the first balancing test.

Science Notebooks and *ScienceFusion*

In many ways, the *ScienceFusion* worktexts are Science Notebooks in themselves. Students are encouraged to write answers directly in the text and to annotate the text for better understanding. However, a separate Science Notebook can still be an invaluable part of your student's learning experience with *ScienceFusion*. Student uses for a Science Notebook along with the worktext include:

▶ writing answers for the Unit Review

▶ writing responses to the Think Outside the Book features in each lesson

▶ planning for and writing answers to the Citizen Science feature in each unit

▶ working through answers before writing them in the worktext

▶ writing all answers if you choose not to have students work directly in the worktext

▶ taking notes on additional materials you present outside of the worktext

▶ making observations and recording data from Daily Demos and additional activities provided in the Teacher Edition

▶ collecting data and writing notes for labs performed from the Lab Manual

▶ making notes and writing answers for Digital Lessons and Virtual Labs

▶ collecting data and writing answers for the Project-Based Videos

The Benefits (for You and Your Students) of Science Notebooking

No doubt, it takes time and effort to help students set up and maintain Science Notebooks, not to mention the time it takes you to review them and provide meaningful feedback. The payoff is well worth it. Here's why:

Keeping a Science Notebook:

▶ leads each learner to engage with ideas

▶ engages students in writing—an active, thinking, analytical process

▶ causes students to organize their thinking

▶ provides students with multiple opportunities and modes to process new information

▶ makes learning experiences more personal

▶ provides students with a record of their own progress and accomplishments

▶ doubles as a study guide for formal assessments

▶ creates an additional vehicle for students to improve their reading and writing skills

As you and your students embrace Science Notebooking, you will surely find it to be an engaging, enriching, and very valuable endeavor.

Using the *ScienceFusion* Worktext

Research shows that an interactive text teaches students how to relate to content in a personal, meaningful way. They learn how to be attentive, energetic readers who reach a deep level of comprehension. Still, the worktext format may be new to you and your students. Below are some answers to questions—both pedagogical and practical—you may have about *ScienceFusion's* worktext format.

How does the worktext format help my students learn?

▶ In this format, your students will interact with the text and visuals on every page. This will teach them to read expertly, to think critically, and to communicate effectively—all skills that are crucial for success in the 21st century.

▶ The use of images and text on every page of the *ScienceFusion* worktext accommodates both visual and verbal learners. Students are engaged by the less formal, magazine-like presentation of the content.

▶ By the end of the school year, the worktexts become a record of the knowledge and skills your students learned in class. Students can use their books as a study guide to prepare for tests.

What are some features that make the *ScienceFusion* worktext different from a regular textbook?

Some of the special features of the *ScienceFusion* worktext include these prompts for writing directly in the worktext:

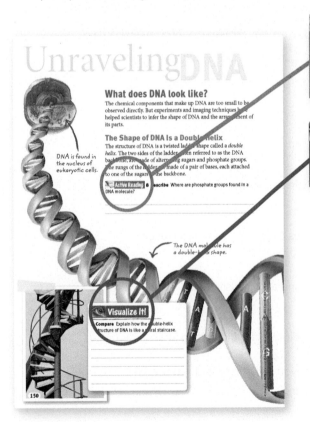

Active Reading

Annotation prompts and questions throughout the worktext teach students how to analyze and interact with content as they read.

Visualize It!

Questions and completion prompts that accompany images help develop visual literacy.

Engage Your Brain

Math problems, with on-page guidance, allow students to understand the relationships between math and science and to practice their math skills.

Do the Math

Interesting questions and activities on the lesson opener pages help prepare students for the lesson content.

Are my students really supposed to write directly in the book?

Yes! Write-on lines are provided for students to answer questions on-page, while the student is reading. Additional prompts are given for students to annotate the pages. You can even encourage your students to experiment with their own systems of annotation. More information can be found in "A How-To Manual for Active Reading" in the Look It Up! Section at the end of the Student Edition and Teacher Edition.

You might wish to encourage your students to write in the worktexts using pencils so that they can more easily revise their answers and notes as needed.

We will have to use the same set of worktexts for several years. How can students use the worktexts if they can't write in them?

Though *ScienceFusion* is set up in a worktext format, the books can still be used in a more traditional fashion. Simply tell your students that they cannot write in the textbooks but should instead use their Science Notebooks for taking notes and answering questions. (See the article titled "Science Notebooking" for more information about using Notebooks with *ScienceFusion*.)

How do I grade my students' answers in the worktext?

The pages in the worktext are conveniently perforated so that your students can turn in their work. Or you may wish for your students to leave the pages in the book, but turn in the books to you on a daily or weekly basis for you to grade them.

The Lesson Reviews and Unit Reviews are designed so students can turn in the pages but still keep their annotated pages for reference when moving on to the next lesson or unit or for review before a lesson or unit test.

TIPS

- Tour the classroom while students are writing in their worktexts. Address any issues you see immediately or make note of items that need to be addressed with students later.

- Have students do 'self checks' and 'partner checks.' Choose a question in the worktext, and have all students check their responses. Or, have students trade their worktext with a partner to check each other's responses.

- Once a week, have students copy five questions and their responses from the worktext onto a sheet of notebook paper. You can review student answers to ensure they're using the worktext correctly without having students turn in worktext pages or the books themselves.

- Use a document camera to show students correct worktext answers.

- Every two weeks, review and grade one class's worth of student worktext answers per day. Or, grade a class's worktexts while the students are taking a test.

Pacing Guide

You have options for covering the lesson materials: you may choose to follow the digital path, the print path, or a combination of the two. Customize your Pacing Guide to plan print, inquiry, digital, and assessment mini-blocks based on your teaching style and classroom needs.

Pressed for Time? Follow the faster-paced compressed schedule.

	Total Days			Customize Your Pacing Guide			
	Traditional 1 = 45 min	Block 1 = 90 min	Compressed (T/B)	Print Path	Inquiry Labs & Activities	Digital Path	Review & Assess
UNIT 1 Earth's Water							
Unit Project	3	1.5	3 (1.5)				
Lesson 1 Water and Its Properties	4	2	3 (1.5)				
Lesson 2 The Water Cycle	5	2.5	4 (2)				
Lesson 3 Surface Water and Groundwater	5	2.5	4 (2)				
Unit Review	2	1	1 (0.5)				
Total Days for Unit 1	19	9.5	15 (7.5)				
UNIT 2 Oceanography							
Unit Project	3	1.5	3 (1.5)				
Lesson 1 Earth's Oceans and the Ocean Floor	5	2.5	4 (2)				
Lesson 2 Ocean Waves	5	2.5	4 (2)				
Lesson 3 Ocean Currents	6	3	5 (2.5)				
Unit Review	2	1	1 (0.5)				
Total Days for Unit 2	21	10.5	17 (8.5)				

	Total Days			Customize Your Pacing Guide				
	Traditional 1 = 45 min	Block 1 = 90 min	Compressed (T/B)	Print Path	Inquiry Labs & Activities	Digital Path	Review & Assess	

UNIT 3 Earth's Atmosphere								
Unit Project	3	1.5	3 (1.5)					
Lesson 1 The Atmosphere	4	2	3 (1.5)					
Lesson 2 Energy Transfer	6	3	5 (2.5)					
Lesson 3 Wind in the Atmosphere	5	2.5	4 (2)					
Unit Review	2	1	1 (0.5)					
Total Days for Unit 3	20	10	16 (8)					

UNIT 4 Weather and Climate								
Unit Project	3	1.5	3 (1.5)					
Lesson 1 Elements of Weather	4	2	3 (1.5)					
Lesson 2 Clouds and Cloud Formation	5	2.5	4 (2)					
Lesson 3 What Influences Weather?	6	3	5 (2.5)					
Lesson 4 Severe Weather and Weather Safety	6	3	5 (2.5)					
Lesson 5 Weather Maps and Weather Prediction	6	3	5 (2.5)					
Lesson 6 Climate	6	3	5 (2.5)					
Lesson 7 Climate Change	7	4	6 (3)					
Unit Review	2	1	1 (0.5)					
Total Days for Unit 4	45	23	37 (18.5)					

Teacher Notes

The Big Idea and Essential Questions

This Unit was designed to focus on this Big Idea and Essential Questions.

Big Idea Water moves through Earth's atmosphere, oceans, and land in a cycle and is essential for life on Earth.

Lesson	ESSENTIAL QUESTION	Student Mastery	 Professional Development	Lesson Overview
LESSON 1 Water and Its Properties	*What makes water so important?*	To describe water's structure, its properties, and its importance to Earth's systems	Content Refresher, TE p. 6	TE p. 12
LESSON 2 The Water Cycle	*How does water change state and move around on Earth?*	To describe the water cycle and the different processes that are part of the water cycle on Earth	Content Refresher, TE p. 7	TE p. 26
LESSON 3 Surface Water and Groundwater	*How does fresh water flow on Earth?*	To explain the processes involved in the flow of water, both above and below the ground	Content Refresher, TE p. 8	TE p. 44

©Ron Watts/Corbis

 **Professional Development**   Science Background

Use the keywords at right to access

- Professional Development from **The NSTA Learning Center**
- **SciLinks** for additional online content appropriate for students and teachers

Keywords

water   water cycle

NSTA National Science Teachers Association

SciLINKS THE WORLD'S A CLICK AWAY

Options for Instruction

Two parallel paths provide coverage of the Essential Questions, with a strong **Inquiry** strand woven into each. Follow the **Print Path,** the **Digital Path,** or your customized combination of print, digital, and inquiry.

	LESSON 1 Water and Its Properties	LESSON 2 The Water Cycle	LESSON 3 Surface Water and Groundwater
Essential Questions	What makes water so important?	How does water change state and move around on Earth?	How does fresh water flow on Earth?
Key Topics	• Importance and Distribution of Water • Structure of Water • States of Water • Properties of Water	• Water Cycle and Change of State • Water in the Atmosphere • Water in the Oceans and on Land • Transport of Matter and Energy	• Surface Water • Groundwater
Print Path	Teacher Edition pp. 12–24 Student Edition pp. 4–13	Teacher Edition pp. 26–39 Student Edition pp. 14–25	Teacher Edition pp. 44–57 Student Edition pp. 30–41
Inquiry Labs	Lab Manual **Quick Lab** Reaching the Dew Point **Quick Lab** Compare Densities	Lab Manual **Exploration Lab** Changes in Water 🖳 Virtual Lab How Does Water Move Through the Water Cycle?	Lab Manual **Quick Lab** Modeling Groundwater **Quick Lab** Model a Stream **S.T.E.M. Lab** Aquifers and Development
Digital Path	Digital Path TS661765	Digital Path TS661210	Digital Path TS661777

UNIT 1
Unit Projects

Citizen Science Project
Conserving Water

Teacher Edition **p. 11**

Student Edition
pp. 2–3

Unit Assessment
Formative Assessment
Strategies RTI
Throughout TE

Lesson Reviews SE

Unit PreTest

Summative Assessment
Alternative Assessment
(1 per lesson) RTI

Lesson Quizzes

Unit Tests A and B

Unit Review RTI
(with answer remediation)

Practice Tests
(end of module)

Project-Based Assessment
See the Assessment Guide for quizzes and tests.

Go Online to edit and create quizzes and tests.

Response to Intervention
See RTI teacher support materials on p. PD6.

Differentiated Instruction

English Language Proficiency

Strategies for **English Language Learners (ELL)** are provided for each lesson, under the Explain tabs.

LESSON 1 *Synonym Study,* TE p. 17

LESSON 2 *Water Cycle Processes,* TE p. 31

LESSON 3 *Card Game,* TE p. 49

Vocabulary strategies provided for all students can also be particularly helpful for ELL. Use different strategies for each lesson or choose one or two to use throughout the unit. Vocabulary strategies can be found under the Explain tab for each lesson (TE pp. 17, 31, and 49).

Leveled Inquiry

Inquiry labs, activities, probing questions, and daily demos provide a range of inquiry levels. Preview them under the Engage and Explore tabs, starting on TE pp. 14, 28, and 46.

Levels of **Inquiry**

DIRECTED inquiry	**GUIDED** inquiry	**INDEPENDENT** inquiry
introduces inquiry skills within a structured framework.	develops inquiry skills within a supportive environment.	deepens inquiry skills with student-driven questions or procedures.

Each long lab has two inquiry options:

LESSON 2 **Exploration Lab** *Changes in Water*

LESSON 3 **S.T.E.M. Lab** *Aquifers and Development*

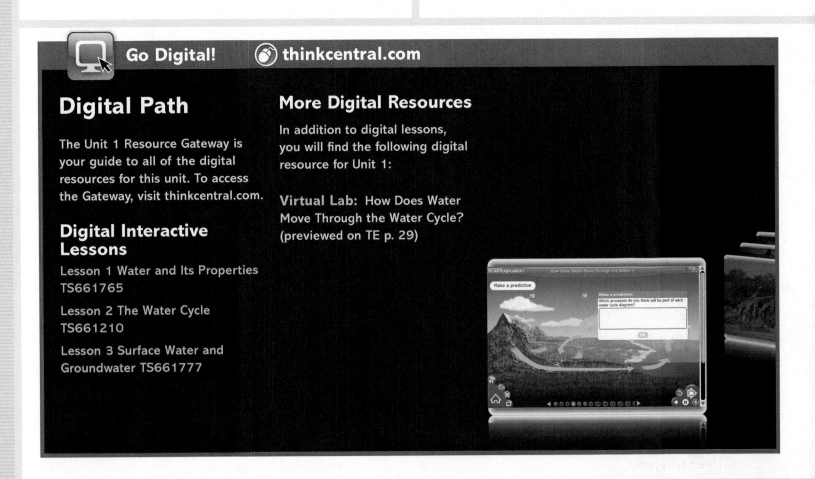

Go Digital! thinkcentral.com

Digital Path

The Unit 1 Resource Gateway is your guide to all of the digital resources for this unit. To access the Gateway, visit thinkcentral.com.

Digital Interactive Lessons

Lesson 1 Water and Its Properties TS661765

Lesson 2 The Water Cycle TS661210

Lesson 3 Surface Water and Groundwater TS661777

More Digital Resources

In addition to digital lessons, you will find the following digital resource for Unit 1:

Virtual Lab: How Does Water Move Through the Water Cycle? (previewed on TE p. 29)

Response to Intervention

Response to Intervention (RTI) is a process for identifying and supporting students who are not making expected progress toward essential learning goals. The following *ScienceFusion* components can be used to provide strategic and intensive intervention.

Component	Location	Strategies and Benefits
STUDENT EDITION Active Reading prompts, Visualize It!, Think Outside the Book	**Throughout each lesson**	Student responses can be used as screening tools to assess whether intervention is needed.
TEACHER EDITION Formative Assessment, Probing Questions, Learning Alerts	**Throughout each lesson**	Opportunities are provided to assess and remediate student understanding of lesson concepts.
TEACHER EDITION Extend Science Concepts	**Reinforce and Review, TE pp. 18, 32, 50** **Going Further, TE pp. 18, 32, 50**	Additional activities allow students to reinforce and extend their understanding of lesson concepts.
TEACHER EDITION Evaluate Student Mastery	**Formative Assessment, TE pp. 19, 33, 51** **Alternative Assessment, TE pp. 19, 33, 51**	These assessments allow for greater flexibility in assessing students with differing physical, mental, and language abilities as well as varying learning and communication modes.
TEACHER EDITION Unit Review Remediation	**Unit Review, TE pp. 58–60**	Includes reference back to Lesson Planning pages for remediation activities and assignments.
INTERACTIVE DIGITAL LESSONS and VIRTUAL LABS	**thinkcentral.com** **Unit 1 Gateway** **Lesson 1 TS661765** **Lesson 2 TS661210** **Lesson 3 TS661777**	Lessons and labs make content accessible through simulations, animations, videos, audio, and integrated assessment. Useful for review and reteaching of lesson concepts.

Content Refresher

Professional Development

Water and Its Properties

ESSENTIAL QUESTION
What makes water so important?

1. Importance and Distribution of Water

Students will learn about the distribution of water and why water is important.

Earth is the only planet in our solar system with a large amount of liquid water. Earth's four named oceans are all connected to form one huge ocean that covers roughly 70% of the planet's surface. Only 3% of all water on Earth is freshwater. Of that 3% freshwater, 75% is ice.

Water plays several important roles on Earth. Because of the presence of liquid water, Earth can support life. All living things, including humans, require water at some point in their lives for survival. Water plays a key role in Earth's weather and in the shaping of Earth's landscape through weathering, erosion, and deposition. Water is essential to human activities including farming, industry, power production, and household activities such as bathing and cleaning.

2. Structure of Water

Students will learn the chemical structure of water.

The familiar chemical formula H_2O is the molecular representation of water. It is thus named because a water molecule consists of two hydrogen atoms and one oxygen atom. An important characteristic of the water molecule is that it is polar. This means that since the two hydrogen atoms carry a small positive charge and the oxygen atom carries a small negative charge, it has opposite charges at one or more positions within a single molecule.

3. States of Water

Students will learn that water can exist in three states.

Water can exist in three states, or forms. They include liquid water, solid ice, or gaseous water vapor. Liquid water has a definite volume, but it does not have a definite shape. Solid water, or ice, has both a definite volume and definite shape. In ice, the molecules are more spread out than they are in liquid water. Because of this, water is unique in that it is less dense as a solid than as a liquid. Therefore, ice floats in liquid water. Water vapor is an invisible gas that does not have a definite shape nor definite volume. It can either expand or be compressed to fill available space.

4. Properties of Water

Students will become familiar with four properties that result from water's polarity.

Water's polarity causes several properties that make it unique.

- Water has high cohesion, which means that water molecules are attracted to each other. This characteristic results in water's tendency to bead up into droplets whenever possible.

- Water also has high adhesion, which means that it is attracted to other polar molecules. This characteristic results in water soaking into several substances, such as paper towels.

- Water has a high specific heat, which means that the amount of energy needed to change the temperature of water by 1 degree Celsius is relatively high compared to many substances. This characteristic of water is key to water's role in weather and climate.

- Water is known as a universal solvent because it dissolves many substances, such as minerals. This characteristic allows water to transport important substances around the Earth system and also within organisms.

©Image Plan/Corbis

 COMMON MISCONCEPTIONS **RTI**

WATER VAPOR Students often mistakenly think that water vapor is visible. Water vapor is an invisible gas mostly found in the atmosphere.

This misconception is addressed in the Quick Lab on p. 15 and on p. 22.

Lesson 3 Surface Water and Groundwater   Make a simple groundwater model by filling a locking plastic bag with water. Place the sealed bag between a layer of gravel and and a layer of soil in a clear plastic container. Water can be poured on top to filter down into the ground to show the zones of saturation. The "aquifer" can be opened by putting a straw down into the bag to illustrate how water for a well can be accessed.

Lesson 2

The Water Cycle

ESSENTIAL QUESTION
How does water change state and move around on Earth?

1. Water Cycle and Change of State

Water changes and moves.

The water cycle is the continuous movement of water between the atmosphere, land, oceans, and living things. Water changes from one state to another in the processes of the water cycle. The scientific use of the word *water* includes solid and gaseous water as well as liquid water.

Water changes state when sufficient energy is absorbed or released. In water's solid state, molecules of water are held almost stationary. But when energy is absorbed by the ice, the molecules move more rapidly. They break from their fixed positions and slide past each other in the fluid form of a liquid. When more energy is absorbed by liquid water, the water changes from a liquid to a gas. Because the additional energy causes the movement of molecules in liquid water to speed up, the molecules collide more frequently with each other. Such collisions can cause the molecules to move so rapidly that the fastest moving molecules escape from the liquid to form invisible water vapor in a process called evaporation.

The energy that is absorbed or released by a substance during a change of state is called latent heat. When liquid water evaporates, the water absorbs energy from the environment. When water vapor changes back into a liquid through the process of condensation, energy is released to the surrounding air and the molecules move closer together. Likewise, latent heat is absorbed when ice thaws, and latent heat is released when water freezes. There's a large change in density and energy between gas and solid and liquid. Sometimes, changes in state alter the temperature of a substance in surprising ways. For example, when water condenses, it releases energy, increasing the temperature.

2. Water in the Atmosphere

Water is in the air around us.

Water reaches the atmosphere by the processes of evaporation, transpiration, and sublimation. Transpiration is the process by which plants release water vapor into the air.

Ice usually changes into a liquid before changing into a gas. However, ice can change directly into water vapor without becoming a liquid through the process of sublimation. When the air is dry and the temperature is below freezing, ice and snow may sublime into water vapor. Water vapor can also deposit directly into ice without becoming a liquid.

3. Water in the Oceans and on Land

Water moves in currents, runoff, and ice flows.

Water circulates in ocean currents. Winds that blow across the surface of Earth's oceans push water across Earth's surface, causing horizontal, stream-like movements of water called surface currents. Surface currents can be several hundred meters deep and can flow several thousand kilometers across oceans.

The currents transfer, or distribute, energy from one part of Earth to another. Both warm-water and cold-water currents travel from one part of the ocean to another. Water near the equator absorbs energy from sunlight. Then, warm-water currents carry this energy to other parts of the ocean.

4. Transport of Matter and Energy

The water cycle carries more than water.

The water cycle transports matter and energy. Examples of matter transported by the water cycle include water itself as it moves around Earth, matter that is dissolved in liquid water, and matter such as sediment that can be suspended and carried in flowing water. Examples of the ways in which the water cycle transports energy include warm ocean currents warming air along cooler coastlines and water that evaporates from a warm ocean surface carrying heat energy into the atmosphere.

Content Refresher (continued)

Professional Development

Lesson 3

Surface Water and Groundwater

ESSENTIAL QUESTION

How does fresh water flow on Earth's surface and below ground?

1. Surface Water

Students will learn how water collects on Earth's surface, and why this water is important.

Earth has abundant water, but nearly all of it (97%) is salt water in the ocean. This water is unusable by land plants and animals. If one were to place a human blood cell in salt water, water would rush out of the cell due to osmosis, causing the cell to shrivel and die. Only about 3% of Earth's water is in the form of fresh, liquid water, the form that we can use.

Surface water results from precipitation. The precipitation flows across the surface as *runoff*, which then gathers in streams, rivers, lakes, and other bodies of water. Some surface water soaks into the ground, where it becomes groundwater.

Due to gravity, water flows downhill across Earth's surface. As it flows, it weathers and erodes the rocks and soil over which it flows, carving out a path, called a *channel*. Over time, channels become wider and deeper; the more rapid the flow of the water, the more effective it is at erosion.

High in mountains or hills, runoff gathers in small streams, which in turn gather together to form larger streams, which flow together to form a river. A small stream or river that feeds a larger river or a lake is called a *tributary*.

Mountain streams often move rapidly and have great erosive power. This is because they have a steep *gradient*, or slope. As a stream flows over flatter lands, it slows down and loses energy; at this point, the *stream load*, or amount of material carried in the stream, may be reduced by deposition along the river's shore or floor.

The area that supplies all the water to a river and its tributaries is called a *watershed*. A watershed can be compared to a large sink. Precipitation that falls anywhere in the watershed will flow downward and eventually reach the mouth of the river. Watersheds are separated by divides; in the United States, a long divide (the continental divide) along the Rocky Mountains separates the Mississippi River Basin from streams that flow toward the Pacific Ocean.

2. Groundwater

Students will learn how groundwater collects and how groundwater is useful.

Groundwater collects in the spaces between rock and soil particles and in the cracks of rocks. It sinks downward until it reaches a layer of impermeable rock (such as clay) and then gathers above this layer. The upper part of the soil that is filled with water is called the *water table*. The water table can reach the surface at lakes, rivers, and wetlands.

An *aquifer* is a rock layer that contains groundwater. To tap this water, people dig wells down from the surface. The base of a well will readily fill with water if the aquifer has the proper qualities. A productive aquifer is usually made of material that has high porosity, meaning there are many pores between the particles that make up the material; the pores allow the material to hold water. The aquifer should also have high permeability, meaning that the pores are connected and water can flow through them.

Aquifers gain water that seeps down from the surface, a process called *recharge*. Aquifers also lose water that seeps out of the ground or flows onto the surface, processes called *discharge*. Human actions, especially the use of wells, have been draining many aquifers. In the southwestern United States, for example, where the climate is hot and dry, aquifers have been tapped extensively to supply water to expanding cities and farms. The draining of aquifers not only causes less water to be available but can also lead to land subsidence, or sinking.

©Ken Thomas

Teacher Notes

Advance Planning

These activities may take extended time or special conditions.

Unit 1

Project Conserving Water, p. 11
    survey and plan

Graphic Organizers and Vocabulary pp. 17, 18, 31, 32, 49, 50
    ongoing with reading

Lesson 3

Daily Demo Rock Spaces, p. 47
    small and large pebbles

Exploration Lab Aquifers and Development, p. 47
    collect local soil and other materials in advance

Differentiated Instruction (Basic) River Load, p. 49
    collect grass, soil, and other materials in advance

UNIT 1

Earth's Water

Big Idea
Water moves through Earth's atmosphere, oceans, and land in a cycle and is essential for life on Earth.

Waterfalls show the important role gravity plays in moving Earth's water.

What do you think?
Fresh water is found in ponds, lakes, streams, rivers, and underground in aquifers. Where does the water in your school come from?

Humans rely on water to stay healthy.

What Do You Think?

Encourage students to consider how important water is to life on Earth.

Ask: What are some ways in which people use water? Sample answers: for drinking, bathing, brushing teeth, cooking, and cleaning

Ask: Why should we conserve fresh water? Sample answer: Even though water is a renewable resource, supplies of fresh water are limited. Conserving water helps to ensure that there will be enough water in the future.

Ask: Where are some places on Earth that you would find water in either its solid, liquid, or gaseous form? Sample answers: rivers, lakes, oceans, glaciers, icebergs, clouds, the air, underground

Probing Questions GUIDED Inquiry

Synthesizing How does a stream like the one shown in the image contribute to the formation of beaches that are miles away? Moving water in streams and rivers breaks down rock particles into sediments. The water carries the sediments as it flows downstream. Eventually the sediments are deposited where the stream or river meets an ocean. Wave action will eventually push the sediments up onto the shoreline to form sandy beaches.

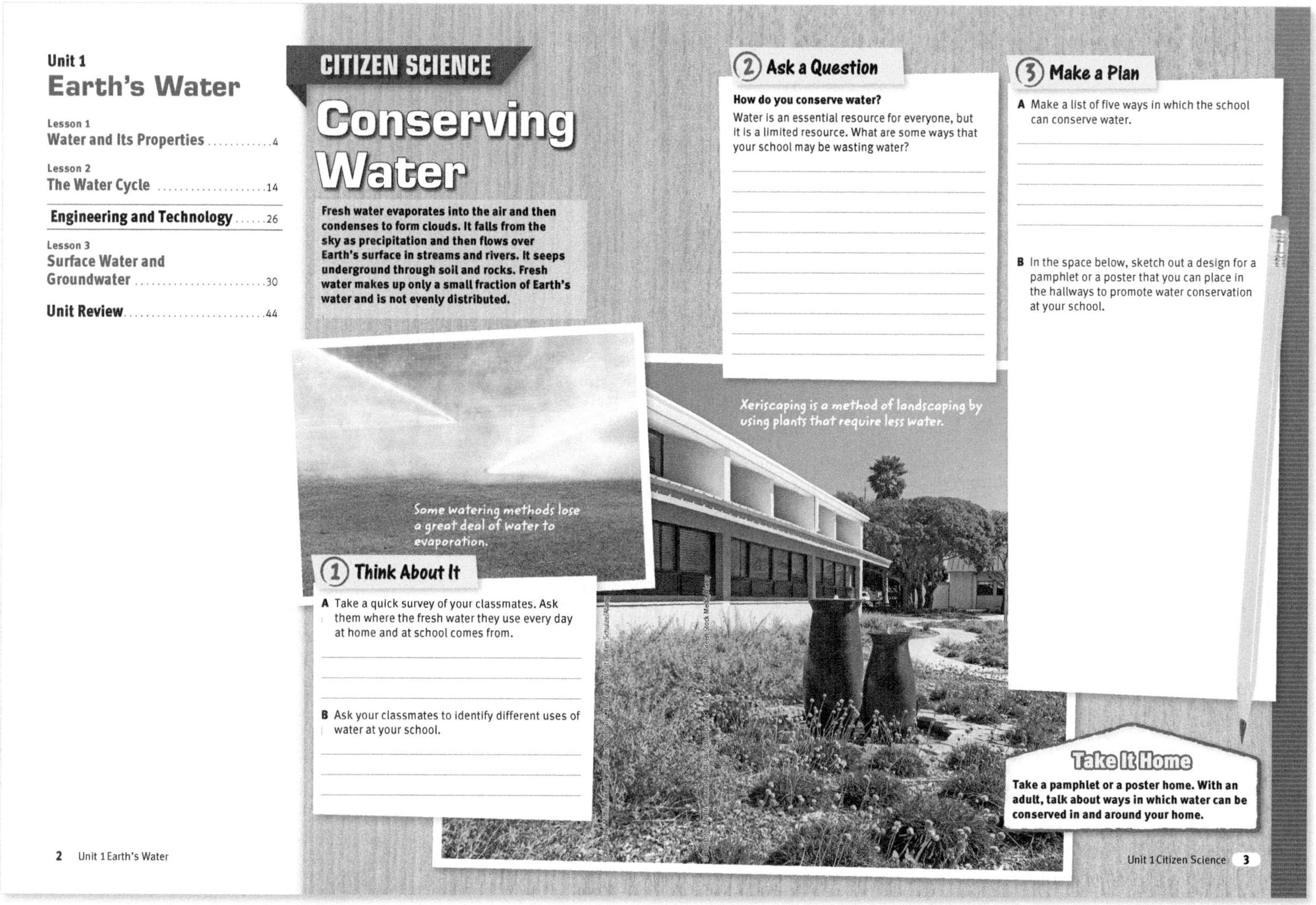

Unit 1
Earth's Water

CITIZEN SCIENCE

Conserving Water

Fresh water evaporates into the air and then condenses to form clouds. It falls from the sky as precipitation and then flows over Earth's surface in streams and rivers. It seeps underground through soil and rocks. Fresh water makes up only a small fraction of Earth's water and is not evenly distributed.

Some watering methods lose a great deal of water to evaporation.

Xeriscaping is a method of landscaping by using plants that require less water.

1 Think About It

A Take a quick survey of your classmates. Ask them where the fresh water they use every day at home and at school comes from.

B Ask your classmates to identify different uses of water at your school.

2 Ask a Question

How do you conserve water?
Water is an essential resource for everyone, but it is a limited resource. What are some ways that your school may be wasting water?

3 Make a Plan

A Make a list of five ways in which the school can conserve water.

B In the space below, sketch out a design for a pamphlet or a poster that you can place in the hallways to promote water conservation at your school.

Take It Home

Take a pamphlet or a poster home. With an adult, talk about ways in which water can be conserved in and around your home.

2   Unit 1 Earth's Water

Unit 1 Citizen Science   3

CITIZEN SCIENCE

Unit Project Conserving Water

1. Think About It

Student surveys should focus on identifying the source of the water used in their homes and at the school. If students don't know the water source, have them research it on the Internet.

2. Ask a Question

Encourage students to think of places where water is used on campus, such as bubblers, bathrooms, and lawns. Remind students to consider not only their own water use, but also ways in which school employees use water in places like the cafeteria. Discuss uses of water that may result in waste.

Optional Online rubric: Class Discussion

3. Make a Plan

A. Students should list five reasonable ways in which the school can conserve water. These can be actions that students can take, or actions that school employees can take.

B. Pamphlets or posters should clearly communicate the issues surrounding water conservation.

Optional Online rubric: Posters and Displays

Take It Home

Ask students to provide a note from an adult confirming that the student discussed the topic with him or her. Ask students to share some of the ideas that resulted from brainstorming with adults.

Water and Its Properties

Essential Question What makes water so important?

 **Professional Development**

For more detailed information about the topics in this lesson, refer to the Content Refresher in the Unit Opener pages.

Opening Your Lesson

Begin the lesson by assessing students' prerequisite and prior knowledge.

Prerequisite Knowledge

- Living things need water.
- Water has an important role in weather.
- Water can be in the form of a solid (ice), a liquid, or a gas (water vapor).

Accessing Prior Knowledge

Ask: What happens to living things, such as plants and animals, if they don't get enough water? Sample answer: Animals get dehydrated and plants wither. This may prevent them from functioning.

Ask: What are some things that we use water for? Sample answers: for drinking; for cleaning; for bathing; for watering plants

Customize Your Opening

- ☐ **Accessing Prior Knowledge,** above
- ☐ **Print Path** Engage Your Brain, SE p. 5 #1–2
- ☐ **Print Path** Active Reading, SE p. 5 #3–4
- ☐ **Digital Path** Lesson Opener

Key Topics/Learning Goals	Supporting Concepts
Importance and Distribution of Water 1 Explain water's importance to Earth's surface and weather, and to living organisms, including humans. 2 Describe the distribution of water on Earth.	• Water shapes Earth's surface and weather. • Water is vital for life, and every living thing is partly made up of water. Humans need access to clean water in order to stay healthy. Contaminated water sources are a major public health problem in many countries. • About 70% of Earth is covered by water. About 3% of that is fresh water; the rest is salt water.
Structure of Water 1 Describe the structure of water. 2 Explain why water is a polar molecule.	• Water is made of two hydrogen atoms and one oxygen atom. The formula is H_2O. • A water molecule is polar because each hydrogen atom has a small positive charge and the oxygen atom has a small negative charge.
States of Water 1 Describe the three states of water on Earth. 2 Describe the properties of water in each of these three states.	• Most water on Earth occurs as a liquid, which exists mainly on and below Earth's surface. Water also occurs on Earth as a gas called water vapor, and as a solid in the form of ice or snow. • Liquid water takes the shape of its container. Water vapor fills available space and also takes the shape of its container. Molecules in liquid water are closer together than those of solid water. Therefore ice is less dense than liquid water.
Properties of Water 1 Explain the properties of water.	• The properties of water include cohesion, adhesion, specific heat, nature as a solvent, and nature as a transporter of vital substances through organisms.

Options for Instruction

Two parallel paths provide coverage of the Essential Questions, with a strong **Inquiry** strand woven into each.
Follow the **Print Path,** the **Digital Path,** or your customized combination of print, digital, and inquiry.

Print Path
Teaching support for the Print Path appears with the Student Pages.

Inquiry Labs and Activities

Digital Path
Digital Path shortcut: TS661765

Watered Down, SE pp. 6–7
What are some of water's roles on Earth?
• Influencing Weather
• Shaping Earth's Surface
• Supporting Life
• Supporting Human Activities

Activity
Water Sport

Earth's Water
Interactive Graphics

Water's Importance
Slideshow

Molecular Attraction, SE p. 8
What is the structure of a water molecule?
What makes water a polar molecule?

Activity
The Elements of Water

Water's Structure
Video

Water Is a Polar Molecule
Interactive Graphics

Molecular Attraction, SE p. 9
What states of water occur on Earth?

Quick Lab
Reaching the Dew Point

Quick Lab
Compare Densities

Activity
United States of Water

Water's States
Interactive Graphics

More about Water's States
Interactive Graphics

The Universal Solvent,
SE pp. 10–11
What are four properties of water?

Activity
Property Signs

Daily Demo
Presenting Properties

Cohesion and Adhesion
Video

Specific Heat and Universal Solvent
Interactive Images

Options for Assessment

See the Evaluate page for options, including Formative Assessment, Summative Assessment, and Unit Review.

Engage and Explore

Activities and Discussion

Activity *Property Signs*

Properties of Water

 small groups
 varied
 DIRECTED inquiry

Display Organize students into groups of four. Assign each member of the group one of the four properties of water: cohesion, adhesion, specific heat, and solvent. Each student should research the property and make a display that describes the property using written paragraphs, drawings, diagrams, and examples. When students are finished, have them combine the four posters into one big class display that describes the four properties of water.

Variation If you have an uneven number of students for this activity, you can have one or two groups of three and direct the group members to work together to complete the fourth property poster.

⊙ *Optional Online rubric: Posters and Displays*

Probing Questions *Life Without Water?*

Importance and Distribution of Water

 whole class
 10 min
inquiry DIRECTED inquiry

Predicting Have students discuss the importance of fresh water to their lives. **Ask:** What might happen if the only water you had access to was polluted? Sample answers: I would get sick. I wouldn't be able to get clean. I wouldn't be able to drink clean water. **Ask:** Imagine that all the fresh water on Earth disappears. What would be some of the effects of this? Sample answers: Plants would die and eventually people wouldn't have anything to eat. You wouldn't have anything to drink. You'd get very sick.

Activity *United States of Water*

Introducing Key Topics

 individuals
 30–45 min
 INDEPENDENT inquiry

Direct students to write and illustrate a story about a water molecule and its experiences with other water molecules as it changes from a liquid state, to a solid state, and to a gaseous state. Encourage students to describe the conditions under which water exists in each of the three states and the characteristics of groups of water molecules in each of the three states. Also, encourage students to represent accurately the structure of a water molecule in their stories.

⊙ *Optional Online rubric: Written Pieces*

Activity *The Elements of Water*

Structure of Water

 individuals or pairs
 10–15 min
 GUIDED inquiry

Models Provide students with toothpicks and gumdrops, foam balls, or some other objects that will work well for modeling the structure of a water molecule. Make sure that students use one colored object for the oxygen atom and another color for the two hydrogen atoms. **Ask:** What types of charges do the atoms that make up water have? The hydrogen atoms have a positive charge; the oxygen atom has a negative charge. **Ask:** Why is water also called H_2O? Water is called H_2O because it is made of two hydrogen atoms and one oxygen atom.

To extend the activity, students can use models to compare the structure of liquid water and solid water (ice). This may help demonstrate why ice is less dense than liquid water.

Customize Your Labs

📖 *See the Lab Manual for lab datasheets.*

⊙ *Go Online for editable lab datasheets.*

(tr) ©PhotoDisc/Getty Images; (br) ©Corbis

Levels of  **Inquiry**

DIRECTED inquiry
introduces inquiry skills within a structured framework.

GUIDED inquiry
develops inquiry skills within a supportive environment.

INDEPENDENT inquiry
deepens inquiry skills with student-driven questions or procedures.

Labs and Demos

Quick Lab *Comparing Densities*

States of Water, Properties of Water

👥 small groups
🕐 25 min
(Inquiry) **DIRECTED** inquiry

Students will compute the densities of solid water (ice) and liquid water.

PURPOSE **To compare the properties of water in its liquid and solid state**

MATERIALS

- balance
- calculator
- graduated cylinder, 250 mL
- ice cube
- paper clip (unbent)
- water, cold

Quick Lab *Reaching the Dew Point*

States of Water

👥 small groups
🕐 10 min
(Inquiry) **DIRECTED** inquiry

Students will observe how water vapor condenses on the outside of a cup filled with cold water.

PURPOSE **To observe how water changes from a gas to a liquid**

MATERIALS

- cup, plastic
- ice cubes (1–2)
- water, room temperature

Daily Demo *Presenting Properties*

Engage

Properties of Water

👥 whole class
🕐 25 min
(Inquiry) **GUIDED** inquiry

Use this demo after introducing students to the properties of water.

PURPOSE **To demonstrate the properties of water**

MATERIALS

- beaker and Bunsen burner or an electric tea kettle
- cup
- eye dropper
- paper towels
- salt
- water

1 Place a few drops of water on a desk. Have students examine the droplets at eye level so they can see that the water forms a rounded droplet. **Ask:** What property of water is being demonstrated? cohesion

2 Heat the water. Once it has started to boil and release steam, **Ask:** What property of water is being demonstrated? specific heat Tell students that water freezes at 0 °C and boils at 100 °C. Substances with lower or higher specific heats freeze and boil at different temperatures.

3 Pour a small amount of water onto the desk. Place a corner of a paper towel next to the spill. Point out that the water starts to immediately soak into the paper towel. **Ask:** What property of water is being demonstrated? adhesion

4 Pour a small amount of salt into a cup and then add warm water. Stir the water until the salt dissolves. **Ask:** What property of water is being demonstrated? its nature as a good solvent

---

Activities and Discussion

☐ **Activity** Property Signs
☐ **Probing Questions** Life Without Water?
☐ **Activity** United States of Water
☐ **Activity** The Elements of Water

Labs and Demos

☐ **Quick Lab** Compare Densities
☐ **Quick Lab** Reaching the Dew Point
☐ **Daily Demo** Presenting Properties

Your Resources

_____

_____

_____

Explain Science Concepts

	📖 Print Path	💻 Digital Path
Key Topics		

Importance and Distribution of Water

☐ **Watered Down,** SE pp. 6–7
- Do the Math, #5
- Active Reading (Annotation strategy), #6
- Visualize It!, #7

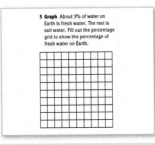

5 Graph About 3% of water on Earth is fresh water. The rest is salt water. Fill out the percentage grid to show the percentage of fresh water on Earth.

☐ **Earth's Water**
Describe the distribution of water on Earth.

☐ **Water's Importance**
Explain the importance of water on Earth.

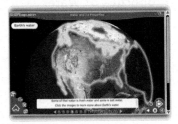

Structure of Water

☐ **Molecular Attraction,** SE p. 8
- Visualize It!, #8

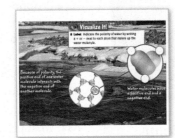

☐ **Water's Structure**
Describe the structure of water.

☐ **Water Is a Polar Molecule**
Explain why water is a polar molecule.

States of Water

☐ **Molecular Attraction,** SE p. 9
- Active Reading (Annotation strategy), #9
- Visualize It!, #10

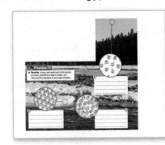

☐ **Water's States**
Identify the three states of water.

☐ **More about Water's States**
Identify the properties of water in each of the three states.

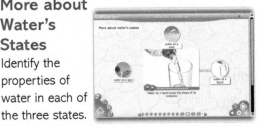

Properties of Water

☐ **The Universal Solvent,** SE pp. 10–11
- Visualize It!, #11
- Summarize, #12
- Think Outside the Book, #13

☐ **Cohesion and Adhesion**
Identify cohesion and adhesion as two properties of water.

☐ **Specific Heat and Universal Solvent**
Describe the specific heat of water and explain why water is called the "universal solvent."

Basic *Water Web*

Properties of Water | individuals
🕐 15 min

Main Idea Web Direct students to fill out a Main Idea Web to help them organize the properties of water. They can use *Water has unique properties* as the main idea in the center of the web. Then each branch can represent one of the four properties discussed in the lesson. Encourage students to include examples, explanations, illustrations, and key words on the next level of branches.

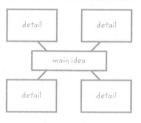

 Optional Online resource: Main Idea Web support

Advanced *Distribution Graphs*

Importance and Distribution of Water | individuals or pairs
🕐 varied

Circle Graphs Allow students to use information in the lesson and additional research to determine how much of Earth's surface is covered with water. Students will then use these data to make a circle graph that represents this information. For additional graphs, have students show the percentage of Earth's water that is fresh and the percentage of fresh water that is liquid. Challenge students to combine all of the information into one circle graph.

 Optional Online resources: Graphing Data, Circle Graph support

ELL *Synonym Study*

Introducing Key Topics | 👥 individuals or pairs
🕐 20 min ·

Three-column Chart The terms *properties, states,* and *structures* may be challenging for EL learners. Each of these terms has several synonyms that are more approachable. Have students make a three-column chart with each of the three terms at the top. Below each term, have students list synonyms, such as *traits, features,* or *qualities* for *properties; shape, form,* or *condition* for *state;* and *design, arrangement,* or *formation* for *structure.* Students may benefit from adding pictures to their lists.

 Optional Online resource: Three-column Chart support

polarity   cohesion   adhesion
specific heat   solvent

Previewing Vocabulary

👥 small groups, then whole class   🕐 15 min

Word Relationships Students may gain a better understanding of the vocabulary words if they study words that are related to the vocabulary terms. As a class, brainstorm a list of words related to some of the terms, such as *dissolve, poles, north pole, south pole, cohesive,* and *adhere.* Assign words to small groups and have them find definitions and example sentences that they will share with the class.

Reinforcing Vocabulary

👥 individuals   🕐 ongoing

Word Triangle As students encounter new vocabulary, have them complete Word Triangles for each term. To make a Word Triangle, have students draw a triangle and split it into three sections. In the bottom third, students will write the term and its definition; in the middle third, students will write a sentence using the term; and in the top third, students will draw an illustration of the term.

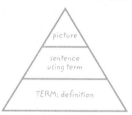

 Optional Online resource: Word Triangle support

Customize Your Core Lesson

Core Instruction
☐ **Print Path** choices
☐ **Digital Path** choices

Vocabulary
☐ **Previewing Vocabulary** Word Relationships
☐ **Reinforcing Vocabulary** Word Triangle

Your Resources

Differentiated Instruction
☐ **Basic** Water Web
☐ **Advanced** Distribution Graphs
☐ **ELL** Synonym Study

Extend Science Concepts

Reinforce and Review

Activity *Water Sport*

Synthesizing Key Topics   small groups
 15–20 min

Competitive Game

1 Split the class into teams of four or five students.

2 Present comprehension questions to each team. If a group answers a question correctly, they earn a point. If they miss a question, the next group gets a chance to answer.

3 Use the following questions and other comprehension questions from the lesson.

- True or False: All living things need water. True
- About what percentage of Earth is covered in water? 70%
- About what percentage of the water on Earth is fresh? 3%
- What is the chemical formula for water? H_2O
- Which two elements make up water? hydrogen and oxygen
- Why is water considered a polar molecule? It has a positive charge at two ends and a negative charge at another end.
- What are three states of water? solid/ice, liquid/liquid water, gas/water vapor
- What are four properties of water? high cohesion, high adhesion, high specific heat, universal solvent

Variation If individual white boards are available, each group can answer each question by writing their responses on white boards and holding up their responses at the same time when prompted.

FoldNote

Synthesizing Key Topics   individuals
ongoing

Layered Book Have students create a Layered Book FoldNote to cover the four key topic areas—*Importance and Distribution of Water, Structure of Water, States of Water,* and *Properties of Water.* As students read the lesson, encourage them to use the Layered Book to take notes.

Online resource: Layered Book support

Going Further

Language Arts Connection

Synthesizing Key Topics   individuals
varied

Water Poetry Share with students a few poems related to water. Have students write their own poems about water that integrate some of the ideas from the lesson. If students are struggling, encourage them to try an acrostic poem or a haiku. Encourage volunteers to read their poems to the rest of the class.

Physical Science Connection

Structure of Water   individuals or pairs
varied

Molecule Research Point out to students that water is just one example of a molecule. Remind students that molecules are made of atoms that have bonded together. Have students research the chemical formulas and molecular structures of other common substances, such as table salt, sugar, baking soda, or carbon dioxide, and then create a poster showing the formulas and structures of one or more molecules.

Customize Your Closing

⬛ *See the Assessment Guide for quizzes and tests.*

⬛ *Go Online to edit and create quizzes and tests.*

Reinforce and Review

☐ **Activity** Water Sport

☐ **FoldNote** Layered Book

☐ **Print Path** Visual Summary, SE p. 12

☐ **Digital Path** Lesson Closer

Evaluate Student Mastery

Formative Assessment

See the teacher support below the Student Pages for additional Formative Assessment questions.

Instruct students to summarize the key topics from the lesson. **Ask:** Why is water important? Sample answer: It shapes Earth's physical structures and weather. It is essential for all living things. **Ask:** How would you describe water's structure? It is made of two hydrogen atoms and one oxygen atom. **Ask:** What are the three states in which water exists on Earth? liquid: liquid water; solid: ice; gas: water vapor **Ask:** What are four of water's properties? It has high cohesion, high adhesion, high specific heat, and easily dissolves many substances.

Reteach

Formative assessment may show that students need reinforcement for certain topics. The resources below are recommended for reteaching. If students were introduced to a topic through the Print Path, you can also use the Digital Path to reteach, and vice versa.
🎧 *Can be assigned to individual students*

Importance and Distribution of Water
FoldNote Layered Book 🎧

Structure of Water
Activity The Elements of Water 🎧

States of Water
Quick Lab Comparing Densities
Activity United States of Water 🎧

Properties of Water
Basic Water Web 🎧

Summative Assessment

Alternative Assessment
Water Profile

🌐 *Online resources: student worksheet, optional rubrics*

Water and Its Properties

Mix and Match: *Water Profile*
Mix and match ideas to show what you've learned about water and its properties.

1. Work on your own, with a partner, or with a small group.
2. Choose one information source from Column A, two topics from Column B, and one option from Column C. Check your choices.
3. Have your teacher approve your plan.
4. Submit or present your results.

A. Choose One Information Source	B. Choose Two Things to Analyze	C. Choose One Way to Communicate Each Choice from the Analysis
___ magazine photo that includes water usage	___ uses of water	___ diagram or illustration
___ observations of the states of water	___ importance of water	___ colors or symbols marked on a visual, with a key
___ observations of weather	___ distribution of water	___ model, such as drawings or descriptions connected by strings
___ observations of water usage at home	___ structure of water	
___ observation of water's interaction with other substances	___ states of water	___ booklet, such as a field guide, travel brochure, playbook, or set of menus
___ photographs of water around a community	___ properties of water	___ game
___ illustration of a water molecule		___ story, song, or poem, with supporting details
___ video that discusses topics related to water		___ skit, chant, or dance, with supporting details
___ print or audio description that includes topics related to water		___ multimedia presentation
___ digital simulation of a concept related to water		

Going Further
☐ Language Arts Connection
☐ Physical Science Connection

Formative Assessment
☐ Strategies Throughout TE
☐ Lesson Review SE

Summative Assessment
☐ Alternative Assessment Water Profile
☐ Lesson Quiz
☐ Unit Tests A and B
☐ Unit Review SE End-of-Unit

Your Resources

_____

_____

Lesson ①

Water and Its Properties

ESSENTIAL QUESTION

What makes water so important?

By the end of this lesson, you should be able to describe water's structure, its properties, and its importance to Earth's systems.

Not all liquids form round droplets, but water does. Water's unique properties have to do with the way water molecules interact.

✋ **Lesson Labs**

Quick Labs
• Reaching the Dew Point
• Compare Densities

🧠 Engage Your Brain

1 Predict Check T or F to show whether you think each statement is true or false.

T F

☐ ☐ Most of the water on Earth is fresh water.

☐ ☐ Water exists in three different states on Earth.

☐ ☐ Water can dissolve many different substances, such as salt.

☐ ☐ Flowing water can be used to generate electricity.

2 Identify The drawing below shows a water molecule. What do each of the three parts represent?

_____

_____

📖 Active Reading

3 Synthesize You can often define an unknown word if you know the meaning of its word parts. Use the word parts and sentence below to make an educated guess about the meaning of the word *cohesion*.

Word part	Meaning
co-	with, together
-hesion	sticking, joined

Example sentence
When water forms droplets, it is displaying the property of cohesion.

Cohesion: _____

_____

_____

Vocabulary Terms

• polarity   • specific heat
• cohesion   • solvent
• adhesion

4 Apply As you learn the definition of each vocabulary term in this lesson, create your own definition or sketch to help you remember the meaning of the term.

4 Unit 1 Earth's Water

Lesson 1 Water and Its Properties 5

Answers

Answers for 1–3 should represent students' current thoughts, even if incorrect.

1. False; True; True; True

2. Each part represents an atom that makes up the water molecule. The two blue parts represent hydrogen, and the larger red part represents oxygen.

3. Sample answer: *Cohesion* means sticking together.

4. Students should define or sketch each vocabulary term in the lesson.

Opening Your Lesson

Discuss student responses to items 1 and 2 to assess students' prerequisite knowledge and to estimate what they already know about water and its properties.

Prerequisites Students should already know that water is essential for life and good health in humans, plants, and other animals, as well as water's role in weather. Students should also know that water freezes into ice and evaporates into a gas.

Building Reading Skills

SQ3R Present the SQ3R—Survey, Question, Read, Recite, Review—reading comprehension strategy to students. Model the first two steps as you introduce the lesson. Point out that surveying the lesson means quickly scanning the material for headers, images, bold words, and other information that provide insight without reading the entire lesson. Explain that the next step is asking questions, such as "What is this lesson about?" or "What am I going to learn about?" Direct students to try out the first two steps and then ask volunteers to share their ideas. As you continue with the lesson, remind students to implement "3R" of the method.

🌐 *Optional Online resource: SQ3R support*

Watered Down

Supporting Life

Every living thing is largely made up of water, and nearly all biological processes use water. All of an organism's cellular chemistry depends on water. Water regulates temperature and helps transport substances. Without water, animals and plants would dry up and die.

For humans, clean water is vital for good health. People must have clean water to drink in order to survive. Contaminated water sources are a major public health problem in many countries. Contaminated water is also harmful to plants, animals, and can affect crops that provide food for humans.

Supporting Human Activities

Clean drinking water is necessary for all humans. Many humans use water at home for bathing, cleaning, and watering lawns and gardens.

More fresh water is used in industry than is used in homes. Over 20% of the fresh water used by humans is used for industrial purposes—to manufacture goods, cool power stations, clean industrial products, extract minerals, and generate energy by using hydroelectric dams.

More water is used for agriculture than industry. Most water used for agriculture is used to irrigate crops. It is also used to care for farm animals.

What are some of water's roles on Earth?

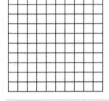

Do the Math

You Try It

5 Graph About 3% of water on Earth is fresh water. The rest is salt water. Fill out the percentage grid to show the percentage of fresh water on Earth.

Water shapes Earth's surface and influences Earth's weather. Water is also vital for life. In fact, you are over 70% water. You depend on clean, fresh drinking water to maintain that 70% of you. But a limited amount of fresh water is available on Earth. Only 3% of Earth's water is drinkable. Of this 3% of water that is drinkable, over 75% is frozen in the polar icecaps and is not readily available for our use. Therefore, it is important that we protect our water resources.

Influencing Weather

Active Reading 6 Identify As you read, underline four different forms of water that fall on Earth's surface.

All weather is related to water. Water constantly moves from Earth's surface to the atmosphere, where it may form clouds. Water falls back to Earth's surface again as rain, snow, hail, or sleet. Weather also depends on the amount of moisture in the air.

Shaping Earth's Surface

Over time, water can completely reshape a landscape. Water slowly wears away rock and carries away sediment and soil. Flowing rivers and pounding ocean waves are also examples of water shaping Earth's surface. Frozen water shapes Earth's surface, too. Glaciers, for example, scrape away rock and soil, depositing the sediment elsewhere when the glacier melts.

Visualize It!

7 List List at least four roles of water in this scene.

6   Unit 1 Earth's Water

© Houghton Mifflin Harcourt Publishing Company • Image Credits: ©Scott Barrow/Corbis

7

Answers

5. Students should mark three squares "fresh water" and 97 squares "salt water."

6. *See students' pages for annotations.*

7. Sample answer: Water makes up the clouds and the rain. Water is shaping the shoreline and is being used for fishing and boating. The lake is necessary for the survival of the local plants and animals.

Building Math Skills

After students have completed the graph in the Do the Math activity, explain that one of the ways that graphics can be helpful is to give readers a representation of an idea that is easier to show than to tell about. Ask students to explain what a reader could quickly conclude after seeing their graphics. Sample answer: A reader should be able to quickly conclude that only a very small amount of the water on Earth is fresh water; the rest is salt water.

Formative Assessment

Ask: What percentage of Earth's water is fresh water? 3% **Ask:** What percentage of Earth's fresh water is frozen? 75% **Ask:** What four roles does water have on Earth? Sample answer: Water influences weather, it shapes the landscape by breaking down and carrying away rock, it is vital for all living things, and it supports human activities, such as farming, industry, and recreational activities.

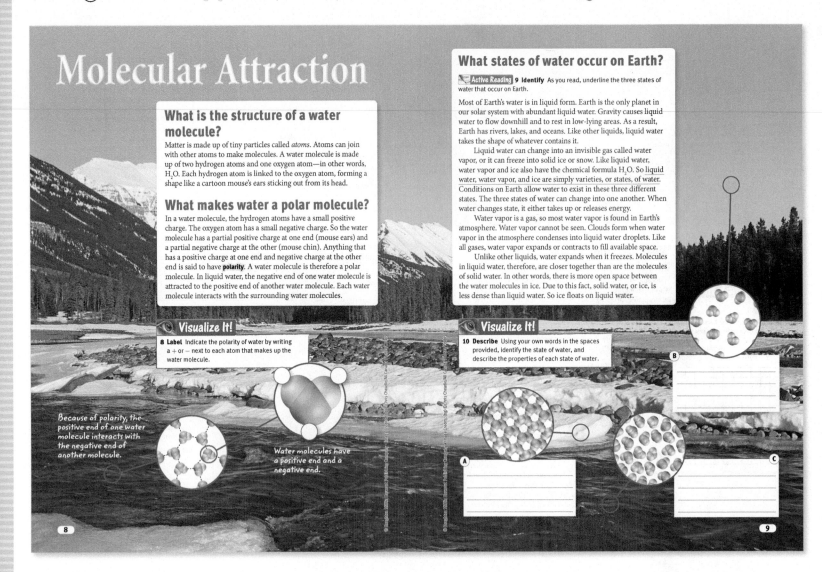

Molecular Attraction

What is the structure of a water molecule?

Matter is made up of tiny particles called *atoms*. Atoms can join with other atoms to make molecules. A water molecule is made up of two hydrogen atoms and one oxygen atom—in other words, H_2O. Each hydrogen atom is linked to the oxygen atom, forming a shape like a cartoon mouse's ears sticking out from its head.

What makes water a polar molecule?

In a water molecule, the hydrogen atoms have a small positive charge. The oxygen atom has a small negative charge. So the water molecule has a partial positive charge at one end (mouse ears) and a partial negative charge at the other (mouse chin). Anything that has a positive charge at one end and negative charge at the other end is said to have **polarity**. A water molecule is therefore a polar molecule. In liquid water, the negative end of one water molecule is attracted to the positive end of another water molecule. Each water molecule interacts with the surrounding water molecules.

🅥 Visualize It!

8 Label Indicate the polarity of water by writing a + or − next to each atom that makes up the water molecule.

Because of polarity, the positive end of one water molecule interacts with the negative end of another molecule.

Water molecules have a positive end and a negative end.

8

What states of water occur on Earth?

Active Reading **9 Identify** As you read, underline the three states of water that occur on Earth.

Most of Earth's water is in liquid form. Earth is the only planet in our solar system with abundant liquid water. Gravity causes liquid water to flow downhill and to rest in low-lying areas. As a result, Earth has rivers, lakes, and oceans. Like other liquids, liquid water takes the shape of whatever contains it.

Liquid water can change into an invisible gas called water vapor, or it can freeze into solid ice or snow. Like liquid water, water vapor and ice also have the chemical formula H_2O. So liquid water, water vapor, and ice are simply varieties, or states, of water. Conditions on Earth allow water to exist in these three different states. The three states of water can change into one another. When water changes state, it either takes up or releases energy.

Water vapor is a gas, so most water vapor is found in Earth's atmosphere. Water vapor cannot be seen. Clouds form when water vapor in the atmosphere condenses into liquid water droplets. Like all gases, water vapor expands or contracts to fill available space.

Unlike other liquids, water expands when it freezes. Molecules in liquid water, therefore, are closer together than are the molecules of solid water. In other words, there is more open space between the water molecules in ice. Due to this fact, solid water, or ice, is less dense than liquid water. So ice floats on liquid water.

🅥 Visualize It!

10 Describe Using your own words in the spaces provided, identify the state of water, and describe the properties of each state of water.

B

A

C

9

Answers

8. Students should draw a + above the hydrogen atoms and a − below the oxygen atom.

9. *See students' pages for annotations.*

10. A. Ice is a solid. It is less dense than water, so it floats on water; B. Water vapor is a gas, so it expands or contracts to fill available space; C. Liquid water flows downhill and takes the shape of whatever it is in.

Building Reading Skills

Summarizing Point out to students that summarizing is a useful skill when reading sections of a lesson. Explain that a summary includes the most important ideas from text but does not include every detail. Have students orally summarize the section describing the structure of a water molecule to a partner. Then, ask volunteers to share with the class. Sample answer: Water is a molecule made of two atoms of hydrogen and one atom of oxygen. Water is a polar molecule because its hydrogen atoms have a positive charge and its oxygen atoms have a negative charge.

🌐 *Optional Online resource: Summarizing support*

Learning Alert 🚧 MISCONCEPTION 🚧

Water Vapor Is Invisible Students are drawn to hands-on and visual examples, so they may mistakenly believe that clouds, fog, and steam are examples of water vapor. Point out to students that although these examples do float in the air, as water vapor does, they are actually examples of liquid water that are suspended in tiny droplets in the air. Emphasize that water vapor is invisible. **Ask:** How do you know that clouds and steam are not actually water vapor? You can see clouds and steam, but water vapor is an invisible gas, so they cannot be water vapor.

The Universal Solvent

What are four properties of water?

The polarity of water molecules affects the properties of water. This is because water's polarity affects how water molecules interact with one another and with other types of molecules.

It Sticks to Itself

The property that holds molecules of a substance together is **cohesion**. Water molecules stick together tightly because of their polarity, so water has high cohesion. Because of cohesion, water forms droplets. And water poured gently into a glass can fill it above the rim because cohesion holds the water molecules together. Some insects can walk on still water because their weight does not break the cohesion of the water molecules.

It Sticks to Other Substances

The property that holds molecules of different substances together is **adhesion**. Polar substances other than water can attract water molecules more strongly than water molecules attract each other. These substances are called "wettable" because water adheres, or sticks, to them so tightly. Paper towels, for example, are wettable. Water drops roll off unwettable, or "waterproof," surfaces, which are made of non-polar molecules.

Visualize It!

11 Label Identify each photo as representing either adhesion or cohesion. Then write captions explaining the properties of water shown by each photo.

(A)

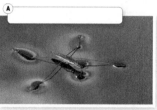

(B)

These stalactites formed as water dripped down and left dissolved minerals behind.

pull lar ruh tee

It Can Absorb Large Amounts of Energy

The energy needed to heat a substance by a particular amount is called its **specific heat**. As water is warmed, its molecules are separated a little as the water expands. The attraction between polar water molecules means that separating them takes a great deal of energy, so the specific heat of water is very high. Because of its high specific heat, water can absorb more energy than many other substances can.

Warm water stores more energy than cold water does. And water vapor stores much more energy than liquid water does. The stored energy is released when warm water cools and when water vapor cools to form liquid. This ability of water to store and release heat is very important in weather and climate.

It Dissolves Many Things

A liquid that dissolves substances is called a **solvent**. Because of its polarity, water dissolves many substances. Therefore, water is often called the universal solvent. Salt, or NaCl, is a familiar substance that water dissolves.

Water as a solvent is very important to living things. Water transports vital dissolved substances through organisms. And most of the chemical reactions that take place inside organisms involve substances dissolved in water.

Only this one doesn't dissolve quickly in water.

12 Summarize What characteristic of water accounts for its properties of adhesion, cohesion, high specific heat, and nature as a solvent?

Think Outside the Book Inquiry

13 Apply Water dissolves a substance until the water becomes saturated and can dissolve no more of the substance. Starting with 100 ml water, determine how much salt or sugar can be dissolved before the solution is saturated.

(11)

Answers

11. A. Cohesion; Sample caption: The insect does not sink into the water because the cohesion of water molecules forms a strong surface. B. Adhesion; Sample caption: Water droplets adhere to the spider web.

12. polarity

13. Student output should include the quantity of salt or sugar that was used to saturate the solution. Answers will vary depending on the temperature of the water.

Building Reading Skills

Student Vocabulary Point out to students that there are several new vocabulary terms in this section of the lesson. Remind students that context clues can usually be found in the text surrounding a word. Have students locate some of the context clues that can help them better understand the meanings of the highlighted terms. cohesion: force that holds molecules of a substance together, stick together, forms droplets; adhesion: holds molecules of different substances together, attract water molecules, "wettable"; specific heat: energy needed to heat a substance by a particular amount, absorb more energy; solvent: liquid that dissolves substances, universal solvent

🌎 Optional Online resource: Student Vocabulary support

Probing Question   GUIDED Inquiry

Recognizing What are some examples of vital substances that are transported by water in organisms? Sample answers: salts, vitamins, dissolved oxygen and carbon dioxide, macromolecules such as proteins, fats, and carbohydrates If students have difficulty thinking of materials that are transported through the body, point out that blood is made of plasma, a clear, yellowish fluid that is 90% water. **Ask:** What are some examples of vital substances that are transported in the blood?

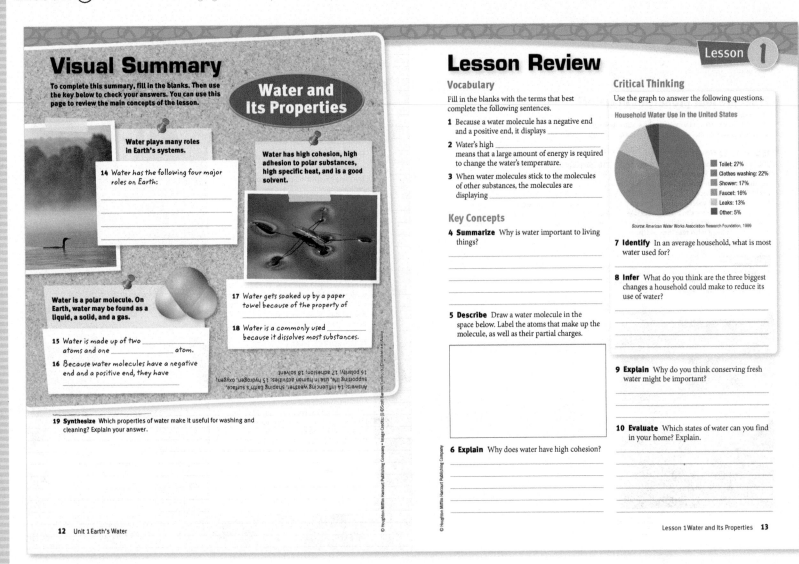

Visual Summary Answers

14. influencing weather; shaping Earth's surface; supporting life; use in human activities

15. hydrogen; oxygen

16. polarity

17. adhesion

18. solvent

19. Sample answer: Water's ability to dissolve substances helps it dissolve and carry away dirt. Its ability to adhere to other molecules also helps it remove stains.

Lesson Review Answers

1. polarity

2. specific heat

3. adhesion

4. Sample answer: All living things are made up mostly of water. Water is used for many biological processes.

5. Student drawings should resemble the illustration of a water molecule in the Visual Summary.

6. Its molecules are polar, so the oppositely charged ends of the molecules are attracted to one another.

7. toilet flushing

8. Sample answer: using a low-flow toilet or flushing less; using a low-flow showerhead or limiting bathing time/frequency; watering the garden only at night

9. Sample answer: Earth has a very limited supply of fresh water, and fresh water is necessary for the survival of living things.

10. Sample answer: Liquid water flows from the faucets in my home. Solid water, or ice, is found in the freezer in the kitchen. Water vapor is invisible, but it is in the air throughout the house. Sometimes the water vapor condenses on the bathroom mirror or on the windows and then is visible as liquid water.

The Water Cycle

Essential Question How does water change state and move around on Earth?

Professional Development

For more detailed information about the topics in this lesson, refer to the Content Refresher in the Unit Opener pages.

Opening Your Lesson

Begin the lesson by assessing students' prerequisite and prior knowledge.

Prerequisite Knowledge

- Knowledge that water can be solid, liquid, or gas
- Understanding of the everyday definition of *atmosphere*

Accessing Prior Knowledge

Ask: Where on Earth can you find water? Sample answers: oceans; lakes; glaciers; snow; clouds; rain; the air around us

Ask: Are all of your answers to the first question examples of liquid water only? Sample answer: No, there is also ice and water vapor in our list.

Customize Your Opening

- ☐ **Accessing Prior Knowledge,** above
- ☐ **Print Path** Engage Your Brain, SE p. 15, #1–2
- ☐ **Print Path** Active Reading, SE p. 15, #3–4
- ☐ **Digital Path** Lesson Opener

Key Topics/Learning Goals	Supporting Concepts
Water Cycle and Change of State 1 Define *water cycle*. 2 List the states of matter and describe how changes of state occur.	• The water cycle is the movement of water on Earth. • The three states of matter are solid, liquid, and gas. Melting, freezing, evaporation, condensation, sublimation, and deposition are processes by which matter changes states.
Water in the Atmosphere 1 Define and describe three ways that water reaches the atmosphere. 2 Define and describe *condensation* and *precipitation*.	• Water reaches the atmosphere by evaporation (liquid water turning to water vapor), transpiration (plants releasing water vapor), and sublimation (ice turning to water vapor). • Water vapor can condense to form droplets of liquid water in the atmosphere. • Precipitation is any form of water, such as rain or snow, that falls to Earth's surface.
Water in the Oceans and on Land 1 Describe what happens to water after it falls to Earth.	• Water circulates in ocean currents. • Water flows as runoff over Earth's land. • Water seeps into the ground. • Water is stored in snow and ice.
Transport of Matter and Energy 1 List and provide examples of two things that the water cycle transports.	• The water cycle transports matter and energy. Examples of matter transported by the water cycle include water itself, matter that is dissolved in water, and sediment that can be suspended in water. The water cycle transports energy as water changes state and as the movement of water brings energy to different parts of Earth.

Options for Instruction

Two parallel paths provide coverage of the Essential Questions, with a strong **Inquiry** strand woven into each. Follow the **Print Path,** the **Digital Path,** or your customized combination of print, digital, and inquiry.

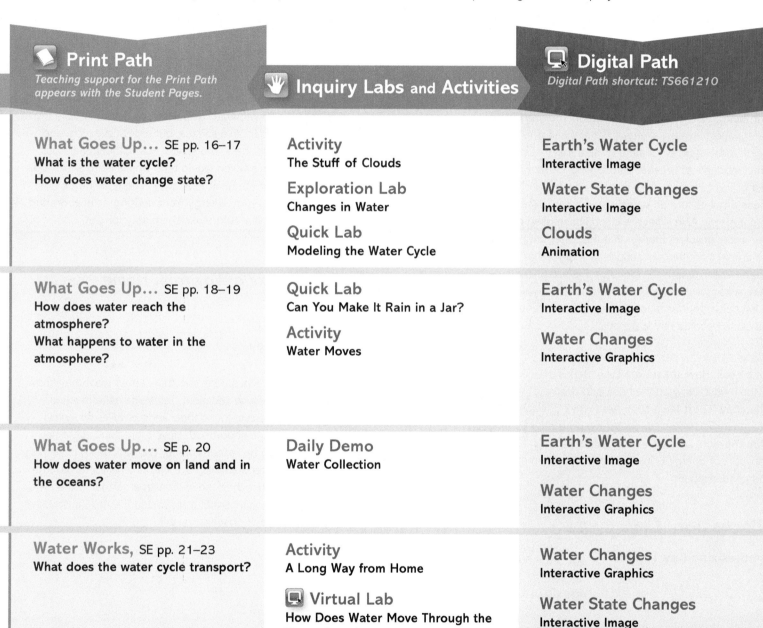

Print Path
Teaching support for the Print Path appears with the Student Pages.

Inquiry Labs and Activities

Digital Path
Digital Path shortcut: TS661210

What Goes Up... SE pp. 16–17
What is the water cycle?
How does water change state?

Activity
The Stuff of Clouds

Exploration Lab
Changes in Water

Quick Lab
Modeling the Water Cycle

Earth's Water Cycle
Interactive Image

Water State Changes
Interactive Image

Clouds
Animation

What Goes Up... SE pp. 18–19
How does water reach the atmosphere?
What happens to water in the atmosphere?

Quick Lab
Can You Make It Rain in a Jar?

Activity
Water Moves

Earth's Water Cycle
Interactive Image

Water Changes
Interactive Graphics

What Goes Up... SE p. 20
How does water move on land and in the oceans?

Daily Demo
Water Collection

Earth's Water Cycle
Interactive Image

Water Changes
Interactive Graphics

Water Works, SE pp. 21–23
What does the water cycle transport?

Activity
A Long Way from Home

Virtual Lab
How Does Water Move Through the Water Cycle?

Water Changes
Interactive Graphics

Water State Changes
Interactive Image

Options for Assessment

See the Evaluate page for options, including Formative Assessment, Summative Assessment, and Unit Review.

Engage and Explore

Activities and Discussion

Activity *The Stuff of Clouds*

Engage

Introducing Key Topics

 whole class
🕐 15 min
 GUIDED inquiry

Ask students to cup their hands and breathe onto their palms. Explain that their breath contains water vapor. Their hands feel warm because water vapor releases energy (to their hands) as it condenses (onto their hands). **Ask:** What state of matter is water vapor? a gas Next, direct students to breathe onto a glass or mirror. Tell them that the mist or fog on the glass or mirror is made up of tiny water droplets. These droplets formed when water vapor in their breath condensed on the mirror. **Ask:** What are clouds composed of? Sample answer: tiny water droplets Explain that the water droplets in clouds are like the droplets on the cool surface of the glass or mirror. **Ask:** Where did the water droplets in clouds come from? They condensed from water vapor in the air. Explain that when the air temperature in the vicinity of a cloud is below freezing, the water droplets that make up the cloud become tiny ice crystals.

GUIDED inquiry Give each student a wet cotton ball. Have them wipe it on the inside of their wrist, blow on the spot, and describe what they feel. It feels cool. **Ask:** Why? Energy was absorbed when the water evaporated from the skin. Discuss with students how the transport of energy is involved in evaporation and condensation.

Discussion *Circle Cycles*

Synthesizing Key Topics

 individuals
🕐 10 min
 GUIDED inquiry

After discussing the parts of the water cycle, challenge students to show the simplest and most common path through the cycle (evaporation from the ocean, condensation, precipitation back into the ocean). Encourage students to use the words *evaporation, condensation,* and *precipitation* as they discuss the topic. When the diagram is finished, illustrate for students more complex paths of the water cycle (including transpiration and runoff).

Probing Question *Reflectors*

Water Cycle and Change of State

 whole class
🕐 15 min
 GUIDED inquiry

Predicting Remind students that most of the energy to turn liquid or solid water into water vapor comes originally from the sun. Sunlight warms Earth's surface, but snow cover, fog, and clouds reflect sunlight back into space. Have students discuss whether the reflecting action would tend to make the snow, fog, or clouds stay or vanish. Sample answer: The reflecting of the sun would keep the sun's energy from melting or evaporating these reflectors, so it would make them stay longer.

Activity *A Long Way from Home*

Engage

Transportation of Matter and Energy

 individuals, pairs, whole class
🕐 15 min
 GUIDED inquiry

Think, Pair, Share Ask students to think about what they know about how glaciers move sediment. Tell students to imagine that a rock that is usually found thousands of miles away has been found in their neighborhood. Have them think about how the water cycle may be responsible for the rock being in such a strange location. After students have had time to think, have them form pairs and discuss their thoughts with a partner and draw a diagram showing the steps that transported the rock. Invite pairs of students to share their scenarios with the class.

©PhotoDisc/Getty Images

Customize Your Labs

📄 *See the Lab Manual for lab datasheets.*

💿 *Go Online for editable lab datasheets.*

Levels of **Inquiry**

DIRECTED inquiry
introduces inquiry skills within a structured framework.

GUIDED inquiry
develops inquiry skills within a supportive environment.

INDEPENDENT inquiry
deepens inquiry skills with student-driven questions or procedures.

Labs and Demos

Daily Demo *Water Collection*

Synthesizing Key Topics

👥 whole class
🕐 20 min
Inquiry GUIDED inquiry

PURPOSE **To model water runoff**

MATERIALS

- marker, water soluble
- paper, blank newsprint
- spray bottle of water
- tray

1 Crumple a sheet of paper and spread it in the tray. Tell students that the paper represents a hilly area of land. Add large dots of marker to different areas of the paper.

2 **Observing** Use the sprayer to mist the "hill." Have students observe the flow of the water. Have them compare the results with their predictions. Have them describe how the water moves. Sample answers: The water flows downhill in different directions. It pools at the bottom of hills.

Exploration Lab *Changes in Water*

Water Cycle and Change of State

👥 small groups
🕐 45 min
Inquiry DIRECTED or GUIDED inquiry

Students will observe water in a closed container.

PURPOSE **To explain how the water cycle influences weather**

MATERIALS

- balance or scale
- bottle, plastic, with cap
- hot plate
- ice
- marker, permanent
- pan
- tongs

Quick Lab *Can You Make It Rain in a Jar?*

PURPOSE **To model condensation and precipitation**

See the Lab Manual or go Online for planning information.

Quick Lab *Modeling the Water Cycle*

PURPOSE **To describe how water moves through the Earth's systems in the water cycle**

See the Lab Manual or go Online for planning information.

🖥 Virtual Lab *How Does Water Move Through the Water Cycle?*

Transport of Matter and Energy

👥 flexible
🕐 45 min
Inquiry GUIDED inquiry

Students model water movement in the water cycle.

PURPOSE **To explore how water transports matter and energy through the water cycle**

Activities and Discussion

☐ **Activity** The Stuff of Clouds
☐ **Discussion** Circle Cycles
☐ **Probing Question** Reflectors
☐ **Activity** A Long Way from Home

Labs and Demos

☐ **Daily Demo** Water Collection
☐ **Exploration Lab** Changes in Water
☐ **Quick Lab** ... Rain in a Jar?
☐ **Quick Lab** Modeling the Water Cycle
☐ **Virtual Lab** How Does Water... ?

Your Resources

Explain Science Concepts

	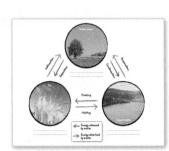 **Print Path**	🖥 **Digital Path**

Water Cycle and Change of State

☐ **What Goes Up...**, SE pp. 16–17
- Visualize It!, #5
- Active Reading (Annotation strategy), #6
- Visualize It!, #7

☐ **Earth's Water Cycle**
Explore different processes that make up the water cycle.

☐ **Clouds**
See the difference between water vapor and cloudy air.

Water in the Atmosphere

☐ **What Goes Up...**, SE pp. 18–19
- Do the Math, #8
- Visualize It!, #9
- Visualize It!, #10
- Summarize, #11

☐ **Earth's Water Cycle**
Explore different processes that make up the water cycle.

☐ **Water Changes**
Explore the processes in which water changes between gas, liquid, and solid forms in the enviroment.

Water in the Oceans and on Land

☐ **What Goes Up...**, SE p. 20
- Active Reading, #12
- Visualize It!, #13

☐ **Earth's Water Cycle**
Explore different processes that make up the water cycle.

☐ **Water Changes**
Explore the processes in which water changes between gas, liquid, and solid forms in the enviroment.

Transport of Matter and Energy

☐ **Water Works**, SE pp. 21–23
- Think Outside the Book, #14
- Visualize It!, #15
- Visualize It!, #16–17
- Think Outside the Book, #18

☐ **Water Changes**
Explore the processes in which water changes between gas, liquid, and solid forms in the enviroment.

☐ **Water State Changes**
Learn how energy is released or absorbed as water changes state.

Basic *Water Changes State*

Water Cycle and Change of State

 individuals

🕐 20 min

Concept Map As students complete the lesson, have them develop a Concept Map for the water cycle. Instruct students to write *Water* in the large oval. If students need help, tell them to surround the center oval with the states of water and use the labeled arrows to explain the relationships. Then have them add labeled arrows and more ovals if they wish to show how water changes state. As students encounter new information in the lesson, they can add more ovals and arrows to show how energy is involved and how the changes of state are connected to the water cycle.

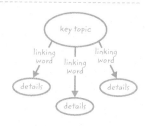

Advanced *Biosphere*

Synthesizing Key Topics

 individuals or pairs

🕐 15 min

Design Biosphere 2 was a totally enclosed environment that mimicked Earth's environment. Have individuals or pairs design their own biosphere that artificially reproduces the water cycle. Have them create sketches or charts to show how their water cycle would work and how it would mimic Earth's water cycle.

ELL *Water Cycle Processes*

Synthesizing Key Topics

 individuals

🕐 30 min

Four Corners To help students differentiate between the processes that make up the water cycle, play Four Corners. Label corners of the room as follows: *evaporation, condensation, precipitation, other.* Ask questions and provide examples and definitions for

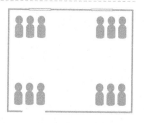

the parts of the water cycle. Have students move to the corner of the room that corresponds to the part of the cycle they think answers the question. If they think the answer is *transpiration* or *sublimation,* have them move to the *other* corner and provide an answer when prompted.

water cycle   evaporation   transpiration

sublimation   condensation   precipitation

Previewing Vocabulary

👥 whole class   🕐 15 min

Word Origins Discuss the meaning of the suffix *-ation.* Explain that it means "action" or "the action of." Then discuss the following words:
- **Condensation** comes from a Latin word meaning "become dense."
- **Evaporation** comes from a Latin word meaning "to disperse, or break up, in steam or vapor."
- **Precipitation** comes from a Latin word meaning "falling from a height."
- **Transpiration** comes from two Latin words, one meaning "breathe," and the other meaning "through."
- **Sublimation** comes from a Latin word meaning "lifting up."

Reinforcing Vocabulary

👥 individuals, then pairs   🕐 15 min

Four Square Have students complete a Four Square diagram for each term. They can fill in the boxes around the center with the term's definition, characteristics of the process, an example that illustrates the term, and a nonexample of the term.

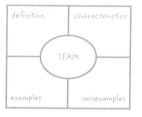

Customize Your Core Lesson

Core Instruction
☐ **Print Path** choices
☐ **Digital Path** choices

Vocabulary
☐ **Previewing Vocabulary** Word Origins
☐ **Reinforcing Vocabulary** Four Square

Your Resources

_____

_____

Differentiated Instruction
☐ **Basic** Water Changes State
☐ **Advanced** Biosphere
☐ **ELL** Water Cycle Processes

Extend Science Concepts

Reinforce and Review

Activity *Water Moves*

Synthesizing Key Topics

 whole class

15 min

GUIDED inquiry

Idea Wheel On the board, draw a large circle with a smaller circle inside. In the smaller, center circle of the wheel, write the main idea of the lesson—*Water Moves*. Then divide the outer ring into four sections. Discuss how water moves with students and fill in the four sections with their ideas and explanations. For each of the labeled sections, have students suggest details that describe the process listed. Point out that there are more than four ways that water moves. Additional examples that students come up with can be listed next to the Idea Wheel. Students who are interested can create their own Idea Wheels with many more sections that address additional ways that water moves.

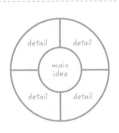

Optional Online resource: Idea Wheel support

Graphic Organizer

Synthesizing Key Topics

 individuals

ongoing

Mind Map After students have studied the lesson, ask them to create a Mind Map with the following terms: *water cycle, evaporation, condensation, transpiration, precipitation, sublimation, iceberg, groundwater.* Encourage students to use drawings, examples, and explanations in their Mind Maps.

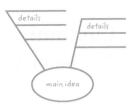

Optional Online resource: Mind Map support

Going Further

Language Arts Connection

Water in the Atmosphere

 individuals

30 min

Water Haiku Have students write a haiku about some part of the water cycle. Explain that a haiku is a short descriptive poem that is only three lines long. The first line has words totaling five syllables; the second line has seven syllables; the third line has five syllables. Present an example, such as the following:

Lacey white snowflakes

Drifting slowly to our Earth

Silent as they fall.

Encourage students to include a simple illustration with their haikus. Display the poems in the classroom.

Botany Connection

Synthesizing Key Concepts

whole class

15 min

Discussion Review the process of transpiration, which occurs in plants. Explain that the stomata allow not only for the release of water vapor, but also for the exchange of gases. Point out that stomata open during the day, allowing water vapor and oxygen to be released into the air. At the same time, carbon dioxide from the air is taken into the plant. At night the stomata close. Encourage students to think about what they know about photosynthesis as they discuss why they think the stomata close at night. In addition, have them discuss how plants replace the water they lose through transpiration, and how this relates to the water cycle.

Customize Your Closing

See the Assessment Guide for quizzes and tests.

Go Online to edit and create quizzes and tests.

Reinforce and Review

☐ **Activity** Water Moves

☐ **Graphic Organizer** Mind Map

☐ **Print Path** Visual Summary, SE p. 24

☐ **Print Path** Lesson Review, SE p. 25

☐ **Digital Path** Lesson Closer

Evaluate Student Mastery

Formative Assessment

See the teacher support below the Student Pages for additional Formative Assessment questions.

Challenge students to make a simple labeled drawing of the water cycle. Have students include in their drawings the three ways in which water enters the atmosphere. evaporation, transpiration, sublimation Have students explain how the water cycle transports energy. Energy is either released or absorbed when water changes state, and this energy moves when the water moves, such as when water vapor rises into the atmosphere.

Reteach

Formative assessment may show that students need reinforcement for certain topics. The resources below are recommended for reteaching. If students were introduced to a topic through the Print Path, you can also use the Digital Path to reteach, and vice versa.

🎧 *Can be assigned to individual students*

Water Cycle and Change of State
Activity The Stuff of Clouds 🎧

Exploration Lab Changes in Water

Water in the Atmosphere
Quick Lab Can You Make It Rain in a Jar? 🎧

Water in the Oceans and on Land
Daily Demo Water Collection 🎧

Transport of Matter and Energy
Activity A Long Way from Home

Summative Assessment

Alternative Assessment
The Water Cycle

◉ *Online resources: student worksheet, optional rubrics*

The Water Cycle

Points of View: *The Water Cycle*
Your class will work together to show what you've learned about the water cycle from several different viewpoints.

1. Work in groups as assigned by your teacher. Each group will be assigned to one or two viewpoints.

2. Complete your assignment, and present your perspective to the class.

 Examples List examples of three things transported by the water cycle. Describe how they are transported.

 Illustrations Draw a diagram that shows the water cycle. In your drawing, include at least two examples of ways water changes state during the cycle. Share your drawing with the class.

 Analysis Describe the three processes by which water moves into the atmosphere. Which process accounts for most of the water moving into the atmosphere?

 Observations Look out a window at a landscape, or look at a picture of landscape. Think about the water cycle and the different forms that water takes in the cycle. In what three states of matter can water exist? Identify one or more forms of water that are present outside or that are pictured in the photograph.

 Calculations Use the National Weather Service's Web site (http://water.weather.gov/) to find statistics about yearly precipitation amounts in your state. Roughly how many inches of precipitation fell on your state last year? Roughly how much precipitation fell on your state four years ago? During which year did more precipitation fall on your state?

Going Further
- ☐ Language Arts Connection
- ☐ Botany Connection

Formative Assessment
- ☐ Strategies Throughout TE
- ☐ Lesson Review SE

Summative Assessment
- ☐ Alternative Assessment The Water Cycle
- ☐ Lesson Quiz
- ☐ Unit Tests A and B
- ☐ Unit Review SE End-of-Unit

Your Resources

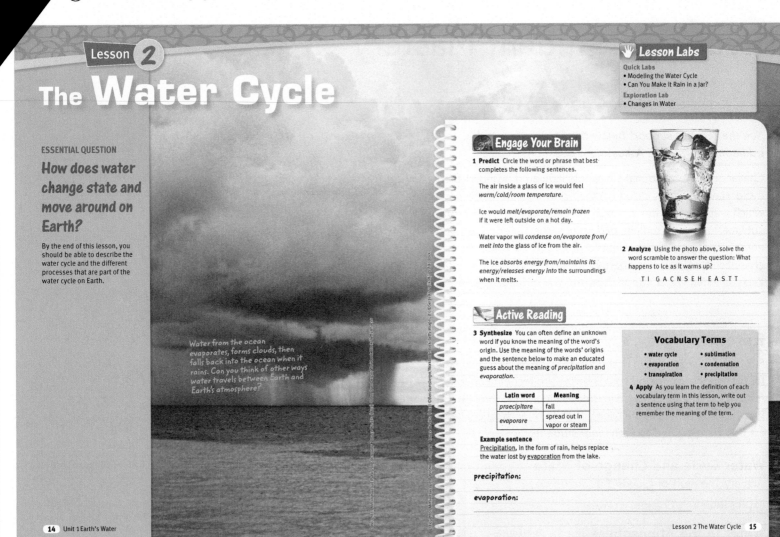

Lesson 2

The Water Cycle

ESSENTIAL QUESTION

How does water change state and move around on Earth?

By the end of this lesson, you should be able to describe the water cycle and the different processes that are part of the water cycle on Earth.

Water from the ocean evaporates, forms clouds, then falls back into the ocean when it rains. Can you think of other ways water travels between Earth and Earth's atmosphere?

Lesson Labs

Quick Labs
• Modeling the Water Cycle
• Can You Make It Rain in a Jar?

Exploration Lab
• Changes in Water

Engage Your Brain

1 Predict Circle the word or phrase that best completes the following sentences.

The air inside a glass of ice would feel *warm/cold/room temperature*.

Ice would *melt/evaporate/remain frozen* if it were left outside on a hot day.

Water vapor will *condense on/evaporate from/ melt into* the glass of ice from the air.

The ice *absorbs energy from/maintains its energy/releases energy into* the surroundings when it melts.

2 Analyze Using the photo above, solve the word scramble to answer the question: What happens to ice as it warms up?

TI GACNSEH EASTT

_____

Active Reading

3 Synthesize You can often define an unknown word if you know the meaning of the word's origin. Use the meaning of the words' origins and the sentence below to make an educated guess about the meaning of *precipitation* and *evaporation*.

Latin word	Meaning
praecipitare	fall
evaporare	spread out in vapor or steam

Example sentence
Precipitation, in the form of rain, helps replace the water lost by evaporation from the lake.

precipitation: _____

evaporation: _____

Vocabulary Terms

• water cycle   • sublimation
• evaporation   • condensation
• transpiration   • precipitation

4 Apply As you learn the definition of each vocabulary term in this lesson, write out a sentence using that term to help you remember the meaning of the term.

14   Unit 1 Earth's Water

Lesson 2 The Water Cycle   15

Answers

Answers for 1–3 should reflect students' current thoughts, even if incorrect.

1. cold; melt; condense on; absorbs energy from

2. It changes state.

3. Sample answer: Precipitation is any form of water that falls from the sky. Evaporation is when water becomes water vapor and spreads into the air.

4. Students' annotations will vary.

Opening Your Lesson

Discuss responses to item 3 to assess students' familiarity with vocabulary terms pertaining to the water cycle.

Prerequisites Students should be familiar with the states of matter—solid, liquid, and gas.

Difficult Concepts Have students identify which state of matter applies to each of the following descriptions:

• The water sample has a definite volume and takes the shape of its container. liquid
• The water sample has no definite volume and spreads out to fill its container. gas
• The water sample has a definite volume and a definite shape. solid

Interpreting Visuals

Have students examine the photo of the glass of water containing ice. Ask students if they have ever noticed the outside of a cold drink having water drops on it. Explain that droplets form when warmer air outside the glass contacts the cold glass. Water vapor in the air then condenses into liquid water on the outside of the glass.

What goes up...

What is the water cycle?

Movement of water between the atmosphere, land, oceans, and even living things makes up the **water cycle**. Rain, snow, and hail fall on the oceans and land because of gravity. On land, ice and water flow downhill. Water flows in streams, rivers, and waterfalls such as the one in the photo, because of gravity. If the land is flat, water will collect in certain areas forming ponds, lakes, and marshland. Some water will soak through the ground and collect underground as groundwater. Even groundwater flows downhill.

Water and snow can move upward if they turn into water vapor and rise into the air. Plants and animals also release water vapor into the air. In the air, water vapor can travel great distances with the wind. Winds can also move the water in the surface layer of the ocean by creating ocean currents. When ocean currents reach the shore or colder climates, the water will sink if it is cold enough or salty enough. The sinking water creates currents at different depths in the ocean. These are some of the ways in which water travels all over Earth.

👁 Visualize It!

5 Analyze What is the relationship between gravity and water in this image?

16

How does water change state?

Water is found in three states on Earth: as liquid water, as solid water ice, and as gaseous water vapor. Water is visible as a liquid or a solid, but it is invisible as a gas in the air. Water can change from one state to another as energy is absorbed or released.

Water absorbs energy from its surroundings as it *melts* from solid to liquid. Water also absorbs energy when it *evaporates* from liquid to gas, or when it *sublimates* from solid to gas. Water releases energy into its surroundings when it *condenses* from gas to liquid. Water also releases energy when it *freezes* from liquid to solid, or *deposits* from gas to solid. No water is lost during these changes.

6 Identify As you read, underline each process in which energy is absorbed or released.

👁 Visualize It!

7 Analyze Under each photo, write an example of where you might find water in that state of matter.

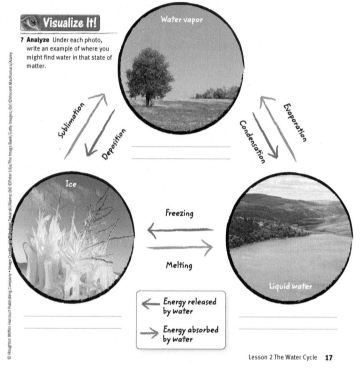

Water vapor

Sublimation

Deposition

Evaporation

Condensation

Ice

Freezing

Melting

Liquid water

→ Energy released by water

→ Energy absorbed by water

Lesson 2 The Water Cycle   **17**

Answers

5. Sample answer: Gravity forces the water to flow downhill. Therefore, a waterfall has formed as the water flows over the cliff.

6. *See students' pages for annotations.*

7. Sample answers: Water vapor: in the air above a forest; Ice: in the mountains; Liquid water: in a lake

Probing Questions   GUIDED Inquiry

Identifying **Ask:** As water vapor condenses to form various types of precipitation, what change in state occurs? Gas changes to liquid (rain) or solid (snow, hail). What energy change occurs? Energy is released.

Interpreting Visuals

Help students interpret the diagram showing the processes by which water changes state. **Ask:** When water vapor changes directly to ice, what is the change in state called? deposition What is the change of state when liquid water becomes water vapor? evaporation Which arrow in the diagram indicates that a change in the state of water releases energy? the blue inner arrows

Learning Alert

Water Cycle Many students think that the processes of evaporation, condensation, and precipitation are the complete water cycle. Make sure students understand that the flow of water on land and underground is also part of the water cycle. Point out that as water moves in the water cycle, the total amount of water in Earth's system stays the same.

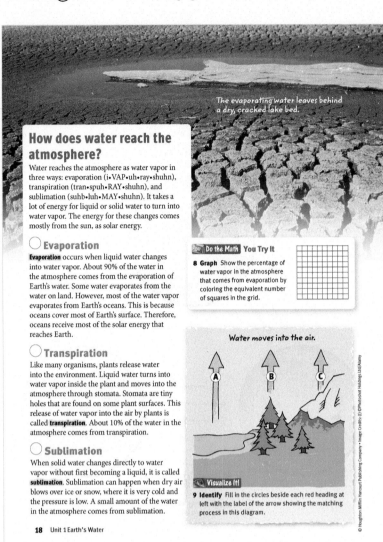

The evaporating water leaves behind a dry, cracked lake bed.

How does water reach the atmosphere?

Water reaches the atmosphere as water vapor in three ways: evaporation (i•VAP•uh•ray•shuhn), transpiration (tran•spuh•RAY•shuhn), and sublimation (suhb•luh•MAY•shuhn). It takes a lot of energy for liquid or solid water to turn into water vapor. The energy for these changes comes mostly from the sun, as solar energy.

○ Evaporation

Evaporation occurs when liquid water changes into water vapor. About 90% of the water in the atmosphere comes from the evaporation of Earth's water. Some water evaporates from the water on land. However, most of the water vapor evaporates from Earth's oceans. This is because oceans cover most of Earth's surface. Therefore, oceans receive most of the solar energy that reaches Earth.

○ Transpiration

Like many organisms, plants release water into the environment. Liquid water turns into water vapor inside the plant and moves into the atmosphere through stomata. Stomata are tiny holes that are found on some plant surfaces. This release of water vapor into the air by plants is called **transpiration**. About 10% of the water in the atmosphere comes from transpiration.

○ Sublimation

When solid water changes directly to water vapor without first becoming a liquid, it is called **sublimation**. Sublimation can happen when dry air blows over ice or snow, where it is very cold and the pressure is low. A small amount of the water in the atmosphere comes from sublimation.

18 Unit 1 Earth's Water

Do the Math **You Try It**

8 Graph Show the percentage of water vapor in the atmosphere that comes from evaporation by coloring the equivalent number of squares in the grid.

Water moves into the air.

Ⓐ **Ⓑ** **Ⓒ**

Visualize It!

9 Identify Fill in the circles beside each red heading at left with the label of the arrow showing the matching process in this diagram.

What happens to water in the atmosphere?

Water reaches the atmosphere as water vapor. In the atmosphere, water vapor mixes with other gases. To leave the atmosphere, water vapor must change into liquid or solid water. Then the liquid or solid water can fall to Earth's surface.

○ Condensation

Remember, **condensation** (kahn•den•SAY•shuhn) is the change of state from a gas to a liquid. If air that contains water vapor is cooled enough, condensation occurs. Some of the water vapor condenses on small particles, such as dust, forming little balls or tiny droplets of water. These water droplets float in the air as clouds, fog, or mist. At the ground level, water vapor may condense on cool surfaces as dew.

○ Precipitation

In clouds, water droplets may collide and "stick" together to become larger. If a droplet becomes large enough, it falls to Earth's surface as precipitation (pri•sip•i•TAY•shuhn). **Precipitation** is any form of water that falls to Earth from clouds. Three common kinds of precipitation shown in the photos are rain, snow, and hail. Snow and hail form if the water droplets freeze. Most rain falls into the oceans because most water evaporates from ocean surfaces and oceans cover most of Earth's surface. But winds carry clouds from the ocean over land, increasing the amount of precipitation that falls on land.

Water returns to Earth's surface.

Ⓓ **Ⓔ**

Visualize It!

10 Identify Fill in the circle beside each red heading at left with the label of the arrow showing the matching process in this diagram.

11 Summarize Fill in the boxes to describe how precipitation forms.

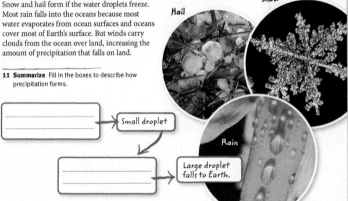

Hail   Snow   Rain

Small droplet

Large droplet falls to Earth.

19

Answers

8. Students should color in 90 squares of the grid.

9. A: Evaporation; B: Transpiration; C: Sublimation

10. D: Condensation; E: Precipitation

11. Water vapor condenses into liquid water.-->Small droplet-->Water droplets collide together, becoming larger droplets.-->Large droplet falls to Earth.

Interpreting Visuals

Ask students what clue in the diagram can help them figure out ways that water can move into the atmosphere as water vapor. arrows that go from the ground up into the atmosphere What happens to water after it falls from clouds? Sample answer: It flows along the ground as runoff; some water sinks into the ground and becomes groundwater.

Probing Questions DIRECTED Inquiry

Hypothesizing Have students form hypotheses about one part of the water cycle. For example, students may hypothesize that water evaporates more quickly from a lake during summer than during winter. Write the hypotheses on the board. If time permits, have the class brainstorm ways that they could test their ideas.

Building Reading Skills

Process Notes Have students use Process Notes to describe the water cycle. In the left column, direct students to list processes that make up the water cycle. In the right column, have them describe each process. They can continue using the Process Notes for the remainder of the lesson.

🌐 *Optional Online resource: Process Notes*

How does water move on land and in the oceans?

After water falls to Earth, it flows and circulates all over Earth. On land, water flows downhill, both on the surface and underground. However, most of Earth's precipitation falls into the oceans. Ocean currents move water around the oceans.

Runoff and Infiltration

All of the water on land flows downhill because of gravity. Streams, rivers, and the water that flows over land are types of *runoff*. Runoff flows downhill toward oceans, lakes, and marshlands.

Some of the water on land seeps into the ground. This process is called *infiltration* (in•fil•TRAY•shuhn). Once underground, the water is called *groundwater*. Groundwater also flows downhill through soil and rock.

Active Reading

12 Compare How do runoff and groundwater differ?

_____

_____

_____

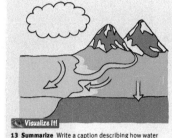

Visualize It!

13 Summarize Write a caption describing how water is moving in the diagram above.

Ice Flow

Much of Earth's ice is stored in large ice caps in Antarctica and Greenland. Some ice is stored in glaciers at high altitudes all over Earth. Glaciers cover about 10% of Earth's surface. Glaciers can be called "rivers of ice" because gravity also causes glaciers to flow slowly downhill. Many glaciers never leave land. However, some glaciers flow to the ocean, where pieces may break off, as seen in the photo, and float far out to sea as icebergs.

Ocean Circulation

Winds move ocean water on the surface in great currents, sometimes for thousands of miles. At some shores, or if the water is very cold or salty, it will sink deep into the ocean. This movement helps create deep ocean currents. Both surface currents and deep ocean currents transport large amounts of water from ocean to ocean.

Icebergs can be carried over long distances by ocean currents.

20 Unit 1 Earth's Water

Water Works

What does the water cycle transport?

In the water cycle, each state of water has some energy in it. This energy is released into or absorbed from its surroundings as water changes state. The energy in each state of water is then transported as the water moves from place to place. Matter is also transported as water and the materials in the water move all over Earth. Therefore, the water cycle moves energy and matter through Earth's atmosphere, land, oceans, and living things.

Think Outside the Book

14 Apply With a classmate, discuss how the water cycle transfers energy.

Energy

Energy is transported in the water cycle through changes of state and by the movement of water from place to place. For example, water that evaporates from the ocean carries energy into the atmosphere. This movement of energy can generate hurricanes. Also, cold ocean currents can cool the air along a coastline by absorbing the energy from the air and leaving the air cooler. This energy is carried away quickly as the current continues on its path. Such processes affect the weather and climate of an area.

Matter

Earth's ocean currents move vast amounts of water all over the world. These currents also transport the solids in the water and the dissolved salts and gases. Rivers transfer water from land into the ocean. Rivers also carry large amounts of sand, mud, and gravel as shown below. Rivers form deltas and floodplains, where some of the materials from upstream collect in areas downstream. Rivers also carve valleys and canyons, and carry the excess materials downstream. Glaciers also grind away rock and carry the ground rock with them as they flow.

Visualize It!

15 Identify What do rivers, such as the ones in the photo, transport?

Lesson 2 The Water Cycle 21

Answers

12. They differ in location. Runoff flows on Earth's surface and groundwater flows beneath Earth's surface.

13. Water flows on land, underground, and in the oceans.

14. Students should be able to articulate how energy is transported over large distances in one of the three common states of water on Earth and how the amount of energy in the water changes during changes of state.

15. energy, water, dissolved salts and gases, sand, mud, and gravel

Formative Assessment

Ask: How does the water cycle move energy and matter? Energy can be transported through changes of state and by water moving from one place to another. How does it move matter? Sample answer: Water itself is moved during all parts of the water cycle. Rivers, oceans, or glaciers can carry sediment and dissolved matter; icebergs can carry matter into the ocean.

Learning Alert

Energy Students may have a hard time understanding how energy is used in the water cycle. Point out that many parts of the water cycle can be likened to things you can do in your kitchen every day, such as boiling or freezing water. Ask students to explain how energy from appliances are used to cause a change of state.

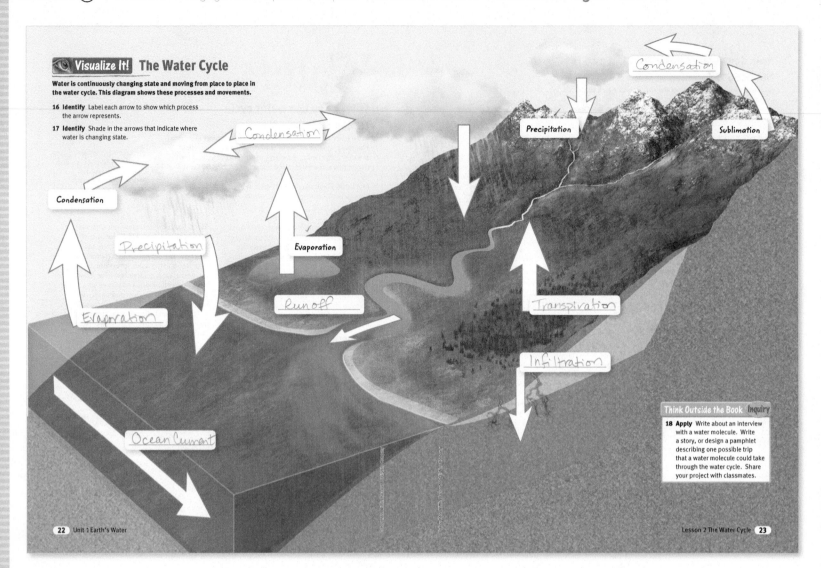

Visualize It! The Water Cycle

Water is continuously changing state and moving from place to place in the water cycle. This diagram shows these processes and movements.

16 Identify Label each arrow to show which process the arrow represents.

17 Identify Shade in the arrows that indicate where water is changing state.

Condensation

Condensation

Precipitation

Sublimation

Condensation

Precipitation

Evaporation

Run off

Transpiration

Evaporation

Infiltration

Ocean Current

Think Outside the Book Inquiry

18 Apply Write about an interview with a water molecule. Write a story, or design a pamphlet describing one possible trip that a water molecule could take through the water cycle. Share your project with classmates.

22   Unit 1 Earth's Water

Lesson 2 The Water Cycle   23

Answers

16. Evaporation: arrow pointing up from ocean. Precipitation: arrow pointing down from clouds. Transpiration: arrow pointing up from trees. Condensation: arrows pointing into clouds. Runoff: arrow in the river. Infiltration: arrow moving from land surface to underground. Ocean current: arrow in the ocean pointing toward the reader.

17. All arrows showing evaporation and condensation should be shaded in.

18. Answers will vary, but students should trace a plausible path through the water cycle shown in the diagram.

Learning Alert

Many students think of the water cycle as working in a circle with the same few steps repeated again and again. The diagram shows that this is not the case—many parts of the cycle are occurring at the same time and the diagram looks nothing like a circle. Point this out to students. **Ask:** Why do students tend to think of the water cycle as something that happens in a circular pattern with the same few steps repeated again and again? Sample answer: Other cycles, such as the life cycle of a frog or butterfly or the cycle of seasons, work in a circular way with the same few steps repeated again and again. How does this diagram show that the water cycle is different? Sample answers: The arrows do not form a circle; the steps do not always go in the same directions; sometimes the cycle seems to move backward; some steps are sometimes not included at all.

Interpreting Visuals

Ask: How does the diagram represent the movement of energy and matter? Sample answers: The transport of energy and water is represented by the arrows; some steps represent movement of other matter such as sediment, which is shown by the brown color at the mouth of the river.

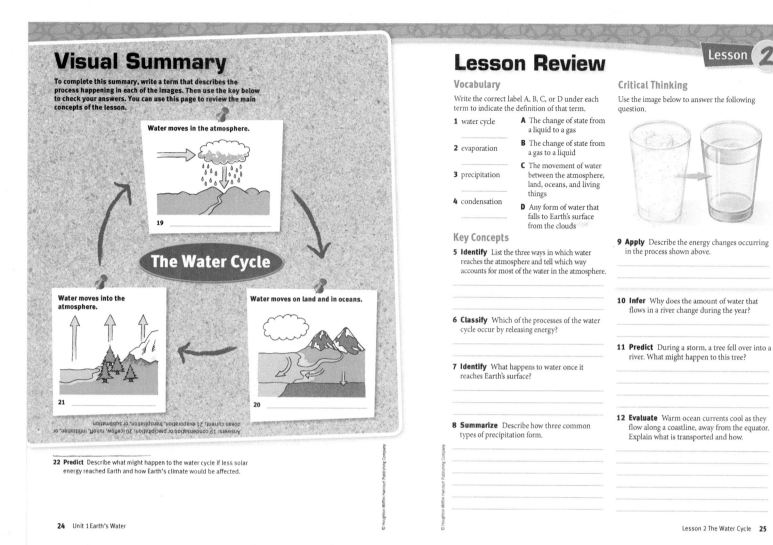

Visual Summary Answers

19. condensation or precipitation

20. iceflow, runoff, infiltration, or ocean current

21. evaporation, transpiration, or sublimation

22. The amount of water and energy transported by the water cycle would slow down and Earth would be colder.

Lesson Review Answers

1. C

2. A

3. D

4. B

5. Evaporation, transpiration and sublimation; most of the water in the atmosphere comes from evaporation.

6. condensation, precipitation, freezing, and depositing

7. On land, water flows downhill. In the oceans, water flows in ocean currents.

8. Water vapor condenses on small particles forming water droplets. In clouds, water droplets collide together, forming larger droplets. Large droplets fall as rain and if cold enough, as snow or hail.

9. The ice is absorbing energy as it melts from ice to liquid water.

10. because of changing amounts of rain and runoff that flow into the river

11. The river might carry the tree downstream. The tree may be deposited along the river, in a delta, or in the ocean.

12. The ocean currents transport energy as they move away from the equator. On reaching cooler coastlines, this energy moves into the cooler atmosphere, warming that air up while cooling down itself.

S.T.E.M. Engineering & Technology

Analyzing Water Power

Purpose To identify inputs, outputs, feedback, and controls in a system

Learning Goals
- Analyze a hydroelectric power plant as a system.
- Identify inputs, outputs, and feedback in a system.
- Examine how controls are used to regulate a system.

Academic Vocabulary
hydroelectric, power plant, input, output, feedback, mechanical energy, electrical energy

Prerequisite Knowledge
- Basic understanding of the water cycle
- Knowledge of energy transfer

21st Century SKILLS

Theme: Financial, Economic, Business, and Entrepreneurial Literacy

Activities focusing on 21st Century Skills are included for this feature and can be found on the following pages.

These activities focus on the following skills:
- **Critical Thinking and Problem Solving**
- **Media Literacy**
- **Leadership and Responsibility**

You can learn more about the 21st Century Skills in the front matter of this Teacher's Edition.

Content Refresher

 Professional Development

Hydroelectric Power Water has been used for power for thousands of years. Long ago, people used rivers to turn paddle wheels to grind grain. The first use of water to produce electricity occurred in the United States in 1880. A water turbine powered 16 lamps in Grand Rapids, Michigan.

Today, seven percent of all electricity in the United States comes from hydroelectric power plants. Seventy-five percent of all renewable energy in the United States comes from hydroelectric power generation. Washington, Oregon, and California produce more than half of all hydroelectric power in the United States. The largest hydroelectric facility in the United States is the Grand Coulee Dam in Grand Coulee, Washington.

A hydroelectric dam impounds water in a reservoir. The reservoir acts much like a battery, storing water to be released as needed to generate power at periods of high demand. When power is needed, water is released through a huge pipe called a penstock. The penstock carries water to a propeller-like turbine, which is turned by the moving water. The shaft of the turbine extends upward into a generator. As the shaft spins, it causes wire coils inside the generator to spin within a magnetic field. This produces an electric current. In a hydroelectric dam, turbines convert the energy of flowing water into mechanical energy, and generators convert this mechanical energy into electricity.

Environmental Impacts of Hydroelectric Power Hydroelectric dams do not pollute, but they can have environmental consequences. Hydroelectric dams can obstruct fish migrations. For example, the Grand Coulee prevents salmon and other fish from migrating upstream to spawn. Water turbines can kill fish. And reservoirs formed by dams flood a large area. This means that people and wildlife that inhabit the area must move, and plant life is killed.

Hydroelectric facilities can also change natural water temperatures, water chemistry, and water flow, which can cause changes to the environment and organisms that live in the environment.

S.T.E.M. Engineering & Technology

Evaluating Technological Systems

Skills
✓ Identify inputs
✓ Identify outputs
Identify system processes
✓ Evaluate system feedback
✓ Apply system controls
✓ Communicate results

Objectives
• Analyze a hydroelectric power plant as a system.
• Identify the inputs and outputs of a system.
• Identify and evaluate feedback in a system.
• Examine how controls are used to regulate a system.

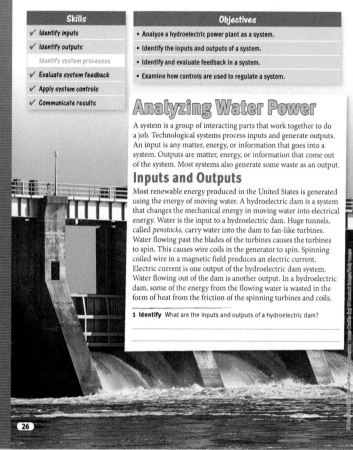

Analyzing Water Power

A system is a group of interacting parts that work together to do a job. Technological systems process inputs and generate outputs. An input is any matter, energy, or information that goes into a system. Outputs are matter, energy, or information that come out of the system. Most systems also generate some waste as an output.

Inputs and Outputs

Most renewable energy produced in the United States is generated using the energy of moving water. A hydroelectric dam is a system that changes the mechanical energy in moving water into electrical energy. Water is the input to a hydroelectric dam. Huge tunnels, called *penstocks,* carry water into the dam to fan-like turbines. Water flowing past the blades of the turbines causes the turbines to spin. This causes wire coils in the generator to spin. Spinning coiled wire in a magnetic field produces an electric current. Electric current is one output of the hydroelectric dam system. Water flowing out of the dam is another output. In a hydroelectric dam, some of the energy from the flowing water is wasted in the form of heat from the friction of the spinning turbines and coils.

1 Identify What are the inputs and outputs of a hydroelectric dam?

"Workers use bicycles or tricycles to travel from one turbine to the next over the length of the dam because the turbines are so large."

Feedback and Control

Feedback is information from one step in a process that affects a previous step in the process. Feedback can be used to regulate a system by applying controls. In a hydroelectric dam system, information about how much electricity is produced is sent back into the system. This information is used to regulate the amount of electricity that is produced. When more electricity is needed, giant gates, called *sluice gates,* are opened to allow water to flow. When less electricity is required, some gates are closed. The sluice gates act as the control in this system.

2 Analyze In the image below, place the terms *input, output,* and *control* in the boxes that correspond to the correct part of the hydroelectric dam system.

Reservoir — Sluice gates — Dam — Generator — Power plant — Transformer — Penstock — Turbine — Power transmission cables — Downstream outlet

A / B / C

Water flowing through a dam spins a turbine. This spins a generator, which produces electric current. Transformers convert the current so that it can be used in homes, businesses, and factories.

✋ You Try It!
Now it's your turn to identify inputs, outputs, feedback, and controls.

26 / 27

Answers

1. The input is water; the outputs are electric current and water.

2. A. control; B. input; C. output

Evaluating Technological Systems

 You Try It!

Now it's your turn to identify inputs, outputs, feedback and controls in a system that uses water power. Working with a partner, think of another way that you could use moving water to do a job. For example, flowing water in water mills has been used to spin large cutting blades in saw mills or to grind grain in flour mills. You can use one of these systems or use your imagination to create your own system that uses moving water to do a job.

(1) Identify Inputs

In the oval below, enter a name for your system. Recall that inputs can be matter, energy, or information. List the inputs into your system on the lines above the arrows. If there are more than three inputs, you can add more arrows.

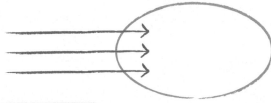

(2) Identify Outputs

As with the inputs, the outputs of a system can be matter, energy, or information. Keep in mind that most systems also generate some waste as an output. In the oval, write the name of your system. Use the arrows below to list the outputs of your system. If there are more than three outputs, you can add more arrows.

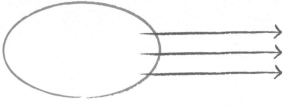

(3) Evaluate System Feedback

Now, consider which steps in your system could be used as feedback to regulate the system. Which outputs need to be monitored and why?

(4) Apply System Controls

Using the feedback you identified in the last step, propose one or more controls for your system that will keep the system working properly.

(5) Communicate Results

In the space below, draw a sketch of the system you developed. Label the inputs, outputs, feedback and controls.

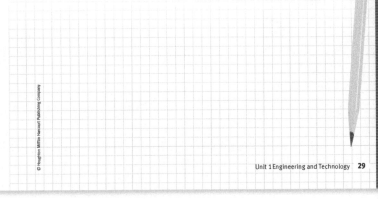

© Houghton Mifflin Harcourt Publishing Company

Answers

1. Sample answer: Water-powered saw mill; Inputs: logs, water

2. Sample answer: Water-powered saw mill; Outputs: water, motion of saw blade, boards, sawdust, heat from friction

3. Sample answer: the number of boards being produced or the speed of the blade could be used as feedback. If too many boards are cut the mill might not be able to sell them all. If the blade spins too fast it may be unsafe.

4. Sample answer: Using feedback about the number of boards, the control could automatically stop logs from being fed into the mill. Using feedback about the blade speed, a brake could be used if the blade starts spinning too fast.

5. Students' sketches should illustrate the system they chose, and should demonstrate an understanding of the inputs, outputs, feedback and control in their system.

21st Century SKILLS

Learning and Innovation Skills

 small groups   ⏱ 15 min

Critical Thinking and Problem Solving Have small groups work together to identify the inputs, outputs, feedback, and controls of other groups' systems. Encourage groups to analyze how the parts of the whole interact with each other to produce the overall outcome. Invite group members to listen to each other and to evaluate evidence and ideas. Have them draw conclusions based on the best analysis of each system. Last, have the groups reflect critically on their learning experience and share their ideas with the class.

Information, Media, and Technology Skills

 pairs   ⏱ 30 min

Media Literacy Invite pairs of students to create a digital presentation about their system that explains the inputs, outputs, feedback, and controls. Encourage groups to use the most appropriate media-creation tools, and to think about the audience and purpose of their presentation as they prepare it. Last, have groups share their presentation with the class or with another class.

Life and Career Skills

 small groups   ⏱ 45 min

Leadership and Responsibility Invite small groups of students to think about how an energy system of their choosing can be improved (for example, to make it less harmful to the environment, or to make it less costly to operate). Students may want to look at tidal energy, wave power, ocean thermal energy, geothermal energy, or wind energy. Let students work together to develop a campaign to influence and guide others toward their goal. Students should do their best to leverage the strengths of individual group members to accomplish their common goal. Encourage students to share their plan with the class or the school.

Differentiated Instruction

Basic *Inputs and Outputs*

 individuals   ⏱ 15 min

Invite students to write a story that describes the inputs, outputs, feedback, and control of a simple technological system, such as an oven or crock pot. Have students underline every input in red and every output in blue, circle the feedback, and draw a rectangular box around the control. Remind students that some things are both inputs and outputs.

ELL *Feedback Loops*

 pairs   ⏱ 10 min

Have students work in pairs to model a feedback loop. One partner will be blindfolded, and will drop marbles into a plastic bottle-top funnel, several at a time. Make sure the neck of the funnel is just large enough to allow one marble to pass through at a time. When the funnel gets full and a marble spills off the top, have the other partner place that marble into the blindfolded partner's open hand. The blindfolded partner will stop adding marbles until the level of marbles in the funnel drops below a line marked on the funnel. When this happens, the non-blindfolded partner removes the feedback marble from the blindfolded partner's hand. Then the blindfolded partner resumes adding marbles to the funnel. Ask students which partner represents the system. Which partner represents the control? What item is the feedback?

Customize Your Feature

☐ **21st Century Skills** Learning and Innovation Skills

☐ **21st Century Skills** Information, Media, and Technology Skills

☐ **21st Century Skills** Life and Career Skills

☐ **Basic** Inputs and Outputs

☐ **ELL** Feedback Loops

Surface Water and Groundwater

Essential Question How does fresh water flow on Earth?

 **Professional Development**

For more detailed information about the topics in this lesson, refer to the Content Refresher in the Unit Opener pages.

Opening Your Lesson

Begin the lesson by assessing students' prerequisite and prior knowledge.

Prerequisite Knowledge

- The processes of the water cycle replenish fresh water on Earth.
- Rivers change Earth's surface as they erode and deposit material.

Accessing Prior Knowledge

Use the SQ3R strategy to preview the lesson and determine what students already know about surface water and groundwater. Explain what the abbreviation SQ3R stands for (survey, question, read, recite, and review) and guide students in using the strategy.

🌐 *Optional Online resource: SQ3R support*

Customize Your Opening

- ☐ **Accessing Prior Knowledge,** above
- ☐ **Print Path** Engage Your Brain, SE p. 31, #1–2
- ☐ **Print Path** Active Reading, SE p. 31, #3–4
- ☐ **Digital Path** Lesson Opener

Key Topics/Learning Goals

Surface Water

1 Explain where surface water comes from and why living things depend on it.
2 Explain the relationship between rivers and the tributaries.
3 Explain how stream load, gradient, and flow describe river processes.
4 Explain the various processes carried on within river systems.
5 Describe watersheds and their structure, and explain how water flow is affected.
6 Describe how humans use the water in watersheds.

Groundwater

1 Explain what groundwater is and how it forms.
2 Define water table and aquifer.
3 Describe the effects of porosity and permeability.
4 Identify how humans use groundwater.
5 Determine how aquifers are discharged and recharged.

Supporting Concepts

- Water that collects on the ground or in a body of water is called surface water. It provides habitat for wildlife and accounts for most human water usage.
- Tributaries are smaller streams that feed into rivers, forming river systems.
- The materials carried by a stream, other than the water itself, make up the stream load. A stream's flow or discharge is the volume of water that flows down the stream within a given time; the steeper the gradient of a stream, the faster the water will travel.
- Rivers transport sediment and dissolved materials.
- A watershed is the land a river system drains. Streams, rivers, lakes, ponds, and groundwater feed a watershed.
- Humans use water for recreation, transportation, industry, and irrigation.

- Groundwater is water that is under Earth's surface, in spaces in rocks, or in soil.
- A water table is the top of the saturated area within soil. An aquifer is a rock layer that stores groundwater.
- Porosity is the percentage of rock composed of pore spaces; permeability measures how easily groundwater flows through an aquifer.
- Groundwater is used for drinking, irrigation, and industry.
- When surface water reaches the water table, it recharges aquifers.

Options for Instruction

Two parallel paths provide coverage of the Essential Questions, with a strong **Inquiry** strand woven into each. Follow the **Print Path,** the **Digital Path,** or your customized combination of print, digital, and inquiry.

 Print Path
Teaching support for the Print Path appears with the Student Pages.

 Inquiry Labs and Activities

Digital Path
Digital Path shortcut: TS661777

Print Path	Inquiry Labs and Activities	Digital Path
Getting Your Feet Wet, SE pp. 32–33 **Where on Earth is fresh water found?**	**Activity** Raft Trip	**Water Cycle** Interactive Graphics
Cry Me a River, SE pp. 34–35 **How does water move on Earth's surface?**	**Activity** Map River Systems	**River Processes** Video
Making a Splash, SE p. 38 **How do people use surface water and groundwater?**	**Quick Lab** Model a Stream	**River Erosion** Slideshow
		Surface Water Used by Humans Slideshow
In Deep Water, SE pp. 36–37 **How does groundwater flow?**	**Daily Demo** Rock Spaces	**Aquifers** Video
Making a Splash, SE p. 38 **How do people use surface water and groundwater?**	**Exploration Lab** Aquifers and Development	**Aquifers** Interactive Graphics
	Quick Lab Modeling Groundwater	
	Activity O, Impermeable Clay!	

Options for Assessment

See the Evaluate page for options, including Formative Assessment, Summative Assessment, and Unit Review.

Engage and Explore

Activities and Discussion

Activity *Raft Trip*

Introducing Key Topics

 pairs
🕐 30 min
 INDEPENDENT inquiry

Have pairs of students locate the nearest river to their town or city on a map. Have them plan a rafting trip down the river that will take them to the nearest ocean. Students can use markers to trace their route on the map. Afterward, engage students with these questions: What interesting places would you pass along your trip? How long do you think your trip would last? What places could you reach and not reach by river?

Probing Questions *Not a Drop to Drink*

Groundwater

 small groups/whole class
🕐 15 min
 GUIDED inquiry

Explain that groundwater supplies in many areas are being used up faster than they can be replenished by rainwater and runoff. In response, some communities are enacting mandatory water conservation measures. Have students form small groups to debate whether water conservation should be enforced. Groups can debate each other, defending their stances with facts. Sample answer: Yes, it should be enforced because water can be a nonrenewable resource if it is used up faster than it is replaced. No, because people have a right to use water they pay for.

Activity *Map River Systems*

Surface Water

 pairs
🕐 45 min
 DIRECTED inquiry

Have pairs of students research and make a poster that illustrates the river systems and drainage basins of North America. Encourage them to use arrows indicating the direction of flow in major rivers and to draw the divides that separate each drainage basin. How have people affected the river systems?

Activity *O, Impermeable Clay!*

Groundwater

 individuals or pairs
🕐 15 min
 GUIDED inquiry

Provide students with modeling clay. Allow them to mold various shapes out of it and see whether water can pass through. Experiment with different shapes and thicknesses; do any of these changes affect the clay's ability to hold in the water? Explain that clay has very low permeability—in fact, few natural materials have lower hydraulic conductivity. Explain that natural clay has a different composition, but the effect would be similar. Challenge students to brainstorm situations when a layer of nearly impermeable material would be desirable (for example, as the bottom layer of an aquifer; to hold in liquids that pool beneath a landfill; as a core within a dam).

©Corbis

Customize Your Labs

 See the Lab Manual for lab datasheets.

 Go Online for editable lab datasheets.

Labs and Demos

Daily Demo *Rock Spaces*

Groundwater

👥 whole class
🕐 15 min
Inquiry **GUIDED** inquiry

PURPOSE **To show that water moves more easily through rocks with greater permeability**

MATERIALS

- small pebbles (less than 4 mm diameter)
- large pebbles (larger than 4 mm diameter)
- two sand sifters
- 250 mL beaker
- water
- two plastic containers

Layer small pebbles in a sand sifter. Layer the larger pebbles in a second sand sifter. **Ask:** Which kind of rock has larger spaces between the rocks? large pebbles **Ask:** Which kind of rock do you think water will move through more easily? large pebbles Have volunteers hold the sifters over the plastic containers. Pour equal amounts of water into each sifter. Measure how much water flowed into each container. **Ask:** What is the relationship between spaces between rocks and the movement of water underground? Water moves more easily in underground areas that have large spaces between rocks.

Quick Lab *Model a Stream*

Surface Water

👥 individuals
🕐 15 min
Inquiry **DIRECTED** inquiry

See the Lab Manual or go Online for planning information.

Exploration Lab *Aquifers and Development*

Groundwater

👥 small groups
🕐 30 min
Inquiry **DIRECTED** inquiry

PURPOSE **To simulate the reduction in groundwater recharge caused by development**

MATERIALS

- 2 aquariums
- golf balls
- cotton cloth
- plastic container
- clear plastic wrap
- food coloring
- granite sample
- limestone sample
- sand
- local soil
- water

See the Lab Manual or go Online for planning information.

Quick Lab *Modeling Groundwater*

Groundwater

👥 pairs
🕐 10 min
Inquiry **DIRECTED** inquiry

PURPOSE **To model the flow and storage of groundwater**

MATERIALS

- bowl
- pencil
- small gravel
- water (16 oz)
- 8-oz paper cup

See the Lab Manual or go Online for planning information.

Activities and Discussion

- ☐ **Activity** Raft Trip
- ☐ **Activity** Map River Systems
- ☐ **Activity** O, Impermeable Clay!
- ☐ **Probing Questions** Not a Drop to Drink

Labs and Demos

- ☐ **Daily Demo** Rock Spaces
- ☐ **Exploration Lab** Aquifers and Development
- ☐ **Quick Lab** Model a Stream
- ☐ **Quick Lab** Modeling Groundwater

Your Resources

_____

_____

_____

_____

Explain Science Concepts

	Print Path	**Digital Path**
Key Topics		

Surface Water

Print Path

☐ **Getting Your Feet Wet,** SE pp. 32–33
- Active Reading (Annotation strategy), #5
- Active Reading (Annotation strategy), #6
- Visualize It!, #7

☐ **Cry Me a River,** SE pp. 34–35
- Visualize It!, #8
- Active Reading, #9
- Active Reading, #10

☐ **Making a Splash,** SE p. 38
- Active Reading (Annotation strategy), #14

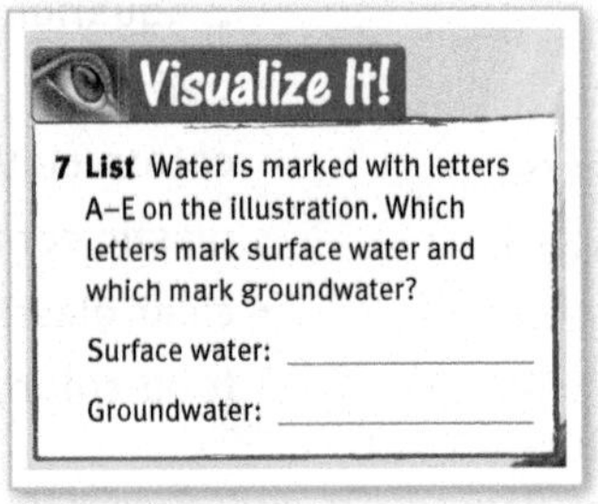

Visualize It!

7 List Water is marked with letters A–E on the illustration. Which letters mark surface water and which mark groundwater?

Surface water: _____

Groundwater: _____

Digital Path

☐ **Water Cycle**
Investigate the water cycle

☐ **River Processes**
Explore stream load, gradient, and flow

☐ **River Erosion**
Investigate watersheds

☐ **Surface Water Used by Humans**
Explore human use of surface water

Groundwater

Print Path

☐ **In Deep Water,** SE pp. 36–37
- Visualize It!, #11
- Visualize It!, #12
- Think Outside the Book, #13

☐ **Making a Splash,** SE p. 38
- Active Reading (Annotation strategy), #14

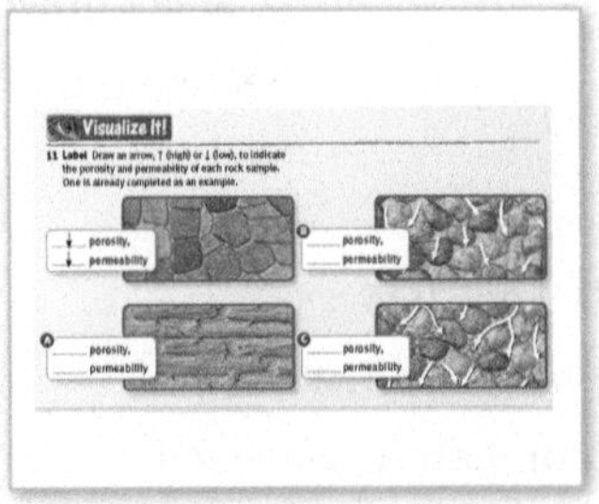

Digital Path

☐ **Aquifers**
Investigate aquifers

☐ **Aquifers**
Explore how porosity and permeability affect water movement in an aquifer

Differentiated Instruction

Basic *River Load*

Surface Water

 small groups
🕐 10 min

Let students model how rivers and streams pick up and drop their loads. Tell students to place small sticks, grass, and bits of rock and soil on one end of a long rectangular pan. Give students a small hose attached to a faucet. Have them run water into the pan to model erosion, transport, and deposition. Encourage students to alter the force of the water to observe how the volume and speed of flowing water affects its ability to pick up sediments.

Advanced *Desalination*

Groundwater

👥 individuals or pairs
🕐 ongoing

Tell students that much of Australia's groundwater is stored in artesian formations (sloping layers of permeable rock between layers of impermeable rock) that are fed by a vast underground aquifer called the Great Artesian Basin. Most of this groundwater is too salty for people to drink or to use for irrigation. Have students find out and report on how the water could be processed in a desalination plant.

ELL *Card Game*

Surface Water

 small groups
🕐 20 min

Have students play a card game to help them learn key vocabulary terms. Organize students into groups of three and assign each group several vocabulary terms. Distribute index cards to each group. Have one student in each group write one vocabulary term on each card. Have a second student draw an illustration for each vocabulary word on a card. Have a third student write one definition on a card. When students are finished, have groups exchange cards and try to match the term with the definition and the illustration.

Lesson Vocabulary

surface water	groundwater	water table
channel	tributary	watershed
divide	aquifer	

Previewing Vocabulary

 whole class
🕐 15 min

Multiple-meaning Words Point out that some words have everyday meanings and scientific meanings. *Divide,* for example, can be a verb that means to separate something into parts. In this lesson, it is a noun that refers to an area of higher ground that separates one watershed from another. Ask students to scan the lesson for other scientific words with multiple meanings. Discuss strategies to determine the meaning of these words, such as using context clues.

Reinforcing Vocabulary

👥 whole class
🕐 15 min

Water Words Help students visualize key vocabulary terms through simple demonstrations. Take students outside to a soil-covered area. Use a garden hose to demonstrate the concepts of surface water, runoff, channel, tributary, and divide. Have students observe how some of the water runs off the surface and seeps into the soil to become groundwater.

Customize Your Core Lesson

Core Instruction
☐ **Print Path** choices
☐ **Digital Path** choices

☐ **Reinforcing Vocabulary**
    Water Words

Vocabulary
☐ **Previewing Vocabulary**
    Multiple-meaning Words

Differentiated Instruction
☐ **Basic** River Load
☐ **Advanced** Desalination
☐ **ELL** Card Game

Your Resources

_____

_____

Extend Science Concepts

Reinforce and Review

Activity *Surface Water and Groundwater*

Synthesizing Key Topics

 whole class
 20 min

Carousel Review Use this strategy to review content with students:

1 Write four different questions on four separate charts. Set up one chart in each corner of the room. Possible questions include: How does groundwater form? What is the relationship between porosity and storage space in an aquifer? How does recharge differ from discharge? How do people use groundwater?

2 Arrange students into small groups. Assign each group a chart.

3 Have each group discuss and answer the question on their chart. After five minutes, direct groups to rotate to the next chart. Students should read the answer from the previous group and then add their own answer to the question.

4 Continue rotating groups until students have responded to the questions on all charts. At that point, groups should return to their original charts.

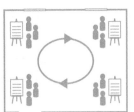

5 Have students review and discuss the answers to their original question. Monitor student discussions to identify any misconceptions or to clarify concepts.

Graphic Organizer

Synthesizing Key Topics

 individuals
 15 min

Cause and Effect Chain Have students make a cause-and-effect chain to explain the relationship between precipitation and fresh water on Earth. Students should recognize that precipitation falls to Earth's surface and runs off into bodies of water to form surface water or seeps into the ground to become groundwater.

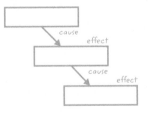

🜊 *Optional Online resource: Cause and Effect Chain support*

Going Further

Math Connection

Synthesizing Key Topics

 individuals
 20 min

Display Water Data Ask students to find out more information about how water is used in the United States. Tell students to compile their data into circle graphs. They should show the percentage of water used by each type of consumer. As an added challenge, have students create circle graphs showing water usage for another country. Students can then compare water usage trends among countries.

Real World Connection

Synthesizing Key Topics

individuals
20 min

Investigate Local Water Sources Encourage students to find out where their drinking water comes from. Students can conduct research online or contact county officials by mail or e-mail. Students should then draw posters that illustrate the path their drinking water takes from a rain cloud to local water sources to a faucet at school. Take the opportunity to discuss the need to clean water both before and after it is used. If time permits, arrange for a tour of a local water treatment plant.

Customize Your Closing

🜊 *See the Assessment Guide for quizzes and tests.*

🜊 *Go Online to edit and create quizzes and tests.*

Reinforce and Review

☐ **Activity** Carousel Review

☐ **Graphic Organizer** Cause and Effect Chain

☐ **Print Path** Visual Summary, SE p. 40

☐ **Digital Path** Lesson Closer

Evaluate Student Mastery

See the teacher support below the Student pages for additional Formative Assessment questions.

Ask the following questions to assess student mastery of the material. **Ask:** What can happen to rainwater that enters a storm drain on your street? Answer: It can drain into local rivers, streams, and lakes. **Ask:** How does permeability relate to the usefulness of an aquifer? Answer: Permeability is a measure of how easily water can flow through an aquifer. High permeability means that the pores in an aquifer are connected, allowing water to flow easily. So a useful aquifer has high permeability.

Reteach

Formative assessment may show that students need reinforcement for certain topics. The resources below are recommended for reteaching. If students were introduced to a topic through the Print path, you can also use the Digital Path to reteach, or vice versa.
🎧 *Can be assigned to individual students*

Surface Water
Activity Map River Systems 🎧
Quick Lab Model a Stream 🎧

Groundwater
Daily Demo Rock Spaces
Quick Lab Modeling Groundwater

Alternative Assessment
Surface Water

⏱ *Online resources: student worksheet; optional rubrics*

Surface Water and Groundwater

Points of View: *Surface Water*
Your class will work together to show what you've learned about surface water from several different viewpoints.

1. Work in groups as assigned by your teacher. Each group will be assigned to one or two viewpoints.

2. Complete your assignment, and present your perspective to the class.

 Vocabulary Make a word wall on the bulletin board that includes vocabulary terms related to surface water. Write the definition of each term on different-colored cards. Use arrows to show interrelationships among the words.

 Examples Use a video camera to record examples of surface water in your area. Include a narration that identifies the bodies of water and describes how they are replenished by the water cycle.

 Illustrations Draw an illustration of a watershed. Label the watershed, divide, main river channel, and tributaries. Include captions that describe the parts of your watershed.

 Analysis You are a hydrologist, a scientist who studies water systems. You have been asked to analyze the factors that affect the flow of a local stream. Write a brief report describing how plants, soil type, and topography affect stream flow.

 Calculations You've been asked to help develop a water conservation plan at school. Research or estimate how much water is used for common activities, such as drinking, cooking, cleaning, flushing toilets, and landscaping. Create a plan that reduces current water usage by at least 20 percent.

 Models Use a stream table to model the processes of erosion and deposition in river systems. Put sand or other sediments into the stream table. Record your observations of how the sediments are eroded and deposited at the mouth of your model river.

Going Further
☐ Math Connection
☐ Real World Connection
☐ Print Path Why It Matters,
  SE p. 39

Formative Assessment
☐ Strategies Throughout TE
☐ Lesson Review SE

Summative Assessment
☐ Alternative Assessment Surface Water
☐ Lesson Quiz
☐ Unit Tests A and B
☐ Unit Review SE End-of-Unit

Your Resources

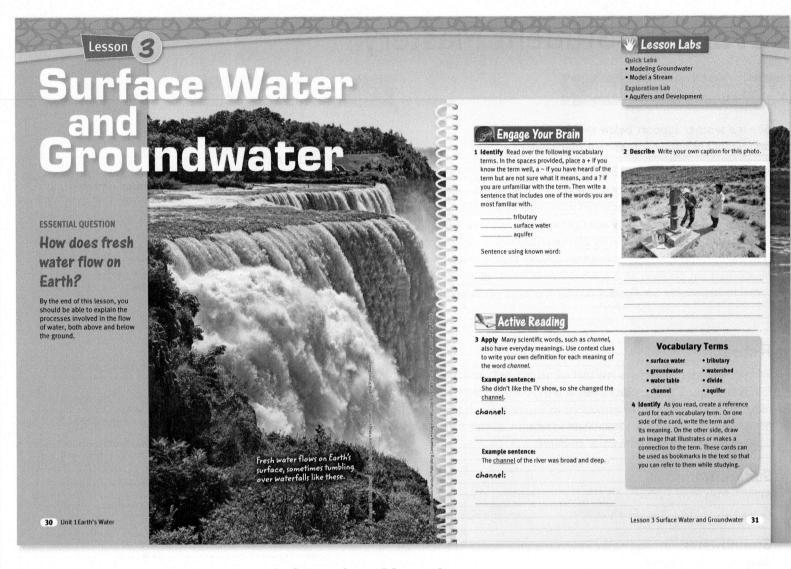

Lesson **3**

Surface Water and Groundwater

ESSENTIAL QUESTION

How does fresh water flow on Earth?

By the end of this lesson, you should be able to explain the processes involved in the flow of water, both above and below the ground.

Fresh water flows on Earth's surface, sometimes tumbling over waterfalls like these.

30 Unit 1 Earth's Water

Lesson Labs

Quick Labs
• Modeling Groundwater
• Model a Stream

Exploration Lab
• Aquifers and Development

Engage Your Brain

1 Identify Read over the following vocabulary terms. In the spaces provided, place a + if you know the term well, a ~ if you have heard of the term but are not sure what it means, and a ? if you are unfamiliar with the term. Then write a sentence that includes one of the words you are most familiar with.

_____ tributary
_____ surface water
_____ aquifer

Sentence using known word:
_____
_____
_____

2 Describe Write your own caption for this photo.

_____
_____
_____
_____

Active Reading

3 Apply Many scientific words, such as *channel*, also have everyday meanings. Use context clues to write your own definition for each meaning of the word *channel*.

Example sentence:
She didn't like the TV show, so she changed the channel.

channel:
_____
_____

Example sentence:
The channel of the river was broad and deep.

channel:
_____
_____

Vocabulary Terms

• surface water   • tributary
• groundwater   • watershed
• water table   • divide
• channel   • aquifer

4 Identify As you read, create a reference card for each vocabulary term. On one side of the card, write the term and its meaning. On the other side, draw an image that illustrates or makes a connection to the term. These cards can be used as bookmarks in the text so that you can refer to them while studying.

Lesson 3 Surface Water and Groundwater 31

Answers

Answers for 1–3 should represent students' current thoughts, even if incorrect.

1. Sample answer: +; ~; ?; The Ohio River is a tributary of the Mississippi River.

2. Sample answer: Water pumps can be used to bring fresh water to the surface.

3. Sample answer: a specific frequency for TV signals;

   the bed of a river

4. Students' annotations will vary.

Opening Your Lesson

After students have answered item 2, have them exchange sentences with a partner to expand their knowledge of vocabulary terms.

Prerequisites Students should already know that Earth is mainly covered by water, and that most of this water is salty and unsuitable for living things to drink. They also should understand the processes of the water cycle, specifically how precipitation replenishes stores of surface water and groundwater. In addition, students should understand how flowing water erodes and deposits sediments.

Learning Alert

Headwaters Tell students that some streams and rivers are fed by springs, as shown in the photo. Many streams, however, form at higher elevations. Water from precipitation and melting snow flows together into gullies that enlarge over time to form a stream channel. The area where water flows together to form a stream is called the stream's headwaters.

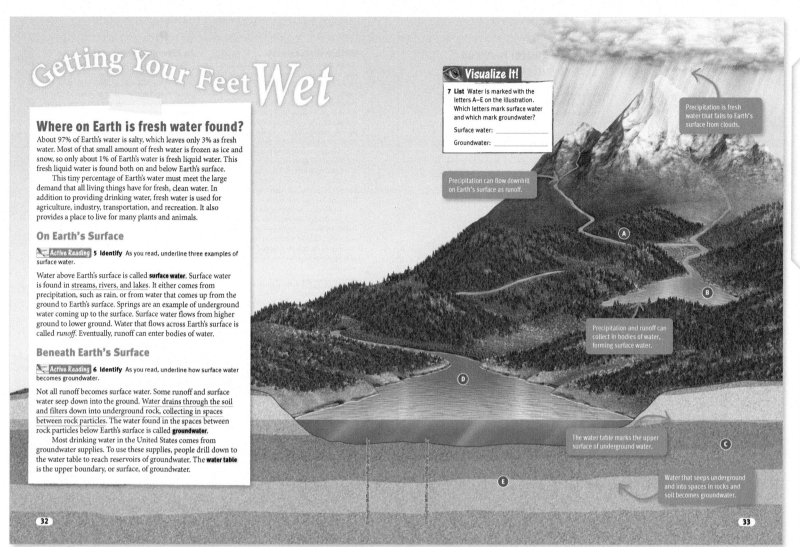

Getting Your Feet Wet

Where on Earth is fresh water found?

About 97% of Earth's water is salty, which leaves only 3% as fresh water. Most of that small amount of fresh water is frozen as ice and snow, so only about 1% of Earth's water is fresh liquid water. This fresh liquid water is found both on and below Earth's surface.

This tiny percentage of Earth's water must meet the large demand that all living things have for fresh, clean water. In addition to providing drinking water, fresh water is used for agriculture, industry, transportation, and recreation. It also provides a place to live for many plants and animals.

On Earth's Surface

Active Reading **5 Identify** As you read, underline three examples of surface water.

Water above Earth's surface is called **surface water**. Surface water is found in streams, rivers, and lakes. It either comes from precipitation, such as rain, or from water that comes up from the ground to Earth's surface. Springs are an example of underground water coming up to the surface. Surface water flows from higher ground to lower ground. Water that flows across Earth's surface is called *runoff*. Eventually, runoff can enter bodies of water.

Beneath Earth's Surface

Active Reading **6 Identify** As you read, underline how surface water becomes groundwater.

Not all runoff becomes surface water. Some runoff and surface water seep down into the ground. Water drains through the soil and filters down into underground rock, collecting in spaces between rock particles. The water found in the spaces between rock particles below Earth's surface is called **groundwater**.

Most drinking water in the United States comes from groundwater supplies. To use these supplies, people drill down to the water table to reach reservoirs of groundwater. The **water table** is the upper boundary, or surface, of groundwater.

Visualize It!

7 List Water is marked with the letters A–E on the illustration. Which letters mark surface water and which mark groundwater?

Surface water: _____

Groundwater: _____

Precipitation is fresh water that falls to Earth's surface from clouds.

Precipitation can flow downhill on Earth's surface as runoff.

Precipitation and runoff can collect in bodies of water, forming surface water.

The water table marks the upper surface of underground water.

Water that seeps underground and into spaces in rocks and soil becomes groundwater.

32

33

Answers

5. See students' pages for annotations.

6. See students' pages for annotations.

7. Surface water: A, B, D;
   Groundwater: C, E

Learning Alert

Caves of Water? Students might think that groundwater is stored in vast underground lakes or rivers. This is rarely the case. Most groundwater is stored in spaces in rock and soil similar to the way water is stored in a sponge. Do a simple demonstration to reinforce this concept. Place a dry sponge on a dish. Have students observe while you spray the sponge with water. **Ask:** What happened to the water? It seeped into the sponge. Relate students' observations to the movement of water into spaces between rocks and soil underground. Students may have observed water stored between grains of sand at the beach; if so, ask them to describe what they saw.

Interpreting Visuals

Have students study the diagram and trace the movement of water from clouds to Earth's surface. Point out that precipitation flows into bodies of surface water. **Ask:** What keeps these bodies of water from overflowing each time it rains or snows? Some surface water seeps into the ground as groundwater, and some evaporates back into the atmosphere.

Cry Me a River

How does water move on Earth's surface?

As precipitation falls on Earth's surface, it flows from higher to lower areas. The water that does not seep below the surface flows together and forms streams. The water erodes rocks and soil, eventually forming channels. A **channel** is the path that a stream follows. Over time, a channel gets wider and deeper, as the stream continues to erode rock and soil.

A **tributary** is a smaller stream that feeds into a river and eventually into a river system. A river system is a network of streams and rivers that drains an area of its runoff.

Visualize It!

8 Identify Label *tributary*, *river*, *divide*, and *stream load* in the spaces provided on the illustration.

Within Watersheds

A **watershed** is the area of land that is drained by a river system. Streams, rivers, flood plains, lakes, ponds, wetlands, and groundwater all contribute water to a watershed. Watersheds are separated from one other by a ridge or an area of higher ground called a **divide**. Precipitation that falls on one side of a divide enters one watershed while the precipitation that falls on the other side of a divide enters another watershed.

The largest watershed in the United States is the Mississippi River watershed. It has hundreds of tributaries. It extends from the Rocky Mountains, in the west, to the Appalachian Mountains, in the east, and down the length of the United States, from north to south.

Many factors affect the flow of water in a watershed. For example, plants slow runoff and reduce erosion. The porosity and permeability of rocks and sediment determine how much water can seep down into the ground. The steepness of land affects how fast water flows over a watershed.

Active Reading 9 State Which land feature separates watersheds?

In Rivers and Streams

Gradient is a measure of the change in elevation over a certain distance. In other words, gradient describes the steepness, or slope, of the land. The higher the gradient of a river or stream, the faster the water moves. The faster the water moves, the more energy it has to erode rock and soil.

A river's *flow* is the amount of water that moves through the river channel in a given amount of time. Flow increases during a major storm or when warm weather rapidly melts snow. An increase in flow causes an increase in a river's speed.

Materials carried by a stream are called *stream load*. Streams with a high flow carry a larger stream load. The size of the particles depends on water speed. Faster streams can carry larger particles. Streams eventually deposit their stream loads where the speed of the water decreases. This commonly happens as streams enter lakes and oceans.

Active Reading 10 Summarize How would an increase in gradient affect the speed of water?

Answers

8. A. divide; B. tributary; C. load; D. river

9. a divide

10. It would make the water move faster.

Building Reading Skills

Main Idea and Detail Notes Remind students that the main idea is the most important concept in a paragraph or section of text. Often, it is found in the heading or in the first sentence of a paragraph. Other times, readers must figure out the main idea by studying supporting details. Supporting details contain information that supports the main idea. Ask students to draw a two-column chart. The first column should be titled "Main Ideas." The second column should be titled "Detail Notes." As they read, ask them to fill in the main idea and detail notes for selected paragraphs or sections of text.

🌐 *Optional Online resource: Main Idea and Detail Notes support*

Probing Questions

Design an Experiment Have students develop a testable question concerning the relationship between vegetation and the flow of water in a watershed. A sample question might be: How do plant roots affect rates of soil erosion in a watershed? Students should develop step-by-step procedures to test their questions. They should include the materials they would use, as well as any necessary safety precautions. Review their procedures. If feasible, allow students to carry out their experiments.

In Deep Water

How does groundwater flow?

Although you can see some of Earth's fresh water in streams and lakes, you cannot see the large amount of water that flows underground as groundwater. Earth has much more fresh groundwater than fresh surface water.

It Trickles Down from Earth's Surface

Water from precipitation or streams may seep below the surface and become groundwater. Groundwater is either stored or it flows underground. It can enter back into streams and lakes, becoming surface water again. An **aquifer** is a body of rock or sediment that stores groundwater and allows it to flow.

Recall that the water table is the upper surface of underground water. The water table can rise or fall depending on the amount of water in the aquifer. In wet regions, the water table can be at or just beneath the soil's surface. In wetland areas, the water table is above the soil's surface.

It Fills Tiny Spaces Underground

An aquifer stores water in open spaces, or *pores*, between particles of rock or sediment. The storage space in an aquifer is measured by *porosity*, the percentage of the rock that is composed of pore space. The greater the pore space is, the higher the porosity is. A cup of gravel, for example, has higher porosity than a cup of sand does.

Permeability is a measure of how easily water can flow through an aquifer. High permeability means that many pores in the aquifer are connected, so water can flow easily. Aquifers with both high porosity and high permeability are useful as a water resource.

Visualize It!

11 Label Draw an arrow, ↑ (high) or ↓ (low), to indicate the porosity and permeability of each rock sample. One is already completed as an example.

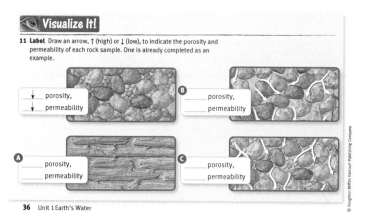

___ porosity, ___ permeability

B ___ porosity, ___ permeability

A ___ porosity, ___ permeability

C ___ porosity, ___ permeability

36 Unit 1 Earth's Water

It Is Recharged and Discharged

Surface water that trickles down into the ground can reach the water table and enter an aquifer. This process is called *recharge*, and occurs in an area called the *recharge zone*.

Where the water table meets the surface, water may pool to form a wetland or may flow out as a spring. The process by which groundwater becomes surface water is called *discharge* and happens in *discharge zones*. Discharge can feed rivers, streams, and lakes. Groundwater is also discharged where water is extracted from wells that are drilled down into the water table. Through discharge and recharge, the same water circulates between surface water and groundwater.

Visualize It!

12 Label On the illustration below, write a caption for *discharge zone* and for *aquifer*.

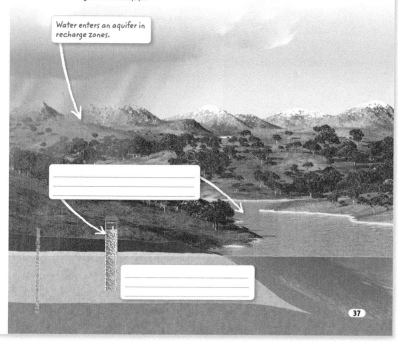

Water enters an aquifer in recharge zones.

37

Think Outside the Book Inquiry

13 Debate During times of little or no rainfall, many communities have regulations limiting water use. Imagine that you live in a community with a depleted aquifer. As a class, develop a set of regulations that you think residents should follow. Start by brainstorming as many uses of water as you can. Then decide which uses should be regulated and to what extent.

Answers

11. A. ↑ porosity, ↓ permeability;
    B. ↑ porosity, ↑ permeability;
    C. ↓ porosity, ↑ permeability

12. Sample answer: aquifer: Water fills and flows through an underground aquifer; discharge zone: Water leaves an aquifer in discharge zones, such as wells and surfaces from which water evaporates.

13. Student output should include a set of regulations for community water use. They may suggest regulating activities such as washing cars or watering lawns. They may propose recycling waste water, increasing water rates, or offering educational programs about water conservation for residents.

Formative Assessment

Ask: How can you reach water in an aquifer? by digging a well **Ask:** Should the well reach several feet above or several feet below the water table? Explain your answer. It should reach several feet below the water table so that it can access water in the aquifer. **Ask:** What can change the level of the water table in an area? Sample answer: A drought might cause the water table to fall. A heavy rainfall might cause the water table to rise.

Learning Alert

Difficult Concepts Students may have difficulty understanding the meaning of the word *permeability*. Tell them to think of it as how quickly the rock will refill with water.

Making a Splash

Active Reading

14 Identify As you read this page, underline how water is used in a typical home.

How do people use surface water and groundwater?

About 75% of all the fresh water used in the United States comes from surface water. The other 25% comes from groundwater. But surface water and groundwater are connected. In human terms, they are one resource. People use this freshwater resource in many different ways.

These rafters enjoy the exhilaration of river rapids.

For Drinking and Use at Home

Groundwater is an important source of drinking water. Surface water is used for drinking, too. Fresh water is also used in many other ways in homes. In a typical home, about 50% of all water used is for washing clothes, bathing, washing dishes, and flushing toilets. About 33% is used to water lawns and gardens. The rest is used for drinking, cooking, and washing hands.

For Agriculture

Activities like growing crops and raising livestock use about 40% of fresh water used in the United States. These activities account for about 70% of all groundwater use. A little over half the water used in agriculture comes from surface water. A little less than half comes from groundwater.

For Industry

Almost half of the fresh water used in the United States is used for industry. Only about 20% of this water comes from groundwater. The rest is surface water. About 40% of water used in industry helps cool elements in power plants.

For Transportation and Recreation

Surface water is also used to transport products and people from place to place. In addition, people use rivers, streams, and lakes for swimming, sailing, kayaking, water skiing, and other types of recreation.

Why It Matters

Troubled Waters

EYE ON THE ENVIRONMENT

Each hour, about 15,114 babies are born around the world. The human population has skyrocketed over the last few hundred years. But the amount of fresh water on Earth has remained roughly the same. The limited supply of fresh water is an important resource that must be managed so that it can meet the demands of a growing population.

Scientists are developing technologies for obtaining clean, fresh water to meet global needs. Here, a boy uses a water purifier straw that filters disease-causing microbes and certain other contaminants from surface water. The straw is inexpensive and can filter 700 L of water before it needs to be replaced—that's about how much water the average person drinks in one year.

Like many places on Earth, Zimbabwe is experiencing severe water shortages. The country has been plagued by droughts since the 1980s. Scientists estimate that about 1 billion people around the world do not have an adequate supply of clean, fresh water.

Extend   Inquiry

15 Infer Most of Earth is covered by water. How can we be experiencing shortages of drinking water?

16 Research Find out which diseases are caused by microbes found in untreated surface water. How might the water purifier straw reduce the number of people getting these diseases?

17 Recommend Conserving water is one way to ensure adequate supplies of drinking water. Work with a group to develop a plan to reduce water use at school. Present your plan to the class. As a class, select the best aspects of each group's plan. Combine the best suggestions into a document to present to the school administration.

Answers

14. *See students' pages for annotations.*

15. Sample answer: Most water on Earth is salt water, which humans cannot drink.

16. Sample answer: Microbes in untreated surface water may cause diarrhea, dysentery, typhoid, and cholera. Rates of these diseases would go down with widespread use of the straw.

17. Student output should include thoughtful and practical suggestions for reducing water use, such as using low-flow or water-reducing faucets and toilets, putting mulch around shrubs and other plants to reduce water loss and the need to water plants, and regularly checking drinking fountains, toilets, and faucets for leaks.

Learning Alert

Making Predictions Before students read the page titled *Making a Splash,* ask them to predict how most water is used in the United States. After students read the page, discuss their predictions. Were their predictions accurate? Did they realize how much water was used for agriculture and industry? Lead students to understand that they use water in many indirect ways, such as when they eat food that was grown in an irrigated field or turn on a television powered by electricity generated by a coal-burning or nuclear power plant.

Why It Matters

Tell students there are nearly seven billion people on Earth. **Ask:** About what percentage of the world's population does not have an adequate supply of clean, fresh water? about 14 percent **Ask:** How might your life change if you did not have access to clean, fresh water? Sample answer: I would not be able to take showers every day. I might be sick because I would not have clean water to drink. **Ask:** In addition to new technology, what else can be done to increase access to clean water? Sample answer: People can conserve water.

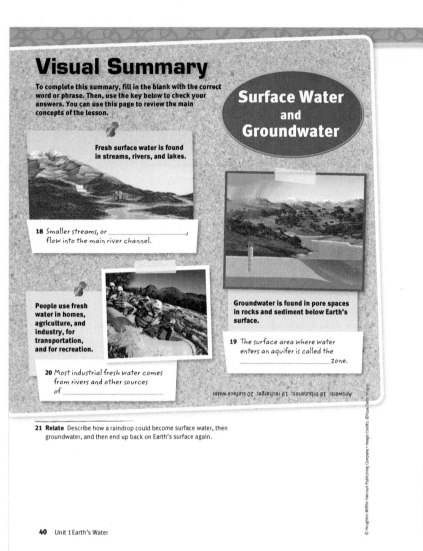

Visual Summary

To complete this summary, fill in the blank with the correct word or phrase. Then, use the key below to check your answers. You can use this page to review the main concepts of the lesson.

Surface Water and Groundwater

Fresh surface water is found in streams, rivers, and lakes.

18 Smaller streams, or _____, flow into the main river channel.

People use fresh water in homes, agriculture, and industry, for transportation, and for recreation.

Groundwater is found in pore spaces in rocks and sediment below Earth's surface.

19 The surface area where water enters an aquifer is called the _____ zone.

20 Most industrial fresh water comes from rivers and other sources of _____

Answers: 18 tributaries; 19 recharge; 20 surface water

21 Relate Describe how a raindrop could become surface water, then groundwater, and then end up back on Earth's surface again.

40 Unit 1 Earth's Water

Lesson Review

Lesson 3

Vocabulary
In your own words, define the following terms.

1 surface water

2 watershed

3 groundwater

4 water table

5 aquifer

Key Concepts

6 Identify What three factors describe the movement of surface water in streams and rivers?

7 Explain How does the gradient of a river affect its flow?

8 Describe How quickly would groundwater flow through rock with high porosity and high permeability? Explain your answer.

Critical Thinking

9 Conclude An area's rate of groundwater recharge exceeds its rate of groundwater discharge. What can you conclude about the area's groundwater supply?

Use this graph to answer the following questions.

Average Water-Level Changes in the High Plains Aquifer by State (1950-2005)

10 Analyze What has happened to the amount of water in the High Plains Aquifer over time?

11 Infer What might account for the changes described in question 10?

Lesson 3 Surface Water and Groundwater 41

Visual Summary Answers

18. tributaries
19. recharge
20. surface water
21. Sample answer: After a rainstorm, a raindrop enters the rivers, streams, lakes, and other surface water. It then could trickle down into the ground and into an aquifer. This groundwater could reach the surface again, through a well or spring, or another place the water table meets the surface.

Lesson Review Answers

1. water that collects on the ground or in a body of water
2. the area of land that is drained by a river system
3. water in the pores of underground rock
4. the topmost limit of the ground that is saturated with water
5. the rock layer that stores groundwater
6. gradient (steepness or slope of the land), flow, and stream load
7. The higher the gradient, the faster the river flows.

8. It would flow fast because there is high pore space (high porosity) and the water can flow easily (high permeability).
9. It is likely high because water is being replenished faster than it is being depleted.
10. It has decreased.
11. Sample answer: increases in population, increases in water use, prolonged periods of dry weather

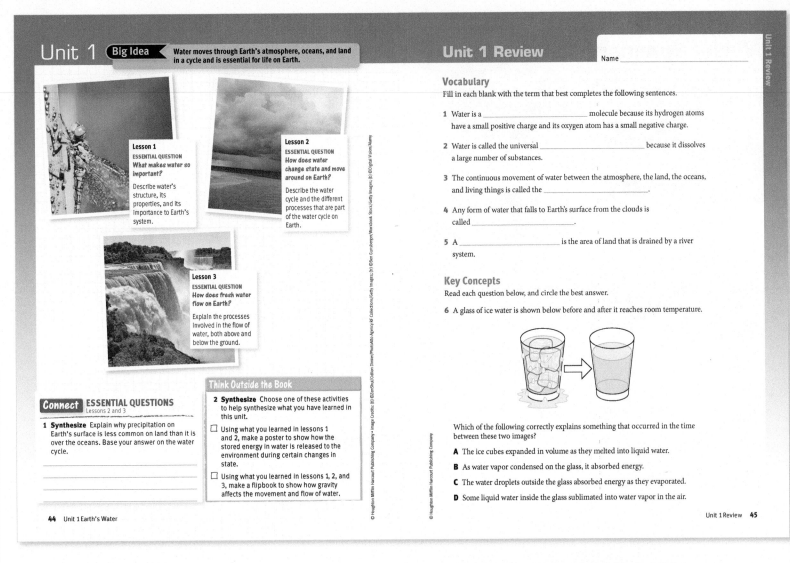

Unit 1

Big Idea — Water moves through Earth's atmosphere, oceans, and land in a cycle and is essential for life on Earth.

Lesson 1
ESSENTIAL QUESTION
What makes water so important?
Describe water's structure, its properties, and its importance to Earth's system.

Lesson 2
ESSENTIAL QUESTION
How does water change state and move around on Earth?
Describe the water cycle and the different processes that are part of the water cycle on Earth.

Lesson 3
ESSENTIAL QUESTION
How does fresh water flow on Earth?
Explain the processes involved in the flow of water, both above and below the ground.

Connect ESSENTIAL QUESTIONS
Lessons 2 and 3

1 Synthesize Explain why precipitation on Earth's surface is less common on land than it is over the oceans. Base your answer on the water cycle.

Think Outside the Book

2 Synthesize Choose one of these activities to help synthesize what you have learned in this unit.

☐ Using what you learned in lessons 1 and 2, make a poster to show how the stored energy in water is released to the environment during certain changes in state.

☐ Using what you learned in lessons 1, 2, and 3, make a flipbook to show how gravity affects the movement and flow of water.

44   Unit 1 Earth's Water

Unit 1 Review

Name _____

Vocabulary
Fill in each blank with the term that best completes the following sentences.

1 Water is a _____ molecule because its hydrogen atoms have a small positive charge and its oxygen atom has a small negative charge.

2 Water is called the universal _____ because it dissolves a large number of substances.

3 The continuous movement of water between the atmosphere, the land, the oceans, and living things is called the _____.

4 Any form of water that falls to Earth's surface from the clouds is called _____.

5 A _____ is the area of land that is drained by a river system.

Key Concepts
Read each question below, and circle the best answer.

6 A glass of ice water is shown below before and after it reaches room temperature.

Which of the following correctly explains something that occurred in the time between these two images?

A The ice cubes expanded in volume as they melted into liquid water.

B As water vapor condensed on the glass, it absorbed energy.

C The water droplets outside the glass absorbed energy as they evaporated.

D Some liquid water inside the glass sublimated into water vapor in the air.

Unit 1 Review   45

Unit Summary Answers

1. Oceans cover a greater amount of Earth's surface than land does. Therefore, a greater amount of condensation and precipitation take place over Earth's ocean than Earth's land.

2. Option 1: Posters should show that the stored energy of water is released 1) when water vapor changes from a gas to a liquid during *condensation*; 2) when liquid water changes to a solid during *freezing*; and 3) when water vapor changes from a gas to a solid during *deposition*. Option 2: Flipbooks should show that when precipitation becomes too heavy to be held in Earth's atmosphere, it falls to Earth's surface in the form of rain, snow, sleet, or hail. On Earth's surface, gravity causes liquid water to run downhill. This process, in which water flows over land, is called *runoff*. When runoff flows into a stream or river, it moves downhill within the stream or river channel. Gravity also causes liquid water on land or in rivers and streams to move downward into pore spaces within rock or sediment. This process is called *infiltration*. This water eventually enters an aquifer, within which gravity causes groundwater to move downhill.

Unit Review [Response to Intervention]

A Quick Grading Chart follows the Answers. See the Assessment Guide for more detail about correct and incorrect answer choices. Refer back to the Lesson Planning pages for activities and assignments that can be used as remediation for students who answer questions incorrectly.

Answers

1. polar The answer is polar because polar molecules have a net positive charge in one or more areas and a net negative charge in one or more areas. (Lesson 1)

2. solvent The answer is solvent because a solvent is a liquid that dissolves other substances. (Lesson 1)

3. water cycle This is the correct definition of the water cycle. (Lesson 2)

4. precipitation The answer is precipitation and cannot be condensation because clouds, fog, and mist are already made up of tiny droplets of condensed water vapor. (Lesson 2)

6th

nued

hs most correctly shows the approximate proportions of
on the surface of the earth?

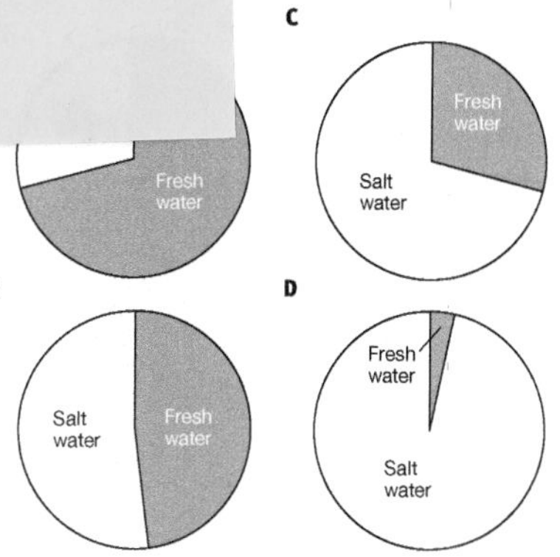

8 Which of the following is not a way that water reaches Earth's atmosphere?

A condensation
C sublimation
B evaporation
D transpiration

9 Which of the following correctly explains why icebergs float in the ocean?

A Ice is less dense than liquid water because water contracts when it freezes, filling in open space between molecules.

B Ice is less dense than liquid water because there is more open space between molecules in ice than in liquid water.

C Ice is more dense than liquid water because there is less open space between molecules in ice than in water.

D Water is a polar molecule, so the net positive electrical charges in the water repel the net positive electrical charges inside the iceberg.

Name ______________________

10 A certain percentage of water that falls to Earth's surface as precipitation does not become surface water or groundwater and does not evaporate back into the atmosphere. Which of the following most likely explains what happens to this water?

A The water falls into the ocean, where it evaporates back into the atmosphere.

B The water is stored as snow and ice on Earth's surface.

C The water molecules are broken down into hydrogen and oxygen atoms.

D The water is absorbed and used by plants.

11 Which of the following is an incorrect statement about the flow of water through watersheds?

A A watershed can be fed by groundwater.

B The boundary separating two watersheds is called a divide.

C Plant life often alters the flow of water in a watershed by causing erosion.

D The gradient of the land can affect the flow of water through a watershed.

12 Which of the following is the name for all the materials carried by a stream other than the water itself?

A discharge
C gradient
B flow
D stream load

Critical Thinking

Answer the following questions in the space provided.

13 Give two examples of the importance of water to human activities, explaining how the water is used.

Answers *(continued)*

5. watershed This is the accepted definition of the term watershed. A watershed is also sometimes called a drainage basin. (Lesson 3)
6. Answer C is correct because evaporating water does absorb energy. (Lesson 2)
7. Answer D is correct because approximately 3% of the water on the surface of the Earth is fresh water. Students don't need to know this exact percent, but they should understand that the vast majority is salt water. (Lesson 1)
8. Answer A is correct because condensation is a way in which water becomes a liquid and becomes separate from the gases in the atmosphere. (Lesson 2)
9. Answer B is correct because water expands when it freezes, allowing more open space between molecules in ice than in water. (Lesson 1)
10. Answer B is correct because a significant amount of precipitation on Earth is stored as snow and ice, which means that this water is not moving through the water cycle. (Lesson 2)
11. Answer C is correct because plant life most often affects the flow by preventing erosion. (Lesson 3)
12. Answer D is correct because the stream load is all the materials carried by a river other than the water itself. (Lesson 3)
13. Key Elements:
    - identifies two human activities that use water, and explains how the water is used (e.g., *Agriculture uses water to grow plants that humans and farm animals eat; Electrical power generation requires water to cool the power plants that create electricity; Public health requires water for human hygiene to keep people and their surroundings clean; Human survival requires that humans consume clean water to survive;* etc.) (Lesson 1)

Unit 1 Review continued

14 The diagram below shows the changes among the three states of water.

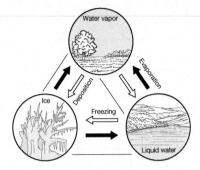

Energy absorbed / released by water

Energy absorbed / released by water

Fill in each of the three blank lines with the correct term for the change of state shown by the arrows. In the key, circle the correct word to show whether water absorbs or releases energy in the changes of state shown by that type of arrow.

Connect ESSENTIAL QUESTIONS
Lessons 1, 2, and 3

Answer the following question in the space provided.

15 Describe what happens to a molecule of water as it moves through the water cycle along any path you choose. Be sure to mention the movement of the water molecule, any changes of state, and the absorption or release of energy.

48   Unit 1 Earth's Water

© Houghton Mifflin Harcourt Publishing Company

Answers (continued)

14. Key Elements:
    - (clockwise from top left) Sublimation; Condensation; Melting; (key) released; absorbed. (Lesson 2)

15. Key Elements:
    - demonstrates an understanding of the water cycle (e.g., *The water molecule starts in the ocean. It absorbs energy as it evaporates into the atmosphere. It releases energy as it condenses and forms a cloud. It precipitates in the mountains as snow and later absorbs energy as it melts. It then flows into a river, infiltrates the soil, and goes below ground. As part of groundwater, it eventually travels back to the ocean.*)
    - correctly identifies changes of state in each stage of the cycle (e.g., *evaporates into the atmosphere, condenses into a cloud, sublimates from ice to water vapor in the atmosphere*, etc.)
    - correctly identifies the energy change related to each change in state (e.g., *releasing or absorbing energy*) (Lesson 1–3)

Quick Grading Chart

Use the chart below for quick test grading. The lesson correlations can help you target reteaching for missed items.

Item	Answer	Cognitive Complexity	Lesson
1.	—	Low	1
2.	—	Low	1
3.	—	Low	2
4.	—	Low	2
5.	—	Low	3
6.	C	Moderate	2
7.	D	Moderate	1
8.	A	Low	2
9.	B	Low	1
10.	B	High	2
11.	C	Moderate	3
12.	D	Low	3
13.	—	Moderate	1
14.	—	Moderate	2
15.	—	Moderate	1–3

Cognitive Complexity refers to the demand on thinking associated with an item, and may vary with the answer choices, the number of steps required to arrive at an answer, and other factors, but not the ability level of the student.

The Big Idea and Essential Questions

This Unit was designed to focus on this Big Idea and Essential Questions.

> **Big Idea** The oceans are a connected system of water in motion that transports matter and energy around Earth's surface.

Lesson	ESSENTIAL QUESTION	Student Mastery	PD Professional Development	Lesson Overview
LESSON 1 Earth's Oceans and the Ocean Floor	*What lies within and beneath Earth's oceans?*	To describe the properties and physical features of Earth's oceans	Content Refresher, TE p. 66	TE p. 72
LESSON 2 Ocean Waves	*How does an ocean wave form and move?*	To describe the characteristics of ocean waves and what happens as they move through the ocean	Content Refresher, TE p. 67	TE p. 88
LESSON 3 Ocean Currents	*How does water move in the ocean?*	To describe the movement of ocean water, explain what factors influence this movement, and explain why ocean circulation is important in Earth's system	Content Refresher, TE p. 68	TE p. 104

©Sean Davey/Aurora Photos/Corbis

 **Professional Development** Science Background

Use the key words at right to access

- Professional Development from **The NSTA Learning Center**
- **SciLinks** for additional online content appropriate for students and teachers

Keywords

ocean currents   ocean waves

oceans

 **National Science Teachers Association**

 **SciLINKS** THE WORLD'S A CLICK AWAY

Options for Instruction

Two parallel paths provide coverage of the Essential Questions, with a strong **Inquiry** strand woven into each. Follow the **Print Path,** the **Digital Path,** or your customized combination of print, digital, and inquiry.

	LESSON 1 Earth's Oceans and the Ocean Floor	**LESSON 2** Ocean Waves	**LESSON 3** Ocean Currents
Essential Questions	*What lies within and beneath Earth's oceans?*	*How does an ocean wave form and move?*	*How does water move in the ocean?*
Key Topics	• Earth's Oceans • Salinity and Temperature • Density • Studying the Ocean Floor and Its Features	• Properties of Ocean Waves • Ocean Wave Formation • Ocean Wave Movement • Waves at the Shore	• Surface Currents in the Ocean • Deep Currents in the Ocean • Upwelling • Ocean Circulation
Print Path	**Teacher Edition** pp. 72–85 **Student Edition** pp. 52–63	**Teacher Edition** pp. 88–101 **Student Edition** pp. 66–77	**Teacher Edition** pp. 104–118 **Student Edition** pp. 80–93
Inquiry Labs	**Lab Manual** **Exploration Lab** Measuring Salinity **Quick Lab** Evaporation Rates **Quick Lab** Ocean Density	**Lab Manual** **Exploration Lab** Wave Movement **Quick Lab** Making Waves **Quick Lab** Factors in Wave Formation	**Lab Manual** **Quick Lab** Can Messages Travel on Ocean Water? Virtual Lab Ocean Currents
Digital Path	**Digital Path** TS661375	**Digital Path** TS661385	**Digital Path** TS661360

UNIT 2
Unit Projects

 Citizen Science Project
Immersion Learning

Teacher's Edition **p. 71**

Student Edition
pp. 50–51

Unit Assessment
Formative Assessment
Strategies
Throughout TE

Lesson Reviews SE

Unit PreTest

Summative Assessment
Alternative Assessment
(1 per lesson) RTI

Lesson Quizzes

Unit Tests A and B

Unit Review RTI

(with answer remediation)

Practice Tests (end of module)

Project-Based Assessment
See the Assessment Guide for quizzes and tests.

Go Online to edit and create quizzes and tests.

Response to Intervention

See RTI teacher support materials on p. PD7.

Differentiated Instruction

English Language Proficiency

Strategies for **English Language Learners (ELL)**
are provided for each lesson, under the Explain tabs.

> LESSON 1 *Contrasting Ocean Research Methods,* TE p. 77
>
> LESSON 2 *Tsunamis,* TE p. 93
>
> LESSON 3 *Understanding Deflection,* TE p. 109

Vocabulary strategies provided for all students can also be a
particular help for ELL. Use different strategies for each lesson
or choose one or two to use throughout the unit. Vocabulary
strategies can be found under the Explain tab for each lesson
(TE pp. 77, 93, and 109).

Leveled Inquiry

Inquiry labs, activities, probing questions, and daily demos
provide a range of inquiry levels. Preview them under the
Engage and Explore tabs starting on TE pp. 74, 90, and 106.

Levels of **Inquiry**	DIRECTED inquiry	GUIDED inquiry	INDEPENDENT inquiry
	introduces inquiry skills within a structured framework.	develops inquiry skills within a supportive environment.	deepens inquiry skills with student-driven questions or procedures.

Each long lab has two inquiry options:

> LESSON 1 **Exploration Lab** *Measuring Salinity*
>
> LESSON 2 **Exploration Lab** *Wave Movement*

Go Digital! ⟐ thinkcentral.com

Digital Path

The Unit 2 Resource Gateway is
your guide to all of the digital
resources for this unit. To access
the Gateway, visit thinkcentral.com.

Digital Interactive Lessons

Lesson 1 Earth's Oceans and the
Ocean Floor TS661375

Lesson 2 Ocean Waves TS661385

Lesson 3 Ocean Currents
TS661360

More Digital Resources

In addition to digital lessons,
you will find the following digital
resources for Unit 1:

People in Science: Evan B.
Forde

Virtual Lab: Ocean Currents
(previewed on TE p. 107)

RTI ▶ Response to Intervention

Response to Intervention (RTI) is a process for identifying and supporting students who are not making expected progress toward essential learning goals. The following *ScienceFusion* components can be used to provide strategic and intensive intervention.

Component	Location	Strategies and Benefits
STUDENT EDITION Active Reading prompts, Visualize It!, Think Outside the Book	**Throughout each lesson**	Student responses can be used as screening tools to assess whether intervention is needed.
TEACHER EDITION Formative Assessment, Probing Questions, Learning Alerts	**Throughout each lesson**	Opportunities are provided to assess and remediate student understanding of lesson concepts.
TEACHER EDITION Extend Science Concepts	**Reinforce and Review, TE pp. 78, 94, 110** **Going Further, TE pp. 78, 94, 110**	Additional activities allow students to reinforce and extend their understanding of lesson concepts.
TEACHER EDITION Evaluate Student Mastery	**Formative Assessment, TE pp. 79, 95, 111** **Alternative Assessment, TE pp. 79, 95, 111**	These assessments allow for greater flexibility in assessing students with differing physical, mental, and language abilities as well as varying learning and communication modes.
TEACHER EDITION Unit Review Remediation	**Unit Review, TE p. 120–122**	Includes reference back to Lesson Planning pages for remediation activities and assignments.
INTERACTIVE DIGITAL LESSONS and VIRTUAL LABS	**thinkcentral.com** **Unit 2 Gateway** **Lesson 1 TS661375** **Lesson 2 TS661385** **Lesson 3 TS661360**	Lessons and labs make content accessible through simulations, animations, videos, audio, and integrated assessment. Useful for review and reteaching of lesson concepts.

Content Refresher

Professional Development

Earth's Oceans and the Ocean Floor

ESSENTIAL QUESTION

What lies within and beneath Earth's oceans?

1. Earth's Oceans

Students will learn that there are five main oceans that make up Earth's global ocean.

Earth is often called the "Water Planet." This is because nearly 70 percent of Earth's surface is covered by water. Of this water, 97 percent is salt water. The global ocean is divided into five bodies of water. The largest is the Pacific Ocean, which contains nearly 50 percent of Earth's ocean water. The Atlantic Ocean is the second-largest ocean. Earth's third-largest ocean is the Indian Ocean, most of which is located in the Southern Hemisphere. Earth's two smallest oceans are the Southern Ocean, located near Antarctica, and the Arctic Ocean, located near the North Pole and largely covered by ice for much of the year.

2. Salinity and Temperature

Students will learn why the salinity and temperature of ocean water vary.

The key factor distinguishing ocean water from fresh water is salinity. In general, the salinity of ocean water is about 3.5 percent (35 g of salt per kilogram of ocean water). However, salinity varies slightly from one location to another as a result of the water cycle and climate variations. The water cycle can lower salinity in regions with heavy precipitation. By contrast, it can increase salinity in regions with increased evaporation.

Ocean water temperature also varies with location. Surface water temperatures are largely affected by latitude. Climate variations also have an effect on surface water temperatures.

Depth also affects ocean water temperature. Scientists divide the ocean into three temperature layers based on depth: the surface layer, the thermocline, and the deep zone. The temperature in the deep zone averages between 2 °C and 4 °C.

3. Density

Students will learn how temperature and salinity affect the density of ocean water.

Pure water has a density of 1.0 g/cm³. However, because ocean water contains dissolved salts, it is denser than pure water and typically has a density between 1.020 g/cm³ and 1.029 g/cm³. The density of the water increases as its salinity increases.

Ocean water becomes denser as its temperature decreases. Different masses of ocean water may have different densities as a result of temperature and salinity variations. These density differences cause the movement of some ocean currents.

4. Studying the Ocean Floor and Its Features

Students will learn about tools used to study the ocean floor, features of the ocean floor, and their formation.

Sonar, satellites, underwater vessels, and deep-sea drilling and dredging are some of the methods used by scientists to study the ocean floor. Sonar uses sound waves to map the ocean floor. Satellites orbiting Earth use measurements of variations in gravity to provide detailed data about the oceans. Scientists use both piloted and remotely operated underwater vessels to make observations. Deep-sea drilling can provide core samples of the ocean sediment and rock that can be analyzed.

Ocean floor features are often divided into two large regions: the continental margin and the deep-ocean basin. The continental margin is the region nearest to the coastlines of the continents. This region is generally divided into three areas: the continental shelf, the continental slope, and the continental rise. Deep-ocean basins rest between the edges of the continental margins. They are made up of abyssal plains and areas formed by tectonic plate interactions. The abyssal plains are the flattest places on Earth.

Features that rise above the ocean floor are mid-ocean ridges, volcanoes, and seamounts. Mid-ocean ridges are mountain chains on the ocean floor. A seamount is a submerged volcano. Subducting plates can form long, narrow depressions in the ocean floor called ocean trenches. The deepest of these is the Mariana Trench. In 1960, Jacques Piccard and Don Walsh became the first to reach the Mariana Trench.

Lesson 2 Ocean Waves   This activity can demonstrate how water moves as a wave passes: Energy is represented by a ball. Students should stand in a line and pass the ball. As each student receives the ball, he or she jumps up a few inches. Upon landing, the student passes the ball to the next person. Students can see how the water (students) moves up and down but stays in place as the wave energy moves through the medium.

Lesson 2

Ocean Waves

ESSENTIAL QUESTION

How does an ocean wave form and move?

1. Properties of Ocean Waves

Students will learn that ocean waves are energy traveling along the boundary between ocean water and the atmosphere.

A wave in the ocean has the same basic shape as many other types of waves. The high point of a wave is the crest, and the low point is the trough. Halfway between the crests and troughs, the water level is neutral, or at a level the water would occupy if there were no waves. The vertical distance between the halfway point of the wave and the trough or the crest is its amplitude. The horizontal distance between successive crests or troughs is the wavelength.

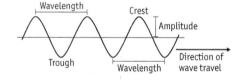

Students will learn to describe wave period and calculate wave speed.

Wave period is the number of waves produced in a given amount of time. You can measure the wave period by counting how many waves pass a fixed point in a period of time. The equation below is known as the wave equation. In the equation, *v* stands for velocity and *f* for frequency.

wave speed (v) = wavelength (λ) × wave period (f)

2. Ocean Wave Formation

Students will learn that most ocean waves derive their energy and motion from the wind.

The size and speed achieved by a wave depend on three factors: the wind speed, the length of time the wind has

blown, and the fetch. The fetch is the distance that the wind can blow across open water. As the amount of energy transferred from the wind to the water increases, the height and steepness of the waves increase as well.

3. Ocean Wave Movement

Students will learn that ocean waves transport energy, not water.

When the wind blows over the ocean, it transfers kinetic energy from molecules of air to molecules of water. Though the waves appear to transport water as they travel, they actually cause the water in any given spot to revolve around a fixed center. Water particles rising to the tops of their paths form the crest of a wave, while those heading down form the trough.

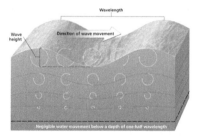

4. Waves at the Shore

Students will learn what happens when an ocean wave reaches the shore.

When a wave approaches the shore, the water becomes shallower. The wave touches the bottom, which slows down the speed of the wave. The slightly faster waves further out catch up, shortening the wavelength. As the speed and length of the wave diminishes, the wave grows taller. Finally, the wave cannot support itself and breaks, causing the water to move onto the shore and transfer its energy.

Tsunamis can be caused when huge amounts of water are displaced by an earthquake, landslide, volcanic eruption, or comet or meteorite strike. The resulting displacement of water can create an immense, destructive wave, such as the great Indian Ocean Tsunami of 2004.

Content Refresher (continued)

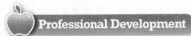
Professional Development

Lesson 3

Ocean Currents

ESSENTIAL QUESTION
How does water move in the ocean?

1. Surface Currents in the Ocean

Surface currents are stream-like movements of water at or near the ocean's surface.

Ocean currents are stream-like movements of water. Surface currents in the ocean can extend hundreds of meters below the surface and can reach thousands of kilometers in length. One example of a surface current is the Gulf Stream.

There are three different factors that play a role in determining surface currents: global winds, the Coriolis effect, and continental deflection. Global winds determine the direction of surface currents. The Coriolis effect is caused by Earth's rotation and is responsible for a curve in direction of ocean currents. Continental deflection occurs when a current runs into a landmass and the current is deflected in another direction.

2. Deep Currents in the Ocean

Currents that occur deep in the ocean are caused by differences in water density.

Density differences in water cause deep ocean currents to form. When the density of water changes, it can rise or sink. Cold water is denser than warm water, and water with high salinity is denser than water with low salinity. When water at the ocean's surface becomes denser, it sinks, and warmer, less dense water rises. Cold, sinking water forms deep currents.

Surface currents and deep currents together can form convection currents.

Differences in water density can cause convection currents to form in the ocean. These currents are made up of both surface and deep currents. When surface water becomes denser, it sinks and becomes a deep current. The water in deep currents can rise to the surface to form surface currents. Convection currents can be vertical, circular, or cyclical.

3. Upwelling

Upwelling occurs when dense, cold water rises and brings nutrients to the ocean's surface.

When winds blow surface currents away from shore, the warm surface water can be replaced by cold, nutrient-rich water from deep in the ocean. This process is called upwelling. Upwelling is important for ocean life. The nutrients that rise to the surface feed organisms called phytoplankton and zooplankton. These organisms in turn provide food for other organisms.

4. Ocean Circulation

As ocean currents travel, they move energy and matter.

Ocean currents carry a large amount of matter and energy around the world. The water at the ocean's surface absorbs energy from the sun, which warms the water. Ocean currents carry this energy from the equator to the poles.

Ocean currents also transport matter around the world. Ocean water contains dissolved solids such as sodium chloride. Water absorbs gases such as nitrogen and oxygen from the atmosphere and transports them to different places. Animals and plants can also be transported by ocean currents.

 COMMON MISCONCEPTIONS RTI

THE EQUATOR Students may believe that Earth is hotter near the equator than it is at the poles because it is closer to the sun. In fact, the equator receives more direct sunlight than the poles, which makes the equator warmer throughout the year.

This misconception is addressed in the Basic Differentiated Instruction on p. 109 and on p. 115.

Teacher Notes

Advance Planning

These activities may take extended time or special conditions.

Unit 2

Project Immersion Learning, p. 71
   research and learning plan

Graphic Organizers and Vocabulary pp. 77, 78, 93, 94, 109, 110
   ongoing with reading

Lesson 1

Quick Lab Evaporation Rates, p. 75
   requires observations over multiple days

Exploration Lab Measuring Salinity, p. 75
   prepare materials in advance

Lesson 3

Daily Demo Model the Coriolis Effect, p. 107
   lazy Susan

UNIT 2

Oceanography

Big Idea
The oceans are a connected system of water in motion that transports matter and energy around Earth's surface.

Ocean waves carry a tremendous amount of energy, which surfers use to travel back to shore.

What do you think?
Day and night, ocean waves strike shorelines around the world. Is it possible to harvest the energy of ocean waves?

Waves crashing ashore can destroy structures and erode rock.

49

What Do You Think?

Encourage students to think about characteristics of the oceans.

Ask: What words do you think describe the oceans? Sample answers: big, salty, powerful, deep, full of life, cold, dark

Ask: Describe how energy travels in the oceans. Sample answer: Energy travels by waves throughout the oceans.

Ask: How can you tell that water in the ocean is on the move? Sample answer: Objects that are in the ocean often float along currents and move great distances.

Learning Alert

Ocean Currents Introduce students to the concept of ocean currents by explaining that the oceans contain large "rivers" of flowing water that move in predictable patterns. Surface currents, which affect the uppermost ten percent of ocean water, are powered mostly by the winds. Deep currents result from differences in water density, as cold, dense water sinks and less dense water rises. Explain to students that currents transport warm and cold water around the globe and have a significant impact on the climate of different regions. Ask students to think about how currents in the ocean are like the circulatory system in the human body. Sample answer: They both distribute resources throughout a system.

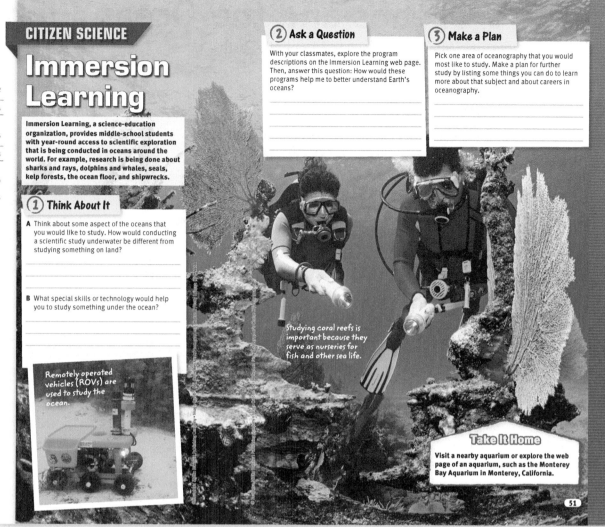

CITIZEN SCIENCE

Immersion Learning

Immersion Learning, a science-education organization, provides middle-school students with year-round access to scientific exploration that is being conducted in oceans around the world. For example, research is being done about sharks and rays, dolphins and whales, seals, kelp forests, the ocean floor, and shipwrecks.

1 Think About It

A Think about some aspect of the oceans that you would like to study. How would conducting a scientific study underwater be different from studying something on land?

_____

_____

B What special skills or technology would help you to study something under the ocean?

_____

_____

Remotely operated vehicles (ROVs) are used to study the ocean.

2 Ask a Question

With your classmates, explore the program descriptions on the Immersion Learning web page. Then, answer this question: How would these programs help me to better understand Earth's oceans?

_____

_____

_____

3 Make a Plan

Pick one area of oceanography that you would most like to study. Make a plan for further study by listing some things you can do to learn more about that subject and about careers in oceanography.

_____

_____

_____

Studying coral reefs is important because they serve as nurseries for fish and other sea life.

Take It Home

Visit a nearby aquarium or explore the web page of an aquarium, such as the Monterey Bay Aquarium in Monterey, California.

50 Unit 2 Oceanography

51

CITIZEN SCIENCE

Unit Project **Immersion Learning**

1. Think About It

A. Sample answer: I would like to learn about sharks. It would be more difficult to study sharks than a land animal because you have to be underwater with sharks.

B. Sample answers: swimming, scuba diving, using a submarine, using robotic vehicles, using underwater lights and cameras

2. Ask a Question

Help students navigate to the Immersion Learning web page. Students should preview the contents of the programs on the web page and should predict what they will learn about.

3. Make a Plan

Students should present a plan that identifies an area of study and specific steps they can take to learn more about that area.

Take It Home

Ask students to share some of the things they learned by visiting an aquarium or an aquarium's web page. Encourage students to describe specific exhibits or organisms found at the aquarium and to share ideas about why aquariums are important.

Optional Online rubric: Class Discussion

Earth's Oceans and the Ocean Floor

Essential Question What lies within and beneath Earth's oceans?

 Professional Development

For more detailed information about the topics in this lesson, refer to the Content Refresher in the Unit Opener pages.

Opening Your Lesson

Begin the lesson by assessing students' prerequisite and prior knowledge.

Prerequisite Knowledge

- Tectonic plate movement
- Buoyancy

Accessing Prior Knowledge

Ask: How might tectonic plate movements affect Earth's oceans? Sample answer: Tectonic plate movements can cause new features to form on the ocean floor, changing the depths of the oceans; tectonic plate movements change the positions of continents, causing oceans to become wider or narrower in some areas.

Ask: What is buoyancy? Sample answer: an upward force that keeps an object immersed in or floating on a liquid

Customize Your Opening

- ☐ **Accessing Prior Knowledge,** above
- ☐ **Print Path** Engage Your Brain, SE p. 53, #1–2
- ☐ **Active Reading** SE p. 53, #3–4
- ☐ **Digital Path** Lesson Opener

Key Topics/Learning Goals	Supporting Concepts
Earth's Oceans 1 Describe the characteristics of Earth's global ocean. 2 Identify Earth's main oceans.	• The global ocean covers almost ¾ of Earth's surface and can be more than 11 km deep. • The global ocean contains five oceans: the Pacific Ocean, Atlantic Ocean, Indian Ocean, Southern Ocean, and Arctic Ocean.
Salinity and Temperature 1 Explain sources of ocean salts and why salinity varies. 2 Explain how location affects ocean water temperature. 3 Describe the three main ocean temperature layers.	• Dissolved salts move from land into oceans by rivers, undersea volcanoes, and vents. • Latitude and depth affect ocean temperature. • Ocean water is warmest at the surface and near the equator, and colder near the poles. • The temperature layers are the surface zone, the thermocline layer, and the deep zone.
Density 1 Identify two factors that affect ocean water density. 2 Relate differences in density to movement of ocean water.	• Temperature and salinity determine ocean water density. Water can become denser due to cooling, increased salinity, or both. • Density differences in ocean water cause the movement of some ocean currents.
Studying the Ocean Floor and Its Features 1 Determine how the ocean floor is studied. 2 Identify the two main regions of the ocean floor. 3 Describe features of the ocean floor.	• People study the ocean floor with sonar, dredging, drilling, vessels, and satellites. • The two main regions are the continental margin and the deep-ocean basin. • Tectonic plate movements form ocean floor features such as mid-ocean ridges and trenches. • An abyssal plain is a large, flat area covered by fine sediment. • Seamounts are submerged volcanoes.

Options for Instruction

Two parallel paths provide coverage of the Essential Questions, with a strong **Inquiry** strand woven into each.
Follow the **Print Path**, the **Digital Path,** or your customized combination of print, digital, and inquiry.

Print Path
Teaching support for the Print Path appears with the Student Pages.

Inquiry Labs and Activities

Digital Path
Digital Path shortcut: TS661375

Print Path	Inquiry Labs and Activities	Digital Path
Feelin' Blue, SE p. 54 **What are Earth's five main oceans?**	**Daily Demo** The Global Ocean **Activity** Graphing Earth's Water	**Earth's Oceans** Interactive Image
Feelin' Blue, SE p. 54–55 **What are some characteristics of ocean water?** • Salinity • Temperature	**Exploration Lab** Measuring Salinity **Quick Lab** Evaporation Rates	**Salinity** Interactive Images **Temperature** Interactive Images
Feelin' Blue, SE p. 56 **What are some characteristics of ocean water?** • Density	**Quick Lab** Ocean Density **Daily Demo** Modeling Density	**Temperature, Salinity, and Density** Interactive Images
Seeing the Sea, SE pp. 57–58 **How is the ocean floor studied?** • With Sonar; With Satellites; In Underwater Vessels; With Deep-Sea Drilling **In Deep Water,** SE pp. 59–61 **Two main regions of the ocean floor** • Continental Margin; Deep-Ocean Basin **What are ocean floor features?** • Mid-Ocean Ridge; Abyssal Plains; Trenches; Seamounts; Volcanoes	**Activity** Submersible Role Play	**Studying the Ocean Floor** Slideshow **Ocean Floor Features** Interactive Graphics

Options for Assessment

See the Evaluate page for options, including Formative Assessment, Summative Assessment, and Unit Review.

Engage and Explore

Activities and Discussion

Activity *Graphing Earth's Water*

Earth's Oceans

 individuals
 15 min
 GUIDED inquiry

To illustrate how much of Earth's surface is covered by water in general and by ocean water in particular, have students develop two circle graphs. Have students use a compass to draw two circles on a sheet of paper. Then ask them to shade an area representing 70 percent in the first circle and label it *Water, 70 percent*. Have them label the remaining section *Land, 30 percent*. Next, direct students to shade and label the second circle to show that 97 percent of Earth's water is ocean water and only three percent is fresh water. Students should title both graphs.

Activity *Submersible Role Play*

Studying the Ocean Floor and Its Features

 pairs
 45 min
 GUIDED inquiry

Tell students that the Mariana Trench is the deepest part of the world's oceans. Next, explain that there has been only one manned expedition to the bottom of the Mariana Trench that took place over 50 years ago. Don Walsh and Jacques Piccard made the descent in the bathyscaphe Trieste on January 23, 1960. Direct students to form pairs and conduct research on how the Trieste was designed, details about the descent, what the men saw, and why they made their ascent early. Then encourage students to role play the journey of Walsh and Piccard. Invite interested students to share their reenactments for the class.

Labs and Demos

Daily Demo *The Global Ocean*

Earth's Oceans

 whole class
 10 min
 DIRECTED inquiry

PURPOSE **To show how Earth's oceans are connected**

MATERIALS

• large globe

1 **Compare** Display a large globe and point out the locations of Earth's individual oceans. **Ask:** Which ocean is largest? Smallest? Pacific Ocean; Arctic Ocean

2 **Describe** Spin the globe slowly and point out places where the oceans connect to form one large global ocean. **Ask:** How could you show that the global ocean is one connected body of water? Sample answer: Draw a line to connect the oceans.

Daily Demo *Modeling Density*

Density

 whole class
 15 min
 GUIDED inquiry

PURPOSE **To show how liquids form layers based on densities**

MATERIALS

• corn oil, 50 mL
• graduated cylinder, large
• maple syrup, 50 mL
• tap water, 50 mL

1 Identify each liquid and explain that maple syrup is the densest liquid and corn oil is the least dense.

2 Pour the maple syrup into the large graduated cylinder.

3 **Predicting Ask:** What do you think will happen when the corn oil is added to the container holding the maple syrup? Sample answer: The corn oil will form a layer on top of the maple syrup. Add the corn oil to the graduated cylinder as students observe.

4 **Predicting Ask:** What will happen when the water is added to the cylinder? Sample answer: It will form a layer between the corn oil and maple syrup. Add the water to the graduated cylinder to let students check the accuracy of their predictions.

Levels of **Inquiry**

DIRECTED inquiry
introduces inquiry skills within a structured framework.

GUIDED inquiry
develops inquiry skills within a supportive environment.

INDEPENDENT inquiry
deepens inquiry skills with student-driven questions or procedures.

Quick Lab *Evaporation Rates*

Salinity and Temperature

 small groups
🕐 20 min, then 5 min/day for 10 days
Inquiry **DIRECTED** inquiry

Students use table salt to explore how dissolved minerals affect water evaporation rates.

PURPOSE **To model how minerals affect evaporation rates**

MATERIALS

- aluminum pie pans, 3 per group
- balance
- beaker, 500 mL
- glass stir rod
- permanent marker
- ruler
- salt
- water
- safety goggles
- lab apron

Exploration Lab *Measuring Salinity*

Salinity and Temperature

 pairs
🕐 90 min
Inquiry **DIRECTED or GUIDED** inquiry

Students create a simple hydrometer, measure salinity levels, and answer questions.

PURPOSE **To explore why ocean salinity varies and understand how a hydrometer works**

MATERIALS

- balance
- ball bearings, 5 or 6
- buckets, 4
- clay, modeling
- filter paper
- graduated cylinder, 100 mL
- markers, permanent
- rod, stirring
- salt
- saltwater solutions
- scissors
- spatula
- straw
- water, tap

Quick Lab *Ocean Density*

Density

 pairs
🕐 25 min
Inquiry **GUIDED** inquiry

Students will form hypotheses about the effects of temperature and salinity on the density of water, then test them.

PURPOSE **To explore factors that can affect ocean density**

MATERIALS

- buckets, 4
- cups, clear plastic, 3
- food coloring
- salt
- spoon
- water

Customize Your Labs

📋 *See the Lab Manual for lab datasheets.*

🌐 *Go Online for editable lab datasheets.*

Activities and Discussion

☐ **Activity** Graphing Earth's Water

☐ **Activity** Submersible Role Play

Labs and Demos

☐ **Daily Demo** The Global Ocean

☐ **Daily Demo** Modeling Density

☐ **Quick Lab** Evaporation Rates

☐ **Exploration Lab** Measuring Salinity

☐ **Quick Lab** Ocean Density

Your Resources

_____

_____

_____

Explain Science Concepts

	 Print Path	 Digital Path
Key Topics		

Earth's Oceans

☐ **Feelin' Blue,** SE p. 54

☐ **Earth's Oceans**
Learn about the features of Earth's oceans.

Salinity and Temperature

☐ **Feelin' Blue,** SE p. 54–55
- Active Reading (Annotation strategy), #5
- Visualize It!, #6

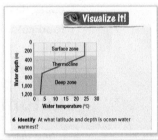

☐ **Salinity**
Learn about salinity in Earth's oceans.

☐ **Temperature**
Explore how temperature and salinity vary in Earth's oceans.

Density

☐ **Feelin' Blue,** SE p. 56
- Visualize It!, #7
- Summarize, #8

☐ **Temperature, Salinity, and Density**
Investigate how temperature and salinity determine density.

☐ **Temperature, Salinity, and Currents**
Explore how density differences in ocean water causes some ocean currents.

Studying the Ocean Floor and Its Features

☐ **Seeing the Sea,** SE pp. 57–58
- Visualize It!, #9
- Visualize It!, #10

☐ **In Deep Water,** SE pp. 59–61
- Active Reading, #11
- Visualize It!, #12
- Active Reading (Annotation Strategy), #13
- Think Outside the Book, #14

☐ **Studying the Ocean Floor**
Learn about different ways people explore the ocean floor.

☐ **Ocean Floor Features**
Investigate regions and features of the ocean floor.

Basic *Charting the Ocean Floor*

Studying the Ocean Floor and Its Features individuals   25–30 min

Three-Column Chart Have students create a Three-Column Chart. In the left column, they should list these ocean features: *mid-ocean ridge, abyssal plains, ocean trenches, seamounts,* and *volcanoes.* In the center column, they should describe the main characteristics of each feature and the key factors that play a role in its formation. Encourage students to draw labeled sketches that show the main characteristics of each ocean floor feature in the third column of the chart.

⊕ *Optional Online resource: Three-Column Chart support*

Advanced *Demonstrating Salinity Increases*

Salinity and Temperature individuals or pairs   ongoing

Ask students to design an experiment to demonstrate why salinity in the oceans is likely to increase in areas where evaporation rates are high. Have students develop a list of the materials they will need and write out a step-by-step procedure for their experiment. After receiving teacher approval for their design, encourage students to conduct their experiment as a class demonstration.

⊕ *Optional Online rubrics: Design Your Own Investigations: Experiments*

ELL *Contrasting Ocean Research Methods*

Studying the Ocean Floor and Its Features pairs   25 min

Double-Door Fold To aid comprehension of the uses of sonar and satellite mapping of ocean features, have ELL students work with a partner to develop a double-door fold to show the differences between the two technologies. Completed folds should  indicate that satellite mapping can cover a greater area than sonar. Also, satellite mapping uses images gathered by satellites, while sonar mapping makes use of pulses of sound sent through the water.

⊕ *Online resource: Double-Door Fold support*

salinity	continental margin	mid-ocean ridge
thermocline	deep-ocean basin	ocean trench

Previewing Vocabulary

 whole class   15 min

Prefixes Ask students what they think the prefix *mid* means. Sample answer: middle Remind students that they can use prefixes to help them understand what a new word or phrase means. Next, tell students that the prefix *thermo* means "warm" or "hot." Ask students to list other words they know with these prefixes. Finally, encourage volunteers to define the vocabulary terms *thermocline* and *mid-ocean ridge.* Prompt: Tell students that *cline* means "gradient of change."

Reinforcing Vocabulary

 individuals   ongoing

Key Term Fold To help students remember the vocabulary terms introduced in this lesson, have them develop a key term fold for the six vocabulary terms. Students can write each vocabulary term on the front of the tabs and the definition of each term under the appropriate tab.

⊕ *Online resource: Key Term Fold support*

Customize Your Core Lesson

Core Instruction
- ☐ **Print Path** choices
- ☐ **Digital Path** choices

Vocabulary
- ☐ **Previewing Vocabulary** Prefixes
- ☐ **Reinforcing Vocabulary** Key Term Fold

Differentiated Instruction
- ☐ **Basic** Charting the Ocean Floor
- ☐ **Advanced** Demonstrating Salinity Increases
- ☐ **ELL** Contrasting Ocean Research Methods

Your Resources

_____

_____

Extend Science Concepts

Reinforce and Review

Activity *Describing Earth's Oceans*

Synthesizing Key Topics small groups
🕐 40–45 min

Jigsaw Divide the class into four groups. Assign each group a key topic from the lesson: Earth's Oceans, Salinity and Temperature, Density of Ocean Water, and Studying the Ocean Floor and Its Features. Have members of each group work together to become experts on their topic as it relates to the Essential Question, "What lies within and beneath Earth's oceans?" Have students work together in their groups until all students are confident that they can teach what they have learned. Reassign students to four new mixed groups that include experts for each topic. Have individuals in each mixed group share their expertise with other students in the group until all students are able to explain how each key topic relates to the Essential Question.

⏱ *Optional Online resource: Jigsaw support*

Graphic Organizer

Synthesizing Key Topics individuals
🕐 ongoing

Cluster Diagram After students have studied the lesson, ask them to create a cluster diagram using the following terms: *continental margin, deep-ocean basin, mid-ocean ridge, ocean trenches,* and *abyssal plain.* Encourage students to include in their diagrams any additional related terms and concepts that they can think of.

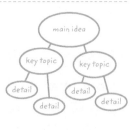

⏱ *Optional Online resource: Cluster Diagram support*

Going Further

Environmental Science Connection

Salinity and Temperature individuals
🕐 varies

Ocean Surface Temperatures Ocean surface temperatures are also affected by surface currents and by the upward movement of colder water from deeper in the ocean, or upwelling. For example, surface waters of the Pacific Ocean near the West Coast of the United States stay fairly cool all summer, whereas those near the East Coast are comparatively warmer. Invite students to research surface ocean currents along the coastlines of the United States and present their findings to the class.

Physical Science Connection

Synthesizing Key Topics whole class
🕐 10 min

Sound Waves in the Ocean Sonar uses the travel time of sound waves to measure ocean depth. The average speed of sound in water is about 1500 m/s. However, the speed of sound waves changes with water temperature. Sound waves travel faster in warm water than in cold. Scientists have developed a technique called *Acoustic Thermometry of Ocean Climate* (ATOC) to measure the time sound takes to travel a known distance through the ocean. Using ATOC, oceanographers can determine the average temperature of areas of the ocean. **Ask:** How is sonar used differently from ATOC? Sample answer: Sonar is used to determine ocean depth. ATOC uses known depth data and the speed of sound in water at different temperatures to gather temperature data of ocean water.

Customize Your Closing

🔖 *See the Assessment Guide for quizzes and tests.*

⏱ *Go Online to edit and create quizzes and tests.*

Reinforce and Review

- ☐ **Activity** *Describing Earth's Oceans*
- ☐ **Graphic Organizer** Cluster Diagram
- ☐ **Print Path** Visual Summary, SE p. 62
- ☐ **Print Path** Lesson Review, SE p. 63
- ☐ **Digital Path** Lesson Closer

Evaluate Student Mastery

See the teacher support below the Student Pages for additional Formative Assessment questions.

Have students review the different types of ocean floor features, their locations, and how they formed. **Ask:** What are the three divisions of the continental margin and how are they distinguished from each other? Sample answer: The continental margin is made up of the continental shelf, the continental slope, and the continental rise. The divisions are based on depth and changes in slope. **Ask:** What types of ocean floor features form at subducting plates and diverging plates? Ocean trenches form at subducting plates; mid-ocean ridges form at diverging plates.

Reteach

Formative assessment may show that students need reinforcement for certain topics. The resources below are recommended for reteaching. If students were introduced to the topic through the Print Path, you can also use the Digital Path to reteach, and vice versa.

🎧 *Can be assigned to individual students*

Earth's Oceans
Activity Graphing Earth's Water 🎧

Salinity and Temperature
Exploration Lab Measuring Salinity

Density
Daily Demo Modeling Density

Exploring the Ocean Floor and Its Features
Activity Submersible Role Play

Alternative Assessment
Describing Earth's Oceans

🔘 *Online resources: student worksheet; optional rubrics*

Earth's Oceans and the Ocean Floor

Take Your Pick: *Describing Earth's Oceans*
Complete the activities to show what you've learned about Earth's

1. Work on your own, with a partner, or with a small group.
2. Choose items below for a total of 10 points. Check your choices.
3. Have your teacher approve your plan.
4. Submit or present your results.

2 Points

_____ **Mnemonics** Create a mnemonic device to help your classmates recall the names of Earth's oceans and their sizes from largest to smallest. Use words that share the same first letter as the ocean.

_____ **Modeling Temperature Zones** Use modeling clay to make a model of a cross section of the ocean's three temperature zones. Attach index cards to identify each zone and its characteristics.

_____ **Mapping Earth's Oceans** Draw an outline map of the world that shows the locations of Earth's continents and each of its five oceans. Label the names of the continents and oceans on your map.

5 Points

_____ **Making Models** Use a balloon and permanent markers to make a model that shows how latitude affects ocean surface temperatures. Label the equator and poles on your model and draw outlines of the continents. Use different colored markers to show different surface water temperatures. Include a key that explains what each color represents.

_____ **Exploring the Ocean Floor** Imagine that you are an oceanographer conducting a deep-sea study. Write a short story that describes the vehicle you use and the ocean floor features you observe.

_____ **Diagramming Cause and Effect** Develop a cause and effect diagram that explains how salinity and temperature can cause the density of ocean water to decrease.

_____ **Make a Table** Develop a table that compares and contrasts the types of information that oceanographers can learn using sonar, satellites, underwater vessels and deep-sea drilling.

8 Points

_____ **Illustrating Ocean Floor Features** Develop an illustration that shows the different parts of the continental margin as well as each of the ocean floor features you have learned about. Include labels and captions to identify each feature and a brief description of how it forms.

_____ **Modeling Ocean Floor Features** Use modeling clay to make a three-dimensional model that shows the different parts of the continental margin and the four main types of ocean floor features. Use index cards to identify and describe each feature shown on your model.

Going Further
☐ Environmental Science Connection
☐ Physical Science Connection

Formative Assessment
☐ Strategies Throughout TE
☐ Lesson Review SE

Summative Assessment
☐ Alternative Assessment Describing Earth's Oceans
☐ Lesson Quiz
☐ Unit Tests A and B
☐ Unit Review SE End-of-Unit

Your Resources

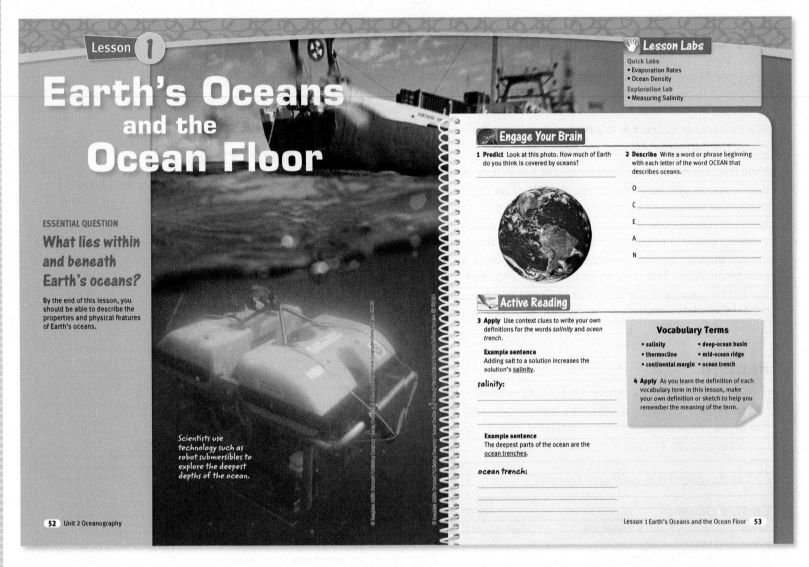

Answers

Answers for 1–3 should represent students' current thoughts, even if incorrect.

1. About three-fourths of Earth is covered by oceans.

2. Sample answer: O = open seas; C = continental margin; E = erupting undersea volcanoes; A = Atlantic Ocean; N = not drinkable water

3. Sample answer: Salinity means how much salt is in a solution; ocean trench means a deep canyon in the ocean floor.

4. Students should define or sketch each vocabulary term in the lesson.

Opening Your Lesson

Discuss student interpretations of the photograph (item 1) and descriptions of oceans (item 2) to assess students' prerequisite knowledge and to estimate what they already know about key topics.

Prerequisites Earth's crust is made up of tectonic plates that continuously move, thereby causing changes to Earth's surface; buoyancy is an upward force exerted by a fluid that opposes an object's weight.

Accessing Prior Knowledge The SQ3R strategy asks students to think about what they are about to read by **S**urveying the material, **Q**uestioning it, **R**eading it, **R**eciting it, and then **R**eviewing it. Introduce the strategy by explaining what each letter stands for, and then allow students to work with a partner to undertake the first two steps in order to preview this lesson. Students can use the last three steps as they work through the lesson.

🌐 *Optional Online resource: SQ3R Strategy support*

Feelin' Blue

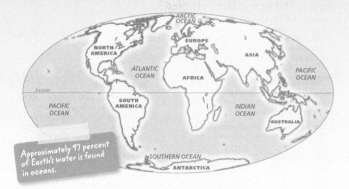

ARCTIC OCEAN

NORTH AMERICA

EUROPE

ASIA

ATLANTIC OCEAN

AFRICA

PACIFIC OCEAN

Equator

PACIFIC OCEAN

SOUTH AMERICA

INDIAN OCEAN

AUSTRALIA

SOUTHERN OCEAN

ANTARCTICA

Approximately 97 percent of Earth's water is found in oceans.

What are Earth's five main oceans?

You can see on the map above that the continents are like huge islands surrounded by one vast, interconnected global ocean. Almost three-fourths of Earth is covered by ocean water. In places, the global ocean is more than 11 km deep.

Earth's global ocean is divided into five main oceans. The largest is the Pacific Ocean. It contains about half of Earth's water. The Atlantic Ocean is next in size. It stretches in a north-south direction. The third-largest ocean, the Indian Ocean, is found mainly in the Southern Hemisphere. The Southern Ocean is located near Antarctica. The smallest ocean, the Arctic Ocean, is nearly covered by ice much of the year.

What are some characteristics of ocean water?

Active Reading

5 **Identify** As you read, underline characteristics of ocean water.

Like all matter, ocean water has both chemical and physical properties. Its chemical characteristics include **salinity**, or the amount and type of dissolved salts, and the amount and type of gases in the seawater. Its physical characteristics include temperature and density.

54 Unit 2 Oceanography

© Houghton Mifflin Harcourt Publishing Company

Salinity

On average, one kilogram of seawater contains about 35 g of dissolved salts. Thus, the overall salinity of seawater is about 3.5 percent.

Dissolved salts come from different sources. Water flowing on or under Earth's surface weathers rocks and carries calcium, magnesium, and sodium ions into the ocean. Underwater volcanoes and vents release solutions that are the source of chloride ions.

Over time, the salinity of seawater has remained relatively steady. However, it does vary from place to place. The salinity of water near the ocean's surface can be lower than average in areas where freshwater streams enter the ocean or where abundant precipitation falls into the ocean. Conversely, salinity can be higher than average in areas where rates of evaporation are high.

The white substance isn't snow. Above, a woman breaks apart salt that is left behind as water evaporates from these shallow, salty pools in Sri Lanka.

Temperature

Ocean water temperature varies by latitude, by depth, and by season. There are three distinct temperature layers by depth. The top layer, or surface zone, is the warmest layer. This layer is heated by the sun. The thermocline is the next zone. In the **thermocline**, water temperature drops with increased depth faster than it does in other layers. The deep zone is the deepest layer, and the coldest.

By latitude, the warmest surface water is near the equator. The coldest is near the poles. But the surface zone is generally warmer than deeper water regardless of latitude. Surface water is warmest in summer and coldest in winter. Driven by winds and density differences, both surface currents and deep currents travel through the global ocean, distributing energy in the form of heat.

Visualize It!

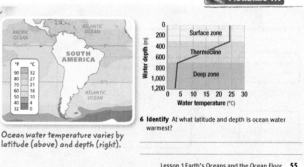

Ocean water temperature varies by latitude (above) and depth (right).

6 **Identify** At what latitude and depth is ocean water warmest?

Lesson 1 Earth's Oceans and the Ocean Floor 55

© Houghton Mifflin Harcourt Publishing Company • Image Credits: ©Lindsay Hebberd/Corbis

---

Answers

5. *See students' pages for annotations.*

6. near equator; at surface

Learning Alert

Robinson Projection Direct students to examine the map at the top of page 54 in their textbooks. Tell students that this is an example of a special type of map developed by Arthur H. Robinson in the 1960s. This type of map strikes a compromise; in order to show the whole Earth as a flat image, some areas, most notably the poles, are distorted.

Interpreting Visuals

Use these questions to help students interpret the map and diagram that show how water temperature varies with latitude and depth. **Ask:** What general relationship exists between surface water temperatures and latitude? Sample answer: Surface water temperatures decrease as latitude increases. **Ask:** How are depth and temperature related? Sample answer: Water is warmest near the surface and coldest in the deep zone.

Formative Assessment

Ask: From largest to smallest, what five oceans make up Earth's global ocean? Pacific Ocean, Atlantic Ocean, Indian Ocean, Southern Ocean, and Arctic Ocean

Ask: What factors determine the chemical characteristics of ocean water? the dissolved solids and gases that make up the water

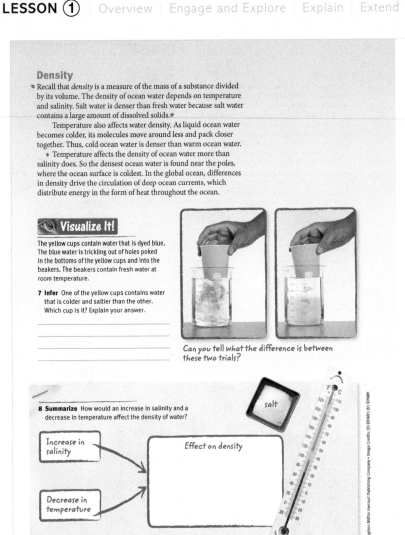

Density

• Recall that *density* is a measure of the mass of a substance divided by its volume. The density of ocean water depends on temperature and salinity. Salt water is denser than fresh water because salt water contains a large amount of dissolved solids.•

   Temperature also affects water density. As liquid ocean water becomes colder, its molecules move around less and pack closer together. Thus, cold ocean water is denser than warm ocean water.

   • Temperature affects the density of ocean water more than salinity does. So the densest ocean water is found near the poles, where the ocean surface is coldest. In the global ocean, differences in density drive the circulation of deep ocean currents, which distribute energy in the form of heat throughout the ocean.

Visualize It!

The yellow cups contain water that is dyed blue. The blue water is trickling out of holes poked in the bottoms of the yellow cups and into the beakers. The beakers contain fresh water at room temperature.

7 Infer One of the yellow cups contains water that is colder and saltier than the other. Which cup is it? Explain your answer.

Can you tell what the difference is between these two trials?

8 Summarize How would an increase in salinity and a decrease in temperature affect the density of water?

Increase in salinity → Effect on density ← Decrease in temperature

56 Unit 2 Oceanography

Seeing the Sea

How is the ocean floor studied?

As you learned earlier in this lesson, the ocean is 11 km deep in some places. People cannot safely dive down to such extreme depths. So what lies at the deepest, darkest part of the ocean? How do scientists learn about the ocean floor? They use technology such as sonar, drills, underwater exploration vessels, and satellites.

Visualize It!

Differences in the times that sound waves take to return to the ship allow scientists to calculate the depth and shapes of ocean floor features.

9 Describe Draw arrows in the boxes to show the directions in which the sound waves are moving.

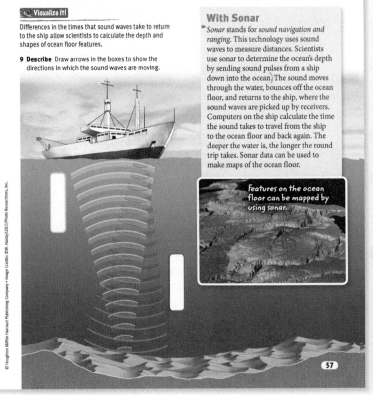

With Sonar

Sonar stands for *sound navigation and ranging*. This technology uses sound waves to measure distances. Scientists use sonar to determine the ocean's depth by sending sound pulses from a ship down into the ocean. The sound moves through the water, bounces off the ocean floor, and returns to the ship, where the sound waves are picked up by receivers. Computers on the ship calculate the time the sound takes to travel from the ship to the ocean floor and back again. The deeper the water is, the longer the round trip takes. Sonar data can be used to make maps of the ocean floor.

Features on the ocean floor can be mapped by using sonar.

57

Answers

7. The cup on the right. The blue water is sinking to the bottom, so it must be denser than the water on the left, which is spreading out.

8. Both an increase in salinity and a decrease in temperature would cause an increase in the density of water.

9. Students should draw an arrow pointing up in the yellow box and an arrow pointing down in the red box.

Probing Questions DIRECTED Inquiry

Applying The ocean is divided into three zones based upon temperature differences. **Ask:** In which of these zones is the densest ocean water located? Why? Sample answer: The densest ocean water will be in the deep zone because this zone contains the coldest ocean water, and cold water is denser than warm water.

Learning Alert

Sea or Ocean Students might find the terms *sea* and *ocean* confusing. In some cases, the words are interchangeable, but the terms can also mean different things. Parts of the global ocean that are partly surrounded by land are known as seas. The Mediterranean Sea is an example of a sea that is part of the global ocean. Seas that are completely landlocked, such as the Caspian Sea, are not part of the global ocean. Challenge students to identify on a map landlocked seas and seas that are part of the global ocean.

Interpreting Visuals

To make sure that students understand how sonar is used to map the ocean floor, direct them to mark with an "X" the location on the visual that would require the greatest amount of time for a sound wave to be reflected back to the surface. Students should mark with an "X" the lowest part of the depression shown in the illustration.

Visualize It! Inquiry

10 Justify Which technologies would you use to explore the underwater landscape shown in this illustration? Explain why you chose these technologies.

_____

_____

_____

_____

_____

_____

With Satellites

Satellites can measure variations in the height of the ocean's surface. The features of the ocean floor can affect the height of the water above them. Scientists can use satellite data to make maps of the sea floor. Satellites can gather data from much larger areas than sonar can. Satellites can also measure other features, such as the ocean's surface temperature, with a high degree of accuracy.

In Underwater Vessels

Just as astronauts explore space by using rockets, scientists use underwater vessels to explore the oceans. Some vessels have pilots and can carry researchers. Other vessels are remotely operated. Remotely operated vehicles, or ROVs, are "flown" from the surface by remote control. ROVs can be used to explore the ocean at depths that are too dangerous for piloted vessels to explore.

With Deep-Sea Drilling

Scientists can collect cores, or long tubes of rock and sediment, from the sea floor. Cores are drilled using equipment on large ships. By studying the layers of rock and sediment in the cores, scientists learn about the history of Earth. For example, through drilling, scientists have found evidence of sea-floor spreading, which occurs where tectonic plates move apart.

58

In Deep Water

What are the two main regions of the ocean floor?

Picture yourself in a piloted research vessel deep below the ocean surface. What would you see on the ocean floor? The ocean floor is not all flat. It has features that include the world's longest mountain chain and deep canyons. The two main regions of the ocean floor are the continental margin and the deep-ocean basin.

The Continental Margin

The **continental margin** is the edge of the continent that is covered by the ocean. The continental margin is divided into the continental shelf, the continental slope, and the continental rise. These divisions are based on depth and changes in slope.

The continental shelf is a relatively flat underwater extension of the continent, which is the land that is above water. The shelf ends at a steeply sloping region, the continental slope. The ocean floor eventually becomes a more gently sloping terrain. This gently sloping area is the continental rise.

The Deep-Ocean Basin

The **deep-ocean basin** begins at the end of the continental margin. It extends under the deepest parts of the ocean. The deep-ocean basin includes narrow depressions and flat, smooth plains.

Active Reading 11 Apply Imagine the ocean is a giant swimming pool. Which region would be the shallow end, and which region would be the deep end?

_____

_____

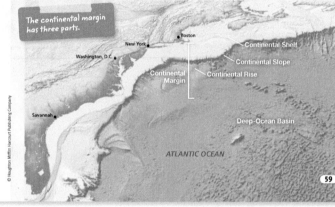

The continental margin has three parts.

Boston
New York
Washington, D.C.
Continental Margin
Savannah
Continental Shelf
Continental Slope
Continental Rise
Deep-Ocean Basin
ATLANTIC OCEAN

59

Answers

10. Student response should include a description of which technologies they would use to explore the underwater landscape in the illustration and an explanation of why those technologies were chosen.

11. The continental margin would be the shallow end, and the deep-ocean basin would be the deep end.

Building Reading Skills

Main Idea Web Students can use a main idea web to organize the information they are learning as they read about the methods scientists use to study the ocean floor.

Formative Assessment

Ask: What are four ways that scientists study the ocean floor and what kind of information does each method provide? Sample answer: Sonar can be used to determine the depth of regions of the ocean and to map its topography; satellites can be used to map underwater features over large areas and to measure temperature variations; underwater vessels can be used to make direct observations of ocean floor features or to explore these features remotely; deep-sea drilling can be used to obtain core samples of the ocean floor and analyze their makeup.

Interpreting Visuals

Have students look at the map showing the parts of the continental margin and the deep-ocean basin. **Ask:** How does the continental shelf differ from the continental slope? Sample answer: The continental shelf is the shallow ocean region that meets the shoreline. The continental slope is the region of the continental margin marked by a steep incline where water depth increases greatly.

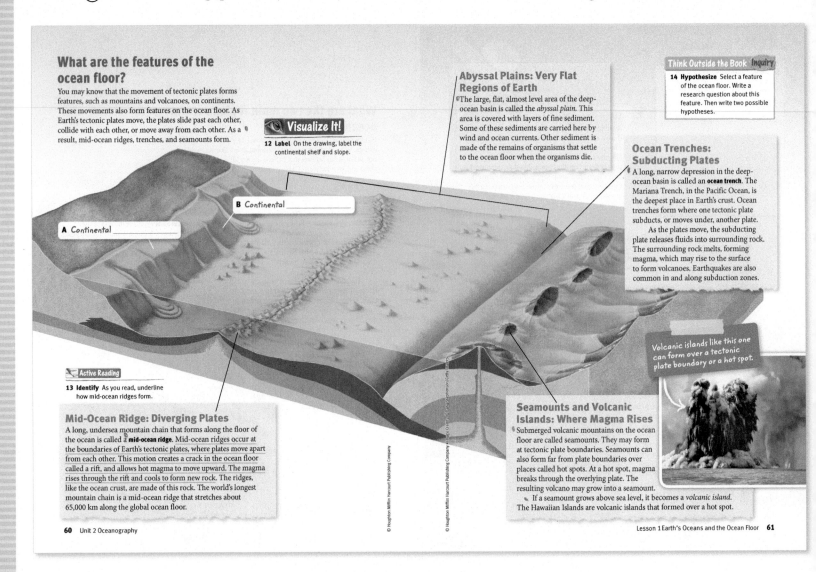

What are the features of the ocean floor?

You may know that the movement of tectonic plates forms features, such as mountains and volcanoes, on continents. These movements also form features on the ocean floor. As Earth's tectonic plates move, the plates slide past each other, collide with each other, or move away from each other. As a result, mid-ocean ridges, trenches, and seamounts form.

Visualize It!

12 Label On the drawing, label the continental shelf and slope.

B Continental _____

A Continental _____

Active Reading

13 Identify As you read, underline how mid-ocean ridges form.

Mid-Ocean Ridge: Diverging Plates

A long, undersea mountain chain that forms along the floor of the ocean is called a **mid-ocean ridge**. Mid-ocean ridges occur at the boundaries of Earth's tectonic plates, where plates move apart from each other. This motion creates a crack in the ocean floor called a rift, and allows hot magma to move upward. The magma rises through the rift and cools to form new rock. The ridges, like the ocean crust, are made of this rock. The world's longest mountain chain is a mid-ocean ridge that stretches about 65,000 km along the global ocean floor.

Abyssal Plains: Very Flat Regions of Earth

The large, flat, almost level area of the deep-ocean basin is called the *abyssal plain*. This area is covered with layers of fine sediment. Some of these sediments are carried here by wind and ocean currents. Other sediment is made of the remains of organisms that settle to the ocean floor when the organisms die.

Ocean Trenches: Subducting Plates

A long, narrow depression in the deep-ocean basin is called an **ocean trench**. The Mariana Trench, in the Pacific Ocean, is the deepest place in Earth's crust. Ocean trenches form where one tectonic plate subducts, or moves under, another plate.

As the plates move, the subducting plate releases fluids into surrounding rock. The surrounding rock melts, forming magma, which may rise to the surface to form volcanoes. Earthquakes are also common in and along subduction zones.

Seamounts and Volcanic Islands: Where Magma Rises

Submerged volcanic mountains on the ocean floor are called seamounts. They may form at tectonic plate boundaries. Seamounts can also form far from plate boundaries over places called hot spots. At a hot spot, magma breaks through the overlying plate. The resulting volcano may grow into a seamount. If a seamount grows above sea level, it becomes a *volcanic island*. The Hawaiian Islands are volcanic islands that formed over a hot spot.

Volcanic islands like this one can form over a tectonic plate boundary or a hot spot.

© Houghton Mifflin Harcourt Publishing Company
© Houghton Mifflin Harcourt Publishing Company

Think Outside the Book Inquiry

14 Hypothesize Select a feature of the ocean floor. Write a research question about this feature. Then write two possible hypotheses.

Answers

12. A. continental shelf; B. continental slope
13. *See students' pages for annotations.*
14. Sample answer: Research question: How does a volcanic island change over time? Possible hypotheses might be that the island grows if volcanic activity continues and that the island is eroded over time by water and wind.

Building Reading Skills

Cause and Effect Encourage students to examine the text regarding mid-ocean ridges and trenches to identify cause-and-effect relationships. Invite volunteers to share examples with the class.

Interpreting Visuals

Have students look at the diagram of ocean floor features. Point out to students that many of the features of the ocean floor are similar to those that occur on Earth's surface. Challenge students to identify features on Earth's surface that share similar characteristics to topographic features on the ocean floor. Sample answers: Mid-ocean ridges are similar to mountain ranges on Earth's surface; abyssal plains are similar to plains; and seamounts are similar to volcanic mountains.

Learning Alert

Island Formation Not all islands are volcanic islands. Islands can form by the growth of coral. Many barrier islands form as a result of deposition. Continental islands are formed by parts of the continental shelf that rise above sea level. Great Britain and Madagascar are examples of continental islands.

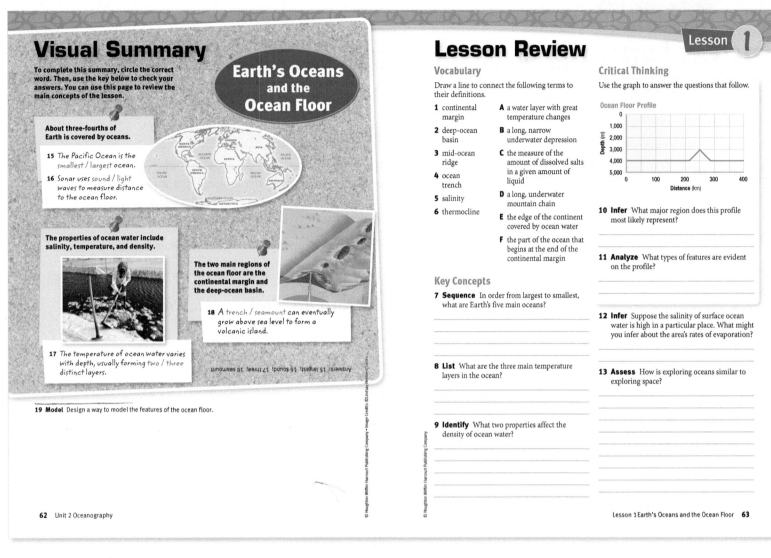

Visual Summary

Earth's Oceans and the Ocean Floor

To complete this summary, circle the correct word. Then, use the key below to check your answers. You can use this page to review the main concepts of the lesson.

About three-fourths of Earth is covered by oceans.

15 The Pacific Ocean is the smallest / largest ocean.

16 Sonar uses sound / light waves to measure distance to the ocean floor.

The properties of ocean water include salinity, temperature, and density.

17 The temperature of ocean water varies with depth, usually forming two / three distinct layers.

The two main regions of the ocean floor are the continental margin and the deep-ocean basin.

18 A trench / seamount can eventually grow above sea level to form a volcanic island.

Answers: 15 largest; 16 sound; 17 three; 18 seamount

19 **Model** Design a way to model the features of the ocean floor.

62 Unit 2 Oceanography

Lesson Review

Lesson 1

Vocabulary

Draw a line to connect the following terms to their definitions.

1 continental margin
2 deep-ocean basin
3 mid-ocean ridge
4 ocean trench
5 salinity
6 thermocline

A a water layer with great temperature changes

B a long, narrow underwater depression

C the measure of the amount of dissolved salts in a given amount of liquid

D a long, underwater mountain chain

E the edge of the continent covered by ocean water

F the part of the ocean that begins at the end of the continental margin

Key Concepts

7 **Sequence** In order from largest to smallest, what are Earth's five main oceans?

8 **List** What are the three main temperature layers in the ocean?

9 **Identify** What two properties affect the density of ocean water?

Critical Thinking

Use the graph to answer the questions that follow.

Ocean Floor Profile

10 **Infer** What major region does this profile most likely represent?

11 **Analyze** What types of features are evident on the profile?

12 **Infer** Suppose the salinity of surface ocean water is high in a particular place. What might you infer about the area's rates of evaporation?

13 **Assess** How is exploring oceans similar to exploring space?

Lesson 1 Earth's Oceans and the Ocean Floor 63

Visual Summary Answers

15. largest
16. sound
17. three
18. seamount
19. Student output should include the three parts of the continental margin (the continental shelf, slope, and rise), as well as features found in the deep-ocean basins (ocean trenches, abyssal plains, seamounts, and mid-ocean ridges).

Lesson Review Answers

1. E; 2. F; 3. D; 4. B; 5. C; 6. A
7. Pacific Ocean, Atlantic Ocean, Indian Ocean, Southern Ocean, Arctic Ocean
8. surface zone, thermocline, deep zone
9. salinity and temperature
10. the deep-ocean basin
11. abyssal plains and mid-ocean ridge
12. They are high.
13. Humans cannot safely explore the deepest parts of the ocean or remain in space for long periods of time. Scientists use technology, including robots, to explore places they cannot go themselves, such as the ocean floor and distant planets.

Understanding a Bathymetric Map

Purpose To learn to use a bathymetric map

Learning Goals
- Understand how to interpret a bathymetric map.
- Draw a bathymetric profile using the depth information on a bathymetric map.

Informal Vocabulary
topographic map, bathymetric map, contour map

Prerequisite Knowledge
- General understanding of Earth's oceans and ocean floors

Discussion *Comparing Bathymetric Maps with Other Maps*

 whole class   🕐 15 min

Inquiry GUIDED inquiry

Have students think about what they already know about contour maps. **Ask:** What is a contour map? Sample answer: A contour map uses lines to show changes in elevation. **Ask:** What is a topographic map? Sample answer: A topographic map shows features on Earth's surface, such as mountain ranges and valleys. **Ask:** How is a bathymetric map different from a topographic map? Sample answer: A bathymetric map shows features underwater instead of features on dry land. **Ask:** How is a bathymetric map different from a contour map? Sample answer: A bathymetric map is a type of contour map. It uses color to show depth of features on the ocean floor.

🌐 *Optional Online rubric: Class Discussion*

Differentiated Instruction

Basic *Comparing Maps*

👥 pairs   🕐 15 min

Have students compare a bathymetric map with another type of map showing the same region. Have students use a Venn diagram to show how the two maps are alike and different. Invite students to share their observations with the class.

🌐 *Optional Online resource: Venn Diagram support*

Advanced *Bathymetric Profiles*

👥 individuals   🕐 20 min

Have students look at the bathymetric map on the student page to identify an underwater feature that they think is interesting. Then have students draw a line across that area of the map. Finally, have students use graph paper to draw a bathymetric profile of the area where they drew the line. Invite students to explain what their profile shows.

ELL *Ocean Depths*

👥 individuals or pairs   🕐 15 min

Provide students with a simple map showing the boundaries of an ocean or other water body. On the map, include numbers showing the depth of the water in meters near shore and at various other points. Have students select colors to represent different depths and then color their map to show where the water body is deepest and most shallow. Direct students to include a key, so viewers of the map can tell what each color means.

Customize Your Feature

- ☐ **Discussion** Comparing Bathymetric Maps with Other Maps
- ☐ **Basic** Comparing Maps
- ☐ **Advanced** Bathymetric Profiles
- ☐ **ELL** Ocean Depths
- ☐ **Building Reading Skills**
- ☐ **You Try It!**

Think Science

Understanding a Bathymetric Map

Topographic maps are contour maps that illustrate the mountains, valleys, and hills on land. Bathymetric maps are contour maps that illustrate similar features on the ocean floor.

Tutorial

A bathymetric map uses curved contour lines that each represent a specific depth. Colors are also often used to show different depths. Because sea level is at 0 meters, increasing depths are shown by negative numbers. The bathymetric map below shows a part of the Mariana Trench, the deepest known part of the world's ocean.

Bathymetric Map

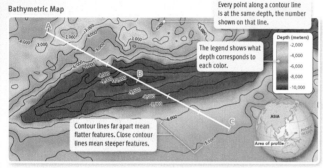

Every point along a contour line is at the same depth, the number shown on that line.

The legend shows what depth corresponds to each color.

Contour lines far apart mean flatter features. Close contour lines mean steeper features.

Bathymetric Profile

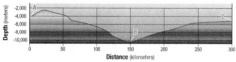

A bathymetric profile shows the change in depth across any chosen reference line on a bathymetric map. This profile details the change in depth across the line ABC shown on the map above. To see how the profile was made, move your finger along the line ABC on the map. Every time you cross a contour line, check that the profile crosses the same depth line on the grid.

64 Unit 2 Oceanography

© Houghton Mifflin Harcourt Publishing Company

You Try It!

Now follow the steps below to draw the profile for this bathymetric map of a region near Monterey Bay, California.

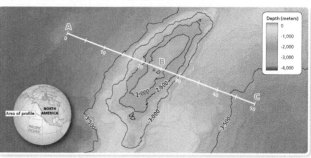

Profile Grid

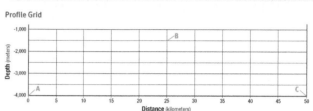

1 List Use the color legend to estimate the depths at points A, B, and C. Record this data in the table below.

Point	Color	Depth
A		
B		
C		

2 Distinguish For each tick mark on the line ABC, place a dot on the corresponding profile grid line at the correct depth.

3 Graph Move your finger along the ABC line on the map and place a dot on the profile grid at the correct depth for each contour line you cross.

4 Draw To complete the profile, connect the dots you plotted.

5 Evaluate Describe the ocean floor feature that you just plotted.

_____

_____

_____

_____

© Houghton Mifflin Harcourt Publishing Company

Unit 2 Think Science **65**

Answers

1.

Point	Color	Depth
A	Dark blue	−4,000 m
B	Light green	−2,000 m
C	Dark Blue	−4,000 m

2. Dots on distance lines should correspond to the approximate depth on the map.

3. Dots on depth lines should correspond to the approximate distance between tick marks on the map.

4. Students' answers should connect all of the plotted dots in a logical order.

5. Sample answer: It is like a small mountain that rises slowly at both ends and steeply near the middle.

Building Reading Skills

Student Vocabulary Explain to students that the Greek word _bathos_ means "depth." The Latin word _metricus_ means "relating to measurement." **Ask:** Based on this knowledge, what do you think _bathymetric_ means? Sample answer: something that measures depth Challenge students to make up other words that use the word part _batho-_ or _-metric_. Have them supply definitions for their made-up words. Sample answer: tempometric, meaning "something that measures speed or tempo"

Think Science **87**

Ocean Waves

Essential Question How does an ocean wave form and move?

Professional Development

For more detailed information about the topics in this lesson, refer to the Content Refresher in the Unit Opener pages.

Opening Your Lesson

Begin the lesson by assessing students' prerequisite and prior knowledge.

Prerequisite Knowledge

- Waves move across the ocean.
- Wind blows across the surface of the ocean.

Accessing Prior Knowledge

Invite students to make a tri-fold FoldNote KWL chart about what they know about ocean waves. Have students put what they know in the first column and what they want to know in the second column. After they have finished the lesson, they can complete the third column with what they learned.

🌐 *Online resource: Tri-fold FoldNote support*

Customize Your Opening

☐ **Accessing Prior Knowledge,** above

☐ **Print Path** Engage Your Brain, SE p. 67

☐ **Print Path** Active Reading, SE p. 67

☐ **Digital Path** Lesson Opener

Key Topics/Learning Goals	Supporting Concepts
Properties of Ocean Waves 1 Explain that an ocean wave results from the transfer of energy from wind to water. 2 Recognize wave parts. 3 Explain wave speed, wavelength, and wave period.	• Ocean waves are caused primarily by wind. • A wave has a crest and a trough. • Wavelength is the distance between waves. • The height of a wave from its rest position to the crest is called the amplitude. • Wave period is the number of waves produced in a given amount of time. • Wave speed is how fast a wave travels.
Ocean Wave Formation 1 Classify ocean waves as mechanical waves. 2 Know that wind energy transers to ocean water. 3 Identify other sources of energy that can form waves.	• A mechanical wave requires a medium, such as air or water, through which to travel. • Mechanical waves carry energy through matter. • As wind passes over the ocean's surface, friction causes the water to ripple.
Ocean Wave Movement 1 Conclude that water does not travel with the energy in a wave. 2 Describe how waves transfer energy to the shore.	• Water does not move with a wave; it rises and falls in circular movements. • Circular motion disappears about half a wavelength below the surface. • Wave energy decreases as water depth increases.
Waves at the Shore 1 Explain why waves break as they reach shallow water. 2 Distinguish a tsunami from other ocean waves.	• Ocean waves transfer energy to the shore; water at the wave bottom slows, but water at the top travels at the original speed. • Waves break as gravity pulls crests down. • A tsunami is a giant ocean wave that forms when a large volume of ocean water is suddenly displaced.

Options for Instruction

Two parallel paths provide coverage of the Essential Questions, with a strong **Inquiry** strand woven into each.
Follow the **Print Path,** the **Digital Path,** or your customized combination of print, digital, and inquiry.

Print Path
Teaching support for the Print Path appears with the Student Pages.

Inquiry Labs and Activities

Digital Path
Digital Path shortcut: TS661385

Catch the Wave, SE pp. 68–69
What are some properties of a wave?
- Size
- Frequency and Wave Period
- Wave Speed

Activity
Modeling Waves

Activity
Wave Questions

Parts of a Wave
Interactive Graphics

Wavelength and Wave Period
Interactive Graphics

Surf's Up!, SE pp. 70–71
What causes ocean waves?
- Wind
- Earthquakes
- Volcanoes
- Landslides
- Meteorites and Asteroids

Quick Lab
Factors in Wave Formation

Quick Lab
Making Waves

Causes of Waves
Video

Doing the Wave, SE p. 72
What happens when a wave moves through the water?
- Energy Travels
- Water Rises and Falls But Stays in the Same Place

Exploration Lab
Wave Movement

Daily Demo
Wave Energy Transfer

Activity
Cartooning Wave Motion

Ocean Waves and Energy
Slideshow

Energy and Waves
Video

Totally Turbulent, SE pp. 74–75
What happens when a wave reaches the shore?
- Energy Decreases with Depth
- It Transfers Energy to the Shore
- It Breaks in Shallow Water
What is a tsunami?

Activity
Saving Lives: Knowledge is Key

Waves in Shallow Water
Interactive Graphics

Tsunami
Video

Options for Assessment

*See the Evaluate page for options, including Formative Assessment,
Summative Assessment, and Unit Review.*

Engage and Explore

Activities and Discussion

Activity *Modeling Waves*

Engage

Introducing Key Concepts

 whole class
 10 min
 GUIDED inquiry

Arrange chairs in a long row and have students sit in the chairs. Then, have the students stand and sit in succession to form a "human wave." Ask students to discuss and then demonstrate how the shape and motion of the wave could be changed. Examples include standing and sitting more quickly to decrease the wave period, or stretching their arms over their heads as they stand and bringing their arms down to their sides as they sit to increase the wave height.

Discussion *Finding Wave Speed*

Properties of Ocean Waves

 small groups or whole class
 10 min
 GUIDED inquiry

Ask students how they would estimate wavelength and wave period if they were in a boat at sea. What visual marks might they use? Sample answer: the number of waves that passed under the boat Make sure students understand that wave period and wave speed are inversely proportional. That is, for a given wavelength, an increase in wave period means a decrease in wave speed. Ask students to state the formula for calculating wave speed. wave speed = wavelength x frequency Invite students to come up with wave speed problems and solve them.

Activity *Saving Lives: Knowledge Is Key*

Waves at the Shore

 pairs
 40 min
 GUIDED inquiry

Ask students if they have heard about the 2004 Indian Ocean tsunami. Explain that the tsunami was triggered by an undersea earthquake and that many people lost their lives in it. Have students form pairs, and tell them that they are going to do a short report on one of the tsunami's heroes—Tilly Smith, a schoolgirl from England. Encourage students to include information on how Tilly learned about tsunamis, what warning signs she recognized, and how many lives she saved. Encourage interested students to make a poster listing the warning signs of an impending tsunami.

Activity *Cartooning Wave Motion*

Ocean Wave Movement

 individuals or pairs
 20 min
 DIRECTED inquiry

Direct students to work together to make a comic strip that shows what happens when a wave moves through water. Their comic strip should contain at least 3 panels and should include an object floating in the water. Remind students that as the wave moves, the object and the water particles move up and down.

©Getty Images

Customize Your Labs

 See the Lab Manual for lab datasheets.

 Go Online for editable lab datasheets.

Levels of **Inquiry**

DIRECTED inquiry	**GUIDED** inquiry	**INDEPENDENT** inquiry
introduces inquiry skills within a structured framework.	develops inquiry skills within a supportive environment.	deepens inquiry skills with student-driven questions or procedures.

Labs and Demos

Daily Demo *Wave Energy Transfer*

Ocean Wave Movement

 whole class
🕐 10 min
Inquiry **DIRECTED** inquiry

PURPOSE **To demonstrate ocean wave movement**

MATERIALS

• marbles or ball bearings, large, 5

1 Line up four of the marbles or ball bearings. Make sure they are all touching.

2 **Predict Ask:** What do you think will happen if I roll the fifth marble and hit the last marble in the line? Sample answer: It will make the other marbles move.

3 Have a volunteer gently roll the fifth marble and hit the end of the lined-up marbles. The marble at the far end of the line will roll away, but the others will not move.

4 Discuss with students how the energy of the rolling marble is transferred to the marble it hits, then to the next marble, and so on until it reaches the last marble, which moves. Tell students that wave energy moves through water the same way.

Quick Lab *Factors in Wave Formation*

PURPOSE **To determine the effect of variables on ocean wave formation**

See the Lab Manual or go Online for planning information.

Exploration Lab *Wave Movement*

Ocean Wave Movement

 small groups
🕐 45 min
Inquiry **GUIDED/INDEPENDENT** inquiry

Students will observe how a bottle near the surface of water and deeper in water moves as waves move through the water.

PURPOSE **To show that waves are traveling energy, not traveling water**

MATERIALS

• aquarium, 9 gal
• pill bottle, plastic
• salt
• water

Quick Lab *Making Waves*

Ocean Wave Formation

 small groups
🕐 15 min
Inquiry **GUIDED** inquiry

Students will form hypotheses, make drawings, then observe a fan blowing on water.

PURPOSE **To demonstrate how waves form**

MATERIALS

• aquarium, 9 gal
• books, optional
• fan, electric
• water

Activities and Discussion

☐ **Activity** Modeling Waves

☐ **Discussion** Finding Wave Speed

☐ **Activity** Saving Lives: Knowledge Is Key

☐ **Activity** Cartooning Wave Motion

Labs and Demos

☐ **Daily Demo** Wave Energy Transfer

☐ **Quick Lab** Factors in Wave Formation

☐ **Exploration Lab** Wave Movement

☐ **Quick Lab** Making Waves

Your Resources

_____

_____

Explain Science Concepts

	📖 Print Path	🖥 Digital Path
Key Topics		
Properties of Ocean Waves	☐ **Catch the Wave,** SE pp. 68–69 • Visualize It!, #5 • Apply, #6 • Do the Math, #7 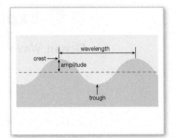	☐ **Parts of a Wave** Learn the parts of a wave. ☐ **Wavelength and Wave Period** Investigate how wavelength and wave period affect wave speed. 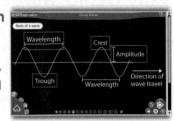
Ocean Wave Formation	☐ **Surf's Up!,** SE pp. 70–71 • Active Reading (Annotation strategy), #8 • Visualize It!, #9 	☐ **Causes of Waves** Explore how ocean waves form.
Ocean Wave Movement	☐ **Doing the Wave,** SE p. 72 • Active Reading, #10 • Visualize It!, #11 	☐ **Ocean Waves and Energy** Learn how the energy in mechanical waves moves. ☐ **Energy and Waves** Learn how energy is transferred in mechanical waves.
Waves at the Shore	☐ **Totally Turbulent,** SE pp. 74–75 • Visualize It!, #15 • Visualize It!, #16 • Think Outside the Book, #17 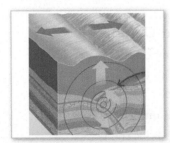	☐ **Waves in Shallow Water** Explore how wave speed and wave height change as waves reach shore. ☐ **Tsunami** Investigate how a tsunami forms and moves.

Differentiated Instruction

Basic *Diagramming Waves*

Properties of Ocean Waves

 individuals or small groups

🕐 varied

Have students write down the following wave characteristics: crest, trough, wavelength, and amplitude. Invite students to use these characteristics to construct diagrams of different sizes of waves, from gentle swells to waves a surfer might enjoy to a giant tsunami. Direct students to make their diagrams on poster board so that they can be shared with the class.

Advanced *Longshore Currents*

Waves at the Shore

 individuals

 15 min

Research After students have learned about what happens when waves reach the shore, prompt them to research longshore currents and their effects on the environment. First, ask students to think about what the difference between a wave and a current might be. Then, discuss with students that while a wave is the movement of energy through water, a current is the steady movement of water itself. Tell students that waves can generate a longshore current. Students should consider how wave action and longshore currents shape beaches and affect other coastal landforms, what human efforts are being made to control the movements of sand and sediment, and why these efforts are being undertaken. Invite students to share what they learn with the class through a multimedia or oral presentation, or through a model of a coastline and a longshore current.

ELL *Tsunamis*

Waves at the Shore

 individuals

🕐 15 min

Concept Map Tsunamis are natural disasters more common in some parts of the world than others. Ask students to develop a concept map for *tsunami*. Encourage students to include information on causes, where tsunamis are most common, crest height, and any other information they would like. Interested students can do research and add that information to their concept maps.

 Optional Online resource: Concept Map support

Lesson Vocabulary

wave	ocean wave	crest
trough	wavelength	wave period
mechanical wave	tsunami	

Previewing Vocabulary

 whole class

🕐 10 min

Word Families In this section there are several terms that contain the word *wave*. Have students create a table for these terms. Tell students that they should complete their tables by writing definitions for these terms in their own words. Students should include the following in their tables: *wave, ocean wave, wavelength, wave period,* and *mechanical wave.*

Reinforcing Vocabulary

 individuals

🕐 ongoing

Word Triangles To help students remember the vocabulary terms in the lesson, have them make word triangles. After they draw the triangle, guide students to write a term and its definition in the bottom section. In the middle section, they should write a sentence in which the term is used correctly. In the top section, direct students to draw a small picture to illustrate the term.

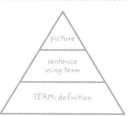

Customize Your Core Lesson

Core Instruction

☐ **Print Path** choices

☐ **Digital Path** choices

Vocabulary

☐ **Previewing Vocabulary** Word Families

☐ **Reinforcing** Word Triangles

Differentiated Instruction

☐ **Basic** Diagramming Waves

☐ **Advanced** Longshore Currents

☐ **ELL** Tsunamis

Your Resources

Extend Science Concepts

Reinforce and Review

Activity *Wave Questions*

Synthesizing Key Topics whole class

🕐 20 min

Inside/Outside Circles Help students review the material by following these steps:

1 After students have read the lesson, give each an index card with a question about material from the text. Students write their answers on the back of the index cards. Check answers to make sure they are correct. Have students adjust incorrect answers.

2 Students pair up and form two circles. One partner is in an inside circle; the other is in an outside circle. The students in the inside circle face out, and the students in the outside circle face in.

3 Each student in the inside circle asks his or her partner the question on the index card. The partner answers. If the answer is incorrect, the student in the inside circle teaches the other student the correct answer. Repeat this step with the outside-circle students asking the questions.

4 Have each student on the outside circle rotate one person to the right. He or she faces a new partner and gets a new question. Students rotate after each pair of questions. (You can vary the rotation by moving more than one person, moving to the left, and so on, but try to make sure that partners are always new.)

Graphic Organizer

Synthesizing Key Topics individuals

🕐 10 min

Cluster Diagram After students have studied the lesson, ask them to create a cluster diagram with the following terms: *wave, ocean wave, crest, trough, wavelength, wave period, mechanical wave, energy.* Tell students to include any other appropriate terms and concepts from the lesson.

🕐 *Optional Online resource: Cluster Diagram*

Going Further

Social Studies Connection

Waves at the Shore individuals or pairs

🕐 20 min

Discussion Beach nourishment, also called beach replenishment, involves dredging huge amounts of sand from the ocean floor and pumping the sand back onto the shoreline to rebuild beaches that have been eroded. This practice is common along the Atlantic and Gulf coasts, but it is controversial. Some people think the natural erosion of beaches should not be disrupted, while others disagree. Invite students to investigate this issue and form their own opinions. Encourage students to share their opinions, and what they are based on, with the class. You can extend this activity by having students form two teams to debate the pros and cons.

Language Arts Connection

Synthesizing Key Topics individuals

🕐 20 min

Write a Wave Haiku The Japanese poetry form haiku is a 3-line poem that has five syllables in the first line, seven syllables in the second line, and five syllables in the last line. Have students write a haiku about waves. Tell them to incorporate what they have learned about how waves form and move. Encourage students to illustrate their work with pen-and-ink drawings.

Customize Your Closing

 See the Assessment Guide for quizzes and tests.

🕐 *Go Online to edit and create quizzes and tests.*

Reinforce and Review

☐ **Activity** Wave Questions

☐ **Graphic Organizer** Cluster Diagram

☐ **Print Path** Visual Summary, SE p. 76

☐ **Print Path** Lesson Review, SE p. 77

☐ **Digital Path** Lesson Closer

Evaluate Student Mastery

Formative Assessment

See the teacher support below the Student Pages for additional Formative Assessment questions.

Ask the following questions to assess student mastery of the material. **Ask:** How can wavelength and frequency be used to calculate speed? To calculate wave speed, you multiply the wave's wavelength by its frequency. **Ask:** How do most waves form? Most waves form when wind blows across the water's surface and transfers energy to the water. **Ask:** Why do waves slow down in shallow water? Waves touch bottom at about one-half their wavelength. Contact with the ocean floor causes the wave to slow down. **Ask:** What factors cause tsunamis? underwater earthquakes, volcanic eruptions, and landslides

Reteach

Formative assessment may show that students need reinforcement for certain topics. The resources below are recommended for reteaching. If students were introduced to a topic through the Print Path, you can also use the Digital Path to reteach, or vice versa.
🎧 *Can be assigned to individual students*

Properties of Ocean Waves
Basic Diagramming Waves 🎧

Ocean Wave Formation
Quick Lab Making Waves

Ocean Wave Movement
Exploration Lab Wave Movement

Waves at the Shore
ELL Tsunamis 🎧

Summative Assessment

Alternative Assessment
Waves

⏱ *Online resources: student worksheet; optional rubrics*

Ocean Waves

Choose Your Meal: *Waves*

1. Work on your own, with a partner, or with a small group.
2. Choose one item from each section of the menu, with an optional dessert. Check your choices.
3. Have your teacher approve your plan.
4. Submit or present your results.

Appetizers

_____ **Model a Wave** Use modeling clay to construct two ocean waves. Label the following parts: crest, trough, wavelength, and amplitude.

_____ **Calculate Wave Speed** Imagine you are on the ocean. You count 4 waves traveling right under your boat in 10 seconds. You estimate the wavelength to be 5 meters. What is the wave speed?

_____ **Predict** Would breakers on a specific beach always form at the same distance from shore? Explain.

Main Dish

_____ **Surf Forecast** Write a script for a weather forecaster describing surf conditions for the next weeks. Tell why the surf will be that way and what effect it may have on beaches.

_____ **Powerpoint Presentation** Create a powerpoint presentation describing how waves move and information about wave size, frequency, and speed.

_____ **Tsunami Preparedness** Think about these regions of the United States: Hawaii, the Pacific Coast, the Gulf Coast, the Florida Atlantic Coast, and the Maine Atlantic Coast. Which are most likely to be affected by a tsunami and why? What safety measures might communities take? Write your answers.

Side Dishes

_____ **Energy Flipbook** Use small pieces of paper or self-sticking notes. Use at least five pages to show the movement of ocean waves. Show how the energy moves, and how the water moves.

_____ **Announce the Action** Create a blow-by-blow sports announcement detailing exactly what is happening as a wave moves, then approaches and hits the shore.

_____ **Wave Education Picture Book** Make a picture book to teach young children how waves form and what happens when waves approach a beach.

Desserts (optional)

_____ **Form a Wave** Act out what happens during a wave. Show how energy moves through the wave, but the particles remain unchanged. You can work alone, with classmates, or use props.

Going Further
- [ ] Social Studies Connection
- [ ] Language Arts Connection
- [ ] **Print Path** Why It Matters, SE p. 73

Formative Assessment
- [ ] Strategies Throughout TE
- [ ] Lesson Review SE

Summative Assessment
- [ ] Alternative Assessment Waves
- [ ] Lesson Quiz
- [ ] Unit Tests A and B
- [ ] Unit Review SE End-of-Unit

Your Resources

_____

_____

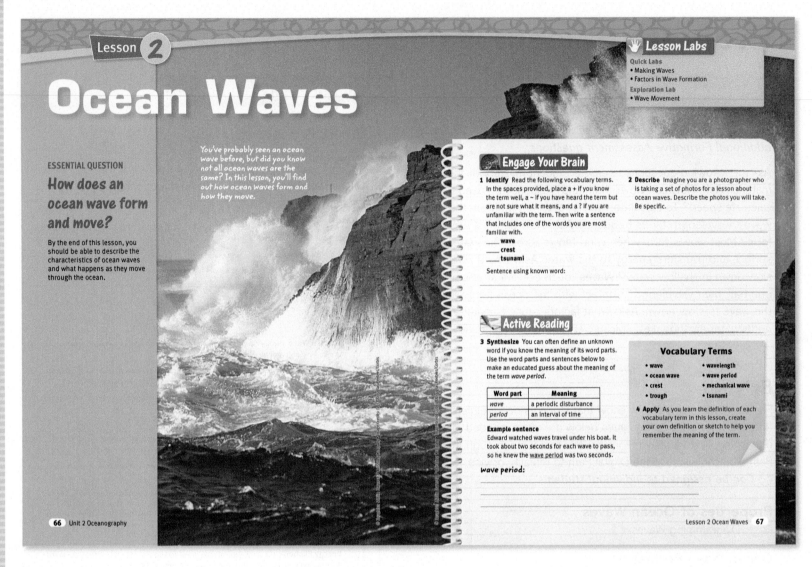

Answers

Answers for 1–3 should represent students' current thoughts, even if incorrect.

1. Sample answer: +; ?; ~; A surfer rides a wave to the shore.

2. Sample answer: I would take photos of waves that are far out in the middle of the ocean and others that are close to shore. I would take photos of different sizes of waves. I would take photos of boats being rocked by the waves.

3. Sample answer: A wave period is the time it takes a wave to pass a particular location.

4. Students should define or sketch each vocabulary term in the lesson.

Opening Your Lesson

Discuss students' responses to item 1 to assess their prerequisite knowledge and to estimate what they already know about ocean waves.

Prerequisites Students should already have some knowledge of how waves move. They should also know that ocean depth decreases closer to the shore. In this lesson, they will build on this knowledge in order to understand ocean waves and the factors that affect them.

Learning Alert

Tsunami The word *tsunami* originally comes from a Japanese word meaning "harbor wave." Tell students that Japan is in an area of the world where tsunamis are more common. The word is said to have been originated by fishermen, who would notice nothing unusual while out at sea, only to return to the harbor to find the area had been devastated by waves.

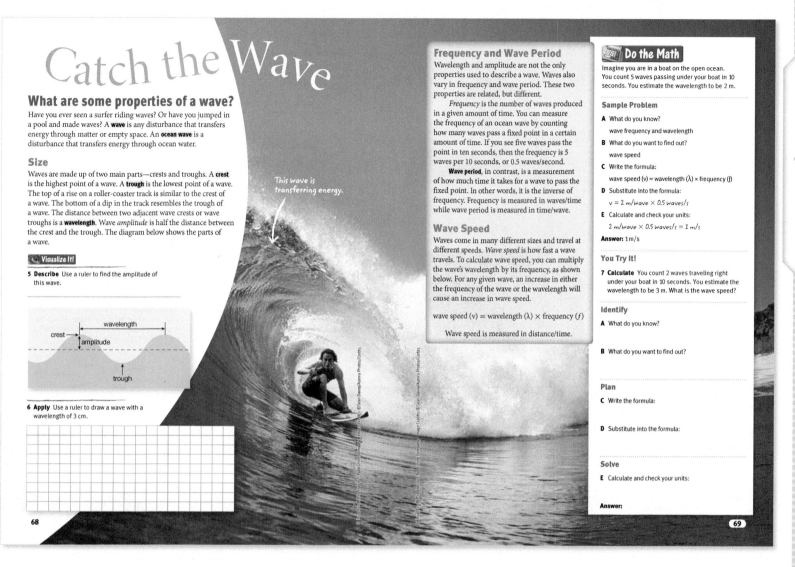

Catch the Wave

What are some properties of a wave?

Have you ever seen a surfer riding waves? Or have you jumped in a pool and made waves? A **wave** is any disturbance that transfers energy through matter or empty space. An **ocean wave** is a disturbance that transfers energy through ocean water.

Size

Waves are made up of two main parts—crests and troughs. A **crest** is the highest point of a wave. A **trough** is the lowest point of a wave. The top of a rise on a roller-coaster track is similar to the crest of a wave. The bottom of a dip in the track resembles the trough of a wave. The distance between two adjacent wave crests or wave troughs is a **wavelength**. Wave *amplitude* is half the distance between the crest and the trough. The diagram below shows the parts of a wave.

Visualize It!

5 Describe Use a ruler to find the amplitude of this wave.

6 Apply Use a ruler to draw a wave with a wavelength of 3 cm.

This wave is transferring energy.

Frequency and Wave Period

Wavelength and amplitude are not the only properties used to describe a wave. Waves also vary in frequency and wave period. These two properties are related, but different.

Frequency is the number of waves produced in a given amount of time. You can measure the frequency of an ocean wave by counting how many waves pass a fixed point in a certain amount of time. If you see five waves pass the point in ten seconds, then the frequency is 5 waves per 10 seconds, or 0.5 waves/second.

Wave period, in contrast, is a measurement of how much time it takes for a wave to pass the fixed point. In other words, it is the inverse of frequency. Frequency is measured in waves/time while wave period is measured in time/wave.

Wave Speed

Waves come in many different sizes and travel at different speeds. *Wave speed* is how fast a wave travels. To calculate wave speed, you can multiply the wave's wavelength by its frequency, as shown below. For any given wave, an increase in either the frequency of the wave or the wavelength will cause an increase in wave speed.

wave speed (v) = wavelength (λ) × frequency (f)

Wave speed is measured in distance/time.

Do the Math

Imagine you are in a boat on the open ocean. You count 5 waves passing under your boat in 10 seconds. You estimate the wavelength to be 2 m.

Sample Problem

A What do you know?
wave frequency and wavelength

B What do you want to find out?
wave speed

C Write the formula:
wave speed (v) = wavelength (λ) × frequency (f)

D Substitute into the formula:
v = 2 m/wave × 0.5 waves/s

E Calculate and check your units:
2 m/wave × 0.5 waves/s = 1 m/s

Answer: 1 m/s

You Try It!

7 Calculate You count 2 waves traveling right under your boat in 10 seconds. You estimate the wavelength to be 3 m. What is the wave speed?

Identify

A What do you know?

B What do you want to find out?

Plan

C Write the formula:

D Substitute into the formula:

Solve

E Calculate and check your units:

Answer:

68   69

Answers

5. 8 mm

6. Students should draw a wave with a wavelength of 3 cm.

7. A. wave frequency and wavelength; B. wave speed; C. wave speed (v) = wavelength (λ) × frequency (f); D. wave speed = 3 m/wave × 0.2 wave/s; E. 3 m × 0.2 s = 0.6 m/s; 0.6 m/s

Interpreting Visuals

Analyzing **Ask:** What is wavelength? the distance between the two crests **Ask:** How did you use the diagram to find this information? Sample answer: I looked at the diagram and found the word *wavelength*. I noticed that the arrow pointed from one crest to the other. **Ask:** What on the diagram shows amplitude? the red dotted line **Ask:** Based on the diagram and the text, what is amplitude? Why do you think so? Sample answer: Amplitude is half the distance from the wave's lowest point to its highest point. I think this because the text says that the amplitude is the maximum distance the wave moves from its rest position, and the diagram shows the red line at the halfway point of the wave's height.

Do the Math

Students might need help calculating the frequency of the wave from the information given in the problem. Remind students that frequency is the number of waves that travel past a fixed point in a certain amount of time. In this problem, two waves travel under the boat in ten seconds. Show students how to use this information to write the fraction ²⁄₁₀. Then review with students how to convert a fraction to a decimal. Demonstrate how to plug the numbers into the formula to find the wave speed. Allow students to use a calculator to check their answer.

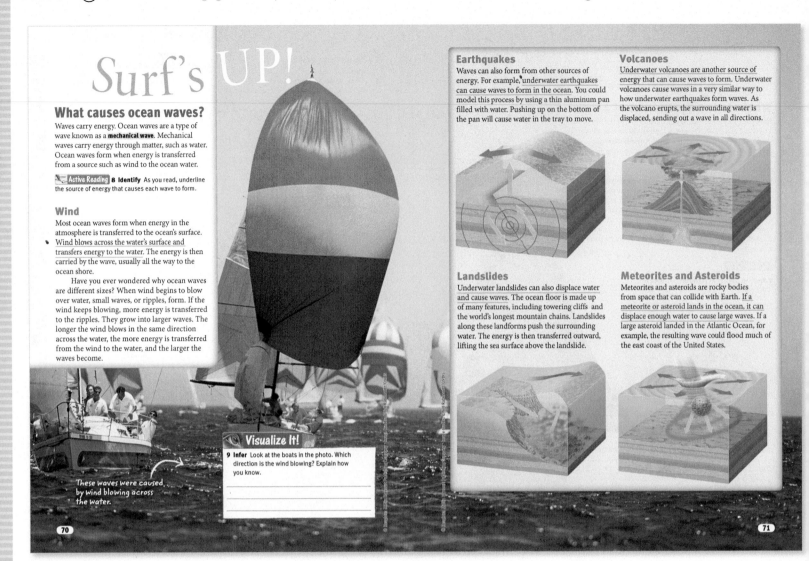

Surf's UP!

What causes ocean waves?

Waves carry energy. Ocean waves are a type of wave known as a **mechanical wave**. Mechanical waves carry energy through matter, such as water. Ocean waves form when energy is transferred from a source such as wind to the ocean water.

Active Reading 8 **Identify** As you read, underline the source of energy that causes each wave to form.

Wind

Most ocean waves form when energy in the atmosphere is transferred to the ocean's surface. Wind blows across the water's surface and transfers energy to the water. The energy is then carried by the wave, usually all the way to the ocean shore.

Have you ever wondered why ocean waves are different sizes? When wind begins to blow over water, small waves, or ripples, form. If the wind keeps blowing, more energy is transferred to the ripples. They grow into larger waves. The longer the wind blows in the same direction across the water, the more energy is transferred from the wind to the water, and the larger the waves become.

These waves were caused by wind blowing across the water.

Visualize It!

9 **Infer** Look at the boats in the photo. Which direction is the wind blowing? Explain how you know.

Earthquakes

Waves can also form from other sources of energy. For example, underwater earthquakes can cause waves to form in the ocean. You could model this process by using a thin aluminum pan filled with water. Pushing up on the bottom of the pan will cause water in the tray to move.

Volcanoes

Underwater volcanoes are another source of energy that can cause waves to form. Underwater volcanoes cause waves in a very similar way to how underwater earthquakes form waves. As the volcano erupts, the surrounding water is displaced, sending out a wave in all directions.

Landslides

Underwater landslides can also displace water and cause waves. The ocean floor is made up of many features, including towering cliffs and the world's longest mountain chains. Landslides along these landforms push the surrounding water. The energy is then transferred outward, lifting the sea surface above the landslide.

Meteorites and Asteroids

Meteorites and asteroids are rocky bodies from space that can collide with Earth. If a meteorite or asteroid lands in the ocean, it can displace enough water to cause large waves. If a large asteroid landed in the Atlantic Ocean, for example, the resulting wave could flood much of the east coast of the United States.

70   71

Answers

8. *See students' pages for annotations.*

9. The wind is blowing from behind the boats. I can tell because the sails are puffed out towards the fronts of the boats.

Building Reading Skills

Main Ideas and Details An important reading strategy is being able to identify the main idea and the supporting details of a passage. Direct students' attention to the question at the top of the page. Have them read it aloud. **Ask:** What will this page be about? the causes of ocean waves Then have students read the page and write down the details in the passage that support the main idea. **Ask:** What is the main cause of most ocean waves? the wind **Ask:** What are several other causes of ocean waves? earthquakes, volcanoes, landslides, and the impacts of meteorites and asteroids

Learning Alert

Mechanical Waves Remind students that ocean waves are not the only type of mechanical waves. Ask them if they can think of another type of mechanical wave. Sample answer: sound waves Students may name types of waves that are not mechanical waves, such as radio waves, light waves, or x-rays. If they do, **ask:** What are the properties of mechanical waves? Sample answer: They transfer energy through matter, but the matter returns to its original state after the wave passes. A mechanical wave must travel through a physical medium such as air, soil, or water. If students have named non-mechanical wave types, **ask:** Can these waves travel through space? Yes Do they require a medium to travel through? No Explain that this makes them non-mechanical waves.

Doing the Wave

What happens when a wave moves through the water?

If you have watched ocean waves, you may have noticed that water seems to move across the ocean's surface. But this movement is only an illusion. Actually, waves don't move water. Instead, they transfer energy through the water.

Energy Travels

As you learned on the previous pages, most waves form when winds blow. Wind transfers energy to the water. As the energy moves through the water, so do the waves. But the water itself does not travel with the energy.

Water Rises and Falls But Stays in the Same Place

Notice in the illustration that the floating seagull remains in approximately the same spot as the wave travels from left to right. The water and the seagull do not move with the wave, but only rise and fall in circular movements. This circular movement of water is generally the greatest at the ocean surface. Wave energy affects surface water to a depth of about half a wavelength. Deeper water is not affected by the energy of surface waves.

Active Reading 10 **Compare** How does the movement of water compare to the movement of energy in a wave?

_____

_____

_____

👁 Visualize It!

11 **Label** Draw an arrow to show the direction of the movement of energy in the waves below.

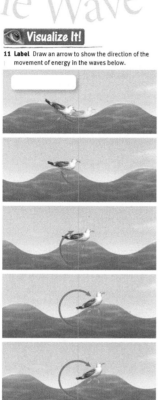

Like the bird in this illustration, water remains in the same place as waves travel through it.

72 Unit 2 Oceanography

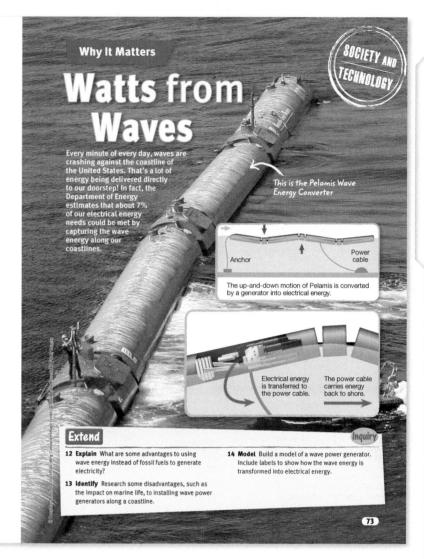

Why It Matters

SOCIETY AND TECHNOLOGY

Watts from Waves

Every minute of every day, waves are crashing against the coastline of the United States. That's a lot of energy being delivered directly to our doorstep! In fact, the Department of Energy estimates that about 7% of our electrical energy needs could be met by capturing the wave energy along our coastlines.

This is the Pelamis Wave Energy Converter

Anchor / Power cable

The up-and-down motion of Pelamis is converted by a generator into electrical energy.

Electrical energy is transferred to the power cable. / The power cable carries energy back to shore.

Extend

Inquiry

12 **Explain** What are some advantages to using wave energy instead of fossil fuels to generate electricity?

13 **Identify** Research some disadvantages, such as the impact on marine life, to installing wave power generators along a coastline.

14 **Model** Build a model of a wave power generator. Include labels to show how the wave energy is transformed into electrical energy.

73

Answers

10. The water moves in a small circle, but the energy is carried forward in a wave.

11. Students should draw an arrow that points to the right.

12. Sample answer: Wave energy is a renewable resource, and no air pollution is caused by using it.

13. Student output should include examples and descriptions of disadvantages of wave power generator use.

14. Student output should include the basic features shown in the diagram on this page, such as the up-and-down motion of the generator that is used to produce electricity.

Formative Assessment

Ask: How does water move as an ocean wave passes by? It rises and falls. **Ask:** What travels with waves? energy

Probing Questions

Applying Tell students that an ocean current is the movement of water itself, while a wave is the movement of energy. Describe the following scenario to students: You are floating in the ocean 1 km from shore, which is north of you. A surface current is flowing east. Are you more likely to travel north with the waves toward the shore or east with the surface current? Ask students to explain their answers. Sample answer: East, because wave energy travels through the water, but the water doesn't travel with the waves.

Why It Matters

Tell students that a device that used wave power to generate electricity was built as early as 1910. Currently, there are numerous technologies being developed and projects being undertaken around the globe to use the power of wave energy for generating electricity or desalinating ocean water. Three Pelamis wave energy converters like the one shown in the photograph were used in the world's first commercial wave farm off the coast of Portugal.

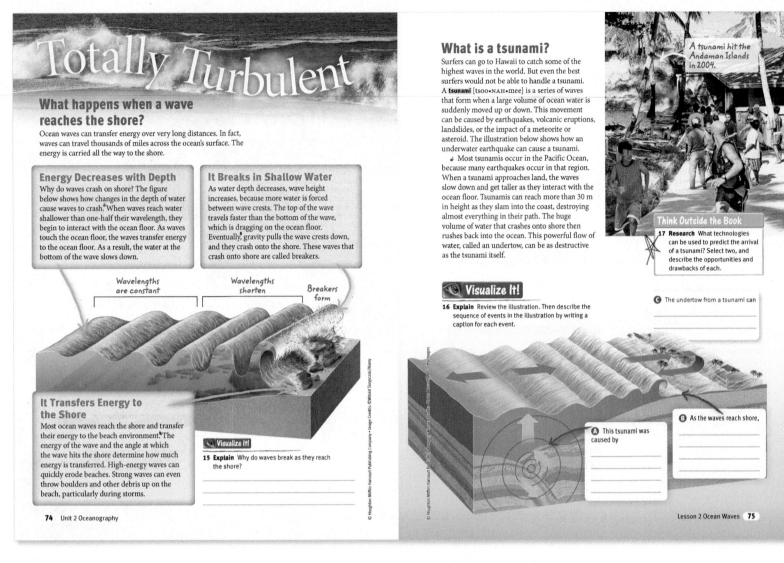

Totally Turbulent

What happens when a wave reaches the shore?

Ocean waves can transfer energy over very long distances. In fact, waves can travel thousands of miles across the ocean's surface. The energy is carried all the way to the shore.

Energy Decreases with Depth

Why do waves crash on shore? The figure below shows how changes in the depth of water cause waves to crash. When waves reach water shallower than one-half their wavelength, they begin to interact with the ocean floor. As waves touch the ocean floor, the waves transfer energy to the ocean floor. As a result, the water at the bottom of the wave slows down.

It Breaks in Shallow Water

As water depth decreases, wave height increases, because more water is forced between wave crests. The top of the wave travels faster than the bottom of the wave, which is dragging on the ocean floor. Eventually, gravity pulls the wave crests down, and they crash onto the shore. These waves that crash onto shore are called breakers.

Wavelengths are constant

Wavelengths shorten

Breakers form

It Transfers Energy to the Shore

Most ocean waves reach the shore and transfer their energy to the beach environment. The energy of the wave and the angle at which the wave hits the shore determine how much energy is transferred. High-energy waves can quickly erode beaches. Strong waves can even throw boulders and other debris up on the beach, particularly during storms.

Visualize It!

15 Explain Why do waves break as they reach the shore?

_____
_____

74 Unit 2 Oceanography

What is a tsunami?

Surfers can go to Hawaii to catch some of the highest waves in the world. But even the best surfers would not be able to handle a tsunami. A **tsunami** [tsoo•NAH•mee] is a series of waves that form when a large volume of ocean water is suddenly moved up or down. This movement can be caused by earthquakes, volcanic eruptions, landslides, or the impact of a meteorite or asteroid. The illustration below shows how an underwater earthquake can cause a tsunami.

Most tsunamis occur in the Pacific Ocean, because many earthquakes occur in that region. When a tsunami approaches land, the waves slow down and get taller as they interact with the ocean floor. Tsunamis can reach more than 30 m in height as they slam into the coast, destroying almost everything in their path. The huge volume of water that crashes onto shore then rushes back into the ocean. This powerful flow of water, called an undertow, can be as destructive as the tsunami itself.

Visualize It!

16 Explain Review the illustration. Then describe the sequence of events in the illustration by writing a caption for each event.

A tsunami hit the Andaman Islands in 2004.

Think Outside the Book

17 Research What technologies can be used to predict the arrival of a tsunami? Select two, and describe the opportunities and drawbacks of each.

C The undertow from a tsunami can
_____

A This tsunami was caused by
_____

B As the waves reach shore,
_____

Lesson 2 Ocean Waves **75**

Answers

15. As water depth decreases, wave height increases, and the bottom of the wave drags on the ocean floor. Eventually, the top of the wave falls over, crashing onto shore.

16. A. the energy from an earthquake that was transferred to the water; B. the wavelength shortens and the wave height increases; C. wash away buildings and property.

17. Student output should demonstrate knowledge of tsunami warning systems. They may discuss both international and regional warning systems involving buoys and seismographs. Students should note that no system as of yet can warn against very sudden tsunamis that strike a few minutes after a quake occurs.

Formative Assessment

Ask: As a wave moves into shallow water, what causes the top of the wave to break and topple over? Contact with the ocean floor causes the wave to slow down and eventually break. **Ask:** What happens to the energy when a wave reaches the shore? The energy is transferred to the shore. **Ask:** Describe factors that cause tsunamis? Tsunamis are giant waves that are caused by underwater earthquakes, volcanic eruptions, and landslides.

Probing Questions

Inferring Some coastlines are more steeply sloped than others. **Ask:** How might wave action on a steeply sloped coastline differ from a gently sloped coastline? The energy of the wave might differ.

Learning Alert

Tsunami vs. Tidal Wave Sometimes tsunamis are referred to as *tidal waves*. This is not accurate because tsunamis are not caused by tides, which are the regular rise and fall of the oceans. Tsunamis are also sometimes referred to as *seismic waves*. This term is not always accurate because they are not always caused by seismic events, such as earthquakes.

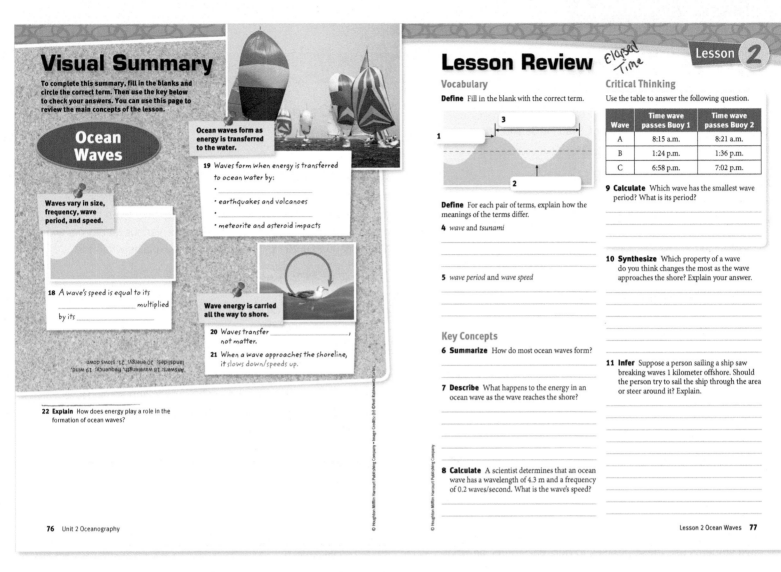

Visual Summary

To complete this summary, fill in the blanks and circle the correct term. Then use the key below to check your answers. You can use this page to review the main concepts of the lesson.

Ocean Waves

Waves vary in size, frequency, wave period, and speed.

18 A wave's speed is equal to its _____ multiplied by its _____

Ocean waves form as energy is transferred to the water.

19 Waves form when energy is transferred to ocean water by:
- •
- • earthquakes and volcanoes
- •
- • meteorite and asteroid impacts

Wave energy is carried all the way to shore.

20 Waves transfer _____, not matter.

21 When a wave approaches the shoreline, it slows down/speeds up.

Answers: 18 wavelength, frequency; 19 wind, landslides; 20 energy; 21 slows down.

22 **Explain** How does energy play a role in the formation of ocean waves?

76   Unit 2 Oceanography

Lesson Review

Elapsed Time

Lesson 2

Vocabulary

Define Fill in the blank with the correct term.

Define For each pair of terms, explain how the meanings of the terms differ.

4 *wave* and *tsunami*

5 *wave period* and *wave speed*

Key Concepts

6 **Summarize** How do most ocean waves form?

7 **Describe** What happens to the energy in an ocean wave as the wave reaches the shore?

8 **Calculate** A scientist determines that an ocean wave has a wavelength of 4.3 m and a frequency of 0.2 waves/second. What is the wave's speed?

Critical Thinking

Use the table to answer the following question.

Wave	Time wave passes Buoy 1	Time wave passes Buoy 2
A	8:15 a.m.	8:21 a.m.
B	1:24 p.m.	1:36 p.m.
C	6:58 p.m.	7:02 p.m.

9 **Calculate** Which wave has the smallest wave period? What is its period?

10 **Synthesize** Which property of a wave do you think changes the most as the wave approaches the shore? Explain your answer.

11 **Infer** Suppose a person sailing a ship saw breaking waves 1 kilometer offshore. Should the person try to sail the ship through the area or steer around it? Explain.

Lesson 2 Ocean Waves   77

Visual Summary Answers

18. wavelength, frequency
19. wind, landslides
20. energy
21. slows down
22. Energy from one medium, such as moving air or crust, must transfer its energy to ocean water. The energy then moves through the water as a wave.

Lesson Review Answers

1. crest
2. trough
3. wavelength
4. Sample answer: A wave is a periodic disturbance as energy is transmitted through a medium, and a tsunami is a series of ocean waves that carry a huge amount of energy.
5. Sample answer: The wave period describes how long it takes a wave to pass a fixed point, while wave speed describes how fast waves are traveling.
6. Most ocean waves form when wind transfers energy to the ocean surface.
7. The bottom of the wave hits the ocean floor, transfers energy, and slows. The slowing water particles pile up, causing the wave's height to grow until the wave crashes back down and transfers the rest of its energy to the beach.
8. 0.86 m/s
9. At 4 minutes, Wave C has the smallest period.
10. Sample answer: The amplitude of the wave. It increases as it nears the shore because of the decreasing water depth.
11. The person should steer the ship around the breaker waves. As water becomes shallower, the wave height increases and the waves may break. Breaking waves could signal a submerged sandbar or reef. A ship could run aground if it encounters such an obstacle.

People in  Science

Evan B. Forde

Purpose To learn about the work of Evan Forde and other oceanographers

Learning Goals
- Identify contributions made by a scientist.
- Recognize that scientists come from different backgrounds.
- Identify jobs in science fields.

Informal Vocabulary
oceanography, submersible

Prerequisite Knowledge
- Understanding of Earth's atmosphere, hydrosphere, and geosphere
- Understanding of the interactions between these different spheres

Activity *Career Quiz*

 small groups   15–30 min

 GUIDED Inquiry

Have students write on separate index cards the following phrases: *What You'll Do, Where You Might Work,* and *Education.* Then have students use these phrases to quiz each other on what oceanographers, geologists, and meteorologists do.

For greater depth, groups can research one of these three professions. Ask them to compare their prior ideas and knowledge about the profession to what they learned in their research.

Basic *Ocean Floor Landforms*

 small groups   30 min

Posters Canyons are one of many types of landforms found on the ocean floor. Assist groups in researching the landforms of the ocean floor. Have each group use what they learn to create a poster. The poster should show images of various landforms with a brief caption under each landform that explains what it is.

Advanced *Tools of the Trade*

 small groups   30–45 min

Quick Research Have groups research the tools used by oceanographers, such as submersibles, nets, and sonar. Have each group focus on a specific tool or type of tool. They can use what they learn to create a page in a catalog of oceanography tools. The catalog entry should include an image of the tool and describe how it works, what it is used for, and how it is operated. Have groups combine their work to form a complete catalog.

ELL *Interview an Oceanographer*

 pairs   15 min

Have students brainstorm questions they would like to ask Evan Forde or another oceanographer. Encourage students to think of a range of questions, from specific questions about what kind of work they do and what instruments they use to do it, to more personal questions about what they enjoy about oceanography. Pairs should then take turns asking each other the questions they brainstormed and making up answers based on the profile of Evan Forde.

Customize Your Feature

- ☐ **Activity** Career Quiz
- ☐ **People in Science** Online
- ☐ **Basic** Ocean Floor Landforms
- ☐ **Advanced** Tools of the Trade
- ☐ **ELL** Interview an Oceanographer
- ☐ **Building Reading Skills**

People in Science

Evan B. Forde
OCEANOGRAPHER

Pillow lava on the ocean floor, seen from **Alvin**

Evan B. Forde is an oceanographer at the Atlantic Oceanographic and Meteorological Laboratory in Miami, Florida. His main areas of study have included looking at the different processes occurring in the U.S. east coast submarine canyons. To study these canyons, Evan became the first African American to participate in research dives in underwater submersibles—machines that can take a human being under water safely—such as Alvin. He is currently studying how conditions in the atmosphere relate to the formation of hurricanes.

Evan graduated with degrees in Geology and Marine Geology and Geophysics from Columbia University in New York City. Along with his scientific research, he is committed to science education. He has developed and taught courses on Tropical Meteorology at the University of Miami. Keeping younger students in mind, he created an oceanography course for middle-school students through the Miami-Dade Public Libraries. Evan speaks often to students about oceanography and the sciences, and is involved with many community youth projects.

Social Studies Connection

Mendocino Canyons
San Francisco
Monterey Canyon
Sur Canyon
CALIFORNIA
Hueneme Canyon
Los Angeles
Santa Monica Canyon
San Diego
Redondo Canyon
Scripps Canyon
La Jolla Canyon

PACIFIC OCEAN

BAJA CALIFORNIA

MEXICO

San Lucas Canyon

Research the Monterey Submarine Canyon shown on the map. Find out its size and if it is still considered one of the largest canyons off the Pacific Coast. Research the kind of organisms that can live there.

Evan B. Forde

78

JOB BOARD

Wind Turbine Technician

What You'll Do: Operate and maintain wind turbine units, including doing repairs and preventative maintenance.

Where You Might Work: You will need to travel often to the different wind farms that have wind turbines. Some technicians may have the chance to travel to wind farms in different countries to complete repairs on wind turbines.

Education: Typically, technicians will graduate from a wind energy program. Technicians should have a solid understanding of math, meteorology, computer, and problem solving skills.

Other Job Requirements: To do these tasks, you will need to climb wind towers as high as 125 meters, so it is helpful if you do not have a fear of heights.

Environmental Engineering Technician

What You'll Do: Help environmental engineers and scientists prevent, control, and get rid of environmental hazards. Inspect, test, decontaminate, and operate equipment used to control and help fix environmental pollution.

Where You Might Work: Offices, laboratories, or industrial plants. Most technicians have to complete field work, so they do spend time working outdoors in all types of weather.

Education: You will need an associate's degree in environmental engineering technology, environmental technology, or hazardous materials information systems technology.

Wind turbine

79

Answers

Social Studies Connection

Students' research should include details about the organisms living in the canyon as well as information about the canyon's size.

Building Reading Skills

Suffixes Ask: What do you think the suffix -*ology* means? science, theory, study The word root *geo* means "earth." What does *geology* mean? the study of earth What other words do you know with the suffix -*ology*? Sample answers: meteorology, technology, paleontology, biology, zoology Help students determine the meaning of other -*ology* words by analyzing the meanings of their word parts. Use a dictionary if necessary.

⊙ *Optional Online resource: Suffixes support*

Ocean Currents

Essential Question How does water move in the ocean?

Professional Development

For more detailed information about the topics in this lesson, refer to the Content Refresher in the Unit Opener pages.

Opening Your Lesson

Begin the lesson by assessing students' prerequisite and prior knowledge.

Prerequisite Knowledge

- Definition of *hydrosphere*
- Gases in the atmosphere
- Definition of *density*

Accessing Prior Knowledge

Ask: What causes wind? the sun's uneven heating of Earth's surface

Ask: What makes up Earth's atmosphere? Sample answer: nitrogen, oxygen, argon, carbon dioxide, and water vapor

Customize Your Opening

- ☐ **Accessing Prior Knowledge,** above
- ☐ **Print Path** Engage Your Brain, SE p. 81 #1–2
- ☐ **Print Path** Active Reading, SE p. 81 #3–4
- ☐ **Digital Path** Lesson Opener

Key Topics/Learning Goals	Supporting Concepts
Surface Currents in the Ocean 1 Define *ocean currents* and *surface currents*. 2 List and describe three things that affect surface currents.	• Ocean currents are streamlike paths of water in the ocean. A surface current is an ocean current near the surface caused by wind. • The Coriolis effect causes surface currents to curve right or left. Continental deflection causes currents to change direction when flowing toward land. Energy from surface winds can transfer to water, causing surface currents.
Deep Currents in the Ocean 1 Define *deep currents* and explain how they form. 2 Define *convection current*. 3 Explain how convection currents transfer energy.	• A deep current is a streamlike movement of ocean water far below the surface. It forms when surface water becomes denser than water below, causing it to sink and become a deep current. • A convection current is any movement of matter resulting from density differences. • Convection currents transfer energy when warm water is moved to colder regions.
Upwelling 1 Define *upwelling*. 2 Explain the importance of upwelling to ocean life.	• Upwelling is the movement of deep, cold, nutrient-rich water to the surface. • Upwelling brings nutrients from the deep ocean to the surface.
Ocean Circulation 1 Describe ocean circulation. 2 Give examples of how ocean currents transport matter and energy.	• Surface and deep currents and upwelling move ocean water through ocean basins. • Matter transported by currents includes water and dissolved solids and gases. Energy is transported from areas near the equator toward Earth's poles.

Options for Instruction

Two parallel paths provide coverage of the Essential Questions, with a strong **Inquiry** strand woven into each.
Follow the **Print Path**, the **Digital Path**, or your customized combination of print, digital, and inquiry.

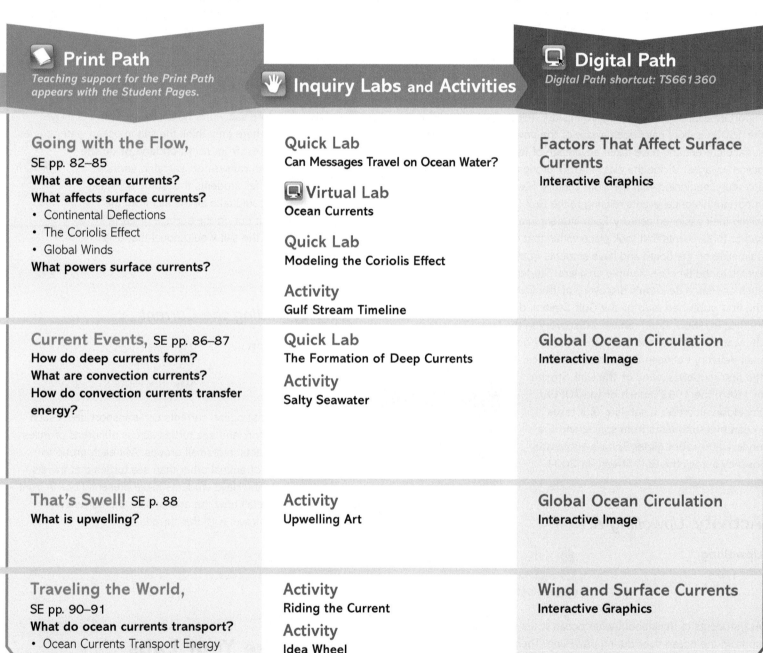

Print Path
Teaching support for the Print Path appears with the Student Pages.

Inquiry Labs and Activities

Digital Path
Digital Path shortcut: TS661360

Going with the Flow,
SE pp. 82–85
What are ocean currents?
What affects surface currents?
- Continental Deflections
- The Coriolis Effect
- Global Winds
What powers surface currents?

Quick Lab
Can Messages Travel on Ocean Water?

Virtual Lab
Ocean Currents

Quick Lab
Modeling the Coriolis Effect

Activity
Gulf Stream Timeline

Factors That Affect Surface Currents
Interactive Graphics

Current Events, SE pp. 86–87
How do deep currents form?
What are convection currents?
How do convection currents transfer energy?

Quick Lab
The Formation of Deep Currents

Activity
Salty Seawater

Global Ocean Circulation
Interactive Image

That's Swell! SE p. 88
What is upwelling?

Activity
Upwelling Art

Global Ocean Circulation
Interactive Image

Traveling the World,
SE pp. 90–91
What do ocean currents transport?
- Ocean Currents Transport Energy
- Ocean Currents Transport Matter

Activity
Riding the Current

Activity
Idea Wheel

Wind and Surface Currents
Interactive Graphics

Options for Assessment

See the Evaluate page for options, including Formative Assessment, Summative Assessment, and Unit Review.

Engage and Explore

Activities and Discussion

Activity *Gulf Stream Timeline*

Engage

Surface Currents in the Ocean

 small groups
🕐 40 min
 GUIDED inquiry

Explain to students that the Gulf Stream has been an interesting and important area of study throughout history. Tell students that since the 1500s, sailors have been aware of the power of the Gulf Stream surface current and have taken advantage of its force to speed up ocean voyages. Divide the class into six groups and assign each group a century, beginning with the 16th century. Have each group research important historical events relating to the Gulf Stream that took place within their assigned century. Each student in a group should record two or three events that took place within that century. Then draw a timeline on the board and have students from each group add events to the timeline. Sample answers: Students may cite events such as Ponce de Leon's discovery of the Gulf Stream in 1513; the first published map of the Gulf Stream, drawn by Athanasius Kircher, in 1665; Ben Franklin's discovery in the late 1780s that the warm waters of the Gulf Stream could be used to speed up mail delivery between England and America; the first modern survey of the Gulf Stream in 1844; the 1992 launch of the TOPEX/Poseidon altimeter, a satellite that takes ocean measurements from space; and the underwater robot glider Spray's successful journey across the Gulf Stream in 2004.

Activity *Upwelling Art*

Upwelling

 individuals
🕐 15 min
 DIRECTED inquiry

Ask students to think about what ocean water looks like when it rises up from the ocean floor during upwelling. Then have each student draw a picture representing this process. Student drawings should include a representation of how upwelling begins and what results as it occurs.

Discussion *Salty Seawater*

Deep Currents in the Ocean

 whole class
🕐 10 min

Tell students that salinity is a measure of dissolved salts or solids in a liquid. Remind them that salt water is denser than fresh water is, and that the more salt water holds, the denser it is. Have students discuss where they think the salt in ocean water comes from. Sample answer: from rocks on land or on the ocean bottom; from rain runoff carrying sodium and chloride ions Tell students that some scientists believe that if we could take all the salt from the ocean and spread it out on the surface of Earth's land, the height of the salt would equal that of a 40-story building.

Activity *Riding the Current*

Ocean Circulation

 small groups
🕐 20 min
 INDEPENDENT inquiry

Remind students that ocean currents can transport items such as coconuts, plankton, and sea turtles across hundreds of miles of ocean. Put students into small groups. Ask each group to research one type of animal other than sea turtles that travels along ocean currents. Have students make presentations in front of the class that detail how the animal uses the current and where the animals travel with the current.

Customize Your Labs

 See the Lab Manual for lab datasheets.

 Go Online for editable lab datasheets.

Levels of **Inquiry**

DIRECTED inquiry
introduces inquiry skills
within a structured
framework.

GUIDED inquiry
develops inquiry skills
within a supportive
environment.

INDEPENDENT inquiry
deepens inquiry skills
with student-driven
questions or procedures.

Labs and Demos

Quick Lab *The Formation of Deep Currents*

Deep Currents in the Ocean

👥 small groups
🕐 two 10 min periods
Inquiry DIRECTED inquiry

Students will model the formation of deep currents as they watch cold water sink in a container of warm water.

PURPOSE **To model and describe formation of deep currents**

MATERIALS

- baking dish, glass
- food coloring
- ice cube tray
- water for ice cubes
- water, hot

Quick Lab *Can Messages Travel on Ocean Water?*

Surface Currents in the Ocean

👥 small groups
🕐 20 min
Inquiry GUIDED inquiry

Students will explore how ocean currents form and how matter is transferred by currents.

PURPOSE **To describe the effect of ocean currents on matter in the ocean**

MATERIALS

- cork or plastic foam ball
- pan, rectangular
- paper fan (optional)
- spoon (optional)
- straw (optional)
- tape

Quick Lab *Modeling the Coriolis Effect*

Surface Currents in the Ocean

👥 pairs
🕐 20 min
Inquiry DIRECTED inquiry

Students will learn how the Coriolis effect influences the path of currents on Earth's surface.

PURPOSE **To model the Coriolis effect and to observe the path of liquid flowing over a spinning sphere**

MATERIALS

- balloon, large, round, light color (2)
- cup, plastic or paper, small
- eyedropper, unbreakable
- food coloring, dark or bright
- newspaper
- piece of string, 15 cm in length (2)

Virtual Lab *Ocean Currents*

Surface Currents in the Ocean

👥 flexible
🕐 45 min
Inquiry GUIDED inquiry

Students measure land and sea temperatures related to surface currents.

PURPOSE **To explore temperatures and ocean currents**

Activities and Discussion

☐ **Activity** Gulf Stream Timeline
☐ **Activity** Upwelling Art
☐ **Discussion** Salty Seawater
☐ **Activity** Riding the Current

Labs and Demos

☐ **Quick Lab** The Formation of… Currents
☐ **Quick Lab** Can Messages Travel on Ocean Water?
☐ **Quick Lab** Modeling… Coriolis Effect
☐ **Virtual Lab** Ocean Currents

Your Resources

Explain Science Concepts

	Print Path	Digital Path
Key Topics		

Print Path

Digital Path

Surface Currents in the Ocean

☐ **Going with the Flow,** SE pp. 82–85
- Active Reading (Annotation strategy), #5
- Visualize It!, #6
- Identify, #7
- Analyze, #8
- Visualize It!, #9

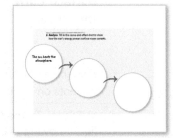

☐ **Factors That Affect Surface Currents**
Learn how wind, continents, and the Coriolis effect affect surface currents.

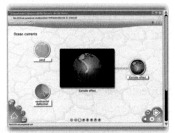

Deep Currents in the Ocean

☐ **Current Events,** SE pp. 86–87
- Active Reading (Annotation strategy), #10
- Visualize It!, #11
- Think Outside the Book, #12
- Inquiry, #13

☐ **Global Ocean Circulation**
Explore why water moves up, down, and across the oceans.

Upwelling

☐ **That's Swell!** SE p. 88
- Active Reading (Annotation strategy), #14
- Predict, #15

☐ **Global Ocean Circulation**
Explore why water moves up, down, and across the oceans.

Ocean Circulation

☐ **Traveling the World,** SE pp. 90–91
- Active Reading (Annotation strategy), #19
- Describe, #20
- List, #21

In the Pacific Ocean, surface currents transport energy from the tropics to latitudes above and below the equator.

☐ **Wind and Surface Currents**
Explore how energy from the sun affects waves and currents.

Basic *Ocean Convection*

Ocean Circulation

 small groups

🕐 varied

Posters To helps students understand why it is warmer at the equator, point out that the equator receives more direct sunlight than the poles, which makes it warmer. Clarify the misunderstanding that this uneven heating is a result of the equator being closer to the sun. In small groups, have students draw posters showing all of the energy sources that warm the ocean and allow warm water to travel in the form of convection currents. Posters should show ocean waters absorbing solar energy and energy from the atmosphere. Posters should also show the ocean's transfer of energy from the equator to the poles.

Advanced *Force of the Atlantic*

Surface Currents in the Ocean

👥 individuals

🕐 varied

Dangerous Journeys Explain to students that in the 1500s and beyond, Spain sent large fleets of ships to South America and Central America to collect valuables such as gold, silver, and gemstones. These ships often used the strong current of the Gulf Stream to return home quickly. The fact that many of these ships were loaded with treasures made them targets for pirates and European raiders. Have students research these expeditions and how they used the Gulf Stream, then write journal entries from the point of view of a sailor on one of the ships.

ELL *Understanding Deflection*

Surface Currents in the Ocean

 individuals

🕐 varied

Bouncing Ball After teaching about continental deflections, hold up a small rubber ball. Tell students that deflection occurs when an object comes in contact with another object and, as a result, changes direction. Demonstrate by bouncing a small rubber ball off the classroom wall. Tell students that this is what happens to surface currents when they come in contact with the continents. To ensure students understand deflection, ask them to offer other examples. Sample answers: a football bouncing off of a goal post; a light beam bouncing off of a mirrored surface

ocean current	surface current	Coriolis effect
deep current	convection current	upwelling

Previewing Vocabulary

 whole class

🕐 10 min

Word Origins Share the following to help students understand and remember terms:
- **Convection** comes from a Latin term that means "the act of carrying."
- **Current** comes from the Latin word *currere* meaning "to run."

Reinforcing Vocabulary

👥 individuals

🕐 ongoing

Cluster Diagram To help students remember terms introduced in this lesson, direct them to make a Cluster Diagram. Students should write the word *currents* in the main circle, then in circles around it they should write the different types of currents. Encourage students to include several details about each type of current.

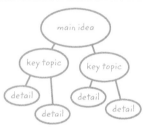

Customize Your Core Lesson

Core Instruction
- ☐ **Print Path** choices
- ☐ **Digital Path** choices

Vocabulary
- ☐ **Previewing Vocabulary** Word Origins
- ☐ **Reinforcing Vocabulary** Cluster Diagram

Your Resources

Differentiated Instruction
- ☐ **Basic** Ocean Convection
- ☐ **Advanced** Force of the Atlantic
- ☐ **ELL** Understanding Deflection

Extend Science Concepts

Reinforce and Review

Activity *Idea Wheel*

Synthesizing Key Topics

 small groups
 25 min

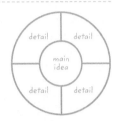

1 Show students a sample Idea Wheel, and explain that students will create an Idea Wheel based on one key topic from the lesson.

2 Divide students into four groups and assign each group a key topic (surface currents in the ocean, deep currents in the ocean, upwelling, and ocean circulation).

3 Have students choose a category or characteristic relating to the assigned key topic for each of the four sections of the Idea Wheel. Then instruct students to fill in each section of the wheel with details related to that category or characteristic.

4 Display student Idea Wheels on a classroom bulletin board and refer to them during a lesson review.

FoldNote

Synthesizing Key Topics

 individuals
varied

Two-Panel Flipchart Have students review the sections on surface currents and deep currents. Then instruct students to complete a Two-Panel Flipchart comparing and contrasting details about the two types of currents.

⌾ *Optional Online resource: Two-Panel Flipchart support*

Going Further

Ecology Connection

Ocean Circulation

 small groups
varied

Polluted Ocean Remind students that the ocean transports energy and matter around the globe. Encourage students to give examples of things that oceans might transport. Sample answer: living organisms, garbage, other pollutants Have students form groups to brainstorm different types of ocean pollutants. Then have them research ways to prevent ocean pollution. Groups should create a visual aid, such as a poster, to show their findings. Have groups present their findings to the class and propose ways that people can help lessen the pollution of the world's oceans.

Health Connection

Synthesizing Key Topics

 whole class
varied

Discussion Tell students that scientists have discovered many treatments for human illnesses in the ocean. Because the human body has developed resistances to some traditional medications, scientists have turned to diverse ocean life for new medical possibilities. Some studies suggest that a natural component in some marine sponges might help the body fight off cancer, and that cone snail venom, which is used to paralyze prey, might be an effective painkiller. Scientists are interested in the unique chemicals contained in these ocean-dwelling creatures and their potential to improve human health and teach scientists more about the processes of the human body.

Customize Your Closing

◆ *See the Assessment Guide for quizzes and tests.*

⌾ *Go Online to edit and create quizzes and tests.*

Reinforce and Review

☐ **Activity** Idea Wheel

☐ **FoldNote** Two-Panel Flip Chart

☐ **Print Path** Visual Summary, SE p. 92

☐ **Print Path** Lesson Review, SE p. 93

☐ **Digital Path** Lesson Closer

Evaluate Student Mastery

See the teacher support below the Student Pages for additional Formative Assessment questions.

Ask: What effect do ocean currents have on the atmosphere? the ocean can release energy into the atmosphere or absorb energy from the atmosphere; currents transport energy around the globe; they transport gases; they release energy into the atmosphere **Ask:** How do ocean currents and upwelling benefit marine life? Upwelling stirs up food and nutrients; currents help sea creatures travel. **Ask:** How do ocean currents help people? Processes such as upwelling help fish thrive, which provides humans with food; currents help humans travel on the ocean.

Reteach

Formative assessment may show that students need reinforcement for certain topics. The resources below are recommended for reteaching. If students were introduced to a topic through the Print Path, you can also use the Digital Path to reteach, and vice versa.

🖲 *Can be assigned to individual students*

Surface Currents in the Ocean
Quick Lab Can Messages Travel on Ocean Water?

Activity Gulf Stream Timeline 🖲

Deep Currents in the Ocean
Quick Lab The Formation of Deep Currents

Upwelling
Activity Upwelling Art 🖲

Ocean Circulation
Activity Riding the Current

Alternative Assessment
Going with the Flow

🔘 *Online resources: student worksheet, optional rubrics*

Ocean Currents

Climb the Pyramid: *Going with the Flow*
Complete the activities to show what you've learned about ocean currents.

1. Work on your own, with a partner, or with a small group.

2. Choose one item from each layer of the pyramid. Check your choices.

3. Have your teacher approve your plan.

4. Submit or present your results.

__ **Affecting Currents**

Create a PowerPoint presentation in which you describe three things that can affect surface ocean currents. In your presentation, include the reasons each factor affects the currents and the way each factor affects currents differently.

__ **The Importance of Upwelling**	__ **Convection Comic**
Imagine that you are a bird that feeds on phytoplankton at the ocean's surface. Present a speech in which you describe upwelling, and explain why upwelling is important to you and other organisms in your ecosystem.	Create a comic strip or flip book in which you show how convection currents work and how they move water. Indicate the warm and cool water in your comic strip or flip book.

__ **A Traveler's Journal**	__ **Puzzling Terms**	__ **A Lesson in Currents**
Imagine that you are a sea turtle who has just traveled hundreds of miles on an ocean current. Write a journal entry in which you describe your travels on the current.	Create a crossword puzzle using at least four terms that describe ocean currents. Include an answer key with your puzzle.	Imagine that one of the science teachers in your grade has to miss class. The teacher has asked you to describe deep ocean currents. Draw at least one image on the board or on a poster to help you describe deep currents.

Going Further
- ☐ Ecology Connection
- ☐ Health Connection
- ☐ **Print Path** Why It Matters, SE p. 89

Formative Assessment
- ☐ **Strategies** Throughout TE
- ☐ **Lesson Review** SE

Summative Assessment
- ☐ Alternative Assessment Going with the Flow
- ☐ Lesson Quiz
- ☐ Unit Tests A and B
- ☐ Unit Review SE End-of-Unit

Your Resources

_____

_____

_____

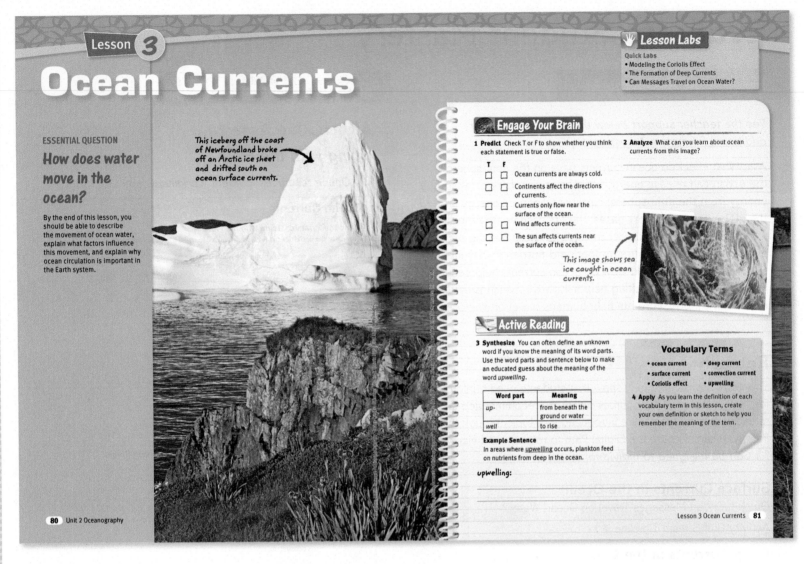

Lesson ③

Ocean Currents

Lesson Labs

Quick Labs
- Modeling the Coriolis Effect
- The Formation of Deep Currents
- Can Messages Travel on Ocean Water?

ESSENTIAL QUESTION

How does water move in the ocean?

By the end of this lesson, you should be able to describe the movement of ocean water, explain what factors influence this movement, and explain why ocean circulation is important in the Earth system.

This iceberg off the coast of Newfoundland broke off an Arctic ice sheet and drifted south on ocean surface currents.

Engage Your Brain

1 Predict Check T or F to show whether you think each statement is true or false.

T	F	
☐	☐	Ocean currents are always cold.
☐	☐	Continents affect the directions of currents.
☐	☐	Currents only flow near the surface of the ocean.
☐	☐	Wind affects currents.
☐	☐	The sun affects currents near the surface of the ocean.

2 Analyze What can you learn about ocean currents from this image?

This image shows sea ice caught in ocean currents.

Active Reading

3 Synthesize You can often define an unknown word if you know the meaning of its word parts. Use the word parts and sentence below to make an educated guess about the meaning of the word *upwelling*.

Word part	Meaning
up-	from beneath the ground or water
well	to rise

Example Sentence
In areas where upwelling occurs, plankton feed on nutrients from deep in the ocean.

upwelling:

Vocabulary Terms
- ocean current
- surface current
- Coriolis effect
- deep current
- convection current
- upwelling

4 Apply As you learn the definition of each vocabulary term in this lesson, create your own definition or sketch to help you remember the meaning of the term.

80 Unit 2 Oceanography

Lesson 3 Ocean Currents 81

Answers

Answers for 1–3 should represent students' current thoughts, even if incorrect.

1. F; T; F; T; T

2. Sample answer: Currents do not necessarily flow in straight lines. Currents can be close to the ocean surface since the ice is near the surface. Water in currents can be cold.

3. Upwelling: the movement of material from the deep ocean to the surface

4. Students should define or sketch each vocabulary term in the lesson.

Opening Your Lesson

Discuss students' answers to items 1 and 2 to assess what students already know about ocean currents, upwelling, and circulation.

Prerequisites Students should already know that the hydrosphere consists primarily of Earth's oceans and that the atmosphere is composed of nitrogen, oxygen, argon, carbon dioxide, and water vapor.

Interpreting Visuals

Have students study the photograph of an iceberg. Tell students that it is common to see icebergs along the coast of Newfoundland from March to July. They originate from the glaciers of western Greenland. Encourage students to explain how they can tell from the photograph that it is spring or summer. There are flowers in the foreground. Encourage students to discuss why icebergs are more common this time of year. Sample answer: During spring and summer, the temperature rises. This could cause icebergs to break off from glaciers.

Going with the Flow

What are ocean currents?

The oceans contain streamlike movements of water called **ocean currents**. Ocean currents that occur at or near the surface of the ocean, caused by wind, are called **surface currents**. Most surface currents reach depths of about 100 m, but some go deeper. Surface currents also reach lengths of several thousand kilometers and can stretch across oceans. An example of a surface current is the Gulf Stream. The Gulf Stream is one of the strongest surface currents on Earth. The Gulf Stream transports, or moves, more water each year than is transported by all the rivers in the world combined.

Infrared cameras on satellites provide images that show differences in temperature. Scientists add color to the images afterward to highlight the different temperatures, as shown below.

Active Reading

5 Identify As you read, underline three factors that affect surface currents.

What affects surface currents?

Surface currents are affected by three factors: continental deflections, the Coriolis effect, and global winds. These factors keep surface currents flowing in distinct patterns around Earth.

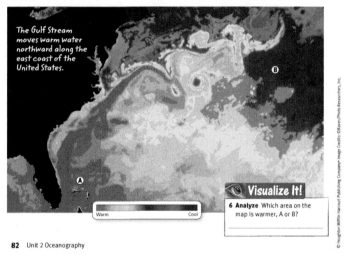

The Gulf Stream moves warm water northward along the east coast of the United States.

Visualize It!

6 Analyze Which area on the map is warmer, A or B?

82 Unit 2 Oceanography

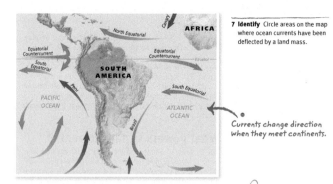

7 Identify Circle areas on the map where ocean currents have been deflected by a land mass.

Currents change direction when they meet continents.

Continental Deflections

If Earth's surface were covered only with water, surface currents would simply travel continually in one direction. However, water does not cover the entire surface of Earth. Continents rise above sea level over about one-third of Earth's surface. When surface currents meet continents, the currents are deflected and change direction. For example, the South Equatorial Current turns southward as it meets the coast of South America.

The Coriolis Effect

Earth's rotation causes all wind and ocean currents, except on the equator, to be deflected from the paths they would take if Earth did not rotate. The deflection of moving objects from a straight path due to Earth's rotation is called the **Coriolis effect** (kawr•ee•OH•lis ih•FEKT). Earth is spherical, so Earth's circumference at latitudes above and below the equator is shorter than the circumference at the equator. But the period of rotation is always 24 hours. Therefore, points on Earth near the equator travel faster than points closer to the poles.

The difference in speed of rotation causes the Coriolis effect. For example, wind and water traveling south from the North Pole actually go toward the southwest instead of straight south. Wind and water deflect to the right because the wind and water move east more slowly than Earth rotates beneath them. In the Northern Hemisphere, currents are deflected to the right. In the Southern Hemisphere, currents are deflected to the left.

The Coriolis effect is most noticeable for objects that travel over long distances, without any interruptions. Over short distances, the difference in Earth's rotational speed from one point to another point is not great enough to cause noticeable deflection.

In the Northern Hemisphere, currents are deflected to the right.

Path of wind without Coriolis effect
Approximate path of wind with Coriolis effect

Lesson 3 Ocean Currents 83

Answers

5. *See students' pages for annotations.*

6. Area A is warmer.

7. Students should draw a circle where the North Equatorial current is deflected by the northern coast of South America, where the South Equatorial current is deflected by the eastern coast of South America, where the Peru currrent is deflected by the western coast of South America, and where the Equatorial Countercurrent is deflected by the northwestern coast of South America.

Building Reading Skills

Main Idea Web Have students complete a Main Idea Web after reading the section about what affects surface currents. Instruct students to use the information in this section of the textbook to fill out their web. Remind students to write the main idea of this section in the middle of their webs and then provide details that support the main idea in each box connected to the main idea.

Interpreting Visuals

Invite students to examine the map of the eastern coast of the United States. Ask volunteers to explain the different colors on the map. Sample answer: The warm colors represent warmer waters; the cool colors represent cooler water. The warmest water is red, and the coldest is deep blue. Encourage students to discuss what effect water temperatures likely have on the climate of the eastern United States. Sample answer: The map shows that the ocean is much warmer along the coast of the southern United States than it is along the northern U.S. coast. This suggests that the weather in the southern region is also much warmer, because the ocean and the atmosphere interact and contribute to the overall climate of each area; the northern U.S. is also at a higher latitude which corresponds to cooler climates.

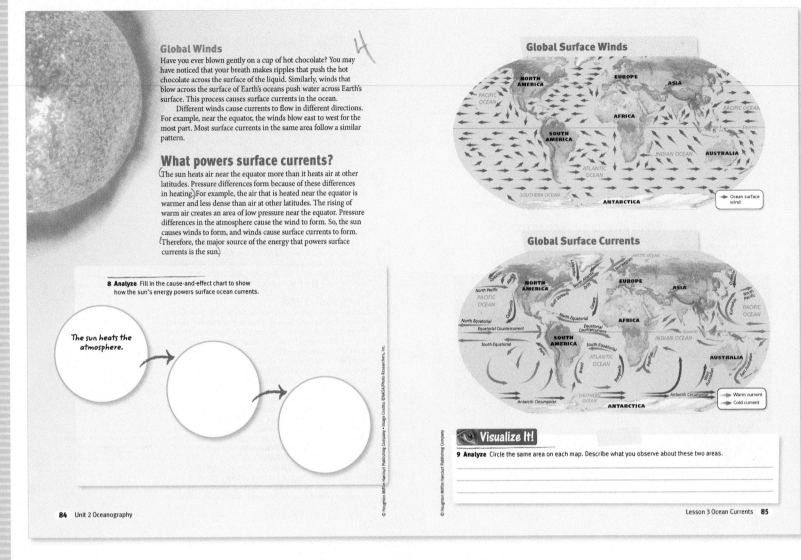

Global Winds

Have you ever blown gently on a cup of hot chocolate? You may have noticed that your breath makes ripples that push the hot chocolate across the surface of the liquid. Similarly, winds that blow across the surface of Earth's oceans push water across Earth's surface. This process causes surface currents in the ocean.

Different winds cause currents to flow in different directions. For example, near the equator, the winds blow east to west for the most part. Most surface currents in the same area follow a similar pattern.

What powers surface currents?

The sun heats air near the equator more than it heats air at other latitudes. Pressure differences form because of these differences in heating. For example, the air that is heated near the equator is warmer and less dense than air at other latitudes. The rising of warm air creates an area of low pressure near the equator. Pressure differences in the atmosphere cause the wind to form. So, the sun causes winds to form, and winds cause surface currents to form. Therefore, the major source of the energy that powers surface currents is the sun.

8 Analyze Fill in the cause-and-effect chart to show how the sun's energy powers surface ocean currents.

The sun heats the atmosphere.

Global Surface Winds

Ocean surface wind

Global Surface Currents

Warm current
Cold current

Visualize It!

9 Analyze Circle the same area on each map. Describe what you observe about these two areas.

84   Unit 2 Oceanography

Lesson 3 Ocean Currents   85

Answers

8. Students should fill in the chart with the terms *Winds form* (middle circle) and *Surface currents form* (right circle).

9. Sample answer: The winds blowing across the bottom of the Global Surface Winds map north of Antarctica match the currents in the same place in the Global Surface Currents map.

Formative Assessment

Ask: How does the sun cause winds to form? Sample answer: The sun warms the atmosphere, creating differences in temperature. The hotter air is less dense and forms areas of low pressure. The cooler air is denser, and it sinks. This movement of the air is wind. **Ask:** How does wind affect ocean currents? Sample answer: When wind blows across the surface of the ocean, it causes the water to move with it, creating surface currents.

Building Reading Skills

Concept Map Direct students to use the sections on global winds and what powers surface currents to create a Concept Map. Have students write *Surface Currents* in the large oval. Ask students to fill in the smaller ovals with details relating to surface currents. Students should also write linking words on the lines connecting the details to the main concept.

Current Events

How do deep currents form?

10 Identify As you read, underline the cause of deep currents.

Movements of ocean water far below the surface are called **deep currents**. Deep currents are caused by differences in water density. *Density* is the amount of matter in a given space or volume. The density of ocean water is affected by salinity (suh•LIN•ih•tee) and temperature. *Salinity* is a measure of the amount of dissolved salts or solids in a liquid. Water with high salinity is denser than water with low salinity. And cold water is denser than warm water. When water cools, it contracts and the water molecules move closer together. This contraction makes the water denser. When water warms, it expands and the water molecules move farther apart. The warm water is less dense, so it rises above the cold water.

When ocean water at the surface becomes denser than water below it, the denser water sinks. The water moves from the surface to the deep ocean, forming deep currents. Deep currents flow along the ocean floor or along the top of another layer of denser water. Because the ocean is so deep, there are several layers of water at any location in the ocean. The deepest and densest water in the ocean is Antarctic Bottom Water, near Antarctica.

Polar region

What are convection currents?

As you read about convection currents, refer to the illustration below. Surface currents and deep currents are linked in the ocean. Together they form convection currents. In the ocean, a **convection current** is a movement of water that results from density differences. Convection currents can be vertical, circular, or cyclical. Think of convection currents in the ocean as a conveyor belt. Surface currents make up the top part of the belt. Deep currents make up the bottom part of the belt. Water from a surface current may become a deep current in areas where water density increases. Deep current water then rises up to the surface in areas where the surface current is carrying low-density water away.

How do convection currents transfer energy?

Convection currents transfer energy. Water at the ocean's surface absorbs energy from the sun. Surface currents carry this energy to colder regions. The warm water loses energy to its surroundings and cools. As the water cools, it becomes denser and it sinks. The cold water travels along the ocean bottom. Then, the cold water rises to the surface as warm surface water moves away. The cold water absorbs energy from the sun, and the cycle continues.

12 Apply Write an interview with a water molecule following a convection current. Be sure to include questions and answers. Can you imagine the temperature changes the molecule would experience?

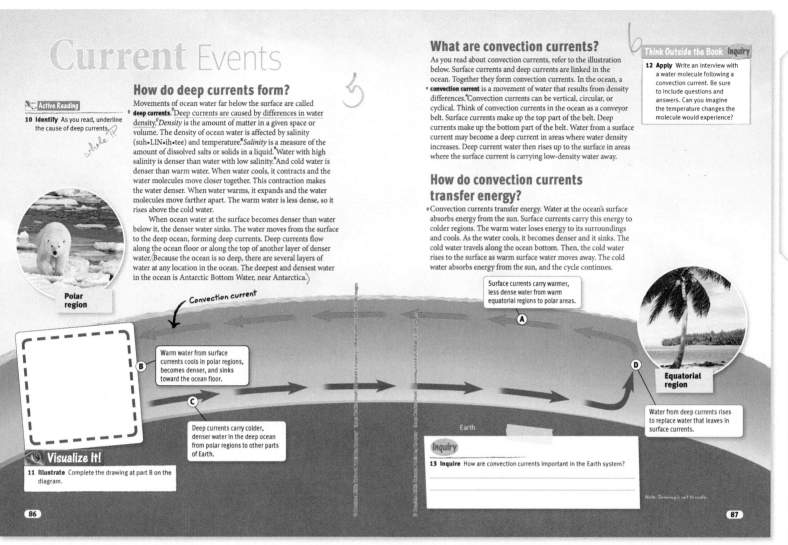

Convection current

Warm water from surface currents cools in polar regions, becomes denser, and sinks toward the ocean floor.

B

C

Deep currents carry colder, denser water in the deep ocean from polar regions to other parts of Earth.

Surface currents carry warmer, less dense water from warm equatorial regions to polar areas.

A

D

Equatorial region

Water from deep currents rises to replace water that leaves in surface currents.

Earth

Visualize It!

11 Illustrate Complete the drawing at part B on the diagram.

Inquiry

13 Inquire How are convection currents important in the Earth system?

Note: Drawing is not to scale.

86

87

Answers

10. *See students' pages for annotations.*

11. The student drawing should show warm water sinking (indicated by a red arrow curving downward). The sinking water cools (indicated by a blue arrow) and then becomes part of the deep current that moves along the ocean floor (the blue arrow curves to the right).

12. Sample answer: I started at the equator, where it was nice and warm. I traveled along the eastern coast of the United States. By the time I reached Canada, the water was getting cold.

13. Convection currents transport energy and matter in the Earth system.

Probing Questions GUIDED Inquiry

Inferring What might happen if the ocean became saltier? What if it lost a great deal of salt? Sample answers: If the ocean became saltier or lost a lot of salt, this might change the flow of deep currents.

Building Reading Skills

Process Notes Have students complete a Process Notes chart after reading the section on how convection currents transfer energy. Instruct students to record the steps for this process on the left side of the chart and to write the details of each step on the right side of the chart.

🌐 *Online resource: Process Notes support*

Learning Alert ✂ MISCONCEPTION ✂

The Equator Students may believe that Earth is hotter near the equator than it is at the poles because this portion of Earth is closer to the sun. In fact, the equator receives more direct sunlight than the poles, which makes the equator warmer throughout the year.

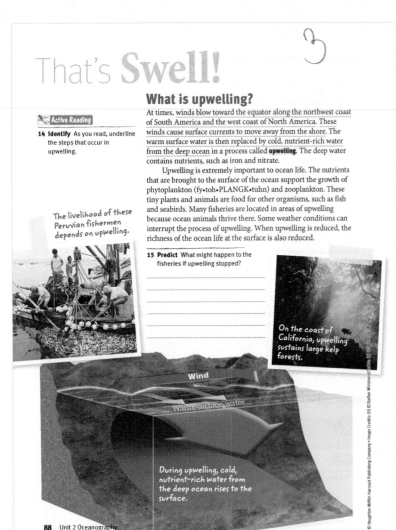

That's Swell!

What is upwelling?

14 Identify As you read, underline the steps that occur in upwelling.

At times, winds blow toward the equator along the northwest coast of South America and the west coast of North America. These winds cause surface currents to move away from the shore. The warm surface water is then replaced by cold, nutrient-rich water from the deep ocean in a process called **upwelling**. The deep water contains nutrients, such as iron and nitrate.

Upwelling is extremely important to ocean life. The nutrients that are brought to the surface of the ocean support the growth of phytoplankton (fy•toh•PLANGK•tuhn) and zooplankton. These tiny plants and animals are food for other organisms, such as fish and seabirds. Many fisheries are located in areas of upwelling because ocean animals thrive there. Some weather conditions can interrupt the process of upwelling. When upwelling is reduced, the richness of the ocean life at the surface is also reduced.

The livelihood of these Peruvian fishermen depends on upwelling.

15 Predict What might happen to the fisheries if upwelling stopped?

_____

_____

_____

_____

_____

On the coast of California, upwelling sustains large kelp forests.

Wind

Warm surface water

During upwelling, cold, nutrient-rich water from the deep ocean rises to the surface.

Why It Matters

Hitching a Ride!

A CHANGING WORLD

What do coconuts, plankton, and sea turtles have in common? They get free rides on ocean currents.

Sprouting Coconuts!
This sprouting coconut may be transported by ocean currents to a beach. This transport explains why coconut trees can grow in several areas.

World Travel
When baby sea turtles are hatched on a beach, they head for the ocean. They can then pick up ocean currents to travel. Some travel from Australia to South America on currents.

Fast Food
Diatoms are a kind of phytoplankton. They are tiny, one-celled plants that form the basis of the food chain. Diatoms ride surface currents throughout the world.

Extend   Inquiry

16 Identify List three organisms transported by ocean currents.

17 Research Investigate the Sargasso Sea. State why a lot of plastic collects in this sea. Find out whether any plastic collects on the shoreline nearest you.

18 Explain Describe how plastic and other debris can collect in the ocean by doing one of the following:
- make a poster
- write a song
- write a poem
- write a short story

Answers

14. See students' pages for annotations.

15. If upwelling stopped, the number of organisms that fish depend on for food might decrease. Fish would have to find other places in the ocean to find food. Fishermen might have to travel farther to find more fish.

Extend

16. Students should list coconuts, plankton, and sea turtles.

17. Surface currents keep the plastic there.

18. Students should explain how plastic and other debris is concentrated by surface currents.

Why It Matters

Phytoplankton are microscopic organisms that make their food via photosynthesis using energy and obtain nutrients in the ocean water. They are the basis of the ocean food chain, which means they are eaten by other very small animals called zooplankton. Small fish eat the zooplankton, large fish eat the smaller fish, and humans and other mammals eat the larger fish. Because phytoplankton depend on sunlight to live, they are found largely in surface waters where the most sunlight exists. Phytoplankton rely on upwelling to provide them with nutrients as they travel the surface currents of the ocean.

Probing Questions GUIDED Inquiry

Predicting Have students look at the illustration of upwelling. How would ocean life be different if upwelling did not occur? Sample answer: If upwelling did not occur, the population of phytoplankton would diminish. Because phytoplankton are at the base of the ocean food chain, organisms that feed on phytoplankton would be forced to move or find alternative food sources, which may be limited.

Traveling the World

What do ocean currents transport?

19 Identify As you read, underline the description of how energy reaches the poles.

Ocean water circulates through all of Earth's ocean basins. The paths are like the main highway on which ocean water flows. If you could follow a water molecule on this path, you would find that the molecule takes more than 1,000 years to return to its starting point! Along with water, ocean currents also transport dissolved solids, dissolved gases, and energy around Earth.

Ocean Currents Transport Energy

Global ocean circulation is very important in the transport of energy in the form of heat. Remember that ocean currents flow in huge convection currents that can be thousands of kilometers long. These convection currents carry about 40% of the energy that is transported around Earth's surface.

Near the equator, the ocean absorbs a large amount of solar energy. The ocean also absorbs energy from the atmosphere. Ocean currents carry this energy from the equator toward the poles. When the warm water travels to cooler areas, the energy is released back into the atmosphere. Therefore, ocean circulation has an important influence on Earth's climate.

In the Pacific Ocean, surface currents transport energy from the tropics to latitudes above and below the equator.

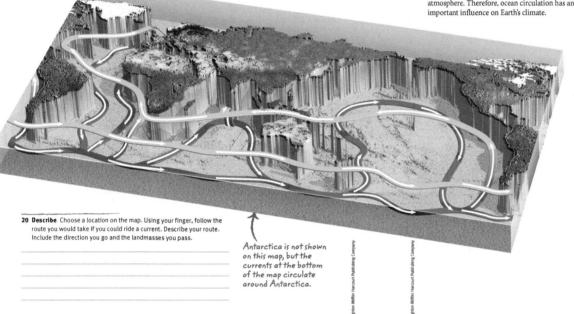

20 Describe Choose a location on the map. Using your finger, follow the route you would take if you could ride a current. Describe your route. Include the direction you go and the landmasses you pass.

Antarctica is not shown on this map, but the currents at the bottom of the map circulate around Antarctica.

Ocean Currents Transport Matter

Besides water, ocean currents transport whatever is in the water. The most familiar dissolved solid in ocean water is sodium chloride, or table salt. Other dissolved solids are important to marine life. Ocean water contains many nutrients—such as nitrogen and phosphorus—that are important for plant and animal growth.

Ocean water also transports gases. Gases in the atmosphere are absorbed by ocean water at the ocean surface. As a result, the most abundant gases in the atmosphere—nitrogen, oxygen, argon, and carbon dioxide—are also abundant in the ocean. Dissolved oxygen and carbon dioxide are necessary for the survival of many marine organisms.

21 List Write three examples of matter besides water that are transported by ocean currents.

Answers

19. See students' pages for annotations.
20. Sample answer: Start at Florida, go north to British Isles, come south, across the equator, past South America, farther south and pick up Antarctica current. Pick up northbound current which heads east across the Pacific Ocean, past Australia and Africa, back to Florida.
21. Any three of sodium chloride (or table salt), nitrogen, phosphorus, gases (or specifically nitrogen, oxygen, carbon dioxide).

Learning Alert

Estuaries Tell students that some ocean currents carry animals to estuaries. Estuaries provide habitats for many types of organisms. They occur when fresh water meets salt water, often where a river empties into the sea. The water in estuaries is brackish, meaning it is a combination of fresh and salt water. Bays, harbors, lagoons, sounds, and inlets are all examples of estuaries. Currents in these areas carry nutrients and other matter from the estuary to the ocean and vice versa.

Interpreting Visuals

Have students look at the two maps of ocean currents. Ask them what they think the different colors used to show currents mean. Sample answer: The different colors indicate that the currents are occurring at different levels. What does it mean when the color on a current route changes? Sample answer: It means that the current is moving to a different depth in the ocean.

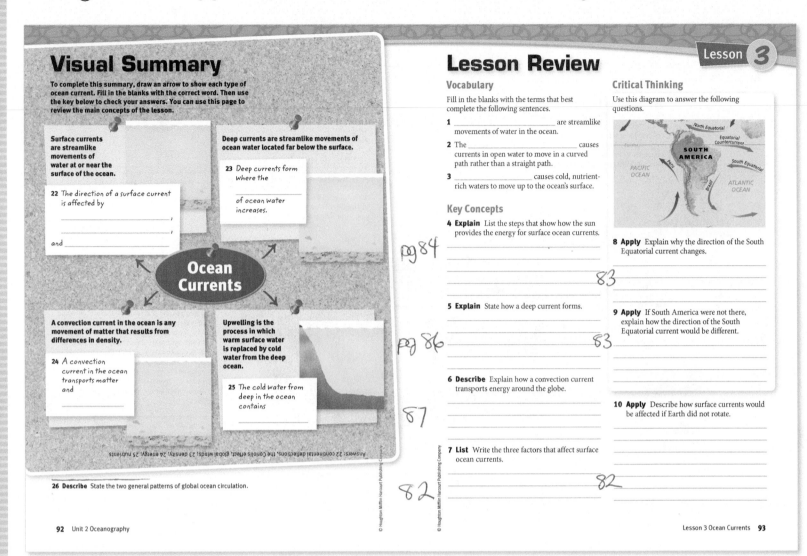

Visual Summary Answers

22. continental deflections; the Coriolis effect; global winds

23. density

24. energy

25. nutrients

26. Ocean currents transport matter and energy around the world; upwelling also transports matter and energy, although upwelling is more localized.

Lesson Review Answers

1. Ocean currents

2. Coriolis effect

3. Upwelling

4. The sun heats the atmosphere. The warmed air rises. The rising air creates an area of low pressure. Pressure differences cause winds to blow. Winds blow on the ocean surface, causing surface ocean currents.

5. Dense ocean water at the surface sinks as it cools. The water moves from the surface to the deep ocean, forming a deep current.

6. Water at the ocean's surface absorbs solar energy. The surface currents carry the energy in the warmed water to colder regions. The warm water loses energy to its surroundings and cools.

7. continental deflection; Coriolis effect; global winds

8. The South Equatorial current meets a landmass (South America) and it is deflected southward.

9. If South America were not there, the South Equatorial current would keep traveling westward.

10. If Earth did not rotate, surface currents would not be deflected. They would just run in a north-south direction or an east-west direction.

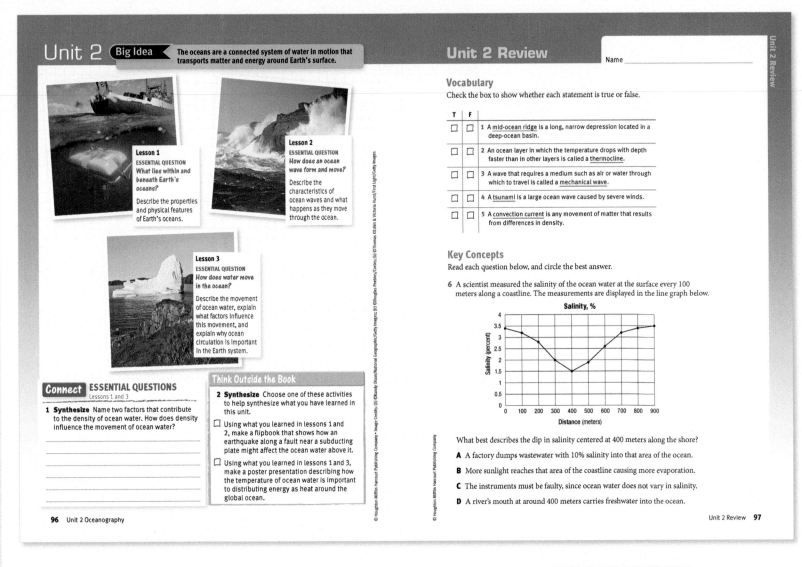

Unit Summary Answers

1. Two factors that contribute to the density of ocean water are salinity and temperature. Denser water sinks, and less dense water rises. This drives deep ocean currents.

2. Option 1: Flipbooks should show an earthquake taking place along a fault below the sea floor. Movement along the fault displaces water, which could cause a wave called a *tsunami* that spreads in concentric circles from the earthquake's epicenter. The tsunami moves quickly across the ocean and slows as it nears land. The tsunami's wavelength shortens as it interacts with the ocean floor, which becomes shallower closer to land. This causes the wave to increase in height and move inland.

   Option 2: Poster presentations should show that the warmest surface waters are found near the equator, because they absorb the most solar energy and energy as heat from the atmosphere. Surface currents carry this warm water away from the equator toward the poles. When the warm water moves into colder regions, it cools as it loses energy as heat into the atmosphere.

Unit Review (Response to Intervention)

A Quick Grading Chart follows the Answers. See the Assessment Guide for more detail about correct and incorrect answer choices. Refer back to the Lesson Planning pages for activities and assignments that can be used as remediation for students who answer questions incorrectly.

Answers

1. False This statement is false because the statement is the definition of an ocean trench. A mid-ocean ridge is a long, undersea mountain range that forms on the ocean floor where two tectonic plates are pulling apart. (Lesson 1)

2. True This statement is true because a thermocline is the layer where temperature changes with depth the fastest. (Lesson 1)

3. True This statement is true because unlike electromagnetic waves, a mechanical wave does require a medium to travel through. (Lesson 2)

7 The picture below shows a method of studying the ocean.

Which of the following best explains this method of studying the ocean?

A A bright beam of white light is being shone down through the ocean to illuminate the ocean floor.

B Sound waves are being sent down through the ocean, and the variation in time taken for the sound waves to return tells how the depth varies.

C A satellite is being used to measure variations in the gravitational field of the Earth, which tells the variation in the depth of the ocean.

D A remotely operated vehicle is being piloted from the ship to take pictures of the ocean floor.

8 Which of the following correctly shows the chain of energy transfers that create surface currents on the ocean?

A solar energy → wind energy → surface currents

B wind energy → solar energy → surface currents

C tidal energy → wind energy → surface currents

D geothermal energy → wind energy → surface currents

9 Looking at a pole at the end of a pier, Maria counted 20 wave crests pass the pole in 10 seconds. She also estimated that the wavelength was 8 pole widths. If the pole is 0.5 meters wide, what was the approximate wave speed?

A 2 m/s   **C** 8 m/s

B 4 m/s   **D** 16 m/s

98 Unit 2 Oceanography

© Houghton Mifflin Harcourt Publishing Company

10 The dashed lines on this map indicate the path of a 2004 tsunami.

December 2004 Tsunami

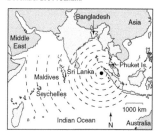

Would an observer standing on a beach on the southeast shore of Sri Lanka have known that a tsunami was coming?

A Yes, because the water would have rushed away from shore.

B No, because the observer was not in the path of the tsunami.

C Yes, because storm clouds would have formed offshore to the southeast.

D No, because the winds that caused the tsunami were from the northeast.

11 Which type of current occurs when the ocean's surface water becomes denser than the water below it and sinks?

A Coriolis current   **C** surface current

B deep current   **D** upwelling

12 The drawing below shows a snapshot of a wave.

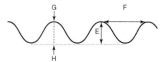

What does the measurement labeled E equal?

A The wave's period   **C** The wave's amplitude

B The wave's wavelength   **D** Twice the wave's amplitude

Unit 2 Review 99

Answers (continued)

4. **False** This statement is false because a tsunami is caused by an earthquake, landslide, or volcanic eruption, not wind. (Lesson 2)

5. **True** This statement is true because convection currents do arise from differences in density. (Lesson 3)

6. **Answer D is correct** because a freshwater source will cause the salinity of ocean water to drop. (Lesson 1)

7. **Answer B is correct** because this describes sonar mapping, which is what is depicted. (Lesson 1)

8. **Answer A is correct** because wind causes surface currents, and solar energy powers the wind. (Lesson 3)

9. **Answer C is correct** because the wavelength is 8(0.5) = 4 meters and the wave period is $^{20}/_{10}$ = 2 waves per second, so wave speed = wavelength × period = 4 × 2 = 8 m/s. (Lesson 2)

10. **Answer A is correct** because a drawback of water away from shore occurs as the tsunami wave builds in height. (Lesson 2)

11. **Answer B is correct** because deep currents are caused by the sinking of ocean water as it becomes more dense than the surrounding water. (Lesson 3)

12. **Answer D is correct** because the amplitude is the distance from the rest point (midpoint between crest and trough) to the crest or trough. (Lesson 2)

13. **Key Elements:**

    • correctly defines upwelling (e.g., *Upwelling is the movement of cold, nutrient-rich water from deep in the ocean to the surface.*)

    • explains importance to ocean life (e.g., *It brings nutrients to the surface, which helps support the organisms that live there.*) (Lesson 3)

14. **Key Elements:**

    • identifies that the salinity would increase (e.g., *The water where the salt was dumped will have higher salinity.*)

    • identifies that the increase in salinity increases the density of the water (e.g., *The higher salinity means that the water becomes more dense.*)

Unit 2 Review continued

Critical Thinking
Answer the following questions in the space provided.

13 Explain what an upwelling is and why it is important to ocean life.

_____
_____
_____
_____

14 Suppose a massive amount of salt was suddenly dumped into one region of the ocean. How would the movement of water be affected in the region of the ocean where the salt was dumped? Be sure to discuss the changes in salinity, density, and the type of ocean current that would result.

_____
_____
_____
_____
_____

Connect ESSENTIAL QUESTIONS
Lessons 1, 2, and 3

Answer the following question in the space provided.

15 Most of the energy that powers ocean waves and ocean currents ultimately comes from the sun. Using what you learned in Lessons 1, 2, and 3, describe how ocean waves and ocean currents transfer solar energy around the globe.

_____
_____
_____
_____
_____
_____

100 Unit 2 Oceanography

© Houghton Mifflin Harcourt Publishing Company

Quick Grading Chart

Use the chart below for quick test grading. The lesson correlations can help you target reteaching for missed items.

Item	Answer	Cognitive Complexity	Lesson
1.	—	Low	1
2.	—	Low	1
3.	—	Low	2
4.	—	Low	2
5.	—	Low	3
6.	D	High	1
7.	B	Moderate	1
8.	A	Moderate	3
9.	C	High	2
10.	A	Moderate	2
11.	B	Moderate	3
12.	D	Moderate	2
13.	—	Moderate	3
14.	—	High	1, 3
15.	—	High	1–3

Cognitive Complexity refers to the demand on thinking associated with an item, and may vary with the answer choices, the number of steps required to arrive at an answer, and other factors, but not the ability level of the student.

Answers (continued)

- identifies that the increase in density means the water will sink (e.g., *Since the mass of water is denser than the water below it, the mass of water will sink.*)
- identifies that a deep current results from a sinking mass of dense water (e.g., *The sinking mass of dense water from the surface creates a deep current in the ocean.*) (Lesson 1, 3)

15. Key Elements:
- correctly identifies that waves are caused by wind, which is powered by solar energy
- explains that waves don't move water, but transfer energy from one part of the ocean to another
- identifies the types of ocean currents that are powered by solar energy
- explains that ocean currents move warm water from warm regions to colder regions (Lesson 1–3)

The Big Idea and Essential Questions

This Unit was designed to focus on this Big Idea and Essential Questions.

Big Idea Earth's atmosphere is a mixture of gases that interacts with solar energy.

Lesson	ESSENTIAL QUESTION	Student Mastery	PD Professional Development	Lesson Overview
LESSON 1 The Atmosphere	*What is the atmosphere?*	To describe the composition and structure of the atmosphere and explain how the atmosphere protects life and insulates Earth	Content Refresher, TE p. 128	TE p. 134
LESSON 2 Energy Transfer	*How does energy move through Earth's system?*	To summarize the three mechanisms by which energy is transferred through Earth's system	Content Refresher, TE p. 129	TE p. 148
LESSON 3 Wind in the Atmosphere	*What is wind?*	To explain how energy provided by the sun causes atmospheric movement, called wind	Content Refresher, TE p. 130	TE p. 168

©Scott Smith/Corbis

 **Professional Development** Science Background

Use the keywords at right to access

- Professional Development from **The NSTA Learning Center**
- **SciLinks** for additional online content appropriate for students and teachers

Keywords

atmosphere   wind

energy transfer in the
    atmosphere

 National Science Teachers Association

 SCi*LINKS*®
THE WORLD'S A CLICK AWAY

Options for Instruction

Two parallel paths provide coverage of the Essential Questions, with a strong **Inquiry** strand woven into each. Follow the **Print Path,** the **Digital Path,** or your customized combination of print, digital, and inquiry.

	LESSON 1 The Atmosphere	**LESSON 2** Energy Transfer	**LESSON 3** Wind in the Atmosphere
Essential Questions	*What is the atmosphere?*	*How does energy move through Earth's system?*	*What is wind?*
Key Topics	• Composition, Air Pressure, and Temperature of the Atmosphere • Structure of the Atmosphere • Life and the Atmosphere	• Temperature, Heat, Thermal Energy, Thermal Expansion • Radiation • Convection • Conduction	• The Movement of Air • Global Winds • Local Winds
Print Path	Teacher Edition pp. 134–146 Student Edition pp. 104–113	Teacher Edition pp. 148–162 Student Edition pp. 114–127	Teacher Edition pp. 168–181 Student Edition pp. 132–143
Inquiry Labs	Lab Manual **Field Lab** Measuring Oxygen in the Air Virtual Lab The Composition and Structure of the Atmosphere	Lab Manual **Quick Lab** The Sun's Angle and Temperature **Quick Lab** Modeling Convection **S.T.E.M. Lab** Heat from the Sun	Lab Manual **Quick Lab** Flying with the Jet Stream **Quick Lab** Rising Heat **Quick Lab** Modeling Air Movement by Convection
Digital Path	Digital Path TS661450	Digital Path TS661150	Digital Path TS661350

UNIT 3
Unit Projects

Citizen Science Project
Clearing the Air

Teacher Edition p. 133

Student Edition
pp. 102–103

Video-Based Project
When the Wind Blows

Unit Assessment
Formative Assessment
Strategies RTI
Throughout TE

Lesson Reviews SE

Unit PreTest

Summative Assessment
Alternative Assessment
(1 per lesson) RTI

Lesson Quizzes

Unit Tests A and B

Unit Review RTI
Practice Tests
(end of module)

Project-Based Assessment
See the Assessment Guide
for quizzes and tests.

Go Online to edit and create
quizzes and tests.

Response to Intervention

See RTI teacher support
materials on p PD7.

Differentiated Instruction

English Language Proficiency

Strategies for **English Language Learners (ELL)** are provided for each lesson, under the Explain tabs.

LESSON 1 *Sphere Terms,* TE p. 139

LESSON 2 *Energy Terms,* TE p. 153

LESSON 3 *Wind Vocabulary Words,* TE p. 173

Vocabulary strategies provided for all students can also be a particular help for ELL. Use different strategies for each lesson or choose one or two to use throughout the unit. Vocabulary strategies can be found in the Explain tab for each lesson (TE pp. 139, 153, and 173).

Leveled Inquiry

Inquiry labs, activities, probing questions, and daily demos provide a range of inquiry levels. Preview them under the Engage and Explore tabs starting on TE pp. 136, 150, and 170.

Levels of **Inquiry**

DIRECTED inquiry	**GUIDED** inquiry	**INDEPENDENT** inquiry
introduces inquiry skills within a structured framework.	develops inquiry skills within a supportive environment.	deepens inquiry skills with student-driven questions or procedures.

Each long lab has two inquiry options:

LESSON 1 **Field Lab** *Measuring Oxygen in the Air*

LESSON 2 **S.T.E.M. Lab** *Heat from the Sun*

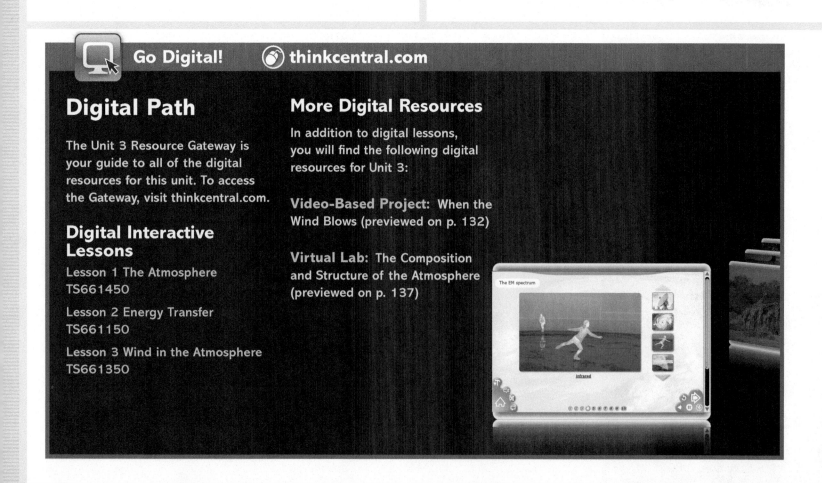

Go Digital! ⊚ thinkcentral.com

Digital Path

The Unit 3 Resource Gateway is your guide to all of the digital resources for this unit. To access the Gateway, visit thinkcentral.com.

Digital Interactive Lessons

Lesson 1 The Atmosphere
TS661450

Lesson 2 Energy Transfer
TS661150

Lesson 3 Wind in the Atmosphere
TS661350

More Digital Resources

In addition to digital lessons, you will find the following digital resources for Unit 3:

Video-Based Project: When the Wind Blows (previewed on p. 132)

Virtual Lab: The Composition and Structure of the Atmosphere (previewed on p. 137)

The EM spectrum

Infrared

RTI Response to Intervention

Response to Intervention (RTI) is a process for identifying and supporting students who are not making expected progress toward essential learning goals. The following *ScienceFusion* components can be used to provide strategic and intensive intervention.

Component	Location	Strategies and Benefits
STUDENT EDITION Active Reading prompts, Visualize It!, Think Outside the Book	**Throughout each lesson**	Student responses can be used as screening tools to assess whether intervention is needed.
TEACHER EDITION Formative Assessment, Probing Questions, Learning Alerts	**Throughout each lesson**	Opportunities are provided to assess and remediate student understanding of lesson concepts.
TEACHER EDITION Extend Science Concepts	**Reinforce and Review, TE pp. 140, 154, 174** **Going Further, TE pp. 140, 154, 174**	Additional activities allow students to reinforce and extend their understanding of lesson concepts.
TEACHER EDITION Evaluate Student Mastery	**Formative Assessment, TE pp. 141, 155, 175** **Alternative Assessment, TE pp. 141, 155, 175**	These assessments allow for greater flexibility in assessing students with differing physical, mental, and language abilities as well as varying learning and communication modes.
TEACHER EDITION Unit Review Remediation	**Unit Review, TE pp. 182–184**	Includes reference back to Lesson Planning pages for remediation activities and assignments.
INTERACTIVE DIGITAL LESSONS and VIRTUAL LABS	**thinkcentral.com** **Unit 3 Gateway** **Lesson 1 TS661450** **Lesson 2 TS661150** **Lesson 3 TS661350**	Lessons and labs make content accessible through simulations, animations, videos, audio, and integrated assessment. Useful for review and reteaching of lesson concepts.

Content Refresher

Professional Development

The Atmosphere

ESSENTIAL QUESTION

What is the atmosphere?

1. Composition, Air Pressure, and Temperature of the Atmosphere

Students will learn about the gases that make up the atmosphere.

Earth's atmosphere is a mixture of gases surrounding the planet. This mixture is commonly called air. Earth's atmosphere is composed mainly of nitrogen (78%) and oxygen (21%). The remaining 1% is made of other gases, such as argon, carbon dioxide, and water vapor. The atmosphere also contains liquids and solids. Clouds are liquid water droplets or solid ice particles. Other particles include salt, dirt, smoke, ash, and dust.

Nitrogen is the most common gas in the atmosphere. It is also essential for plant growth. However, it cannot be used by plants in its atmospheric form. Microscopic bacteria must first change the nitrogen into a usable form. One group of bacteria converts nitrogen into ammonia. Another group combines the ammonia with oxygen to form nitrites. Still another group of bacteria changes the nitrites to nitrates, which can be absorbed by plants.

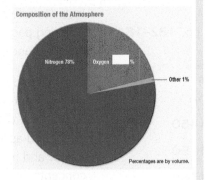
Composition of the Atmosphere

Nitrogen 78%   Oxygen %
Other 1%
Percentages are by volume.

Air pressure is a measure of the force with which air molecules push on a surface. Air pressure is caused by the pull of Earth's gravity on the molecules that make up the atmosphere. Air pressure decreases as distance from Earth's surface increases. Air temperature also changes as altitude increases. Temperature differences result from the way in which energy is absorbed by gases in the atmosphere.

Air density decreases with higher altitude—a fact that can influence the outcome of a baseball game. In areas at high elevations, a baseball can travel about 10% farther than a ball

hit with the same force in an area at sea level. This occurs because the air is less dense at higher elevations. Thus, a double in Atlanta might be a home run in Denver.

2. Structure of the Atmosphere

Students will learn that each layer of the atmosphere has different properties.

The four main layers of Earth's atmosphere are the troposphere, the stratosphere, the mesosphere, and the thermosphere. The troposphere is the lowest layer of Earth's atmosphere. This layer contains almost 90% of the atmosphere's total mass, and most weather occurs in this layer. Temperature decreases as altitude increases in this layer. The stratosphere lies directly above the troposphere. The ozone layer is part of the stratosphere. Temperature increases as altitude increases in this layer. The mesosphere lies above the stratosphere. Temperature decreases as altitude increases in this layer. The thermosphere is the uppermost layer of the atmosphere. Temperature increases with altitude in this layer.

The upper layers of the atmosphere contain a layer called the ionosphere. This layer, which is within the thermosphere, contains ionized particles that can affect certain radio transmissions. AM radio signals bounce off the ionosphere and return to Earth. They can be reflected back and forth in this manner over long distances.

3. Life and the Atmosphere

Students will learn how the atmosphere protects and insulates the planet.

Earth's atmosphere protects living things from harmful solar radiation by reflecting or absorbing most of the electromagnetic radiation that reaches Earth. The ozone layer absorbs harmful ultraviolet radiation. The atmosphere also maintains an average global temperature that can sustain life and that ensures the availability of liquid water. The greenhouse effect is the warming of the surface and lower atmosphere of Earth that occurs when gases in the atmosphere, such as water vapor and carbon dioxide, absorb and reradiate thermal energy.

Lesson 1 The Atmosphere Have students create an illustration of the four atmospheric layers, listing each layer's height above the Earth. Then, have students find images from the Internet or magazines of the following, which students should then place on the correct layer in the illustration: hot-air balloon (5-7 km), clouds (16 km), meteors (48-80 km), the aurora borealis (100-250 km), and the International Space Station (300 km).

Lesson 2

Energy Transfer
ESSENTIAL QUESTION
How does energy move through Earth's system?

1. Temperature, Heat, Thermal Energy, and Thermal Expansion

Students will learn about the relationships among temperature, heat, thermal energy, and thermal expansion.

Temperature is a measure of the average kinetic energy of the particles in an object. Heat is the energy that is transferred between objects that are at different temperatures. Thermal energy is the total kinetic energy of the particles that make up a substance.

When objects that have different temperatures come into contact, energy (as heat) will be transferred from the warmer object to the cooler object until both objects have the same temperature. Different substances (such as metal, rock, water, and air) transfer energy at different rates because each substance has a unique specific heat capacity. Specific heat capacity is a measure of the amount of energy required to increase the temperature of 1 g of a substance by 1 °C. So, some substances require more energy to show an increase in temperature than others. For example, water heats up and cools down more slowly than land does because water has a higher specific heat capacity.

When a substance's temperature increases, the substance's particles have more kinetic energy. As a result, the particles move faster and move farther apart. As the space between particles increases, the substance expands. The increase in volume that results from an increase in temperature is called thermal expansion. When a substance's temperature decreases, the opposite process occurs and the substance contracts.

2. Radiation

Students will learn that radiation transfers energy through space.

Radiation is the transfer of energy as electromagnetic waves. It occurs between objects that are not touching each other. Energy can be transferred through space by radiation. The sun is the source of most energy on Earth. The sun's energy reaches Earth in the form of electromagnetic radiation, mainly as visible light, but also as ultraviolet radiation and other types of waves. The sun's energy is absorbed by rock, water, air, and living things. The energy changes to thermal energy and transfers to other parts of Earth's system. Earth's surface and atmosphere radiate energy back into space as infrared energy.

3. Convection

Students will learn that convection can transfer energy.

Convection is the transfer of energy due to the movement of matter. Convection happens most efficiently in liquids or gases. Convection occurs as a result of uneven heating of matter and the thermal expansion and contraction of substances. Convection currents form where hot matter rises and cooler matter sinks. Cooler water, for example, is denser than warmer water, and so cooler water sinks below warmer water. Convection currents occur in the ocean because of differences in density of ocean water. These currents carry energy throughout Earth's oceans.

4. Conduction

Students will learn that conduction transfers energy from one object to another.

Conduction is the transfer of energy as heat through a material. Substances or objects must be in direct contact in order for conduction to occur. Conduction occurs between the geosphere and the atmosphere where the air makes direct contact with the ground. Conduction occurs within only a few centimeters of the ground surface. Conduction also occurs within the hydrosphere, geosphere, and atmosphere as particles of water, rock, or air touch one another.

Content Refresher (continued)

 Professional Development

Wind in the Atmosphere

ESSENTIAL QUESTION
What is wind?

1. The Movement of Air

Students will learn what causes wind and wind patterns.

The sun warms Earth's atmosphere. Solar heating of the atmosphere is uneven, which results in differences in air temperature. When the sun heats the air, air molecules absorb energy. The molecules in the warming air begin to move faster and spread apart. The molecules in cold air do not move as quickly and are more tightly packed. This is why cold air is denser than warm air and why cold air sinks and warm air rises. Wind is the result of air moving from areas of high pressure to areas of low pressure.

As air heated along the equator flows toward the poles, it creates bands of high and low pressure that stretch across Earth at intervals of 30° of latitude.

Winds within these regions move in predictable paths. These paths, however, are not straight. This is because Earth is rotating. This rotation causes north-bound winds to curve eastward and south-bound winds to curve westward. This phenomenon is referred to as the Coriolis effect. It was discovered in 1835 by French engineer and mathematician Gustave-Gaspard Coriolis.

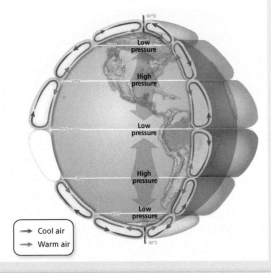

2. Global Winds

Students will learn what causes global winds.

Between each pressure belt, hot and cold air moves in tighter circular patterns known as convection cells. These cells, along with pressure belts and the Coriolis effect, produce wind systems called global winds. The three types of global winds are trade winds, westerlies, and polar easterlies. Trade winds exist in the region between the equator and 30° latitude, and they curve to the west in both hemispheres. Westerlies can be found between 30° and 60° latitude. Though these winds come from the northwest and southwest, Earth's rotation causes them to curve to the east. Polar easterlies, which blow between 60° and the poles, originate in the northeast and southeast but curve to the west.

Two other wind systems, which are weak and sluggish, are the doldrums and the horse latitudes. The doldrums is an area around the equator where air pressure is very low and winds are very calm. The area at about 30° latitude in each hemisphere is called the horse latitudes.

Another type of global wind are jet streams. Jet streams are bands of high-speed winds that often form in the upper troposphere and stretch across large areas of the globe. Airplane pilots often take advantage of these high-speed winds to travel faster.

3. Local Winds

Students will learn what causes local winds.

Just as the sun causes uneven heating of the air, it also causes uneven heating of Earth's surface, which causes local winds. Land heats up faster than water does. A sea breeze occurs when cooler air over water moves onto the land and pushes the warm, less dense air upward. A land breeze occurs at night when cooler air over land moves onto the water and pushes warmer air upward. Valley breezes and mountain breezes are also local winds. As the sun warms the air along mountainsides, warm air moves upward in what is known as a valley breeze. At night, when the mountains cool, cold air moves down into the valley, creating a mountain breeze.

Teacher Notes

Advance Planning

These activities may take extended time or special conditions.

Unit 3

Video-Based Project When the Wind Blows, p. 132
  multiple activities spanning several lessons

Project Clearing the Air, p. 133
  plan and presentation

Graphic Organizers and Vocabulary pp. 139, 140, 153, 154, 173, 174
  ongoing with reading

Lesson 1

Field Lab Measuring Oxygen in the Air, p. 137
  requires three 90-min periods

Lesson 2

S.T.E.M. Lab Heat from the Sun, p. 151
  requires two 45-min periods

Lesson 3

Quick Lab Modeling Air Movement by Convection, p. 171
  15-gallon glass aquarium, ice cubes, incense stick

What Do You Think?

Encourage students to think about how energy is transferred through Earth's atmosphere and why it is important to humans and other organisms on Earth.

Ask: What is Earth's main source of energy? the sun

Ask: How can you tell that energy from the sun is absorbed by surfaces on Earth and transformed into thermal energy? Sample answer: Car surfaces get hot when sitting outside in the sun.

Ask: Air in a room can be warmed as the air contacts radiators and stoves. How is the warmth transferred throughout the room? The warmed air moves throughout the room, and cooler air moves into contact with the radiator or stove.

UNIT 3

Earth's Atmosphere

Big Idea
Earth's atmosphere is a mixture of gases that interacts with solar energy.

Earth's atmosphere is divided into different layers. These clouds have formed in the troposphere, the lowest layer of the atmosphere where most weather occurs.

Wind is the movement of air caused by differences in air pressure.

What do you think?

Like other parts of the Earth system, energy is transferred through Earth's atmosphere. What are the three processes by which energy is transferred through the atmosphere?

101

Video-Based Project

When the Wind Blows

🌀 *Go Online to preview the videos, access teacher support pages, and print student activity worksheets.*

Students build a wind turbine and test its ability to generate electricity.

Activities

1 Researching Wind Energy and Wind-Turbine Construction
2 Designing and Building a Wind Turbine
3 Testing the Wind Turbine, Communicating Results

Unit 3
Earth's Atmosphere

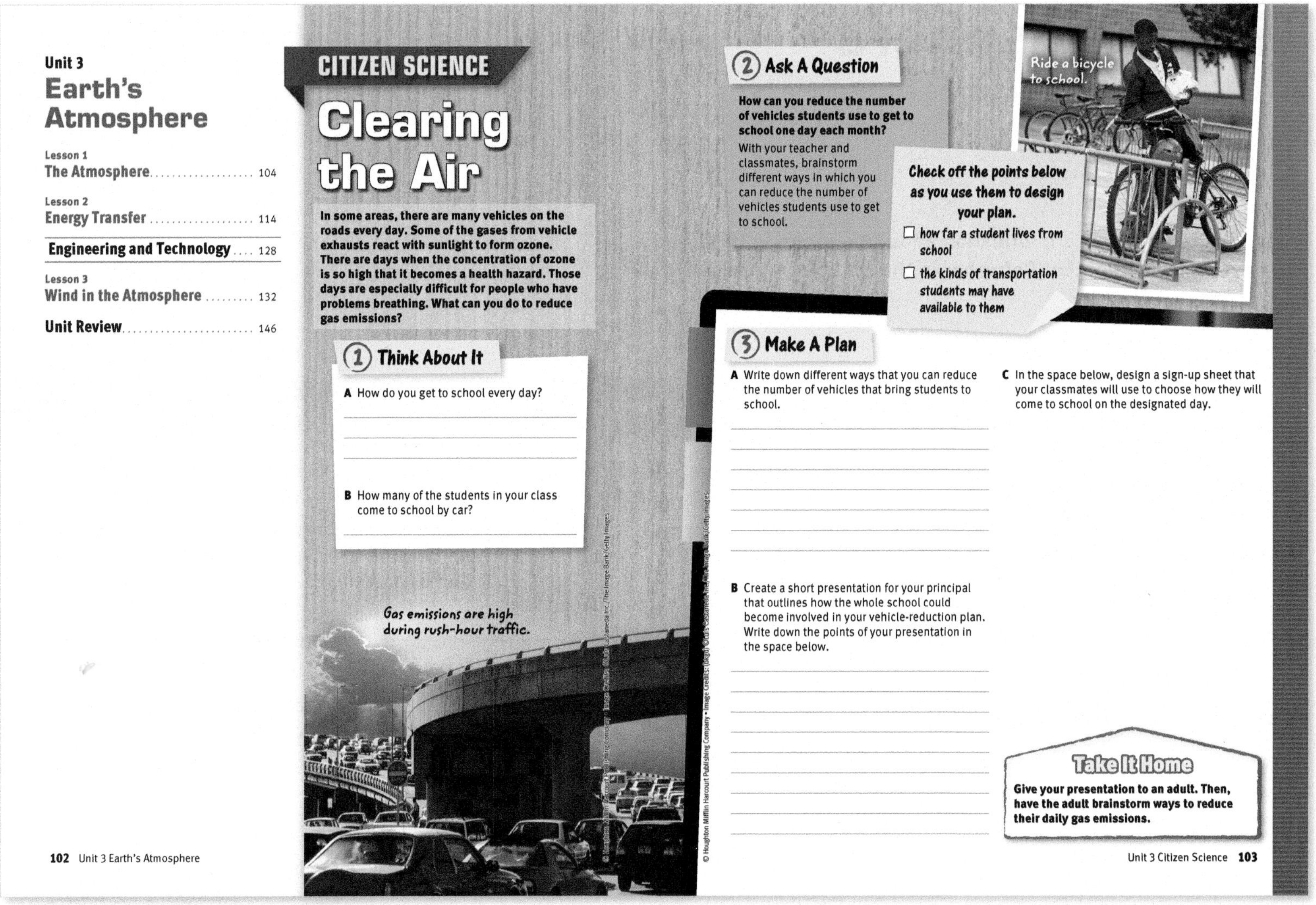

CITIZEN SCIENCE
Clearing the Air

In some areas, there are many vehicles on the roads every day. Some of the gases from vehicle exhausts react with sunlight to form ozone. There are days when the concentration of ozone is so high that it becomes a health hazard. Those days are especially difficult for people who have problems breathing. What can you do to reduce gas emissions?

1 Think About It

A How do you get to school every day?

B How many of the students in your class come to school by car?

Gas emissions are high during rush-hour traffic.

2 Ask A Question

How can you reduce the number of vehicles students use to get to school one day each month?

With your teacher and classmates, brainstorm different ways in which you can reduce the number of vehicles students use to get to school.

Ride a bicycle to school.

Check off the points below as you use them to design your plan.

☐ how far a student lives from school

☐ the kinds of transportation students may have available to them

3 Make A Plan

A Write down different ways that you can reduce the number of vehicles that bring students to school.

B Create a short presentation for your principal that outlines how the whole school could become involved in your vehicle-reduction plan. Write down the points of your presentation in the space below.

C In the space below, design a sign-up sheet that your classmates will use to choose how they will come to school on the designated day.

Take It Home
Give your presentation to an adult. Then, have the adult brainstorm ways to reduce their daily gas emissions.

102 Unit 3 Earth's Atmosphere

Unit 3 Citizen Science 103

CITIZEN SCIENCE

Unit Project Clearing the Air

1. Think About It

A. Answers should reflect how students get to school.

B. Answers will depend on the answers of classmates.

2. Ask a Question

Students' answers will vary.

3. Make a Plan

A. Answers may include cycling, walking, carpooling, or taking the bus.

B. Students should be able to clearly articulate the problem and their proposed solution. Good presentations will take into account the logistics of transporting students from different areas and the transportation options available. Presentations could also summarize potential reductions in gas emissions.

C. The sign-up sheet might include columns for the students' names, the way they will come to school, and who they will be coming with (other students, parents, etc.).

Take It Home

Ask students to provide a note from an adult confirming that the student gave him or her the presentation. Ask students to share some of the ideas that resulted from brainstorming with adults.

Optional Online rubric: Oral Presentations

The Atmosphere

Essential Question What is the atmosphere?

Professional Development

For more detailed information about the topics in this lesson, refer to the Content Refresher in the Unit Opener pages.

Opening Your Lesson

Begin the lesson by assessing students' prerequisite and prior knowledge.

Prerequisite Knowledge

- The Earth system
- Definition of a gas
- The atmosphere and biosphere

Accessing Prior Knowledge

Ask: What is the atmosphere? Sample answer: It is a layer of gases surrounding Earth. It contains oxygen and other gases needed for life.

Ask: How does the atmosphere affect temperatures on Earth? Sample answers: The gases in the atmosphere keep Earth from getting too hot or too cold.

Customize Your Opening

☐ **Accessing Prior Knowledge,** above

☐ **Print Path** Engage Your Brain, SE p. 105 #1–2

☐ **Print Path** Active Reading, SE p. 105 #3–4

☐ **Digital Path** Lesson Opener

Key Topics/Learning Goals	Supporting Concepts
Composition, Air Pressure, and Temperature of the Atmosphere 1 Define *atmosphere*. 2 Identify the main components of Earth's atmosphere. 3 Define *air pressure*. 4 Describe how air pressure changes with altitude. 5 Explain why temperature changes as altitude increases.	• Earth's atmosphere is a mixture of gases and is commonly called air. • Earth's atmosphere is composed mainly of nitrogen and oxygen. The remaining 1% is other gases. • The atmosphere contains liquids and solids, including salt, dirt, smoke, ash, and dust. • Air pressure is caused by gravity. • Air pressure decreases as distance from Earth's surface increases. • Air temperature changes as altitude increases.
Structure of the Atmosphere 1 List the four main layers of the atmosphere. 2 Identify the properties of each layer of Earth's atmosphere.	• The troposphere is the lowest layer of Earth's atmosphere. Temperature decreases as altitude increases in this layer. • The stratosphere lies directly above the troposphere; it contains the ozone layer. Temperature increases with altitude here. • The mesosphere is above the stratosphere. Temperature decreases with altitude here. • The thermosphere is the uppermost layer. Temperature increases with altitude here.
Life and the Atmosphere 1 Describe how the atmosphere protects life. 2 Describe how the atmosphere insulates the planet.	• Earth's atmosphere protects life by reflecting or absorbing most of the sun's radiation. • The ozone layer protects life by absorbing harmful ultraviolet radiation. • The atmosphere maintains temperatures suitable for life and available liquid water. • The greenhouse effect is the warming of the surface and lower atmosphere of Earth.

Options for Instruction

Two parallel paths provide coverage of the Essential Questions, with a strong **Inquiry** strand woven into each. Follow the **Print Path,** the **Digital Path,** or your customized combination of print, digital, and inquiry.

 Print Path
Teaching support for the Print Path appears with the Student Pages.

 Inquiry Labs and Activities

 Digital Path
Digital Path shortcut: TS661450

Print Path	Inquiry Labs and Activities	Digital Path
Up and Away!, SE pp. 106–107 **What Is Earth's atmosphere?** • A Mixture of Gases and Small Particles **How do pressure and temperature change in the atmosphere?**	**Quick Lab** Modeling Air Pressure **Quick Lab** Modeling Air Pressure Changes with Altitude **Field Lab** Measuring Oxygen in the Air 🖥 **Virtual Lab** The Composition and Structure of the Atmosphere	**Atmospheric Layers** Interactive Image **Air Has Mass** Diagram
Look Way Up, SE pp. 108–109 **What are the layers of the atmosphere?** • Thermosphere • Mesosphere • Stratosphere • Troposphere	**Activity** Drawing the Atmosphere **Activity** Atmospheric Review	**Atmospheric Layers** Interactive Image **Air Has Mass** Diagram
Here Comes the Sun, SE pp. 110–111 **How does the atmosphere protect life on Earth?** • By Absorbing or Reflecting Harmful Radiation • By Maintaining the Right Temperature Range	**Daily Demo** The Greenhouse Effect **Activity** Greenhouse Temperatures	**The Greenhouse Effect** Animation **Ozone and Oxygen** Interactive Image

Options for Assessment

See the Evaluate page for options, including Formative Assessment, Summative Assessment, and Unit Review.

Engage and Explore

Activities and Discussion

Activity *Role-Playing the Atmosphere*

Engage

Composition, Air Pressure, and Temperature of the Atmosphere

 whole class
🕐 10 min
Inquiry **GUIDED** inquiry

Tell students to imagine they are a gas in the atmosphere. Because the atmosphere is 78% nitrogen, 21% oxygen, and 1% other gases, students should figure out how many students they need for each role. Assign parts. Students who are nitrogen should write a large *N* on a sheet of paper. Students who are oxygen should write an *O* on a sheet of paper. Have one student be all other gases, and write *argon, carbon dioxide, water vapor, and other gases* on a sheet of paper. Then invite the gases to move around and mix, as they might in the atmosphere.

Activity *Drawing the Atmosphere*

Structure of the Atmosphere

 pairs or small groups
 15 min
Inquiry **GUIDED** inquiry

Invite students to make a poster that shows the layers of the atmosphere. Make sure students label each layer and describe the characteristics of each layer.

 Optional Online rubric: Posters and Displays

Activity *Greenhouse Temperatures*

Life and the Atmosphere

 Individuals, then pairs
🕐 10 min
Inquiry **GUIDED** inquiry

Think, Pair, Share Give students 3 minutes to write down how greenhouse gases affect temperatures on Earth. Next, have students list what they think would happen if the concentration of greenhouse gases increased, decreased, or stayed the same. Have each student choose one example from the list. Pairs of students should explain the examples to each other and identify how the amount of greenhouse gases can cause temperature change. Call on pairs to share their ideas.

Labs and Demos

Daily Demo *The Greenhouse Effect*

Engage

Life and the Atmosphere

👥 whole class
🕐 20 min
Inquiry **GUIDED** inquiry

PURPOSE **To show how the greenhouse effect can affect temperature**

MATERIALS

- heat lamp, light source, or sunny windowsill
- jars or cups (2)
- plastic wrap
- thermometers (2)
- water
- white paper

Explain that the atmosphere allows some solar energy to reach Earth and warm it. That energy is trapped by the atmosphere. Without the atmosphere, the energy would be lost, and Earth would be much colder. To demonstrate this concept, follow these steps:

1 Fill each cup half full with water. Measure the temperature of the water in each cup. Record the temperature.

2 Put a sheet of white paper on top of one cup. Put plastic wrap on the other to make a tight seal. Cut a slit in the paper and plastic wrap, so that you can slip a thermometer into the cup. Place the cups in the sun (or under a light source).

3 Check the temperatures in 15 min. Invite students to explain what happened. Sample answer: The white paper reflected light, so the water absorbed less energy. The plastic wrap let light energy through to warm the water, then trapped the heat.

Customize Your Labs

 See the Lab Manual for lab datasheets.

 Go Online for editable lab datasheets.

Levels of **Inquiry**

DIRECTED inquiry introduces inquiry skills within a structured framework.

GUIDED inquiry develops inquiry skills within a supportive environment.

INDEPENDENT inquiry deepens inquiry skills with student-driven questions or procedures.

   ## Quick Lab *Modeling Air Pressure*

Composition, Air Pressure, and Temperature of the Atmosphere

 individuals
🕐 10 min
Inquiry DIRECTED inquiry

Students invert plastic cups filled with water and covered with index cards, make observations, and form hypotheses.

PURPOSE **To describe how air pressure can hold water inside a cup**

MATERIALS

• cup, plastic
• index card
• lab apron
• sink, bucket, or plastic tub
• water

   ## Quick Lab *Modeling Air Pressure Changes with Altitude*

Composition, Air Pressure, and Temperature of the Atmosphere

👥 small groups
🕐 30 min
Inquiry DIRECTED inquiry

Students model how air pressure changes with altitude by modeling air pressure with a stack of magazines.

PURPOSE **To describe how air pressure changes with altitude**

MATERIALS

• magazines (15)
• ruler, metric
• scale, bathroom

  ## Field Lab *Measuring Oxygen in the Air*

Composition, Air Pressure, and Temperature of the Atmosphere

👥 pairs
🕐 three 90-min periods
Inquiry DIRECTED / GUIDED inquiry

Students observe steel wool oxidation to determine the percentage of oxygen in the local environment.

PURPOSE **To measure the percentage of oxygen in the air**

MATERIALS

• beakers, 500 mL (2)
• graduated cylinder
• marker, permanent
• matches
• scissors
• steel wool
• stopwatch
• syringe, plastic
• ring stand with clamp (2)
• ruler, metric
• tape, masking
• test tubes (2)
• tweezers
• vinegar, 30 mL
• water, 1 L

  ## Virtual Lab *Composition and Structure of the Atmosphere*

Composition, Air Pressure, and Temperature of the Atmosphere

👥 flexible
🕐 45 min
Inquiry GUIDED inquiry

Students examine the composition and structure of the atmosphere.

PURPOSE **To explore the composition and structure of the atmosphere**

Activities and Discussion

☐ **Activity** Role-Playing the Atmosphere
☐ **Activity** Drawing the Atmosphere
☐ **Activity** Greenhouse Temperatures

Labs and Demos

☐ **Daily Demo** The Greenhouse Effect
☐ **Quick Lab** Modeling Air Pressure
☐ **Quick Lab** Air Pressure Changes . . .
☐ **Field Lab** Oxygen in the Air
☐ **Virtual Lab** . . . the Atmosphere

Your Resources

Explain Science Concepts

	📖 Print Path	**💻 Digital Path**
Key Topics		
Composition, Air Pressure, and Temperature of the Atmosphere	☐ **Up and Away!,** SE pp. 106–107 • Visualize It!, #5 • Active Reading (Annotation strategy), #6 • Inquiry, #7 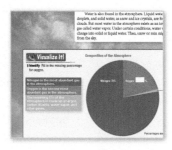	☐ **Atmospheric Layers** Explore how temperature and air pressure change through the layers of the atmosphere. ☐ **Air Has Mass** Learn how the mass of air above a location is related to air pressure. 
Structure of the Atmosphere	☐ **Look Way Up,** SE pp. 108–109 • Think Outside the Book, #8 • Visualize It!, #9 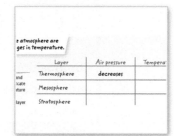	☐ **Atmospheric Layers** Explore how temperature and air pressure change through the layers of the atmosphere. ☐ **Air Has Mass** Learn how the mass of air above a location is related to air pressure.
Life and the Atmosphere	☐ **Here Comes the Sun,** SE pp. 110–111 • Visualize It!, #10 • Active Reading, #11 • Visualize It!, #12	☐ **The Greenhouse Effect** See the positive and negative effects of greenhouse gases on temperatures. ☐ **Ozone and Oxygen** Learn the relationship between two important gases. 

Basic *Gas Molecules in the Atmosphere*

Composition, Air Pressure, and Temperature of the Atmosphere

 individuals
🕐 10 min

Have students draw a diagram that shows the relative number of gas molecules in the atmosphere. Have students draw dots to represent gas molecules. Drawings should show many more gas molecules lower in the atmosphere, and that gas molecules are fewer and farther apart as you move higher into the atmosphere.

Advanced *Graphing Air Temperature and Pressure*

Composition, Air Pressure, and Temperature of the Atmosphere

 individuals
🕐 15 min

Have students research information on how temperature changes with altitude, and how air pressure changes with altitude. Encourage them to create a line graph to show what they discovered. Direct them to graph two lines of different colors. One line should show what happens to temperatures in the atmosphere as altitude increases. The other should show what happens to air pressure as altitude increases. Remind students to include a key. Display graphs around the classroom.

 Optional Online resource: Line Graph support

ELL *Sphere Terms*

Structure of the Atmosphere

 individuals or pairs
🕐 15 min

Illustrating Sphere Words Have students, individually or in pairs, draw a diagram that shows the relationship of each of the following "sphere" terms: *atmosphere, stratosphere, troposphere, thermosphere,* and *mesosphere.* Have students label each term in the diagram, and briefly describe what the term means.

Lesson Vocabulary

atmosphere	mesosphere	ozone layer
air pressure	stratosphere	greenhouse effect
thermosphere	troposphere	

Previewing Vocabulary

 whole class
🕐 10 min

Word Parts Explain that analyzing Word Parts can help readers figure out the meanings of words. **Ask:** What is a *sphere*? Sample answer: a round object

- If *atmos-* means "vapor," or "breath," what does *atmosphere* mean? Sample answer: air we breathe surrounding the globe
- If *tropo* means "change," or "turn," what does *troposphere* mean? Sample answer: a layer around Earth in which some change occurs
- If *thermo-* means "heat" or "hot," what does **thermosphere** mean? Sample answer: the hot layer surrounding Earth

Reinforcing Vocabulary

 individuals
🕐 ongoing

Four Square Students can draw boxes divided into 4 parts with a circle in the middle, then write each term in the circle. Students should then fill in surrounding cells with the information shown.

 Optional Online resource: Four Square support

Customize Your Core Lesson

Core Instruction
- ☐ **Print Path** choices
- ☐ **Digital Path** choices

Vocabulary
- ☐ **Previewing Vocabulary** Word Parts
- ☐ **Reinforcing Vocabulary** Four Square

Your Resources

Differentiated Instruction
- ☐ **Basic** Gas Molecules in the Atmosphere
- ☐ **Advanced** Graphing Air Temperature and Pressure
- ☐ **ELL** Sphere Terms

Extend Science Concepts

Reinforce and Review

Activity *Atmospheric Review*

Synthesizing Key Topics
 whole class
🕐 20 min

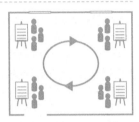

Carousel Review Help students review the material by following these steps:

1 Arrange chart or notebook paper in different parts of the room. On each paper, write a question about the lesson content. Use the questions below, or develop your own.

  • What is Earth's atmosphere?
  • How do temperature and air pressure relate to Earth's atmosphere?
  • What are the layers of Earth's atmosphere?
  • How does the atmosphere protect us?

2 Divide students into small groups and assign each group a chart. Give each group a different colored marker.

3 Groups review their question, discuss the answer, and write a response.

4 After 5 to 10 min, each group rotates to the next station. Groups put a check by each answer they agree with, comment on answers they don't agree with, and add their own answers. Continue until all groups have reviewed all charts.

5 Groups share information with the class.

Graphic Organizer

Synthesizing Key Topics
 individuals
🕐 10 min

Idea Wheel Have students draw a large circle with a small circle inside. Inside the small circle, students write *The Atmosphere*. They then divide the outer ring into sections (as many as needed). Students then label outer sections with characteristics or details related to the atmosphere. Write details in an Idea Wheel on the board.

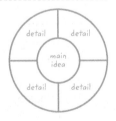

🕐 *Optional Online resource: Idea Wheel support*

Going Further

Real World Connection

Life and the Atmosphere
 individuals
🕐 20 min

Research Project Have interested students conduct research to find out what changes have taken place in the ozone layer over the South Pole in the past 30 years. Encourage students to describe any trends they notice, offer possible causes for these trends, discuss the impact these trends might have on people, and offer potential solutions for any problems these trends might cause. Ask interested students to share their reports with the class.

Fine Arts Connection

Structure of the Atmosphere
👥 individuals
🕐 20 min

Writing a Poem Invite interested students to write a poem or song about the layers of the atmosphere. Encourage them to include details about each layer, such as density, whether temperature rises or drops with altitude, and any other details, such as where airplanes tend to fly, where the ozone layer exists, and where greenhouse gases can be found. Allow students time to share their poem or song with the class. Have students leave their poem or song in a class library to help future students remember the layers of the atmosphere.

Customize Your Closing

🔖 *See the Assessment Guide for quizzes and tests.*

🕐 *Go Online to edit and create quizzes and tests.*

Reinforce and Review

☐ **Activity** Atmospheric Review
☐ **Graphic Organizer** Idea Wheel
☐ **Print Path** Visual Summary, SE p. 112
☐ **Print Path** Lesson Review, SE p. 113
☐ **Digital Path** Lesson Closer

Evaluate Student Mastery

See the teacher support below the Student pages for additional Formative Assessment questions.

Ask: How would the temperature on Earth be affected if the amount of greenhouse gases in the atmosphere changed? Sample answer: If the amount of greenhouse gases increased, Earth's temperature would increase because more energy would be trapped. If greenhouse gases decreased, temperature would also decrease because more energy would escape.
Ask: Beginning with the layer closest to Earth's surface, what are the layers of the atmosphere? troposphere, stratosphere, mesosphere, and thermosphere **Ask:** What is the atmosphere mostly composed of? It is mostly nitrogen and oxygen.

Reteach

Formative assessment may show that students need reinforcement for certain topics. The resources below are recommended for reteaching. If students were introduced to a topic through the Print Path, you can also use the Digital Path to reteach, or vice versa.
🎧 *Can be assigned to individual students*

Composition, Air Pressure and Temperature of the Atmosphere
Graphic Organizer Idea Wheel 🎧
Quick Lab Modeling Air Pressure 🎧

Structure of the Atmosphere
Activity Drawing the Atmosphere 🎧

Life and the Atmosphere
Daily Demo The Greenhouse Effect

Alternative Assessment
Design a Travel Brochure for Another Planet
🔊 *Online resources: student worksheet, optional rubrics*

The Atmosphere

Tic-Tac-Toe: *Design a Travel Brochure for Another Planet*
Imagine that you are a real estate agent who wants to sell a piece of property on another world. Create a travel brochure that shows the traits the property has that makes it appealing to humans.

1. Work on your own, with a partner, or with a small group.
2. Choose three quick activities from the game. Check the boxes you plan to complete. They must form a straight line in any direction.
3. Have your teacher approve your plan.
4. Do each activity, and turn in your results.

__ Plant Contribution	__ Graph the Atmosphere	__ Clean Air
Plants contribute oxygen to the atmosphere. Describe why plants grow so well in this place and why this is beneficial to the buyer.	Make a graph of the atmosphere that shows what the temperature is at different altitudes.	Write a persuasive paragraph that describes the beneficial air qualities of the place.
__ Safety	__ Ozone	__ Make a Visual
List the qualities of the atmosphere that make it safe and comfortable for people to live on this planet.	Write a poem describing the ozone layer, what it does to protect the world, and any ways in which it is different from the ozone layer of Earth.	Draw a pie chart that shows the percentages of different types of gases in the atmosphere of the planet.
__ Sketch	__ Advertising	__ Journal Entries
Make a sketch that shows the different layers of the atmosphere. Are they the same as or different from the layers of Earth's atmosphere? How? What occurs in each layer?	Write an advertisement to convince people to move to this world for its healthful air qualities. Compare the atmosphere on this world with the atmosphere on Earth.	Write four journal entries from different times of year that show how the atmosphere protects people from harmful radiation and how it keeps the world at a comfortable temperature year round.

Going Further
☐ **Real World Connection**
☐ **Fine Arts Connection**

Formative Assessment
☐ **Strategies** Throughout TE
☐ **Lesson Review** SE

Summative Assessment
☐ **Alternative Assessment** Design a Travel Brochure for Another Planet
☐ **Lesson Quiz**
☐ **Unit Tests A and B**
☐ **Unit Review** SE End-of-Unit

Your Resources

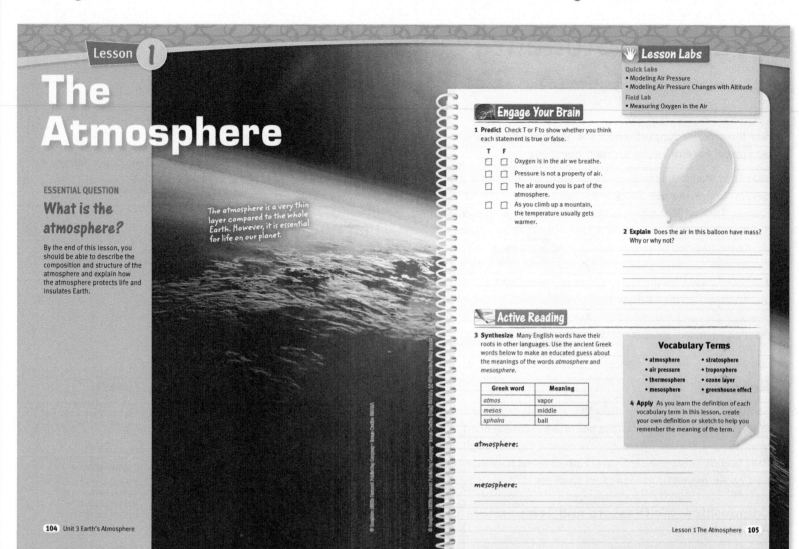

Answers

Answers for 1–3 should represent students' current thoughts, even if incorrect.

1. T; F; T; F

2. Yes. Air is matter, and all matter has mass.

3. Sample answers: a ball of vapor; the middle of a ball

4. Students should define or sketch each vocabulary term in the lesson.

Opening Your Lesson

Discuss students' answers to item 1 to assess their understanding of the atmosphere. Most students should realize that the air we breathe is part of the atmosphere, and that the atmosphere contains oxygen.

Prerequisites Students should already have some general knowledge of the atmosphere, as well as how the atmosphere interacts with the biosphere, hydrosphere, geosphere, and cryosphere.

Learning Alert

Oxygen in the Atmosphere Remind students, if necessary, that the oxygen we breathe and the oxygen in the atmosphere are the same gas. Explain to students that oxygen is released into the atmosphere by green plants and by some other small living organisms. Oxygen gas, nitrogen gas, and a few other gases make up the atmosphere. Most of the nitrogen on Earth is in the atmosphere; however, the human body contains 3% nitrogen by mass. Nitrogen is also found in soil and plays an important part in plant growth. Additionally, nitrogen plays an important role in digestion, growth, and metabolism.

Up and Away!

What is Earth's atmosphere?

The mixture of gases that surrounds Earth is the **atmosphere**. This mixture is most often referred to as air. The atmosphere has many important functions. It protects you from the sun's damaging rays and also helps to maintain the right temperature range for life on Earth. For example, the temperature range on Earth allows us to have an abundant amount of liquid water. Many of the components of the atmosphere are essential for life, such as the oxygen you breathe.

A Mixture of Gases and Small Particles

As shown below, the atmosphere is made mostly of nitrogen gas (78%) and oxygen gas (21%). The other 1% is other gases. The atmosphere also contains small particles such as dust, volcanic ash, sea salt, and smoke. There are even small pieces of skin, bacteria, and pollen floating in the atmosphere!

Water is also found in the atmosphere. Liquid water, as water droplets, and solid water, as snow and ice crystals, are found in clouds. But most water in the atmosphere exists as an invisible gas called water vapor. Under certain conditions, water vapor can change into solid or liquid water. Then, snow or rain might fall from the sky.

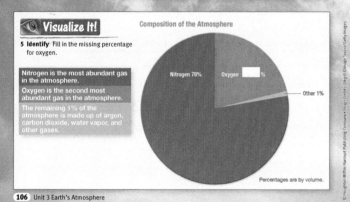

Visualize It!

5 Identify Fill in the missing percentage for oxygen.

Nitrogen is the most abundant gas in the atmosphere.

Oxygen is the second most abundant gas in the atmosphere.

The remaining 1% of the atmosphere is made up of argon, carbon dioxide, water vapor, and other gases.

Composition of the Atmosphere

Nitrogen 78%   Oxygen ___%   Other 1%

Percentages are by volume.

106   Unit 3 Earth's Atmosphere

How do pressure and temperature change in the atmosphere?

The atmosphere is held around Earth by gravity. Gravity pulls gas molecules in the atmosphere toward Earth's surface, causing air pressure. **Air pressure** is the measure of the force with which air molecules push on an area of a surface. At sea level, air pressure is over 1 lb for every square centimeter of your body! That is like carrying a 1-liter bottle of water on the tip of your finger!

However, air pressure is not the same throughout the atmosphere. Although there are many gas molecules that surround you on Earth, there are fewer and fewer gas molecules in the air as you move away from Earth's surface. So, as altitude increases, air pressure decreases.

As altitude increases, air temperature also changes. These changes are mainly due to the way solar energy is absorbed in the atmosphere. Some parts of the atmosphere are warmer because they contain a high percentage of gases that absorb solar energy. Other parts of the atmosphere contain less of these gases and are cooler.

Active Reading

6 Identify As you read, underline what happens to temperature and to pressure as altitude increases.

Inquiry

7 Explain Why does a mountain climber need an oxygen supply at very high altitudes, even though the air still contains 21% oxygen?

At high altitudes such as the top of Mount Everest, air pressure and temperature are lower than they are at sea level.

107

Answers

5. Oxygen is 21%.

6. *See students' pages for annotations.*

7. Because there are much fewer molecules of oxygen at very high altitudes

Probing Questions GUIDED (Inquiry)

Synthesizing Have students look at the pie chart. **Ask:** What is the percentage of nitrogen in the atmosphere? 78% **Ask:** Because the atmosphere is denser closer to Earth's surface, is there more nitrogen close to the Earth's surface than at the top of a mountain? Yes. **Ask:** Does that mean that the percentage of nitrogen at the top of a mountain changes? No. There is less nitrogen at the top of a mountain, but there are also less oxygen and other gases. So the atmosphere always contains 78% nitrogen. **Ask:** At the top of a mountain, are the gas molecules closer together or farther apart than at the base of the mountain? They are farther apart. **Ask:** Why are they farther apart? because there is less air pressure pushing them closer together

Learning Alert

Water Vapor Students may think that water vapor is the same as steam or fog. Remind students that water vapor is invisible, unlike steam and fog. Steam is water droplets. When invisible water vapor in the atmosphere condenses, it becomes water droplets (clouds, fog, and rain) or frozen water (snow, sleet, or hail).

Look Way Up

What are the layers of the atmosphere?

Earth's atmosphere is divided into four layers, based on temperature and other properties. As shown at the right, these layers are the troposphere (TROH•puh•sfir), stratosphere (STRAT•uh•sfir), mesosphere (MEZ•uh•sfir), and thermosphere (THER•muh•sfir). Although these names sound complicated, they give you clues about the layers' features. *Tropo-* means "turning" or "change," and the troposphere is the layer where gases turn and mix. *Strato-* means "layer," and the stratosphere is where gases are layered and do not mix very much. *Meso-* means "middle," and the mesosphere is the middle layer. Finally, *thermo-* means "heat," and the thermosphere is the layer where temperatures are highest.

Think Outside the Book

8 Describe Research the part of the thermosphere called the ionosphere. Describe what the aurora borealis is.

The aurora borealis occurs in the thermosphere.

108

Thermosphere
The **thermosphere** is the uppermost layer of the atmosphere. The temperature increases as altitude increases because gases in the thermosphere absorb high-energy solar radiation. Temperatures in the thermosphere can be 1,500 °C or higher. However, the thermosphere feels cold. The density of particles in the thermosphere is very low. Too few gas particles collide with your body to transfer heat energy to your skin.

Mesosphere
The **mesosphere** is between the thermosphere and stratosphere. In this layer, the temperature decreases as altitude increases. Temperatures can be as low as –120 °C at the top of the mesosphere. Meteoroids begin to burn up in the mesosphere.

Stratosphere
The **stratosphere** is between the mesosphere and troposphere. In this layer, temperatures generally increase as altitude increases. Ozone in the stratosphere absorbs ultraviolet radiation from the sun, which warms the air. An ozone molecule is made of three atoms of oxygen. Gases in the stratosphere are layered and do not mix very much.

Troposphere
The **troposphere** is the lowest layer of the atmosphere. Although temperatures near Earth's surface vary greatly, generally, temperature decreases as altitude increases. This layer contains almost 80% of the atmosphere's total mass, making it the densest layer. Almost all of Earth's carbon dioxide, water vapor, clouds, air pollution, weather, and life forms are in the troposphere.

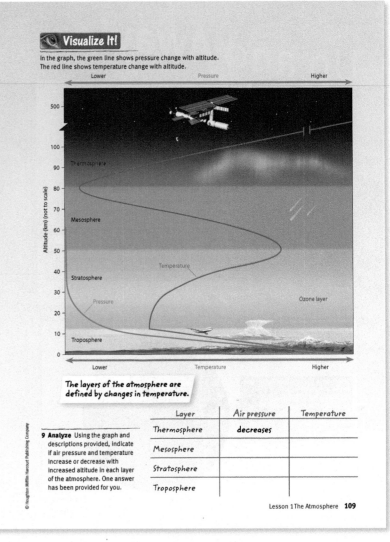

Visualize It!

In the graph, the green line shows pressure change with altitude. The red line shows temperature change with altitude.

The layers of the atmosphere are defined by changes in temperature.

9 Analyze Using the graph and descriptions provided, indicate if air pressure and temperature increase or decrease with increased altitude in each layer of the atmosphere. One answer has been provided for you.

Layer	Air pressure	Temperature
Thermosphere	decreases	
Mesosphere		
Stratosphere		
Troposphere		

Lesson 1 The Atmosphere **109**

Answers

8. Answers will vary. Students can describe the properties of this layer and formation of charged particles. The link can be made between the charged particles and production of the aurora borealis. Students may also mention the ionosphere's role in short-wave radio transmission.

9. Thermosphere: air pressure decreases, temperature increases

   Mesosphere: air pressure decreases, temperature decreases

   Stratosphere: air pressure decreases, temperature increases

   Troposphere: air pressure decreases, temperature decreases

Interpreting Visuals

Ask: What does the red line in the troposphere show? It shows that temperatures decrease as altitude increases. **Ask:** What does the green line show? air pressure **Ask:** What does the visual show about air pressure? Air pressure decreases with altitude. **Ask:** Does temperature decrease with altitude? No. In the stratosphere and thermosphere, air temperature increases with altitude. **Ask:** Where does air temperature decrease with altitude? in the troposphere and the mesosphere **Ask:** What does the temperature line look like as it goes through the four layers of the atmosphere? Sample answer: It zigzags. Temperature decreases, then increases, then decreases, then increases. **Ask:** In what layer is the ozone layer? the stratosphere **Ask:** In what layer is the aurora borealis? the thermosphere **Ask:** In what layer do meteoroids burn up? the mesosphere **Ask:** In what layer do you find clouds and weather? the troposphere

Probing Questions DIRECTED Inquiry

Analyzing Jet planes fly near the top of the troposphere. Is it more important to heat or cool the passenger cabins at this altitude? How do you know? Sample answer: The top of the troposphere is the coldest part of the troposphere, so it is important to heat the cabins. It is higher than the tops of mountains, so it must be cold.

Here Comes   the Sun ...

How does the atmosphere protect life on Earth?

The atmosphere surrounds and protects Earth. The atmosphere provides the air we breathe. It also protects Earth from harmful solar radiation and from space debris that enters the Earth system. In addition, the atmosphere controls the temperature on Earth.

By Absorbing or Reflecting Harmful Radiation

Earth's atmosphere reflects or absorbs most of the radiation from the sun. The **ozone layer** is an area in the stratosphere, 15 km to 40 km above Earth's surface, where ozone is highly concentrated. The ozone layer absorbs most of the solar radiation. The thickness of the ozone layer can change between seasons and at different locations. However, as shown at the left, scientists have observed a steady decrease in the overall volume of the ozone layer over time. This change is thought to be due to the use of certain chemicals by people. These chemicals enter the stratosphere, where they react with and destroy the ozone. Ozone levels are particularly low during certain times of the year over the South Pole. The area with a very thin ozone layer is often referred to as the "ozone hole."

By Maintaining the Right Temperature Range

Without the atmosphere, Earth's average temperature would be very low. How does Earth remain warm? The answer is the greenhouse effect. The **greenhouse effect** is the process by which gases in the atmosphere, such as water vapor and carbon dioxide, absorb and give off infrared radiation. Radiation from the sun warms Earth's surface, and Earth's surface gives off infrared radiation. Greenhouse gases in the atmosphere absorb some of this infrared radiation and then reradiate it. Some of this energy is absorbed again by Earth's surface, while some energy goes out into space. Because greenhouse gases keep energy in the Earth system longer, Earth's average surface temperature is kept at around 15°C (59°F). In time, all the energy ends up back in outer space.

Active Reading **11 List** Name two examples of greenhouse gases.

Visualize It!

South Pole
Fall 1979

Less ozone   More ozone

South Pole
Fall 2008

10 Compare How did the ozone layer over the South Pole change between 1979 and 2008?

The Greenhouse Effect

Greenhouse gas molecules absorb and emit infrared radiation.

Atmosphere without Greenhouse Gases	Atmosphere with Greenhouse Gases
Without greenhouse gases in Earth's atmosphere, radiation from Earth's surface is lost directly to space. **Average Temperature: -18°C**	With greenhouse gases in Earth's atmosphere, radiation from Earth's surface is lost to space more slowly, which makes Earth's surface warmer. **Average Temperature: 15°C**

sunlight   infrared radiation

The atmosphere is much thinner than shown here.

Visualize It!

12 Illustrate Draw your own version of how greenhouse gases keep Earth warm.

Answers

10. There is a much larger area of the ozone layer that has become thinner.

11. water vapor and carbon dioxide

12. Students' drawings should indicate that energy is aborbed by greenhouse gases and that this energy is reradiated through the atmosphere to keep Earth warm.

Probing Questions GUIDED Inquiry

Synthesizing Greenhouse gases make up less than 1% of the gases in the atmosphere. Greenhouse gases can be found in all of the layers of Earth's atmosphere. Which layer do you think contains the greatest quantity of greenhouse gases? Why? Sample answer: The troposphere has the greatest air pressure of all the layers of the atmosphere, so most of the greenhouse gas molecules would be in the troposphere. In the other layers, the gas molecules are much farther apart because the air pressure is lower, so there are fewer greenhouse gas molecules.

Formative Assessment

Ask: How do air pressure and temperature change in the atmosphere? Sample answers: Air pressure decreases with altitude. Temperature decreases with altitude in the troposphere and mesosphere. It increases with altitude in the stratosphere and thermosphere. **Ask:** How does the atmosphere protect the planet? Sample answer: The atmosphere absorbs or reflects harmful radiation and keeps the planet at a temperature at which life can exist.

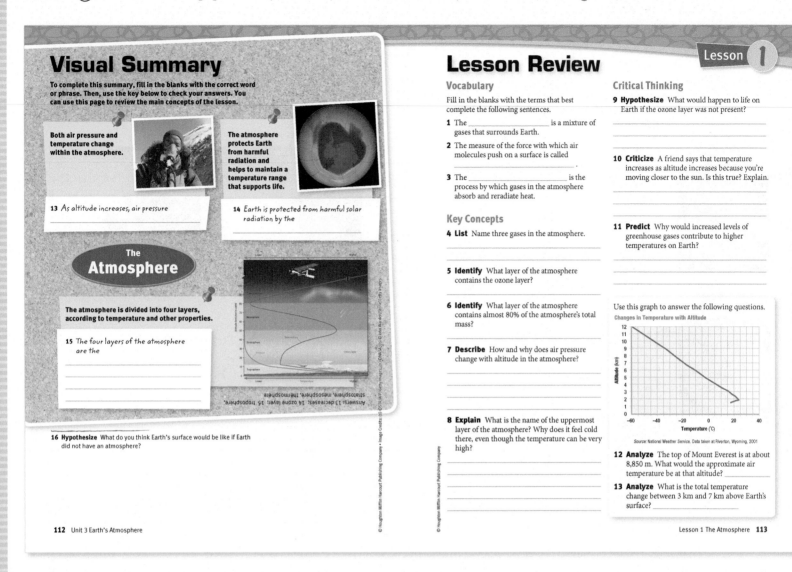

Visual Summary

To complete this summary, fill in the blanks with the correct word or phrase. Then, use the key below to check your answers. You can use this page to review the main concepts of the lesson.

Both air pressure and temperature change within the atmosphere.

The atmosphere protects Earth from harmful radiation and helps to maintain a temperature range that supports life.

13 As altitude increases, air pressure _____

14 Earth is protected from harmful solar radiation by the _____

The Atmosphere

The atmosphere is divided into four layers, according to temperature and other properties.

15 The four layers of the atmosphere are the _____

Answers: 13 decreases; 14 ozone layer; 15 troposphere, stratosphere, mesosphere, thermosphere

16 Hypothesize What do you think Earth's surface would be like if Earth did not have an atmosphere?

112 Unit 3 Earth's Atmosphere

Lesson Review

Vocabulary

Fill in the blanks with the terms that best complete the following sentences.

1 The _____ is a mixture of gases that surrounds Earth.

2 The measure of the force with which air molecules push on a surface is called _____.

3 The _____ is the process by which gases in the atmosphere absorb and reradiate heat.

Key Concepts

4 List Name three gases in the atmosphere.

5 Identify What layer of the atmosphere contains the ozone layer?

6 Identify What layer of the atmosphere contains almost 80% of the atmosphere's total mass?

7 Describe How and why does air pressure change with altitude in the atmosphere?

8 Explain What is the name of the uppermost layer of the atmosphere? Why does it feel cold there, even though the temperature can be very high?

Critical Thinking

9 Hypothesize What would happen to life on Earth if the ozone layer was not present?

10 Criticize A friend says that temperature increases as altitude increases because you're moving closer to the sun. Is this true? Explain.

11 Predict Why would increased levels of greenhouse gases contribute to higher temperatures on Earth?

Use this graph to answer the following questions.
Changes in Temperature with Altitude

Source: National Weather Service. Data taken at Riverton, Wyoming, 2001

12 Analyze The top of Mount Everest is at about 8,850 m. What would the approximate air temperature be at that altitude? _____

13 Analyze What is the total temperature change between 3 km and 7 km above Earth's surface? _____

Lesson 1 The Atmosphere 113

Visual Summary Answers

13. decreases

14. ozone layer

15. troposphere, stratosphere, mesosphere, and thermosphere

16. Overall, it would be cold because the greenhouse effect would not occur. Also, there would be bombardment of solar energy and radiation during daylight. So, life would have difficulty existing on Earth.

Lesson Review Answers

1. atmosphere

2. air pressure

3. greenhouse effect

4. Sample answer: nitrogen, oxygen, carbon dioxide

5. stratosphere

6. troposphere

7. Air pressure decreases with altitude because there is less gravitational force acting on gas molecules the farther you move away from Earth's surface.

8. Thermosphere; it feels cold because the density of particles that transfer energy as heat is very low.

9. Life, as we know it, would no longer exist since there would be no protection from harmful solar radiation and no greenhouse effect to keep Earth warm.

10. No. Different amounts of gases absorb solar radiation in Earth's atmospheric layers, which causes temperatures to increase or decrease.

11. Greenhouse gases absorb energy, which is reradiated through the atmosphere to warm Earth. If the amount of greenhouse gases increases, this would cause increased warming of Earth.

12. about −35 °C

13. The total change is about 35 °C.

Energy Transfer

Essential Question How does energy move through Earth's system?

 **Professional Development**

For more detailed information about the topics in this lesson, refer to the Content Refresher in the Unit Opener pages.

Opening Your Lesson

Begin the lesson by assessing students' prerequisite and prior knowledge.

Prerequisite Knowledge

- "Spheres" of Earth's system, including the atmosphere, hydrosphere, cryosphere, geosphere, and biosphere
- How the greenhouse effect influences Earth's temperature

Accessing Prior Knowledge

Ask: When you put something hot in the refrigerator, what happens? Sample answer: The hot object becomes cold.

Ask: Where does the energy from the hot object go? Sample answers: It is transferred from the object to the air inside the refrigerator. The cooling system then transfers the energy from the inside of the refrigerator to outside the refrigerator.

Customize Your Opening

☐ **Accessing Prior Knowledge,** above

☐ **Print Path** Engage Your Brain, SE p. 115 # 1–2

☐ **Print Path** Active Reading, SE p. 115 # 3–4

☐ **Digital Path** Lesson Opener

Key Topics/Learning Goals	Supporting Concepts
Temperature, Heat, Thermal Energy, Thermal Expansion 1 Define key terms. 2 Describe what happens when objects at different temperatures come into contact.	• Temperature measures the kinetic energy of an object. Heat is energy transferred between objects. Thermal energy is the total kinetic energy of a substance. Thermal expansion is when temperature increases and particles move faster and farther apart. • When objects of different temperatures come into contact, energy is transferred (as heat) from the warmer to the cooler object.
Radiation 1 Summarize the process of radiation. 2 Identify the main source of energy on Earth's surface. 3 Identify examples of radiation on Earth.	• Radiation is the transfer of energy as electromagnetic waves. Radiation can occur between objects that are not touching. • The sun is Earth's main source of energy. • Energy from the sun is absorbed by rocks, water, air, and living things. That energy changes to thermal energy and is transferred to other parts of Earth's system.
Convection 1 Summarize the process of convection. 2 Identify examples of convection on Earth.	• Convection is the transfer of energy due to movement of matter. Convection occurs as a result of uneven heating of matter and thermal expansion and contraction. • Convection occurs most efficiently in liquids or gases, but also in solids, such as Earth's mantle. Convection currents form when hot matter rises and cool matter sinks.
Conduction 1 Summarize conduction. 2 Identify examples of conduction on Earth.	• Conduction is the transfer of energy through a material. Objects must touch for conduction to occur. • Conduction occurs as water, rock, and air particles touch and transfer energy.

Options for Instruction

Two parallel paths provide coverage of the Essential Questions, with a strong **Inquiry** strand woven into each.
Follow the **Print Path,** the **Digital Path,** or your customized combination of print, digital, and inquiry.

 **Print Path**
Teaching support for the Print Path appears with the Student Pages.

 Inquiry Labs and **Activities**

Digital Path
Digital Path shortcut: TS661150

Print Path	Inquiry Labs and Activities	Digital Path
Hot and Cold, SE pp. 116–117 **How are energy and temperature related?** **What is thermal expansion?** **Getting Warm,** SE pp. 118–119 **What is heat?** **Why can the temperatures... differ?**	**Activity** Three Types of Energy Transfer	**Define Heat** Interactive Image **Thermal Expansion** Interactive Images **Temperature** Interactive Graphics
Heat, SE pp. 120–121 **How is energy transferred by radiation?** **Where does radiation occur on Earth?**	**Quick Lab** The Sun's Angle and Temperature **Quick Lab** How Does Color Affect Temperature? **S.T.E.M. Lab** Heat from the Sun	**Methods of Transfer** Animation **Radiation** Interactive Images
Heating Up, SE pp. 122–123 **How is energy transferred by convection?** **Where does convection occur on Earth?**	**Quick Lab** Modeling Convection **Activity** Alike and Different	**Radiation** Interactive Images **Convection** Interactive Graphics
Ouch!, SE pp. 124–125 **How is energy transferred by conduction?** **Where does conduction occur...?**	**Activity** Energy Transfer Game **Daily Demo** Transfer Energy	**Methods of Transfer** Animation **Conduction** Interactive Image

Options for Assessment

See the Evaluate page for options, including Formative Assessment, Summative Assessment, and Unit Review.

Engage and Explore

Activities and Discussion

Activity *Diagramming Energy Transfer*

 Engage

Radiation

 pairs or small groups
🕐 15 min
 GUIDED inquiry

Have student groups draw a diagram or sketch that shows how energy from the sun is absorbed by the atmosphere, geosphere, and hydrosphere. Then this energy is changed into thermal energy and reradiated into Earth's system or back into space. Display student diagrams for reference throughout the lesson.

Activity *Alike and Different*

Synthesizing Key Topics

 pairs or small groups
🕐 10 min
 GUIDED inquiry

Venn Diagram Invite students to draw a Venn diagram to compare convection and conduction. Where the circles overlap, they should list characteristics shared by the two types of energy transfer. Where the circles do not overlap, they should list ways the types of energy transfer are different.

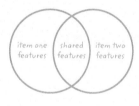

item one features | shared features | item two features

⏱ *Optional Online resource: Venn Diagram support*

Activity *Three Types of Energy Transfer*

Synthesizing Key Topics

 whole class
🕐 10 min
 GUIDED inquiry

Write Fast! Give students examples of energy transfer, and have them quickly write whether each example is convection, conduction, or radiation. For example, warming a pan on the stove (conduction), warm water rising in a pond (convection), the hot sun on your face (radiation), and so on.

Labs and Demos

⏱ S.T.E.M. Lab *Heat from the Sun*

Synthesizing Key Topics

 small groups
🕐 2 45-min periods
 GUIDED or **INDEPENDENT** inquiry

Students will explore how the energy from the sun affects the temperature of air, water, and land.

PURPOSE To build a landscape model and heat it to monitor how the sun affects temperature.

MATERIALS

* clay, modeling
* container, plastic
* gravel
* heat lamp
* paper, blank
* salt
* sand
* soil, potting
* thermometers (3)
* stopwatch
* tray
* water

⏱ ▢ Quick Lab *How Does Color Affect Temperature?*

PURPOSE To compare how different-colored objects absorb and radiate energy

See the Lab Manual or go Online for planning information.

Customize Your Labs

 See the Lab Manual for lab datasheets.

 Go Online for editable lab datasheets.

Levels of **Inquiry**

DIRECTED inquiry	GUIDED inquiry	INDEPENDENT inquiry
introduces inquiry skills within a structured framework.	develops inquiry skills within a supportive environment.	deepens inquiry skills with student-driven questions or procedures.

Daily Demo *Transfer Energy*

Synthesizing Key Topics

 pairs or small groups
10 min
 GUIDED inquiry

PURPOSE **To show the three ways energy can be transferred**

MATERIALS

- **colored wax, small pieces**
- **copper rod**
- **flame**
- **tongs to hold the hot metal rod**

To help students understand the different concepts of conduction, convection, and radiation, place a small amount of wax at various spots on a copper rod. Explain that the wax will melt when the rod transfers energy to the wax through conduction. Because you will be warming the rod at only one end, the atoms in the copper rod will transfer energy by conduction to the atoms at the other end of the rod. Ask students to predict what will happen to the wax when the rod is warmed on one end. Then, heat one end of the copper rod. The wax closest to the flame will melt first, and the wax farthest away will melt last, as energy finally reaches that point.

Then move the rod into and out of the flame to demonstrate radiation. Explain that when the rod is not touching the flame, energy is still being transferred to the rod through radiation. Have students summarize each type of energy transfer.

Note: Convection can be demonstrated by placing the wax above the flame; hot air rises and warms the wax. Radiation can be demonstrated by placing the wax to the side of the flame; radiation travels in all directions.

Quick Lab *Modeling Convection*

Convection

 small groups
20 min
 DIRECTED inquiry

Students will model a convection current, draw a diagram of what they observe, and relate their model to energy transfer in Earth's system.

PURPOSE **To observe and diagram convection currents**

MATERIALS

- **beaker, large**
- **hot plate**
- **paper, colored**
- **water, cold**

Quick Lab *The Sun's Angle and Temperature*

Radiation

 pairs
20 min
DIRECTED inquiry

Students will explore how the angle of the sun's rays influences temperatures on Earth.

PURPOSE **To describe the relationship between the angle of the sun and temperatures on Earth**

MATERIALS

- **adhesive putty**
- **globe**
- **lamp**
- **thermometers (2)**

Activities and Discussion

- ☐ **Activity** Diagramming Energy Transfer
- ☐ **Activity** Alike and Different
- ☐ **Activity** Three Types of Energy Transfer

Labs and Demos

- ☐ **S.T.E.M. Lab** Heat from the Sun
- ☐ **Quick Lab** How Does Color... ?
- ☐ **Daily Demo** Transfer Energy
- ☐ **Quick Lab** Modeling Convection
- ☐ **Quick Lab** The Sun's Angle . . .

Your Resources

Explain Science Concepts

	Print Path	Digital Path
Key Topics		

Temperature, Heat, Thermal Energy, Thermal Expansion

Print Path:

☐ **Hot and Cold,** SE pp. 116–117
- Visualize It!, #5
- Predict, #6
- Inquiry, #7

☐ **Getting Warm,** SE pp. 118–119
- Active Reading (Annotation strategy), #8
- Visualize It!, #9
- Predict, #10

Digital Path:

☐ **Define Heat**
Learn about energy, heat, and temperature.

☐ **Temperature**
Learn about measuring temperature.

Radiation

Print Path:

☐ **Heat,** SE pp. 120–121
- Visualize It!, #11
- Summarize, #12
- Think Outside the Book, #13

Digital Path:

☐ **Radiation**
Learn how radiation can cause a change in temperature.

Convection

Print Path:

☐ **Heating Up,** SE pp. 122–123
- Visualize It!, #14
- Active Reading, #15
- Visualize It!, #16

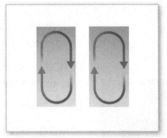

Digital Path:

☐ **Convection**
Explore the ways moving matter carries energy to different locations.

Conduction

Print Path:

☐ **Ouch!,** SE pp. 124–125
- Active Reading, #17
- Visualize It! #18
- Summarize, #19

Digital Path:

☐ **Conduction**
Explore how energy can travel through a material or between materials.

Differentiated Instruction

Basic *Specific Heat*

Temperature, Heat, Thermal Energy, Thermal Expansion

 individuals
🕐 10 min

If students have trouble understanding the concept of specific heat, ask them to think about pizza just out of the oven. Ask students which part of the pizza—the crust or the cheese—is cool enough to touch first. The crust will be cool enough to touch first. Tell students that water has a relatively high specific heat, which means it heats up more slowly than other substances, such as sand. Because it has a high specific heat, water also cools off much more slowly than substances with a lower specific heat. Ask students to think about whether the cheese or the crust has a higher specific heat. Sample answer: the cheese cools more slowly than the crust, so the cheese must have a higher specific heat than the crust.

Advanced *Electromagnetic Radiation*

Radiation

 individuals
🕐 15 min

Quick Research Encourage interested students to research the electromagnetic spectrum. Invite students to make posters or some other type of display that explains the electromagnetic spectrum, including types of radiation we cannot see, such as infrared, ultraviolet, and x-rays. Display student projects in the classroom.

🌐 *Optional Online rubric: Posters and Displays*

ELL *Energy Terms*

Synthesizing Key Topics

 pairs
🕐 15 min

Word Triangles Have pairs of students write a difficult word from this lesson and its definition in the bottom section. In the middle section, have them work together to write a sentence in which the word is used correctly. In the top section, have them draw a small picture to illustrate and help them remember the word.

picture
sentence using term
TERM: definition

🌐 *Optional Online resource: Word Triangle support*

Lesson Vocabulary

temperature   thermal energy   thermal expansion

heat   radiation   convection

conduction

Previewing Vocabulary

 whole class
🕐 10 min

Word Parts Explain that analyzing word parts can help readers figure out the meanings of words.

• If *duct-* means "to lead," how can you remember what *conduction* means? Energy is led from one object to another.

• If *vect-* means "to carry," how can you remember what convection means? Convection currents carry energy in a circle.

Reinforcing Vocabulary

 individuals
🕐 ongoing

Frame Game Invite students to write a vocabulary term in the center of a frame. Then have students decide which information to frame the vocabulary term with. They can use examples, a definition, descriptions, illustrations, parts, sentences, or whatever makes sense to help them remember the word. Have them make a new frame for each term.

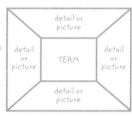

Customize Your Core Lesson

Core Instruction

☐ **Print Path** choices

☐ **Digital Path** choices

Vocabulary

☐ **Previewing Vocabulary** Word Parts

☐ **Reinforcing Vocabulary** Frame Game

Your Resources

Differentiated Instruction

☐ **Basic** Specific Heat

☐ **Advanced** Electromagnetic Radiation

☐ **ELL** Energy Terms

_____

_____

Extend Science Concepts

Reinforce and Review

Activity *Energy Transfer Game*

Synthesizing Key Topics   whole class 🕐 15 min

Three Corners Pick three corners of the classroom to represent radiation, convection, and conduction. Label each corner. Read the following relationships to students. After each one, ask the students to stand in the corner they think describes the relationship. Give each student in the correct corner a point. You can continue the game with additional examples provided by student volunteers.

1 A metal rod is heated at one end until the other end becomes hot. conduction

2 A hand placed on a hot mug becomes warm. conduction

3 The warm water in the ocean rises, and cooler water sinks. convection

4 An ice cube in your hand melts. conduction

5 The sun warms the dirt in your garden. radiation

6 The air is cooler near the bottom bunk than the top bunk. convection

7 Butter dropped into a hot pan melts. conduction

8 You feel warmth standing near a heater. radiation

Graphic Organizer

Synthesizing Key Topics   individuals 🕐 10 min

Pyramid FoldNote Have students make a Pyramid FoldNote. On one side of the pyramid, they should write key ideas about radiation. On another side of the pyramid, they should write key ideas about conduction. On the third side of the pyramid, they should write key ideas about convection.

⟳ *Online resource: Pyramid support*

Going Further

Engineering Connection

Synthesizing Key Topics   individuals 🕐 20 min

Rube Goldberg Device Ask students if they have ever heard of a Rube Goldberg device. Invite students to explain what this is, or if no one knows, explain that a Rube Goldberg device is an overly complicated machine that performs a simple function, such as toasting a piece of bread. Examples of Rube Goldberg devices can easily be found online. Encourage interested students to design their own Rube Goldberg devices. Their complicated machines should somehow transfer energy to perform the function. For example, wax could hold a string in place. Radiation from the sun melts the wax, which causes the string to be set free. Student designs can be drawn or actually built. Display drawings and devices around the classroom.

Real World Connection

Synthesizing Key Topics   individuals 🕐 20 min

Solar Energy Invite interested students to conduct research to find out how solar energy works. What parts of the process use radiation, what parts use conduction or convection? Let students explain their findings to the class.

Customize Your Closing

📄 *See the Assessment Guide for quizzes and tests.*

⟳ *Go Online to edit and create quizzes and tests.*

Reinforce and Review

☐ **Activity** Three Corners

☐ **Graphic Organizer** Pyramid FoldNote

☐ **Print Path** Visual Summary, SE p. 126

☐ **Print Path** Lesson Review, SE p. 127

☐ **Digital Path** Lesson Closer

Evaluate Student Mastery

Formative Assessment

See the teacher support below the Student Pages for additional Formative Assessment questions.

Ask: What is the difference between thermal energy and heat? Thermal energy is the total kinetic energy in a substance. It depends on temperature and on the number of particles in a substance. Heat is the energy transferred between objects that are at different temperatures. Describe three ways energy is transferred. Radiation is electromagnetic energy from the sun or some other source; convection is the transfer of energy through movement of matter caused by the uneven heating of matter; conduction transfers energy through direct contact.

Reteach

Formative assessment may show that students need reinforcement for certain topics. The resources below are recommended for reteaching. If students were introduced to a topic through the Print Path, you can also use the Digital Path to reteach, and vice versa.
🎧 *Can be assigned to individual students*

Temperature, Heat, Thermal Energy, Thermal Expansion
Basic Specific Heat

Radiation
Quick Lab How Does Color Affect Temperature? 🎧

Convection
Quick Lab Modeling Convection

Conduction
Activity Three Types of Energy Transfer

Summative Assessment

Alternative Assessment
Transfer of Energy

🌐 *Online resources: student worksheet, optional rubrics*

Energy Transfer

Climb the Pyramid: *Energy Transfer*
Energy can be transferred in several ways. Climb the pyramid to show how much you understand about the transfer of energy.

1. Work on your own, with a partner, or with a small group.
2. Choose one item from each layer of the pyramid. Check your choices.
3. Have your teacher approve your plan.
4. Submit or present your results.

__ **Specific Heat**
Imagine that you bite into a slice of a hot blackberry pie. The filling and the crust are at the same temperature. Explain why the filling burns your mouth but the crust does not.

__ **Thermal Energy**	__ **Thermal Expansion**
Explain how a cup of tea and a gallon of tea that are at the same temperature can have different thermal energies.	Draw a diagram that explains thermal expansion.

__ **Too Warm**	__ **Too cold**	__ **Warm up**
Suppose your room is too warm. Explain which process—radiation, conduction, or convection—would work best to cool it.	Suppose your hands are cold. Explain how you could warm them through conduction.	Suppose you are a cold-blooded snake. Explain which process—radiation, conduction, or convection—could warm you up.

Going Further
☐ Engineering Connection
☐ Real World Connection

Formative Assessment
☐ Strategies Throughout TE
☐ Lesson Review SE

Summative Assessment
☐ Alternative Assessment Transfer of Energy
☐ Lesson Quiz
☐ Unit Tests A and B
☐ Unit Review SE End-of-Unit

Your Resources

_____   _____

_____   _____

Answers

Answers for 1–3 should represent students' current thoughts, even if incorrect.

1. Sample answers: a fire, an ice cube, light, temperature

2. Sample answer: My hands would get hot. This would happen because heat would come from the hot chocolate.

3. Sample answer: A race that comes before a final race.

   Sample answer: A way to make a house or room warmer.

   Sample answer: A type of energy that makes things warm.

4. Students' annotations will vary.

Opening Your Lesson

Discuss students' answers to item 2 to assess their understanding of energy transfer from object to object. Most students should realize that their hands would become warm as energy is transferred from the mug to their hands.

Prerequisites Students should already have some general knowledge of the spheres of the Earth system, including the atmosphere and biosphere. They should also understand how the greenhouse effect influences temperatures on Earth.

Learning Alert

Energy Transfer Remind students, if necessary, that energy is transferred from one object to another as heat, not coldness. Some students may think that if you place an ice pack next to a sandwich in a lunchbox then the coldness is transferred from the ice pack to the sandwich. In fact, energy is transferred from the warmer sandwich to the cooler ice pack, which makes the ice warmer and the sandwich cooler. It may seem as if coldness is being transferred, but in reality energy is moving from a warmer to a colder object, and this transfer of energy makes the sandwich cool down.

Hot and Cold

How are energy and temperature related?

All matter is made up of moving particles, such as atoms or molecules. When particles are in motion, they have kinetic energy. Because particles move at different speeds, each has a different amount of kinetic energy.

Temperature (TEMM•per•uh•choor) is a measure of the average kinetic energy of particles. The faster a particle moves, the more kinetic energy it has. As shown below, the more kinetic energy the particles of an object have, the higher the temperature of the object. Temperature does not depend on the number of particles. A teapot holds more tea than a cup. If the particles of tea in both containers have the same average kinetic energy, the tea in both containers is at the same temperature.

Thermal energy is the total kinetic energy of particles. A teapot full of tea at a high temperature has more thermal energy than a teapot full of tea at a lower temperature. Thermal energy also depends on the number of particles. The more particles there are in an object, the greater the object's thermal energy. The tea in a teapot and a cup may be at the same temperature, but the tea in the pot has more thermal energy because there is more of it.

Visualize It!

5 Analyze Which container holds particles with the higher average kinetic energy?

particle motion
Celsius

particle motion
Celsius

116 Unit 3 Earth's Atmosphere

© Houghton Mifflin Harcourt Publishing Company

What is thermal expansion?

When the temperature of a substance increases, the substance's particles have more kinetic energy. Therefore, the particles move faster and move apart. As the space between the particles increases, the substance expands. The increase in volume that results from an increase in temperature is called **thermal expansion**. Most substances on Earth expand when they become warmer and contract when they become cooler. Water is an exception. Cold water expands as it gets colder and then freezes to form ice.

Thermal expansion causes a change in the density of a substance. *Density* is the mass per unit volume of a substance. When a substance expands, its mass stays the same but its volume increases. As a result, density decreases. Differences in density that are caused by thermal expansion can cause movement of matter. For example, air inside a hot-air balloon is warmed, as shown below. The air expands as its particles move faster and farther apart. As the air expands, it becomes less dense than the air outside the balloon. The less-dense air inside the balloon is forced upward by the colder, denser air outside the balloon. This same principle affects air movement in the atmosphere, water movement in the oceans, and rock movement in the geosphere.

Inquiry

7 Apply Why would an increase in the temperature of the oceans contribute to a rise in sea level?

6 Predict What might happen to the hot-air balloon if the air inside it cooled down?

When the air in this balloon becomes hotter, it becomes less dense than the surrounding air. So, the balloon goes up, up, and away!

Lesson 2 Energy Transfer 117

© Houghton Mifflin Harcourt Publishing Company • Image Credits: (r) ©Rion Crabtree/Photographer's Choice RF/Getty Images; (br) ©Photo by Andreas Rentz/Getty Images

---

Answers

5. The particles in the hot drink (on the left) have a higher average kinetic energy.

6. The balloon might begin to sink toward the ground.

7. An increase in the temperature of the water in the oceans would cause thermal expansion of the water. This would cause an increase in volume of the water. The increased volume of water would cause the water levels of the oceans to rise.

Probing Questions GUIDED Inquiry

Synthesizing Is it possible for a cup of tea and a teapot that is full of tea to have the same thermal energy? Explain. Yes, it is possible if the tea in the cup were very hot and the tea in the teapot were not as hot. Even though there is more tea in the teapot, if it is cooler than the tea in the cup, it could still have less thermal energy. If a teaspoon of water and a cup of water have the same temperature, do they have the same kinetic energy? Yes. Which do you think will cool down faster, the teaspoon of water or the cup of water? Why? the teaspoon of water because it has much less water to cool When the teaspoon of water cools down more than the cup of water, will it still have the same kinetic energy as the cup of water? No, because it is now cooler than the cup of water. Which would have more thermal energy? the cup of water because it has more particles and it is hotter

Learning Alert

Motion of Matter Remind students that particles in all states of matter are in motion. Ask students if they think metal would have kinetic energy. Sample answer: Yes, the atoms in metal are moving. They just move more slowly than molecules in water or air. What happens when the kinetic energy of metal increases? Its temperature increases.

Getting Warm

What is heat?

8 Identify As you read, underline the direction of energy transfer between objects that are at different temperatures.

You might think of the word *heat* when you imagine something that feels hot. But heat also has to do with things that feel cold. In fact, heat is what causes objects to feel hot or cold. You may often use the word *heat* to mean different things. However, in this lesson, the word *heat* has only one meaning. **Heat** is the energy that is transferred between objects that are at different temperatures.

Energy Transferred Between Objects

When objects that have different temperatures come into contact, energy will be transferred between them until both objects reach the same temperature. The direction of this energy transfer is always from the object with the higher temperature to the object with the lower temperature. When you touch something cold, energy is transferred from your body to that object. When you touch something hot, like the pan shown below, energy is transferred from that object to your body.

Visualize It!

9 Predict Draw an arrow to show the direction in which energy is transferred between the pan and the oven mitts.

This pan is being removed from the oven and is very hot.

118   Unit 3 Earth's Atmosphere

Why can the temperatures of land, air, and water differ?

When the same amount of energy is being transferred, some materials will get warmer or cooler at a faster rate than other materials. Suppose you are walking along a beach on a sunny day. You may notice that the land feels warmer than the air and the water, even though they are all exposed to the same amount of energy from the sun. This is because the land warms up at a faster rate than the water and air do.

Specific Heat

The different rates at which materials become warmer or cooler are due to a property called *specific heat*. A substance that has a high specific heat requires a lot of energy to show an increase in temperature. A substance with a lower specific heat requires less energy to show the same increase in temperature. Water has a higher specific heat than land. So, water warms up more slowly than land does. Water also cools down more slowly than land does.

10 Predict Air has a lower specific heat than water. Once the sun goes down, will the air or the water cool off faster? Why?

_____
_____
_____

The temperatures of land, water, and air may differ— even when they are exposed to the same amount of energy from the sun.

119

Answers

8. *See students' pages for annotations.*

9. Arrows should indicate that energy is transferred from the pan to the oven mitt.

10. The air will cool off faster because it has a lower specific heat than water.

Learning Alert

Transfer of Heat Energy Students may not completely understand the movement of heat energy. Explain that heat is energy that is transferred between objects that have different temperatures. These objects must be in direct contact. Make it clear that the direction of energy transfer is always from the hotter object to the cooler object. Also explain that energy transfer will continue until both objects reach the same temperature.

Probing Questions   GUIDED (Inquiry)

Analyzing If something with a high specific heat and something with a low specific heat start out at the same temperature and are then exposed to the same amount of energy, which will warm up first? the one with the low specific heat Which one will retain the energy longest? the one with high specific heat In the fall, why might the ocean water near the shore be warm even though the air temperature is cool? because the water cools off slowly In the early summer, why might water in a lake be cold even though the sun is shining and the air temperature is warm? because the water heats up more slowly than the air

Heat

How is energy transferred by radiation?

On a summer day, you can feel warmth from the sun on your skin. But how did that energy reach you from the sun? The sun transfers energy to Earth by radiation. **Radiation** is the transfer of energy as electromagnetic (ee•LEK•troh•mag•NEH•tik) waves. Radiation can transfer energy between objects that are not in direct contact with each other. Many objects other than the sun also radiate energy as light and heat. These include a hot burner on a stove and a campfire, shown below.

Electromagnetic Waves

Energy from the sun is called *electromagnetic radiation*. This energy travels in waves. You are probably familiar with one form of radiation called *visible light*. You can see the visible light that comes from the sun. Electromagnetic radiation includes other forms of energy, which you cannot see. Most of the warmth that you feel from the sun is infrared radiation. This energy has a longer wavelength and lower energy than visible light. Higher-energy radiation includes x-rays and ultraviolet light.

Energy from the sun is transferred through space.

Visualize It!

11 Analyze Write a caption for the campfire photo on the right. Make sure the caption relates the image to radiation.

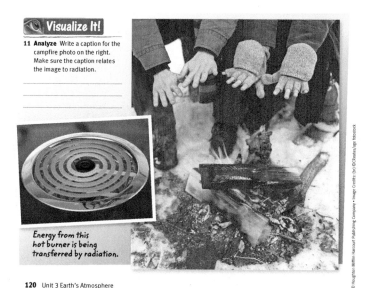

Energy from this hot burner is being transferred by radiation.

Where does radiation occur on Earth?

We live almost 150 million km from the sun. Yet almost all of the energy on Earth is transmitted from the sun by radiation. The sun is the major source of energy for processes at Earth's surface. Receiving that energy is absolutely vital for life on Earth. The electromagnetic waves from the sun also provide energy that drives the water cycle.

When solar radiation reaches Earth, some of the energy is reflected and scattered by Earth's atmosphere. But much of the energy passes through Earth's atmosphere and reaches Earth's surface. Some of the energy that Earth receives from the sun is absorbed by the atmosphere, geosphere, and hydrosphere. Then, the energy is changed into thermal energy. This thermal energy may be reradiated into the Earth system or into space. Much of the energy is transferred through Earth's systems by the two other ways—convection and conduction.

Think Outside the Book

13 Apply Research ultraviolet radiation from the sun and its role in causing sunburns.

12 Summarize Give two examples of what happens when energy from the sun reaches Earth.

© Houghton Mifflin Harcourt Publishing Company • Image Credits: (br) ©CKieatus/age fotostock

© Houghton Mifflin Harcourt Publishing Company

120 Unit 3 Earth's Atmosphere

Lesson 2 Energy Transfer 121

Answers

11. Sample answer: A campfire feels warm because of the transfer of energy by radiation.

12. Sample answer: The sun's energy is absorbed by the geosphere and hydrosphere. The sun's energy can also be reflected by the atmosphere.

13. Student answers should focus on the ultraviolet wavelengths and how damaging this high-energy radiation can be.

Probing Questions GUIDED (Inquiry)

Analyzing When the sun transfers energy to a rock, is this an example of radiation? Why? Sample answer: Yes, energy is transferred from the sun to an object that is not in contact with the sun. When you put a pan on a burner, is that radiation? Sample answer: No, the burner is touching the pan. Energy is transferred by conduction, not radiation. What are some other examples of radiation? Sample answers: when a heater or campfire warms you up, when you can feel the warmth coming from a lightbulb

Formative Assessment

Ask: What is the difference between temperature and thermal energy? Sample answers: Temperature measures the average kinetic energy of moving particles (that is, how fast the particles move). Thermal energy measures the total kinetic energy of the substance. **Ask:** Can something small have more thermal energy than something big? yes, if the smaller object is very hot **Ask:** If two things are exactly the same size, must they have the same thermal energy? No, if one is warmer than the other, it will have more thermal energy. **Ask:** If two things are exactly the same temperature, must they have the same thermal energy? No, if they are different sizes, the bigger one will have more thermal energy.

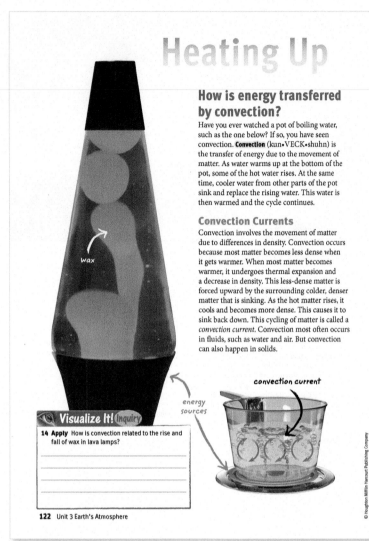

Heating Up

How is energy transferred by convection?

Have you ever watched a pot of boiling water, such as the one below? If so, you have seen convection. **Convection** (kun•VECK•shuhn) is the transfer of energy due to the movement of matter. As water warms up at the bottom of the pot, some of the hot water rises. At the same time, cooler water from other parts of the pot sink and replace the rising water. This water is then warmed and the cycle continues.

Convection Currents

Convection involves the movement of matter due to differences in density. Convection occurs because most matter becomes less dense when it gets warmer. When most matter becomes warmer, it undergoes thermal expansion and a decrease in density. This less-dense matter is forced upward by the surrounding colder, denser matter that is sinking. As the hot matter rises, it cools and becomes more dense. This causes it to sink back down. This cycling of matter is called a *convection current*. Convection most often occurs in fluids, such as water and air. But convection can also happen in solids.

wax

convection current

energy sources

Visualize It! Inquiry

14 Apply How is convection related to the rise and fall of wax in lava lamps?

122 Unit 3 Earth's Atmosphere

Where does convection occur on Earth?

If Earth's surface is warmer than the air, energy will be transferred from the ground to the air. As the air becomes warmer, it becomes less dense. This air is pushed upward and out of the way by cooler, denser air that is sinking. As the warm air rises, it cools and becomes denser and begins to sink back toward Earth's surface. This cycle moves energy through the atmosphere.

Convection currents also occur in the ocean because of differences in the density of ocean water. More dense water sinks to the ocean floor, and less dense water moves toward the surface. The density of ocean water is influenced by temperature and the amount of salt in the water. Cold water is denser than warmer water. Water that contains a lot of salt is more dense than less-salty water.

Energy produced deep inside Earth heats rock in the mantle. The heated rock becomes less dense and is pushed up toward Earth's surface by the cooler, denser surrounding rock. Once cooled near the surface, the rock sinks. These convection currents transfer energy from Earth's core toward Earth's surface. These currents also cause the movement of tectonic plates.

Active Reading **15 Name** What are three of Earth's spheres in which energy is transferred by convection?

_____

_____

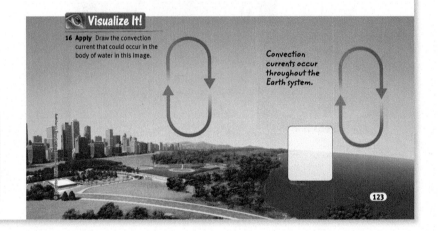

Visualize It!

16 Apply Draw the convection current that could occur in the body of water in this image.

Convection currents occur throughout the Earth system.

123

Answers

14. The wax is warmed from below by a lightbulb. This causes the density of the wax to decrease and the wax to rise in the lamp. When the wax gets to the top, it cools and its density increases. The wax then sinks back down.

15. The three spheres are the atmosphere, geosphere, and hydrosphere.

16. Diagrams should appear like convection currents to illustrate movement of cool water downward, and warm water upward.

Building Reading Skills

Main Idea/Details Explain that heads can help you figure out main ideas and important points about a topic. What is the first important point that is made? Energy is transferred by convection currents. Find some important details in the paragraphs that support this main idea. Heat changes the density of most matter. When matter is less dense, it rises. When it cools, it becomes heavier and sinks back toward the heat source. This cycling is a convection current.

Probing Questions   GUIDED Inquiry

Analyzing How do you think energy is transferred in the air during convection? The warm Earth transfers energy to the air at Earth's surface. The warm air expands and rises. But as it rises, it transfers energy to cooler air around it. So the warm air becomes cooler and denser and begins to sink. Then the process repeats itself. Explain what happens when a pot of water boils. Sample answer: Plumes of hot, less-dense water rise rapidly to the top of the pot. Then they cool and sink to the bottom of the pot, pushing hotter, less-dense water to the top of the pot. Do you think a convection current would be stronger when temperature differences are greater? Why? Yes, there will be a bigger difference in the densities of the hot and cold matter, which will make the hot matter rise faster.

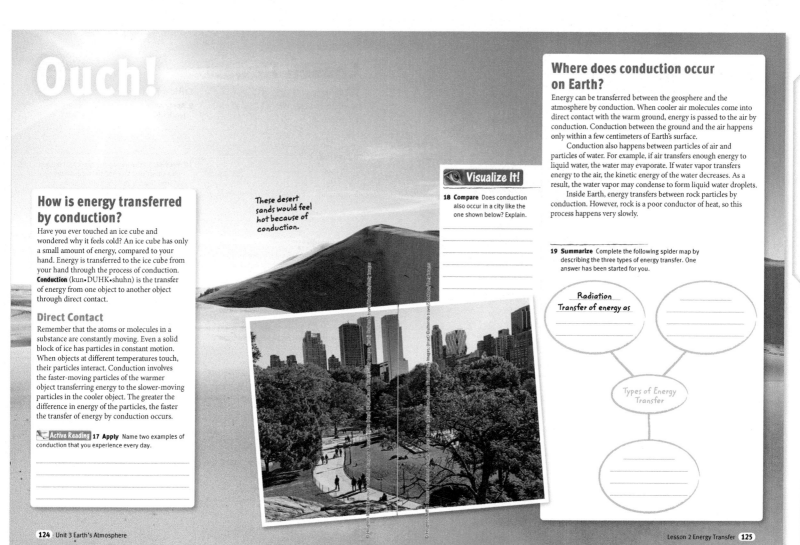

Ouch!

How is energy transferred by conduction?

Have you ever touched an ice cube and wondered why it feels cold? An ice cube has only a small amount of energy, compared to your hand. Energy is transferred to the ice cube from your hand through the process of conduction. **Conduction** (kun•DUHK•shuhn) is the transfer of energy from one object to another object through direct contact.

Direct Contact

Remember that the atoms or molecules in a substance are constantly moving. Even a solid block of ice has particles in constant motion. When objects at different temperatures touch, their particles interact. Conduction involves the faster-moving particles of the warmer object transferring energy to the slower-moving particles in the cooler object. The greater the difference in energy of the particles, the faster the transfer of energy by conduction occurs.

Active Reading **17 Apply** Name two examples of conduction that you experience every day.

These desert sands would feel hot because of conduction.

👁 **Visualize It!**

18 Compare Does conduction also occur in a city like the one shown below? Explain.

Where does conduction occur on Earth?

Energy can be transferred between the geosphere and the atmosphere by conduction. When cooler air molecules come into direct contact with the warm ground, energy is passed to the air by conduction. Conduction between the ground and the air happens only within a few centimeters of Earth's surface.

Conduction also happens between particles of air and particles of water. For example, if air transfers enough energy to liquid water, the water may evaporate. If water vapor transfers energy to the air, the kinetic energy of the water decreases. As a result, the water vapor may condense to form liquid water droplets.

Inside Earth, energy transfers between rock particles by conduction. However, rock is a poor conductor of heat, so this process happens very slowly.

19 Summarize Complete the following spider map by describing the three types of energy transfer. One answer has been started for you.

Radiation
Transfer of energy as

Types of Energy Transfer

Answers

17. Student answers should be examples of energy transfer between objects at different temperatures through direct contact.

18. Yes, it does. Energy can be transferred from the warm surface of Earth, such as from the pavement or ground, to the cooler air molecules.

19. Radiation: the transfer of energy as electromagnetic waves through space

    Convection: the transfer of energy due to the movement of matter

    Conduction: the transfer of energy between objects by direct contact

Probing Questions GUIDED *Inquiry*

Synthesizing Deep-fried ice cream is ice cream rolled in a coating, sometimes crushed corn flakes, then fried in a large amount of oil. How is it possible to make deep-fried ice cream without melting the ice cream? Use information from this lesson. Sample answer: The coated ice cream is cooked by conduction, which is more rapid when two temperatures are very different. The oil is very hot, and the crushed corn flakes are very cold, so heat conducts very rapidly. The crust of the dessert is getting hot as it fries, but it takes a while longer for the energy to reach the inside of the dessert, and so there is not enough time for the ice cream to melt before it is removed from the hot oil.

Formative Assessment

Ask: What is an example of energy transfer by conduction? Sample answer: When a hot potato touches your tongue, energy is conducted to your tongue. **Ask:** When you put an ice cube in juice, does energy move from the cold ice cube to the warm juice? No, energy is transferred from the warm juice to the ice, cooling the juice, and warming the ice.

Visual Summary

To complete this summary, fill in the blanks with the correct word or phrase. Then, use the key below to check your answers. You can use this page to review the main concepts of the lesson.

Energy Transfer

Heat is the energy that is transferred between objects that are at different temperatures.

20 The particles in a hot pan have _____ kinetic energy than the particles in a cool oven mitt.

Energy can be transferred in different ways.

21 The three ways that energy can be transferred are labeled in the image as

A: _____

B: _____

C: _____

Answers: 20 more; 21 A: radiation, B: conduction, C: convection

22 Apply What type of energy transfer is responsible for making you feel cold when you are swimming in cool water? Explain your answer.

126 Unit 3 Earth's Atmosphere

Lesson Review

Lesson 2

Vocabulary

In your own words, define the following terms.

1 radiation

2 convection

3 conduction

Key Concepts

4 Compare What is the difference between temperature, thermal energy, and heat?

5 Describe What is happening to a substance undergoing thermal expansion?

6 Explain What is the main source of energy for most processes at Earth's surface?

7 Summarize What happens when two objects at different temperatures touch? Name one place where it occurs in Earth's system.

8 Identify What is an example of convection in Earth's system?

Critical Thinking

9 Apply Why can metal utensils get too hot to touch when you are cooking with them?

10 Predict You are doing an experiment outside on a sunny day. You find the temperature of some sand is 28°C. You also find the temperature of some water is 25°C. Explain the difference in temperatures.

Use this image to answer the following questions.

11 Analyze Name one example of where energy transfer by radiation is occurring.

12 Analyze Name one example of where energy transfer by conduction is occurring.

13 Analyze Name one example of where energy transfer by convection is occurring.

Lesson 2 Energy Transfer 127

Visual Summary Answers

20. more

21. A: radiation; B: conduction; C: convection

22. Conduction is responsible. My skin would be in direct contact with water that is at a lower temperature than my skin. Therefore, energy would transfer from my skin to the water, making me feel cold.

Lesson Review Answers

1. Sample answer: transfer of energy as electromagnetic waves through space

2. Sample answer: transfer of energy due to movement of matter

3. Sample answer: transfer of energy between two objects in direct contact

4. Temperature: measure of average kinetic energy; Thermal energy: total kinetic energy; Heat: transfer of energy between objects that are at different temperatures

5. As the temperature of a substance increases, the space between the particles increases. This causes the substance to expand.

6. the sun

7. energy is transferred; from the ground to the air just above it

8. Student answers should include an example from the atmosphere, geosphere, or hydrosphere.

9. The energy from cooking can transfer to the metal spoon by conduction (direct contact with something hot) or radiation (if near something hot).

10. Water has a higher specific heat than sand. Therefore, it takes longer for it to increase in temperature.

11. burner to air; oven element to inside of oven

12. burner to pot; pot to contents; oven rack to pan; pan to bread

13. in the pot; in the oven

Building a Wind Turbine

Purpose To learn how the need for clean energy has driven a technological solution

Learning Goals

- Relate the need for clean energy to technological development.
- Design a technological solution to a problem.
- Test and modify a prototype to achieve the desired result.

Informal Vocabulary

machine, wind turbine, design

Prerequisite Knowledge

- Basic understanding of how wind is generated in the atmosphere
- Basic understanding of how gears work

Materials

assorted wind turbine parts

fan

gears

small bulb

small motor

socket

Teacher Note Small electric motors can be purchased from most lab suppliers. This activity may be done in several class periods as a long-term project.

Caution! Students should wear goggles at all times during this activity. Remind students to use caution with the glass bulb and the electrical items. Remind students to notify a teacher if a bulb is broken. Students should not attempt to clean up a broken bulb themselves.

Content Refresher

Professional Development

Wind Generators Most wind generators in modern wind farms are horizontal-axis wind turbines (HAWTs). HAWTs have the main rotor shaft and electrical generator at the top of a tower, and must be pointed into the wind. Small turbines are pointed by simple wind vanes, while large turbines generally use a wind sensor and a motor. Most HAWTs have gears that turn the slow rotation of the blades into a faster rotation to drive the electrical generator. The advantages of HAWTs are their efficiency, reliability, and low noise vibration.

The key advantage of vertical-axis wind turbines (VAWTs) is that the turbine does not need to be pointed into the wind to be effective. This is an advantage at sites where the wind direction is highly variable. With a vertical axis, the generator and gearbox can be placed near the ground, so the tower doesn't need to support them, and they are more accessible for maintenance. A gearbox is commonly used to step up the speed of the generator. All turbines are equipped with shut-down features to avoid damage at high wind speeds.

21st Century SKILLS   Theme: Environmental Literacy

Activities focusing on 21st Century Skills are included for this feature and can be found on the following pages.

These activities focus on the following skills:

- **Initiative and Self-Direction**
- **Media Literacy**
- **Communication and Collaboration**

You can learn more about the 21st Century Skills in the front matter of this Teacher's Edition.

S.T.E.M.   Engineering & Technology

Engineering Design Process

Skills
Identify a need
Conduct research
✓ Brainstorm solutions
✓ Select a solution
Design a prototype
✓ Build a prototype
✓ Test and evaluate
✓ Redesign to improve
✓ Communicate results

Objectives
• Explain how a need for clean energy has driven a technological solution.
• Describe two examples of wind-powered generators.
• Design a technological solution to a problem.
• Test and modify a prototype to achieve the desired result.

Building a Wind Turbine

During the Industrial Revolution, machines began to replace human and animal power for doing work. From agriculture and manufacturing to transportation, machines made work faster and easier. However, these machines needed fuel. Fossil fuels, such as coal, oil, and gasoline, powered the Industrial Revolution and are still used today. But burning fossil fuels produces waste products that harm the environment. In addition, fossil fuels will eventually run out. As a result, we need to better understand alternative, renewable sources of energy.

Brainstorming Solutions

There are many sources of energy besides fossil fuels. One of the most abundant renewable sources is wind. A wind turbine is a device that uses energy from the wind to turn an axle. The turning axle can be attached to other equipment to do jobs such as pumping water, cutting lumber, or generating electricity. To generate electricity, the axle spins magnets around a coiled wire. This causes electrons to flow in the wire. Flowing electrons produce an electric current. Electric current is used to power homes and businesses or electrical energy can be stored in a battery.

1 Brainstorm What are other possible sources of renewable energy that could be used to power a generator?

HAWTs must be pointed into the wind to work. A motor turns the turbine to keep it facing the wind. HAWT blades are angled so that wind strikes the front of the blades, and then pushes the blades as it flows over them. Because wind flows over the blades fairly evenly, there is little vibration. So HAWTs are relatively quiet, and the turbines last a long time.

Wind direction

Blade moves counterclockwise

The Modern Design

There are two general types of modern wind turbines. A horizontal-axis wind turbine (HAWT) has a main axle that is horizontal, and a generator at the top of a tall tower. A vertical-axis wind turbine (VAWT) has a main axle that is vertical, and a generator at ground level. The blades are often white or light gray, to blend with the clouds. Blades can be more than 40 meters (130 ft) long, supported by towers more than 90 meters (300 ft) tall. The blade tips can travel more than 320 kilometers (200 mi) per hour!

2 Infer What problems may have been encountered as prototypes for modern wind turbines were tested?

VAWTs do not need to be pointed into the wind to work. The blades are made so that one blade is pushed by the wind while the other returns against the wind. But because each blade moves against the wind for part of its rotation, VAWTs are less efficient than HAWTs. They also tend to vibrate more and, as a result, make more noise.

Wind direction

Blade moves against the wind

Blade moves with the wind

✋ You Try It!

Now it's your turn to design a wind turbine that will generate electricity and light a small bulb.

Answers

1. Answers will vary. Sample answer: water, geothermal energy, solar energy, animal or human power

2. Answers will vary. Sample answer: People may have been disturbed by the noise, vibrations may have caused arms of windmills to fly off, people may have been injured by falling windmills or flying blades, animals or birds may have been injured by spinning blades.

Engineering Design Process

✋ You Try It!

Now it's your turn to design an efficient wind turbine that will generate enough electricity to light a small bulb.

① Brainstorm solutions

Brainstorm ideas for a wind turbine that will turn an axle on a small motor. The blades must turn fast enough so that the motor generates enough electricity to light a small bulb. Fill in the table below with as many ideas as you can for each part of your wind turbine. Circle each idea you decide to try.

Materials
- ✓ assorted wind turbine parts
- ✓ fan
- ✓ gears
- ✓ small bulb
- ✓ small motor
- ✓ socket

Type of axis	Shape of turbine	Attaching axis to motor	Control speed

② Select a solution

From the table above, choose the features for the turbine you will build. In the space below, draw a model of your wind turbine idea. Include all the parts and show how they will be connected.

③ Build a prototype

Now build your wind turbine. As you built your turbine, were there some parts of your design that could not be assembled as you had predicted? What parts did you have to revise as you were building the prototype?

④ Test and evaluate

Point a fan at your wind turbine and see what happens. Did the bulb light? If not, what parts of your turbine could you revise?

⑤ Redesign to improve

Choose one part to revise. Modify your design and then test again. Repeat this process until your turbine lights up the light bulb.

⑥ Communicate results

Which part of the turbine seemed to have the greatest effect on the brightness of the light bulb?

Answers

1. Answers will vary. Students should list several possibilities for each design item and then circle the item they finally choose.

2. Students should draw a wind turbine and show how it will be attached to the small motor.

3. Answers will vary. Students should describe any parts they had to modify as they built their turbine.

4. Answers will vary depending on whether the bulb lights or not. If not, students should describe the parts they could modify.

5. Answers will vary depending on students' designs. Students should describe the modifications they made at each step until the bulb lit.

6. Answers will vary depending on students' designs.

21st Century SKILLS

Life and Career Skills

 individuals   🕐 varied

Initiative and Self-Direction Most people support the idea of wind power, but when wind farms are proposed for specific communities, local opposition is often intense. Have interested students use the Internet to research reasons for local opposition to wind farms. Encourage students to work independently to define the focus of their research, set goals, monitor their time, and develop a brief presentation.

Information, Media, and Technology Skills

 individuals   🕐 varied

Media Literacy Encourage students to use the Internet or library resources to find newspaper articles or news video about wind power. Then, have students choose one news item and answer the following questions. When was the news published? What is the source of the news item? Is the source credible? What was the main point of the news item? Was any information missing from the news item that would have helped readers or viewers to better understand the issue?

Learning and Innovation Skills

🏃 small groups   🕐 varied

Communication and Collaboration Organize students into groups of four to participate in a classroom discussion that explores the advantages and disadvantages of different energy sources. Assign each group a different energy source, such as wind, the sun, hydroelectric power, or natural gas. Have two students in each group work together to research the advantages of using the energy source, and have two students research the disadvantages of using the energy source. After all groups have completed their research, each group should report on the advantages and disadvantages associated with their energy source. Once all groups have presented, students should rank the energy sources in order from most promising to least promising, based on the information they heard.

Differentiated Instruction

Basic *Wind-Powered Device*

 individuals or pairs   🕐 25 min

For hundreds of years, windmills have been used for tasks such as grinding grain, pumping water, and cutting lumber. Have students brainstorm designs for a wind-powered device that could accomplish one of these tasks. Then have students select a design and draw a sketch showing how their device would work.

Advanced *Energy Output Modeling*

 pairs or small groups   🕐 35 min

Encourage interested students to design a method to test the energy output of the wind turbine created in this activity. Students should explore multiple options commonly used to measure electrical output and discuss the merits of each.

ELL *Energy Transfer Technology*

 partners   🕐 15 min

After students have read the feature, have them explain to a partner in their own words how energy is transferred by wind. Then ask students to describe how that energy can be harnessed by technology such as a wind turbine. If necessary, have students draw a model of a wind turbine and use the drawing as a visual reference as they explain how turbines work.

Customize Your Feature

- [ ] **21st Century Skills** Life and Career Skills
- [ ] **21st Century Skills** Information, Media, and Technology Skills
- [ ] **21st Century Skills** Learning and Innovation Skills
- [ ] **Basic** Wind-Powered Device
- [ ] **Advanced** Energy Output Modeling
- [ ] **ELL** Energy Transfer Technology

Wind in the Atmosphere

Essential Question What is wind?

 **Professional Development**

For more detailed information about the topics in this lesson, refer to the Content Refresher in the Unit Opener pages.

Opening Your Lesson

Begin the lesson by assessing students' prerequisite and prior knowledge.

Prerequisite Knowledge

- Characteristics of four layers of the atmosphere
- Heat capacity in air, water, and land

Accessing Prior Knowledge

Ask: What are the four layers of the atmosphere? How are they defined? the thermosphere, mesosphere, stratosphere, and troposphere; they are defined by changes in temperature

Ask: Why do the temperatures of land, air, and water differ? They have different heat capacities, causing them to heat up and cool down at different rates.

Customize Your Opening

☐ **Accessing Prior Knowledge,** above

☐ **Print Path** Engage Your Brain, SE p. 133 #1–2

☐ **Print Path** Active Reading, SE p. 133 #3–4

☐ **Digital Path** Lesson Opener

Key Topics/Learning Goals

The Movement of Air

1 Explain why air moves and identify the source of energy that causes air movement.

2 Illustrate how convection cells in Earth's atmosphere cause high- and low-pressure belts at Earth's surface.

3 Summarize the Coriolis effect.

Global Winds

1 List two factors that produce global winds.

2 Identify and locate the three major global wind systems. Describe winds where global pressure belts meet.

3 Define *jet streams*.

Local Winds

1 Explain how differences in the way land and water absorb and release energy cause local winds, such as sea, land, valley, and mountain breezes.

Supporting Concepts

- Wind is air movement from an area of higher pressure to one of lower pressure. Air moves due to density differences from uneven heating of Earth's surface. The sun warms Earth and causes the circulation of air.

- Rising and sinking air in the atmosphere forms convection cells, which create high- and low-pressure belts on Earth.

- The Coriolis effect is the curving of the path of a moving object as a result of Earth's rotation. Winds curve to the right in the Northern Hemisphere; left in the Southern.

- Pressure belts and the Coriolis effect produce global winds.

- The major wind systems are the easterlies, westerlies, and trade winds. Polar easterlies blow east to west. Mid-latitude westerlies blow west to east. Tropical trade winds blow east to west. The doldrums and horse latitudes are zones with weak, variable winds located at 30° north and south latitudes and the equator.

- Jet streams are bands of high-speed winds in the upper troposphere.

- Local winds move short distances and are variable in direction. Most local winds are caused by differences in pressure, in turn caused by uneven heating of Earth's surface. Land and water absorb and release energy differently, resulting in local air pressure differences which cause sea and land breezes and mountain and valley breezes.

Options for Instruction

Two parallel paths provide coverage of the Essential Questions, with a strong **Inquiry** strand woven into each.
Follow the **Print Path**, the **Digital Path**, or your customized combination of print, digital, and inquiry.

Print Path *Teaching support for the Print Path appears with the Student Pages.*	**Inquiry Labs and Activities**	 **Digital Path** *Digital Path shortcut: TS661350*
Blow It Out! SE pp. 134–135 **What causes wind?** • Areas of High and Low Pressure **How does Earth's rotation affect wind?**	**Quick Lab** Rising Heat **Quick Lab** Modeling Air Movement by Convection **Daily Demo** Air Pressure and Wind **Activity** Trivia Game	**Why Air Moves** Interactive Graphics
Blowin' Around, SE pp. 136–138 **What are examples of global winds?** • Trade Winds • Westerlies • Polar Easterlies • The Doldrums and Horse Latitudes • The Jet Streams	**Activity** Journey of a Trade Wind **Quick Lab** Flying with the Jet Stream	**Global Winds** Interactive Image **Jet Streams** Interactive Images
Feelin' Breezy, SE pp. 140–141 **What are examples of local winds?** • Sea and Land Breezes • Valley and Mountain Breezes	**Activity** Wind Direction	**Local Winds** Interactive Images

Options for Assessment

See the Evaluate page for options, including Formative Assessment, Summative Assessment, and Unit Review.

Engage and Explore

Activities and Discussion

Discussion *Jet Streams and Weather*

Global Winds

 whole class
 20 min
 GUIDED inquiry

Discuss with students how jet streams can affect the weather in a certain area. Remind students that jet streams follow boundaries between hot and cold air. Point out that jet streams shift to areas of varying temperatures during the different seasons. Also mention that jet streams exist for different amounts of time in different areas. Have students brainstorm ways in which these factors allow jet streams to affect the weather. Make a list of students' ideas on the board, and then rule out any ideas that do not explain this phenomenon. Be sure to explain why these suggestions are incorrect, and replace these with correct explanations of how jet streams affect weather around the world.

Activity *Journey of a Trade Wind*

Global Winds

 small groups
 15 min
 DIRECTED inquiry

Role Play Have students form small groups to create presentations about trade winds. Ask students to use role-playing in their presentations. Presentations should describe how a trade wind can change as it moves from one region into another, and how it becomes another type of wind. Presentations should be accompanied by narration to describe the characteristics of the wind in each region. Students should move around and use gestures and props to portray the different global winds.

 Optional Online rubric: Oral Presentations

Activity *Wind Direction*

Local Winds

 pairs
 20 min
 DIRECTED inquiry

Point out to students that wind direction can make all the difference when classifying a local wind. Tell students that they will make wind vanes to help them determine the direction from which the wind is blowing. Have pairs of students draw large arrows on manila folders. Instruct them to draw the back end as wide as the widest part of the front of the arrow. Have students cut out their arrows, and tape a washer to one side of the pointy end of the arrow. Have students hold their arrows with two fingers until the arrows are balanced horizontally. Then punch a hole in this spot and have students thread and tie a piece of string through it. Take students outside and have each pair tie their arrow to a tree. Tell students that their arrows will always point in the direction the wind is coming from.

Discussion *Studying the Wind*

The Movement of Air

 individuals or pairs
 20 min
 DIRECTED inquiry

Have students pretend they are scientists who must study the wind. Have them discuss what they would want to study about the wind. Sample answers: speed, temperature, direction, Have students discuss why a scientist might want to study the wind. Sample answers: to predict weather, to explain seasonal changes in air temperature, to predict wind speed and strength for travel purposes

Customize Your Labs

 See the Lab Manual for lab datasheets.

 Go Online for editable lab datasheets.

Levels of  **DIRECTED** inquiry   **GUIDED** inquiry   **INDEPENDENT** inquiry

introduces inquiry skills within a structured framework.   develops inquiry skills within a supportive environment.   deepens inquiry skills with student-driven questions or procedures.

Labs and Demos

Quick Lab *Rising Heat*

The Movement of Air

👥 small groups
🕐 10 min
Inquiry **DIRECTED** inquiry

Students will explore how heat is transferred in the atmosphere.

PURPOSE **To describe how convection currents transfer heat through the atmosphere**

MATERIALS

- feather, soft (2)
- hot plate
- heat-resistant gloves
- lab apron
- safety goggles

Quick Lab *Flying with the Jet Stream*

Global Winds

👥 pairs
🕐 20 min
Inquiry **DIRECTED** inquiry

Students will determine the relationship between the jet stream and the speed of a jet flying with or against the jet stream.

PURPOSE **To describe the relationship between the jet stream and ground speed**

MATERIALS

- calculator
- paper
- pencil

Daily Demo *Air Pressure and Wind*

The Movement of Air

👥 whole class
🕐 20 min
Inquiry **GUIDED** inquiry

PURPOSE **To model how air temperature affects density and speed**

MATERIALS

- balloons (2)
- plastic bottles, 2 L (2)
- plastic tub of cold water
- plastic tub of hot water

1 **Observing** Fill the two bottles with tepid water. **Ask:** Do you see any differences between the bottles? No, the bottles look the same. Remind students that wind is caused by temperature changes that change the density of the air in the atmosphere.

2 Place a balloon over the mouth of each bottle to trap the air inside. Place one bottle in each tub of water. What is happening inside the bottles? The cold water is cooling the air in the bottle. The hot water is warming the air in the bottle.

3 Why is the balloon in the hot water inflating? The air is rising, causing the balloon to inflate. Why does the balloon in the cold water remain deflated? The cold air is sinking, and as it does, it pulls the balloon into the bottle.

Quick Lab *Modeling Air Movement by Convection*

PURPOSE **To describe the formation of convection currents**

See the Lab Manual or go Online for planning information.

Activities and Discussion

☐ **Discussion** Jet Streams and Weather
☐ **Activity** Journey of a Trade Wind
☐ **Activity** Wind Direction
☐ **Discussion** Studying the Wind

Labs and Demos

☐ **Quick Lab** Rising Heat
☐ **Quick Lab** Flying with the Jet Stream
☐ **Daily Demo** Air Pressure and Wind
☐ **Quick Lab** Modeling Air Movement by Convection

Your Resources

Explain Science Concepts

	Print Path	Digital Path

Key Topics		

The Movement of Air

Print Path

☐ **Blow It Out!** SE pp. 134–135
- Visualize It!, #5
- Active Reading (Annotation strategy), #6
- Visualize It!, #7

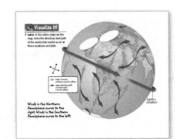

Digital Path

☐ **Why Air Moves**
See how uneven energy from sunlight and other effects produce wind.

Global Winds

Print Path

☐ **Blowin' Around,** SE pp. 136–138
- Active Reading, #8
- Think Outside the Book, #9
- Visualize It!, #10
- Active Reading (Annotation strategy), #11
- Visualize It!, #12

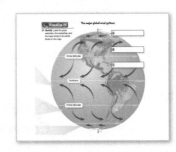

Digital Path

☐ **Global Winds**
Explore the Easterlies, Westerlies, and Trade Winds.

☐ **Jet Streams**
Learn about the jet streams and their effects.

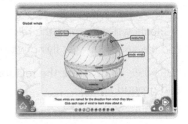

Local Winds

Print Path

☐ **Feelin' Breezy,** SE pp. 140–141
- Active Reading (Annotation strategy), #16
- Visualize It!, #17
- Visualize It!, #18

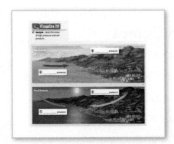

Digital Path

☐ **Local Winds**
Explore how local wind patterns form.

Differentiated Instruction

Basic *Trade Winds and Travel*

Synthesizing Key Topics

 individuals
🕐 varied

Investigate Have students look up how sailors in the past used the trade winds to help them reach their various destinations. Ask students to take notes about what routes sailors took to use the trade winds and how lack of modern technologies made travel on the oceans more difficult. Students should share the details of their research in a class discussion.

Basic *Illustrated Sea Breezes*

Local Winds

 small groups
🕐 varied

Posters Have students work in groups to design posters illustrating the formation of a sea breeze. Posters should show temperature differences and wind direction, which are both essential elements to the formation of a sea breeze. Groups should then explain the processes illustrated in their posters.

Advanced *Beyond the Book*

Global Winds

 small groups
🕐 varied

Oral Presentation Explain to students that sometimes low-level jet streams form much closer to Earth than normal jet streams, which occur at the upper level of the troposphere. Have students research the conditions under which a low-level jet stream may form. Students should present their findings, including visual aids, to the class as a group.

ELL *Wind Vocabulary Words*

Synthesizing Key Topics

 individuals
🕐 varied

Vocabulary Cards Have ELL students create flash cards for vocabulary words. Students should write the word on the front of the card. Ask students to draw a picture on the back of the card that will help them remember the meaning of the word. Ask students to practice saying the word aloud, and correct any errors in pronunciation.

Lesson Vocabulary

wind   Coriolis effect   global wind

jet stream   local wind

Previewing Vocabulary

 individuals   🕐 15 min

Magnet Words Provide each student with three Magnet Word handouts. On the overhead, model filling out the Magnet Word sheet for the first vocabulary term. Then ask students to complete the remaining handouts for two other vocabulary words. Ask students to volunteer phrases from their individual sheets to create a comprehensive overview of each term.

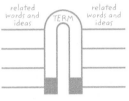

Reinforcing Vocabulary

 individuals   🕐 ongoing

Four Square To help students fully understand the vocabulary words, have them complete a Four Square for each term. Four Square sheets will include the word, a definition, characteristics, examples, and nonexamples.

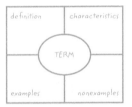

🌐 *Optional Online resource: Four Square support*

Customize Your Core Lesson

Core Instruction

☐ **Print Path** choices

☐ **Digital Path** choices

Vocabulary

☐ **Previewing Vocabulary** Magnet Words

☐ **Reinforcing Vocabulary** Four Square

Your Resources

Differentiated Instruction

☐ **Basic** Trade Winds and Travel

☐ **Basic** Illustrated Sea Breezes

☐ **Advanced** Beyond the Book

☐ **ELL** Wind Vocabulary Words

Extend Science Concepts

Reinforce and Review

Activity *Trivia Game*

Synthesizing Key Topics   whole class
   🕐 25–30 min

Wind Trivia Separate the class into two teams and arrange chairs so that each team is sitting in a circle. Walk back and forth between the two teams, posing questions to each one. Starting with the student closest to you, go around the circles and ask questions, one at a time, so that each student has a chance to answer. If a student answers a question correctly, he or she earns a point for the team. If a student answers incorrectly, ask the other team the same question as a toss-up, meaning students on the team can discuss the question briefly and elect a person to provide the agreed-upon answer. Consider offering an incentive to the winning team, such as an extra point on a test or a classroom prize.

Graphic Organizer

Synthesizing Key Topics   whole class
   🕐 ongoing

Cluster Diagram Place a Cluster Diagram on the overhead projector and write the word *wind* in the center. Provide students with blank copies of the Cluster Diagram. Ask students to volunteer words and phrases to fill in the bubbles of the Cluster Diagram. Students should fill in the words on their handouts as you fill in the words on the overhead.

🔘 *Optional Online resource: Cluster Diagram support*

Going Further

Astronomy Connection

The Movement of Air   small groups
   🕐 varied

Organize Data Tell students that Earth is not the only planet with wind. Other planets in our solar system also have winds. Some blow hard enough to blow a hot air balloon across the U.S. in under 30 minutes. Some can attain temperatures hot enough to  melt rocks. Have student groups look up information about winds on two of the eight planets: Mercury, Venus, Earth, Mars, Jupiter, Saturn, Uranus, and Neptune. Have students record information on average wind speed, average wind temperature, and other interesting facts about winds on these planets. Then have each student create a Two-Panel Flipchart FoldNote to compare the characteristics of the winds on the two different planets.

🔘 *Online resource: Two-Panel Flip Chart support*

Environmental Science Connection

Synthesizing Key Topics   whole class
   🕐 varied

Wind Power Tell students that environmental scientists have designed machines that can produce electricity using the power of the wind. **Ask:** Have you ever seen a giant structure with long blades that spin in the air? These structures are called wind turbines. Their blades spin with the power of wind, generating electricity for use in a community. Discuss the benefits and limitations of wind power with students.

Customize Your Closing

 See the Assessment Guide for quizzes and tests.

🔘 *Go Online to edit and create quizzes and tests.*

Reinforce and Review

- ☐ **Activity** Trivia Game
- ☐ **Graphic Organizer** Cluster Diagram
- ☐ **Print Path** Visual Summary, SE p. 142
- ☐ **Print Path** Lesson Review, SE p. 143
- ☐ **Digital Path** Lesson Closer

Evaluate Student Mastery

See the teacher support below the Student Pages for additional Formative Assessment questions.

Ask: How does temperature affect winds all over the globe? Sample answer: The temperature of air affects its movement. As air heats, air molecules begin to move more quickly and farther apart. Hot air, which is less dense, begins to rise into the atmosphere. As the air rises, it begins to cool. As air molecules in cold air pack more closely, the dense air begins to sink. The cold air sinks to Earth's surface. Sinking, cold, dense air causes an area of high pressure. This denser air moves to areas where the air pressure is lower. The moving air is wind.

Reteach

Formative assessment may show that students need reinforcement for certain topics. The resources below are recommended for reteaching. If students were introduced to a topic through the Print Path, you can also use the Digital Path to reteach, and vice versa.

🎧 *Can be assigned to individual students*

The Movement of Air
Discussion Studying the Wind 🎧

Daily Demo Air Pressure and Wind

Global Winds
Activity Understanding Global Winds 🎧

Quick Lab Flying with the Jet Stream

Local Winds
Activity Wind Direction 🎧

Alternative Assessment
Wind Formation

🔘 *Online resources: student worksheet, optional rubrics*

Wind in the Atmosphere

Points of View: *Wind Formation*
Your class will work together to show what you've learned about wind in the atmosphere from several different viewpoints.

1. Work in groups as assigned by your teacher. Each group will be assigned to one or two viewpoints.

2. Complete your assignment, and present your perspective to the class.

 Vocabulary Write sentences to show what you know about wind formation. Use these terms in your sentences: *Coriolis effect, convection cells,* and *global pressure belts.*

 Illustrations Show how convection cells in Earth's atmosphere cause high- and low-pressure belts at Earth's surface.

 Analysis Describe how global wind systems are affected by global pressure belts and the Coriolis effect.

 Observations Spend some time outside making observations about the wind. Then use what you already know to decide whether your area is affected by sea and land breezes, valley and mountain breezes, or other local winds.

 Details Explain what wind is, sources of energy that cause atmospheric movement, why air moves, how convection cells affect wind, and the Coriolis effect.

Going Further
- ☐ Astronomy Connection
- ☐ Environmental Science Connection
- ☐ Print Path Why It Matters, SE p. 139

Your Resources

Formative Assessment
- ☐ Strategies Throughout TE
- ☐ Lesson Review SE

Summative Assessment
- ☐ Alternative Assessment Wind Formation
- ☐ Lesson Quiz
- ☐ Unit Tests A and B
- ☐ Unit Review SE End-of-Unit

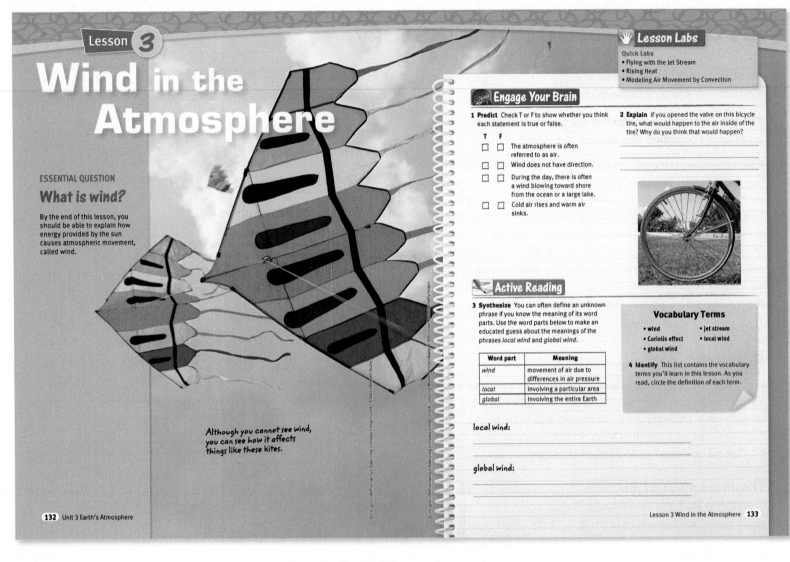

Lesson ③

Wind in the Atmosphere

ESSENTIAL QUESTION

What is wind?

By the end of this lesson, you should be able to explain how energy provided by the sun causes atmospheric movement, called wind.

Although you cannot see wind, you can see how it affects things like these kites.

132 Unit 3 Earth's Atmosphere

Lesson Labs

Quick Labs
• Flying with the Jet Stream
• Rising Heat
• Modeling Air Movement by Convection

Engage Your Brain

1 Predict Check T or F to show whether you think each statement is true or false.

T F
☐ ☐ The atmosphere is often referred to as air.
☐ ☐ Wind does not have direction.
☐ ☐ During the day, there is often a wind blowing toward shore from the ocean or a large lake.
☐ ☐ Cold air rises and warm air sinks.

2 Explain If you opened the valve on this bicycle tire, what would happen to the air inside of the tire? Why do you think that would happen?

_____
_____

Active Reading

3 Synthesize You can often define an unknown phrase if you know the meaning of its word parts. Use the word parts below to make an educated guess about the meanings of the phrases *local wind* and *global wind*.

Word part	Meaning
wind	movement of air due to differences in air pressure
local	involving a particular area
global	involving the entire Earth

local wind:
_____

global wind:
_____

Vocabulary Terms

• wind   • jet stream
• Coriolis effect   • local wind
• global wind

4 Identify This list contains the vocabulary terms you'll learn in this lesson. As you read, circle the definition of each term.

Lesson 3 Wind in the Atmosphere 133

Answers

Answers for 1–3 should represent students' current thoughts, even if incorrect.

1. T; F; T; F

2. Sample answer: The air would come rushing out of the tire because the air is under higher pressure in the tire.

3. Sample answers: the movement of air in a particular area; the movement of air across Earth

4. Students' annotations will vary.

Opening Your Lesson

Discuss students' answers to items 1 and 2 to assess students' preconceptions and prerequisite knowledge, and to estimate what they already know about the key topics.

Preconceptions Students may think of the word *local* as relating specifically to a nearby community and the wind as a force that forms and dissipates within a small area.

Prerequisites Students should already know the four layers of the atmosphere; that changes in air pressure are caused by gravity's pull on gas molecules; that solar energy is responsible for changes in air temperature; and how specific heat capacity influences differences in temperature between air, water, and land.

Interpreting Visuals

Have students study the photograph of the kites. Point out that the kites are flying at different heights in the atmosphere. Invite students to offer ideas about how the different heights might affect the kites differently. Sample answer: The air might be moving faster or slower at different heights, causing the kite to move faster or slower; the air might be warmer or cooler (higher or lower density) at different heights, causing the air to put more or less pressure on the kite.

Blow It Out!

What causes wind?

The next time you feel the wind blowing, you can thank the sun! The sun does not warm the whole surface of the Earth in a uniform manner. This uneven heating causes the air above Earth's surface to be at different temperatures. Cold air is more dense than warmer air is. Colder, denser air sinks. When denser air sinks, it places greater pressure on the surface of Earth than warmer, less-dense air does. This results in areas of higher air pressure. Air moves from areas of higher pressure toward areas of lower pressure. The movement of air caused by differences in air pressure is called **wind**. The greater the differences in air pressure, the faster the air moves.

Areas of High and Low Pressure

Cold, dense air at the poles creates areas of high pressure at the poles. Warm, less-dense air at the equator forms an area of lower pressure. This pressure gradient results in global movement of air. However, instead of moving in one circle between the equator and the poles, air moves in smaller circular patterns called *convection cells*, shown below. As air moves from the equator, it cools and becomes more dense. At about 30°N and 30°S latitudes, a high-pressure belt results from the sinking of air. Near the poles, cold air warms as it moves away from the poles. At around 60°N and 60°S latitudes, a low-pressure belt forms as the warmed air is pushed upward.

Active Reading

6 Identify As you read, underline how air movement in the Northern Hemisphere is influenced by the Coriolis effect.

How does Earth's rotation affect wind?

Pressure differences cause air to move between the equator and the poles. If Earth was not rotating, winds would blow in a straight line. However, winds are deflected, or curved, due to Earth's rotation, as shown below. The apparent curving of the path of a moving object from an otherwise straight path due to Earth's rotation is called the **Coriolis effect** (kawr•ee•OH•lis ih•FEKT). This effect is most noticeable over long distances.

Because each point on Earth makes one complete rotation every day, points closer to the equator must travel farther and, therefore, faster than points closer to the poles do. When air moves from the equator toward the North Pole, it maintains its initial speed and direction. If the air travels far enough north, it will have traveled farther east than a point on the ground beneath it. As a result, the air appears to follow a curved path toward the east. Air moving from the North Pole to the equator appears to curve to the west because the air moves east more slowly than a point on the ground beneath it does. Therefore, in the Northern Hemisphere, air moving to the north curves to the east and air moving to the south curves to the west.

Visualize It!

5 Identify In the white oval area on the map, draw the convection cell that was left out. Use a pencil to indicate warm air and a pen to indicate cool air.

The warming and cooling of air produces pressure belts every 30° of latitude.

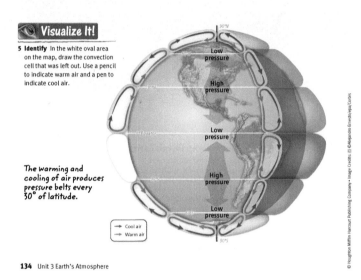

Visualize It!

7 Label In the white ovals on the map, draw the direction and path of the winds that would occur at those locations on Earth.

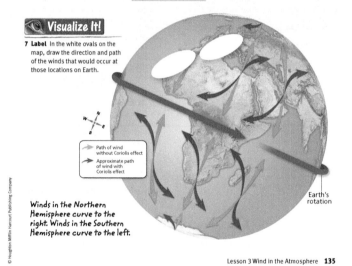

Path of wind without Coriolis effect

Approximate path of wind with Coriolis effect

Winds in the Northern Hemisphere curve to the right. Winds in the Southern Hemisphere curve to the left.

Earth's rotation

Answers

5. Drawings should indicate a convection cell with cool air sinking at 30°S, where it warms and moves back to the equator, and then rises and cools.

6. *See students' pages for annotations.*

7. Drawings should indicate that winds blowing to the north curve to the east and winds blowing to the south curve to the west.

Building Reading Skills

Main Idea Web Have students complete a Main Idea Web after reading "What causes wind?" Instruct students to write the main idea of this section in the middle of the web and then provide details that support the main idea in each of the boxes stemming from the middle.

○ *Optional Online resource: Main Idea Web support*

Probing Questions DIRECTED Inquiry

Predicting How do you think the movement of air would be different if Earth did not rotate? Sample answer: Winds would move straight across Earth instead of curving in a different direction from their intended path.

Blowin' Around

What are examples of global winds?

Recall that air travels in circular patterns called convection cells that cover approximately 30° of latitude. Pressure belts at every 30° of latitude and the Coriolis effect produce patterns of calm areas and wind systems. These wind systems occur at or near Earth's surface and are called **global winds**. As shown at the right, the major global wind systems are the *polar easterlies* (EE•ster•leez), the *westerlies* (WES•ter•leez), and the *trade winds*. Winds such as polar easterlies and westerlies are named for the direction from which they blow. Calm areas include the doldrums and the horse latitudes.

Active Reading

8 Explain If something is being carried by westerlies, what direction is it moving toward?

_____

Think Outside the Book *Inquiry*

9 Model Winds are described according to their direction and speed. Research wind vanes and what they are used for. Design and build your own wind vane.

Trade Winds

The trade winds blow between 30° latitude and the equator in both hemispheres. The rotation of Earth causes the trade winds to curve to the west. Therefore, trade winds in the Northern Hemisphere come from the northeast, and trade winds in the Southern Hemisphere come from the southeast. These winds became known as the trade winds because sailors relied on them to sail from Europe to the Americas.

Westerlies

The westerlies blow between 30° and 60° latitudes in both hemispheres. The rotation of Earth causes these winds to curve to the east. Therefore, westerlies in the Northern Hemisphere come from the southwest, and westerlies in the Southern Hemisphere come from the northwest. The westerlies can carry moist air over the continental United States, producing rain and snow.

Polar Easterlies

The polar easterlies blow between the poles and 60° latitude in both hemispheres. The polar easterlies form as cold, sinking air moves from the poles toward 60°N and 60°S latitudes. The rotation of Earth causes these winds to curve to the west. In the Northern Hemisphere, polar easterlies can carry cold Arctic air over the majority of the United States, producing snow and freezing weather.

© Houghton Mifflin Harcourt Publishing Company

© Houghton Mifflin Harcourt Publishing Company

Visualize It!

10 Identify Label the polar easterlies, the westerlies, and the trade winds in the white boxes on the map.

The major global wind systems

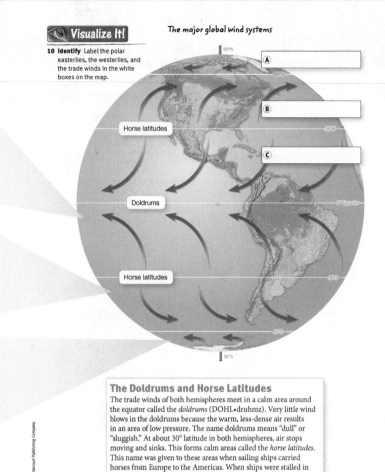

Horse latitudes

Doldrums

Horse latitudes

A

B

C

The Doldrums and Horse Latitudes

The trade winds of both hemispheres meet in a calm area around the equator called the *doldrums* (DOHL•druhmz). Very little wind blows in the doldrums because the warm, less-dense air results in an area of low pressure. The name doldrums means "dull" or "sluggish." At about 30° latitude in both hemispheres, air stops moving and sinks. This forms calm areas called the *horse latitudes*. This name was given to these areas when sailing ships carried horses from Europe to the Americas. When ships were stalled in these areas, horses were sometimes thrown overboard to save water.

136 Unit 3 Earth's Atmosphere

Lesson 3 Wind in the Atmosphere **137**

Answers

8. It is moving toward the east. Student answers may specify northeast or southeast.

9. Answers will vary. This research should help introduce students to the idea of measuring wind direction and strength. It also provides students with hands-on practice, using a weather vane that they build themselves.

10. A: polar easterlies; B: westerlies; C: trade winds

Formative Assessment

Ask: Why are the winds different every 30° latitude across the globe? Sample answer: The changes in air pressure occur every 30° latitude, creating different conditions for wind to form. **Ask:** How does the rotation of Earth affect the different types of global winds? Sample answer: Trade winds traveling northeast and southeast both curve to the west; westerlies traveling northwest and southwest both curve to the east; polar easterlies traveling northeast and southeast; both curve to the west.

Learning Alert

Westerlies and Polar Easterlies Students may mistakenly believe that westerlies and polar easterlies are named after the direction in which they travel instead of the direction from which they come. Draw a compass on the board, and draw and label arrows showing the directions in which each type of wind moves.

Probing Questions GUIDED *Inquiry*

Inferring Why is the air in most regions along the equator less dense than the air at other latitudes? How might this affect the weather at the equator? Sample answer: The air at the equator is less dense because it is warmer than the air at other latitudes. This probably means that weather in this area is hot and not very windy.

The Jet Streams

11 Identify As you read, underline the direction that the jet streams travel.

A flight from Seattle to Boston can be 30 min faster than a flight from Boston to Seattle. Why? Pilots can take advantage of a jet stream. **Jet streams** are narrow belts of high-speed winds that blow from west to east, between 7 km and 16 km above Earth's surface. Airplanes traveling in the same direction as a jet stream go faster than those traveling in the opposite direction of a jet stream. When an airplane is traveling "with" a jet stream, the wind is helping the airplane move forward. However, when an airplane is traveling "against" the jet stream, the wind is making it more difficult for the plane to move forward.

The two main jet streams are the polar jet stream and the subtropical (suhb•TRAHP•i•kuhl) jet stream, shown below. Each of the hemispheres experiences these jet streams. Jet streams follow boundaries between hot and cold air and can shift north and south. In the winter, as Northern Hemisphere temperatures cool, the polar jet stream moves south. This shift brings cold Arctic air to the United States. When temperatures rise in the spring, this jet stream shifts to the north.

Visualize It!

12 Identify Label the polar jet stream and the subtropical jet stream in the Northern Hemisphere.

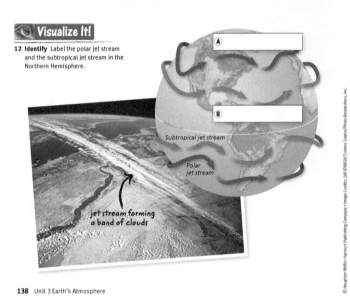

Subtropical jet stream

Polar jet stream

jet stream forming a band of clouds

138 Unit 3 Earth's Atmosphere

Why It Matters

EYE ON THE ENVIRONMENT

Desert Trades

How does some of the Sahara end up in the Americas? Global winds carry it.

Trade Wind Carriers
Trade winds can carry Saharan dust across the Atlantic Ocean to Florida and the Caribbean.

Florida Meets the Sahara
This hazy skyline in Miami is the result of a dust storm. Where did the dust come from? It all started in the Sahara.

Africa

The Sahara
The Sahara is the world's largest hot desert. Sand and dust storms that produce skies like this are very common in this desert.

Extend
Inquiry

13 Explain Look at a map and explain how trade winds carry dust from the Sahara to the Caribbean.

14 Relate Investigate the winds that blow in your community. Where do they usually come from? Identify the wind system that could be involved.

15 Apply Investigate how winds played a role in distributing radioactive waste that was released after an explosion at the Chernobyl Nuclear Power Plant in Ukraine. Present your findings as a map illustration or in a poster.

139

Answers

11. *See students' pages for annotations.*

12. A: polar; B: subtropical

13. Sample answer: The Sahara extends across North Africa near 30°N. In this area, trade winds blow from east to west. Trade winds pick up dust, then carry it to the west and over the Atlantic Ocean toward the Caribbean.

14. Answers will vary with location. For the continental United States, it will be the westerlies or trade winds.

15. Answers should show the spread of radioactivity across at least western Russia and parts of Europe.

Learning Alert

Jet Streams The airplane example in the textbook may guide students to believe that the jet stream begins much higher in the atmosphere than is actually true. Explain to students that jet streams begin at around 20,000 ft (6 to 9 mi) above Earth's surface. This makes them accessible to hot-air ballooners and occasionally to some birds.

Formative Assessment

Ask: Why is it faster to fly in some directions than others? Sample answer: Pilots can sometimes take advantage of the jet stream, which is a high-speed wind that helps them go faster. **Ask:** What are westerlies and polar easterlies? They are global winds. **Ask:** What causes them to curve? the Coriolis effect

Why It Matters

Trade winds actually contribute to the dryness of deserts such as the Sahara. These hot winds prevent moist clouds from forming over the desert, creating an unprotected area fully exposed to the sun. The constant direct sunlight keeps the desert environment very hot and dry. Most of the world's deserts are located between the equator and 30° latitude, in the area of Earth where trade winds blow.

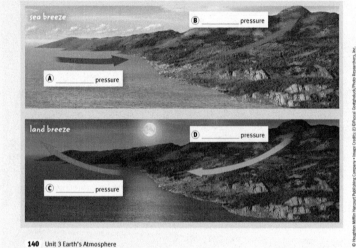

What are examples of local winds?

Active Reading

16 Identify As you read, underline two examples of geographic features that contribute to the formation of local winds.

Local geographic features, such as a body of water or a mountain, can produce temperature and pressure differences that cause local winds. Unlike global winds, local winds are the movement of air over short distances. They can blow from any direction, depending on the features of the area.

Sea and Land Breezes

Have you ever felt a cool breeze coming off the ocean or a lake? If so, you were experiencing a sea breeze. Large bodies of water take longer to warm up than land does. During the day, air above land becomes warmer than air above water. The colder, denser air over water flows toward the land and pushes the warm air on the land upward. While water takes longer to warm than land does, land cools faster than water does. At night, cooler air on land causes a higher-pressure zone over the land. So, a wind blows from the land toward the water. This type of local wind is called a land breeze.

Visualize It!

17 Analyze Label the areas of high pressure and low pressure.

sea breeze

B _____ pressure

A _____ pressure

land breeze

D _____ pressure

C _____ pressure

140 Unit 3 Earth's Atmosphere

Valley and Mountain Breezes

Areas that have mountains and valleys experience local winds called mountain and valley breezes. During the day, the sun warms the air along the mountain slopes faster than the air in the valleys. This uneven heating results in areas of lower pressure near the mountain tops. This pressure difference causes a valley breeze, which flows from the valley up the slopes of the mountains. Many birds float on valley breezes to conserve energy. At nightfall, the air along the mountain slopes cools and moves down into the valley. This local wind is called a mountain breeze.

Visualize It!

18 Analyze Label the areas of high pressure and low pressure.

valley breeze

B _____ pressure

A _____ pressure

mountain breeze

D _____ pressure

C _____ pressure

Lesson 3 Wind in the Atmosphere 141

Answers

16. *See students' pages for annotations.*

17. sea breeze: A: high pressure B: low pressure; land breeze: C: low pressure; D: high pressure

18. valley breeze: A: high pressure; B: low pressure; mountain breeze: C: low pressure; D: high pressure

Interpreting Visuals

Have students examine the illustrations of valley and mountain breezes. Remind students that breezes travel from areas of higher pressure to areas of lower pressure. Ask students to explain what the arrows are indicating. Sample answer: The arrows are indicating the direction that the breezes are traveling. They are moving from areas of higher pressure—that is, colder air—to areas of lower pressure. If the mountain slope heats faster than the valley during the day, creating lower pressure, and cools faster than the valley at night, creating higher pressure, what can you determine about the temperatures in the valley and the temperatures on the mountain slope? Sample answer: The temperatures in the valley don't change as much; the temperatures are less extreme. On the mountain slope, temperatures change a great deal and are more extreme than temperatures in the valley.

Probing Questions GUIDED Inquiry

Inferring What type of weather might a sea breeze carry onto land? Why? Sample answer: wet weather, such as rain, because the breeze collects moisture as it passes over the ocean; temperature change, because the air over water can be warmer or colder than the air over land

Visual Summary

To complete this summary, circle the correct word or phrases. Then use the key below to check your answers. You can use this page to review the main concepts of the lesson.

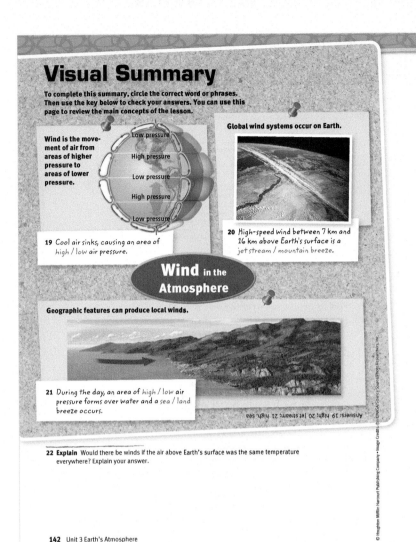

Wind is the movement of air from areas of higher pressure to areas of lower pressure.

Low pressure
High pressure
Low pressure
High pressure
Low pressure

19 Cool air sinks, causing an area of *high / low* air pressure.

Global wind systems occur on Earth.

20 High-speed wind between 7 km and 16 km above Earth's surface is a *jet stream / mountain breeze.*

Wind in the Atmosphere

Geographic features can produce local winds.

21 During the day, an area of *high / low* air pressure forms over water and a *sea / land* breeze occurs.

Answers: 19 high; 20 jet stream; 21 high, sea

22 Explain Would there be winds if the air above Earth's surface was the same temperature everywhere? Explain your answer.

142 Unit 3 Earth's Atmosphere

© Houghton Mifflin Harcourt Publishing Company • Image Credits: (b) ©NASA/Science Source/Photo Researchers, Inc.

Lesson Review

Vocabulary

Fill in the blanks with the term that best completes the following sentences.

1 Another term for air movement caused by differences in air pressure is

2 Pilots often take advantage of the _____, which are high-speed winds between 7 km and 16 km above Earth's surface.

3 The apparent curving of winds due to Earth's rotation is the _____

Key Concepts

4 Explain How does the sun cause wind?

5 Predict If Earth did not rotate, what would happen to the global winds? Why?

6 Explain How do convection cells in Earth's atmosphere cause high- and low-pressure belts?

7 Describe What factors contribute to global winds? Identify areas where winds are weak.

8 Identify Name a latitude where each of the following occurs: polar easterlies, westerlies, and trade winds.

Critical Thinking

9 Predict How would local winds be affected if water and land absorbed and released heat at the same rate? Explain your answer.

10 Compare How is a land breeze similar to a sea breeze? How do they differ?

Use this image to answer the following questions.

11 Analyze What type of local wind would you experience if you were standing in the valley? Explain your answer.

12 Infer Would the local wind change if it was nighttime? Explain.

© Houghton Mifflin Harcourt Publishing Company

Lesson 3 Wind in the Atmosphere 143

Visual Summary Answers

19. high

20. jet stream

21. high; sea

22. If the air above Earth's surface was a uniform temperature, there would not be differences in air density. Therefore, areas of differing air pressure would not occur. Because wind is the movement of air from areas of higher pressure to areas of lower pressure, it means there would not be any global winds.

Lesson Review Answers

1. wind

2. jet streams

3. Coriolis effect

4. The uneven heating of Earth's surface by the sun causes differences in air temperature and density. This forms areas of different air pressure, which causes wind.

5. The global winds would only travel north and south between the equator and the poles due to lack of Coriolis effect.

6. Convection cells from rising and sinking of air create high-pressure belts at 90° and 30° north and south, and low-pressure belts at the equator and 60° north and south.

7. Convection cells and pressure belts cause wind, and the Coriolis effect causes winds to follow curved paths over long distances. Winds are weak at the equator and at 30°N and 30°S latitude.

8. Sample answer: easterlies: 75°N; westerlies: 45°N; trade winds: 20°N

9. This would eliminate or reduce local winds.

10. Both occur near water. Land breezes occur at night and move from land to water. Sea breezes occur during the day and move from water to land.

11. A valley breeze; moves up the slope (high to low pressure) during the day.

12. Yes, mountain breeze, from mountain top to the valley (high to low pressure) would occur.

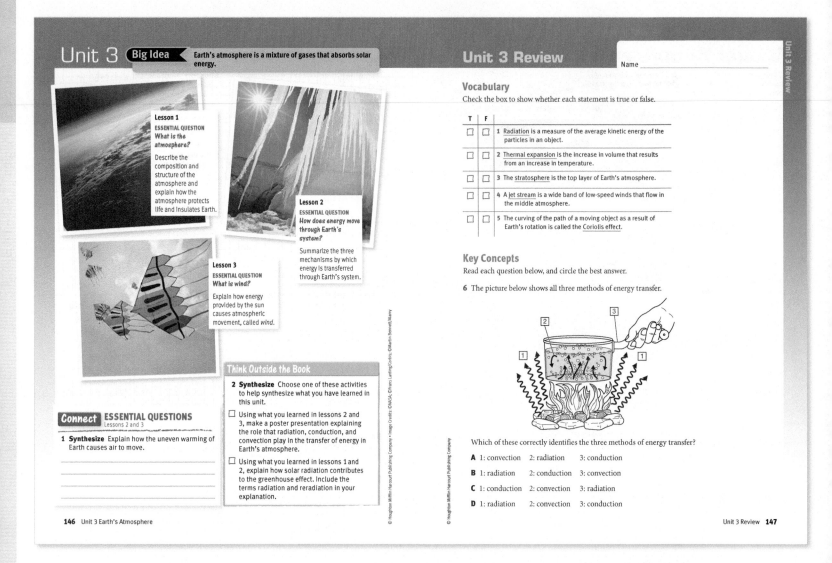

Unit 3   Big Idea   Earth's atmosphere is a mixture of gases that absorbs solar energy.

Lesson 1
ESSENTIAL QUESTION
What is the atmosphere?
Describe the composition and structure of the atmosphere and explain how the atmosphere protects life and insulates Earth.

Lesson 2
ESSENTIAL QUESTION
How does energy move through Earth's system?
Summarize the three mechanisms by which energy is transferred through Earth's system.

Lesson 3
ESSENTIAL QUESTION
What is wind?
Explain how energy provided by the sun causes atmospheric movement, called *wind*.

Connect ESSENTIAL QUESTIONS Lessons 2 and 3

1 Synthesize Explain how the uneven warming of Earth causes air to move.

Think Outside the Book

2 Synthesize Choose one of these activities to help synthesize what you have learned in this unit.

☐ Using what you learned in lessons 2 and 3, make a poster presentation explaining the role that radiation, conduction, and convection play in the transfer of energy in Earth's atmosphere.

☐ Using what you learned in lessons 1 and 2, explain how solar radiation contributes to the greenhouse effect. Include the terms radiation and reradiation in your explanation.

146   Unit 3 Earth's Atmosphere

Unit 3 Review   Name _____

Vocabulary
Check the box to show whether each statement is true or false.

T	F	
☐	☐	**1** Radiation is a measure of the average kinetic energy of the particles in an object.
☐	☐	**2** Thermal expansion is the increase in volume that results from an increase in temperature.
☐	☐	**3** The stratosphere is the top layer of Earth's atmosphere.
☐	☐	**4** A jet stream is a wide band of low-speed winds that flow in the middle atmosphere.
☐	☐	**5** The curving of the path of a moving object as a result of Earth's rotation is called the Coriolis effect.

Key Concepts
Read each question below, and circle the best answer.

6 The picture below shows all three methods of energy transfer.

Which of these correctly identifies the three methods of energy transfer?

A 1: convection   2: radiation   3: conduction

B 1: radiation   2: conduction   3: convection

C 1: conduction   2: convection   3: radiation

D 1: radiation   2: convection   3: conduction

Unit 3 Review   147

Unit Summary Answers

1. The sun does not warm Earth's surface uniformly. Uneven warming of Earth's surface causes air pressure to differ from place to place. Air moves as wind across Earth's surface from areas of high pressure to areas of low pressure.

2. Option 1: Poster presentations should include the following: Sunlight warms the ground by the process of *radiation*. The warm ground warms the air above it by the process of *conduction*. In the process of *convection*, cool, dense air sinks downward and pushes warm, less dense air out of the way. The warm air rises and carries energy upward. In addition, students might cite this as an example of thermal expansion.

   Option 2: Radiation from the sun reaches Earth's surface and warms it. The energy as heat is emitted into the atmosphere. Some of this energy escapes into space, but greenhouse gases also trap some of this energy. This energy is reradiated back toward Earth as heat. Note that some students may substitute the term infrared radiation for heat. Heat is the transfer of energy between two objects at different temperatures.

Unit Review   Response to Intervention

A Quick Grading Chart follows the Answers. See the Assessment Guide for more detail about correct and incorrect answer choices. Refer back to the Lesson Planning pages for activities and assignments that can be used as remediation for students who answer questions incorrectly.

Answers

1. False This statement is false because this is the definition of temperature. Radiation is the transfer of energy by electromagnetic waves. (Lesson 2)

2. True This statement is true because thermal expansion does refer to the expansion of an object when its temperature increases. When an object cools down, it contracts. (Lesson 2)

3. False This statement is false because the stratosphere is the second lowest layer of Earth's atmosphere; the thermosphere is the top layer. (Lesson 1)

7 Which of these is not a way in which energy is transferred to Earth from the sun?

A conduction   **C** visible light

B infrared radiation   **D** x-rays

8 A plastic spoon that has a temperature of 78° F is placed into a bowl of soup that has a temperature of 84° F. Which of these correctly describes what will happen?

A Energy as heat moves from the spoon to the soup.

B Energy as heat does not move, because the spoon is plastic.

C Energy as heat moves from the soup to the spoon.

D Energy as heat does not move, because the temperature difference is too small.

9 Refer to the diagram of winds and currents below to answer the question.

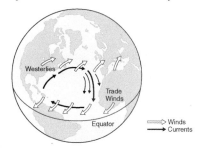

Which of the following best explains the curvature of the arrows for the westerlies and the trade winds?

A The ocean currents create winds flowing in a similar direction to the current.

B The Coriolis effect causes the winds to curve that way because the Earth rotates from left to right.

C The Coriolis effect causes the winds to curve that way because the Earth rotates from right to left.

D The sun is shining and warming the air from the right side of this diagram.

10 An astronomer studying planets outside our solar system has analyzed the atmospheres of four planets. Which of these planets' atmospheres would be most able to support a colony of humans?

A Planet A: 76% Nitrogen, 23% Oxygen, 1% Other

B Planet B: 82% Nitrogen, 11% Oxygen, 7% Other

C Planet C: 78% Nitrogen, 1% Oxygen, 21% Other

D Planet D: 27% Nitrogen, 3% Oxygen, 70% Other

11 Refer to the picture below to answer the question.

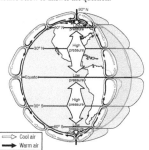

Which of the following is most responsible for the moving bands of air around Earth that are shown in the picture above?

A conduction   **C** Coriolis effect

B convection   **D** greenhouse effect

12 Which of the following describes the general pattern of winds near the equator?

A Winds are generally weak because the equator is a region where low and high air pressure atmospheric bands come together.

B Winds are generally strong because the equator is a region where low and high air pressure atmospheric bands come together.

C Winds are generally strong because the equator is a region of mostly high air pressure.

D Winds are generally weak because the equator is a region of mostly low air pressure.

Answers *(continued)*

4. False This statement is false because a jet stream is a narrow band of high-speed winds that blows in the upper atmosphere. (Lesson 3)

5. True This statement is true because the Coriolis effect does make winds and currents on Earth curve due to the rotation of the Earth. Winds and currents that travel long distances across Earth's surface curve to the right in the Northern Hemisphere and to the left in the Southern Hemisphere. (Lesson 3)

6. Answer D is correct because the flame radiates energy to the pot, convection circulates the boiling water, and conduction moves heat to the handle. (Lesson 2)

7. Answer A is correct because conduction does not transfer energy from the sun to the Earth since conduction requires direct contact between objects. (Lesson 2)

8. Answer C is correct because energy as heat moves from things that are at a higher temperature to things that are at a lower temperature. (Lesson 2)

9. Answer B is correct because the Coriolis effect makes the winds curve to the right from their north-to-south or south-to-north direction in the northern hemisphere. (Lesson 3)

10. Answer A is correct because this composition is the closest one to Earth's atmosphere. (Lesson 1)

11. Answer B is correct because this is showing convection cells around the globe. (Lesson 2)

12. Answer D is correct because this describes the area near the equator sometimes called the doldrums. (Lesson 3)

13. Key Elements:
    - draws an arrow pointing in towards land
    - correctly explains that the movement of wind is from higher air pressure to lower air pressure and correctly names sea breeze (Lesson 3)

14. Key Elements:
    - correctly names the troposphere and describes that the temperature and air pressure both decrease rapidly while moving up

Quick Grading Chart

Use the chart below for quick test grading. The lesson correlations can help you target reteaching for missed items.

Item	Answer	Cognitive Complexity	Lesson
1.	—	Low	2
2.	—	Low	2
3.	—	Low	1
4.	—	Low	3
5.	—	Low	3
6.	D	Low	2
7.	A	Moderate	2
8.	C	Moderate	2
9.	B	Moderate	3
10.	A	Moderate	1
11.	B	Moderate	2
12.	D	Moderate	3
13.	—	Moderate	3
14.	—	High	1
15.	—	High	1–3

Cognitive Complexity refers to the demand on thinking associated with an item, and may vary with the answer choices, the number of steps required to arrive at an answer, and other factors, but not the ability level of the student.

Unit 3 Review continued

Critical Thinking
Answer the following questions in the space provided.

13 The picture below shows a situation that causes local winds.

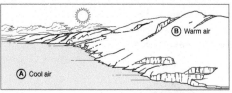
(B) Warm air
(A) Cool air

Draw an arrow on the picture to show which way the wind will blow. Describe why the wind blows in that direction and name this type of local wind.

14 Suppose you were a superhero that could fly up through the atmosphere while feeling the temperature and air pressure change around you. Describe your trip in a paragraph, naming the four main atmospheric layers and telling how the temperature and air pressure change as you pass through each.

Connect ESSENTIAL QUESTIONS
Lessons 1, 2, and 3

Answer the following question in the space provided.

15 Explain how Earth gets energy from the sun and what the atmosphere does with that energy to help life survive on Earth.

150 Unit 3 Earth's Atmosphere

Answers *(continued)*

- correctly names the stratosphere and describes that the temperature rises while the air pressure continues to decrease
- correctly names the mesosphere and describes that the temperature and air pressure both decrease while moving up
- correctly names the thermosphere and describes that the temperature rises again while the air pressure still decreases (Lesson 1)

15. Key Elements:

- names radiation as the method of energy transfer from the sun to Earth
- explains that the atmosphere filters out harmful radiation
- explains that the atmosphere insulates Earth to stabilize temperature
- explains that wind is created by solar energy and convection
- describes how winds in the atmosphere move energy from the sun around Earth (Lesson 1–3)

The Big Idea and Essential Questions

This Unit was designed to focus on this Big Idea and Essential Questions.

Big Idea — Air pressure, temperature, air movement, and humidity in the atmosphere affect both weather and climate.

Lesson	ESSENTIAL QUESTION	Student Mastery	(PD) Professional Development	Lesson Overview
LESSON 1 Elements of Weather	*What is weather and how can we describe different types of weather conditions?*	To describe elements of weather and explain how they are measured	Content Refresher, TE p. 192	TE p. 202
LESSON 2 Clouds and Cloud Formation	*How do clouds form, and how are clouds classified?*	To describe the formation and classification of clouds	Content Refresher, TE p. 193	TE p. 216
LESSON 3 What Influences Weather?	*How do the water cycle and other global patterns affect local weather?*	To explain how global patterns in Earth's system influence weather	Content Refresher, TE p. 194	TE p. 234
LESSON 4 Severe Weather and Weather Safety	*How can humans protect themselves from hazardous weather?*	To describe the major types of hazardous weather and the ways human beings can protect themselves from hazardous weather and from sun exposure	Content Refresher, TE p. 195	TE p. 250
LESSON 5 Weather Maps and Weather Prediction	*What tools do we use to predict weather?*	To understand how meteorologists forecast the weather using weather maps and other data	Content Refresher, TE p. 196	TE p. 266
LESSON 6 Climate	*How is climate affected by energy from the sun and variations on Earth's surface?*	To describe the main factors that affect climate and explain how scientists classify climates	Content Refresher, TE p. 197	TE p. 284
LESSON 7 Climate Change	*What are the causes and effects of climate change?*	To describe climate change and the causes and effects of climate change	Content Refresher, TE p. 198	TE p. 300

©Burton McNeely/Getty Images

 **Professional Development** Science Background

Use the keywords at right to access

- Professional Development from **The NSTA Learning Center**
- **SciLinks** for additional online content appropriate for students and teachers

Keywords
climate
clouds
weather
weather safety

National Science Teachers Association

SCiLINKS.
THE WORLD'S A CLICK AWAY

Options for Instruction

Two parallel paths provide coverage of the Essential Questions, with a strong **Inquiry** strand woven into each. Follow the **Print Path,** the **Digital Path,** or your customized combination of print, digital, and inquiry.

	LESSON 1 Elements of Weather	**LESSON 2** Clouds and Cloud Formation	**LESSON 3** What Influences Weather?
Essential Questions	*What is weather and how can we describe different types of weather conditions?*	*How do clouds form, and how are clouds classified?*	*How do the water cycle and other global patterns affect local weather?*
Key Topics	• Elements of Weather • Measuring Elements of Weather	• Introduction to Clouds • Cloud Formation • Cloud Classification • Fog	• How the Water Cycle Influences Weather • How Patterns in the Atmosphere Affect Weather • How Patterns in the Ocean Influence Weather
Print Path	Teacher Edition pp. 202–214 Student Edition pp. 154–163	Teacher Edition pp. 216–229 Student Edition pp. 164–175	Teacher Edition pp. 234–248 Student Edition pp. 180–193
Inquiry Labs	Lab Manual **Field Lab** Comparing Different Ways to Estimate Wind Speed **Quick Lab** Investigate the Measurement of Rainfall **Quick Lab** Classifying Features of Different Types of Clouds	Lab Manual **Quick Lab** How Does a Cloud Form? **Quick Lab** Out of Thin Air	Lab Manual **Quick Lab** Analyze Weather Patterns **Quick Lab** Coastal Climate Model **Exploration Lab** Modeling El Niño
Digital Path	Digital Path TS661221	Digital Path TS661466	Digital Path TS661222

LESSON 4	LESSON 5	LESSONS 6, 7, and
Severe Weather and Weather Safety	Weather Maps and Weather Prediction	UNIT 4 Unit Projects
How can humans protect themselves from hazardous weather?	**What tools do we use to predict weather?**	*See the next page*
• Hazardous Weather • Safety and Weather	• Introduction to Weather Forecasting • Weather Forecasting Data • Weather Maps • Weather Forecasts	

		Unit Assessment
Teacher Edition pp. 250–264	Teacher Edition pp. 266–280	*See the next page*
Student Edition pp. 194–207	Student Edition pp. 208–221	

Lab Manual **Quick Lab** Sun Protection **Exploration Lab** Preparing for Severe Weather Virtual Lab When Severe Weather Strikes	Lab Manual **Quick Lab** Watching the Weather **Quick Lab** Cloud Cover Virtual Lab Forecasting the Weather
Digital Path TS661510	Digital Path TS661288

Options for Instruction

Two parallel paths provide coverage of the Essential Questions, with a strong **Inquiry** strand woven into each. Follow the **Print Path,** the **Digital Path,** or your customized combination of print, digital, and inquiry.

	LESSON 6 Climate	LESSON 7 Climate Change	UNIT 4 Unit Projects
Essential Questions	**How is climate affected by energy from the sun and variations on Earth's surface?**	**What are the causes and effects of climate change?**	Citizen Science Project **Exit Strategy** Teacher Edition p. 201 Student Edition pp. 152–153
Key Topics	• Climate vs. Weather • Solar Energy and Climate • Other Factors That Affect Climate • Climate Zones	• Natural Climate Change • Climate Change and Human Activity • Reducing Climate Change	

Print Path

Teacher Edition pp. 284–298	Teacher Edition pp. 300–315
Student Edition pp. 224–237	Student Edition pp. 238–253

Inquiry Labs

Lab Manual **Quick Lab** Determining Climate **Quick Lab** … the Sun's Rays **Field Lab** How Land Features Affect Climate	Lab Manual **Quick Lab** Greenhouse Effect **Quick Lab** Graphing Sunspots

Digital Path

Digital Path TS661230	Digital Path TS661645

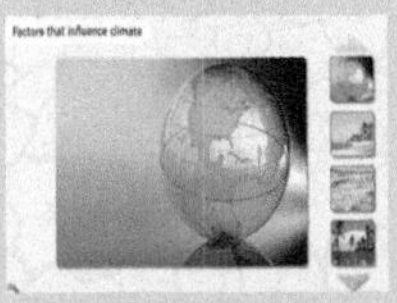

Unit Assessment

Formative Assessment

Strategies RTI
Throughout TE

Lesson Reviews SE

Unit PreTest

Summative Assessment

Alternative Assessment (1 per lesson) RTI

Lesson Quizzes

Unit Tests A and B

Unit Review RTI
(with answer remediation)

Practice Tests (end of module)

Project-Based Assessment

See the Assessment Guide for quizzes and tests.

Go Online to edit and create quizzes and tests.

Response to Intervention

See RTI teacher support materials on p. PD6.

Teacher Notes

Differentiated Instruction

English Language Proficiency

Strategies for **English Language Learners (ELL)** are provided for each lesson, under the Explain tabs.

LESSON 1 *Organizing Ideas,* TE p. 207

LESSON 2 *Cloud Cartoons,* TE p. 221

LESSON 3 *Air Masses and Weather,* TE p. 239

LESSON 4 *Safety Brochure,* TE p. 255

LESSON 5 *Two-Panel Flip Chart,* TE p. 271

LESSON 6 *Key Ideas,* TE p. 289

LESSON 7 *Note Taking,* TE p. 305

Vocabulary strategies provided for all students can also be a particular help for ELL. Use different strategies for each lesson or choose one or two to use throughout the unit. Vocabulary strategies can be found under the Explain tabs for each lesson (TE pp. 207, 221, 239, 255, 271, 289, and 305).

Leveled Inquiry

Inquiry labs, activities, probing questions, and daily demos provide a range of inquiry levels. Preview them under the Engage and Explore tabs starting on TE pp. 204, 218, 236, 252, 268, 286, and 302.

Levels of **Inquiry**

DIRECTED inquiry	**GUIDED** inquiry	**INDEPENDENT** inquiry
introduces inquiry skills within a structured framework.	develops inquiry skills within a supportive environment.	deepens inquiry skills with student-driven questions or procedures.

Each long lab has two inquiry options:

LESSON 1 **Field Lab** *Comparing Different Ways to Estimate Wind Speed*

LESSON 3 **Exploration Lab** *Modeling El Niño*

LESSON 4 **Exploration Lab** *Preparing for Severe Weather*

LESSON 6 **Field Lab** *How Land Features Affect Climate*

Go Digital! thinkcentral.com

Digital Path

The Unit 4 Resource Gateway is your guide to all of the digital resources for this unit. To access the Gateway, visit thinkcentral.com.

Digital Interactive Lessons

Lesson 1 Elements of Weather TS661221

Lesson 2 Clouds and Cloud Formation TS661466

Lesson 3 What Influences Weather? TS661222

Lesson 4 Severe Weather and Weather Safety TS661510

Lesson 5 Weather Prediction and Weather Maps TS661288

Lesson 6 Climate TS661230

Lesson 7 Climate Change TS661645

More Digital Resources

In addition to digital lessons, you will find the following digital resources for Unit 4:

Video-Based Project: Tornado Warning (previewed on TE p. 200)

People in Science: J. Marshall Shepherd

Virtual Labs: When Severe Weather Strikes (previewed on TE p. 253) Forecasting the Weather (previewed on TE p. 269)

RTI ▸ Response to Intervention

Response to Intervention (RTI) is a process for identifying and supporting students who are not making expected progress toward essential learning goals. The following *ScienceFusion* components can be used to provide strategic and intensive intervention.

Component	Location	Strategies and Benefits
STUDENT EDITION Active Reading prompts, Visualize It!, Think Outside the Book	**Throughout each lesson**	Student responses can be used as screening tools to assess whether intervention is needed.
TEACHER EDITION Formative Assessment, Probing Questions, Learning Alerts	**Throughout each lesson**	Opportunities are provided to assess and remediate student understanding of lesson concepts.
TEACHER EDITION Extend Science Concepts	**Reinforce and Review, TE pp. 208, 222, 240, 256, 272, 290, 306** **Going Further, TE pp. 208, 222, 240, 256, 272, 290, 306**	Additional activities allow students to reinforce and extend their understanding of lesson concepts.
TEACHER EDITION Evaluate Student Mastery	**Formative Assessment, TE pp. 209, 223, 241, 257, 273, 291, 307** **Alternative Assessment, TE pp. 209, 223, 241, 257, 273, 291, 307**	These assessments allow for greater flexibility in assessing students with differing physical, mental, and language abilities as well as varying learning and communication modes.
TEACHER EDITION Unit Review Remediation	**Unit Review, TE pp. 316–319**	Includes reference back to Lesson Planning pages for remediation activities and assignments.
INTERACTIVE DIGITAL LESSONS and VIRTUAL LABS	**thinkcentral.com** **Unit 4 Gateway** **Lesson 1 TS661221** **Lesson 2 TS661466** **Lesson 3 TS661222** **Lesson 4 TS661510** **Lesson 5 TS661288** **Lesson 6 TS661230** **Lesson 7 TS661645**	Lessons and labs make content accessible through simulations, animations, videos, audio, and integrated assessment. Useful for review and reteaching of lesson concepts.

Content Refresher

Professional Development

Elements of Weather

ESSENTIAL QUESTION

What is weather and how can we describe different types of weather conditions?

1. Elements of Weather

Weather is the condition of the atmosphere at a given time. Elements of weather are the characteristics we observe and measure. Elements of weather include temperature, humidity, precipitation, air pressure, wind, and visibility.

Precipitation

Precipitation is any form of water that falls to Earth's surface from clouds. Precipitation of any kind originates from a cloud. Precipitation can form when below-freezing temperatures inside a cloud cause water vapor to change into ice crystals. Air temperature determines which type of precipitation falls to Earth's surface.

Relative Humidity

Relative humidity is a ratio of the water vapor in the air to the amount of vapor needed to saturate the air. In other words, relative humidity measures how close the air is to reaching the dew point. For example, at 25 °C, the dew point is reached at 20 g of water vapor per 1 kg of air. If air that is 25 °C holds 5 g of water vapor, the relative humidity is expressed as 5/20, or 25%. Relative humidity increases as vapor enters the air. It also increases if moisture in the air remains constant but the temperature decreases. Conversely, if the temperature increases as the vapor in the air remains constant, the relative humidity will decrease.

2. Measuring Elements of Weather

Instruments used to measure elements of weather include thermometers for air temperature, psychrometers for relative humidity, rain gauges for precipitation, barometers for air pressure, anemometers for wind speed, and wind vanes or windsocks for wind direction.

Measuring Air Pressure

Air pressure is the measure of the force with which air molecules push on a surface. Gravity causes the molecules that make up air to be pulled toward Earth's surface. The weight of air above an area produces the pressure at that location. As altitude increases, air pressure decreases. Meteorologists use barometers to measure air pressure. The type of barometer most commonly used today is called an aneroid barometer. Inside an aneroid barometer is a sealed metal container from which most of the air has been removed to form a partial vacuum. Changes in atmospheric pressure cause the sides of the container to bend inward or bulge out. These changes move a pointer on a scale. Aneroid barometers can keep a continuous record of atmospheric pressure.

Measuring Winds

One way to estimate wind strength without actually using an instrument to measure wind speed is to use the Beaufort wind scale, devised in 1806 by Admiral Sir Francis Beaufort. Originally designed for sailing ships, this scale divides wind speed into 13 levels by observing the effects of winds of different speeds on the sea or on objects on land such as flags, trees, and structures. At force 0 on the scale, the sea is as smooth as a mirror. Force 12 means a hurricane is in progress.

  COMMON MISCONCEPTIONS **RTI**

AIR PRESSURE Students often think that air pressure acts only in a downward direction. They have difficulty with the concept that air pressure exerts an equal force in all directions on objects on Earth's surface.

This misconception is addressed in the Discussion on p. 204.

Lesson 1 Elements of Weather When teaching lessons about weather, I encourage students to write a story, make a video, or draw a comic strip about their most interesting weather experience. In their words, pictures, or reenactments, they need to use the lesson vocabulary and concepts correctly. By choosing their own format, students can showcase their strengths and interests in a fun and educational way.

Lesson 2

Clouds and Cloud Formation
ESSENTIAL QUESTION
How do clouds form, and how are clouds classified?

1. Clouds and Climate

Students will learn about the composition of clouds and explain how clouds affect climate.

A cloud is a collection of small water droplets or ice crystals suspended in the air. Clouds appear white because water droplets or ice crystals within them scatter the light that impinges on them in all directions.

Precipitation, such as rain, hail, sleet, or snow, falls from clouds when the water droplets or ice crystals become too heavy for the air to support. Only certain types of clouds produce precipitation.

Clouds affect Earth's climate in important ways. Clouds high in the atmosphere trap heat that radiates from Earth's surface and keep this heat from escaping into space. Low clouds reflect solar radiation before the radiation reaches Earth's surface.

2. Cloud Formation

Students will learn how clouds form.

Cloud formation, like other processes in the water cycle, depends on solar energy. Solar energy causes water to evaporate from Earth's surface. Water that evaporates rises into the atmosphere and cools, causing clouds to form. Clouds return water to Earth's surface as precipitation in the form of rain, snow, sleet, or hail.

The gaseous state of water is water vapor. Water vapor is present in the air up to approximately 10 km from Earth's surface (the tropopause), and sometimes higher. Water molecules are constantly changing state. If there are more molecules leaving a liquid surface (such as a water droplet) than there are molecules arriving, there is an overall net evaporation. Similarly, if more molecules are arriving than

leaving, there is a net condensation. At a higher temperature, water molecules have more energy and therefore can escape a liquid surface more readily than they can at a lower temperature. At a lower temperature, they have less energy, and therefore can less readily escape the liquid surface. At a certain temperature, called the *dew point*, the rate of evaporation is less than the rate of condensation. As a result, droplets can grow and a cloud may form.

Evaporation is also influenced by the shape of the boundary (molecules can more easily escape from highly curved shapes, such as those of water drops) and whether there are other substances within the droplet. Molecules also escape more readily from liquids than from solids. The presence of condensation nuclei, such as tiny solid particles of dust, soil, or smoke, also contributes to condensation.

Several processes can cause air to rise, expand, and cool. In *frontal lifting*, a mass of warm air advances or is wedged above a mass of cold air. In *orographic lifting*, warm air rises as it is forced upward by an obstacle, such as a mountain.

3. Cloud Classification

Students will learn to classify clouds.

Three basic shapes of clouds are stratus, cumulus, and cirrus. *Stratus* means "layer." Stratus clouds are thin, flat, and have ill-defined edges. They are the lowest clouds and form fog when they appear at Earth's surface. *Cumulus* means "heap." Cumulus clouds are thick and fluffy on top and generally flat on the bottom. Dark, thick cumulus clouds produce stormy weather. *Cirrus* means "curl." Cirrus clouds form high in the atmosphere. They are made of ice crystals and appear white and feathery. They do not produce precipitation that reaches Earth's surface and are associated with calm weather.

Clouds are also classified by altitude. Low clouds form closest to Earth's surface. Middle clouds form between 2,000 m and 6,000 m above Earth's surface. The prefix *alto-* identifies middle clouds. High clouds form above 6,000 m and are made of ice crystals. The prefix *cirro-* identifies high clouds.

Clouds of vertical development may rise high into the atmosphere. Cumulonimbus clouds, which produce thunderstorms, are a common example of these clouds.

Content Refresher (continued)

Professional Development

What Influences Weather?

ESSENTIAL QUESTION

How do the water cycle and other global patterns affect local weather?

1. How the Water Cycle Influences Weather

The sun drives the water cycle, and the water cycle drives weather. The processes of evaporation, condensation, and precipitation make up the water cycle.

The amount of water in the air is measured as humidity. Clouds, fog, and various forms of precipitation can affect visibility.

2. How Patterns in the Atmosphere Affect Weather

Air Masses and Fronts

An air mass tends to take on the temperature and moisture characteristics of the land or water below it. When an air mass moves into a region, it brings temperature and moisture conditions that affect the new location.

Changes in weather are caused by the interaction of air masses. When air masses with different temperature and moisture characteristics meet, a front forms. Fronts are named for the advancing air mass. A cold front occurs when cold air moves under warm air and pushes the warm air up. Thunderstorms, heavy rain, or snow can accompany cold fronts. A warm front occurs when warm air moves over colder air that is leaving an area and often brings drizzly rain. A stationary front forms when warm and cold air masses that have similar air densities move toward each other.

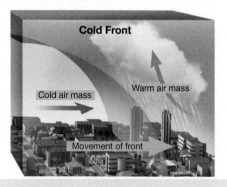

Cold Front

Cold air mass

Warm air mass

Movement of front

Pressure Systems

A high-pressure system forms when an air mass cools. The molecules are pushed closer together, and the air becomes denser and sinks. High-pressure systems often bring dry, clear weather. Low-pressure systems occur when air masses join, rise, and cool, forming clouds, rain, and stormy weather.

Global Winds and Jet Streams

Earth's curvature causes unequal heating of the surface by the sun. Because air moves from areas of high pressure to areas of low pressure, regional wind belts exist. Hot equatorial air rises and produces a low-pressure belt. Cold air near the poles sinks and produces high-pressure belts. Due to the Coriolis effect, wind belts curve in both hemispheres.

The jet stream is a belt of high-speed winds blowing from west to east around the globe in the upper troposphere and lower stratosphere. A jet stream is typically about a few hundred miles wide. Jet streams can form where air masses of different temperatures and air pressures meet. Warm air is less dense than cold air, and these density differences cause air pressure differences. Air moves from areas of high pressure to areas of low pressure, creating wind. The fastest winds, such as the polar jet stream, occur at high altitudes. The polar jet stream can pull cold air down from Canada into the United States and pull warm air up into Canada.

3. How Patterns in the Ocean Influence Weather

Land areas close to large bodies of water usually have moderate temperatures. The reason for these moderate temperatures is that water heats up and cools down more slowly than land does. This affects the temperature of the air and therefore the land near large bodies of water.

The temperature of ocean currents is another factor affecting weather. The surface temperature of ocean water affects the temperature of the air above it. Coastal areas close to warm-water surface currents tend to have warmer weather than inland areas at the same latitude and elevation. Coastal areas near cold surface currents tend to have cooler weather than inland areas at the same latitude and elevation. Wind patterns in an area also affect temperature. A region that receives winds from ocean waters has more moderate temperatures than a similar region in which the winds blow from the land.

Severe Weather and Weather Safety

ESSENTIAL QUESTION

How can humans protect themselves from hazardous weather?

1. Hazardous Weather

Thunderstorms

Thunderstorms develop as warm, moist air rises, and water vapor within the air condenses to form a cumulus cloud. As condensation continues, the cloud rises rapidly and becomes a dark cumulonimbus cloud. Heavy rain and hailstones may fall from the cloud, and lightning may strike. While strong updrafts continue to rise, downdrafts form as air is dragged downward by falling precipitation. Thunderstorms dissipate when strong downdrafts stop air currents from rising, causing the supply of water vapor to decrease.

Hurricanes

A hurricane has wind speeds of more than 119 km/h that spiral in toward an intense low-pressure center. A hurricane develops over tropical oceans. It begins as humid air over the ocean rises rapidly. As moisture in the rising warm air condenses, a large amount of energy in the form of latent heat is released. This energy makes the warm air rise more quickly. A fully developed hurricane consists of a series of thick cumulonimbus cloud bands that spiral upward around the center of the storm. The storm surges that accompany hurricanes can flood vast, low-lying coastal areas. Most deaths during hurricanes are caused by drowning.

Tornadoes

A tornado is a destructive, rotating column of air that has very high wind speeds and that is visible as a funnel-shaped cloud. A tornado forms when a thunderstorm meets high-altitude, horizontal winds. These winds cause the rising air to rotate. A storm cloud may develop a rapidly spinning extension that reaches downward and may or may not touch the ground.

2. Safety and Weather

Thunderstorms

Have a storm preparedness kit. Listen to weather updates. Go or stay indoors. Avoid electrical appliances, running water, metal pipes, and phone lines. If outside, avoid tall objects, stay away from bodies of water, and get into a car, if possible.

Hurricanes

Secure loose objects, doors, and windows. Plan an evacuation route. Listen to weather updates. Stay indoors in a small inner room, closet, or hallway without windows; stay away from areas that may have flying debris or other such dangers.

Tornadoes

Plan a safety route. Listen to weather updates. Go or stay indoors. Go to a basement, storm cellar, or small, inner room that has no windows. Stay away from areas that are likely to have flying debris. If outside, lie in a low area.

Sun and Heat Exposure

Heat exhaustion and heat stroke can occur if you have been in the sun too long. Heat stroke and heat exhaustion can best be prevented by wearing light clothing and drinking water, even if you are not thirsty, when you are active in warm weather.

 COMMON MISCONCEPTIONS

LIGHTNING NEVER STRIKES THE SAME SPOT TWICE A common misconception is that if a lightning strike occurs once in a particular location it will not strike that place again. The misconception, or myth, may be strengthened by the common expression "lightning never strikes twice," meaning that a particular misfortune will only occur once.

This misconception is addressed in the Discussion on p. 252 and on p. 259.

Content Refresher (continued)

Professional Development

Lesson 5

Weather Maps and Weather Prediction

ESSENTIAL QUESTION
What tools do we use to predict weather?

1. Introduction to Weather Forecasting

Students will learn that eight elements of weather are observed and forecast.

Meteorology is the scientific study of Earth's atmosphere. Weather forecasting is the analysis of scientific data to predict likely future weather conditions. Scientists observe eight elements of weather to make forecasts: air temperature, humidity, wind direction, wind speed, cloud types and altitudes, precipitation, atmospheric pressure, and visibility. While meteorologists may forecast weather many days into the future, these predictions are not always accurate.

2. Weather Forecasting Data

Students will learn how scientists collect weather data.

Scientists obtain weather data from surface observations (land stations, ships, and buoys), upper-air observations (balloons and airplanes), remotely sensed observations (satellites and radar), and Numerical Weather Prediction models. Instruments at surface weather observation systems observe the weather just above Earth's surface. These instruments record air temperature, humidity, wind direction, wind speed, cloud height, precipitation, atmospheric pressure, and visibility. Weather balloons collect data from the surface up to 20–30 km into the atmosphere. These balloons carry sensing devices that report air temperature, humidity, atmospheric pressure, and wind data. Aircraft also collect upper air data. Satellites provide information about cloud locations, cloud-top temperatures, and cloud-tracked winds between the surface and an altitude of roughly 10 km. Weather radar finds the location, movement, and intensity of precipitation.

3. Weather Maps

Students will learn about types of weather maps.

Weather maps depict both the current and future states of the atmosphere. Surface weather maps show current weather conditions just above Earth's surface for a large area. These maps are based on information gathered from many surface observation locations. A station model shows the location of a weather-recording location or station. Surrounding this circle are symbols and numbers that represent current weather data. A surface weather map shows air pressure and fronts. Lines called *isobars* connect points of equal or constant pressure and form closed circles that represent areas of high and low pressure. Different symbols show types of fronts.

Upper air charts, created from data collected by weather balloons, portray conditions on a pressure level. A pressure level is an undulating surface that has the same pressure everywhere. The ridges and troughs on an upper air chart are associated with high- and low-pressure systems on Earth's surface. These charts can also be used to determine the location of jet streams.

4. Weather Forecasts

Students will learn that weather forecasts can be short-range, medium-range, and long-range.

In general, shorter forecast periods are more accurate than longer-range forecasts.

Meteorologists can use forecasts from complex computer models (Numerical Weather Prediction) to predict where conditions are right for severe weather. They issue a weather advisory when weather conditions will not be a serious hazard but may cause inconvenience. They issue a weather watch when hazardous weather conditions are possible. People should make preparations, have a plan in place, and get updates from a local radio or television station. Meteorologists issue a weather warning when weather conditions pose a threat to life and property. Examples of weather warnings include extreme wind warnings and flood warnings.

Climate

Essential Question

How is climate affected by energy from the sun and variations on Earth's surface?

1. Climate Versus Weather

Annual Precipitation in Three Climates

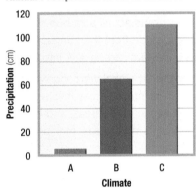

Geography affects climate.

Climate is distinct from weather. Weather denotes conditions from moment to moment, and climate denotes characteristic weather patterns occurring over time.

Some of the geographical factors that affect climate include the following:

- latitude—the distance north or south of the equator
- elevation—the height above sea level
- presence or absence of large bodies of water
- ocean currents, which transfer heat energy between global regions

2. Solar Energy and Climate

Heat from the sun is a key factor of climate.

Energy from the sun hits the equator at the most direct angle. As one moves away from the equator, the sun's energy strikes Earth at less direct angles. The sun's role in the water cycle and air movement also affects climate.

3. Other Factors That Affect Climate

Topography plays a larger role than most realize.

Topography can have just as great an impact as latitude. Mountains may create rain shadows and flat plains allow winds to travel uninterrupted for long distances. As elevation increases, temperature decreases.

Large bodies of water stabilize climate conditions.

Because water heats up and cools down more slowly than land does, it has a stabilizing effect on coastline areas.

Surface currents move warm and cold water.

Like air, water moves in convection currents, meaning cold water moves to places where water is warmer and warm water moves toward colder water. This process affects climate.

4. Climate Zones

Scientists have identified three major climate zones.

Earth is divided into three zones along lines of latitude: polar, temperate, and tropical. Within each zone are subclimates, which are grouped by temperature and precipitation patterns.

 COMMON MISCONCEPTIONS

FREEZING AT THE EQUATOR? Students may assume that all locations along the equator are hot. However, elevation has an enormous impact on temperature; in fact, some equatorial locations at high elevations have fairly chilly average daily temperatures.

This misconception is addressed in the Learning Alert on p. 295.

Content Refresher (continued)

Professional Development

Climate Change

ESSENTIAL QUESTION
What are the causes and effects of climate change?

1. Natural Climate Change

Students will learn the natural factors that have affected climate throughout Earth's history.

Natural climate changes can occur gradually or suddenly. For example, the movement of tectonic plates (large sections of Earth's crust) causes gradual, long-term climate change. Over the past 200 million years, tectonic plate motion caused a huge landmass called *Pangaea* to separate and the continents to move to their present positions. Some continents became warmer, while others, such as Antarctica, became cooler.

Huge volcanic eruptions or asteroid impacts can change Earth's climate relatively suddenly. These events change climate by increasing the amount of particulates in the atmosphere. Particulates are tiny, solid particles suspended in the air. They affect climate by reflecting solar energy back into space and absorbing sunlight, which lowers average temperatures on Earth.

Other natural changes in climate occur in cycles. Sunspot activity varies over an 11-year cycle. El Niño and La Niña are events in the ocean and atmosphere that generally cause year-long changes to climate. These two events tend to occur in an alternating pattern. Ice ages are long periods of cold weather during which ice sheets cover much of Earth. Ice sheets advance and retreat over periods of millions of years.

2. Climate Change and Human Activity

Students will learn how human activity is causing climate change.

The *greenhouse effect* is the process by which greenhouse gases in the atmosphere absorb and reradiate energy as heat back to Earth, which warms Earth's surface and the lower atmosphere.

Greenhouse gases include carbon dioxide, water vapor, methane, and nitrous oxide. In recent years, various human activities have been adding different amounts of greenhouse gases to Earth's atmosphere. Scientists argue that rising levels of greenhouse gases are causing *global warming*, the gradual increase in average global surface temperature.

The burning of fossil fuels and the mass removal of trees, called *deforestation*, are causes of an increasing amount of greenhouse gases. The burning of fossil fuels is a carbon source, meaning it adds carbon dioxide to the atmosphere. Trees and other plants act as a carbon sink, meaning they remove carbon dioxide from the atmosphere. Deforestation converts this important carbon sink into a carbon source.

Scientists predict that global warming will lead to more intense weather. This intensity may involve stronger and more frequent hurricanes in some areas, and longer and more frequent droughts in other areas. Melting glaciers and ice caps could raise global sea levels as much as 60 cm by 2100. Ecosystem changes are also predicted; some species might not adapt as well to the changes and move to geographically different places where conditions are closer to optimal. Higher temperatures and changing rainfall patterns might harm crops.

3. Reducing Climate Change

Students will learn how people can slow the rate of climate change.

Nations, communities, and individuals can all take action to reduce climate change and its effects. Many nations have signed the Kyoto Protocol, agreeing to reduce their carbon dioxide emissions. To fight deforestation, the United Nations began a program called *REDD*, **R**educing **E**missions from **D**eforestation and Forest **D**egradation in Developing Countries.

Clean energy technologies are being researched and used to replace fossil fuels. These technologies include biofuels, solar power, wind power, and water power. Individuals also can take action to reduce greenhouse gases in the atmosphere. Steps individuals can take include recycling waste and reusing products; reducing electricity use; utilizing public transportation, bikes, and carpools; eating locally grown food; and using energy sources that do not release CO_2.

Teacher Notes

Advance Planning

These activities may take extended time or special conditions.

Unit 4

Video-Based Project Tornado Warning, p. 200
multiple activities spanning several lessons

Project Exit Strategy, p. 201
oral presentation and emergency evacuation drill

Graphic Organizers and Vocabulary pp. 207, 208, 221, 222, 239, 240, 255, 256, 271, 272, 289, 290, 305, 306
ongoing with reading

Lesson 1

Activity Tracking Weather, p. 204
record weather data over several days

Activity Weather Tools, p. 204
meteorological instruments

Field Lab Comparing Different Ways to Estimate Wind Speed, p. 205
requires two 45-min periods and outdoor observations

Lesson 2

Activity Charting Clouds, p. 218
record cloud observations and predict weather over one week

Lesson 4

Quick Lab Sun Protection, p. 253
sun-sensitive paper, various sunscreens

Exploration Lab Preparing for Severe Weather, p. 253
requires two 45-min periods

Lesson 6

Field Lab How Land Features Affect Climate, p. 286
requires two 45-min periods and outdoor observations

Differentiated Instruction (Advanced) Climate Data, p. 289
record weather data over two weeks

What Do You Think?

Discuss severe weather and weather safety with students.

Ask: What kinds of severe weather do you know about? Sample answers: hurricanes; tornadoes; thunderstorms; blizzards

Ask: Think about a time when you experienced a severe storm. What was it like? What did you do to stay safe? Sample answer: I remember being in a hurricane. There were strong winds and heavy rain. To stay safe, I stayed inside with my parents.

UNIT 4

Weather and Climate

Strong winds create huge waves that crash on shore.

Big Idea

Air pressure, temperature, air movement, and humidity in the atmosphere affect both weather and climate.

What do you think?

The weather can change very quickly. In severe weather, people and pets can get hurt, and property can be damaged. Can you think of ways to keep people, pets, and property safe?

Warning flags are used to show how safe this beach is.

151

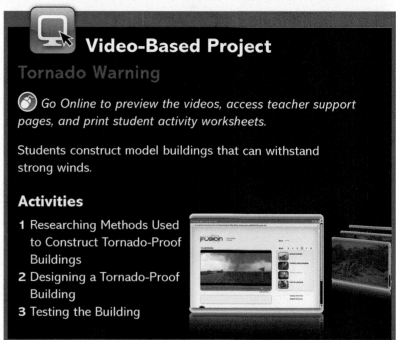

Video-Based Project

Tornado Warning

🔘 *Go Online to preview the videos, access teacher support pages, and print student activity worksheets.*

Students construct model buildings that can withstand strong winds.

Activities

1 Researching Methods Used to Construct Tornado-Proof Buildings

2 Designing a Tornado-Proof Building

3 Testing the Building

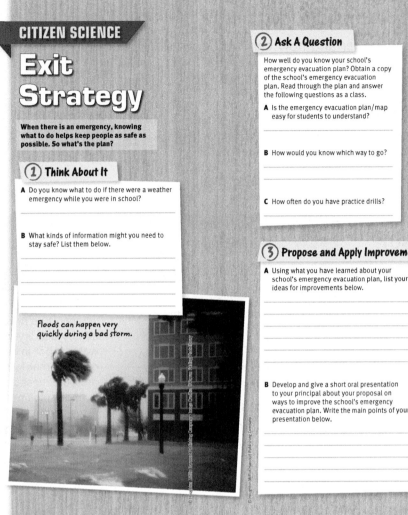

CITIZEN SCIENCE

Exit Strategy

When there is an emergency, knowing what to do helps keep people as safe as possible. So what's the plan?

1 Think About It

A Do you know what to do if there were a weather emergency while you were in school?

B What kinds of information might you need to stay safe? List them below.

Floods can happen very quickly during a bad storm.

2 Ask A Question

How well do you know your school's emergency evacuation plan? Obtain a copy of the school's emergency evacuation plan. Read through the plan and answer the following questions as a class.

A Is the emergency evacuation plan/map easy for students to understand?

B How would you know which way to go?

C How often do you have practice drills?

3 Propose and Apply Improvements

A Using what you have learned about your school's emergency evacuation plan, list your ideas for improvements below.

B Develop and give a short oral presentation to your principal about your proposal on ways to improve the school's emergency evacuation plan. Write the main points of your presentation below.

C As a class, practice the newly improved emergency evacuation plan. Describe how well the improved emergency evacuation plan worked.

EMERGENCY EVACUATION ROUTE

You are here

Take It Home
With an adult, create an emergency evacuation plan for your family or evaluate your family's emergency evacuation plan and propose improvements.

152 Unit 4 Weather and Climate

Unit 4 Citizen Science 153

CITIZEN SCIENCE

Unit Project Exit Strategy

1. Think About It

A. yes or no

B. Students may need to know whether to evacuate the building or to remain inside. If evacuation is required, students would need to know things such as the route to the nearest exit, which exit is equipped for wheelchair use, the location of a meeting point, and how to reach a parent or guardian.

2. Ask a Question

Obtain a copy of the school's evacuation plan, and make copies for students. As a class, discuss the details of the plan, any symbols used on the map, and whether students understand it.

Optional Online rubric: Class Discussion

3. Propose and Apply Improvements

A. Students may suggest: having teachers go over the map and evacuation routes routinely; assigning a few students specific tasks to help organize the class in an emergency; creating a buddy system to help students look out for each other.

B. Students may use the points from A and also include how to communicate the information to the entire student body.

C. Students' answers should reflect their opinion of the exercise.

Optional Online rubric: Oral Presentations

Take It Home

Ask students to provide you with a brief paragraph detailing their family's emergency evacuation plan. This might include the safest routes out of the house, a meeting place, methods of calling each other on the phone, a list of supplies for emergencies, and so on.

Optional Online rubric: Written Pieces

Elements of Weather

Essential Question What is weather and how can we describe different types of weather conditions?

 **Professional Development**

For more detailed information about the topics in this lesson, refer to the Content Refresher in the Unit Opener pages.

Opening Your Lesson

Begin the lesson by assessing students' prerequisite and prior knowledge.

Prerequisite Knowledge

- Density
- Water cycle
- Atmosphere
- Temperature

Accessing Prior Knowledge

Ask: What is the water cycle? the continuous movement of water between the atmosphere, the land, the oceans, and living things What processes are included in this cycle? evaporation, transpiration, sublimation, condensation, precipitation, runoff, infiltration, movement of water on land and in oceans

Ask: What is temperature? how hot or cold something is

Customize Your Opening

- ☐ **Accessing Prior Knowledge,** above
- ☐ **Print Path** Engage Your Brain, SE p. 155, #1–2
- ☐ **Print Path** Active Reading, SE p. 155, #3–4
- ☐ **Digital Path** Lesson Opener

Key Topics/Learning Goals

Elements of Weather

1 Define *weather*.
2 Explain how each of the following relates to weather:
  - Temperature
  - Humidity
  - Precipitation
  - Air pressure
  - Wind direction and speed
  - Visibility

Measuring Elements of Weather

1 Describe how each of these is measured:
  - Temperature
  - Humidity
  - Precipitation
  - Air pressure
  - Wind direction and speed
2 Describe technology that is used in weather data collection.

Supporting Concepts

- Weather is the short-term state of the atmosphere, including temperature, humidity, precipitation, wind, visibility, and air pressure.
- Temperature measures how hot or cold air is. Humidity measures the amount of water vapor in air. Precipitation is any form of water that falls to Earth from clouds. Air pressure measures the force with which air molecules push on a surface. Wind is movement of air caused by differences in air pressure. Visibility is the distance at which objects can be seen with the unaided eye.

- Thermometers measure temperature.
- Humidity is measured with a psychrometer.
- Precipitation is measured by capturing the precipitation in a gauge.
- Air pressure is measured with a barometer.
- Wind direction is measured with a wind vane or windsock.
- Anemometers measure wind speed.
- Stationary weather data collection technology includes ground stations and weather buoys. Moving weather data collection technology includes satellites, airplanes, and ships.

Options for Instruction

Two parallel paths provide coverage of the Essential Questions, with a strong **Inquiry** strand woven into each.
Follow the **Print Path**, the **Digital Path**, or your customized combination of print, digital, and inquiry.

 Print Path
Teaching support for the Print Path appears with the Student Pages.

 Inquiry Labs and **Activities**

Digital Path
Digital Path shortcut: TS661221

Wonder About Weather?
SE pp. 156–158
What is weather?
What is temperature?
What is humidity?
What is precipitation?

The Air Out There, SE pp. 160–161
What is air pressure?
What is wind?
What is visibility?
What are some ways that weather data can be collected?

Daily Demo
Effects of Pressure

Quick Lab
Classifying Features of Different Types of Clouds

Activity
Weather Elements

Elements of Weather
Interactive Image

Visibility
Animation

Wonder About Weather?
SE pp. 156–158
How is temperature measured?
How is humidity measured?
How is precipitation measured?

The Air Out There, SE pp. 160–161
How is air pressure measured?
How is wind measured?
How is visibility measured?
What are some ways that weather data can be collected?

Activity
Tracking Weather

Activity
Weather Tools

Quick Lab
Investigate the Measurement of Rainfall

Field Lab
Comparing Different Ways to Estimate Wind Speed

Elements Measured
Interactive Graphics

Moving or Stationary
Diagram

Options for Assessment

See the Evaluate page for options, including Formative Assessment, Summative Assessment, and Unit Review.

Engage and Explore

Activities and Discussion

Discussion *Pressure All Around*

Elements of Weather

 whole class
🕐 15 min
inquiry **DIRECTED** inquiry

Observing Many students hold the misconception that air pressure pushes only in a downward direction. Show a shoebox with a lid to students. Ask them to discuss where air pressure is pushing on the box. Point to all sides and take the lid off and point to the inside of the box, clarifying that air is pressing equally on all sides. **Ask:** What part of the box are molecules of air pushing on? all parts **Ask:** How do we know that air is pressing on all sides equally? Since air pressure pushes on all parts equally, the box does not implode or explode

Probing Question *Highs and Lows*

Elements of Weather

 pairs, then whole class
🕐 35 min
inquiry **GUIDED** inquiry

Reports Provide students with copies of a local newspaper's weather report. Have student pairs read through the report, charts, and maps, highlighting any use of the words *high* or *low*. Have pairs discuss the meanings of the information provided. Come back together as a class and have pairs explain one of the examples they found. Have students brainstorm other elements of weather that could be described as high or low that were not mentioned in the report. Ask students to describe their examples.

Activity *Tracking Weather*

Measuring Elements of Weather

 small groups, then whole class
🕐 ongoing
inquiry **GUIDED** inquiry

Supply students with daily local weather reports and have each group track a different weather element. One group should also record whether it is cloudy or sunny each day. Then, after several days, encourage students to graph their data. As a challenge, students can pick two atmospheric elements and create a graph that shows how they relate to each other, for example, atmospheric pressure and precipitation or temperature and humidity. Display completed graphs around the classroom, and encourage students to discuss how the various elements seem to relate to one another.

Activity *Weather Tools*

Measuring Elements of Weather

 individuals
🕐 30 min
inquiry **GUIDED** inquiry

If possible, bring in real meteorological instruments for measuring wind speed (anemometer), wind direction (wind vane or windsock), and tools that measure relative humidity, such as a wet-and-dry bulb psychrometer, hair-tension hygrometer, or electric hygrometer. Display the tools in workstations, with labels, so students can examine them and see how they work. Allow students to rotate through the stations to study the instruments. Have students return to their desks and create an illustrated sheet showing each of the tools.

Customize Your Labs

 See the Lab Manual for lab datasheets.

 Go Online for editable lab datasheets.

Labs and Demos

Daily Demo *Effects of Pressure*

Elements of Weather

 whole class
 15 min
Inquiry GUIDED inquiry

PURPOSE **To observe the effects of unequal air pressure**

MATERIALS

- pan, filled with cold water and ice
- soft drink bottle, plastic with cap

1 Pour about an inch of hot water into the bottle. Secure the cap.

2 **Observing** Hold the bottle in the ice water so it is covered. Have students observe what happens. **Ask:** What happened to the bottle? It collapsed inward. What crushed the bottle? Air pressure is greater outside the bottle than it is inside; the air inside cooled and contracted so it took up less space; the water vapor condensed into liquid, which takes up less space.

Quick Lab *Investigate the Measurement of Rainfall*

Measuring Elements of Weather

 pairs
 30 min
Inquiry DIRECTED inquiry

Students investigate how to measure rainfall.

PURPOSE **To understand how a uniform measurement of rainfall can be obtained from different sized areas.**

MATERIALS

- funnels (2 different sizes)
- graduated cylinders
- jars, clear glass (cylinder shaped) (2)
- marker, permanent
- ruler, metric
- scissors
- water
- watering can, sprinkler, or garden hose with sprayer

Quick Lab *Classifying Features of Different Types of Clouds*

Elements of Weather

 pairs
 30 min
Inquiry DIRECTED inquiry

Students build a scale model of different clouds at various altitudes.

PURPOSE **To understand the height range of cloud types**

MATERIALS

- calculator
- cotton balls
- glue, white
- marker
- poster board (preferably blue)
- ruler, metric

Field Lab *Comparing Different Ways to Estimate Wind Speed*

Measuring Elements of Weather

small groups
2 45-min periods
Inquiry DIRECTED inquiry

Students use weather tools to estimate wind speeds.

PURPOSE **To understand the difference between qualitative and quantitative data collection to measure wind speed**

MATERIALS

- cardboard
- cups, clear plastic (3)
- cup, colored plastic (1)
- meterstick
- field notebook
- pencil with eraser
- pushpin
- ruler, metric
- scissors
- stapler
- timer
- marker

Activities and Discussion

- ☐ **Discussion** Pressure All Around
- ☐ **Probing Question** Highs and Lows
- ☐ **Activity** Tracking Weather
- ☐ **Activity** Weather Tools

Labs and Demos

- ☐ **Daily Demo** Effects of Pressure
- ☐ **Quick Lab** Investigate…Rainfall
- ☐ **Quick Lab** Classifying…Clouds
- ☐ **Field Lab** … Estimate Wind Speed

Your Resources

_____

_____

_____

Explain Science Concepts

Key Topics	📖 Print Path	🖥 Digital Path

📖 Print Path

☐ **Wonder About Weather?**
SE pp. 156–158
• Visualize It!, #7
• Explain, #8

☐ **The Air Out There,** SE pp. 160–161
• Active Reading, #14

🖥 Digital Path

☐ **Elements of Weather**
Explore temperature, wind, and other elements of weather.

☐ **Visibility**
Learn about factors that affect visibility.

Elements of Weather

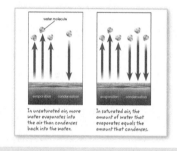

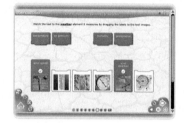

📖 Print Path

☐ **Wonder About Weather?**
SE pp. 156–158
• Visualize It!, #5
• Active Reading (Annotation strategy), #6
• Visualize It!, #9
• Measure, #10

☐ **The Air Out There,** SE pp. 160–161
• Visualize It!, #13
• Visualize It!, #15

🖥 Digital Path

☐ **Elements Measured**
Learn how to measure different elements of weather.

☐ **Moving or Stationary**
See some of the ways to collect sets of weather data.

Measuring Elements of Weather

Differentiated Instruction

Basic *Mnemonic Devices*

Elements of Weather   individuals, then whole class
🕐 25 min

To help students remember the names of different weather tools, encourage students to devise simple memory strategies. Explain that finding an association between the tool and the element it measures can help them remember. Provide the example that *temperature* and *thermometer* both begin with the letter *t*. Have students come up with their own lists of mnemonic devices. Suggest that students create rhymes or imagine visual clues. Have volunteers share their ideas with the rest of the class.

Advanced *Temperature Study*

Measuring Elements of Weather   🧑 individuals
🕐 30 min

Unit Conversion Although scientists usually use Celsius to discuss temperature, most Americans are more familiar with temperatures given in Fahrenheit. Have interested students locate a formula either on the Internet or in a reference book to describe how to convert Fahrenheit to Celsius. Have them create a chart that gives the temperature for several common temperature benchmarks, such as the temperature at which water freezes or boils, the temperature for baking cookies, the temperature outside on a nice day, and several others that students come up with. Then have students write several sentences that uses temperature given in degrees Celsius.

ELL *Organizing Ideas*

Measuring Elements of Weather   🧑 individuals
🕐 20 min

Concept Map Help struggling readers organize information about weather elements and tools by creating Concept Maps. Have students write *Elements of Weather* in the center circle. Encourage them to write the elements mentioned in the lesson in the ovals radiating out. In the next layer, students can write or draw descriptions of the elements and the tools that are used to measure them.

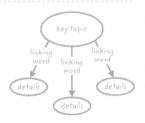

🌐 *Optional Online resource: Concept Map support*

Lesson Vocabulary

weather	humidity	relative humidity
dew point	precipitation	air pressure
wind	visibility	

Previewing Vocabulary

 whole class   🕐 25 min

Word Splash Use the Word Splash strategy to help familiarize students with the terms, and to relate the words and concepts to one another. Draw a large rectangle on the board. Write the word *weather* in the center of the rectangle. Then write the remaining vocabulary terms around the center word. Have students choose four vocabulary terms. For each chosen term, have them write a sentence that predicts how that term relates to the center word.

Reinforcing Vocabulary

🧑 individuals or groups   🕐 20 min

Frame Game To help students learn challenging terms, have them build frames for three or four terms they are struggling with. Have students write the term in the center and include examples, a definition, descriptions, and pictures. Have them use a new frame for each term.

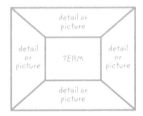

Customize Your Core Lesson

Core Instruction
☐ **Print Path** choices
☐ **Digital Path** choices

Vocabulary
☐ **Previewing Vocabulary**
   Word Splash
☐ **Reinforcing Vocabulary**
   Frame Game

Your Resources

Differentiated Instruction
☐ **Basic** Mnemonic Devices
☐ **Advanced** Temperature Study
☐ **ELL** Organizing Ideas

Extend Science Concepts

Reinforce and Review

Activity *Weather Elements*

Synthesizing Key Topics small groups
🕐 40–45 min

Jigsaw Divide the class into five small groups. Assign each group one of the following topics: Explain temperature and how it can it be measured. Explain humidity and how it can be measured. Explain precipitation and how it can be measured. Explain air pressure and how it can be measured. Explain wind and how it can be measured. Then have each group work to become experts on their topic.

• Have groups work until all students are confident that they can teach what they have learned about their key topic to the members of another group.

• Reassign students to new mixed groups. The groups should include at least one expert from each of the key topics. Have individuals in each mixed group share their expertise with other students in the group. The goal is for all students to be able to explain how each of the key topics relates to the essential question for the lesson.

Graphic Organizer

Synthesizing Key Topics individuals, then pairs
🕐 ongoing

Cluster Diagram After students have studied the lesson, ask them to make a Cluster Diagram. Have them draw a large circle in the middle of a sheet of paper. Direct them to write the word *weather* in the center of the circle. Tell them that this is the main idea. Then have them draw at least four medium-sized circles that are connected to the large circle by lines. Inside each of the smaller circles, have students write a term that is related to the main idea. Suggest the following ideas for students who are stuck: *weather, humidity, relative humidity, dew point, precipitation, air pressure, wind,* and *visibility*. Suggest that students include how the various elements are measured. Then have them pair with a partner to discuss how each term they chose is related to the main word.

🕐 *Optional Online resource: Cluster Diagram support*

Going Further

Engineering Connection

Elements of Weather flexible
🕐 45 min

Timeline Wind is an element of weather that humans have harnessed through the ages. Provide students with the following list of dates and information and have them use it to make an illustrated timeline. Challenge students to find additional important dates in the history of wind power.

• 500–900 CE: The first windmills were developed in Persia.
• About 1300: The first horizontal-axis windmills (like a pinwheel) appeared in western Europe.
• 1888: Charles F. Brush used the first large windmill to generate electricity in Cleveland, Ohio.
• 1979: The first wind turbine rated over 1 megawatt began operating.
• 2007: Wind power provided 5% of the renewable energy used in the United States.

Technology Connection

Synthesizing Key Concepts whole class
🕐 30 min

Discussion Tell students that the use of satellite and radar technology has changed the field of meteorology in dramatic ways. The technology allows meteorologists to observe the patterns of clouds in the skies, which they can use to determine information about weather. Direct students to an online weather map that uses interactive radar and satellite information. Have students discuss how the tools could help meteorologists.

Customize Your Closing

 See the Assessment Guide for quizzes and tests.

🕐 Go Online to edit and create quizzes and tests.

Reinforce and Review

☐ **Activity** Weather Elements

☐ **Graphic Organizer** Cluster Diagram

☐ **Print Path** Visual Summary, SE p. 162

☐ **Print Path** Lesson Review, SE p. 163

☐ **Digital Path** Lesson Closer

Evaluate Student Mastery

Formative Assessment

See the teacher support below the Student Pages for additional Formative Assessment questions.

Have students describe what they can about the current day's weather. Students shouldn't be able to describe each weather element because they are not all observable without the right tools. For these elements, have students describe which tools they would use to gather these data. Sample answers: The temperature and the humidity level today are high. It is not windy. There was precipitation (rain) this morning, but it has stopped. I can see clearly, so visibility is high. I can't tell how high the air pressure is; I need a barometer to measure that.

Reteach

Formative assessment may show that students need reinforcement for certain topics. The resources below are recommended for reteaching. If students were introduced to a topic through the Print Path, you can also use the Digital Path to reteach, and vice versa.
🎧 *Can be assigned to individual students*

Elements of Weather
Discussion Pressure All Around
Daily Demo Effects of Pressure 🎧
Activity Weather Elements

Measuring Elements of Weather
Activity Tracking Weather
Activity Weather Tools

Summative Assessment

Alternative Assessment
Weather Basics

🌐 *Online resources: student worksheet, optional rubrics*

Elements of Weather

Climb the Pyramid: *Weather Basics*
You and your classmates will work together to complete the activities and show what you have learned about the elements of weather.

1. Work on your own, with a partner, or with a small group.
2. Choose one item from each layer of the pyramid. Check your choices.
3. Have your teacher approve your plan.
4. Submit or present your results.

__ **Creating Questions**
Create a ten-question quiz about the elements of weather and the ways these elements are measured. Include five multiple-choice questions and five true-or-false questions. Include questions about temperature, humidity, precipitation, air pressure, wind direction, and visibility. Include the answers to your questions on a separate sheet.

__ **This Just In!**
Imagine your school has just purchased a barometer, a wind sock, a thermometer, and a precipitation gauge. Present a news report that discusses the functions of these tools and the ways they will help students at your school learn about weather.

__ **Measuring Up**
Compose a PowerPoint presentation with at least four slides. On each slide, define one instrument used to measure the elements of weather. Find pictures of each of the featured elements and include them on your slides. Present your work to the class.

__ **Back to the Drawing Board**
Imagine that you just wrote a book about the elements of weather. Design a cover for your book. Be sure to include a descriptive title and an illustration that is appropriate for your topic.

__ **Precipitation Poetry**
Write a four-stanza poem about the four major types of precipitation. Have each stanza of the poem discuss one of the major types. Try to keep all the stanzas at about the same length.

__ **Picturing the Weather**
Create a collage of weather events that are typical for the area in which you live. Try to include as many different weather events as possible. Use pictures from old magazines or pictures from the Internet to complete your collage.

Going Further
- [ ] **Engineering Connection**
- [ ] **Technology Connection**
- [ ] **Print Path** Why It Matters, SE p. 159

Formative Assessment
- [ ] **Strategies** Throughout TE
- [ ] **Lesson Review** SE

Summative Assessment
- [ ] **Alternative Assessment** Weather Basics
- [ ] **Lesson Quiz**
- [ ] **Unit Tests A and B**
- [ ] **Unit Review** SE End-of-Unit

Your Resources

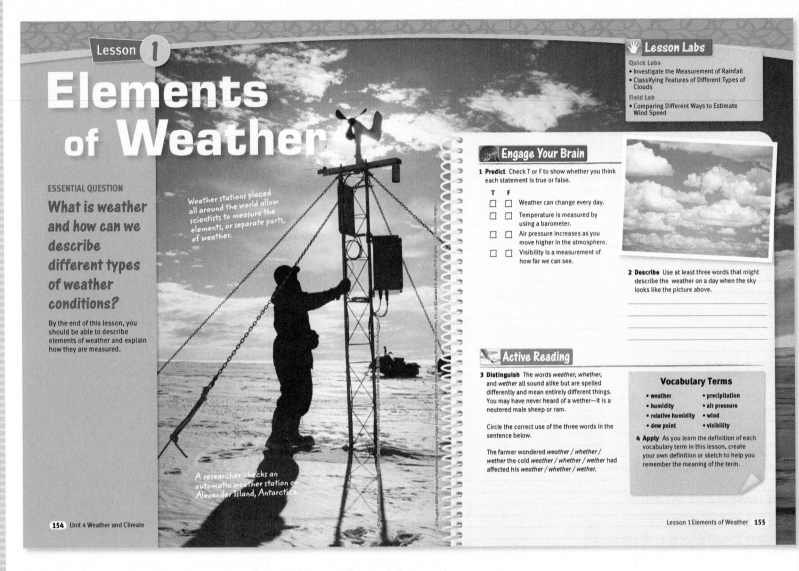

Lesson ①

Elements of Weather

ESSENTIAL QUESTION

What is weather and how can we describe different types of weather conditions?

By the end of this lesson, you should be able to describe elements of weather and explain how they are measured.

Weather stations placed all around the world allow scientists to measure the elements, or separate parts, of weather.

A researcher checks an automatic weather station on Alexander Island, Antarctica.

Lesson Labs

Quick Labs
• Investigate the Measurement of Rainfall
• Classifying Features of Different Types of Clouds

Field Lab
• Comparing Different Ways to Estimate Wind Speed

Engage Your Brain

1 Predict Check T or F to show whether you think each statement is true or false.

T	F	
☐	☐	Weather can change every day.
☐	☐	Temperature is measured by using a barometer.
☐	☐	Air pressure increases as you move higher in the atmosphere.
☐	☐	Visibility is a measurement of how far we can see.

2 Describe Use at least three words that might describe the weather on a day when the sky looks like the picture above.

Active Reading

3 Distinguish The words *weather, whether,* and *wether* all sound alike but are spelled differently and mean entirely different things. You may have never heard of a wether—it is a neutered male sheep or ram.

Circle the correct use of the three words in the sentence below.

The farmer wondered *weather / whether / wether* the cold *weather / whether / wether* had affected his *weather / whether / wether.*

Vocabulary Terms

• weather	• precipitation
• humidity	• air pressure
• relative humidity	• wind
• dew point	• visibility

4 Apply As you learn the definition of each vocabulary term in this lesson, create your own definition or sketch to help you remember the meaning of the term.

154 Unit 4 Weather and Climate

Lesson 1 Elements of Weather 155

Answers

Answers for 1–3 should represent students' current thoughts, even if incorrect.

1. T; F; F; T

2. Sample answer: sunny (or partly cloudy), warm, dry

3. whether; weather; wether

4. Students should define or sketch each vocabulary term in the lesson.

Opening Your Lesson

Discuss responses to item 3 to assess students' ability to distinguish between homophones for *weather*. Point out that the word *whether* has a meaning similar to the word *if*. Tell students that one way to remember the spelling of *weather* is to remember that it refers to conditions in the atmosphere, and contains the letters *a* and *t*. These two letters are also the first two letters of the word *atmosphere*.

Prerequisites Students should be familiar with processes of the water cycle. They should also understand the concepts of temperature and of density (mass per unit volume), especially as it pertains to air pressure.

Assessing Prior Knowledge

Weather Instruments Have students name weather instruments that they have heard of. List their responses on the board. Sample answers: thermometer; rain gauge; wind vane; windsock What can these instruments tell us? thermometer—temperature; rain gauge—precipitation; wind vane or windsock—wind direction

Wonder about Weather?

What is weather?

Weather is the condition of Earth's atmosphere at a certain time and place. Different observations give you clues to the weather. If you see plants moving from side to side, you might infer that it is windy. If you see a gray sky and wet, shiny streets, you might decide to wear a raincoat. People talk about weather by describing factors such as temperature, humidity, precipitation, air pressure, wind, and *visibility* (viz•uh•BIL•i•tee).

What is temperature and how is it measured?

Temperature is a measure of how hot or cold something is. An instrument that measures and displays temperature is called a *thermometer*. A common type of thermometer uses a liquid such as alcohol or mercury to display the temperature. The liquid is sealed in a glass tube. When the air gets warmer, the liquid expands and rises in the tube. Cooler air causes the liquid to contract and fill less of the tube. A scale, often in Celsius (°C) or Fahrenheit (°F), is marked on the glass tube.

Another type of thermometer is an electrical thermometer. As the temperature becomes higher, electric current flow increases through the thermometer. The strength of the current is then translated into temperature readings.

Extreme Weather Facts

Earth's highest recorded temperature was in El Azizia, Libya, on September 1922 at 58 °C (136 °F).

Earth's lowest recorded temperature was in Vostok, Antarctica, on July 1983 at −89 °C (−128 °F).

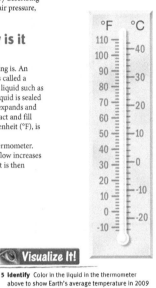

Visualize It!

5 Identify Color in the liquid in the thermometer above to show Earth's average temperature in 2009 (58 °F). Write the Celsius temperature that equals 58 °F on the line below.

156 Unit 4 Weather and Climate

© Houghton Mifflin Harcourt Publishing Company

What is humidity and how is it measured?

As water evaporates from oceans, lakes, and ponds, it becomes water vapor, or a gas that is in the air. The amount of water vapor in the air is called **humidity**. As more water evaporates and becomes water vapor, the humidity of the air increases.

Humidity is often described through relative humidity. **Relative humidity** is the amount of water vapor in the air compared to the amount of water vapor needed to reach saturation. As shown below, when air is saturated, the rates of evaporation and condensation are equal. Saturated air has a relative humidity of 100%. A psychrometer (sy•KRAHM•i•ter) is an instrument that is used to measure relative humidity.

Air can become saturated when evaporation adds water vapor to the air. Air can also become saturated when it cools to its dew point. The **dew point** is the temperature at which more condensation than evaporation occurs. When air temperature drops below the dew point, condensation forms. This can cause dew on surfaces cooler than the dew point. It also can form fog and clouds.

Active Reading

6 Identify Underline the name of the instrument used to measure relative humidity.

Visualize It!

7 Sketch In the space provided, draw what happens in air that is below the dew point.

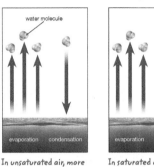

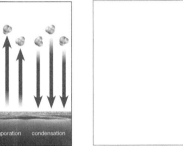

water molecule

evaporation condensation

evaporation condensation

In unsaturated air, more water evaporates into the air than condenses back into the water.

In saturated air, the amount of water that evaporates equals the amount that condenses.

When air cools below its dew point, more water vapor condenses into water than evaporates.

8 Explain Why does dew form on grass overnight?

Lesson 1 Elements of Weather 157

Answers

5. approximately 14 °C

6. *See students' pages for annotations.*

7. Students should draw diagrams showing more condensation arrows/molecules than evaporation arrows/molecules.

8. Because the air temperature at night can cool below the dew point temperature, water vapor condenses onto the grass as dew.

Interpreting Visuals

Help students interpret the textbook diagrams showing the difference in rates of evaporation and condensation between unsaturated air and saturated air. **Ask:** What is the same and what is different about the two diagrams? In both images, water is evaporating, but in the first image, which shows unsaturated air, only a little water is condensing; in the second image of saturated air, more water is condensing. What do the arrows tell us? They show that a process is taking place.

Learning Alert

Temperature Temperature can be a confusing topic for many students. Ask students to explain what temperature is. Sample answer: Temperature is how hot or cold something is. **Ask:** What is the difference between Celsius and Fahrenheit? Sample answer: Like miles and kilometers, they are different units for measuring the same thing.

What is precipitation and how is it measured?

Water vapor in the air condenses not only on Earth's surfaces, but also on tiny particles in the air to form clouds. When this water from the air returns to Earth's surface, it falls as precipitation. **Precipitation** is any form of water that falls to Earth's surface from the clouds. The four main forms of precipitation are rain, snow, hail, and sleet.

Rain is the most common form of precipitation. Inside a cloud, the droplets formed by condensation collide and form larger droplets. They finally become heavy enough to fall as raindrops. Rain is measured with a rain gauge, as shown in the picture below. A funnel or wide opening at the top of the gauge allows rain to flow into a cylinder that is marked in centimeters.

Snow forms when air temperatures are so low that water vapor turns into a solid. When a lot of snow has fallen, it is measured with a ruler or meterstick. When balls or lumps of ice fall from clouds during thunderstorms it is called **hail**. Sleet forms when rain falls through a layer of freezing air, producing falling ice.

Visualize It! *Inquiry*

9 Synthesize What are two ways in which all types of precipitation are alike?

Snow
Snow can fall as single ice crystals or ice crystals can join to form snowflakes.

Rain
Rain occurs when the water droplets in a cloud get so big they fall to Earth.

Sleet
Small ice pellets fall as sleet when rain falls through cold air.

Hail
Hailstones are layered lumps of ice that fall from clouds.

10 Measure How much rain has this rain gauge collected?

158 Unit 4 Weather and Climate

Why It Matters

Watching Clouds

EYE ON THE ENVIRONMENT

Cirrus Clouds

Cumulus Clouds

Stratus Clouds

As you can see above, cirrus (SIR•uhs) clouds appear feathery or wispy. Their name means "curl of hair." They are made of ice crystals. They form when the wind is strong.

Cumulus (KYOOM•yuh•luhs) means "heap" or "pile." Usually these clouds form in fair weather but if they keep growing taller, they can produce thunderstorms.

Stratus (STRAY•tuhs) means "spread out." Stratus clouds form in flat layers. Low, dark stratus clouds can block out the sun and produce steady drizzle or rain.

If you watch the sky over a period of time, you will probably observe different kinds of clouds. Clouds have different characteristics because they form under different conditions. The shapes and sizes of clouds are mainly determined by air movement. For example, puffy clouds form in air that rises sharply or moves straight up and down. Flat, smooth clouds covering large areas form in air that rises gradually.

Extend *Inquiry*

11 Reflect Think about the last time you noticed the clouds. When are you most likely to notice what type of cloud is in the sky?

12 Research Word parts are used to tell more about clouds. Look up the word parts *-nimbus* and *alto-*. What are cumulonimbus and altostratus clouds?

Lesson 1 Elements of Weather 159

Answers

9. Sample answer: made of water, falls to the ground

10. approximately 24 cm

11. Sample answer: when the clouds are getting dark and severe weather is on its way

12. Cumulonimbus clouds are cumulus clouds that produce precipitation. Altostratus clouds are stratus clouds that form at medium altitudes.

Interpreting Visuals

Have students draw lines from parts of the diagram to the sentence in the text that tells more about it. **Ask:** How can putting the text and the diagrams together give you a better idea of the ideas introduced on the page? Sample answer: Having visuals next to explanations and descriptions helps me picture things in my mind.

Probing Questions DIRECTED *Inquiry*

Hypothesizing Have students hypothesize about how water in the atmosphere condenses to form clouds. Point out that water vapor usually condenses on something solid. **Ask:** What solid matter in air could water vapor condense on to form clouds? Sample answers: particles of dust; smoke; pollen; soil particles; in some areas, salt from the ocean

Why It Matters

Ask students to summarize the distinctions between the three cloud types featured. Sample answers: Cirrus clouds are wispy and usually accompany wind. Cumulus clouds are fluffy and usually accompany fair weather. Stratus clouds are dark, spread out, and usually accompany rain.

The Air Out There

What is air pressure and how is it measured?

Scientists use an instrument called a *barometer* (buh•RAHM•i•ter) to measure air pressure. **Air pressure** is the force of air molecules pushing on an area. The air pressure at any area on Earth depends on the weight of the air above that area. Although air is pressing down on us, we don't feel the weight because air pushes in all directions. So, the pressure of air pushing down is balanced by the pressure of air pushing up.

Air pressure and density are related; they both decrease with altitude. Notice in the picture that the molecules at sea level are closer together than the molecules at the mountain peak. Because the molecules are closer together, the pressure is greater. The air at sea level is denser than air at high altitude.

Air pressure and density are lower at a high altitude.

Air pressure and density are higher at sea level.

Visualize It!

13 Identify Look at the photos below and write whether wind direction or wind speed is being measured.

Anemometer

An anemometer measures:

Wind vane

A wind vane measures:

160 Unit 4 Weather and Climate

What is wind and how is it measured?

Wind is air that moves horizontally, or parallel to the ground. Uneven heating of Earth's surface causes pressure differences from place to place. These pressure differences set air in motion. Over a short distance, wind moves directly from higher pressure toward lower pressure.

An anemometer (an•uh•MAHM•i•ter) is used to measure wind speed. It has three or four cups attached to a pole. The wind causes the cups to rotate, sending an electric current to a meter that displays the wind speed.

Wind direction is measured by using a wind vane or a windsock. A wind vane has an arrow with a large tail that is attached to a pole. The wind pushes harder on the arrow tail due to its larger surface area. This causes the wind vane to spin so that the arrow points into the wind. A windsock is a cone-shaped cloth bag open at both ends. The wind enters the wide end and the narrow end points in the opposite direction, showing the direction the wind is blowing.

What is visibility and how is it measured?

Visibility is a measure of the transparency of the atmosphere. Visibility is the way we describe how far we can see, and it is measured by using three or four known landmarks at different distances. Sometimes not all of the landmarks will be visible. Poor visibility can be the result of air pollution or fog.

Poor visibility can be dangerous for all types of travel, whether by air, water, or land. When visibility is very low, roads may be closed to traffic. In areas where low visibility is common, signs are often posted to warn travelers.

Active Reading

14 Explain What are two factors that can affect visibility?

Fog forms as land cools overnight, causing water vapor in the air above the land to condense.

What are some ways to collect weather data?

Many forms of technology are used to gather weather data. The illustration below shows some ways weather information can be collected. Instruments within the atmosphere can make measurements of local weather conditions. Satellites can collect data from above the atmosphere.

Visualize It! (Inquiry)

15 Infer What are the benefits of stationary weather collection? Moving weather collection?

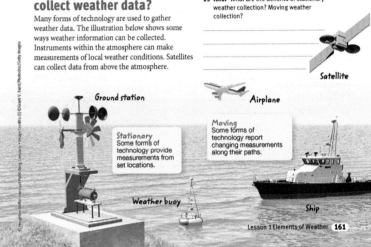

Satellite

Airplane

Ground station

Stationary
Some forms of technology provide measurements from set locations.

Moving
Some forms of technology report changing measurements along their paths.

Weather buoy

Ship

Lesson 1 Elements of Weather 161

Answers

13. wind speed; wind direction

14. air pollution and fog

15. Sample answer: Stationary weather collection provides long-term weather data at specific locations. It is useful for comparison to past measurements. Moving weather collection technology can gather data over a wide area.

Probing Questions GUIDED Inquiry

Inferring What does the fact that most rain starts out as falling ice crystals tell you about temperatures in clouds? Sample answer: Temperatures in clouds are generally colder than temperatures closer to Earth's surface.

Learning Alert 🔲 MISCONCEPTION 🔲

Air Pressure Students may think that air pressure is exerted only in a downward direction. They may have difficulty understanding that air pressure is exerted in all directions. To assess their understanding, have students hold out a hand flat. Ask them if there is more pressure on the back of the hand or on the palm. Responses should indicate an understanding that air is pressing with the same force against every part of the body.

Formative Assessment

Ask students to describe which type of instruments might be found in a ground station. Then have students identify the weather elements that each instrument measures. Sample answers: thermometer to measure air temperature; barometer to measure air pressure; psychrometer to measure relative humidity; rain gauge to measure precipitation; anemometer to measure wind speed; wind vanes to determine wind direction

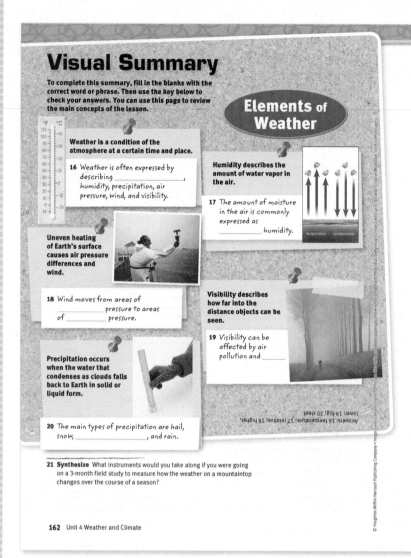

Lesson Review

Lesson 1

Vocabulary

In your own words, define the following terms.

1 weather _____

2 humidity _____

3 air pressure _____

4 visibility _____

Key Concepts

Weather element	Instrument
5 Identify Measures temperature	
	6 Identify Is measured by using a barometer
7 Identify Measures relative humidity	
	8 Identify Is measured by using a rain gauge or meterstick
9 Identify Measures wind speed	

10 List What are four types of precipitation?

Critical Thinking

11 Apply Explain how wind is related to the uneven heating of Earth's surfaces by the sun.

12 Explain Why does air pressure decrease as altitude increases?

13 Synthesize What is the relative humidity when the air temperature is at its dew point?

The weather data below was recorded from 1989–2009 by an Antarctic weather station similar to the station in the photo at the beginning of this lesson. Use these data to answer the questions that follow.

	Jan.	Apr.	July	Oct.
Mean max. temp. (°C)	2.1	−7.4	−9.9	−8.1
Mean min. temp. (°C)	−2.6	−14.6	−18.1	−15.1
Mean precip. (mm)	9.0	18.04	28.5	16.5

14 Identify Which month had the lowest mean minimum and maximum temperatures?

15 Infer The precipitation that fell at this location was most likely in what form?

Visual Summary Answers

16. temperature

17. relative

18. higher; lower

19. fog

20. sleet

21. Sample answer: thermometer, psychrometer, rain gauge, meterstick, barometer, wind vane or windsock, anemometer

Lesson Review Answers

1. Sample answer: the combined factors of temperature, humidity, precipitation, air pressure, wind speed and direction, and visibility in a certain place at a certain time

2. Sample answer: the amount of water vapor in the air

3. Sample answer: the force of air molecules pushing on an area

4. Sample answer: a measure of how far in the distance one can see

5. Thermometer

6. Air pressure

7. Psychrometer

8. Precipitation

9. Anemometer

10. rain, snow, sleet, hail

11. The sun heats up Earth's surface unevenly due to the different types of surfaces (for example, water, land), creating pressure differences. Air moves from areas of higher pressure to areas of lower pressure, creating wind.

12. There is less air above you as you move up in altitude.

13. 100%

14. July

15. snow

John

Clouds and Cloud Formation

Essential Question How do clouds form, and how are clouds classified?

Professional Development

For more detailed information about the topics in this lesson, refer to the Content Refresher in the Unit Opener pages.

Opening Your Lesson

Begin the lesson by assessing students' prerequisite and prior knowledge.

Prerequisite Knowledge

• A general understanding of elements of weather

Accessing Prior Knowledge

Ask: Describe different types of clouds that you have observed. Sample answers: thin and wispy; round and puffy; low and gray; dark with flat tops

Ask: When are you most likely to view clouds? Sample answers: before a rainstorm or snowstorm; during a drizzle; prior to severe weather such as an approaching tornado

Customize Your Opening

☐ **Accessing Prior Knowledge,** above

☐ **Print Path** Engage Your Brain, SE p. 165

☐ **Print Path** Active Reading, SE p. 165

☐ **Digital Path** Lesson Opener

Key Topics/Learning Goals	Supporting Concepts
Introduction to Clouds 1 Briefly state what a cloud is. 2 Explain why clouds are important to climate. 3 Explain why clouds are important to weather.	• A cloud is a collection of small water droplets or ice crystals suspended in the air. • Clouds reflect some solar radiation back into space, which cools Earth's surface. Clouds absorb some heat (infrared radiation) emitted by Earth and radiate it back downward, which warms Earth's surface. • Clouds are the source of precipitation and affect temperatures locally.
Cloud Formation 1 Explain how a cloud forms. 2 Describe dew point. 3 Tell how water droplets form. 4 Describe cooling processes. 5 Tell about solar energy's role in cloud formation.	• Water vapor condenses on particles when the dew point is reached, and droplets form. • Cooling occurs when moist air mixes with air of a different temperature; when a cold air mass or mountains lift a warm air mass; or when an air mass moves over a cold surface. • Earth's surface absorbs solar energy and reradiates it as heat. Air near the surface absorbs it, rises, expands, and cools.
Cloud Classification 1 List two classifications. 2 Describe the basic shapes and the altitude classes. 3 Contrast clouds of vertical development. 4 Describe cloud naming.	• Clouds are classified by shape and altitude. • Shapes: stratus (flat, gray), cumulus (thick, fluffy), and cirrus (white, thin). • Altitude: low clouds (water droplets), middle clouds (water droplets or ice crystals), high clouds (ice crystals), and clouds of vertical development water droplets and ice crystals.
Fog 1 Briefly state what fog is and how fog forms. 2 Describe two ways in which air can cool to form fog.	• Fog is water vapor that has formed near Earth's surface due to the cooling of air close to the ground. • Fog can form if air near the ground cools, or if warm, moist air blows over a cold surface.

Options for Instruction

Two parallel paths provide coverage of the Essential Questions, with a strong **Inquiry** strand woven into each. Follow the **Print Path,** the **Digital Path,** or your customized combination of print, digital, and inquiry.

Print Path
Teaching support for the Print Path appears with the Student Pages.

Inquiry Labs and Activities

Digital Path
Digital path shortcut: TS661466

Print Path	Inquiry Labs and Activities	Digital Path
Head in the Clouds, SE p. 166 **What are clouds?** **How do clouds affect climate?**	**Activity** Solar Insulation	**What Are Clouds?** Interactive Images
Head in the Clouds, SE pp. 167–168 **How do clouds form?** **What is the role of solar energy in cloud formation?** **What processes cool air enough to form clouds?**	**Quick Lab** How Does a Cloud Form? **Quick Lab** Out of Thin Air	**How Clouds Form** Graphic Sequence **Solar Radiation and Clouds** Graphics **More About Cloud Formation** Slideshow
Head in the Clouds, SE p. 169 **What are three cloud shapes?** **I've Looked at Clouds from Both Sides Now,** SE pp. 170–171 **What are the types of clouds based on altitude?**	**Activity** Charting Clouds	**Cloud Types** Interactive Graphics **Classifying Clouds by Altitude** Interactive Graphics
I've Looked at Clouds from Both Sides Now, SE p. 172 **How does fog form?**	**Daily Demo** Form Fog	**Fog** Interactive Images

Options for Assessment

See the Evaluate page for options, including Formative Assessment, Summative Assessment, and Unit Review.

gage and Explore

Activities and Discussion

Probing Questions *Fog*

Engage

Fog

 whole class
 10 min
 GUIDED inquiry

Ask: Where have you seen fog? Students will probably indicate that they have viewed fog around bodies of water and in low places such as valleys. **Ask:** Describe the sensations of being in a thick fog. Sample answers: It feels moist and humid; there is little to no visibility. **Ask:** How does fog burn off? The sun burns off fog, and it becomes invisible once the air temperature increases.

Activity *Charting Clouds*

Cloud Classification

 pairs or small groups
 ongoing
GUIDED inquiry

Have students work together to create a chart that they can use to track clouds and predict weather. They can design the chart on a computer or by hand. They should create five columns for their chart: date, cloud type, morning weather, weather prediction, afternoon weather. In the morning, students should fill in the first four columns. They should note the date and whether the cloud is stratus, cumulus, or cirrus. They should then describe the weather and use the shape of the cloud to predict the weather for that afternoon. In the afternoon, students can fill in the actual weather. Students should track clouds for at least one week. At the end of this period, they can discuss how accurate their predictions were.

Activity *Solar Insulation*

Introduction to Clouds

 small groups
 20 min.
 GUIDED inquiry

Have students work together to simulate how clouds affect climate. Provide each group with a desk lamp. Have them shine the lamp onto a flat surface on which they have placed two thermometers. After 10 minutes, they should record the temperature. Have them cover one thermometer with the paper and set the other on top of the paper. After 10 minutes, they should record the temperature on each thermometer. Was there a difference? If so, what do they think caused the difference?

Take It Home *Cloud Collages*

Cloud Classification

 adult-student pairs
ongoing
GUIDED inquiry

Students and adults work together to create a collage of various clouds. Pairs can take walks around their neighborhood and record details about different types of clouds by making sketches and jotting down notes about shapes and colors. Then they can gather materials to make a collage. Beyond the traditional cotton balls, pairs can use creative collage materials with an emphasis on recycled items such as buttons, cellophane, and lace.

©David R. Frazier/Alamy Images

Customize Your Labs

See the Lab Manual for lab datasheets (including leveled variations) and additional teacher support for the labs.

Go Online for editable lab datasheets and teacher support.

Levels of  **DIRECTED** inquiry   **GUIDED** inquiry   **INDEPENDENT** inquiry

introduces inquiry skills within a structured framework.   develops inquiry skills within a supportive environment.   deepens inquiry skills with student-driven questions or procedures.

Labs and Demos

Daily Demo *Form Fog*

Engage

Fog

👥 whole class
🕐 10 min
Inquiry **DIRECTED** inquiry

PURPOSE **To demonstrate the formation of fog**

MATERIALS

* glass jar
* hot water
* ice cubes
* strainer or small plastic bag

Inquiry **Safety tip:** Be sure that the water is not hot enough to scald.

Fill the jar to the top with hot water. Let the water sit in the jar for 60 seconds. Carefully pour out all of the hot water except for one inch. Place the strainer or plastic bag over the top of the jar. Then add three or four ice cubes to the strainer or bag. Fog will form as the warm, moist air at the bottom of the jar collides with the cold air created by the ice cubes and begins to condense.

🌐 🔲 Quick Lab *How Does a Cloud Form?*

PURPOSE **To describe what happens when air cools to its dew point and to explain how water droplets form**

See the Lab Manual or go Online for planning information.

🌐 🔲 Quick Lab *Out of Thin Air*

Cloud Formation

👥 individuals
🕐 20 min
Inquiry **GUIDED** inquiry

Students put the water into the container and record their observations. Then they add ice cubes and again record their observations, both immediately after adding the ice cubes and again several minutes later. Water droplets will form on the outside of the container.

PURPOSE **To model and observe the formation of water droplets**

MATERIALS

* ice cubes
* plastic container
* room-temperature water

Activities and Discussion

☐ **Probing Questions** Fog
☐ **Activity** Charting Clouds
☐ **Activity** Solar Insulation

Labs and Demos

☐ **Daily Demo** Form Fog
☐ **Quick Lab** How Does a Cloud Form?
☐ **Quick Lab** Out of Thin Air

Your Resources

Explain Science Concepts

	📕 Print Path	💻 Digital Path
Key Topics		
Introduction to Clouds	☐ **Head in the Clouds,** SE p. 166 • Active Reading, #5 • Apply , #6 Active Reading 6 Describe What are two ways in which clouds affect Earth's climate?	☐ **What Are Clouds?** Investigate clouds and their importance.
Cloud Formation	☐ **Head in the Clouds,** SE pp. 167–169 • Conclude, #7 • Active Reading (Annotation strategy)#8 • Visualize It!, #9 • Visualize It!, #10 Active Reading 8 Identify As you read, underline the processes that can cool air enough to form clouds.	☐ **How Clouds Form** Find out how clouds form. ☐ **Solar Radiation and Clouds** Find out why the sun's energy is essential to cloud formation. ☐ **More About Cloud Formation** Investigate the cooling processes that allow clouds to form.
Cloud Classification	☐ **I've Looked at Clouds from Both Sides Now,** SE pp. 170–171 • Active Reading (Annotation strategy) #11 • Think Outside the Book #12 • Visualize It!, #13 Think Outside the Book Inquiry 12 Apply Research cumulonimbus clouds. When you complete your research, consider different materials that might be used to create a model of a cumulonimbus cloud. Then, use your materials to build a model that shows the structure of a cumulonimbus cloud.	☐ **Cloud Types** Investigate classification by shape. ☐ **Classifying Clouds by Altitude** Investigate classification by altitude.
Fog	☐ **I've Looked at Clouds from Both Sides Now,** SE p. 172 • Active Reading (Annotation strategy), #14 • Visualize It!, #15	☐ **Fog** Investigate how fog forms.

Basic *What's On the Way?*

Cloud Formation

 individuals

🕐 15 min

Have students find out more about how people can determine what kind of weather is on the way by understanding the shapes of clouds. Direct students to make a Layered Book FoldNote that can be used as a quick reference guide to clouds and the weather changes they bring.

Advanced *Junior Meteorologists*

Cloud Classification

👥 small groups

🕐 30 min

Have groups of students work together to create a radio broadcast script about clouds that are approaching their region. Each small group should select a type of cloud based on altitude: low, middle, high, or a cloud of vertical development. Then groups should research the cloud that they've selected. Their script should include a description of the cloud, where in the atmosphere the cloud is located, and predictions of weather associated with this cloud. A spokesperson from each group can read the radio broadcast to the class.

ELL *Cloud Cartoons*

Cloud Classification

👥 small groups

🕐 15 min

Give each student in the group the name of a cloud shape along with a brief description. Then challenge students one by one to draw a cartoon on the board depicting his or her cloud. Other students in the group should attempt to guess which cloud shape the student drew.

Lesson Vocabulary

cloud	dew point	stratus cloud
cumulus cloud	cirrus cloud	fog

Previewing Vocabulary

👥 whole class

🕐 15 min

Word Origins Share the following explanations to help students differentiate between the three types of clouds:
- **Stratus** comes from a Latin word meaning "horizontal layer." These low-lying, flat clouds are stretched or spread out parallel to the horizon.
- **Cumulus** is also a Latin word meaning "heap, pile, mass." These fluffy clouds with flat bases resemble a mound of cotton balls.
- **Cirrus** is another Latin word meaning "a lock of hair, tendril, curl, ringlet of hair." These clouds form thin, wispy strands with tufts nicknamed "mares' tails."

Reinforcing Vocabulary

👥 individuals

🕐 ongoing

Word Squares To help students remember the vocabulary terms in the lesson, have them make a Key Term FoldNote containing the vocabulary term, a picture, dictionary definitions, and a sentence using the term that demonstrates its meaning.

TERM	symbol or picture
translation	
my meaning	sentence
dictionary definition	

Customize Your Core Lesson

Core Instruction

☐ **Print Path** choices

☐ **Digital Path** choices

Vocabulary

☐ **Previewing Vocabulary** Word Origins

☐ **Reinforcing Vocabulary** Word Squares

Your Resources

Differentiated Instruction

☐ **Basic** What's on the Way?

☐ **Advanced** Junior Meteorologists

☐ **ELL** Cloud Cartoons

Extend Science Concepts

Reinforce and Review

Activity *Inside/Outside Circles*

Introduction to Clouds   whole class 🕐 20 min

Inside/Outside Circles Help students review the lesson by following these steps:

1 After students have read the lesson, give each an index card with a word from the text on one side and a definition on the other.

2 Students pair up and form two circles. One partner is in an inside circle; the other is in an outside circle. The students in the inside circle face out, and the students in the outside circle face in.

3 Each student in the inside circle asks his or her partner the definition of the vocabulary word on the index card. The partner answers. If the answer is incorrect, the student in the inside circle teaches the other student the correct definition. Repeat this step with the outside-circle students asking the definitions.

4 Have each student on the outside circle rotate one person to the right. He or she faces a new partner and gets a new vocabulary word. Students rotate after each pair of words and definitions. (You can vary the rotation by moving more than one person, moving to the left, and so on, but try to make sure that partners are always new.)

Graphic Organizer

Cloud Formation   individuals 🕐 10 min

Process Chart Have students use a process chart graphic organizer to list the steps involved in cloud formation. Students may check the order of the steps in their textbooks or notes and adjust if needed.

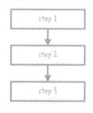

Going Further

Fine Arts Connection

Cloud Classification   whole class 🕐 varies

Create a Mural Have the class work together to plan a classroom mural of all the clouds that they have learned about. Students should discuss the layout of the mural and sketch it out in small scale before they start painting. They can collaborate on poster board that has been hung on a wall. Make sure that a tarp covers the floor to catch any paint drips. Students can label the clouds they've painted.

Language Arts Connection

Fog   small groups 🕐 ongoing

Write and Perform a Skit Invite small groups to write a short skit that is set in the fog. Encourage groups to use the foggy setting as the impetus of the action. When groups have finished writing their skits, provide time for them to perform for the class.

Customize Your Closing

🔷 *See the Assessment Guide for quizzes and tests.*

🌐 *Go Online to edit and create quizzes and tests.*

Reinforce and Review

☐ **Activity** Introduction to Clouds

☐ **Graphic Organizer** Process Chart

☐ **Print Path** Visual Summary, SE p. 174

☐ **Digital Path** Lesson Closer

Evaluate Student Mastery

See the teacher support below the Student Pages for additional Formative Assessment questions.

Ask the following questions to assess student mastery of the material. **Ask:** What are three basic cloud shapes? stratus clouds, cumulus clouds, and cirrus clouds **Ask:** What are four classes of clouds based on altitude? low clouds, middle clouds, high clouds, and clouds of vertical development **Ask:** How do clouds form? Clouds form when rising air is cooled to the dew point temperature and water vapor changes from gas to a liquid.

Reteach

Formative assessment may show that students need reinforcement for certain topics. The resources below are recommended for reteaching. If students were introduced to a topic through the Print path, you can also use the Digital Path to reteach, or vice versa.
🎧 *Can be assigned to individual students*

Introduction to Clouds
Activity Solar Insulation

Cloud Formation
Quick Lab Out of Thin Air

Cloud Classification
Activity Charting Clouds
ELL Cloud Cartoons 🎧

Fog
Daily Demo Form Fog 🎧

Alternative Assessment
Clouds
🌐 *Online resources: student worksheet, optional rubrics*

Clouds and Cloud Formation

Mix and Match: *Clouds*
Mix and match ideas to show what you've learned about clouds based on altitude.

1. Work on your own, with a partner, or with a small group.
2. Choose two information sources from Column A, one topic from Column B, and three options from Column C. Check your choices.
3. Have your teacher approve your plan.
4. Submit or present your results.

A. Choose Two Information Sources	B. Choose One Thing to Analyze	C. Choose Three Ways to Communicate Analysis
___ observations of clouds during a neighborhood walk	___ low clouds, including stratus, stratocumulus, and nimbostratus	___ diagram or chart
___ photographs of clouds under different weather conditions	___ middle clouds, including altocumulus and altostratus	___ model
___ illustration and/or diagram of low, middle, and high clouds	___ high clouds, including cirrus, cirrocumulus, and cirrostratus	___ booklet, such as a weather guide
___ video that includes clouds of vertical development	___ clouds of vertical development, including nimbostratus and cumulonimbus	___ game, such as a cloud quiz
___ print or audio description that includes clouds based on altitude		___ song or poem, with supporting details, using poetic language such as "mares' tails"
___ a reliable source of common cloud classifications from the Internet		___ skit, chant, or dance, with supporting details
		___ multimedia presentation
_____		_____

Going Further
☐ **Fine Arts Connection**
☐ **Language Arts Connection**
☐ **Print Path** Why It Matters, SE p. 173

Formative Assessment
☐ **Strategies** Throughout TE
☐ **Lesson Review** SE

Summative Assessment
☐ **Alternative Assessment** Clouds
☐ **Lesson Quiz**
☐ **Unit Tests A and B**
☐ **Unit Review** SE End-of-Unit

Your Resources

_____   _____

_____   _____

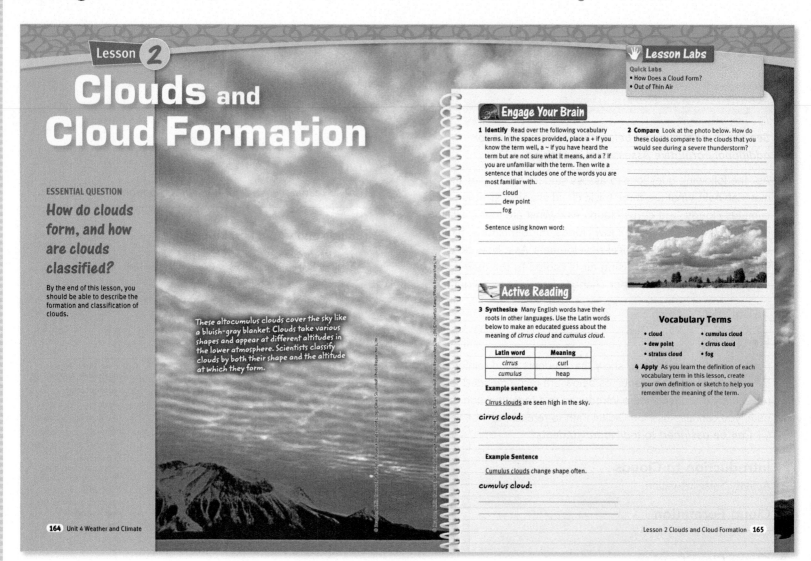

Answers

Answers for 1-3 should represent students' current thoughts, even if incorrect.

1. Answers will vary.

2. Sample answer: These clouds are smaller, whiter, and not as tall as clouds that produce severe thunderstorms.

3. Sample answers: A cirrus cloud will look wispy and curled, similar to hair. A cumulus cloud will look thick and piled up.

4. Students should define or sketch each vocabulary term in the lesson.

Opening Your Lesson

Discuss students' answers to item 1 to assess their understanding of different cloud shapes and the dew point.

Prerequisites Students should already have some understanding of the water cycle, elements of weather, clouds, fog, and climate. In this lesson, they will apply this understanding to the formation and classification of clouds.

Learning Alert

Difficult Concept Emphasize that a cloud is a collection of tiny water droplets and/or ice crystals. Students might have a misunderstanding about what constitutes a cloud. Some might believe that clouds are composed of water vapor, smoke, dust, fog, cotton, or bags of water. This misinformation could be the result of watching cloud formation demonstrations using tea kettles, from materials used for art projects, or from literary and poetic descriptions of clouds.

Head in the Clouds

Storm clouds appear dark gray. They are so full of water droplets that little light can pass through them.

What are clouds?

When you look into the sky, you see the amazing shapes that clouds take and how quickly those shapes change. But, have you ever asked yourself what clouds are made of or how they form? And did you know that there are different types of clouds?

A **cloud** is a collection of small water droplets or ice crystals that are suspended in the air. Clouds are visible because water droplets and ice crystals reflect light. Clouds are most often associated with precipitation. However, the reality is that most cloud types do not produce precipitation.

How do clouds affect climate?

The precipitation that falls from clouds has a significant effect on local climate. In particular, the pattern of precipitation of an area will determine the climate of that area. For instance, a desert is an area that receives less than 25 cm of precipitation a year. But, a tropical rainforest may average 250 cm of precipitation a year.

Clouds also affect temperatures on Earth. About 25% of the sun's energy that reaches Earth is reflected back into space by clouds. Low-altitude clouds, which are thick and reflect more sunlight, help to cool Earth. On the other hand, thin, high-altitude clouds absorb some of the energy that radiates from Earth. Part of this energy is reradiated back to Earth's surface. This warms Earth, because this energy is not directly lost to space.

Active Reading 5 Describe What are two ways in which clouds affect Earth's climate?

6 Apply Sketch a cloud, and write a caption that relates the drawing to the content on this page.

© Houghton Mifflin Harcourt Publishing Company • Image Credits: ©Mike Theiss/National Geographic/Getty Images

166 Unit 4 Weather and Climate

How do clouds form?

Clouds form when water vapor condenses, or changes from a gas to a liquid. For water vapor to condense, two things must happen. Air must be cooled to its dew point, and there must be a solid surface on which water molecules can condense.

Air Cools to the Dew Point

As warm air rises in Earth's atmosphere, it expands and cools. If air rises high enough into the atmosphere, it cools to its dew point. **Dew point** is the temperature at which the rate of condensation equals the rate of evaporation. *Evaporation* is the change of state from a liquid to a gas that usually occurs at the surface of a liquid. Evaporation takes place at the surface of an ocean, lake, stream, or other body of water. Water vapor in the air can condense and form water droplets or ice crystals when the temperature is at or below the dew point.

Water Droplets or Ice Crystals Form on Nuclei

Water molecules condense much more rapidly when there is a solid surface on which to condense. In clouds, tiny solid particles called *cloud condensation nuclei* are the surfaces on which water droplets condense. Examples of cloud condensation nuclei include dust, salt, soil, and smoke.

Clouds are most commonly made of very large numbers of very small water droplets. However, at high altitudes, where temperatures are very cold, clouds are composed of ice crystals.

D Cloud formation takes place.

C Condensation takes place on nuclei.

condensation nucleus 0.0002 millimeter diameter

cloud droplet 0.05 millimeter diameter

B

A Warm air rises, expands, and cools.

7 Conclude Complete the flow chart by filling in the missing information.

© Houghton Mifflin Harcourt Publishing Company

167

Answers

5. Sample answer: Clouds affect climate by moderating temperatures at Earth's surface and by producing precipitation.

6. Students should draw a type of cloud with which they are familiar. Captions will vary depending upon student sketches.

7. B: Air cools to the dew point.

Interpreting Visuals

When clouds are present, does this mean that rain is predicted? No. Clouds don't always foretell rain. Some clouds occur when skies are blue and sunny. Other clouds are accompanied by snow, hail, or sleet.

Probing Questions GUIDED *Inquiry*

Comparing How can the effect of clouds be like a blanket? Clouds trap heat that is escaping from Earth's surface into space, much as a blanket traps body heat. The clouds radiate the heat back to Earth's surface and Earth's lower atmosphere. Clouds keep the temperature from dropping lower than it would if the sky was clear.

What is the role of solar energy in cloud formation?

The water cycle is the movement of water between the atmosphere, land, and ocean. Solar energy drives the water cycle and, therefore, provides the energy for cloud formation.

About 50 percent of the sun's incoming energy is absorbed by land, by water on the land's surface, and by surface waters in the oceans. This absorbed energy causes liquid water at the water's surface to become water vapor, a gas. This process is called evaporation. The water vapor rises into the atmosphere with air that has been warmed near Earth's surface.

Solar energy does not warm the surface of Earth evenly. Unequal heating of Earth's surface causes areas of high pressure and low pressure to form in the atmosphere. Air flows horizontally from areas of high pressure to areas of low pressure. This horizontal movement of air is called *wind*. Wind causes clouds to move around Earth's surface. However, for air to be cooled to its dew point so that clouds can form, the air is pushed up, or is lifted, into the atmosphere.

Visualize It!

9 Compare The images below show two processes by which clouds form when an air mass is lifted. In what ways are these two processes similar? In what ways are these two processes different?

_____

_____

_____

Frontal Lifting

Wind

0 °C
Warm air
-4 °C   Cold air   4 °C
6 °C   10 °C   13 °C
Cold front

Orographic Lifting

4000 m
3000 m   10 °C
2000 m   15 °C
1000 m   20 °C
         30 °C
Sea level   Desert
Ocean

What processes cool air enough to form clouds?

Active Reading **8 Identify** As you read, underline the processes that can cool air enough to form clouds.

There are several ways in which air can be cooled to its dew point. These include frontal and orographic lifting (ohr•uh•GRAF•ik LIFT•ing). Frontal lifting can occur when a warm air mass rises over a cold air mass. Once the rising air cools to its dew point, condensation occurs and clouds form.

Frontal lifting can also occur when a mass of cold air slides under a mass of warm air, pushing the warm air upward. The rising air cools to the dew point. Clouds form that often develop into thunderstorms.

Orographic lifting occurs when an obstacle, such as a mountain range, forces a mass of air upward. Water vapor in the air cools to its dew point and condenses. The clouds that form release large amounts of precipitation as rain or snow as they rise up the mountain. The other side of the mountain receives little precipitation.

What are three cloud shapes?

You have probably noticed the different shapes that clouds take as they move through the sky. Some clouds are thick and puffy. Other clouds are thin and wispy. Scientists use shape as a way to classify clouds. The three classes of clouds based on shape are stratus (STRAT•uhs) clouds, cumulus (KYOOM•yuh•luhs) clouds, and cirrus (SIR•uhs) clouds.

Stratus Clouds

The lowest clouds in the atmosphere are stratus clouds. **Stratus clouds** are thin and flat, and their edges are not clearly defined. *Stratus* is a Latin word that means "layer." Stratus clouds often merge into one another and may look like a single layer that covers the entire sky. Stratus clouds are often gray. Light mist or drizzle may fall from these clouds. Fog is a type of stratus cloud that forms at or near the ground.

Cumulus Clouds

Cumulus is a Latin word that means "heap." **Cumulus clouds** are thick and puffy on top and generally flat on the bottom. These clouds have well-defined edges and can change shape rapidly. Some may tower high into the atmosphere, where the top of the cloud sometimes flattens.

Fair-weather cumulus clouds are bright and white. But cumulus clouds can become dark as more and more water droplets or ice crystals are added to the cloud. Cumulus clouds can produce severe weather. Thunder, lightning, and heavy precipitation are associated with cumulus clouds.

Cirrus Clouds

Cirrus is a Latin word that means "curl." **Cirrus clouds** look feathery, and their ends curl. Cirrus clouds are white.

Cirrus clouds form high in the atmosphere. At the altitudes where cirrus clouds form, there is little water vapor, and temperatures are very cold. As a result, cirrus clouds are made of ice crystals rather than liquid water droplets. They do not produce precipitation that reaches Earth's surface.

Visualize It!

10 Identify Name the three different clouds based on shape.

A _____

B _____

C _____

Answers

8. *See students' pages for annotations.*

9. Frontal and orographic lifting both can cause air to rise, cool to the dew point, and form clouds. However, frontal lifting occurs when two air masses meet, whereas orographic lifting occurs when an air mass encounters some type of large obstacle, such as a mountain range.

10. A: cumulus; B: cirrus; C: stratus

Building Reading Skills

Supporting Main Ideas When discussing frontal and orographic lifting, display photographs of clouds forming from orographic lifting, clouds forming at a cold front, and clouds forming at a warm front. Read the captions of the two images in the student text aloud, using the photographs to point out orographic lifting and frontal lifting.

Formative Assessment

Ask: If you saw thin, wispy clouds through which you could view the sun or moon, which cloud shape would you probably be looking at? Explain your answer. I would be looking at cirrus clouds. Because these clouds are thin and occur at high altitudes during fair weather, you can see the sun or the moon through them.

I've Looked at Clouds from Both Sides Now

11 Identify As you read the text, underline the prefixes associated with each class of cloud. If a class has no prefix, underline that information too.

What are the types of clouds based on altitude?

Scientists classify clouds by altitude as well as shape. The four classes of clouds based on altitude are low clouds, middle clouds, high clouds, and clouds of vertical development. These four classes are made up of 10 cloud types. Prefixes are used to name the clouds that belong to some of these classes.

Low Clouds
Low clouds form between Earth's surface and 2,000 m altitude. Water droplets commonly make up these clouds. The three types of low clouds are stratus, stratocumulus, and nimbostratus. There is no special prefix used to name low clouds. However, *nimbus* means "rain," so *nimbo*stratus clouds are rain clouds.

Middle Clouds
Middle clouds form between 2,000 m and 6,000 m altitude. They are most commonly made up of water droplets, but may be made up of ice crystals. The prefix *alto-* is used to name middle clouds. The two types of middle clouds are altocumulus and altostratus.

High Clouds
High clouds form above 6,000 m altitude. At these high altitudes, air temperature is below freezing. Therefore, high clouds are made up of ice crystals. The prefix *cirro-* is used to name high clouds. Cirrus, cirrocumulus, and cirrostratus are the types of high clouds.

Clouds of Vertical Development
Clouds of vertical development can rise high into the atmosphere. Although the cloud base is at low altitude, cloud tops can reach higher than 12,000 m. Clouds of vertical development are commonly formed by the rapid lifting of moist, warm air, which can result in strong vertical growth. There is no special prefix used to name clouds of vertical development. The two types of clouds of vertical development are cumulus and cumulonimbus.

Cumulonimbus clouds have the greatest vertical development of any cloud type. Air currents within these clouds can move upward at as much as 20 m/s. Cumulonimbus clouds are linked to severe weather and can produce rain, hail, lightning, tornadoes, and dangerous, rapidly sinking columns of air that strike Earth.

Think Outside the Book Inquiry

12 Apply Research cumulonimbus clouds. When you complete your research, consider different materials that might be used to create a model of a cumulonimbus cloud. Then, use your materials to build a model that shows the structure of a cumulonimbus cloud.

170 Unit 4 Weather and Climate

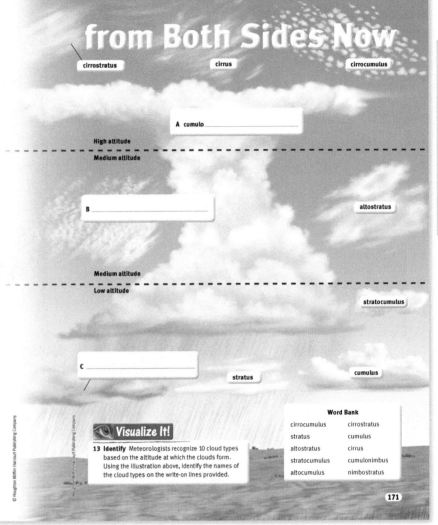

Visualize It!

13 Identify Meteorologists recognize 10 cloud types based on the altitude at which the clouds form. Using the illustration above, identify the names of the cloud types on the write-on lines provided.

Word Bank
cirrocumulus, cirrostratus, stratus, cumulus, altostratus, cirrus, stratocumulus, cumulonimbus, altocumulus, nimbostratus

171

Answers

11. *See students' pages for annotations.*

12. Student models should show a flat-based cloud that rises high into the atmosphere. Models should show the characteristic "anvil" cloud top. Arrows within the cloud should show updrafts and downdrafts. From the dark base of the cloud, students should show heavy precipitation in the form of both rain and hail falling. Lightning should also be present and can be seen at various altitudes within the cloud as well as coming from the cloud base. Some student models may even show a tornado emerging from a rotating wall cloud.

13. A. cumulonimbus; B. altocumulus; C. nimbostratus

Building Math Skills

Ask: Scientists have classified clouds into four main classes based on altitude. Convert feet into meters for each class. Low clouds: near ground level to 6,000 ft 1,830 m; middle clouds: 6,000 ft to 20,000 ft 1,830 m to 6,100 m; high clouds: 20,000 ft to 40,000 ft 6,100 m to 12,200 m; clouds of vertical development: 1,600 ft to more than 39,000 ft 490 m to more than 12,000 m

Probing Questions GUIDED Inquiry

Help students understand different types of clouds based on altitude. **Ask:** How do low clouds differ from high clouds? Because low clouds are close to Earth's surface, they are made up of water droplets. High clouds form at higher altitudes and are made up of ice crystals. **Ask:** What clouds can grow several miles in height? Explain why these clouds signal danger. Cumulonimbus clouds tower more than 12,000 m into the atmosphere. These clouds are accompanied by severe weather, such as thunderstorms, snow showers, hail, and tornadoes.

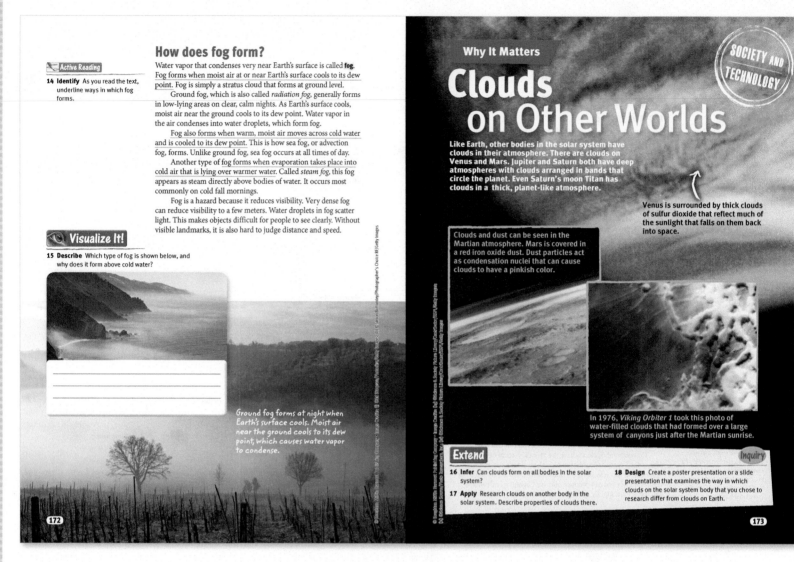

How does fog form?

Active Reading

14 Identify As you read the text, underline ways in which fog forms.

Water vapor that condenses very near Earth's surface is called **fog**. Fog forms when moist air at or near Earth's surface cools to its dew point. Fog is simply a stratus cloud that forms at ground level.

Ground fog, which is also called *radiation fog*, generally forms in low-lying areas on clear, calm nights. As Earth's surface cools, moist air near the ground cools to its dew point. Water vapor in the air condenses into water droplets, which form fog.

Fog also forms when warm, moist air moves across cold water and is cooled to its dew point. This is how sea fog, or advection fog, forms. Unlike ground fog, sea fog occurs at all times of day.

Another type of fog forms when evaporation takes place into cold air that is lying over warmer water. Called *steam fog*, this fog appears as steam directly above bodies of water. It occurs most commonly on cold fall mornings.

Fog is a hazard because it reduces visibility. Very dense fog can reduce visibility to a few meters. Water droplets in fog scatter light. This makes objects difficult for people to see clearly. Without visible landmarks, it is also hard to judge distance and speed.

Visualize It!

15 Describe Which type of fog is shown below, and why does it form above cold water?

Ground fog forms at night when Earth's surface cools. Moist air near the ground cools to its dew point, which causes water vapor to condense.

Why It Matters

Clouds on Other Worlds

SOCIETY AND TECHNOLOGY

Like Earth, other bodies in the solar system have clouds in their atmosphere. There are clouds on Venus and Mars. Jupiter and Saturn both have deep atmospheres with clouds arranged in bands that circle the planet. Even Saturn's moon Titan has clouds in a thick, planet-like atmosphere.

Venus is surrounded by thick clouds of sulfur dioxide that reflect much of the sunlight that falls on them back into space.

Clouds and dust can be seen in the Martian atmosphere. Mars is covered in a red iron oxide dust. Dust particles act as condensation nuclei that can cause clouds to have a pinkish color.

In 1976, *Viking Orbiter 1* took this photo of water-filled clouds that had formed over a large system of canyons just after the Martian sunrise.

Extend

Inquiry

16 Infer Can clouds form on all bodies in the solar system?

17 Apply Research clouds on another body in the solar system. Describe properties of clouds there.

18 Design Create a poster presentation or a slide presentation that examines the way in which clouds on the solar system body that you chose to research differ from clouds on Earth.

172 173

Answers

14. *See students' pages for annotations.*

15. Sample answer: sea fog; Sea fog forms over cold water when warm air that is moving over the water is cooled to its dew point.

16. No, most bodies in the solar system do not have enough mass to have the gravitational attraction needed to capture and maintain an atmosphere in which clouds can form.

17. Student answers will vary depending upon the body in the solar system the student elects to research.

18. Student answers will vary depending upon the body in the solar system the student elects to research.

Learning Alert ⚠ MISCONCEPTION ⚠

Difficult Concept Fog is a cloud that forms near the ground. Billions of water droplets that are suspended in the air form these low-lying clouds. The moisture often rises from a nearby body of water, such as a lake or bay, or from a marsh or damp ground. Fog is denser than mist, which is also composed of water droplets suspended in air. When fog is composed of ice crystals, it is called *ice fog*. Fog reduces visibility to 1 km or less.

Why It Matters

Clouds can appear in the atmospheres of other planets and moons in our solar system. Depending on the mixture of gases surrounding that planet or moon, clouds are often composed of materials other than water. For example, clouds on Venus are composed of sulfur dioxide; Uranus and Neptune have clouds made of methane; and liquid methane makes up the clouds over Saturn's largest moon, Titan. Have students compare and contrast the clouds in the images to clouds on Earth.

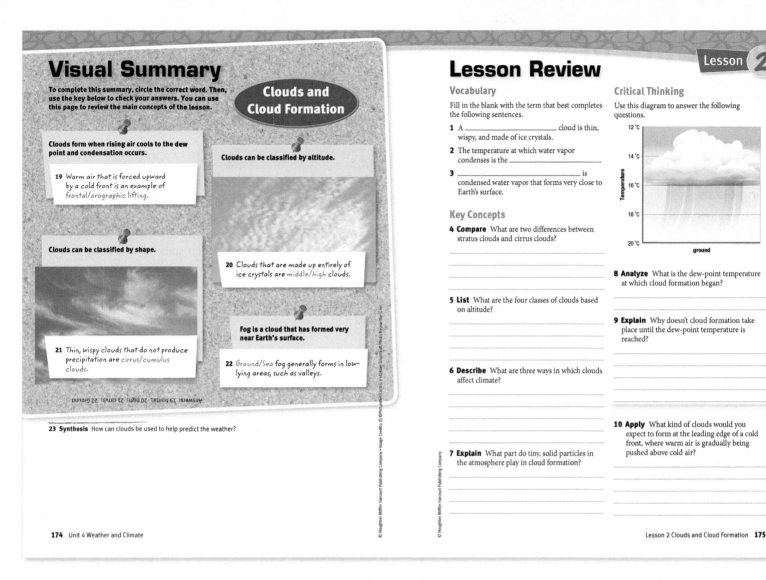

Visual Summary

To complete this summary, circle the correct word. Then, use the key below to check your answers. You can use this page to review the main concepts of the lesson.

Clouds and Cloud Formation

Clouds form when rising air cools to the dew point and condensation occurs.

19 Warm air that is forced upward by a cold front is an example of frontal/orographic lifting.

Clouds can be classified by shape.

21 Thin, wispy clouds that do not produce precipitation are cirrus/cumulus clouds.

Clouds can be classified by altitude.

20 Clouds that are made up entirely of ice crystals are middle/high clouds.

Fog is a cloud that has formed very near Earth's surface.

22 Ground/Sea fog generally forms in low-lying areas, such as valleys.

Answers: 19 frontal; 20 high; 21 cirrus; 22 Ground

23 Synthesis How can clouds be used to help predict the weather?

174 Unit 4 Weather and Climate

Lesson Review

Lesson 2

Vocabulary

Fill in the blank with the term that best completes the following sentences.

1 A _____ cloud is thin, wispy, and made of ice crystals.

2 The temperature at which water vapor condenses is the _____.

3 _____ is condensed water vapor that forms very close to Earth's surface.

Key Concepts

4 Compare What are two differences between stratus clouds and cirrus clouds?

5 List What are the four classes of clouds based on altitude?

6 Describe What are three ways in which clouds affect climate?

7 Explain What part do tiny, solid particles in the atmosphere play in cloud formation?

Critical Thinking

Use this diagram to answer the following questions.

8 Analyze What is the dew-point temperature at which cloud formation began?

9 Explain Why doesn't cloud formation take place until the dew-point temperature is reached?

10 Apply What kind of clouds would you expect to form at the leading edge of a cold front, where warm air is gradually being pushed above cold air?

Lesson 2 Clouds and Cloud Formation 175

Visual Summary Answers

19. frontal
20. high
21. cirrus
22. Ground
23. Sample answer: Some cloud types, such as nimbostratus and cumulonimbus, signal rain in the immediate future. Other cloud types, such as cumulus or cirrus, signal fair weather for at least the near future. Some high clouds can signal the approach of a front.

Lesson Review Answers

1. cirrus
2. dew point
3. Fog
4. Sample answer: Stratus clouds are low clouds. Stratus clouds are made of water droplets. Cirrus clouds are high clouds. Cirrus clouds are made of ice crystals.
5. low clouds; middle clouds; high clouds; clouds of vertical development
6. Clouds help to cool Earth's surface, warm Earth's surface, and deliver precipitation.
7. Sample answer: Water vapor molecules condense more rapidly when they attach to a solid surface.

Condensation nuclei, such as dust, salt, soil, and smoke, act as tiny surfaces on which water vapor condenses to form water droplets.

8. 16° C
9. Cloud formation takes place at the dew point because that is the temperature at which water vapor condenses into water droplets.
10. Sample answer: I would expect clouds of vertical development to form at the leading edge of a cold front as warm air is gradually pushed higher into the atmosphere, which causes vertical cloud growth.

S.T.E.M. Engineering & Technology

Using Data in Systems

Purpose To use weather data as an input to generate a weather map and make weather predictions as an output

Learning Goals

- Analyze weather forecasting as a system.
- Identify the inputs and outputs of a forecasting system.
- Interpret weather data to generate a weather map.

Academic Vocabulary

meteorologist, isobar, barometric pressure, weather fronts

Prerequisite Knowledge

- Basic understanding of the water cycle, Earth's atmosphere, the causes of wind, and wind patterns
- Knowledge of elements of weather

21st Century SKILLS — Theme: Global Awareness

Activities focusing on 21st Century Skills are included for this feature and can be found on the following pages.

These activities focus on the following skills:

- **Communication and Collaboration**
- **Information Literacy**
- **Social and Cross-Cultural Skills**

You can learn more about the 21st Century Skills in the front matter of this Teacher's Edition.

Content Refresher

Professional Development

Weather Forecasting Meteorology is the study of the atmosphere in relation to weather processes and forecasting. Meteorologists use information from a wide variety of sources. One primary data source is observation stations at airports and military bases. Meteorologists can also use satellites, radar, weather balloons, lightning detection networks, and surface sensors to understand temperature, wind, humidity, precipitation, visibility, and cloud cover across the nation.

Satellite imagery can help forecasters monitor developing storms. Radar can reliably track the movement of rain, so meteorologists can generally provide accurate short-term forecasts about when and where it will rain. Snow, however, is more difficult to forecast, since radar cannot detect snow well. Light snow can go entirely undetected by radar.

Weather balloons carry aloft instrument platforms called radiosondes. A radiosonde contains instruments for measuring air pressure, humidity, and temperature at different levels of the atmosphere, from the ground to altitudes of 20 kilometers or higher. A radio transmitter located within the instrument package transmits data to a ground station. The path of a radiosonde as it ascends also provides information about wind direction and speed.

To forecast thunderstorms or tornadoes, scientists use surface and upper-air observations to determine winds, areas of low pressure, and instability. Satellites track the movement of weather systems that might cause this dangerous weather. Computer models can use past data to help determine where such storms might develop today. Radar and satellites can track the storms once they develop.

Computer models can aid weather forecasting, but when the models disagree, it is up to a meteorologist to interpret and draw conclusions from the weather data.

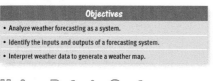

S.T.E.M. Engineering & Technology

Evaluating Technological Systems

Skills
✓ Identify inputs
✓ Identify outputs
✓ Identify system processes
Evaluate system feedback
Apply system controls
✓ Communicate results

Objectives
• Analyze weather forecasting as a system.
• Identify the inputs and outputs of a forecasting system.
• Interpret weather data to generate a weather map.

Using Data in Systems

A system is a group of interacting parts that work together to do a job. Technological systems process inputs and generate outputs. An input is any matter, energy, or information that goes into a system. Outputs are matter, energy, or information that come out of the system. When you use a computer, the data set that is entered is the input. The computer delivers your output on the monitor or the printer.

Weather Data Go Into a System

What do you do if you have an outdoor activity planned tomorrow? You probably check the weather forecast to help you decide what to wear. Meteorologists are scientists who use data from different sources to find out what is happening in the atmosphere. Weather data are the input. The data set is processed by computers that perform complex calculations to generate weather models. Weather forecast systems combine 72 hours of data from weather stations, weather balloons, radar, aircraft, and weather satellites to show what is happening in Earth's atmosphere now and to predict what will happen in the future.

1 Explain How is a television weather forecast part of a technological system?

_____

_____

_____

The atmosphere is a system that can have dramatic outputs. Those outputs are inputs into a weather forecasting system.

Forecast Data Come Out of the System

Weather maps are one type of output from a weather forecasting system. On a weather map you can find information about atmospheric pressure, and about the direction and temperature of moving air. The numbered lines on a weather map are called *isobars*. Isobars connect areas that have the same atmospheric pressure. Isobars center around areas of high and low pressure. An area of high pressure (H) indicates a place where cool, dense air is falling. An area of low pressure (L) indicates a place where warm, less dense air is rising. Pressure differences cause air to move. The leading edge of a cool air mass is called a *cold front*. The leading edge of a warm air mass is called a *warm front*. On a weather map, blue lines with triangles show cold fronts and red lines with half circles show warm fronts.

The direction of the triangles or half circles on a map shows which way a front is moving. Wind direction is described in terms of the direction from which the wind is blowing. A west wind is blowing from west to east.

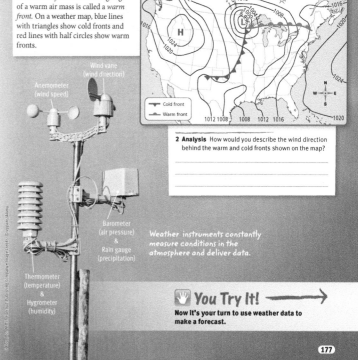

Anemometer (wind speed)

Wind vane (wind direction)

Barometer (air pressure) & Rain gauge (precipitation)

Thermometer (temperature) & Hygrometer (humidity)

Weather instruments constantly measure conditions in the atmosphere and deliver data.

Cold front
Warm front

2 Analysis How would you describe the wind direction behind the warm and cold fronts shown on the map?

_____

_____

_____

✋ You Try It! →

Now it's your turn to use weather data to make a forecast.

Answers

1. The weather forecast is the output of a system that uses weather data as input and processes the data to make predictions.

2. A south wind is blowing behind the warm front. A west to northwest wind is blowing behind the cold front.

Evaluating Technological Systems

✋ You Try It!

Now it's your turn to become part of the weather forecasting system. The table and map on these pages show some weather data for several cities in the United States. You will use those data to analyze weather and make predictions.

1 Identify Inputs

Which information in the table will you use to determine where the high and low pressure areas may be located?

City	Barometric pressure (mbar)	Wind direction	Temperature (°F)
Atlanta	1009	S	63
Chicago	1012	W	36
Cleveland	1006	S	35
Denver	1021	S	34
New York	990	S	58
Billings	1012	SW	28
Spokane	1009	SW	27
Los Angeles	1009	W	68
Dallas	1012	NW	50
Memphis	1012	NW	45
Orlando	1006	S	78
Raleigh	998	S	60

2 Identify Outputs

What outputs from weather stations are included on a weather map?

3 Identify System Processes

How will you process the information in the table and on the map to make predictions? Describe how you will use the inputs to develop an output.

4 Communicate Results

Use data from the table and the map to answer the questions below.

A According to the data in the table, where are the centers of the high and low pressure systems at this time? Mark them on the map using an H or an L.

B Add the temperature listed in the table for each city to the map.

C Imagine that you are a meteorologist in Atlanta and this is the current map. What temperature change would you predict over the next few hours, and why?

D What pressure change would you predict for Denver over the next few days, and why?

Answers

1. barometric pressure for each city

2. high- and low-pressure areas, isobars, temperature, fronts, and the direction in which the fronts are moving

3. Sample answer: Using the pressure and temperature differences and directions in which the fronts are moving, we can predict changes that are likely to occur at cities on the map.

4. A. Students should place an H slightly northeast of Denver. Students should place an L slightly west of New York. *See students' pages for annotations.*

   B. *See students' pages for annotations.*

   C. Sample answer: Based on the information shown on the map, there is a cold front moving toward Atlanta. As the cold front passes Atlanta, the temperature in Atlanta will drop.

   D. Sample answer: The wind in Denver is blowing from the south, so the high-pressure system is likely to move northward, causing the pressure in Denver to decrease.

21st Century SKILLS

Learning and Innovation Skills

 small groups　　 45 min

Communication and Collaboration Have several students work together to write and present a weather skit for a group of younger students. The skit can be fiction or nonfiction but should help the younger students understand how weather forecasters gather data and make predictions. Encourage groups to present their skits in such a way that they can be understood by students of different ages, language proficiencies, and cultural backgrounds. Encourage group members to be flexible, share responsibilities, and make compromises to reach their common goal.

Information, Media, and Technology Skills

 pairs or small groups　　ongoing

Information Literacy Have pairs or small groups select one of the cities featured on their weather map. Challenge students to analyze data from their weather map and develop a forecast of probable weather conditions in that city over the next two or three days. Then have students work together to produce a weather report for television, radio, or the Internet. Students should write text or a script, develop any visuals that are needed, and then create a report using their chosen media.

Life and Career Skills

small groups　　ongoing

Social and Cross-Cultural Skills Invite small groups of students to write a history of how people in earlier times felt about the significance of different weather phenomena. Then have students compare these findings with how people around the world see these same phenomena. What differences or similarities do students notice? Remind students to respond open-mindedly to different ideas and values. Encourage students to share their findings with the class.

Differentiated Instruction

Basic *Comparing Weather Maps*

 individuals　　 20 min

Invite students to draw a second weather map, using a different set of data. Have students compare their two maps and describe how predictions made from each map would differ.

Advanced *Graphing Historical Data*

 individuals or pairs　　ongoing

Invite interested students to research historical weather data for their area and to graph it to show trends. For example, how much rain does the area receive in a given month, or how much snow does it receive in winter, or how have summer temperatures changed over time? Ask students to identify the historical weather data they want to collect and then present the information in a graph that makes the data easy to understand.

ELL *How Weather Travels*

individuals or pairs　　20 min

Have students draw a map that shows how weather moves across a nation (it doesn't have to be the United States). Encourage students to label types of weather, places, and geographical features (mountains, rivers, oceans) on their maps.

Customize Your Feature

- [ ] **21st Century Skills** Learning and Innovation Skills
- [ ] **21st Century Skills** Information, Media, and Technology Skills
- [ ] **21st Century Skills** Life and Career Skills
- [ ] **Basic** Comparing Weather Maps
- [ ] **Advanced** Graphing Historical Data
- [ ] **ELL** How Weather Travels

What Influences Weather?

Essential Question How do the water cycle and other global patterns affect local weather?

 **Professional Development**

For more detailed information about the topics in this lesson, refer to the Content Refresher in the Unit Opener pages.

Opening Your Lesson

Begin the lesson by assessing students' prerequisite and prior knowledge.

Prerequisite Knowledge

- Density
- Earth's atmosphere and the water cycle
- Heat transfer by radiation, convection, and conduction
- Temperature

Accessing Prior Knowledge

Ask: How are density and air pressure related? when one decreases, the other one also decreases

Ask: What is Earth's atmosphere? the thin layer of gases surrounding Earth Define *water cycle.* The continuous movement of water on the surface and in the crust of Earth, through its atmosphere, as well as through living things.

Customize Your Opening

☐ **Accessing Prior Knowledge,** above

☐ **Print Path** Engage Your Brain, SE p. 181, #1–2

☐ **Print Path** Active Reading, SE p. 181, #3–4

☐ **Digital Path** Lesson Opener

Key Topics/Learning Goals	Supporting Concepts
How the Water Cycle Influences Weather 1 Explain ways in which the water cycle influences weather.	• Precipitation is part of the water cycle. • Humidity is a measure of the amount of water in the air, and the evaporation of water into the air is part of the water cycle. • Visibility can be affected by clouds, fog, and precipitation, all part of the water cycle.
How Patterns in the Atmosphere Affect Weather 1 Define *air mass* and *front;* explain how weather is affected by air masses. 2 Describe a cold front and a warm front. 3 Describe a high-pressure and a low-pressure system. 4 Define *jet stream,* and explain how the polar jet stream influences weather.	• An air mass takes on the temperature and moisture characteristics of the land or water below it, then moves to new locations. • A front is the boundary between air masses. • Cold fronts occur when cold air moves under warm air, pushing it up. Warm fronts occur when warm air moves over colder air. • In high-pressure systems, air moves downward and rotates. In low-pressure systems, air rises, cools, and forms clouds. • Stationary fronts cause many days of unchanging weather, usually mild and clear. • The polar jet stream pulls cold air down from Canada into the United States.
How Patterns in the Ocean Influence Weather 1 Describe how ocean currents influence weather.	• The water's surface temperature affects the temperature of the air above it. • Coastal areas affected by warm surface currents tend to have warmer weather than inland areas at same latitude and elevation. • Coastal areas near cold surface currents tend to have cooler weather than inland areas at the same latitude and elevation.

Options for Instruction

Two parallel paths provide coverage of the Essential Questions, with a strong **Inquiry** strand woven into each. Follow the **Print Path,** the **Digital Path,** or your customized combination of print, digital, and inquiry.

 Print Path
Teaching support for the Print Path appears with the Student Pages.

 Inquiry Labs and Activities

🖥 **Digital Path**
Digital Path shortcut: TS661222

Print Path	Inquiry Labs and Activities	Digital Path
Water, Water Everywhere..., SE pp. 182–183 **How does the water cycle affect weather?**	**Activity** Cool Off	**Air Masses** Diagram
Putting Up a Front, SE pp. 184–185 **How do air masses affect weather? Where do fronts form?** **Feeling the Pressure,** SE pp. 186–187 **Pressure systems and how they interact How pressure systems affect us** **Windy Weather,** SE pp. 188–189 **How global wind patterns and jet streams affect weather**	**Daily Demo** Blowing Around **Daily Demo** It's a Breeze **Activity** Air Mass Matters **Quick Lab** Analyze Weather Patterns	**Air Masses** Diagram **The Jet Stream** Animation **Fronts and Weather** Interactive Image **Front Interactions** Interactive Graphics **Air Pressure** Diagram
Ocean Effects, SE pp. 190–191 **How do ocean currents influence weather?** • Cool Ocean Current Lowers Coastal Air Temperatures • Warm Ocean Current Raises Coastal Air Temperatures	**Activity** Sharing Expertise **Quick Lab** Coastal Climate Modeling **Exploration Lab** Modeling El Niño	**Ocean Current Flow** Interactive Image

Options for Assessment

See the Evaluate page for options, including Formative Assessment, Summative Assessment, and Unit Review.

Engage and Explore

Activities and Discussion

Activity *Cool Off*

 Engage

Water Cycle Influences

 pairs
 15 min
 DIRECTED inquiry

Have students work in pairs. Distribute isopropyl alcohol swabs to each team. Have students rub the alcohol swab on an unbroken patch of skin and talk about what they experience. **Ask:** What happens? the alcohol evaporates quickly Have students describe how the swabbed skin feels. cool Then ask them to explain why it feels cool. Sample answer: The alcohol evaporates, and evaporation takes or absorbs energy from the skin. This makes the skin feel cooler.

CAUTION **Students who have skin allergies should not participate.**

Activity *Air Mass Matters*

Patterns in the Atmosphere

 individuals
 15 min
 GUIDED inquiry

Mind Maps Have students create a Mind Map about air masses to help them remember new information. Have them make one leg for each type of air mass. Direct them to fill in the branches with details about the source of the air mass and the direction of its movement. They should also provide information about the type of weather associated with each air mass.

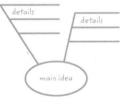

Discussion *Hurricanes*

Water Cycle Influences

 whole class
15 min

Hurricanes cause a lot of destruction. In Florida, hurricane season occurs from June 1 to November 30. Hurricanes gain power as they move across the ocean, sucking up moist tropical air. When they hit land, they slow down and unleash high winds and heavy rains. Have students discuss why they think hurricanes are so destructive, and relate any personal experiences they have had with hurricanes.

Labs and Demos

Daily Demo *Blowing Around*

Patterns in the Atmosphere

 whole class
 20 min
DIRECTED inquiry

PURPOSE **To observe how rotation causes global winds to curve**

MATERIALS

- globe

1 Gather students around a globe. Have a student draw a straight chalk line on the globe from the North Pole to the equator.

2 **Predicting** Have students predict what would happen to the line if it were drawn while the globe was spinning. As you slowly spin the globe, have the student repeat the experiment.

3 What happens to the chalk line? The line curves to the right. Point out that Earth's rotation causes winds to move in curved paths. What is this called? the Coriolis effect

4 How would winds flow if Earth did not rotate? in straight lines

⊘ ◻ **Quick Lab** *Analyze Weather Patterns*

PURPOSE **To explain interactions among Earth's systems**

See the Lab Manual or go Online for planning information

Customize Your Labs

◻ *See the Lab Manual for lab datasheets.*

⊘ *Go Online for editable lab datasheets.*

Levels of **Inquiry**

DIRECTED inquiry	GUIDED inquiry	INDEPENDENT inquiry
introduces inquiry skills within a structured framework.	develops inquiry skills within a supportive environment.	deepens inquiry skills with student-driven questions or procedures.

Daily Demo *It's a Breeze*

Patterns in the Atmosphere

 whole class
🕐 20 min
Inquiry GUIDED inquiry

Use this short demo after you have discussed wind formation resulting from uneven heating of Earth's surface.

PURPOSE **To observe how winds are produced**
MATERIALS

- cardboard sheets taped together
- glass baking pans (2)
- ice
- incense stick and match
- modeling clay, small piece
- pot holder or oven mitt
- sand

1 Have one group of students fill one small glass baking pan with sand. Have another group fill a second baking dish with ice.
2 Heat the dish containing sand in a microwave oven on high for 1 minute until the sand is warm.
3 Place the pans side by side. Use several sheets of cardboard taped together as a screen to surround the pans on three sides.
4 Light an incense stick and place it in a piece of modeling clay between the two pans.
5 **Observing** What do you see? Explain why this happens. The smoke from the incense moves sideways toward the pan with warm sand. The warm sand heats the air above it, decreasing its density, causing the air to rise. The air above the ice is colder and denser. This colder air flows in to take the place of the warm air rising above the sand, creating a breeze.

Quick Lab *Coastal Climate Model*

How Patterns in the Ocean Influence Weather

 small groups
🕐 30 min
Inquiry DIRECTED inquiry

Students will create a model that shows how ocean breezes can cause condensation and precipitation.

PURPOSE **To make a model of factors affecting the climate of coastal areas**
MATERIALS

- fan
- metal pan, shallow
- sink
- thermometer
- water, hot and cold

Exploration Lab *Modeling El Niño*

How Patterns in the Ocean Influence Climate

 small groups
🕐 45 min
Inquiry DIRECTED or GUIDED inquiry

Students construct a model of the ocean using water and oil; then they simulate surface winds and study the effects the winds have on their ocean model.

PURPOSE **To model the relationship between winds and the El Niño**
MATERIALS

- bowl
- container, clear rectangular
- food coloring, blue
- hair dryer
- vegetable oil (200 mL)
- paint, oil-based, red
- spoons (2)
- water
- marker, permanent
- masking tape

Activities and Discussion

☐ **Activity** Cool Off
☐ **Activity** Air Mass Matters
☐ **Discussion** Hurricanes

Labs and Demos

☐ **Daily Demo** Blowing Around
☐ **Quick Lab** Analyze Weather Patterns
☐ **Daily Demo** It's a Breeze
☐ **Quick Lab** Coastal Climate Model
☐ **Exploration Lab** Modeling El Niño

Your Resources

_____

_____

_____

Explain Science Concepts

	📖 **Print Path**	💻 **Digital Path**
Key Topics		

How the Water Cycle Influences Weather

☐ **Water, Water Everywhere!**,
SE pp. 182–183
- Active Reading, #5
- Visualize It!, #6
- Visualize It!, #7

☐ **Air Masses**
Learn how elements of the water cycle and air masses influence weather.

How Patterns in the Atmosphere Affect Weather

☐ **Putting Up A Front,** SE pp. 184–185
- Active Reading (Annotation strategy), #8
- Apply, #9
- Identify, #10
- Infer, #11

☐ **Feeling the Pressure,** SE pp. 186–187
- Visualize It!, #12
- Visualize It!, #13

☐ **Windy Weather,** SE pp. 188–189
- Visualize It!, #14
- Active Reading, #15
- Visualize It!, #16

Warm air rises

☐ **Air Masses**
Learn how elements of the water cycle and air masses influence weather.

☐ **The Jet Stream**
Watch how the jet stream moves.

☐ **Fronts and Weather**
Explore different types of fronts and the weather associated with each.

☐ **Front Interactions**
Explore the relationships between air masses and fronts.

☐ **Air Pressure**
Learn about systems of high and low pressure.

How Patterns in the Ocean Influence Weather

☐ **Ocean Effects,** SE pp. 190–191
- Visualize It!, #17
- Visualize It!, #18
- Visualize It!, #19

☐ **Ocean Current Flow**
Explore the different ocean currents and their influence on weather.

Average Monthly High Temperatures

Differentiated Instruction

Basic *Water Cycle and Weather*

Synthesizing Key Topics individuals   ⏱ 25 min

Diagram Briefly review the water cycle with students. Then have students make a labeled diagram that explains how each of the following parts of the water cycle affects weather: evaporation, condensation, precipitation. Suggest that students provide a separate text box on their drawing for each process. Each box should be large enough for them to write their explanation within it. When their diagrams are complete, ask students to label the part of their diagram that is associated with a low-pressure system (precipitation).

Advanced *Compare Global Winds*

How Patterns in the Atmosphere Affect Weather   individuals   ⏱ 15 min

Comparison Chart Encourage students to create a two-column chart with four rows. Have them label the columns "Latitude" and "Direction." Direct them to label the rows "Trade Winds," "Westerlies," "Polar Easterlies," and "Jet Streams." Have students do research, as needed, to complete their charts with the details that relate to each type of wind.

ELL *Air Masses and Weather*

How Patterns in the Atmosphere Affect Weather   groups   ⏱ 20 min

Cause-and-Effect Chain Help EL learners understand what happens when air masses meet. First discuss the everyday meaning of the term *front* ("forward part"). Have them identify the front part of their desks. Explain the "weather" meaning of the term *front* ("a boundary between two air masses"). Divide the class in two. One group completes a cause-and-effect chain diagram about what happens when a cold air mass moves toward and meets a warm air mass. The other group completes the diagram by describing what happens when a warm air mass moves toward and meets a cold air mass.

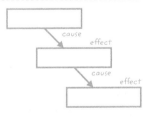

Lesson Vocabulary

air mass   jet stream   front

Previewing Vocabulary

👥 whole class   ⏱ 15 min

Description Wheel To help students remember the different terms introduced in the lesson, have them draw a circle with several radiating spokes. Students write the term in the center of the wheel. On each of the spokes students should write a term or phrase that is descriptive of the center term.

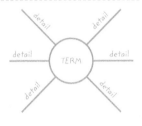

Reinforcing Vocabulary

👥 individuals or groups   ⏱ 20 min

Combination Notes Have students make combination notes to reinforce the vocabulary terms and the concepts associated with them. Have students write the vocabulary term across the top of a piece of paper. Underneath, students can draw two columns. Ask students to write key phrases related to the term in the left column. In the right column, encourage students to draw illustrations or diagrams explaining the key phrases and how they relate to the vocabulary term.

Customize Your Core Lesson

Core Instruction
- ☐ Print Path choices
- ☐ Digital Path choices

Vocabulary
- ☐ Previewing Vocabulary Description Wheel
- ☐ Reinforcing Vocabulary Combination Notes

Your Resources

Differentiated Instruction
- ☐ Basic Water Cycle and Weather
- ☐ Advanced Compare Global Winds
- ☐ ELL Air Masses and Weather

_____

_____

Extend Science Concepts

Reinforce and Review

Activity *Sharing Expertise*

Synthesizing Key Topics   small groups
🕐 40–45 min

Jigsaw Divide the class into three groups. Assign each group a key topic from the lesson.

- Have members of each group work together to become experts on their topic as it relates to the Essential Question, How do the water cycle and global weather patterns affect local weather?
- Have students work together in their groups until all students are confident that they can teach what they have learned about their key topic to the members of another group.
- Reassign students to three new mixed groups. The groups should include experts for each of the key topics. Have individuals in each mixed group share their expertise with other students in the group. The goal is for all students to be able to explain how each of the key topics relates to the Essential Question for the lesson.

Graphic Organizer

How Patterns in the Ocean Influence Weather   individuals
🕐 15 min

Main Idea Web Have students complete Main Idea Webs that show their understanding of how ocean currents influence weather. Have them write this main idea in a central box. Then have them add boxes around this box. In each surrounding box students should write a supporting detail for this concept. Prompt students to include information about how warm-water surface currents and cold-water surface currents affect coastal areas.

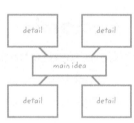

 Optional Online resource: Main Idea Web support

Going Further

Social Studies Connection

How Patterns in the Atmosphere Affect Weather   whole class
🕐 45 min

Discussion The region between the trade winds and the westerlies at about 30° north latitude is called the Horse Latitudes. Explain the origin of the name. In this region, winds are light or calm over vast areas of the ocean, so ships sailing to the New World could be stuck there for weeks at a time. Supposedly, to conserve water, horses carried as cargo were tossed overboard and their carcasses then floated in these waters. Students can refer to the illustration of global wind belts to describe the direction of the westerlies and trade winds. Encourage students to suggest reasons that the winds are so light in this area.

Language Arts Connection

Synthesizing Key Concepts   groups
🕐 varied

Research Project Old proverbs and sayings about the weather began with real observations of atmospheric conditions, for example, "Red sky at morning, sailors take warning; red sky at night, sailors' delight." A red sky can indicate rain or dry weather depending on the time of the day it occurs. Have students work in groups to research weather proverbs and investigate which sayings appear to be reliable. Students can present their findings in a short written paper.

Customize Your Closing

🔖 *See the Assessment Guide for quizzes and tests.*

 Go Online to edit and create quizzes and tests.

Reinforce and Review

☐ **Activity** Sharing Expertise

☐ **Graphic Organizer** Main Idea Web

☐ **Print Path** Visual Summary, SE p. 192

☐ **Print Path** Lesson Review, SE p. 193

☐ **Digital Path** Lesson Closer

Evaluate Student Mastery

Formative Assessment

See the teacher support below the Student Pages for additional Formative Assessment questions.

Have students identify three weather factors that are directly associated with the water cycle. clouds, humidity, precipitation
Ask: What is an air mass and what effect do air masses have on weather? An air mass is a large amount of air with a consistent air temperature and moisture content. As it moves into a region, it brings its temperature and moisture conditions to that region.

Ask: What is a front and how do fronts bring about changes in weather? A front is the boundary between air masses of different densities and different temperatures. When different types of fronts interact it results in weather changes. Finally, elicit the cause of global wind patterns. pressure differences from the uneven heating of Earth's surface and the Coriolis effect

Reteach

Formative assessment may show that students need reinforcement for certain topics. The resources below are recommended for reteaching. If students were introduced to a topic through the Print Path, you can also use the Digital Path to reteach, and vice versa.
🎧 *Can be assigned to individual students*

How the Water Cycle Influences Weather
Activity Cool Off 🎧

How Patterns in the Atmosphere Affect Weather
Activity Air Mass Matters 🎧

How Patterns in the Ocean Influence Weather
Activity Sharing Expertise

Summative Assessment

Alternative Assessment

Weather's Influences

🔾 *Online resource: student worksheet, optional rubrics*

What Influences Weather?

Take Your Pick: *Weather's Influences*

1. Work on your own, with a partner, or with a small group.
2. Choose items below for a total of 10 points. Check your choices.
3. Have your teacher approve your plan.
4. Submit or present your results.

2 Points

_____ **Picturing Currents** Choose a coastal area of the United States and draw a map of it. Add ocean currents to your map. Indicate whether the land is affected by cold or warm currents.

_____ **You Decide** Using a small piece of paper or an index card, write an answer to the following question: *What do you know about air masses and how they affect the weather?*

5 Points

_____ **In Your Own Words** Choose one paragraph or one screen from the Ocean Effects section of your lesson. Rewrite the content in your own words and present it to your class.

_____ **Under Pressure** With a small group, develop and perform a dance that represents both high- and low-pressure systems. In your dance, show how both systems act and what types of weather are associated with each system.

_____ **Making a Cycle** Create a three-dimensional model of how the water cycle influences weather. Use materials such as shoe boxes, cotton balls, paper, and markers. Then write a one-paragraph summary of the ways parts of the water cycle affect weather. Attach the summary to the model.

_____ **A Different Point of View** Write a short fiction story or cartoon from the point of view of the polar jet stream. In your story, have the polar jet stream explain how it affects the weather. Additionally, have the jet stream describe one of its best weather-related memories.

8 Points

_____ **Star Attraction** Suppose you are the owner of a beachside resort. Make a commercial advertising your resort. Include information about how the local weather is affected by ocean currents, weather systems, and weather fronts.

_____ **This Just In!** Present a news report about the visibility in your area. Find your local weather forecast and locate information about visibility. Present this information in your news report. Then present your ideas about why the visibility in your area is high or low. Remember that visibility can be affected by clouds, fog, precipitation, weather systems, and weather fronts.

Going Further
☐ Social Studies Connection
☐ Language Arts Connection

Formative Assessment
☐ Strategies Throughout TE
☐ Lesson Review SE

Summative Assessment
☐ Alternative Assessment Weather's Influences
☐ Lesson Quiz
☐ Unit Tests A and B
☐ Unit Review SE End-of-Unit

Your Resources

_____

_____

Lesson ③

What Influences Weather?

ESSENTIAL QUESTION

How do the water cycle and other global patterns affect local weather?

By the end of this lesson, you should be able to explain how global patterns in Earth's system influence weather.

The weather doesn't always turn out the way you want. But learning about the factors that affect weather can help you plan your next outing.

180 Unit 4 Weather and Climate

Lesson Labs

Quick Labs
• Analyze Weather Patterns
• Coastal Climate Model

Exploration Lab
• Modeling El Niño

Engage Your Brain

1 Predict Check T or F to show whether you think each statement is true or false.

T F
☐ ☐ The water cycle affects weather.
☐ ☐ Air can be warmed or cooled by the surface below it.
☐ ☐ Warm air sinks, cool air rises.
☐ ☐ Winds can bring different weather to a region.

2 Explain How can air temperatures along this coastline be affected by the large body of water that is nearby?

_____
_____
_____

Active Reading

3 Infer A military front is a contested armed frontier between opposing forces. A *weather front* occurs between two air masses, or bodies of air. What kind of weather do you think usually happens at a weather front?

_____
_____
_____

Vocabulary Terms
• air mass
• front
• jet stream

4 Apply As you learn the definition of each vocabulary term in this lesson, create your own definition or sketch to help you remember the meaning of the term.

Lesson 3 What Influences Weather? 181

Answers

Answers for 1–3 should represent students' current thoughts, even if incorrect.

1 T; T; F; T

2. Air temperatures can be cooler or warmer near large bodies of water than inland temperatures at the same latitude because water warms up and cools down more slowly than the land nearby.

3. Sample answer: Stormy weather may form at a weather front where two air masses come together.

4. Students should define or sketch each vocabulary term in the lesson.

Opening Your Lesson

Assessing Prior Knowledge Discuss student responses (items 1 and 2) to assess their prior knowledge of how global patterns in Earth's system influence weather.

Prerequisites Students should know that density is mass per unit of volume of a substance. They should be familiar with the transfer of energy by radiation (infrared radiation from the sun traveling to Earth through the vacuum of space), conduction (warming of air in contact with Earth's heated surface), and convection (rising currents of heated air and sinking cooled air).

Before You Read

SQ3R Help students use the SQ3R strategy. Tell them that before they begin reading a section, they should first survey the headings, keywords, and visuals. Explain that the goal of this exercise is to figure out what that section is about. Suggest that they write questions that they hope will be answered in the text. Then, as they read, they should look for answers to their questions. As they complete a section, have them write the main ideas of the text in their own words. Whenever possible, students should review new information by applying it in a new context or situation.

🌐 *Optional Online resource: SQ3R support*

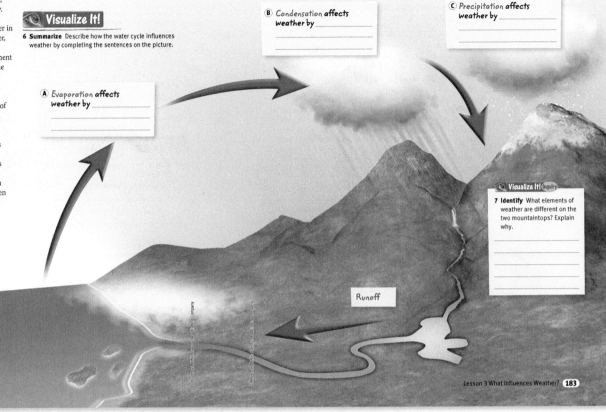

Water, Water Everywhere . . .

How does the water cycle affect weather?

Weather is the short-term state of the atmosphere, including temperature, humidity, precipitation, air pressure, wind, and visibility. These elements are affected by the energy received from the sun and the amount of water in the air. To understand what influences weather, then, you need to understand the water cycle.

The *water cycle* is the continuous movement of water between the atmosphere, the land, the oceans, and living things. In the water cycle, shown to the right, water is constantly being recycled between liquid, solid, and gaseous states. The water cycle involves the processes of evaporation, condensation, and precipitation.

Evaporation occurs when liquid water changes into water vapor, which is a gas. Condensation occurs when water vapor cools and changes from a gas to a liquid. A change in the amount of water vapor in the air affects humidity. Clouds and fog form through condensation of water vapor, so condensation also affects visibility. Precipitation occurs when rain, snow, sleet, or hail falls from the clouds onto Earth's surface.

Active Reading

5 List Name at least 5 elements of weather.

Visualize It!

6 Summarize Describe how the water cycle influences weather by completing the sentences on the picture.

Ⓐ *Evaporation* **affects** weather by _____

Ⓑ *Condensation* **affects** weather by _____

Ⓒ *Precipitation* **affects** weather by _____

Visualize It! Inquiry

7 Identify What elements of weather are different on the two mountaintops? Explain why.

Runoff

182 Unit 4 Weather and Climate

Lesson 3 What Influences Weather? 183

Answers

5. Sample answer: temperature, humidity, precipitation, air pressure, wind, visibility

6. A: increasing water vapor in the air, affecting humidity; B: forming clouds and fog, affecting visibility; C: bringing water in the form of rain, snow, sleet, or hail to the ground

7. There is rain on one mountaintop and snow on the other. The differences in type of precipitation are due to temperature differences.

Interpreting Visuals

Have students use the diagram of the water cycle to explain why the word *continuous* is used to describe the water cycle. Then have them use the diagram to explain why the word *simultaneous* could also be used to describe it. Student explanations should reflect that the processes of the water cycle simultaneously repeat over and over, each at its own rate.

Learning Alert

Water from Living Things Students may not realize that living things contribute to the water cycle. Remind students that the evaporation of water from plants during transpiration and the exhalation of water vapor by animals add moisture to the atmosphere.

Probing Questions   INDEPENDENT Inquiry

Inferring A drought is a long period when there is little or no rainfall in an area. Once a drought occurs, what conditions would make it continue? Sample answer: When rainfall is below normal for a long time, there is less water in lakes and other bodies of water. Less water evaporates, so there is less water vapor in the air. Few clouds form. Clouds are necessary for rain; therefore, a drought could last for a long time.

Putting Up a **Front**

How do air masses affect weather?

8 Identify As you read, underline how air masses form.

You have probably experienced the effects of air masses—one day is hot and humid, and the next day is cool and pleasant. The weather changes when a new air mass moves into your area. An **air mass** is a large volume of air in which temperature and moisture content are nearly the same throughout. An air mass forms when the air over a large region of Earth stays in one area for many days. The air gradually takes on the temperature and humidity of the land or water below it. When an air mass moves, it can bring these characteristics to new locations. Air masses can change temperature and humidity as they move to a new area.

Where do fronts form?

When two air masses meet, density differences usually keep them from mixing. A cool air mass is more dense than a warm air mass. A boundary, called a **front**, forms between the air masses. For a front to form, one air mass must run into another air mass. The kind of front that forms depends on how these air masses move relative to each other, and on their relative temperature and moisture content. Fronts result in a change in weather as they pass. They usually affect weather in the middle latitudes of Earth. Fronts do not often occur near the equator because air masses there do not have big temperature differences.

The boundary between air masses, or front, cannot be seen, but is shown here to illustrate how air masses can take on the characteristics of the surface below them.

Air masses that form above water are moist.

Air masses that form above land are dry.

184

Cold Fronts Form Where Cold Air Moves under Warm Air

Warm air is less dense than cold air is. So, a cold air mass that is moving can quickly push up a warm air mass. If the warm air is moist, clouds will form. Storms that form along a cold front are usually short-lived but can move quickly and bring heavy rain or snow. Cooler weather follows a cold front.

9 Apply If you hear that a cold front is headed for your area, what type of weather might you expect?

_____

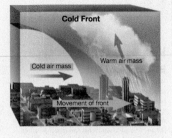

Cold Front

Cold air mass — Warm air mass

Movement of front

Warm Fronts Form Where Warm Air Moves over Cold Air

A warm front forms when a warm air mass follows a retreating cold air mass. The warm air rises over the cold air, and its moisture condenses into clouds. Warm fronts often bring drizzly rain and are followed by warm, clear weather.

10 Identify The rainy weather at the edge of a warm front is a result of

☐ the cold air mass that is leaving.

☐ the warm air rising over the cold air.

☐ the warm air mass following the front.

Warm Front

Warm air mass — Cold air mass

Movement of front

Stationary Fronts Form Where Cold and Warm Air Stop Moving

In a stationary front, there is not enough wind for either the cold air mass or the warm air mass to keep moving. So, the two air masses remain in one place. A stationary front can cause many days of unchanging weather, usually clear.

11 Infer When could a stationary front become a warm or cold front?

_____

Stationary Front

Cold air mass — Warm air mass

Lesson 3 What Influences Weather? **185**

Answers

8. *See students' pages for annotations.*

9. A brief but maybe heavy storm with precipitation, and then cooler weather

10. the warm air rising over the cold air

11. When a warm or cold air mass advances

Probing Questions GUIDED Inquiry

Recognizing Patterns Challenge students to think in reverse. Describe the following weather conditions, then ask students to identify the type of front associated with each kind of weather: clouds form and there may be some brief, stormy weather; cold front; many days of cloudy, wet weather; stationary front drizzly rain over a large area followed by clearing; warm front.

Interpreting Visuals

Have students use the illustrations of fronts to answer these questions. **Ask:**

• Which type of front acts like a wedge as it moves forward and lifts up another front? cold front

• In which type of front do air masses remain separated? stationary front

Learning Alert

Naming Fronts A moving front is named according to the advancing air mass. For example, when colder air is moving forward into warmer air, the weather is described as a cold front. Similarly, if the warm air mass is advancing, it is a warm front.

Feeling the Pressure!

What are pressure systems, and how do they interact?

Areas of different air pressure cause changes in the weather. In a *high-pressure system*, air sinks slowly down. As the air nears the ground, it spreads out toward areas of lower pressure. Most high-pressure systems are large and change slowly. When a high-pressure system stays in one location for a long time, an air mass may form. The air mass can be warm or cold, humid or dry.

In a *low-pressure system*, air rises and so has a lower air pressure than the areas around it. As the air in the center of a low-pressure system rises, the air cools.

The diagram below shows how a high-pressure system can form a low-pressure system. Surface air, shown by the black arrows, moves out and away from high-pressure centers. Air above the surface sinks and warms. The green arrows show how air swirls from a high-pressure system into a low-pressure system. In a low-pressure system, the air rises and cools.

Visualize It!

12 Identify Choose the correct answer for each of the pressure systems shown below.

A high-pressure system can spiral into a low-pressure system, as illustrated by the green arrows below. In the Northern Hemisphere, air circles in the directions shown.

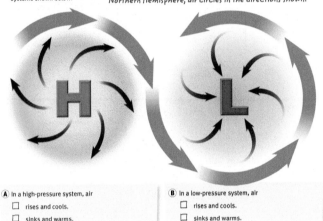

(A) In a high-pressure system, air
- [ ] rises and cools.
- [ ] sinks and warms.

(B) In a low-pressure system, air
- [ ] rises and cools.
- [ ] sinks and warms.

186 Unit 4 Weather and Climate

How do different pressure systems affect us?

When air pressure differences are small, air doesn't move very much. If the air remains in one place or moves slowly, the air takes on the temperature and humidity of the land or water beneath it. Each type of pressure system has it own unique weather pattern. By keeping track of high- and low-pressure systems, scientists can predict the weather.

High-Pressure Systems Produce Clear Weather

High-pressure systems are areas where air sinks and moves outward. The sinking air is denser than the surrounding air, and the pressure is higher. Cooler, denser air moves out of the center of these high-pressure areas toward areas of lower pressure. As the air sinks, it gets warmer and absorbs moisture. Water droplets evaporate, relative humidity decreases, and clouds often disappear. A high-pressure system generally brings clear skies and calm air or gentle breezes.

Low-Pressure Systems Produce Rainy Weather

Low-pressure systems have lower pressure than the surrounding areas. Air in a low-pressure system comes together, or converges, and rises. As the air in the center of a low-pressure system rises, it cools and forms clouds and rain. The rising air in a low-pressure system causes stormy weather.

A low-pressure system can develop wherever there is a center of low pressure. One place this often happens is along a boundary between a warm air mass and a cold air mass. Rain often occurs at these boundaries, or fronts.

Visualize It!

13 Match Label each picture as a result of a high- or low-pressure system. Then, draw a line from each photo to its matching air-pressure diagram.

(A)

(B)

Warm air rises

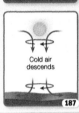
Cold air descends

187

Answers

12. A: sinks and warms; B: rises and cools

13. A: high-pressure system; students should match it to the diagram with air descending. B: low-pressure system; students should match it to the diagram with air rising.

Learning Alert

Air Pressure Some students think that there are two types of air pressure—high and low. Explain that air pressure, like temperature, is a continuum.

Interpreting Visuals

Have students look at the diagrams showing airflow between two pressure systems. Ask students to describe this airflow. The air in a high-pressure system is spiraling outward and moving toward the low-pressure system. Direct students to use a finger to trace along the arrow that shows this movement. Students should trace the path of the arrow that begins above the high-pressure system and moves around the low-pressure system.

Formative Assessment

Ask: How does uneven heating of Earth's surface affect the movement of air between pressure systems? Uneven heating of Earth's surface by the sun causes air above different regions to be warm or cool. **Prompt:** Think about temperature and pressure differences. Sample answer: Temperature differences between air masses result in air pressure differences; pressure differences between adjacent air masses cause air masses to move; air moves from regions of higher pressure to regions of lower pressure.

Windy Weather

How do global wind patterns affect local weather?

Winds are caused by unequal heating of Earth's surface—which causes air pressure differences—and can occur on a global or on a local scale. On a local scale, air-pressure differences affect both wind speed and wind direction at a location. On a global level, there is an overall movement of surface air from the poles toward the equator. The heated air at the equator rises and forms a low-pressure belt. Cold air near the poles sinks and creates high-pressure centers. Because air moves from areas of high pressure to areas of low pressure, it moves from the poles to the equator. At high altitudes, the warmed air circles back toward the poles.

Temperature and pressure differences on Earth's surface also create regional wind belts. Winds in these belts curve to the east or the west as they blow, due to Earth's rotation. This curving of winds is called the *Coriolis effect* (kawr•ee•OH•lis eff•EKT). Winds would flow in straight lines if Earth did not rotate. Winds bring air masses of different temperatures and moisture content to a region.

Visualize It!

14 Apply Trade winds bring
☐ cool air to the warmer equatorial regions.
☐ warm air to the cooler, higher latitudes.

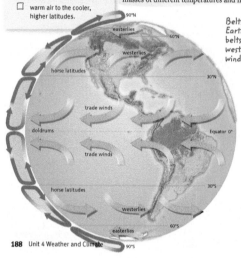

Belts of global winds circle Earth. The winds in these belts curve to the east or west. Between the global wind belts are calm areas.

188 Unit 4 Weather and Climate

How do jet streams affect weather?

Long-distance winds that travel above global winds for thousands of kilometers are called **jet streams**. Air moves in jet streams with speeds that are at least 92 kilometers per hour and are often greater than 180 kilometers per hour. Like global and local winds, jet streams form because Earth's surface is heated unevenly. They flow in a wavy pattern from west to east.

Each hemisphere usually has two main jet streams, a polar jet stream and a subtropical jet stream. The polar jet streams flow closer to the poles in summer than in winter. Jet streams can affect temperatures. For example, a polar jet stream can pull cold air down from Canada into the United States and pull warm air up toward Canada. Jet streams also affect precipitation patterns. Strong storms tend to form along jet streams. Scientists must know where a jet stream is flowing to make accurate weather predictions.

Active Reading
15 Identify What are two ways jet streams affect weather?

_____
_____
_____

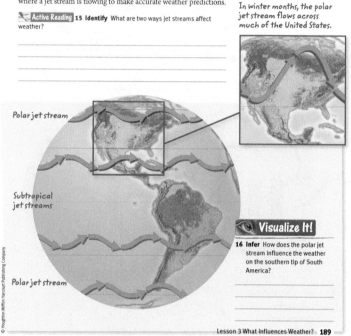

In winter months, the polar jet stream flows across much of the United States.

Visualize It!

16 Infer How does the polar jet stream influence the weather on the southern tip of South America?

_____
_____
_____

Lesson 3 What Influences Weather? 189

Answers

14. cool air to the warmer equatorial regions

15. Jet streams affect temperatures because they can bring cold air down to warmer places and warmer air to colder places. Jet streams affect precipitation because there are often storms along the jet stream itself.

16. The polar jet stream brings colder air from Antarctica to southern South America.

Interpreting Visuals

Have students study the direction of the trade winds indicated by the arrows in both the Northern and Southern Hemispheres on the global wind map. Which way do these winds appear to be blowing? Winds in both hemispheres appear to be blowing west. Why is this? the Coriolis effect Ask students to find the doldrums on the map. What are the trade winds doing where the doldrums are located? They are meeting and appear to be turning west. What type of winds are in the area of the doldrums? very calm and light Based on the paths of the trade winds shown on the map, why do you think the doldrums are so calm? The trade winds from the Northern Hemisphere and Southern Hemisphere come together and meet near the equator. Because they are changing direction, this might cause them to slow.

Formative Assessment

Ask: What are two ways in which the trade winds of the Northern Hemisphere differ from the westerlies of the Northern Hemisphere? They flow in opposite directions from each other and they occur at different latitudes.

What type of weather does a polar jet stream bring? cold weather Why? The polar jet stream can bring down cold air from Canada.

Ocean Effects

How do ocean currents influence weather?

The same global winds that blow across the surface of Earth also push water across Earth's oceans, causing surface currents. Different winds cause currents to flow in different directions. The flow of surface currents moves energy as heat from one part of Earth to another. As the map below shows, both warm-water and cold-water currents flow from one ocean to another. Water near the equator carries energy from the sun to other parts of the ocean. The energy from the warm currents is transferred to colder water or to the atmosphere, changing local temperatures and humidity.

Oceans also have an effect on weather in the form of hurricanes and monsoons. Warm ocean water fuels hurricanes. Monsoons are winds that change direction with the seasons. During summer, the land becomes much warmer than the sea in some areas of the world. Moist wind flows inland, often bringing heavy rains.

Visualize It!

17 Summarize Describe how ocean currents help make temperatures at different places on Earth's surface more similar than they would be if there were no currents.

Surface currents are caused by winds. They distribute energy across Earth's surface, changing local temperature and humidity.

Warm current
Cold current

190 Unit 4 Weather and Climate

© Houghton Mifflin Harcourt Publishing Company

Cool Ocean Currents Lower Coastal Air Temperatures

As currents flow, they warm or cool the atmosphere above, affecting local temperatures. The California current is a cold-water current that keeps the average summer high temperatures of coastal cities such as San Diego around 26 °C (78 °F). Cities that lie inland at the same latitude have warmer averages. The graph below shows average monthly temperatures for San Diego and El Centro, California.

Visualize It!

18 Explain Why are temperatures in San Diego, California, usually cooler than they are in El Centro, California?

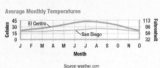
Average Monthly Temperatures
Source: weather.com

Warm Ocean Currents Raise Coastal Air Temperatures

In areas where warm ocean currents flow, coastal cities have warmer winter temperatures than inland cities at similar latitudes. For example, temperatures vary considerably from the coastal regions to the inland areas of Norway due to the warmth of the North Atlantic Current. Coastal cities such as Bergen have relatively mild winters. Inland cities such as Lillehammer have colder winters but temperatures similar to the coastal cities in summer.

Visualize It!

19 Identify Circle the city that is represented by each color in the graph.

■ Lillehammer/Bergen
■ Lillehammer/Bergen

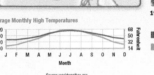
Average Monthly High Temperatures
Source: worldweather.org

© Houghton Mifflin Harcourt Publishing Company

Lesson 3 What Influences Weather? 191

Answers

17. Ocean currents carry heat energy from warm water to colder water or to the atmosphere. Cold-water currents also absorb heat energy from nearby warmer currents and from warmer air.

18. The cold California current keeps San Diego cooler than it would be otherwise.

19. purple line: Bergen; green: line: Lillehammer

Interpreting Visuals

Use the map of global ocean currents to help you explain to students why a southern coastal city in California, such as San Diego, would have cooler summers than a southern inland city in California. The California current, a cool current, flows near the coast and cools air temperatures in coastal cities such as San Diego; cities inland from San Diego have much warmer air because there is no cooling current.

Learning Alert

Warm and Cool The map of global ocean currents shows both warm and cool water currents. Explain that *warm* means "warmer than surrounding waters," and *cool* is "cooler than surrounding waters." Ask where most of the warm water currents originate. near the equator Then have them identify the temperature of currents that flow from the poles. cool

Probing Questions   DIRECTED (Inquiry)

Synthesizing How does heat transfer by convection tend to cause ocean water temperatures to equalize? Warm and cool water currents mix, transferring heat from the warm water to the cool water by convection; cooler water is warmed and warmer water is cooled.

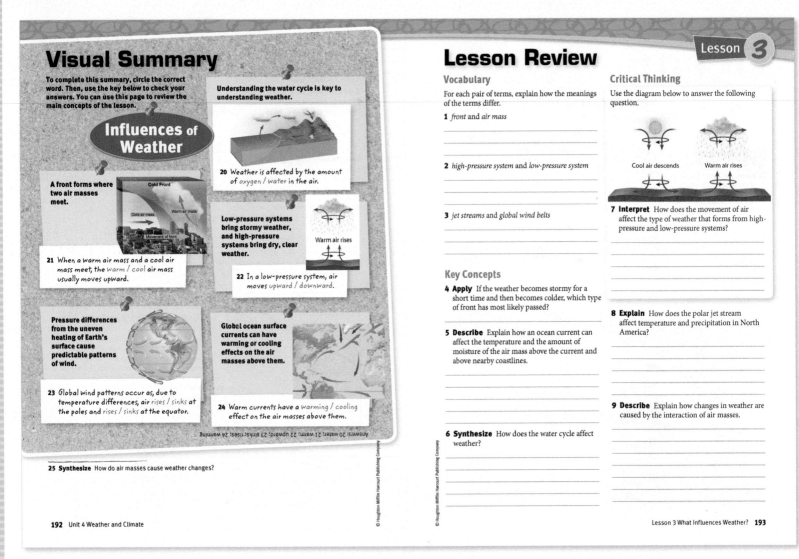

Visual Summary Answers

20. water

21. warm

22. upward

23. sinks; rises

24. warming

25. Moving air masses can bring different temperatures and humidity to an area. Where air masses meet at fronts, weather changes can occur as the air masses interact, possibly causing wind and precipitation.

Lesson Review Answers

1. A front is the boundary between two different air masses.

2. Air sinks in a high-pressure system and brings clear, dry weather. Air rises in a low-pressure system, and brings rainy weather.

3. Jet streams flow above the surface of global wind belts. Global wind belts are predictable worldwide winds.

4. cold front

5. An ocean current can transfer energy to the air above it, warming the air, or it can absorb energy from the air, cooling the air. Water can evaporate, increasing the humidity of the air above the ocean.

6. Through evaporation of water, affecting humidity; condensation of water, affecting clouds, fog, and visibility; and precipitation.

7. In a high-pressure system, cool air sinks and warms, and weather is clear and dry. In low-pressure systems, warm air rises and cools, forming clouds and precipitation.

8. This jet stream brings cold air down to the United States and warm air from the south up to Canada. Storms can form along the polar jet stream.

9. A front where two air masses meet can be stormy due to the rising of warm air and resulting winds, clouds, and precipitation.

Severe Weather and Weather Safety

Essential Question How can humans protect themselves from hazardous weather?

Professional Development

For more detailed information about the topics in this lesson, refer to the Content Refresher in the Unit Opener pages.

Opening Your Lesson

Begin the lesson by assessing students' prerequisite and prior knowledge.

Prerequisite Knowledge

- Air mass
- Air pressure

Accessing Prior Knowledge

Ask: What is an air mass? air that takes on the temperature and moisture characteristics of the land or water below it

Ask: Distinguish between a high-pressure system and a low-pressure system. A high-pressure system is an area where air sinks toward the surface and spreads out toward areas of lower pressure, often bringing dry, clear weather; a low-pressure system is an area of rising air which cools, often resulting in cloudy, rainy, or stormy weather.

Customize Your Opening

☐ **Accessing Prior Knowledge,** above

☐ **Print Path** Engage Your Brain, SE p. 195 #1–2

☐ **Print Path** Active Reading, SE p. 195 #3–4

☐ **Digital Path** Lesson Opener

Key Topics/Learning Goals

Hazardous Weather

1 Define *thunderstorm, hurricane,* and *tornado* and describe how each is formed.

2 Describe the dangers and damaging effects of thunderstorms, tornadoes, and hurricanes.

Safety and Weather

1 Explain how to prepare for hazardous weather such as high winds or heavy rains.

2 Describe how to be safe during a thunderstorm, hurricane, and tornado.

3 Describe how to protect against overexposure to the sun and to stay safe from summer heat.

Supporting Concepts

- Thunderstorms form when humid air near the ground rises, expands, and cools. Lightning can start forest fires, causing damage to property and death. Hail damages crops, cars, and windows.

- Hurricanes are storms with high winds that form as thunderstorms over tropical waters. They spin around low-pressure cells. Hurricane winds can destroy property, and cause flooding from rains and storm surges.

- A tornado is a rotating column of air stretching from a cloud toward the ground. It may form when horizontal winds cause the rising air in a thunderstorm to rotate. Tornadoes destroy homes and cause injury.

- Before a storm, gather emergency supplies and be prepared to evacuate if it is recommended by officials.

- To protect against high winds or heavy rains, secure loose objects outside, cover windows, and stay indoors away from windows.

- To stay safe during storms, find shelter.

- To protect yourself against sun exposure, apply protective sunscreen and wear protective clothing and sunglasses.

- To stay safe during extreme heat, limit outdoor activities, drink water, and know the signs of heat stroke and exhaustion.

Options for Instruction

Two parallel paths provide coverage of the Essential Questions, with a strong **Inquiry** strand woven into each. Follow the **Print Path,** the **Digital Path,** or your customized combination of print, digital, and inquiry.

 Print Path
Teaching support for the Print Path appears with the Student Pages.

 Inquiry Labs and **Activities**

 Digital Path
Digital Path shortcut: TS661510

Take Cover! SE pp. 196–197
What do we know about thunderstorms?

Plan Ahead SE pp. 198–199
What do we know about hurricanes?

Secure Loose Objects!
SE pp. 200–201
What do we know about tornadoes?

Activity
Weather the Storm

Quick Lab
Create Your Own Lightning

Common Types of Weather
Interactive Images

How Storms Form
Video Clips

More on Thunderstorms
Interactive Image

Hurricane Formation
Diagram

Be Prepared! SE pp. 202–203
What can people do to prepare for severe weather?
What can people do to stay safe during thunderstorms?
How can people stay safe during a tornado?
How can people stay safe during a hurricane?

Use Sun Sense! SE pp. 204–205
How can people protect their skin from the sun?
How can people stay protected from summer heat?

Activity
Prepare a Plan

Activity
Stormy Weather Game

Exploration Lab
Preparing for Severe Weather

Quick Lab
Sun Protection

 Virtual Lab
When Severe Weather Strikes

Storm Dangers
Interactive Images

Severe Weather
Interactive Graphics

Sun Overexposure
Image

Heat Injuries
Interactive List

Options for Assessment

See the Evaluate page for options, including Formative Assessment, Summative Assessment, and Unit Review.

~~En~~gage and Explore

Activities and Discussion

Activity *Weather the Storm*

 Engage

Introducing Key Topics

 pairs
 15 min
 DIRECTED inquiry

Write these terms on the board: *thunderstorm with lightning strikes, tornado, hurricane.* Provide pictures showing each type of severe weather and its aftermath. Have students write a brief account to serve as captions for the pictures. The captions should describe the type of storm shown and the type of damage that occurred. Then have students suggest at least one action that a person living in the affected area could carry out in advance of the storm in order to stay safe and to protect his or her property. Have them share their ideas with other student pairs.

Probing Question *Color Me Tornado*

Hazardous Weather

 individuals
 10 min
 GUIDED inquiry

Analyzing Have students think about what they have learned about how tornadoes form. Elicit that they form from thunderstorms and that they start out as funnel clouds, only becoming a tornado once they touch the ground. Point out that as the funnel cloud develops, it is visible as a white or grayish color, like a cloud. Its color becomes darker as it moves along the ground. **Ask:** What causes the initial light color and then the darker color of a tornado? Within the tornado, water vapor in rotating air condenses into liquid water droplets. These droplets are the same as the tiny water droplets that make up clouds, giving the funnel a cloudlike appearance. As the descending funnel cloud begins to pick up dust, dirt, and debris from the ground, it takes on a darker color.

Activity *Prepare a Plan*

Safety and Weather

 whole class
 15 min
 DIRECTED inquiry

Have small groups develop emergency plans for their town in the event of severe weather. Students should pick a type of storm likely to affect their area and consider its effects. Have them decide how to protect residents and public property. Have students write press releases or conduct a press conference, describing the actions to be taken in preparation for the storm.

Discussion *Lightning Strike*

Safety and Weather

 whole class
 15 min
 DIRECTED inquiry

Have students discuss the common misconception that lightning never strikes the same spot twice. Display a photo of the Empire State Building being struck by lighting and explain that it is struck by lightning on average 100 times a year. Have students discuss why this building would be struck so often. Elicit that the Empire State Building is the tallest building in the immediate area. Point out that lighting often strikes the highest point in an area.

Discussion *Heed the Warning*

Safety and Weather

 whole class
 25 min

Tell students that today, almost nobody is surprised by a hurricane. In 2003, the National Weather Service began providing hurricane forecasts five days in advance of Hurricane Katrina's arrival. This allows time for people and resources to be moved to safety. Discuss some of the ways that warnings help people prepare for a storm.

Labs and Demos

Exploration Lab *Preparing for Severe Weather*

Safety and Weather

 small groups
🕐 2 45-min class periods
Inquiry DIRECTED or GUIDED inquiry

Students analyze a severe weather scenario and create an emergency response plan.

PURPOSE **To construct an appropriate emergency response plan**

Quick Lab *Create Your Own Lightning*

Hazardous Weather

 small groups
🕐 15 min
Inquiry DIRECTED inquiry

Students build a device that helps them model static electricity.

PURPOSE **To model lightning using static electricity**

MATERIALS

- wooden dowel, 10 cm long, 1 cm diameter
- aluminum pie pan
- polystyrene foam material
- thumbtack

Quick Lab *Sun Protection*

PURPOSE **To identify how people protect themselves from the sun**

See the Lab Manual or go Online for planning information.

Virtual Lab *When Severe Weather Strikes*

Safety and Weather

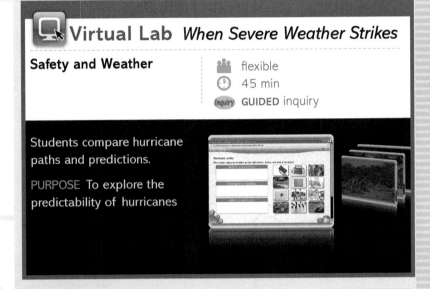

👥 flexible
🕐 45 min
Inquiry GUIDED inquiry

Students compare hurricane paths and predictions.

PURPOSE **To explore the predictability of hurricanes**

Customize Your Labs

📄 *See the Lab Manual for lab datasheets.*

🌐 *Go Online for editable lab datasheets.*

Activities and Discussion

☐ **Activity** Weather the Storm
☐ **Probing Question** Color Me Tornado
☐ **Activity** Prepare a Plan
☐ **Discussion** Lightning Strike
☐ **Discussion** Heed the Warning

Labs and Demos

☐ **Exploration Lab** Preparing for Severe Weather
☐ **Quick Lab** Create Your Own Lightning
☐ **Quick Lab** Sun Protection
☐ **Virtual Lab** When Severe Weather Strikes

Your Resources

Explain Science Concepts

Key Topics	📖 **Print Path**	🖥 **Digital Path**
	☐ **Take Cover!** SE pp. 196–197 • Visualize It! #5 • Visualize It! #6 • Active Reading (Annotation strategy), #7	☐ **Common Types of Weather** Look through different types of weather and the conditions that produce them.
Hazardous Weather	☐ **Plan Ahead!** SE pp. 198–199 • Active Reading (Annotation strategy), #8 • Active Reading, #9 • Think Outside the Book, #10	☐ **How Storms Form** Learn more about how different types of weather are produced.
		☐ **More on Thunderstorms** Learn more about thunderstorms, lightning, hail, and tornadoes.
	☐ **Secure Loose Objects!** SE pp. 200–201 • Think Outside the Book, #11 • Active Reading (Annotation strategy), #12 • Graphic Organizer, #13–14	☐ **Hurricane Formation** Learn where hurricanes form.

Safety and Weather	☐ **Be Prepared!** SE pp. 202–203 • Think Outside the Book, #15 • Apply, #16	☐ **Storm Dangers** Learn about the dangers from lightning, strong winds, storm surges, and flooding.
	☐ **Use Sun Sense!** SE pp. 204–205 • Active Reading (Annotation strategy), #17 • Visualize It!, #18 • Active Reading (Annotation strategy), #19	☐ **Severe Weather** Learn what to do before, during, and after severe weather.
		☐ **Sun Overexposure** Learn about sunburn and other hazards from too much sunlight.
		☐ **Heat Injuries** Learn some of the dangers of hot weather and how to prevent illness.

Basic *Storm Formation*

Hazardous Weather

 small groups

🕐 25 min

Sequence Diagrams After students have completed the lesson, divide the class into three groups. Have the students in one group each complete their own sequence diagram to show the stages in the formation of a thunderstorm. Direct a second group to complete sequence diagrams to show the development of a hurricane. Have a third group use sequence diagrams to describe the formation of a tornado. Then have students reform into three new groups that contain members from each of the original groups. Have the new group members share their diagrams and discuss the sequence of events that lead to each type of weather.

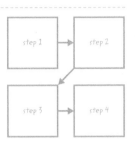

Advanced *Hurricane Paths*

Synthesizing Key Topics

 small groups

🕐 15 min

Research and Share Students can work together to plot the path of a current or past tropical storm that became a hurricane on a map of the Atlantic or Pacific Ocean. They can use symbols or colors to represent different stages of the storm. Ask students to consider the size of the storm as well as the location of its center.

ELL *Safety Brochure*

Safety and Weather

 individuals

🕐 varied

Provide EL students an opportunity to review precautions for hazardous weather as well as those for sun exposure. Have them create a *Storm Safety* brochure that could be distributed to educate family members and friends. Have students provide one page in their brochure for each storm type and list as many safety measures for each storm as they can fit on a page. Have them provide illustrations for their brochure by making drawings or finding suitable images from magazines or the Internet.

thunderstorm	lightning	thunder
hurricane	storm surge	tornado

Previewing Vocabulary

👥 whole class 🕐 ongoing

Word Splash Use the Word Splash strategy to give students an opportunity to understand how the lesson's terms and concepts relate to each other. For example, write the term *thunderstorm* on the board. Around it, write these terms: *lightning, thunder, severe weather, updraft*. Then, for each of the surrounding terms, have students write a sentence that shows how they think that term relates to the term in the center (*thunderstorm*). As they learn about thunderstorms, have them check their predictions. Repeat with other terms.

Reinforcing Vocabulary

👥 individuals or groups 🕐 ongoing

Four Square To help students remember the terms introduced in the lesson, have them complete a four square diagram for each term. Students should write the term in the center oval and fill in the surrounding cells with information that fits the term.

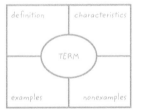

Customize Your Core Lesson

Core Instruction
☐ **Print Path** choices
☐ **Digital Path** choices

Vocabulary
☐ **Previewing Vocabulary** Word Splash
☐ **Reinforcing Vocabulary** Four Square

Your Resources

Differentiated Instruction
☐ **Basic** Storm Formation
☐ **Advanced** Hurricane Paths
☐ **ELL** Safety Brochure

Extend Science Concepts

Reinforce and Review

Activity *Stormy Weather Game*

Synthesizing Key Topics   whole class
🕐 40–45 min

Four Corners Pick four corners of the classroom to represent thunderstorms, hurricanes, tornadoes, or storm surges. Label each corner. Read the following descriptions to students. After each one, ask the students to stand in the corner of the hazardous weather they think is being described. Give each student in the correct corner a point. You can continue the game with additional examples provided by student volunteers.

1 This rise in sea level forms in the ocean during a severe storm and crashes onto shore, endangering lives and causing property damage. storm surge

2 This is an intense local storm during which there are lightning discharges. thunderstorm

3 This violently rotating column of air is seen as a funnel-shaped cloud. tornado

4 This large, rotating tropical weather system has wind speeds of at least 119 km/h. hurricane

Graphic Organizer

Hazardous Weather   individuals
 🕐 15 min
Inquiry **GUIDED** inquiry

Cause and Effect Chain Remind students that hurricanes can lead to storm surges. Have students complete a Cause and Effect Chain to explain the steps leading up to a storm surge, beginning with the ocean getting warm in the summer.

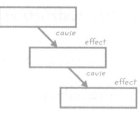

🌐 *Optional Online resource: Cause and Effect Chain support*

Going Further

Math Connection

Hazardous Weather   small groups, whole class, then individuals
 🕐 45 min

Research Project Have students research data on the average annual number of tornadoes that occur by state. Assign approximately five states to each small group to research (try to evenly distribute states that experience the greatest number of tornadoes). Have groups come together as a class to compile their data into one table. Finally, have each student use the table to make a bar graph showing the five states with the fewest and the five states with the greatest annual number of tornadoes.

Social Studies Connection

Safety and Weather   whole class
🕐 15 min

Discussion Discuss with students the importance of the National Weather Service in issuing warnings for upcoming storms. Use the example of a 1938 hurricane that devastated the Northeast. Explain that the storm made a 12-day journey across the Atlantic before slamming into the coast. Neither the U.S. Weather Bureau nor the public knew it was coming. Today almost nobody is surprised by a hurricane because warnings are given early.
Ask: Why is it important to get the earliest warning possible of approaching hazardous weather? It allows time for people and resources to be moved to safety. Have students describe any experiences they have had with advance storm warnings.

Customize Your Closing

🖥 *See the Assessment Guide for quizzes and tests.*

🌐 *Go Online to edit and create quizzes and tests.*

Reinforce and Review

☐ **Activity** Stormy Weather Game

☐ **Graphic Organizer** Cause and Effect Chain

☐ **Print Path** Visual Summary, SE p. 206

☐ **Print Path** Lesson Review, SE p. 207

☐ **Digital Path** Lesson Closer

Evaluate Student Mastery

See the teacher support below the Student Pages for additional Formative Assessment questions.

Ask: What are some safety measures people can take to deal with hazardous weather conditions and storms? Before a storm, gather emergency supplies and prepare a plan to evacuate. Protect from high winds by securing loose objects outdoors and covering windows. Find shelter during a tornado. Protect against sun exposure by applying sunscreen and wearing protective clothing and sunglasses. During summer heat, limit outdoor activities, drink water, and know signs of heat stroke and heat exhaustion.

Reteach

Formative assessment may show that students need reinforcement for certain topics. The resources below are recommended for reteaching. If students were introduced to a topic through the Print Path, you can also use the Digital Path to reteach, and vice versa.

🎧 *Can be assigned to individual students*

Hazardous Weather

Activity Weather the Storm 🎧

Quick Lab Create Your Own Lightning

Safety and Weather

Activity Prepare a Plan 🎧

Exploration Lab Preparing for Severe Weather

Activity Stormy Weather Game

Alternative Assessment
Severe Weather Expert

⊘ *Online resources: student worksheet, optional rubrics*

Severe Weather and Weather Safety		
Climb the Ladder: *Severe Weather Expert*		
1. Work on your own, with a partner, or with a small group.		
2. Choose one item from each rung of the ladder. Check your choices.		
3. Have your teacher approve your plan.		
4. Submit or present your results.		

__ **Outsmarting Storms** Do some research about the average amount of damage that thunderstorms create in the United States every year. Then, write a one-page report about steps Americans can take to reduce the damage created by thunderstorms.	__ **Planning Ahead** Create a three-slide PowerPoint presentation about the steps you should take before, during, and after a severe thunderstorm. Make another three-slide presentation about a tornado. Include at least three pictures, graphs, or illustrations in each presentation.	
__ **Fun (and Safety) in the Sun** Imagine your cousin's family is going on a vacation to the beach. Make a video in which you warn your family members about the dangers of sun exposure and give them advice about staying safe in the sun.	__ **Preparation Persuasion** Pick two items to purchase to help in case of severe weather, such as a battery-run radio, a first-aid kit, a solar-powered flashlight, or a food kit. Make a persuasive argument justifying your choices.	
__ **Picturing Severe Weather** To help students at your cousin's school learn about severe weather events, you and your cousin are making posters. Create a poster that shows and discusses one severe weather event such as a hurricane, storm surge, lightning, or hailstorm.	__ **A Powerful Performance** Perform a song, dance, or skit that shows or talks about tornadoes or other severe weather. Make sure that your audience learns about the movement of tornadoes or the other types of severe weather that you have chosen, and the havoc they can cause.	

Going Further
☐ Math Connection
☐ Social Studies Connection

Formative Assessment
☐ Strategies Throughout TE
☐ Lesson Review SE

Summative Assessment
☐ Alternative Assessment Severe Weather Expert
☐ Lesson Quiz
☐ Unit Tests A and B
☐ Unit Review SE End-of-Unit

Your Resources

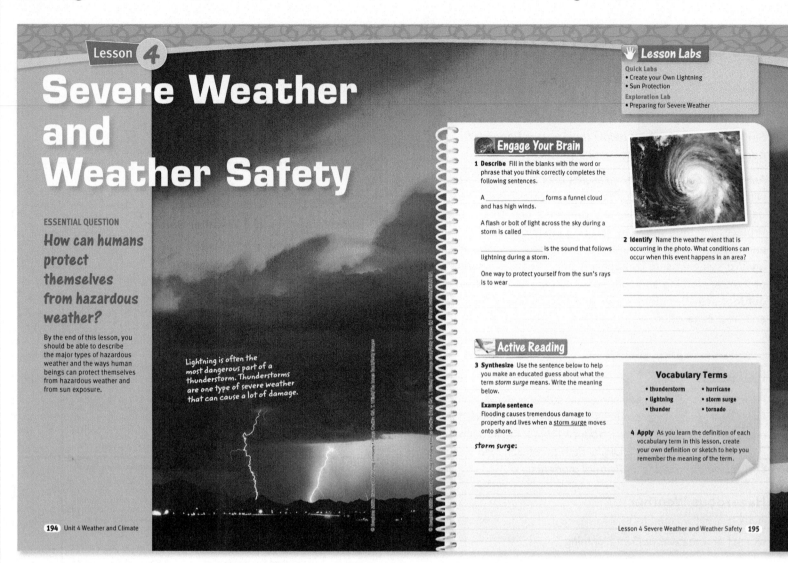

Answers

Answers for 1–3 should represent students' current thoughts, even if incorrect.

1. tornado; lightning; Thunder; sample answer: sunscreen

2. hurricane; Sample answer: high winds, heavy rains, flooding

3. Sample answer: A storm surge is a rise in sea level that causes flooding on shore during a hurricane.

4. Students should define or sketch each vocabulary term in this lesson.

Opening Your Lesson

Discuss student responses to questions 1 and 2 to assess students' prior knowledge about the key topics.

Preconceptions Students may be aware of sunburn but unaware of other effects of overexposure.

Prerequisites Students should be familiar with the fact that energy from the sun and the water cycle are key factors in weather patterns. Students should also be familiar with the concept that energy from the sun strikes Earth and warms it.

Learning Alert

Sunny Day Dangers Although most of the hazardous weather discussed in this lesson involves violent storms and the dangerous conditions they produce, unprotected overexposure to sunlight and prolonged exposure to extreme heat, although less dramatic, pose serious dangers as well.

☑ Take Cover!

What do we know about thunderstorms?

SPLAAAAAT! BOOOOM! The loud, sharp noise of thunder might surprise you, and maybe even make you jump. The thunder may have been joined by lightning, wind, and rain. A **thunderstorm** is an intense local storm that forms strong winds, heavy rain, lightning, thunder, and sometimes hail. A thunderstorm is an example of severe weather. Severe weather is weather that can cause property damage and sometimes death.

Thunderstorms Form from Rising Air

Thunderstorms get their energy from humid air. When warm, humid air near the ground mixes with cooler air above, the warm air creates an updraft that can build a thunderstorm quickly. Cold downdrafts bring precipitation and eventually end the storm by preventing more warm air from rising.

Step 1
In the first stage, warm air rises and forms a cumulus cloud. The water vapor releases energy when it condenses into cloud droplets. This energy increases the air motion. The cloud continues building up.

Step 2
Ice particles may form in the low temperatures near the top of the cloud. As the ice particles grow large, they begin to fall and pull cold air down with them. This strong downdraft brings heavy rain or hail.

Step 3
During the final stage, the downdraft can spread out and block more warm air from moving upward into the cloud. The storm slows down and ends.

👁 **Visualize It!**

5 Describe What role does warm air play in the formation of a thunderstorm?

_____

_____

© Houghton Mifflin Harcourt Publishing Company

196 Unit 4 Weather and Climate

Lightning is a Discharge of Electrical Energy

If you have ever shuffled your feet on a carpet, you may have felt a small shock when you touched a doorknob. If so, you have experienced how lightning forms. **Lightning** is an electric discharge that happens between a positively charged area and a negatively charged area. While you walk around, electrical charges can collect on your body. When you touch someone or something else, the charges jump to that person or object in a spark of electricity. In a similar way, electrical charges build up near the tops and bottoms of clouds as pellets of ice move up and down through the clouds. Suddenly, a flash of lightning will spark from one place to another.

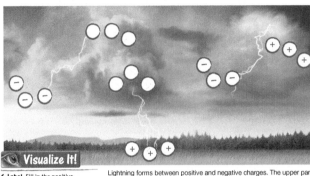

👁 **Visualize It!**

6 Label Fill in the positive and negative charges in the appropriate spaces provided.

Lightning forms between positive and negative charges. The upper part of a cloud usually carries a positive electric charge. The lower part of the cloud carries mainly negative charges. Lightning is a big spark that jumps between parts of clouds, or between a cloud and Earth's surface.

Thunder Is a Result of Rapidly Expanding Air

When lightning strikes, the air along its path is heated to a high temperature. The superheated air quickly expands. The rapidly moving air causes the air to vibrate and release sound waves. The result is **thunder**, the sound created by the rapid expansion of air along a lightning strike.

You usually hear thunder a few seconds after you see a lightning strike, because light travels faster than sound. You can count the seconds between a lightning flash and the sound of thunder to figure out about how far away the lightning is. For every 3 seconds between lightning and its thunder, add about 1 km to the lightning strike's distance from you.

📖 **Active Reading**

7 Identify As you read, underline the explanation of what causes thunder during a storm.

© Houghton Mifflin Harcourt Publishing Company

Lesson 4 Severe Weather and Weather Safety **197**

Answers

5. Warm air rises and fuels the storm.

6. Students draw on page, from top to bottom: positive signs, negative signs.

7. *See students' pages for annotations.*

Learning Alert ⚠️ MISCONCEPTION ⚠️

Lightning Never Strikes Twice A common misconception is that if a lightning strike occurs once in a location, lightning will not strike that place again. Pose this question to students: If a building is struck by lightning, is it safe from lightning in the future? If students respond yes, they likely hold the misconception that lightning never strikes the same place twice. Explain that this concept is a myth and that lightning strikes the highest spot in an area.

Interpreting Visuals

Help students interpret the visual of a thunderstorm formation. **Ask:** Which diagram shows the most severe and dangerous stage of a thunderstorm? Step 2 Compare the first two stages. Why does the cloud become tall? The air rises.

Building Math Skills

Explain the "flash-to-bang" method to calculate distance to a lightning strike. When you see the lightning flash, count the seconds until you hear the bang of thunder. Divide that number by 3. The result is the approximate distance in kilometers that the lighting is from your location. **Ask:** If a lightning flash occurs 21 s before the thunder is heard, how far away did the lightning strike? 21 ÷ 3 = 7 km

☑ Plan Ahead!

What do we know about hurricanes?

A **hurricane** is a tropical low-pressure system with winds blowing at speeds of 119 km/h (74 mi/h) or more—strong enough to uproot trees. Hurricanes are called typhoons when they form over the western Pacific Ocean and cyclones when they form over the Indian Ocean.

Active Reading

8 Identify As you read, underline the definition of *hurricane*.

Hurricanes Need Water to Form and Grow

A hurricane begins as a group of thunderstorms moving over tropical ocean waters. Thunderstorms form in areas of low pressure. Near the equator, warm ocean water provides the energy that can turn a low-pressure center into a violent storm. As water evaporates from the ocean, energy is transferred from the ocean water into the air. This energy makes warm air rise faster. Tall clouds and strong winds develop. As winds blow across the water from different directions into the low-pressure center, the paths bend into a spiral. The winds blow faster and faster around the low-pressure center, which becomes the center of the hurricane.

As long as a hurricane stays above warm water, it can grow bigger and more powerful. As soon as a hurricane moves over land or over cooler water, it loses its source of energy. The winds lose strength and the storm dies out. If a hurricane moves over land, the rough surface of the land reduces the winds even more.

Hurricanes in the Northern Hemisphere usually move westward with the trade winds. Near land, however, they will often move north or even back out to sea.

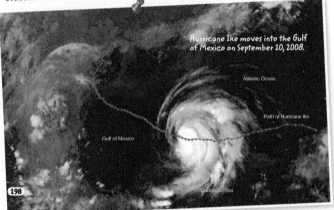

Hurricane Ike moves into the Gulf of Mexico on September 10, 2008.

Atlantic Ocean

Path of Hurricane Ike

Gulf of Mexico

Caribbean Sea

198

Hurricanes Can Cause Extensive Damage

A hurricane can pound a coast with huge waves and sweep the land with strong winds and heavy rains. The storms cause damage and dangerous conditions in several ways. Hurricane winds can lift cars, uproot trees, and tear the roofs off buildings. Hurricanes may also produce tornadoes that can cause even more damage. Heavy rains from hurricanes may make rivers overflow their banks and flood nearby areas. When a hurricane moves into a coastal area, it also pushes a huge mass of ocean water known as a **storm surge**. In a storm surge, the sea level rises several meters, backing up rivers and flooding the shore. A storm surge can be the most destructive and deadliest part of a hurricane. Large waves add to the damage. A hurricane may affect an area for a few hours or a few days, but the damage may take weeks or even months to clean up.

Active Reading

9 Describe What are three of the dangers associated with hurricanes?

_____

_____

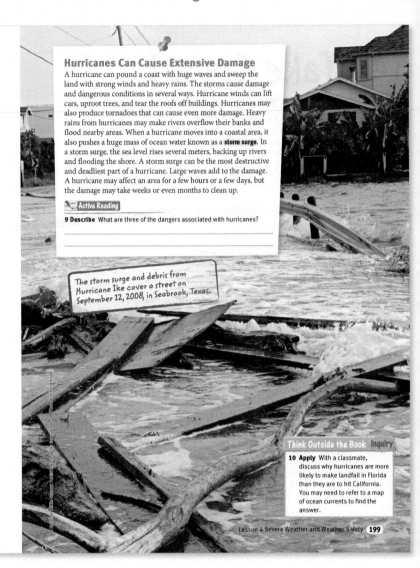

The storm surge and debris from Hurricane Ike cover a street on September 12, 2008, in Seabrook, Texas.

Think Outside the Book Inquiry

10 Apply With a classmate, discuss why hurricanes are more likely to make landfall in Florida than they are to hit California. You may need to refer to a map of ocean currents to find the answer.

Lesson 4 Severe Weather and Weather Safety **199**

Answers

8. *See students' pages for annotations.*

9. Hurricane winds can lift cars, uproot trees, and tear off roofs. Tornadoes can also form and cause damage. Heavy rains and storm surges cause flooding.

10. Florida has warm ocean water while California has a cold current running along its coast.

Learning Alert

Cyclones Before they read the text, ask students if they have heard the word *cyclone*. Explain that this word has several meanings. Students may have heard it used informally to mean "tornado." Point out that meteorologists use the word to refer to a low-pressure system, whether or not that system has hurricane-force winds. It is also used to refer to a hurricane in the western Pacific Ocean.

Probing Questions DIRECTED Inquiry

Inferring How could a map of ocean currents help you predict the path of a hurricane? Ocean current maps show the directions that currents travel. Currents that originate near the equator are likely paths for hurricanes. A hurricane following a current that begins near the equator and heads toward land may make landfall.

Formative Assessment

Ask: Where does a hurricane get energy to form? Heat from the sun causes warm ocean water to evaporate, adding moisture to the already warm air; as warm, moist air rises, water vapor condenses, releasing large amounts of energy. Why do hurricanes slow down when they move from the ocean onto land? When hurricanes make landfall, they lose their source of energy—the warm ocean water—so they slow down.

☑ Secure Loose Objects!

What do we know about tornadoes?

A **tornado** is a destructive, rotating column of air that has very high wind speeds and that is sometimes visible as a funnel-shaped cloud. A tornado forms when a thunderstorm meets horizontal winds at a high altitude. These winds cause the warm air rising in the thunderstorm to spin. A storm cloud may form a thin funnel shape that has a very low pressure center. As the funnel reaches the ground, the higher-pressure air rushes into the low-pressure area. The result is high-speed winds, which cause the damage associated with tornadoes.

Clouds begin to rotate, signaling that a tornado may form.

The funnel cloud becomes visible as the tornado picks up dust from the ground or particles from the air.

The tornado moves along the ground before it dies out.

Think Outside the Book

11 Illustrate Read the description of the weather conditions that cause tornadoes and draw a sketch of what those conditions might look like.

Most Tornadoes Happen in the Midwest

Tornadoes happen in many places, but they are most common in the United States in *Tornado Alley*. Tornado Alley reaches from Texas up through the midwestern United States, including Iowa, Kansas, Nebraska, and Ohio. Many tornadoes form in the spring and early summer, typically along a front between cool, dry air and warm, humid air.

Tornadoes Can Cause Extensive Damage

The danger of a tornado is mainly due to the high speed of its winds. Winds in a tornado's funnel may have speeds of more than 400 km/h. Most injuries and deaths caused by tornadoes happen when people are struck by objects blown by the winds or when they are trapped in buildings that collapse.

Active Reading

12 Identify As you read, underline what makes a tornado so destructive.

13 Summarize In the overlapping sections of the Venn diagram, list the characteristics that are shared by the different types of storms. In the outer sections, list the characteristics that are specific to each type of storm.

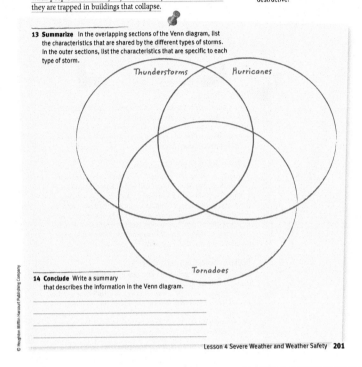

Thunderstorms   Hurricanes

Tornadoes

14 Conclude Write a summary that describes the information in the Venn diagram.

Answers

11. Students will draw on the page a thunderstorm meeting high horizontal winds.

12. *See students' pages for annotations.*

13. All three types of storms involve severe weather, thunderstorms; Thunderstorms and hurricanes involve heavy rains, flooding; Hurricanes and tornadoes involve high-speed winds, rotating clouds; Thunderstorms involve lightning, thunder; Hurricanes involve storm surges, ocean water; Tornadoes involve funnel-shaped clouds.

14. Thunderstorms, hurricanes, and tornadoes are all types of severe weather that can begin as thunderstorms and that can cause extensive damage.

Building Reading Skills

Cause/Effect Describe the atmospheric conditions that cause the formation of a tornado. A thunderstorm meets high-altitude, horizontal winds, which cause the rising air in the thunderstorm to rotate. A storm cloud develops a narrow funnel shape that has a very-low-pressure center; as the funnel reaches the ground, the higher-pressure air rushes into the low-pressure area.

Probing Questions   INDEPENDENT (Inquiry)

Analyzing Have students imagine they are looking at a photograph of a weather-related disaster and must play the role of a weather detective. Explain that the photo shows an aerial view of a group of houses. There is a small, straight path of destruction in which five houses in a row have been completely destroyed. Yet all the houses in front and in back of these houses are untouched. What type of weather event caused this damage? tornado Explain your reasoning. A small path of destruction indicates a tornado; a hurricane affects a much larger area.

☑ Be Prepared!

What can people do to prepare for severe weather?

Severe weather is weather that can cause property damage, injury, and sometimes death. Hail, lightning, high winds, tornadoes, hurricanes, and floods are all part of severe weather. Hailstorms can damage crops and cars and can break windows. Lightning starts many forest fires and kills or injures hundreds of people and animals each year. Winds and tornadoes can uproot trees and destroy homes. Flooding is also a leading cause of weather-related deaths. Most destruction from hurricanes results from flooding due to storm surges.

Think Outside the Book Inquiry

15 Apply Research severe weather in your area and come up with a plan for safety.

Plan Ahead

Have a storm supply kit that contains a battery-operated radio, batteries, flashlights, candles, rain jackets, tarps, blankets, bottled water, canned food, and medicines. Listen to weather announcements. Plan and practice a safety route. A safety route is a planned path to a safe place.

Listen for Storm Updates

During severe weather, it is important to listen to local radio or TV stations. Severe weather updates will let you know the location of a storm. They will also let you know if the storm is getting worse. A *watch* is given when the conditions are ideal for severe weather. A *warning* is given when severe weather has been spotted or is expected within 24 h. During most kinds of severe weather, it is best to stay indoors and away from windows. However, in some situations, you may need to evacuate.

Follow Flood Safety Rules

Sometimes, a place can get so much rain that it floods, especially if it is a low-lying area. So, like storms, floods have watches and warnings. However, little advance notice can usually be given that a flood is coming. A flash flood is a flood that rises and falls very quickly. The best thing to do during a flood is to find a high place to stay until it is over. You should always stay out of floodwaters. Even shallow water can be dangerous because it can move fast.

What can people do to stay safe during thunderstorms?

Stay alert when thunderstorms are predicted or when dark, tall clouds are visible. If you are outside and hear thunder, seek shelter immediately and stay there for 30 min after the thunder ends. Heavy rains can cause sudden, or flash, flooding, and hailstones can damage property and harm living things.

Lightning is one of the most dangerous parts of a thunderstorm. Because lightning is attracted to tall objects, it is important to stay away from trees if you are outside. If you are in an open area, stay close to the ground so that you are not the tallest object in the area. If you can, get into a car. Stay away from ponds, lakes, or other bodies of water. If lightning hits water while you are swimming or wading in it, you could be hurt or killed. If you are indoors during a thunderstorm, avoid using electrical appliances, running water, and phone lines.

How can people stay safe during a tornado?

Tornadoes are too fast and unpredictable for you to attempt to outrun, even if you are in a car. If you see or hear a tornado, go to a place without windows, such as basement, a storm cellar, or a closet or hallway. Stay away from areas that are likely to have flying objects or other dangers. If you are outside, lie in a ditch or low-lying area. Protect your head and neck by covering them with your arms and hands.

How can people stay safe during a hurricane?

If your family lives where hurricanes may strike, have a plan to leave the area, and gather emergency supplies. If a hurricane is approaching your area, listen to weather reports for storm updates. Secure loose objects outside, and cover windows with storm shutters or boards. During a storm, stay indoors and away from windows. If ordered to evacuate the area, do so immediately. After a storm, be aware of downed power lines, hanging branches, and flooded areas.

16 Apply What would you do in each of these scenarios?

Scenario	What would you do?
You are swimming at an outdoor pool when you hear thunder in the distance.	
You and your family are watching TV when you hear a tornado warning that says a tornado has been spotted in the area.	
You are listening to the radio when the announcer says that a hurricane is headed your way and may make landfall in 3 days.	

Answers

15. Sample answer: Plan a quick route to a safe place in the event of a hurricane. Plan what supplies are needed for 3 days without running water or power.

16. 1st scenario: Get out of the pool and go inside a building or car for at least 30 min after the thunder ends.

   2nd scenario: Move to a basement, cellar, or small inner room, closet, or hallway that has no windows. Stay away from areas that are likely to have flying debris or other dangers.

   3rd scenario: Get enough food and water to last for a few days. Board up windows. In the event of a hurricane, stay indoors. Evacuate in advance if ordered to do so by state or federal officials.

Learning Alert

Know the Signs of a Tornado Some tornadoes occur without a tornado warning, so when conditions are right for tornado development, it is wise to stay alert. Besides looking for a clearly visible tornado, there are other things to look and listen for. These include the following: a strong and continuing rotation in the base of a cloud; whirling dust or debris on the ground under a cloud; hail or heavy rain followed by either quiet calmness or a fast, intense wind shift; a loud, continuous roar or rumble, which doesn't fade in a few seconds as thunder does.

Formative Assessment

Ask: What should you do if a hurricane or tornado is approaching your area? Listen to local weather reports. Evacuate if advised; if you remain, stay indoors and away from windows. **Ask:** What items would you keep in a storm preparedness kit? portable radio, fresh batteries, flashlights, rain gear, blankets, bottled water, canned food, and medicine **Ask:** What is the difference between a storm watch and a warning? A *watch* is issued when the conditions are ideal for severe weather; a *warning* is given when severe weather has been spotted or is expected within 24 h.

☑ Use Sun Sense!

How can people protect their skin from the sun?

17 Identify As you read, underline when the sun's ray's are strongest during the day.

Human skin contains melanin, which is the body's natural protection against ultraviolet (UV) radiation from the sun. The skin produces more melanin when it is exposed to the sun, but UV rays will still cause sunburn when you spend too much time outside. It is particularly important to protect your skin when the sun's rays are strongest, usually between 10 A.M and 4 P.M.

Have fun in the sun! Just be sure to protect your skin from harmful rays.

Know the Sun's Hazards

It's easy to notice the effects of a sunburn. Sunburn usually appears within a few hours after sun exposure. It causes red, painful skin that feels hot to the touch. Prolonged exposure to the sun will lead to sunburn in even the darkest-skinned people. Sunburn can lead to skin cancer and premature aging of the skin. The best way to prevent sunburn is to protect your skin from the sun, even on cloudy days. UV rays pass right through clouds and can give you a false feeling of protection from the sun.

Wear Sunscreen and Protective Clothing

Even if you tan easily, you should still use sunscreen. For most people, a sun protection factor (SPF) of 30 or more will prevent burning for about 1.5 h. Babies and people who have pale skin should use an SPF of 45 or more. In addition, you can protect your skin and eyes in different ways. Seek the shade, and wear hats, sunglasses, and perhaps even UV light-protective clothing.

204

How can people protect themselves from summer heat?

Heat exhaustion is a condition in which the body has been exposed to high temperatures for an extended period of time. Symptoms include cold, moist skin, normal or near-normal body temperature, headache, nausea, and extreme fatigue. *Heat stroke* is a condition in which the body loses its ability to cool itself by sweating because the victim has become dehydrated.

Limit Outdoor Activities

When outdoor temperatures are high, be cautious about exercising outdoors for long periods of time. Pay attention to how your body is feeling, and go inside or to a shady spot if you are starting to feel light-headed or too warm.

Drink Water

Heat exhaustion and heat stroke can best be prevented by drinking 6 to 8 oz of water at least 10 times a day when you are active in warm weather. If you are feeling overheated, dizzy, nauseous, or are sweating heavily, drink something cool (not cold). Drink about half a glass of cool water every 15 min until you feel like your normal self.

Drinking water is one of the best things you can do to keep yourself healthy in hot weather.

Visualize It!

18 Describe List all the ways the people in the photo of the beach may have protected themselves from overexposure to the sun.

Know the Signs of Heat Stroke

19 Identify Underline signs of heat stroke in the paragraph below.

Heat stroke is life threatening, so it is important to know the signs and treatment for it. Symptoms of heat stroke include hot, dry skin; higher than normal body temperature; rapid pulse; rapid, shallow breathing; disorientation; and possible loss of consciousness.

What to Do In Case of Heat Stroke

☐ Seek emergency help immediately.

☐ If there are no emergency facilities nearby, move the person to a cool place.

☐ Cool the person's body by immersing it in a cool (not cold) bath or using wet towels.

☐ Do not give the person food or water if he or she is vomiting.

☐ Place ice packs under the person's armpits.

Lesson 4 Severe Weather and Weather Safety **205**

Answers

17. *See students' pages for annotations.*

18. sunscreen, umbrellas, hats, sunglasses, UV-protective clothing

19. *See students' pages for annotations.*

Probing Questions   DIRECTED (Inquiry)

Summarizing A hot, sunny day is a great time to enjoy the outdoors, but there are risks involved in exposure to heat and UV rays. How can a person prepare for being outdoors on a hot, sunny day? Wear sunscreen and protective clothing, drink plenty of water, and move to the shade if you start to feel too hot.

Learning Alert

Sun Protection The UV index is a forecast of the probable intensity of skin-damaging ultraviolet radiation reaching Earth's surface during the noon hour. The index ranges from 0 to more than 11. The greater the UV index is, the higher the risk is of skin-damaging UV radiation. The amount of UV radiation needed to damage skin is dependent on several factors. In general, the darker a person's skin is (that is, the more melanin in the skin), the longer it takes to cause a sunburn. Wear clothing that does not transmit visible light. To determine if clothing will protect you, place your hand between the fabric and a light source. If you can see your hand through the fabric, the garment offers little protection against sun exposure. UV-absorbent sunglasses can help protect your eyes from sun damage. Ideal sunglasses should block 99% to 100% of UVA and UVB radiation. Darker glasses are not necessarily the best. UV protection comes from a chemical applied to the lenses or the material they are made from, not from the color or darkness of the lenses.

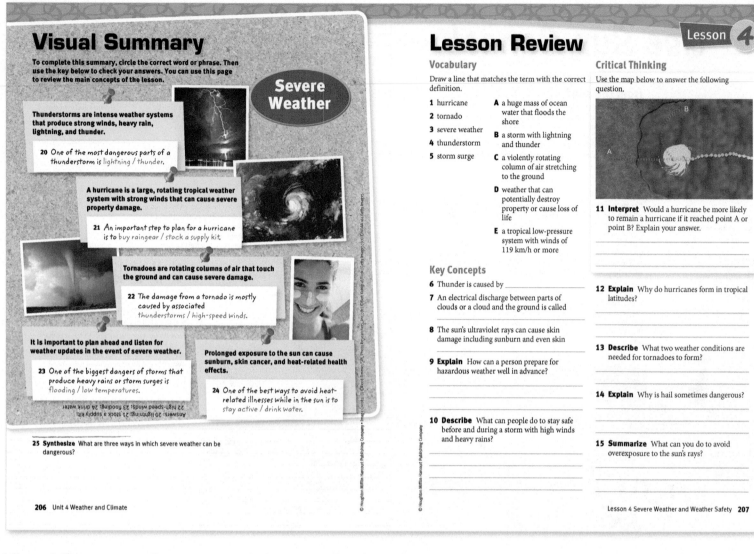

Visual Summary

To complete this summary, circle the correct word or phrase. Then use the key below to check your answers. You can use this page to review the main concepts of the lesson.

Severe Weather

Thunderstorms are intense weather systems that produce strong winds, heavy rain, lightning, and thunder.

20 One of the most dangerous parts of a thunderstorm is lightning / thunder.

A hurricane is a large, rotating tropical weather system with strong winds that can cause severe property damage.

21 An important step to plan for a hurricane is to buy raingear / stock a supply kit.

Tornadoes are rotating columns of air that touch the ground and can cause severe damage.

22 The damage from a tornado is mostly caused by associated thunderstorms / high-speed winds.

It is important to plan ahead and listen for weather updates in the event of severe weather.

23 One of the biggest dangers of storms that produce heavy rains or storm surges is flooding / low temperatures.

Prolonged exposure to the sun can cause sunburn, skin cancer, and heat-related health effects.

24 One of the best ways to avoid heat-related illnesses while in the sun is to stay active / drink water.

Answers: 20 lightning; 21 stock a supply kit; 22 high-speed winds; 23 flooding; 24 drink water.

25 **Synthesize** What are three ways in which severe weather can be dangerous?

206 Unit 4 Weather and Climate

Lesson Review

Lesson 4

Vocabulary

Draw a line that matches the term with the correct definition.

1 hurricane

2 tornado

3 severe weather

4 thunderstorm

5 storm surge

A a huge mass of ocean water that floods the shore

B a storm with lightning and thunder

C a violently rotating column of air stretching to the ground

D weather that can potentially destroy property or cause loss of life

E a tropical low-pressure system with winds of 119 km/h or more

Key Concepts

6 Thunder is caused by _____

7 An electrical discharge between parts of clouds or a cloud and the ground is called _____

8 The sun's ultraviolet rays can cause skin damage including sunburn and even skin _____

9 **Explain** How can a person prepare for hazardous weather well in advance?

10 **Describe** What can people do to stay safe before and during a storm with high winds and heavy rains?

Critical Thinking

Use the map below to answer the following question.

11 **Interpret** Would a hurricane be more likely to remain a hurricane if it reached point A or point B? Explain your answer.

12 **Explain** Why do hurricanes form in tropical latitudes?

13 **Describe** What two weather conditions are needed for tornadoes to form?

14 **Explain** Why is hail sometimes dangerous?

15 **Summarize** What can you do to avoid overexposure to the sun's rays?

Lesson 4 Severe Weather and Weather Safety 207

Visual Summary Answers

20. lightning

21. stock a supply kit

22. high-speed winds

23. flooding

24. drink water

25. Sample answer: High winds can cause flying debris or destroy shelters, heavy rain can cause flooding, and lightning can cause injury or death.

Lesson Review Answers

1. E

2. C

3. D

4. B

5. A

6. expanding air

7. lightning

8. cancer

9. Plan a safe route to leave the area and gather enough emergency supplies to last several days.

10. Secure loose objects outside and cover windows before the storm, stay indoors away from windows during the storm.

11. Point B, because it needs warm water for energy. It will die out if it moves over land to point A.

12. because the water in tropical waters is warm enough to fuel a hurricane

13. a thunderstorm and high-altitude horizontal winds

14. Hail can damage property and harm living things.

15. Wear sunscreen, sunglasses, hats, and UV-protective clothing, find shade, do not remain in the sun for long periods of time, avoid outdoors between 10 am and 4 pm, and apply sunscreen often.

Weather Maps and Weather Prediction

Essential Question What tools do we use to predict weather?

 Professional Development

For more detailed information about the topics in this lesson, refer to the Content Refresher in the Unit Opener pages.

Opening Your Lesson

Begin the lesson by assessing students' prerequisite and prior knowledge.

Prerequisite Knowledge

- A general understanding of the structure of Earth's atmosphere
- A general understanding of elements of weather

Accessing Prior Knowledge

Ask: What are some reasons to listen to a weather forecast? Sample answers: to figure out if you need an umbrella; to plan for a hiking or camping trip

Ask: What kinds of information do you hear in a weather forecast? Sample answers: whether rain or snow is likely; what the temperature will be; whether it will be clear or cloudy; how windy it will be

Customize Your Opening

- ☐ **Accessing Prior Knowledge,** above
- ☐ **Print Path** Engage Your Brain, SE p. 209
- ☐ **Print Path** Active Reading, SE p. 209
- ☐ **Digital Path** Lesson Opener

Key Topics/Learning Goals	Supporting Concepts
Introduction to Weather Forecasting 1 Distinguish *meteorology* from other sciences. 2 Describe *weather forecasting*.	• *Meteorology* is the scientific study of Earth's atmosphere. • Weather forecasting is the analysis of scientific data to make predictions.
Weather Forecasting Data 1 Explain how different forms of weather data are obtained. 2 Describe the observation of surface weather, and how to get upper air data. 3 Describe data from satellites. 4 Explain what kind of weather data radar provides.	• Data for weather forecasts are obtained by ground stations, radar, balloons and aircraft, and satellites. • Automated weather observation systems observe weather just above Earth's surface. • Weather data from the middle- to upper levels of the atmosphere are obtained by weather balloons, aircraft, and satellites. • Weather radar is used to track precipitation.
Weather Maps 1 List types of weather maps. 2 Describe surface weather maps and what they show. 3 Explain station models. 4 Explain upper air charts.	• Weather maps include depictions of the current and future states of the atmosphere. • Surface weather maps show current weather conditions, air pressure, and fronts. • A station model shows current weather at a weather recording location or station. • Upper air charts show wind and pressure.
Weather Forecasts 1 List eight weather elements. 2 Compare types of forecasts. 3 List three types of hazardous weather forecasts.	• Weather elements include: air temperature, humidity, wind, cloud types, precipitation, atmospheric pressure, and visibility. • Short-, medium-, and long-term forecasts predict weather for different spans of time. • Hazardous weather forecasts include weather advisories, watches, and warnings.

Options for Instruction

Two parallel paths provide coverage of the Essential Questions, with a strong **Inquiry** strand woven into each.
Follow the **Print Path,** the **Digital Path,** or your customized combination of print, digital, and inquiry.

 Print Path
Teaching support for the Print Path appears with the Student Pages.

 Inquiry Labs and Activities

 Digital Path
Digital Path shortcut: TS661288

Print Path	Inquiry Labs and Activities	Digital Path
Cloudy **with** *a chance* **of...,** SE p. 210 **What is weather forecasting?** **What weather elements are forecast?**	**Quick Lab** Watching the Weather **Activity** Working Against Weather	**Forecasting the Weather** Interactive Graphics **Elements of Weather** Interactive Images
What's Going on *up There?,* SE pp. 212–213 **How are weather data collected?** • By Ground Stations • By Radar • By Balloons and Aircraft • By Satellites	**Daily Demo** **Barometer Prediction** **Activity** **Tools of the Trade**	**Types of Weather Instruments** Interactive Images **Land-based or Not?** Interactive Images
What's Going on *up There?,* SE pp. 214–217 **What kinds of symbols and maps are used to analyze the weather?** • Station Models • Surface Weather Maps • Upper Air Charts	**Activity** **Responding to Weather Maps**	**Station Models** Interactive Images **Weather Symbols** Interactive Graphics
The National Weather Service..., SE pp. 218–219 **What are types of weather forecasts?** • Short- and Medium-Range Forecasts • Long-Range Weather Forecasts • Hazardous Weather Forecasts	**Quick Lab** **Cloud Cover** 🖥 **Virtual Lab** **Forecasting the Weather**	**Types of Forecasts** Video **Severe Weather** Interactive Images

Options for Assessment

See the Evaluate page for options, including Formative Assessment, Summative Assessment, and Unit Review.

Engage and Explore

Activities and Discussion

Probing Questions *Predicting the Weather*

Introducing Key Topics

 whole class
 10 min
 GUIDED inquiry

Ask: What clues tell you that the weather is going to change? Sample answers: dark storm clouds, wind, the sky getting lighter, a sudden drop or rise in temperature **Ask:** What might happen if a weather forecast is inaccurate? Sample answers: Students could indicate that they might be caught in a thunderstorm without a raincoat and umbrella; they might have to cancel an outdoor sports event; or the temperature is too hot for their daily jog.

Activity *Tools of the Trade*

Weather Forecasting Data

 small groups
 30 min
 GUIDED inquiry

Have students work together to research different tools that meteorologists use to observe current weather conditions. Assign each group a meteorological instrument such as an anemometer, barometer, rain gauge, thermometer, or weather vane. Students should research the instrument that their group was assigned. Then, each group should work together to create a classroom presentation. Ask them to include background on how the tool was created, how it is used, and why the information the tool records is important. Students should also include visuals such as photographs of the tools in action. Each group can give its meteorological instrument presentation to the class.

Activity *Working Against Weather*

Introduction to Weather Forecasting

 individuals
 20 min
 GUIDED inquiry

Think, Pair, Share Give students three minutes to write down as many examples as they can about how weather affects various occupations. Remind students to consider a variety of jobs, both indoors and outdoors, and a range of hazardous weather conditions. After three minutes, have each student choose three examples from his or her list and discuss the examples with a partner. Each student should explain why he or she selected each occupation and tell how hazardous weather conditions can mean the difference between profit or loss, success or failure, or life or death. Call on pairs to share an example with the class and discuss how or why they chose their examples.

Take It Home *Tomorrow's Weather in My Neighborhood*

Weather Forecasts

 adult-student pairs
 ongoing
GUIDED inquiry

Students and adults watch a weather report, taking notes on the next day's weather for three days in a row. Pairs should pay attention to the symbols and maps used. They should record the type and amount of precipitation predicted, air temperature highs and lows, wind speed and direction, cold and warm fronts, and cloud cover. They should record this data and then check it the following day to see if it was correct.

Customize Your Labs

 See the Lab Manual for lab datasheets.

 Go Online for editable lab datasheets.

Labs and Demos

Daily Demo *Barometer Prediction*

Weather Forecasting Data

 whole class
 10 min, then ongoing
 GUIDED inquiry

PURPOSE To show how a barometer can be used to predict weather

MATERIALS

• barometer

1 Show students the barometer. **Ask:** What does a barometer measure? atmospheric pressure

2 **Analyze Ask:** Why are barometers useful for predicting weather? Sample answer: If air pressure stays the same or changes, you can tell if the weather will stay the same or change.

3 **Predict Ask:** What do you think it means if the barometer shows atmospheric pressure falling quickly? Sample answer: A low pressure system is moving in. **Ask:** What kind of weather would this predict? Sample answer: wet or stormy weather

4 Write the following information on the board:

Barometric Readings and Weather they indicate

Over 30.20	29.80–30.20	Under 29.80
Rising or Steady: fair weather	**Rising or Steady:** same as present	**Rising or Steady:** clearing, cooler
Slowly Falling: fair weather	**Slowly Falling:** not much change	**Slowly Falling:** precipitation
Quickly Falling: cloudy, warmer	**Quickly Falling:** precipitation likely	**Quickly Falling:** stormy

Hang the barometer in the classroom, and leave the information on the board. Students can check the barometer over the next few days, make predictions based on the information, and see if their predictions are correct.

Quick Lab *Cloud Cover*

Weather Forecasts

 pairs
15 min
DIRECTED inquiry

Students will observe cloud cover and simulate the cover using paper. They will then estimate the percentage of cloud cover.

PURPOSE To estimate cloud cover to predict weather

MATERIALS

• **paper, blue and white** • scissors

Quick Lab *Watching the Weather*

PURPOSE To use knowledge of station models and weather symbols to interpret a weather map

See the Lab Manual or go Online for planning information.

Virtual Lab *Forecasting the Weather*

Weather Forecasts

flexible
45 min
GUIDED inquiry

Students use weather maps to forecast weather.

PURPOSE To use weather data to make forecasts

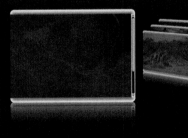

Activities and Discussion

☐ **Probing Questions** Predicting the Weather

☐ **Activity** Tools of the Trade

☐ **Take It Home** Tomorrow's Weather

☐ **Activity** Working Against Weather

Labs and Demos

☐ **Daily Demo** Barometer Prediction

☐ **Quick Lab** Cloud Cover

☐ **Quick Lab** Watching the Weather

☐ **Virtual Lab** Forecasting the Weather

Your Resources

Explain Science Concepts

Key Topics	📝 Print Path	🖥 Digital Path
Introduction to Weather Forecasting	☐ *Cloudy* with *a chance of...* SE p. 210 • Infer, #5 • Visualize It!, #6 🔍 **Visualize It!** **6 Apply** Identify three elements of weather that appear in this beach scene.	☐ **Forecasting the Weather** Learn about how meteorologists forecast the weather. **Elements of Weather** Learn which elements of weather are measured in order to accurately forecast the weather.
Weather Forecasting Data	☐ **What's Going on** *up There?* SE pp. 212–213 • Visualize It!, #10 • Visualize It!, #11 • Active Reading, #12 • Think Outside the Book, #13 🔍 **Visualize It!** **10 Apply** Which town is experiencing the most severe weather? **11 Apply** In which town is it raining lightly?	☐ **Types of Weather Instruments** Explain how weather data are obtained by different instruments.
Weather Maps	☐ **What's Going on** *up There?* SE pp. 214–217 • Active Reading, #14 • Visualize It!, #15 • Visualize It!, #16 • Visualize It!, #17 • Visualize It!, #18 • Visualize It!, #19 🔍 **Visualize It!** **15 Observe** Where are the temperature and dew point recorded on a station model?	☐ **Station Models** Explore station models and symbols. **Weather Symbols** Explore weather symbols and their meanings.
Weather Forecasts	☐ **The National Weather Service has issued a severe storm warning,** SE pp. 218–219 • Infer, #20 • Active Reading, #21 • Visualize It!, #22	☐ **Types of Forecasts** Compare short-range, medium-range, and long-range forecasts. ☐ **Severe Weather** Identify three types of hazardous weather forecasts.

Differentiated Instruction

Basic *Weather Symbol Chart*

Weather Maps

 individuals
🕐 10 min

After students have learned about station plots, have them create a chart of common weather symbols showing different types of precipitation or conditions that cause reduced visibility. Remind them that some pictograms have more than one symbol, such as the different representations for light, moderate, and heavy snow.

Advanced *Making a Weather Map*

Weather Maps

 individuals or pairs
🕐 20 min

Invite students to collect local weather data and data from other areas around your state. Tell students that they can find a great deal of weather data online, from news stations and the National Weather Service. They can also find weather data in newspapers. Direct students to use this data to make a weather map of your state. Remind students to include information on temperature, precipitation, and fronts, and to include a key. Display completed maps around the room.

ELL *Two-Panel Flip Chart*

Weather Forecasting Data

 individuals or pairs
🕐 10 min

Have students, individually or in pairs, make a two-panel flip chart. They should collate blank pages, including a piece of heavy cardboard as the final page so the chart can stand up. Then they can insert string or rings to bind the pages together at the top. Ask students to use the flip chart to compare two different ways that weather data is collected, such as radar and satellites.

🌐 *Online Resource: Two-Panel Flip Chart support*

Lesson Vocabulary

weather forecasting   meteorology   station model

Previewing Vocabulary

 whole class
🕐 10 min

Everyday Language vs. Scientific Meaning Remind students that a term's usage in everyday language is often very different from its strict scientific meaning. For example, the term *station model* in everyday language could refer to the model of a train station. In meteorology, however, it refers to group of meteorological symbols that represent the weather at a particular observing station. Familiarize students with scientific dictionaries, either in print or online, and have them search for lesson vocabulary and other scientific terms.

Reinforcing Vocabulary

 individuals
🕐 ongoing

Four Square To help students remember the different terms introduced in the lesson, have them draw a 2-by-2 matrix with a circle at the center. Students place a term in the circle and then fill in the surrounding cells with the types of information shown.

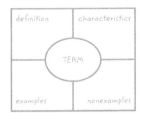

Customize Your Core Lesson

Core Instruction
☐ Print Path choices
☐ Digital Path choices

Vocabulary
☐ Previewing Vocabulary
Everyday Language vs. Scientific Meaning

☐ Reinforcing Vocabulary
Four Square

Differentiated Instruction
☐ Basic Weather Symbol Chart
☐ Advanced Making a Weather Map
☐ ELL Two-Panel Flip Chart

Your Resources

Extend Science Concepts

Reinforce and Review

Activity *Responding to Weather Maps*

Synthesizing Key Topics   whole class
⏱ 20 min

Card Responses Help students review the material by following these steps: Hand out index cards, and have students make answer cards for questions you will ask. Cards should say *true* on one side, *false* on the other. Ask the following questions, or other questions that you create: At a signal from you, students hold up their cards. Be clear about the signal so everyone answers at the same time.

1 An isobar is a tool used to predict weather. false

2 A weather watch is issued when severe weather will definitely occur. false

3 Surface maps are often included in TV weather forecasts. true

4 A station model collects weather data. false

5 Meteorologists collect data on cloud types. true

6 Doppler radar is used mainly to measure cloud cover. false

7 A radiosonde measures conditions in the upper atmosphere. true

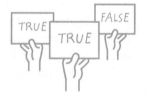

8 Upper air weather charts are always changing. true

Graphic Organizer

Weather Forecasts   individuals
⏱ 10 min

Idea Wheel After students have studied the lesson, have them draw a large circle with a smaller circle inside. They should divide the outer ring into three sections labeled: *advisories, watches, warnings.* The smaller, center circle contains the main topic: *types of hazardous weather forecasts.* Students can fill in each of the three outer rings with details related to each type of hazardous weather forecast.

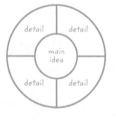

Going Further

Music Connection

Weather Forecasting Data   pairs or small groups
⏱ 20 min

Eye of the Storm Song Invite pairs or groups of students to write a song about Hurricane Hunters flying into the eye of a storm located above their neighborhood. Their lyrics could describe the bumpy ride, the thick thunderstorm, the crew's bravery, and information about the hurricane being tracked. Students can add sound effects that represent the hurricane. Encourage students to perform their song for the class.

Fine Arts Connection

Weather Forecasting Data   individuals
⏱ 30 min

Weather Vane Design Invite students to design a weather vane. Remind students that when the wind hits the larger back end of the weather vane, it turns so the arrow points in the direction the wind is coming from. Students can create weather vanes using everyday materials such as straws, posterboard, paper clips, and dowels.

Customize Your Closing

🪨 *See the Assessment Guide for quizzes and tests.*

🧭 *Go Online to edit and create quizzes and tests.*

Reinforce and Review

☐ **Activity** Responding to Weather Maps

☐ **Graphic Organizer** Idea Wheel

☐ **Print Path** Visual Summary, SE p. 220

☐ **Print Path** Lesson Review, SE p. 221

☐ **Digital Path** Lesson Closer

Evaluate Student Mastery

Formative Assessment

See the teacher support below the Student pages for additional Formative Assessment questions.

Ask the following questions to assess student mastery of the material. **Ask:** What are eight elements of weather that meteorologists collect data on? air temperature, humidity, wind direction, wind speed, cloud types and altitudes, precipitation, atmospheric pressure, and visibility **Ask:** What type of information would weather radar record? movement of storms, cloud locations, precipitation and air motion **Ask:** When would the National Weather Service issue a weather advisory? Answer: when anticipated weather conditions could cause inconvenience if caution is not used

Reteach

Formative assessment may show that students need reinforcement for certain topics. The resources below are recommended for reteaching. If students were introduced to a topic through the Print path, you can also use the Digital Path to reteach, or vice versa.
🎧 *Can be assigned to individual students*

Introduction to Weather Forecasting
Activity Working Against Weather 🎧

Weather Forecasting Data
Activity Tools of the Trade 🎧

Weather Maps
Basic Weather Symbol Chart 🎧

Weather Forecast
Quick Lab Cloud Cover

Summative Assessment

Alternative Assessment
Weather Trackers

💿 *Online resources: student worksheet, optional rubrics*

Weather Maps and Weather Prediction

Tic-Tac-Toe: *Weather Trackers*
Your team of student assistants is spending a week with a meteorologist investigating the science behind a variety of weather conditions.

1. Work with a partner or with a small group.
2. Choose three quick activities from the game. Check the boxes you plan to complete. They must form a straight line in any direction.
3. Have your teacher approve your plan.
4. Do each activity, and turn in your results.

__ Becoming a Meteorologist	__ Weather High Up	__ Weather Crawl
Create a brochure explaining what a meteorologist does and what the basic requirements are for succeeding in this career.	Imagine that you are an airplane pilot. You are trying to convince your co-pilot to use an upper-air chart to plan your next flight. Write an e-mail to him explaining what types of information the chart can provide, and why this information is useful.	Design a weather crawl that will scroll across the bottom of the TV screen in moving banner format. How will you make this small screen space eye-catching?
__ Satellite Sonnet	__ Forecasting the Future	__ Teaching Plan
Write a poem describing the images that a satellite sent back to a ground station from its position hundreds of kilometers above Earth.	Write a skit that shows the effects a short-term forecast that predicts stormy weather has on a variety of people in different occupations.	Design a plan to teach a primary school class what symbols on a surface weather map mean. You should include a key for the symbols, an example of a surface weather map, and a written plan for explaining the map.
__ Competition	__ Disaster Plan	__ Nor'easter Report
Storm chasers are preparing to capture a tornado on film. There is a spot available for assistants from one school in your state. Write a persuasive e-mail detailing why your team is best suited for the job.	Design a poster that the National Weather Service will use to advertise hazardous weather forecasts, what they mean, and what people should do when they hear them.	Strong winds are blowing in from the northeast, dumping heavy rain and snow along the Atlantic Coast and creating high surf that will result in coastal flooding. Write an urgent news report that will be broadcast on the radio.

Going Further

☐ Music Connection
☐ Fine Arts Connection
☐ **Print Path** Why It Matters, SE p. 211

Your Resources

Formative Assessment

☐ Strategies Throughout TE
☐ Lesson Review SE

Summative Assessment

☐ Alternative Assessment Weather Trackers
☐ Lesson Quiz
☐ Unit Tests A and B
☐ Unit Review SE End-of-Unit

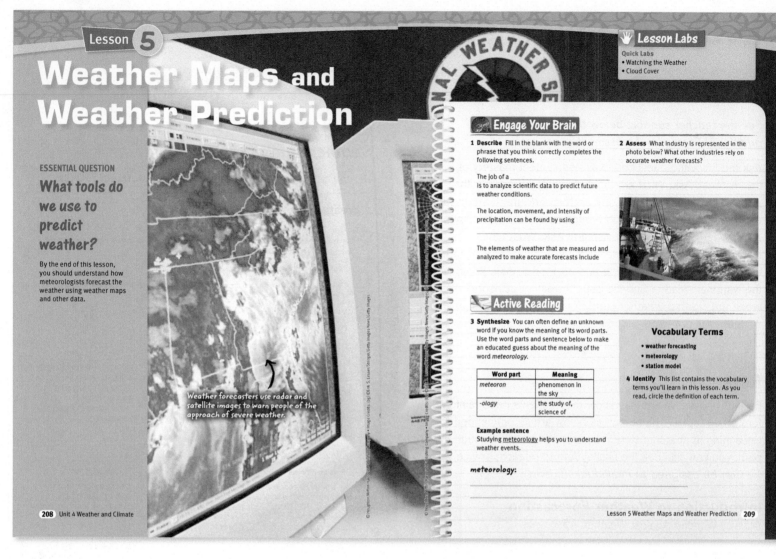

Answers

Answers for 1–3 should represent students' current thoughts, even if incorrect.

1. weather forecaster; radar; Sample answers: temperature, air pressure, wind speed, relative humidity/dew point, cloud type, cloud cover/visibility, wind direction, and precipitation

2. commercial fishing (or shipping); sample answers of other industries include agriculture, recreation, aviation, construction, landscaping

3. Meteorology is the study of phenomena in the sky.

4. Students should define and sketch each vocabulary term in the lesson.

Opening Your Lesson

Discuss students' answers to item 1 to assess their understanding of a weather forecaster's job, how storms are tracked, and what elements of weather are forecast.

Prerequisites Students should already have some understanding of elements of weather and basic weather measurements, such as temperature. In this lesson, they will apply this understanding to how weather maps and other data are used to predict weather.

Learning Alert

Uses of Radar Students might be familiar with how radar is used to pinpoint the location, speed, and course of an object such as aircraft and speeding traffic. The same system can also detect the motion of rain drops and forecast their future position and intensity. Radar was first used during World War II to detect enemy airplanes, ships, and submarines. Radio waves sent into the air bounced off of these objects, allowing soldiers to "see" for hundreds of miles, even in the dark. Today, Doppler radars use radio waves to measure the distance and direction of rain drops and ice crystals. The movement of rain drops and ice crystals gives a picture of wind direction. A series of radar scans can depict the motion of thunderstorms or a line of precipitation. One of radar's most important applications is the Tornado Vortex Signature, which can locate strong wind rotation within a thunderstorm.

Cloudy with *a chance* of ...

What is weather forecasting?

Looking at the weather outdoors in the morning helps you to decide what clothes to wear that day. Different observations give clues to the current weather. The leaves in the trees may be moving if it is windy. If the sky is gray and the streets are shiny, it may be raining.

Checking the weather forecast also helps determine how the weather might change. **Weather forecasting** is the analysis of scientific data to predict future weather conditions.

What elements of weather are forecast?

Weather forecasters study the elements of weather to make detailed predictions. The study of weather and Earth's atmosphere is called **meteorology** [mee•tee•uh•RAHL•uh•jee]. Scientists who study meteorology are called *meteorologists*.

Eight elements of weather are observed around the clock. These elements are air temperature, humidity, wind direction, wind speed, clouds, precipitation, atmospheric pressure, and visibility. Using these eight elements to make accurate weather forecasts helps people stay safe and comfortable. To make the best predictions, meteorologists need accurate data.

5 Infer Forest firefighters need accurate and detailed weather forecasts. What weather elements would these firefighters be most interested in? Explain.

_____

_____

_____

_____

👁 Visualize It!

6 Apply Identify three elements of weather that appear in this beach scene.

A _____

B _____

C _____

210 Unit 4 Weather and Climate

Why It Matters

SOCIETY AND TECHNOLOGY

The Hurricane Hunters

Flying in stormy weather can be an uncomfortable and frightening experience. Yet, some pilots are trained to fly into the most intense storms. The Hurricane Hunters of the National Oceanic and Atmospheric Administration (NOAA) fly right into the eye of tropical storms and hurricanes to collect valuable data. Weather forecasters use the data to predict a storm's path and intensity.

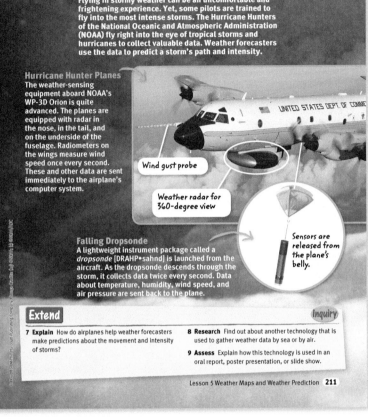

Hurricane Hunter Planes
The weather-sensing equipment aboard NOAA's WP-3D Orion is quite advanced. The planes are equipped with radar in the nose, in the tail, and on the underside of the fuselage. Radiometers on the wings measure wind speed once every second. These and other data are sent immediately to the airplane's computer system.

Wind gust probe

Weather radar for 360-degree view

Sensors are released from the plane's belly.

Falling Dropsonde
A lightweight instrument package called a *dropsonde* [DRAHP•sahnd] is launched from the aircraft. As the dropsonde descends through the storm, it collects data twice every second. Data about temperature, humidity, wind speed, and air pressure are sent back to the plane.

Extend   Inquiry

7 Explain How do airplanes help weather forecasters make predictions about the movement and intensity of storms?

8 Research Find out about another technology that is used to gather weather data by sea or by air.

9 Assess Explain how this technology is used in an oral report, poster presentation, or slide show.

Lesson 5 Weather Maps and Weather Prediction 211

Answers

5. Sample answer: Because high temperatures, strong winds, and dry conditions increase the risk of wildfire, firefighters would be interested in air temperature, humidity, wind speed, wind direction, and precipitation.

6. A: wind speed and wind direction; B: clouds; C: precipitation

7. Instruments on or released from aircraft can monitor atmospheric conditions within storms. This data can help predict a storm's intensity and path.

8. Sample answer: Students may research weather balloons, ships, or satellites.

9. Students' presentations should show which weather elements the technology observes and records and explain how.

Interpreting Visuals

The people in this photograph are leaving because of an oncoming storm. **Ask:** What are some other outdoor activities that are dependent upon weather conditions? Sample answers: skiing; tennis; sailing

Why It Matters

Before satellites were used to locate storms, routine flights were made to locate developing storms. Although satellites now provide an enormous amount of information, there are still some types of information that they cannot provide, such as the atmospheric pressure in a hurricane or its wind speed. Hurricane hunters furnish this information, which is essential to predicting storm development and movement.

Probing Questions   DIRECTED Inquiry

Comparing The *MS Polarfront* is a ship stationed in the North Atlantic. This weather ship, the last of its kind, is used to forecast the weather. Why is an aircraft more efficient in monitoring weather than a ship? Sample answer: Aircraft can move much faster and can launch weather-sensing equipment into storms.

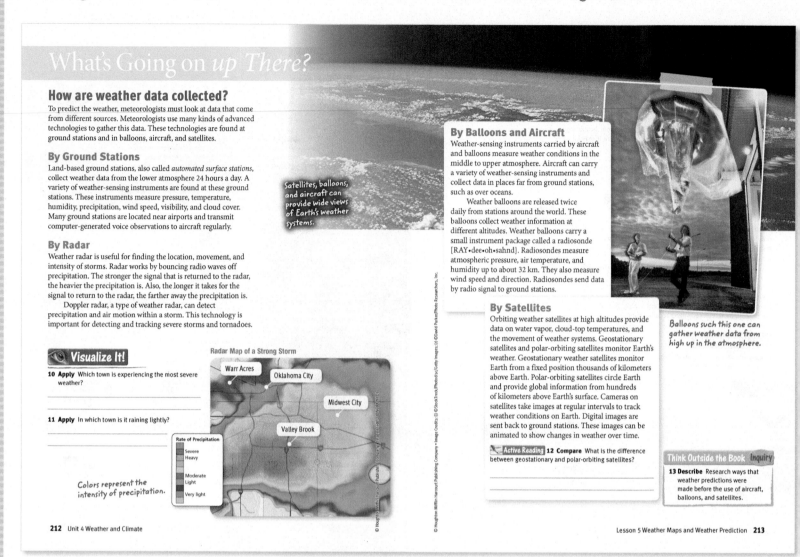

What's Going on *up There?*

How are weather data collected?

To predict the weather, meteorologists must look at data that come from different sources. Meteorologists use many kinds of advanced technologies to gather this data. These technologies are found at ground stations and in balloons, aircraft, and satellites.

By Ground Stations

Land-based ground stations, also called *automated surface stations*, collect weather data from the lower atmosphere 24 hours a day. A variety of weather-sensing instruments are found at these ground stations. These instruments measure pressure, temperature, humidity, precipitation, wind speed, visibility, and cloud cover. Many ground stations are located near airports and transmit computer-generated voice observations to aircraft regularly.

By Radar

Weather radar is useful for finding the location, movement, and intensity of storms. Radar works by bouncing radio waves off precipitation. The stronger the signal that is returned to the radar, the heavier the precipitation is. Also, the longer it takes for the signal to return to the radar, the farther away the precipitation is.

Doppler radar, a type of weather radar, can detect precipitation and air motion within a storm. This technology is important for detecting and tracking severe storms and tornadoes.

Satellites, balloons, and aircraft can provide wide views of Earth's weather systems.

👁 Visualize It!

10 Apply Which town is experiencing the most severe weather?

_____

11 Apply In which town is it raining lightly?

_____

Radar Map of a Strong Storm

Warr Acres · Oklahoma City · Midwest City · Valley Brook

Rate of Precipitation
- Severe
- Heavy
- Moderate
- Light
- Very light

Colors represent the intensity of precipitation.

By Balloons and Aircraft

Weather-sensing instruments carried by aircraft and balloons measure weather conditions in the middle to upper atmosphere. Aircraft can carry a variety of weather-sensing instruments and collect data in places far from ground stations, such as over oceans.

Weather balloons are released twice daily from stations around the world. These balloons collect weather information at different altitudes. Weather balloons carry a small instrument package called a radiosonde [RAY·dee·oh·sahnd]. Radiosondes measure atmospheric pressure, air temperature, and humidity up to about 32 km. They also measure wind speed and direction. Radiosondes send data by radio signal to ground stations.

By Satellites

Orbiting weather satellites at high altitudes provide data on water vapor, cloud-top temperatures, and the movement of weather systems. Geostationary satellites and polar-orbiting satellites monitor Earth's weather. Geostationary weather satellites monitor Earth from a fixed position thousands of kilometers above Earth. Polar-orbiting satellites circle Earth and provide global information from hundreds of kilometers above Earth's surface. Cameras on satellites take images at regular intervals to track weather conditions on Earth. Digital images are sent back to ground stations. These images can be animated to show changes in weather over time.

🌊 Active Reading
12 Compare What is the difference between geostationary and polar-orbiting satellites?

_____

Balloons such this one can gather weather data from high up in the atmosphere.

Think Outside the Book Inquiry

13 Describe Research ways that weather predictions were made before the use of aircraft, balloons, and satellites.

Answers

10. Valley Brook is experiencing the most severe weather.

11. Warr Acres is experiencing light rain.

12. Geostationary satellites stay in the same position over Earth, while polar-orbiting satellites orbit Earth.

13. Student answers will vary. Student research should show various ways in which weather observations were made based on ground observations of different elements of weather.

Building Reading Skills

Combination Notes When exploring how weather data are collected on the ground, at sea, and in the air, encourage students to develop combination notes to help them remember the information. Direct students to make two columns. Have them write details from the text in the left column and draw sketches to help them remember what they have learned in the right column.

🌐 *Optional Online resource: Combination Notes support*

Learning Alert

Satellites Students may think that geostationary satellites are somehow fixed above Earth in a single spot, and that is why they appear stationary. Explain that, in fact, geostationary satellites are constantly orbiting Earth at a very high altitude. However, because they orbit Earth in about the same amount of time it takes Earth to revolve once, to an observer on the ground it appears as if the satellite is somehow miraculously staying in a fixed position.

What kinds of symbols and maps are used to analyze the weather?

In the United States, meteorologists with the National Weather Service (NWS) collect and analyze weather data. The NWS prepares weather maps and station models to make weather data easy to use and understand.

Station Models

A **station model** is a set of meteorological symbols that represent the weather at a particular observing station. Station models are often shown on weather maps. Placing many station models on a map makes it possible to see large weather patterns, such as fronts.

A station model is a small circle that is surrounded by a set of symbols and numbers that represent current weather data at a specific location. Key weather elements shown on a station model are temperature, wind speed and direction, cloud cover, air pressure, and dew point. Note that the pointer, or wind barb, for wind direction points *into* the wind.

Active Reading

14 Identify What are the key weather elements shown by a station model?

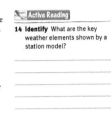

Visualize It!

15 Observe Where are the temperature and dew point recorded on a station model?

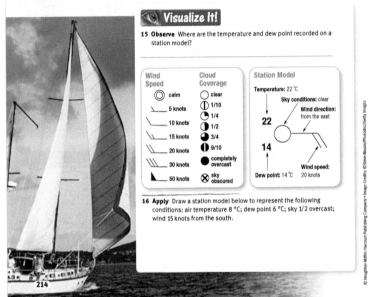

16 Apply Draw a station model below to represent the following conditions: air temperature 8 °C; dew point 6 °C; sky 1/2 overcast; wind 15 knots from the south.

Surface Weather Maps

Meteorologists commonly use surface weather maps to show forecasts on television. A surface weather map displays air pressure and the locations of fronts. Precipitation may also be shown.

Air pressure is shown by using isobars. Isobars are lines that connect points of equal air pressure and are marked in units called *millibars*. Isobars form closed loops. The center of these loops is marked with either a capital H (high) or L (low). A capital H represents a center of high pressure, and a capital L represents a center of low pressure.

Fronts are also shown on surface weather maps. Blue lines with blue triangles are cold fronts. Red lines with red half circles are warm fronts. Stationary fronts alternate between blue and red.

Visualize It!

17 Apply What type of front has recently passed through this area?

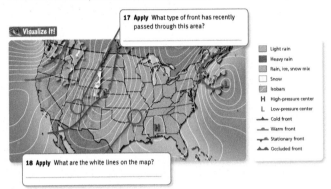

Light rain
Heavy rain
Rain, ice, snow mix
Snow
Isobars
H High-pressure center
L Low-pressure center
Cold front
Warm front
Stationary front
Occluded front

18 Apply What are the white lines on the map?

Upper-Air Charts

Another type of weather map used to analyze weather is the upper-air chart. Upper-air charts are based on data collected by instruments carried into the atmosphere by weather balloons.

Upper-air charts show wind and air pressure at middle and upper levels of Earth's atmosphere. Information from upper air charts indicates if and where weather systems will form, and if these systems will move, remain stationary, or fall apart. In addition, these charts are used to determine the position of jet streams. Airlines and airplane pilots use upper-air charts to determine flight paths and possible areas of turbulence.

Lesson 5 Weather Maps and Weather Prediction **215**

Answers

14. temperature, wind speed and direction, cloud cover, air pressure, and dew point

15. on the left; the temperature is recorded above the dew point

16. The center circle should be half-darkened on the right-hand side of the circle. The wind barb should be pointing toward the south and have a full-length, outer angled line and a half-length, inner angled line coming off of the barb. The number 8 should be in the northwest corner of the station model, and the number 6 should be directly below the 8 in the southwest corner of the station model.

17. a cold front

18. isobars

Formative Assessment

Ask: What is a station model? A station model is a set of meteorological symbols that is used to represent the weather at a particular observing station. If you saw a line on a surface weather map alternating from blue with triangles to red with half-circles, what would this indicate? It would indicate a stationary front, with two different air masses that remain at a standstill.

Building Math Skills

Scientists have created a key that includes cloud coverage symbols ranging from no clouds to completely overcast. Within this range are symbols depicting various fractions of cloud coverage. Write the following problems on the board and encourage students to figure out the equivalent fractions for the following cloud coverages:

$\frac{1}{10} = \frac{x}{20}$ $\frac{2}{20}$

$\frac{1}{4} = \frac{x}{12}$ $\frac{3}{12}$

$\frac{1}{2} = \frac{x}{10}$ $\frac{5}{10}$

$\frac{3}{4} = \frac{x}{8}$ $\frac{6}{8}$

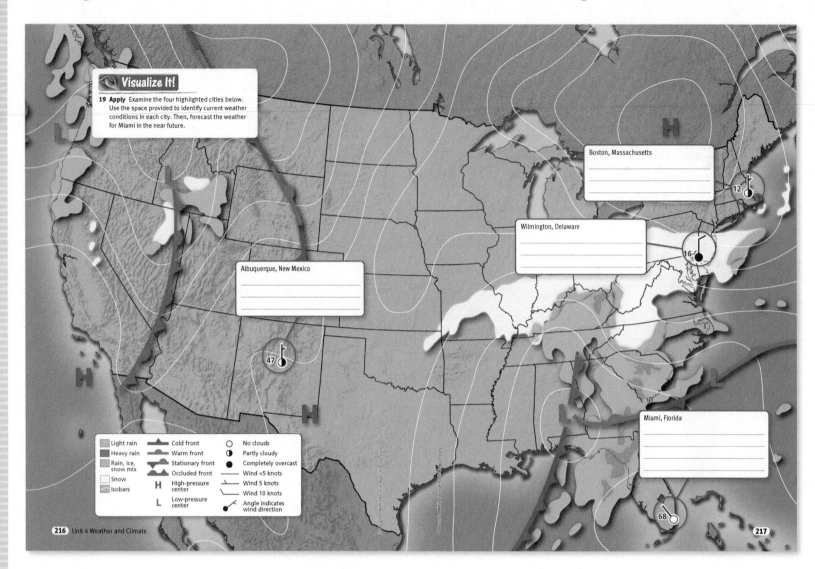

Answers

19. Boston: currently 12 degrees and partly cloudy with north winds at 5 knots; Wilmington: currently 16 degrees and overcast, snowing with north winds at 10 knots; Miami: currently 68 degrees with clear skies, northwest winds at <5 knots; prediction: increasing clouds and rain with cooler temperatures; Albuquerque: currently 47 degrees and partly cloudy with north winds at 5 knots.

Interpreting Visuals

If students are having difficulty predicting weather for Miami, direct them to look for the symbol that indicates cloud cover. **Ask:** What does the white circle tell you? that the sky is currently clear **Ask:** What direction does the line coming off the circle point to? northwest **Ask:** What does this tell you? that the wind is coming from the northwest **Ask:** What type of front do you see located to the northwest of Miami? a cold front **Ask:** What type of precipitation is occurring to the northwest of Miami, and how can you tell? Sample answer: It is raining lightly northwest of Miami. I can tell because the area is shaded light green. **Ask:** Using this information, what type of weather will Miami likely have in the near future? How can you tell? Sample answer: Miami will likely become cooler, become more overcast, and receive light rain. I can tell because the wind symbol indicates that the wind is blowing from the northwest, so whatever weather is to the northwest of Miami will likely move into the Miami area. There is a cold front and light rain to the northwest, so this is what will probably move into the Miami area. If necessary, repeat this process with another city on the map to help students become more familiar with what they should be looking for.

What are some types of weather forecasts?

As supercomputers have become faster in recent years, forecasts have also improved. Increasing amounts of weather data can be combined to create more accurate forecasts. The NWS, NOAA, and local meteorologists use computer models to develop short-range, medium-range, and long-range forecasts. These forecasts are made available to the public by radio, television, newspaper, and the Internet.

Short-Range and Medium-Range Weather Forecasts

Short-range weather forecasts make predictions about the weather 0 to 3 days into the future. Medium-range weather forecasts predict weather conditions between 3 days and 7 days into the future. Temperature, wind, cloud cover, and precipitation are predicted with different degrees of accuracy.

Weather forecasting is an imperfect science. Many variables affect weather, and all of these variables are changing constantly. In general, short-term forecasts are more accurate than forecasts made for longer periods of time. Yet, given the continuous changes that occur in the atmosphere, even short-range forecasts cannot always be accurate.

20 Infer Why is it important for the farmer to know the long-range forecast?

Long-Range Weather Forecasts

Most people want to know what the weather will be like in the near future. However, some people need to know what the weather will be like over a longer time period. The NWS issues long-range forecasts for periods of time that range from weeks to months into the future. Using sea surface temperatures and high-level winds, forecasters can make general predictions about the future. For example, they can predict if the weather will be warmer or colder or wetter or drier than average for a certain region. However, they cannot predict the temperature or if it will rain on a particular day.

Some meteorologists prepare specialized forecasts for farmers.

218   Unit 4 Weather and Climate

Hazardous Weather Forecasts

An important job of meteorologists is to warn the public about severe weather. This information is shown as a weather "crawl" at the bottom of a television screen. The NWS issues three types of hazardous weather forecasts: weather advisories, weather watches, and weather warnings.

A weather advisory is issued when the expected weather conditions will not be a serious hazard but may cause inconvenience if caution is not used. When severe weather conditions are possible over a large geographic area, a weather watch is issued. People should prepare and have a plan of action in place in case a storm threatens. A weather warning is issued when weather conditions that pose a threat to life and property are happening or are about to happen. People who live in the path of the storm need to take immediate action.

Active Reading   **21 Compare** What is the difference between a weather watch and a weather warning?

The National Weather Service issues weather advisories, weather watches, and weather warnings to inform the public about hazardous weather.

Visualize It!

22 Compose Write a caption for the photo based on a hazardous weather forecast.

219

Answers

20. Sample answer: Farmers need to know the long-term weather forecast to plan planting and harvesting schedules.

21. A weather watch is issued for large geographic areas that could possibly experience severe weather. A weather warning is issued when severe weather is occurring or will definitely occur. Immediate action to protect life or property is necessary in the warning area.

22. Sample answer: Residents board up the windows of a house based on a hurricane warning.

Learning Alert

Forecast Accuracy Remind students that even using information provided by the most modern, fastest supercomputer centers, meteorologists can't always accurately forecast day-to-day weather. A variety of computer models developed and implemented by specialists aid, rather than replace, human weather forecasters. Meteorologists take measurements and make observations; these data are run through computer models to obtain a forecast. The meteorologist combines this computer forecast with other methods, such as weather statistics from previous years, along with complex rules that the atmosphere follows, to make predictions. Combining methods helps meteorologists select the most likely outcome.

Probing Questions   GUIDED Inquiry

Applying Think about hazardous weather forecasts that might be broadcast in your area. What precautions could you take for severe weather? Sample answer: If a hurricane was predicted, I would stay indoors away from windows. My family has an emergency kit with extra water, food, matches and candles, flashlights and batteries, and a battery-powered radio. We would listen to the emergency broadcast to see if we needed to follow an evacuation route to a safer location.

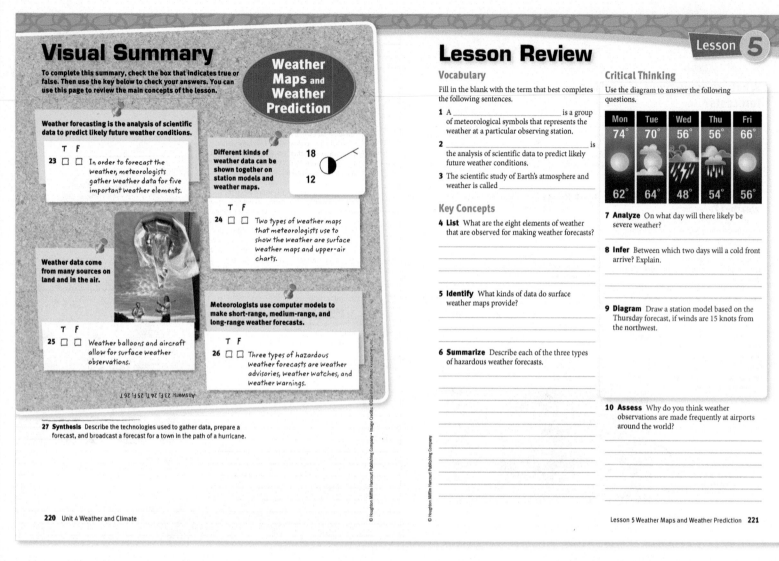

Visual Summary Answers

23. F

24. T

25. F

26. T

27. Sample answer: Aircraft, satellites, and radar are used to collect data about storm path, wind speed, and precipitation. Weather maps are used to help convey this information, and special warnings are issued via TV, radio, and the Internet.

Lesson Review Answers

1. station model

2. Weather forecasting

3. meteorology

4. air temperature, humidity, wind direction, wind speed, cloud types and altitudes, precipitation, atmospheric pressure, and visibility

5. air pressure, the locations of fronts, and precipitation

6. Weather advisory: when the expected weather conditions will not be a serious hazard but may cause inconvenience if caution is not used. Weather watch: when hazardous weather conditions are possible for a large area. Weather warning: when weather conditions that pose a threat to life and property will occur or are occurring.

7. Wednesday

8. The front will arrive between Tuesday and Wednesday. A cold front often brings storms, precipitation, and a drop in temperature.

9. *See students' pages for annotations.*

10. Sample answer: Weather has a big effect on airline safety and efficiency. Pilots and controllers need information about changing weather to ensure the safety of passengers.

J. Marshall Shepherd

Purpose To learn about the work of Dr. J. Marshall Shepherd and other meteorologists

Learning Goals
- Identify contributions made by a scientist.
- Recognize that scientists come from different backgrounds.
- Identify jobs in science fields.

Informal Vocabulary
instrument, satellite, radar

Prerequisite Knowledge
- Weather
- Severe weather
- Climate

Activity *Make a Rain Gauge*

 individuals

 ongoing

 DIRECTED Inquiry

Like Dr. Shepherd, students can make their own weather instruments. Provide students with clear plastic soda bottles, scissors, masking tape, markers, and rulers. First, students should cut off the top part of their bottle. Alternatively, students could use wide-mouth glass jars. Then have them run a strip of tape up one side of the bottle and use the ruler to measure inches, starting from the bottom. They should draw a line at each inch mark and label the lines. Encourage students to put their rain gauges outside the next time it rains and measure how much rain falls, using the scale on the tape. Advise students to place rocks or other heavy objects around their gauges to prevent them from tipping over.

For greater depth, have students record rainfall amounts for a month and make a chart to display their findings.

Differentiated Instruction

Basic *Impacts of Weather*

 individuals, then pairs, then whole class

 25 min

Think, Pair, Share These pages list many fields and occupations in which meteorology is used. Have individual students brainstorm why meteorology might be useful in these fields or in others that they can think of. Then have students pair up and share their ideas. Encourage them to try to think of more uses of meteorology and eliminate any uses that don't make sense. Finally, encourage pairs to share their ideas with the class.

Advanced *Children's Book*

 pairs or small groups

 30 min

Have each group choose a weather topic that they learned about in this unit. Each group should then write and illustrate a children's book that explains the topic so a younger student could understand it. Encourage them to be creative but to make sure their explanations are factually accurate. If possible, have groups share their finished books with students in a younger grade.

ELL *Meteorology Words*

 pairs

10 min

Cluster Diagram To help students understand the relationships between the meteorology-related words on these pages, have pairs of students create Cluster Diagrams. Pairs should write *meteorology* in a large center circle. Then they should write words related to *meteorology* in medium-sized circles connected to the large circle. They can then add words that give more specific details in small circles connected to the medium circles.

Customize Your Feature

☐ **Activity** Make a Rain Gauge
☐ **People in Science** Online

☐ **Basic** Impacts of Weather
☐ **Advanced** Children's Book
☐ **ELL** Meteorology Words
☐ **Social Studies Connection**
☐ **Building Reading Skills**

People in Science

J. Marshall Shepherd
METEOROLOGIST AND CLIMATOLOGIST

Dr. Marshall Shepherd, who works at the University of Georgia, has been interested in weather since he made his own weather-collecting instruments for a school science project. Although the instruments he uses today, like computers and satellites, are much larger and much more powerful than the ones he made in school, they give him some of the same information.

In his work, Dr. Shepherd tries to understand weather events, such as hurricanes and thunderstorms, and relate them to current weather and climate change. He once led a team that used space-based radar to measure rainfall over urban areas. The measurements confirmed that the areas downwind of major cities experience more rainfall in summer than other areas in the same region. He explained that the excess heat retained by buildings and roads changes the way the air circulates, and this causes rain clouds to form.

While the most familiar field of meteorology is weather forecasting, research meteorology is also used in air pollution control, weather control, agricultural planning, climate change studies, and even criminal and civil investigations.

J. Marshall Shepherd

Social Studies Connection

An almanac is a type of calendar that contains various types of information, including weather forecasts and astronomical data, for every day of the year. Many people used almanacs before meteorologists started to forecast the weather. Use an almanac from the library or the Internet to find out what the weather was on the day that you were born.

JOB BOARD

Atmospheric Scientist

What You'll Do: Collect and analyze data on Earth's air pressure, humidity, and winds to make short-range and long-range weather forecasts. Work around the clock during weather emergencies like hurricanes and tornadoes.

Where You Might Work: Weather data collecting stations, radio and television stations, or private consulting firms.

Education: A bachelor's degree in meteorology, or in a closely related field with courses in meteorology, is required. A master's degree is necessary for some jobs.

Snow Plow Operator

What You'll Do: In areas that receive snowfall, prepare the roads by spreading a mixture of sand and salt on the roads when snow is forecast. After a snowfall, drive snow plows to clear snow from roads and walkways.

Where You Might Work: For public organizations or private companies in cities and towns that receive snowfall.

Education: In most states, there is no special license needed, other than a driver's license.

Airplane Pilot

What You'll Do: Fly airplanes containing passengers or cargo, or for crop dusting, search and rescue, or fire-fighting. Before flights, check the plane's control equipment and weather conditions. Plan a safe route. Pilots communicate with air traffic control during flight to ensure a safe flight and fill out paperwork after the flight.

Where You Might Work: Flying planes for airlines, the military, radio and tv stations, freight companies, flight schools, farms, national parks, or other businesses that use airplanes.

Education: Most pilots will complete a four-year college degree before entering a pilot program. Before pilots become certified and take to the skies, they need a pilot license and many hours of flight time and training.

222 | 223

Social Studies Connection

Tell students that the information in an almanac is generally found in tables organized by date. Encourage students to also look at the almanac's predictions for future weather. Do they think these predictions will come true?

Building Reading Skills

Three-Column Chart Have students use a Three-Column Chart to compare and contrast the occupations listed on the job board. Students might make comparisons of the tools used in each job, the places where the jobs are set, the level of education required for the job, and the degree to which the job is related to meteorology. Ask students to use their charts to determine which job they would like best.

Optional Online resource: Three-Column Chart support

Climate

Essential Question How is climate affected by energy from the sun and variations on Earth's surface?

Professional Development

For more detailed information about the topics in this lesson, refer to the Content Refresher in the Unit Opener pages.

Opening Your Lesson

Begin the lesson by assessing students' prerequisite and prior knowledge.

Prerequisite Knowledge

- Definitions of *convection currents, air pressure, temperature, precipitation, wind, humidity, condensation,* and *evaporation*
- Understanding the water cycle

Accessing Prior Knowledge

Ask: How is the average temperature and precipitation here different from other places? Sample answer: It is warmer here than Alaska and wetter than in a desert.

Ask: How does the sun affect temperature? The sun makes temperature increase.

Ask: Have you seen a photograph of a mountain that shows snow on the top but not at the bottom? Why is this? Sample answer: The top must be colder.

Customize Your Opening

- ☐ **Accessing Prior Knowledge,** above
- ☐ **Print Path** Engage Your Brain, SE p. 225 #1–2
- ☐ **Print Path** Active Reading, SE p. 225 #3–4
- ☐ **Digital Path** Lesson Opener

Key Topics/Learning Goals	Supporting Concepts
Climate vs. Weather 1 Distinguish between climate and weather. 2 Identify the two main factors that determine climate.	• Weather is the atmospheric condition at a particular time and place. Climate comprises the typical weather conditions in an area. • Climate is mostly determined by temperature and precipitation.
Solar Energy and Climate 1 Define *latitude* and state why latitude affects climate. 2 Explain the effect of sun's energy on precipitation, winds. 3 Describe how winds can affect climate.	• Latitude is the distance in degrees north or south from the equator. It determines how much solar energy an area receives. • The water cycle is driven by the sun's energy; it determines precipitation. • Winds transfer energy and affect precipitation by carrying water vapor.
Other Factors That Affect Climate 1 Explain the effects of topography and elevation on climate. 2 Explain how mountains affect precipitation. 3 Explain the effect of large bodies of water and surface currents on climate.	• Topography affects wind movement, temperature, and precipitation. • As elevation increases, temperature usually decreases. • Rain-shadow effect: rainy conditions exist on one side of a mountain, dry on the other. • Water absorbs and releases energy more slowly than land which affects climate at coastlines; surface currents carry warm or cool water, which affects the air temperature.
Climate Zones 1 Explain how latitude is related to air temperature. 2 Locate the polar, temperate and tropical climate zones.	• The higher the latitude, the colder the climate tends to be. • The tropical climate zone is near the equator, the polar climate zone is near the poles, and the temperate climate zone is at mid-latitudes. Each zone contains sub-zones.

Options for Instruction

Two parallel paths provide coverage of the Essential Questions, with a strong **Inquiry** strand woven into each. Follow the **Print Path,** the **Digital Path,** or your customized combination of print, digital, and inquiry.

Print Path
Teaching support for the Print Path appears with the Student Pages.

Inquiry Labs and Activities

Digital Path
Digital Path shortcut: TS661230

Print Path	Inquiry Labs and Activities	Digital Path
How's the Climate? SE pp. 226–227 **What determines climate?** • Temperature, Precipitation	**Quick Lab** Determining Climate	**Weather and Climate** Interactive List
Here Comes the Sun! SE pp. 228–229 **The sun's energy affects climate** • Latitude Affects the Amount of Solar Energy an Area Receives and Its Climate • The Sun Powers the Water Cycle • The Sun Powers Wind	**Quick Lab** The Angle of the Sun's Rays **Daily Demo** Angle of the Sun's Rays	**Factors that Influence Climate** Interactive Graphics
Latitude Isn't Everything, SE pp. 230–231 **How Earth's features affect climate** • Topography Can Affect Winds • Elevation Influences Temperature **Waterfront Property,** SE pp. 232–233 **How do large bodies of water and ocean currents affect climate?**	**Daily Demo** Condensation Demonstration **Quick Lab** Factors That Affect Climate **Field Lab** How Land Features Affect Climate **Activity** Here and There	**Factors that Influence Climate** Interactive Graphics **Currents and Climate** Animation
Zoning Out, SE pp. 234–235 **What are the three major climate zones?** • Temperate, Polar, Tropical	**Activity** Climate Circle	**Major Climate Zones** Animation

Options for Assessment

See the Evaluate page for options, including Formative Assessment, Summative Assessment, and Unit Review.

Engage and Explore

Activities and Discussion

Activity *Here and There*

Introducing Key Topics

 individuals or pairs
🕐 35 min
(Inquiry) **GUIDED** inquiry

Assign a different city to each individual or pair. Try to choose cities from a broad range of climate conditions and make sure the conditions are different from the climate of the students' community. Have students research the climates of their assigned city and that of their own community. Students can look online or in an encyclopedia or atlas for information. Encourage students to find the average rainfall and temperature of the two locations. Have students record information in a Two-Panel Flip Chart, which they can share with the class. Encourage students to think about factors that affect the climates and climate zones.

 Online Resource: Two-Panel Flip Chart

Probing Question *Studying Climate*

Climate vs. Weather

 whole class
🕐 10–15 min
(Inquiry) **GUIDED** inquiry

Analyzing Remind students of the differences between weather and climate. Tell students that weather is measured using a variety of instruments, such as thermometers and barometers. Ask students what they think the main tool scientists use to study weather and why. **Prompt:** Studying climate requires analyzing data. Sample answer: Scientists need to make generalizations to study climate; therefore they probably use math to analyze data about the weather.

Discussion *What's the Difference?*

Climate vs. Weather

 whole class
🕐 25 min

The difference between weather and climate can be confusing. Have students discuss the relationship between weather and climate. As they discuss, record key words, ideas, and examples that help show the relationship between weather and climate.

Labs and Demos

Quick Lab *The Angles of the Sun's Rays*

 Engage

Solar Energy and Climate

 small groups
🕐 30 min
(Inquiry) **DIRECTED** inquiry

Students model the angles at which the sun's light strikes their location and use a flashlight to model how different angles produce more or less concentrated light.

PURPOSE To show the relationship between light angle and heat

MATERIALS

- flashlight
- globe or map showing student location and latitude
- meterstick
- paper, tabloid or larger (3 sheets)
- protractor
- tape

Field Lab *How Land Features Affect Climate*

Other Factors That Affect Climate

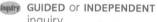 small groups
🕐 2 45-min periods
(Inquiry) **GUIDED** or **INDEPENDENT** inquiry

Students determine how microclimates are affected by land features.

PURPOSE To investigate how land features cause microclimates on Earth's surface

MATERIALS

- thermometer
- weather data-collecting instruments
- stopwatch

Customize Your Labs

🗂 *See the Lab Manual for lab datasheets.*

🖰 *Go Online for editable lab datasheets.*

Daily Demo *Condensation Demonstration*

Engage

Other Factors That Affect Climate

 whole class
 20–25 min
Inquiry GUIDED inquiry

PURPOSE **To demonstrate how cooling air causes condensation**

MATERIALS

- cup, styrofoam or ceramic
- hot water
- small plate

1 Ask students to explain what they understand about the role condensation plays in the rain shadow effect. Sample answer: when air hits a mountain, it is forced up the side of the mountain. Because air temperature cools with increasing elevation, the air cools and condenses. This can produce rain.

2 Tell students that you are going to demonstrate condensation. Fill the cup halfway with hot water and hold the plate an inch or two above the cup.

3 After two or three minutes, remove the plate. Show students the underside of the plate and ask them what they observe. water droplets

4 **Analyzing** Why did water droplets form? the plate is cooler than the cup of hot water

5 **Applying** How does this apply to the rain shadow effect? Air cooled when it rose and hit the cooler plate, and water droplets formed. Air cools as it travels up the side of a mountain, causing condensation and sometimes rain.

Quick Lab *Factors That Affect Climate*

Other Factors That Affect Climate

 small groups
🕐 30 min
Inquiry DIRECTED inquiry

Students add soil to one container and water to another then measure how fast each absorbs and releases heat.

PURPOSE **To determine whether land or water absorbs heat faster and to explain how this affects climate**

MATERIALS

- container, 2
- heat lamp
- meter stick
- soil
- stopwatch

- thermometer, celsius, 2
- water
- lab aprons
- safety goggles

Quick Lab *Determining Climate*

Climate vs. Weather

 small groups
🕐 30 min
Inquiry DIRECTED inquiry

Students research and interpret data about weather in your state over the past five years to make generalizations about the climate in the state.

PURPOSE **To make generalizations about the climate of your state**

MATERIALS

- colored pencils
- graph paper

- research materials, including almanacs and the Internet

Activities and Discussion

☐ **Activity** Here and There
☐ **Probing Question** Studying Climate
☐ **Discussion** What's the Difference?

Labs and Demos

☐ **Quick Lab** … the Sun's Rays

☐ **Field Lab** How Land Features Affect Climate
☐ **Daily Demo** Condensation Demonstration
☐ **Quick Lab** Factors… Affect Climate
☐ **Quick Lab** Determining Climate

Your Resources

_____

_____

Explain Science Concepts

Key Topics	📖 Print Path	🖥 Digital Path
Climate vs. Weather	☐ **How's the Climate?** SE pp. 226–227 • Active Reading (Annotation strategy), #5 • Visualize It!, #6 • Visualize It!, #7 • Think Outside the Book, #8	☐ **Weather and Climate** Learn the differences between weather and climate.
Solar Energy and Climate	☐ **Here Comes the Sun!** SE pp. 228–229 • Active Reading (Annotation strategy), #9 • Visualize It!, #10 • Visualize It!, #11	☐ **Factors that Influence Climate** Explore how latitude, elevation, and other factors affect the climate of a location.
Other Factors That Affect Climate	☐ **Latitude Isn't Everything…,** SE pp. 230–231 • Active Reading (Annotation strategy), #12 • Visualize It!, #13 • Visualize It!, #14 • Infer, #15 ☐ **Waterfront Property,** SE pp. 232–233 • Visualize It!, #16 • Summarize, #17 • Visualize It!, #18	☐ **Factors that Influence Climate** Explore how latitude, elevation, and other factors affect the climate of a location. ☐ **Currents and Climate** See how warm or cool water can affect a climate.
Climate Zones	☐ **Zoning Out,** SE pp. 234–235 • Active Reading (Annotation strategy), #19 • Visualize It!, #20 • Two-Column Chart, #21 • Visualize It!, #22	☐ **Major Climate Zones** Learn about polar, temperate, and tropical climates.

Differentiated Instruction

Basic *Climate Factors*

Synthesizing Key Topics

 individuals
🕐 ongoing

Remind students that climate and weather are complex topics, and that more than one factor must be considered. Encourage students to make a chart titled "Factors that Affect Climate." Have them list each factor as they read about it, then write a description of exactly how that factor can affect climate.

Advanced *Climate Data*

Climate versus Weather

 pairs
🕐 ongoing

Have student pairs choose two cities in the United States that are in different climate zones; for example, Anchorage, Alaska, and Mobile, Alabama. Have them use a national news source to keep track of the temperature and precipitation in these two cities for two weeks. Encourage students to use their data to make line graphs, one showing temperature changes, the other, precipitation. Make sure the graphs have two lines—one for each city. Students should then do some research to find out about the climates in the cities. Encourage students to write a short paragraph comparing the usual climates of their cities to the recent weather in their cities based on their research and the graphed data.

ELL *Key Ideas*

Synthesizing Key Topics

 pairs
🕐 25 min

Cluster Diagram To help EL learners organize the most important details in the lesson, have them create a Cluster Diagram. Help students develop a main idea phrase for the center circle, such as "Climate is affected by many factors" or "Climate is the long-term weather pattern of an area." Have students then fill in the rest of the diagram with supporting details.

🌐 *Optional Online resource: Cluster Diagram*

Lesson Vocabulary

weather	latitude	elevation
climate	topography	surface current

Previewing Vocabulary

 whole class
🕐 15 min

Word Origins Share the following to help students remember terms:
- **Climate** comes from the Greek *klima*, meaning "region or zone."
- **Latitude** comes from the Latin *latus*, meaning "wide."
- **Topography** comes from the Greek words *topos*, which means "place," and *graph*, which means "write."
- **Elevation** comes from the Latin *elevare*, meaning "lift up or raise."

Reinforcing Vocabulary

👤 individuals
🕐 ongoing

Word Triangle Have students complete Word Triangles for each term. Students will draw a triangle and split it into three sections. In the bottom third, students write the word and its definition; in the middle third, students write a sentence using the term; and in the top third, students will draw an illustration of the term.

🌐 *Optional Online resource: Word Triangle*

Customize Your Core Lesson

Core Instruction
- ☐ **Print Path** choices
- ☐ **Digital Path** choices

Vocabulary
- ☐ **Previewing Vocabulary** Word Origins
- ☐ **Reinforcing Vocabulary** Word Triangle

Your Resources

Differentiated Instruction
- ☐ **Basic** Climate Factors
- ☐ **Advanced** Climate Data
- ☐ **ELL** Key Ideas

Extend Science Concepts

Reinforce and Review

Activity *Climate Circle*

Synthesizing Key Topics   whole class   🕐 20 min

Inside/Outside Circles

1   Pass out questions on index cards to students. Have them write the answers on the back of the card. Check students' answers to make sure they are correct. Have students adjust incorrect answers.

2   Have students pair up and form two circles. One partner is in an inside circle, the other is in an outside circle. The students in the inside circle face out, and the students in the outside circle face in.

3   Each student in the inside circle asks his or her partner the question on the index cards. If the partner's answer is incorrect, the student in the inside circle teaches the other student the correct answer. Repeat this step with the outside-circle students asking the questions.

4   Have each student on the outside circle rotate one person to the right. He or she faces a new partner and gets a new question. Students rotate after each pair of questions.

Sample Questions

- True or False: Climate and weather are the same thing. false
- True or False: The only thing that affects climate is latitude. false
- How does elevation affect climate? The higher an area's elevation, the colder it will probably be.
- Are places near large bodies of water warmer or colder during the winter? warmer
- A(n) _____ causes one side of a mountain to get a lot of rain and the other side to be very dry. rain shadow
- What are the three major climate zones? tropical, polar, temperate

FoldNotes

Synthesizing Key Topics   individuals   🕐 ongoing

Layered Book Have students use a Layered Book FoldNote to take notes on the four key topic areas—*Climate vs. Weather; Solar Energy and Climate; Other Factors That Affect Climate; Climate Zones.*

🕐 *Online resource: Layered Book*

Going Further

Social Studies Connection

Synthesizing Key Topics   pairs   🕐 30 min

Map Study Explain to students that different kinds of maps can reveal a lot of information about the factors that affect a region's climate. Have students look at different types of U.S. maps. Useful maps could include a topographical map, an ocean currents map, a map showing latitude, and a map showing the type of terrain, such as grassland, forest, or desert. Have students analyze the factors that affect specific regions' climates. For example, **Ask:** What might account for the mild weather in California? or What factors affect the climate of Florida?

Life Science Connection

Climate Zones   pairs   🕐 25 min

Research Project Explain to students that climate has a huge impact on ecosystems and that organisms are adapted to the climates where they thrive. Have students research an ecosystem, such as a desert ecosystem, a rainforest ecosystem, or a polar ecosystem. Then have them prepare a poster that describes the climate of the ecosystem including the climate zone it is found in. Posters should include examples of plants and animals that thrive in the ecosystem and explain how they are adapted to that specific climate.

🕐 *Optional Online rubric: Written Pieces*

Customize Your Closing

🔲 *See the Assessment Guide for quizzes and tests.*

🕐 *Go Online to edit and create quizzes and tests.*

Reinforce and Review

☐ **Activity** Climate Circle

☐ **FoldNote** Layered Book

☐ **Print Path** Visual Summary, SE p. 236

☐ **Print Path** Lesson Review, SE p. 237

☐ **Digital Path** Lesson Closer

Evaluate Student Mastery

Formative Assessment

See the teacher support below the Student Pages for additional Formative Assessment questions.

Describe the climatic conditions of the area where students live. Explain that climate is predictable, although the weather conditions vary from day to day. State the average temperature and precipitation of the area. **Ask:** How do factors like energy from the sun, topography, large bodies of water, and surface currents affect the climate of the region where we live? Responses will vary but should account for latitude, topography and elevation, proximity to large bodies of water, and ocean currents.

Reteach

Formative assessment may show that students need reinforcement for certain topics. The resources below are recommended for reteaching. If students were introduced to a topic through the Print Path, you can also use the Digital Path to reteach and vice versa.
🎧 *Can be assigned to individual students*

Climate vs. Weather
Discussion What's the Difference?

Solar Energy and Climate
Quick Lab The Angles of the Sun's Rays

Other Factors That Affect Climate
Quick Lab Factors that Affect Climate

Field Lab How Land Features Affect Climate 🎧

Climate Zones
Activity Here and There 🎧

Summative Assessment

Alternative Assessment
Climate Factors Anywhere in the World

🔘 *Online resources: student worksheet, optional rubrics.*

Climate

Climb the Pyramid: *Climate Factors Anywhere in the World*

1. Work on your own, with a partner, or with a small group.
2. Choose one item from each layer of the pyramid. Check your choices.
3. Have your teacher approve your plan.
4. Submit or present your results.

__ **City Creator**
Invent two locations with very different climates. On a poster, describe the climatic conditions of each city, including temperature and precipitation conditions. Explain what factors affect the climate in your two cities. You may include information about latitude, topography, elevation, large bodies of water, and ocean currents. Posters may include illustrations and other visuals.

__ **Climate Journal**
Select a region and gather information about its climate. Demonstrate what you've learned about the climate by imagining you are a person who lives in that climate and keeping a journal that describes the weather for one day out of each month. Be sure to include information about temperature and precipitation and also indicate the factors that affect the climate in the region.

__ **Where in the World?**
Research a place that seems to have a confused climate zone. Are there freezing places in the tropical zone or hot places in polar or temperate zones? Create a poster describing the unexpected climate in the location you have chosen. Explain the factors that affect the region's climate. Posters can include diagrams, maps, and other visuals.

__ **Fighting Factors**
Write a skit in which each of the factors that affects climate is a character. Imagine that the factors are having a discussion about which of them has the greatest impact on climate. Write dialogue for each factor to help them make their cases.

__ **Climate Poem**
Select a city or region with a climate that interests you. Research the climate conditions there and the factors that cause them. Write a poem about this place that describes the climate and the different factors that affect it.

__ **Compare Cities**
Select two cities with different climates for which there is temperature and precipitation data available. Write a paragraph that compares the average monthly temperature and precipitation for each city. Graph your data if you want to help visualize it.

Going Further
☐ Social Studies Connection
☐ Life Science Connection

Formative Assessment
☐ Strategies Throughout TE
☐ Lesson Review SE

Summative Assessment
☐ Alternative Assessment Climate Factors Anywhere in the World
☐ Lesson Quiz
☐ Unit Tests A and B
☐ Unit Review SE End-of-Unit

Your Resources

Answers

Answers for 1–3 should represent students' current throughts, even if incorrect.

1. F; T; F; T

2. If sunlight were blocked for long periods of time, the temperature on Earth's surface would be colder, and without sunlight coming in, it may become cold enough to start an ice age.

3. Sample answer: Topography is about writing or representing the features of a place.

4. Students should define or sketch each vocabulary term in the lesson.

Opening Your Lesson

Discuss student responses to item 1 to assess their prerequisite knowledge and to estimate what they already know about the key topics.

Prerequisites Students should already be familiar with the water cycle and the term *precipitation*. Students should also be familiar with convection currents and the concept that warm air and water move in currents to areas where the air or water is cooler.

Use the strategy below to assess students' prior knowledge about climate.

Anticipation Guide To help students self-assess their prior knowledge about climate, you may wish to have them create an Anticipation Guide. Explain to students that an Anticipation Guide is a tool with which they can record their ideas before reading a section. Then they can check to see if they were right after they read. To complete an Anticipation Guide, have students first fill in the statement columns with ideas about climate. These statements can be self-generated, generated through class discussion, or generated by the teacher. Then have students write in the next column whether they agree or disagree with the statement. Finally, as students read the lesson, they can fill in the last column indicating whether the text agrees or disagrees with the statement.

🌐 *Optional Online resource: Anticipation Guide*

How's the **Climate?**

What determines climate?

5 Identify As you read, underline two elements of weather that are important in determining climate.

Weather conditions change from day to day. **Weather** is the condition of Earth's atmosphere at a particular time and place. **Climate**, on the other hand, describes the weather conditions in an area over a long period of time. For the most part, climate is determined by temperature and precipitation (pree•SIP•uh•tay•shuhn). But what factors affect the temperature and precipitation rates of an area? Those factors include latitude, wind patterns, elevation, locations of mountains and large bodies of water, and nearness to ocean currents.

Temperature

Temperature patterns are an important feature of climate. Although the average temperature of an area over a period of time is useful information, using only average temperatures to describe climate can be misleading. Areas that have similar average temperatures may have very different temperature ranges.

A temperature range includes all of the temperatures in an area, from the coldest temperature extreme to the warmest temperature extreme. Organisms that thrive in a region are those that can survive the temperature extremes in that region. Temperature ranges provide more information about an area and are unique to the area. Therefore, temperature ranges are a better indicator of climate than are temperature averages.

Visualize It!

6 Infer How might the two different climates shown below affect the daily lives of the people who live there?

_____
_____
_____
_____
_____

Polar region

Desert region

226

Precipitation

Precipitation, such as rain, snow, or hail, is also an important part of climate. As with temperature, the average yearly precipitation alone is not the best way to describe a climate. Two places that have the same average yearly precipitation may receive that precipitation in different patterns during the year. For example, one location may receive small amounts of precipitation throughout the year. This pattern would support plant life all year long. Another location may receive all of its precipitation in a few months of the year. These months may be the only time in which plants can grow. So, the pattern of precipitation in a region can determine the types of plants that grow there and the length of the growing season. Therefore, the pattern of precipitation is a better indicator of the local climate than the average precipitation alone.

Think Outside the Book Inquiry

8 Apply With a classmate, discuss what condition, other than precipitation, is likely related to better plant growth in the temperate area shown directly below than in the desert on the bottom right.

Visualize It!

7 Interpret Match the climates represented in the bar graph below to the photos by writing A, B, or C in the blank circles.

Annual Precipitation in Three Climates

○ There are enough resources in the area for plants to thickly cover the ground.

○ Some plants that grow in deserts have long roots to reach the water deep underground.

○ Conditions in a tropical forest allow lots of plants to grow quickly and closely together.

Lesson 6 Climate **227**

Answers

5. *See students' pages for annotations.*

6. Students' answers should accurately relate to each of the photos. Students may mention how hard it is to get water in the desert or how people have to make sure that they keep cool enough. The opposite would be true of the photo in which a polar climate is shown.

7. *B:* temperate; *A:* desert; *C:* tropical forest

8. A smaller temperature range in the temperate region above probably allows for better plant growth than the larger temperature range in the desert.

Building Reading Skills

Text Structure: Comparison/Contrast How are weather and climate the same? How are they different? Sample answer: Both weather and climate are related to conditions in the atmosphere including temperature and precipitation. However, weather varies from day to day, but climate describes the conditions over a longer period of time.

Building Math Skills

Using average annual ranges of temperature and precipitation to interpret climate can be misleading. Give students an example of two cities, such as New York City and Portland, Oregon, that have fairly similar average annual temperatures and precipitation amounts, but have quite different climates. **Ask:** What does this example illustrate? Sample answer: Because different locations can have similar average ranges of temperatures and precipitation amounts, but very different climatic conditions, it is important to consider extremes of temperature and precipitation. Challenge students to pick two cities, then determine average annual precipitation and temperature for each. List the results each of the students arrived at on the board, grouping cities with similar annual temperature and precipitation together. Then encourage students to consider whether cities with similar averages also share similar climates. Ask them to explain why or why not.

Here Comes the Sun!

How is the sun's energy related to Earth's climate?

9 Identify As you read, underline how solar energy affects the climate of an area.

The climate of an area is directly related to the amount of energy from the sun, or *solar energy*, that the area receives. This amount depends on the latitude (LAHT•ih•tood) of the area. **Latitude** is the angular distance in degrees north and south from the equator. Different latitudes receive different amounts of solar energy. The available solar energy powers the water cycle and winds, which affect the temperature, precipitation, and other factors that determine the local climate.

Latitude Affects the Amount of Solar Energy an Area Receives and that Area's Climate

Latitude helps determine the temperature of an area, because latitude affects the amount of solar energy an area receives. The figure below shows how the amount of solar energy reaching Earth's surface varies with latitude. Notice that the sun's rays travel in lines parallel to one another. Near the equator, the sun's rays hit Earth directly, at almost a 90° angle. At this angle, the solar energy is concentrated in a small area of Earth's surface. As a result, that area has high temperatures. At the poles, the sun's rays hit Earth at a lesser angle than they do at the equator. At this angle, the same amount of solar energy is spread over a larger area. Because the energy is less concentrated, the poles have lower temperatures than areas near the equator do.

10 Analyze What is the difference between the sun's rays that strike at the equator and the sun's rays that strike at the poles?

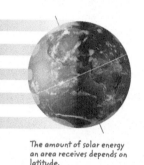

Drawing is not to scale.

The amount of solar energy an area receives depends on latitude.

228   Unit 4 Weather and Climate

The Sun Powers the Water Cycle

It is easy to see how the water cycle affects weather and climate. For example, when it rains or snows, you see precipitation. In the water cycle, energy from the sun warms the surface of the ocean or other body of water. Some of the liquid water evaporates, becoming invisible water vapor, a gas. When cooled, some of the vapor condenses, turning into droplets of liquid water and forming clouds. Some water droplets collide, becoming larger. Once large enough, they fall to Earth's surface as precipitation.

11 Apply Using the figure below, explain how the water cycle affects the climate of an area.

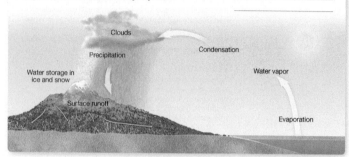

Clouds

Precipitation

Condensation

Water vapor

Water storage in ice and snow

Surface runoff

Evaporation

The Sun Powers Wind

The sun warms Earth's surface unevenly, creating areas of different air pressure. As air moves from areas of higher pressure to areas of lower pressure, it is felt as wind, as shown below. Global and local wind patterns transfer energy around Earth's surface, affecting global and local temperatures. Winds also carry water vapor from place to place. If the air cools enough, the water vapor will condense and fall as precipitation. The speed, direction, temperature, and moisture content of winds affect the climate and weather of the areas they move through.

Warm, less dense air rises, creating areas of low pressure.

Cold, more dense air sinks, creating areas of high pressure.

Wind forms when air moves from a high-pressure area to a low-pressure area.

Warm surface

Cool surface

229

Answers

9. *See students' pages for annotations.*

10. The sun's rays are concentrated in a smaller area at the equator than at the poles.

11. The water cycle can affect the amount of precipitation in an area. In the figure, water evaporating from the ocean is transported inland, where it condenses into clouds and falls as precipitation.

Interpreting Visuals

The arrows in the diagram of the sun and Earth represent energy from the sun. What concept does the diagram help you understand? The equator receives more direct rays from the sun than places farther from the equator.

Learning Alert

Hours of Daylight Students may believe that length of daylight does not vary by locale. Using a globe and a lamp or sunny window, model how Earth's tilt causes its polar regions to have 24-h daylight at midsummer and 24-h darkness at midwinter. Make the point that other regions of the globe have different amounts of daylight and darkness compared with these polar extremes, even on the same day.

Formative Assessment

Ask: Why is it usually warmer at Earth's equator than at its poles? The equator receives more direct energy from the sun than anywhere else on Earth; the solar energy that the poles receive is more indirect. **Ask:** Besides heating Earth's surface, how else does solar energy affect climate? Solar energy also drives the water cycle, which affects precipitation; the sun's uneven heating of Earth's surfaces also causes winds, which affect temperature and precipitation.

Latitude Isn't Everything

How do Earth's features affect climate?

12 Identify As you read, underline how topography affects the climate of a region.

On land, winds have to flow around or over features on Earth's surface, such as mountains. The surface features of an area combine to form its **topography** (tuh•POG•ruh•fee). Topography influences the wind patterns and the transfer of energy in an area. An important aspect of topography is elevation. **Elevation** refers to the height of an area above sea level. Temperature changes as elevation changes. Thus, topography and elevation affect the climate of a region.

Topography Can Affect Winds

Even the broad, generally flat topography of the Great Plains gives rise to unique weather patterns. On the plains, winds can flow steadily over large distances before they merge. This mixing of winds produces thunderstorms and even tornadoes.

Mountains can also affect the climate of an area, as shown below. When moist air hits a mountain, it is forced to rise up the side of the mountain. The rising air cools and often releases rain, which supports plants on the mountainside. The air that moves over the top of the mountain is dry. The air warms as it descends, creating a dry climate, which supports desert formation. Such areas are said to be in a *rain shadow*, because the air has already released all of its water by the time that it reaches this side of the mountain.

Visualize It!

13 Apply Circle the rain gauge in each set that corresponds to how much rain each side of the mountain is likely to receive.

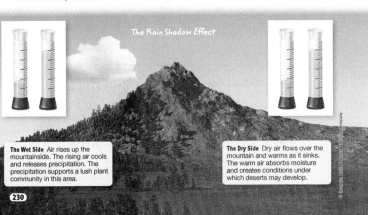

The Rain Shadow Effect

The Wet Side Air rises up the mountainside. The rising air cools and releases precipitation. The precipitation supports a lush plant community in this area.

The Dry Side Dry air flows over the mountain and warms as it sinks. The warm air absorbs moisture and creates conditions under which deserts may develop.

230

Elevation Influences Temperature

Elevation has a very strong effect on the temperature of an area. If you rode a cable car up a mountain, the temperature would decrease by about 6.5 °C (11.7 °F) for every kilometer you rose in elevation. Why does it get colder as you move higher up? Because the lower atmosphere is mainly warmed by Earth's surface that is directly below it. The warmed air lifts to higher elevations, where it expands and cools. Even close to the equator, temperatures at high elevations can be very cold. For example, Mount Kilimanjaro in Tanzania is close to the equator, but it is still cold enough at the peak to support a permanent glacier. The example below shows how one mountain can have several types of climates.

Visualize It!

14 Apply Circle the thermometer that shows the most likely temperature for each photo at different elevations.

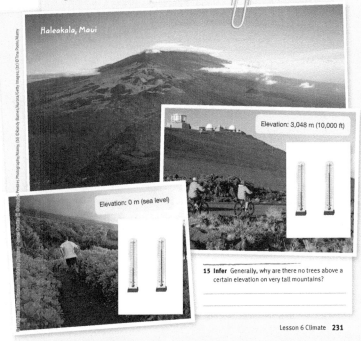

Effects of Elevation

Haleakala, Maui

Elevation: 3,048 m (10,000 ft)

Elevation: 0 m (sea level)

15 Infer Generally, why are there no trees above a certain elevation on very tall mountains?

Lesson 6 Climate 231

Answers

12. *See students' pages for annotations.*

13. wet side: the rain gauge that is more full on the right should be circled; on the dry side: the rain gauge that is less full on the left should be circled

14. at 3048 m: the thermometer showing the lower temperature should be circled; at 0 m: the thermometer showing the higher temperature should be circled

15. Above a certain elevation on tall mountains, it is too cold for trees to grow.

Learning Alert ⚡ MISCONCEPTION ⚡

Freezing at the Equator? Students probably think that all places on the equator are hot. This is true for many locations on the equator. However, elevation has a tremendous impact on temperature. Ask students whether they believe that locations around the equator are all hot. If they answer yes, remind them that elevation has a big impact on temperature and that there are some places on the equator that regularly experience freezing temperatures. Mount Cayambe, which is located on the equator in Ecuador, is 5,790 m (19,000 ft) tall and has an average daytime temperature of 2 °C (36 °F) and an average nighttime temperature of −10 °C (14 °F).

Building Reading Skills

Text Structure: Sequence Have students use clue words such as *first, next, then,* and *finally* to describe the sequence involved in a rain-shadow effect. Sample answer: First, moisture rises from oceans into air; then, winds move the moisture toward land and it moves up the sides of mountains; next, as the air cools, the moisture is released from the clouds as precipitation; finally, the air moves over the mountains, but because the air is warm and descending, any remaining moisture is not released, so the other side of the mountain receives no rain.

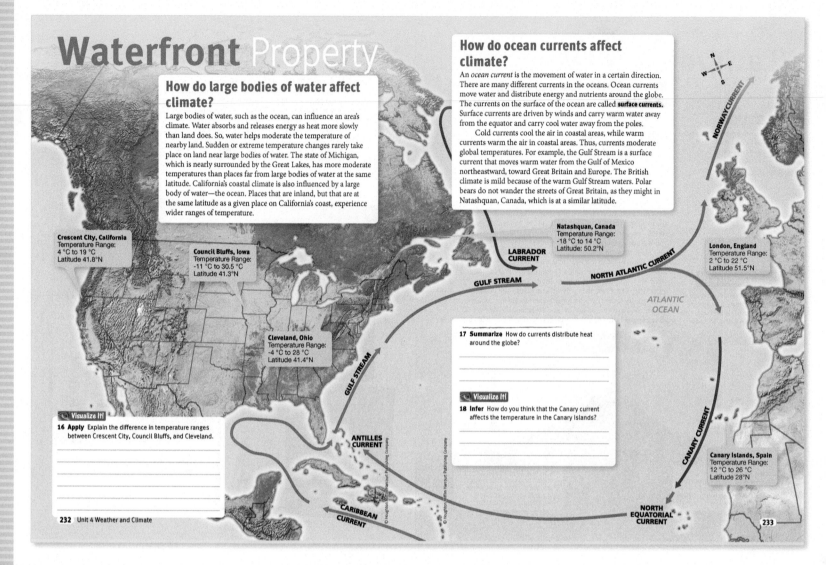

Waterfront Property

How do large bodies of water affect climate?

Large bodies of water, such as the ocean, can influence an area's climate. Water absorbs and releases energy as heat more slowly than land does. So, water helps moderate the temperature of nearby land. Sudden or extreme temperature changes rarely take place on land near large bodies of water. The state of Michigan, which is nearly surrounded by the Great Lakes, has more moderate temperatures than places far from large bodies of water at the same latitude. California's coastal climate is also influenced by a large body of water—the ocean. Places that are inland, but that are at the same latitude as a given place on California's coast, experience wider ranges of temperature.

How do ocean currents affect climate?

An *ocean current* is the movement of water in a certain direction. There are many different currents in the oceans. Ocean currents move water and distribute energy and nutrients around the globe. The currents on the surface of the ocean are called **surface currents.** Surface currents are driven by winds and carry warm water away from the equator and carry cool water away from the poles.

Cold currents cool the air in coastal areas, while warm currents warm the air in coastal areas. Thus, currents moderate global temperatures. For example, the Gulf Stream is a surface current that moves warm water from the Gulf of Mexico northeastward, toward Great Britain and Europe. The British climate is mild because of the warm Gulf Stream waters. Polar bears do not wander the streets of Great Britain, as they might in Natashquan, Canada, which is at a similar latitude.

Crescent City, California
Temperature Range:
4 °C to 19 °C
Latitude 41.8°N

Council Bluffs, Iowa
Temperature Range:
-11 °C to 30.5 °C
Latitude 41.3°N

Cleveland, Ohio
Temperature Range:
-4 °C to 28 °C
Latitude 41.4°N

Natashquan, Canada
Temperature Range:
-18 °C to 14 °C
Latitude: 50.2°N

London, England
Temperature Range:
2 °C to 22 °C
Latitude 51.5°N

Canary Islands, Spain
Temperature Range:
12 °C to 26 °C
Latitude 28°N

LABRADOR CURRENT
GULF STREAM
NORTH ATLANTIC CURRENT
NORWAY CURRENT
CANARY CURRENT
ANTILLES CURRENT
CARIBBEAN CURRENT
NORTH EQUATORIAL CURRENT
ATLANTIC OCEAN

16 Apply Explain the difference in temperature ranges between Crescent City, Council Bluffs, and Cleveland.

17 Summarize How do currents distribute heat around the globe?

18 Infer How do you think that the Canary current affects the temperature in the Canary Islands?

© Houghton Mifflin Harcourt Publishing Company

232 Unit 4 Weather and Climate

233

Answers

16. Sample answer: Council Bluffs has the largest temperature range because it is not near water. Crescent City has the smaller temperature range than Cleveland because Crescent City is on the Pacific, which is a larger body of water than Lake Erie.

17. Ocean currents move warm water away from the equator and cold water away from the poles.

18. The colder Canary current would cool down the temperature in the Canary Islands.

Interpreting Visuals

Have students study the map. **Ask:** What does the map showing ocean currents help you better understand? Sample answer: The map helps me better understand how water travels from one place to another; it helps me understand how ocean currents can affect a region's temperature.

Formative Assessment

Vancouver, British Columbia, has a relatively mild climate despite being at the same latitude as many Canadian cities that experience frigid weather. Vancouver is located near the Pacific Ocean on the west coast of North America. **Ask:** What factors might account for Vancouver's mild climate? Sample answer: Vancouver is at a low elevation; Vancouver is near a large body of water.

Building Reading Skills

Context Clues: Contrast Point out the sentence with the word *inland* near the bottom of the paragraph on large bodies of water. Have students read that sentence and the previous sentence. Ask students to use context clues to figure out what *inland* means. *Inland* means "away from the ocean."

Zoning Out

What are the three major climate zones?

Earth has three major types of climate zones: tropical, temperate, and polar. These zones are shown below. Each zone has a distinct temperature range that relates to its latitude. Each of these zones has several types of climates. These different climates result from differences in topography, winds, ocean currents, and geography.

 Active Reading

19 Identify Underline the factor that determines the temperature ranges in each zone.

21 Summarize Fill in the table for either the factor that affects climate or the effect on climate the given factor has.

Factor	Effect on climate
Latitude	*warmer @ equator - colder @ poles b/c sunlight most concentrated @ equator + dispersed @ poles*
elevation	Cooler temperatures as you travel up a tall mountain
Winds	*redistributes energy as heat + moisture*
proximity to H₂O	Moderates weather so that highs and lows are less extreme
Surface ocean currents	*moderates coastal temp.*
Topography	Impacts wind patterns and the transfer of energy in an area

Temperate

Temperate climates have an average temperature below 18 °C (64 °F) in the coldest month and an average temperature above 10 °C (50 °F) in the warmest month. There are five temperate zone subclimates: marine west coast climates, steppe climates, humid continental climate, humid subtropical climate, and Mediterranean climate. The temperate zone is characterized by lower temperatures than the tropical zone. It is located between the tropical zone and the polar zone.

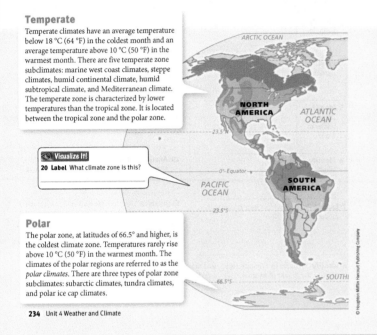

Visualize It!

20 Label What climate zone is this?

Polar

The polar zone, at latitudes of 66.5° and higher, is the coldest climate zone. Temperatures rarely rise above 10 °C (50 °F) in the warmest month. The climates of the polar regions are referred to as the *polar climates.* There are three types of polar zone subclimates: subarctic climates, tundra climates, and polar ice cap climates.

234 Unit 4 Weather and Climate

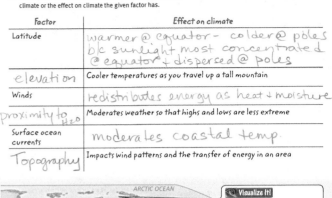

Visualize It!

22 Label What climate zone is this?

Tropical

Climates that are characterized by high temperatures and are located in the equatorial region are referred to as *tropical climates.* These climates have an average monthly temperature of at least 18 °C (64 °F), even during the coldest month of the year. Within the tropical zone, there are three subclimates: rain forest climates, desert climates, and savanna climates.

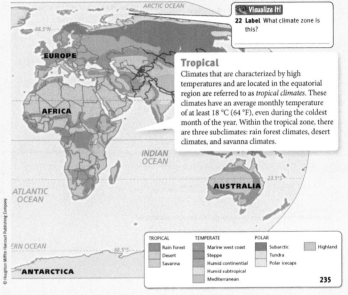

TROPICAL	TEMPERATE	POLAR	
Rain forest	Marine west coast	Subarctic	Highland
Desert	Steppe	Tundra	
Savanna	Humid continental	Polar icecaps	
	Humid subtropical		
	Mediterranean		

235

Answers

19. *See students' pages for annotations.*

20. tropical

21. Students should fill in the table as follows: It's warmer at the equator and colder at the poles because sunlight is most concentrated at the equator and most dispersed at the poles. (first row, right); elevation (second row, left); redistributes energy as heat and moisture around Earth (third row, right); proximity to large bodies of water (fourth row, left); moderates coastal temperatures (fifth row, right); topography (sixth row, left).

22. polar

Interpreting Visuals

Have students list some places on the map that fall into each of the three climate zones. Sample answers: polar: Alaska, Greenland, Antarctica; temperate: United States, Australia, China; tropical: Colombia, Costa Rica, Ethiopia

Building Reading Skills

Main Idea and Details What is the main idea of this section? Sample answer: Earth is divided into three major climate zones. Which details support the main idea? Sample answers: The three zones are polar, temperate, and tropical; the zones are divided along lines of latitude; the coldest zone is polar; the warmest is tropical; and the climate of the temperate zone is located between the polar zone and the tropical zone.

Probing Questions GUIDED (Inquiry)

Synthesizing Not all places within a climate zone experience the same climate. What factors account for these variations? The climate zones are based on lines of latitude only. However, many other factors affect climate, including topography, elevation, proximity to large bodies of water, and surface currents.

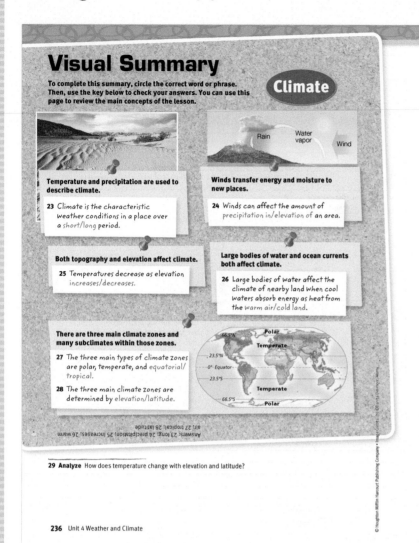

Visual Summary

To complete this summary, circle the correct word or phrase. Then, use the key below to check your answers. You can use this page to review the main concepts of the lesson.

Climate

Temperature and precipitation are used to describe climate.

23 Climate is the characteristic weather conditions in a place over a short/long period.

Winds transfer energy and moisture to new places.

24 Winds can affect the amount of precipitation in/elevation of an area.

Both topography and elevation affect climate.

25 Temperatures decrease as elevation increases/decreases.

Large bodies of water and ocean currents both affect climate.

26 Large bodies of water affect the climate of nearby land when cool waters absorb energy as heat from the warm air/cold land.

There are three main climate zones and many subclimates within those zones.

27 The three main types of climate zones are polar, temperate, and equatorial/tropical.

28 The three main climate zones are determined by elevation/latitude.

Answers: 23 long; 24 precipitation; 25 increases; 26 warm air; 27 tropical; 28 latitude

29 **Analyze** How does temperature change with elevation and latitude?

236 Unit 4 Weather and Climate

Lesson Review

Vocabulary

In your own words, define the following terms.

1 topography

2 climate

Key Concepts

Fill in the table below.

Factor	Effect on Climate
3 **Identify** Latitude	
4 **Identify** Elevation	
5 **Identify** Large bodies of water	
6 **Identify** Wind	

7 **Explain** What provides Great Britain with a moderate climate? How?

8 **Identify** What are two characteristics used to describe the climate of an area?

Critical Thinking

Use the image below to answer the following question.

9 **Explain** Location A receives nearly 200 cm of rain each year, while Location B receives only 30 cm. Explain why Location A gets so much more rain. Use the words *rain shadow* and *precipitation* in your answer.

10 **Analyze** What climate zone are you in if the temperatures are always very warm? Where is this zone located on Earth?

11 **Analyze** How does the sun's energy affect the climate of an area?

Lesson 6 Climate 237

Visual Summary Answers

23. long
24. precipitation
25. increases
26. warm air
27. tropical
28. latitude
29. The temperature decreases with increasing elevation or latitude.

Lesson Review Answers

1. *Topography* is the combination of the surface features of a region.

2. *Climate* describes the long-term weather conditions for an area.

3. It affects how the sun's energy is dispersed over an area, due to the curve of Earth's surface, thus affecting the temperature of the area.

4. Temperature decreases as elevation increases.

5. Can warm up and cool down the air above nearby land, creating a more moderate climate for that area

6. Transfers energy around Earth's surface and also affects levels of precipitation in an area

7. The Gulf Stream is a warm surface current that warms up the air near Great Britain as it flows by.

8. Temperature and precipitation

9. Location A gets more rain because the rising moist air releases precipitation in the form of rain as it cools. The remaining dry air moves over the mountain and warms as it sinks toward location B, which is in the rain shadow.

10. Tropical, near the equator

11. The sun's energy powers the water cycle and the wind, so it can affect the temperatures and the levels of precipitation in an area, thus affecting the local climate.

Climate Change

Essential Question What are the causes and effects of climate change?

 Professional Development

For more detailed information about the topics in this lesson, refer to the Content Refresher in the Unit Opener pages.

Opening Your Lesson

Begin the lesson by assessing students' prerequisite and prior knowledge.

Prerequisite Knowledge

- A general understanding of climate
- A general understanding of seasonal weather patterns
- A general understanding of the greenhouse effect and the negative impact of human activity on the atmosphere

Accessing Prior Knowledge

Have students develop an Anticipation Guide to preview the content of the lesson and to assess their prior knowledge about climate change.

Customize Your Opening

- ☐ **Accessing Prior Knowledge,** above
- ☐ **Print Path** Engage Your Brain, SE p. 239
- ☐ **Print Path** Active Reading, SE p. 239
- ☐ **Digital Path** Lesson Opener

Key Topics/Learning Goals

Natural Climate Change

1. Explain that Earth's climate has naturally varied throughout geologic history.
2. Identify examples of natural events that cause changes in Earth's climate.

Climate Change and Human Activity

1. Explain that human activities increase levels of greenhouse gases in the atmosphere and contribute to global warming.
2. Identify some predicted effects of climate change linked to global warming.

Reducing Climate Change

1. Identify ways that humans can reduce the rate of global warming.
2. Recognize that global warming is a global issue and involves economic, political, and scientific factors.

Supporting Concepts

- Geologic evidence shows that Earth's climate has changed over time, and many ice ages have occurred. Natural climate changes occur both suddenly and gradually over time.
- Tectonic plate movements cause gradual climate changes as continents move.
- Sudden climate changes are caused by asteroid impacts, ocean temperature changes, and volcanic eruptions.

- Certain human activities, such as burning fossil fuels, increase greenhouse gases such as carbon dioxide, methane, and nitrous oxide. Land clearing reduces the number of plants, which eliminate CO_2 from the atmosphere through photosynthesis.
- Scientists use computer models to predict future changes in climate, including higher temperatures in most parts of the world, reduction in Arctic sea ice, shrinking glaciers, retreat of Greenland ice sheets, changes in rainfall patterns, rising sea levels, and more severe storms.

- Humans can slow the rate of global warming by reducing greenhouse gas emissions and removing greenhouse gases from the atmosphere.
- By conserving energy, increasing energy efficiency, and using alternative energy resources, we can reduce our dependence on fossil fuels. However, the cost of these new technologies presents a challenge to some countries.

Options for Instruction

Two parallel paths provide coverage of the Essential Questions, with a strong **Inquiry** strand woven into each.
Follow the **Print Path,** the **Digital Path,** or your customized combination of print, digital, and inquiry.

 Print Path
Teaching support for the Print Path appears with the Student Pages.

 Inquiry Labs and Activities

Digital Path
Digital Path shortcut TG661645

The Temps are a–Changin',
SE pp. 240–243
What are some natural causes of climate change?
What are some causes of repeating patterns of climate change?

Activity
Volcanic Eruption News Brief

Quick Lab
Graphing Sunspots

Natural Climate Variations
Interactive Graphics

Natural Causes of Climate Change
Slideshow

Is It Getting HOTTER?,
SE pp. 244–248
How do humans affect climate?
• By Burning Fossil Fuels
• By Deforestation
What are some predicted effects of climate change?
• Effects on the Atmosphere
• Effects on the Hydrosphere and Cryosphere
• Effects on the Biosphere
How are climate predictions made?

Daily Demo
Icecaps Melting

Quick Lab
Greenhouse Effect

Activity
The Global Warming Debate

Deforestation and Climate Change
Video

Global Temperatures
Graphic Sequence

Effects of Global Climate Change
Interactive Images

Think Clean and Green,
SE pp. 249–251
How can people reduce their impact on climate change?
What are some economic and political issues related to climate change?

Activity
Book It!

We Can Slow Climate Change
Interactive Graphics

Humans Affecting Climate Change
Interactive Images

Options for Assessment

See the Evaluate page for options, including Formative Assessment, Summative Assessment, and Unit Review.

Engage and Explore

Activities and Discussion

Activity *Volcanic Eruption News Brief*

Engage

Natural Climate Change

 small groups
 varies
 GUIDED inquiry

In June 1991, Mount Pinatubo erupted, spewing millions of tons of soot and ash and huge amounts of sulfur dioxide into the atmosphere. Within a year, average global temperatures dropped about 0.5 °C, and many regions experienced a harsher winter and cooler summer. Other eruptions have had similar effects. Perhaps the most notable is the "year without a summer" that followed the 1815 eruption of Mount Tambora in Indonesia. Have students form groups to investigate major volcanic eruptions throughout history and prepare a timeline documenting the effects on climate. Then have each group write and produce a radio broadcast, news brief, or webcast about the effects of volcanic eruptions on climate change.

Activity *The Global Warming Debate*

Climate Change and Human Activity

 small groups
varies
GUIDED inquiry

While many climatologists think that human activities are inducing global warming, some remain skeptical. Given the variety of other factors known to influence climate and the evidence that climates have changed in the past without human influence, these scientists do not think that increasing greenhouse gases are solely responsible for the temperature increases during the last century. Ask students to research different sides of this issue. Then, have groups choose a position on the issue. Conduct a debate between groups that hold opposing positions for the rest of the class.

Discussion *Natural vs. Human Causes*

Synthesizing Key Topics

 whole class
 20 min
 GUIDED inquiry

Lead a class discussion focusing on the differences between natural and human causes of climate change.

Activity *Book It!*

Engage

Reducing Climate Change

 individuals
 varied
 INDEPENDENT inquiry

Ask students to make a FoldNote Booklet about how humans are making efforts to reduce their effect on the planet, particularly in the area of climate change. They can begin compiling information for their booklets by reviewing the lesson, but should be encouraged to find out more information from other reliable sources. They can include text and illustrations in their booklets.

Customize Your Labs

🔷 *See the Lab Manual for lab datasheets.*

🔵 *Go Online for editable lab datasheets.*

 Levels of **Inquiry**

DIRECTED inquiry	GUIDED inquiry	INDEPENDENT inquiry
introduces inquiry skills within a structured framework.	develops inquiry skills within a supportive environment.	deepens inquiry skills with student-driven questions or procedures.

Labs and Demos

Daily Demo *Icecaps Melting*

 Engage

Synthesizing Key Topics

 whole class
 10 min
DIRECTED inquiry

PURPOSE **To model the effects of global warming on the polar icecaps**

MATERIALS

- bowl of water
- modeling clay
- ice cubes

Sea levels may rise if icecaps melt, but only if those icecaps cover land, as the Antarctic ice sheet does. Fill a bowl with water, and add a few ice cubes to simulate floating icecaps. Mark the water level. Ask students to predict what will happen when the ice melts. Then let the ice melt, observing any changes as the ice melts. (The water level should stay the same.) Repeat with the same level of water, but with an island made of clay in the bowl. Place the ice cubes on the clay, and mark the water level; ask for predictions again. Let the ice melt, and observe how the water level rises.

Quick Lab *Greenhouse Effect*

Climate Change and Human Activity

 pairs
30 min
GUIDED inquiry

PURPOSE **To describe how sunlight affects air temperature; to model the greenhouse effect**

MATERIALS

- 2 clear plastic jars
- clear plastic wrap
- 2 rubber bands
- 4 thermometers
- white tissue paper
- transparent tape

Students wrap a jar in plastic wrap. They measure and record the temperature of the air around the jar at the beginning of the experiment and 15 minutes later. Then they measure and record the temperature inside the jar. Direct them to repeat the measurement every three minutes.

Quick Lab *Graphing Sunspots*

Natural Climate Change

 individuals
30 min
GUIDED inquiry

PURPOSE **To make connections between sunspot data and climate change; to analyze and graph data**

See the Lab Manual or go Online for planning information.

Activities and Discussion

☐ **Activity** Volcanic Eruption News Brief
☐ **Activity** The Global Warming Debate
☐ **Activity** Book It!
☐ **Discussion** Natural vs. Human Causes

Labs and Demos

☐ **Daily Demo** Icecaps Melting
☐ **Quick Lab** Greenhouse Effect
☐ **Quick Lab** Graphing Sunspots

Your Resources

Explain Science Concepts

Key Topics	Print Path	Digital Path
Natural Climate Change	☐ **The Temps are a–Changin',** SE pp. 240–243 • Visualize It!, #5 • Visualize It!, #6 • Active Reading, #7 • Do the Math, #8 • Visualize It!, #9 • Active Reading, #10 	☐ **Natural Climate Variations** Learn about natural climate variations. ☐ **Natural Causes of Climate Change** Explore the natural causes of climate change. 
Climate Change and Human Activity	☐ **Is It Getting HOTTER?,** SE pp. 244–248 • Active Reading, #11 • Active Reading, #12 • Visualize It!, #13 • Visualize It!, #14 • Infer, #15 • Infer, #16 • Active Reading (Annotation strategy), #17 • Visualize It!, #18 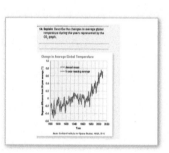	☐ **Deforestation and Climate Change** Find out how deforestation contributes to global warming. ☐ **Global Temperatures** See how the amount of carbon dioxide in the atmosphere has changed over the years. 
Reducing Climate Change	☐ **Think Clean and Green,** SE pp. 249–251 • Do the Math, #19 • Do the Math, #20 • Summarize, #21 • Active Reading (Annotation strategy), #22 • Think Outside the Book, #23 • Predict, #24 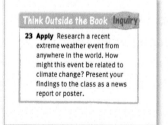	☐ **We Can Slow Climate Change** Find out how climate change might be slowed. ☐ **Humans Affecting Climate Change** Learn about how global warming is a worldwide issue involving economic, social, political, and scientific factors.

Basic *Write it Out*

Synthesizing Key Topics

 individuals

🕐 35 min

Ask students to synthesize their understanding of the causes of climate change by writing a paragraph explaining how the climate can change because of natural and human activity and how we can work to stop or reverse the change related to human activity.

Basic *Jigsaw*

Synthesizing Key Topics

 small groups

🕐 40 min

Form small groups of four students each. Assign each student a section in this lesson to become an expert about. Have them study the section and additional resources available in the classroom, and teach the rest of their group about their section. Encourage group members to take notes and ask questions to make sure they know all there is to know about each section by the end of the lesson. Students can serve as section experts throughout the lesson, and other students can seek out these experts when they need additional information about a section.

Advanced *Test Questions*

Synthesizing Key Topics

 individuals

🕐 varied

To help students stay involved with the text, ask them to think of and write possible test questions while they are reading the text. Then have students review by asking other students their questions. After the question-and-answer session, collect all of the questions. Tell students you are going to use some of their questions for a test or quiz—and do so.

ELL *Note-Taking*

Synthesizing Key Topics

 pairs

🕐 40 min

Have students work in pairs to go back through the lesson content and take notes. Have them write down the titles of each section, the question heads, and any other subheads. Then have them jot down important features from each of these subsections.

ice age   greenhouse effect   global warming

Previewing Vocabulary

 whole class

🕐 10 min

Adjective Forms Point out that each of the vocabulary terms contains an adjective, or a word that is used to modify or tell more about the noun that follows it. On the board, underline *ice* in *ice age*, *greenhouse* in *greenhouse effect*, and *global* in *global warming*. Point out that *ice* and *greenhouse* are nouns that are acting as adjectives, but the word *globe* has been changed into an adjective form (*global*) with the addition of the suffix *-al*.

Reinforcing Vocabulary

 individuals

🕐 30 min

Word Triangles To help students remember the vocabulary terms introduced in this lesson, have them complete a Word Triangle graphic organizer for each. In the bottom, they should write the definition of the term; in the center, they should write a sentence using the term; in the top, they should draw a picture illustrating the term.

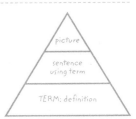

Customize Your Core Lesson

Core Instruction

- [ ] **Print Path** choices
- [ ] **Digital Path** choices

Vocabulary

- [ ] **Previewing Vocabulary** Adjective Forms
- [ ] **Reinforcing Vocabulary** Word Triangle

Your Resources

Differentiated Instruction

- [ ] **Basic** Write It Out
- [ ] **Basic** Jigsaw
- [ ] **Advanced** Test Questions
- [ ] **ELL** Note-Taking

_____

_____

Extend Science Concepts

Reinforce and Review

Activity *Climate Change Review*

Synthesizing Key Topics
  small groups
🕐 20 min

Carousel Review Set up chart paper in four corners of the room. Write one of the following questions on each piece of paper.

1 Name several natural causes of climate change. Volcanic eruptions; meteor or asteroid strikes; tectonic plate motion

2 Name several human causes of climate change. Greenhouse gas emissions; deforestation

3 Name a greenhouse gas. Methane, carbon dioxide, nitrous oxide, water vapor

4 How can humans reduce climate change? Recycling; reducing greenhouse gas emissions

Split the class into small groups, and provide each group with a different color marker. Assign each group to a corner and a question. Give each group five minutes to answer their question. When the time is up (or if everyone has finished), have them rotate to the next question. All groups should answer all four questions. Finally, take some time to check each group's answer by reviewing the material as a class.

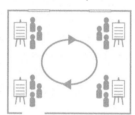

Graphic Organizer

Synthesizing Key Topics
  individuals
🕐 35 min

Mind Map After students have studied the lesson, ask them to create a mind map for the following terms: *ice age, greenhouse effect, global warming.*

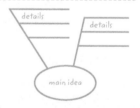

Going Further

Earth Science Connection

Natural Climate Change
 individuals or pairs
🕐 varies

The sun is a variable star; its energy output varies over time. During the last 200 to 300 years, the sun's brightness has increased about 0.4 percent. According to studies, this increase is too weak to explain global warming. However, changes in the number and duration of sunspots—the dark, cooler regions on the surface of the sun—also correlate with changes in Earth's temperature. Have students research the topic of the sun's brightness and prepare a short report or project describing its effects on global temperatures.

◎ *Optional Online rubric: Written Pieces*

Language Arts Connection

Synthesizing Key Topics
 individuals
🕐 15 min

Key Word Scan Test students' ability to find definitions of key terms by playing this game. Tell students that they will have to come up with a question based on a definition you give. For example, if you say, "an increase in the average temperature of Earth's atmosphere," students would ask, "What is global warming?"

Customize Your Closing

📷 *See the Assessment Guide for quizzes and tests.*

◎ *Go Online to edit and create quizzes and tests.*

Reinforce and Review

☐ **Activity** Climate Change Review

☐ **Graphic Organizer**

☐ **Print Path** Visual Summary, SE p. 252

☐ **Digital Path** Lesson Closer

Evaluate Student Mastery

Formative Assessment

See the teacher support below the Student Pages for additional Formative Assessment questions.

Describe or have students review human causes of climate change and what we can do to reduce the rate of global warming. **Ask:** How do human actions impact changes in Earth's climate? Describe some of the things that we can do to reduce the rate and effects of global warming. Sample answer: Human activity, such as burning fossil fuels and increasing the emissions of greenhouse gases into the atmosphere, can speed up the effects of global warming. Humans can reduce and slow these effects by recycling, walking instead of driving, and finding cleaner energy sources.

Reteach

Formative assessment may show that students need reinforcement for certain topics. The resources below are recommended for reteaching. If students were introduced to a topic through the Print Path, you can also use the Digital Path to reteach, and vice versa.
🎧 *Can be assigned to individual students*

Natural Climate Change
Quick Lab Graphing Sunspots 🎧

Climate Change and Human Activity
Quick Lab Greenhouse Effect 🎧

Reducing Climate Change
Advanced Test Questions

Activity Book It! 🎧

Summative Assessment

Alternative Assessment
Causes of Climate Change

🎧 *Online resources: student worksheet, optional rubrics*

Climate Change

Points of View: *Causes of Climate Change*
Complete the activity to show what you've learned about climate change.

1. Work in groups as assigned by your teacher. Each group will be assigned to one or two viewpoints.

2. Complete your assignment, and present your perspective to the class.

 Terms The terms *global warming, greenhouse gas, emissions, eruptions,* and *atmosphere* all relate to climate change. Write a short story that explains how clearing a forest in order to build a skyscraper contributes to global warming.

 Examples List examples of three ways that natural events can affect global temperatures.

 Illustrations Draw an illustration to show the potential effects of climate change on the hydrosphere, cryosphere, or biosphere.

 Analysis Both human activity and natural events can cause changes in the global climate. Why is it important to lessen human impact on the environment if natural changes will take place anyway?

 Details What are some specific things young people can do to reduce the speed of global warming and other changes to global climate?

 Models Describe an action that young people can take to reduce climate change, then outline how this action might be implemented at your school.

Going Further
☐ Earth Science Connection
☐ Language Arts Connection

Formative Assessment
☐ Strategies Throughout TE
☐ Lesson Review SE

Summative Assessment
☐ Alternative Assessment Causes of Climate Change
☐ Lesson Quiz
☐ Unit Tests A and B
☐ Unit Review SE End-of-Unit

Your Resources

Lesson **7**

Climate Change

ESSENTIAL QUESTION

What are the causes and effects of climate change?

By the end of this lesson, you should be able to describe climate change and the causes and effects of climate change.

Temperatures are rising in the Arctic. Warmer temperatures cause the ice sheets to freeze later and melt sooner. With less time on the ice to hunt for seals, polar bears are struggling to survive.

238 Unit 4 Weather and Climate

Lesson Labs

Quick Labs
• Greenhouse Effect
• Graphing Sunspots

Engage Your Brain

1 Predict Check T or F to show whether you think each statement is true or false.

T	F	
☐	☐	There have been periods on Earth when the climate was colder than the climate is today.
☐	☐	The ocean does not play a role in climate.
☐	☐	Earth's climate is currently warming.
☐	☐	Humans are contributing to changes in climate.

2 Describe Write your own caption relating this photo to climate change.

_____

_____

Active Reading

3 Apply Many scientific terms, such as *greenhouse effect*, also have everyday meanings. Use context clues to write your own definition for the words *greenhouse* and *effect*.

Example sentence
The greenhouse is filled with tropical plants that are found in Central America.

greenhouse:

_____

_____

Example sentence
What are some of the effects of staying up too late?

effect:

_____

_____

Vocabulary Terms
• ice age
• greenhouse effect
• global warming

4 Identify As you read, create a reference card for each vocabulary term. On one side of the card, write the term and its meaning. On the other side, draw an image that illustrates or makes a connection to the term. These cards can be used as bookmarks in the text so that you can refer to them while studying.

Lesson 7 Climate Change **239**

Answers

Answers for 1–3 should represent students' current thoughts, even if incorrect.

1. true; false; true; true

2. Student answers will vary. Sample answer: If Earth's climate grows warmer, there will be more icebergs as the ice sheets break up.

3. Sample answer: A greenhouse is a building in which plants are kept warm. An effect is the result of an action.

4. Students should define or sketch each vocabulary term in the lesson.

Opening Your Lesson

Discuss student answers to item 1 to assess students' prerequisite knowledge and to estimate what they already know about key topics.

Preconceptions Climate change is driven by both natural and human activities. Humans can take action to reduce the rate of climate change and its effects.

Prerequisites Students should already understand climate and seasonal weather patterns, as well as the benefits of the greenhouse effect and the ozone layer.

Accessing Prior Knowledge

SQ3R The SQ3R (online toolkit) strategy asks students to think about what they are about to read by **S**urveying the material, **Q**uestioning it, **R**eading it, **R**eciting it, and then **R**eviewing it. Introduce the strategy by explaining what each letter stands for, and then use the transparency to demonstrate the strategy for students. Allow them to work with a partner as they employ the SQ3R strategy in previewing this lesson.

You may prefer to use an Anticipation Guide to determine what students already know about climate change.

🌐 *Optional online resource: SQ3R, Anticipation Guide*

The Temps are a–Changin'

What are some natural causes of climate change?

The weather conditions in an area over a long period of time are called *climate*. Natural factors have changed Earth's climate many times during our planet's history. Natural changes in climate can be long-term or short-term.

Movement of Tectonic Plates

Tectonic plate motion has contributed to long-term climate change over billions of years. And Earth's plates are still moving!

The present continents once fit together as a single landmass called *Pangaea* (pan•JEE•uh). Pangaea began to break up about 200 million years ago. By 20 million years ago, the continents had moved close to their current positions. Some continents grew warmer as they moved closer to the equator. Other continents, such as Antarctica, moved to colder, higher latitudes.

The eruption of Mt. Pinatubo sent ash and gases as high as 34 km into the atmosphere.

Climate Change After Mt. Pinatubo Eruption

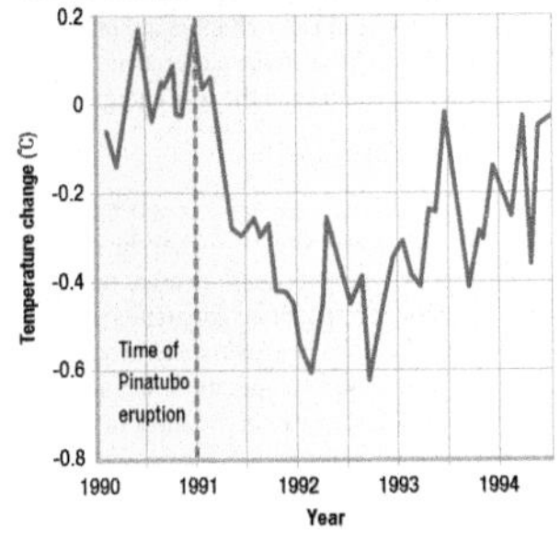

This graph shows the *change* in average global temperature, not the actual temperature.

Source: Goddard Institute for Space Studies, NASA, 1997

Visualize It!

5 Infer Today, Antarctica is the coldest desert on Earth. But fossils of trees and dinosaurs have been found on this harsh continent. Explain how life could thrive on ancient Antarctica.

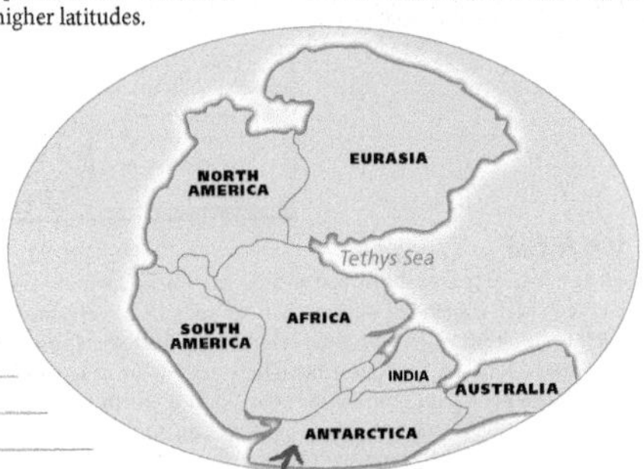

_____

_____

_____

_____

Tethys Sea

Antarctica was part of the supercontinent Pangaea about 250 million years ago. Antarctica is located at the South Pole today.

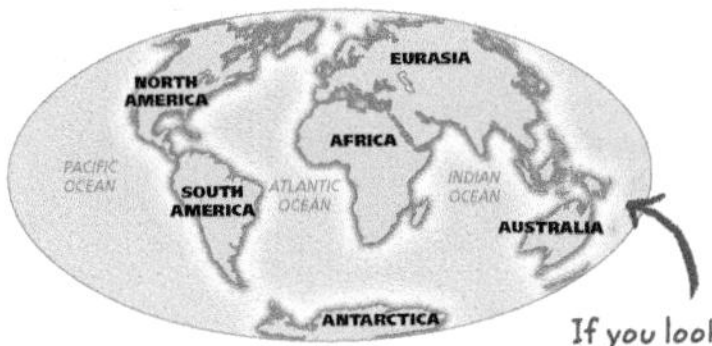

If you look closely at the current shapes of the continents, you can see how they once fit together to form Pangaea.

Particles in the Atmosphere

Short-term changes in climate can be due to natural events that send *particulates* into the atmosphere. Particulates are tiny, solid particles that are suspended in air or water. They absorb some of the sun's energy and reflect some of the sun's energy back into space. This process temporarily lowers temperatures on Earth.

Where do particulates come from? Asteroid impacts throw large amounts of dust into the atmosphere. Dust from the asteroid that struck near Mexico around 65 million years ago would have blocked the sun's rays. This reduction in sunlight may have limited photosynthesis in plants. The loss of plant life may have caused the food chain to collapse and led to dinosaur extinction.

Volcanic eruptions also release enormous clouds of ash and gases into the atmosphere. Particulates from large eruptions can circle Earth. The average global surface temperature fell by about 0.5 °C for several years after the 1991 eruption of Mt. Pinatubo in the Philippines. Twenty million tons of sulfur dioxide and 5 m³ of ash were blasted into the atmosphere. The sulfur-rich gases combined with water to form an Earth-cooling haze.

Active Reading **7 Describe** Give one example of a long-term and one example of a short-term change in climate caused by natural factors.

_____

_____

Visualize It!

6 Analyze What happened to global temperatures after the eruption of Mt. Pinatubo? How long did this effect last?

_____

_____

_____

240 Unit 4 Weather and Climate

Lesson 7 Climate Change 241

Answers

5. Antarctica once had a warmer climate because it was closer to the equator.

6. Average global temperatures decreased for several years.

7. An example of long-term climate change is tectonic plate motion, which changes the climate of continents. An example of a short-term change is a volcanic eruption that releases particulates into the atmosphere.

Probing Questions GUIDED Inquiry

Evaluating Understanding Earth's systems can help scientists understand natural causes of climate change. How do you think knowledge of Earth's systems gives us insight into how and why these changes occur? Explain your thoughts.

Building Reading Skills

Concept Map Students can use a concept map to organize the information they are learning as they read. Ask them to draw and complete a concept map about climate change as they read through this chapter.

Learning Alert 🚧 MISCONCEPTION 🚧

Causes of Natural Climate Change Students may think that climate change can only occur as a result of human activities. Yet human activity is only one cause of climate change. Explain that there are natural causes, and highlight examples cited in the text, such as volcanic eruptions.

During El Niño years, heavy rains fall in the usually dry southwestern United States. This rain can cause floods that wash out roads.

What are some causes of repeating patterns of climate change?

From day to day, or even year to year, the weather can change quite a lot. Some of these changes are relatively unpredictable, but others are due to predictable patterns or cycles. These patterns are the result of changes in the way energy is distributed around Earth.

Sun Cycles

Most of Earth's energy comes from the sun. And the output from the sun is very slightly higher during times of higher sunspot activity. Sunspots are dark areas on the sun that appear and disappear. Sunspot activity tends to increase and decrease in a cycle that lasts approximately 11 years. The effect of this sunspot cycle on global temperatures is not dramatic. But studies show a possible link between the sunspot cycle and global rain patterns.

El Niño and La Niña

Changes in ocean temperature also affect climate. During El Niño years, ocean temperatures are higher than usual in the tropical Pacific Ocean. The warmer water causes changes in global weather patterns. Some areas are cooler and wetter than normal. Other areas are warmer and dryer than normal.

The opposite effect occurs during La Niña years. Ocean temperatures are cooler than normal in the equatorial eastern Pacific Ocean. El Niño and La Niña conditions usually alternate, and both can lead to conditions such as droughts and flooding.

📱 Do the Math

8 Calculate About what percentage of years are El Niño years, with warmer than average ocean temperatures? About what percentage are La Niña years? About what percentage are neither El Niño or La Niña years?

Cycles of El Niño and La Niña

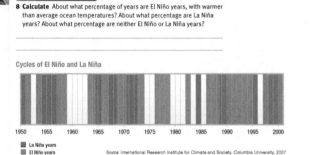

- ■ La Niña years
- ■ El Niño years

Source: International Research Institute for Climate and Society, Columbia University, 2007

242   Unit 4 Weather and Climate

🔍 Visualize It!

During the last 2 million years, continental ice sheets have expanded far beyond the polar regions. There have been multiple advances of ice sheets (glacial periods) and retreats of ice sheets (interglacial periods). The timeline shows recent glacial and interglacial periods.

Cycles of the Recent Ice Age

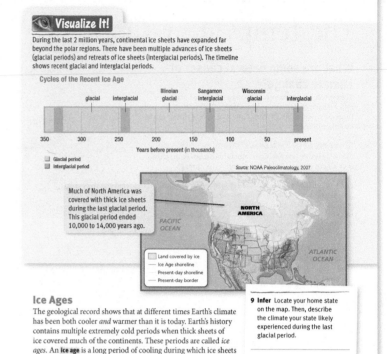

□ Glacial period
■ Interglacial period

Source: NOAA Paleoclimatology, 2007

Much of North America was covered with thick ice sheets during the last glacial period. This glacial period ended 10,000 to 14,000 years ago.

- ☐ Land covered by ice
- — Ice Age shoreline
- — Present-day shoreline
- — Present-day border

Ice Ages

The geological record shows that at different times Earth's climate has been both cooler *and* warmer than it is today. Earth's history contains multiple extremely cold periods when thick sheets of ice covered much of the continents. These periods are called *ice ages.* An **ice age** is a long period of cooling during which ice sheets spread beyond the polar regions. The exact cause of ice ages is not fully understood. Some hypotheses propose that ice ages include changes in Earth's orbit, shifts in the balance of incoming and outgoing solar radiation, and changes in heat exchange rates between the equator and the poles.

Geologic evidence indicates that ice ages occur over widely spaced intervals of time—approximately every 200 million years. Each ice age lasts for millions of years. The most recent ice age began about 2 million years ago, with its peak about 20,000 years ago. Large ice sheets still cover Greenland and Antarctica.

📖 Active Reading   10 List What are some possible causes of ice ages?

9 Infer Locate your home state on the map. Then, describe the climate your state likely experienced during the last glacial period.

Lesson 7 Climate Change   **243**

Answers

8. 24 of 51 years are El Niño years (47%); 14 of 51 years are La Niña years (27%); and 13 of 51 years are neither El Niño or La Niña years (25%)

9. Student answers will vary depending on where they live.

10. changes in Earth's orbit, shifts in the balance of incoming and outgoing solar radiation, changes in heat exchange rates between the equator and the poles

Interpreting Visuals

Have students look at the image of recent ice age cycles. Ask them to pay special attention to the cooling (glacial periods) and warming (interglacial periods) trends. Discuss whether they think another ice age will occur and, if they do, when.

Building Reading Skills

Idea Wheel Have students make an Idea Wheel graphic organizer about repeating patterns of climate change. In the smaller, central ring, have them write the main idea: *Repeating Patterns of Climate Change.* Ask students to label the sections with the different patterns: *movement of tectonic plates, particles in atmosphere, sun cycles, El Niño and La Niña,* and *ice ages.* In each section, have them then describe the pattern.

🌐 *Optional online resource: Idea Wheel graphic organizer*

Formative Assessment

Ask: How can natural events cause climate change? Give one example. Sample Answer: A volcanic eruption may release particulates into the atmosphere that block sunlight and keep it from reaching Earth.

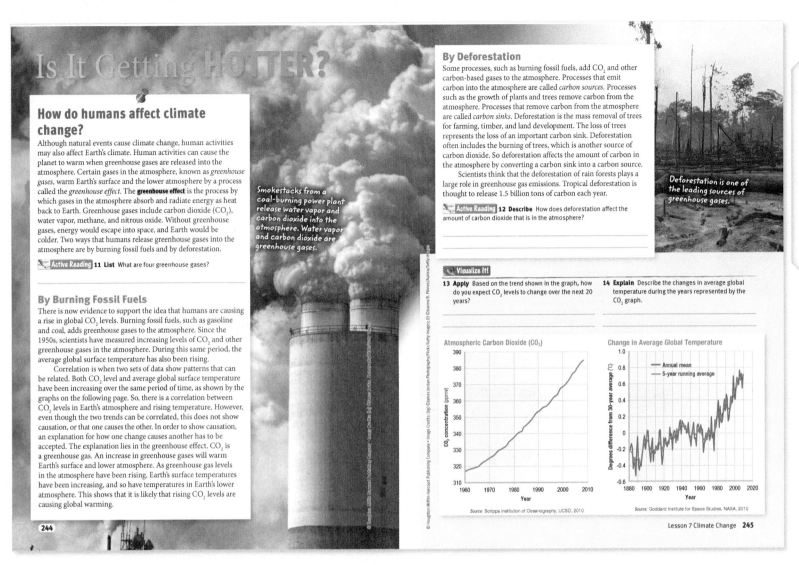

Is It Getting HOTTER?

How do humans affect climate change?

Although natural events cause climate change, human activities may also affect Earth's climate. Human activities can cause the planet to warm when greenhouse gases are released into the atmosphere. Certain gases in the atmosphere, known as *greenhouse gases*, warm Earth's surface and the lower atmosphere by a process called the *greenhouse effect*. The **greenhouse effect** is the process by which gases in the atmosphere absorb and radiate energy as heat back to Earth. Greenhouse gases include carbon dioxide (CO_2), water vapor, methane, and nitrous oxide. Without greenhouse gases, energy would escape into space, and Earth would be colder. Two ways that humans release greenhouse gases into the atmosphere are by burning fossil fuels and by deforestation.

Active Reading 11 List What are four greenhouse gases?

By Burning Fossil Fuels

There is now evidence to support the idea that humans are causing a rise in global CO_2 levels. Burning fossil fuels, such as gasoline and coal, adds greenhouse gases to the atmosphere. Since the 1950s, scientists have measured increasing levels of CO_2 and other greenhouse gases in the atmosphere. During this same period, the average global surface temperature has also been rising.

Correlation is when two sets of data show patterns that can be related. Both CO_2 level and average global surface temperature have been increasing over the same period of time, as shown by the graphs on the following page. So, there is a correlation between CO_2 levels in Earth's atmosphere and rising temperature. However, even though the two trends can be correlated, this does not show causation, or that one causes the other. In order to show causation, an explanation for how one change causes another has to be accepted. The explanation lies in the greenhouse effect. CO_2 is a greenhouse gas. An increase in greenhouse gases will warm Earth's surface and lower atmosphere. As greenhouse gas levels in the atmosphere have been rising, Earth's surface temperatures have been increasing, and so have temperatures in Earth's lower atmosphere. This shows that it is likely that rising CO_2 levels are causing global warming.

Smokestacks from a coal-burning power plant release water vapor and carbon dioxide into the atmosphere. Water vapor and carbon dioxide are greenhouse gases.

By Deforestation

Some processes, such as burning fossil fuels, add CO_2 and other carbon-based gases to the atmosphere. Processes that emit carbon into the atmosphere are called *carbon sources*. Processes such as the growth of plants and trees remove carbon from the atmosphere. Processes that remove carbon from the atmosphere are called *carbon sinks*. Deforestation is the mass removal of trees for farming, timber, and land development. The loss of trees represents the loss of an important carbon sink. Deforestation often includes the burning of trees, which is another source of carbon dioxide. So deforestation affects the amount of carbon in the atmosphere by converting a carbon sink into a carbon source.

Scientists think that the deforestation of rain forests plays a large role in greenhouse gas emissions. Tropical deforestation is thought to release 1.5 billion tons of carbon each year.

Active Reading 12 Describe How does deforestation affect the amount of carbon dioxide that is in the atmosphere?

Deforestation is one of the leading sources of greenhouse gases.

Visualize It!

13 Apply Based on the trend shown in the graph, how do you expect CO_2 levels to change over the next 20 years?

14 Explain Describe the changes in average global temperature during the years represented by the CO_2 graph.

Atmospheric Carbon Dioxide (CO_2)

Source: Scripps Institution of Oceanography, UCSD, 2010

Change in Average Global Temperature

— Annual mean
— 5-year running average

Source: Goddard Institute for Space Studies, NASA, 2010

244

Lesson 7 Climate Change 245

Answers

11. carbon dioxide; methane; nitrous oxide; water vapor

12. Deforestation destroys plants and trees that remove CO_2 from the atmosphere. Burning trees increases the amount of CO_2 that is released into the atmosphere.

13. Carbon dioxide levels will likely continue to increase over the next 20 years.

14. Temperatures appear to increase sharply from 1960 to present. Temperatures are now about 0.8 degree warmer than in 1960.

Building Reading Skills

Concept Map Using the concept map strategy in the online toolkit, have students explain the term *deforestation*. Give them time to share their maps with the class or small groups.

Probing Questions DIRECTED *Inquiry*

Application What is the greenhouse effect? How is it positive? How is it negative? The greenhouse effect is the warming of Earth's surface and lower atmosphere. It occurs because greenhouse gases absorb and reradiate energy from Earth's surface. Without the greenhouse effect, Earth would be much colder. The release of large amounts of greenhouse gases into the atmosphere can raise the average global surface temperature.

Using Annotations

Text Structure: Main Idea/Details As students complete the graphic organizer in this section, have them find specific examples of sources for each of the greenhouse gases. Ask them to include their examples with their tables as a visual reminder of each gas.

What are some predicted effects of climate change?

Data show that the world's climate has been warming in recent years. **Global warming** is a gradual increase in average global temperature. Global warming will affect global weather patterns, global sea level, and life on Earth.

Effects on the Atmosphere

Studies show that the average global surface temperature has increased by about 0.3 °C to 0.8 °C over the last 100 years. Even small changes in temperature can greatly affect weather and precipitation. Scientists predict that warming will generate more severe weather. Predictions suggest that storms will be more powerful and occur more frequently. It has also been predicted that as much as half of Earth's surface may be affected by drought.

Effects on the Hydrosphere and Cryosphere

Much of the ice on Earth occurs in glaciers in mountains, arctic sea ice, and ice sheets that cover Greenland and Antarctica. As temperatures increase, some of this ice will melt. A 2010 report observed record-setting hot temperatures, which resulted in record ice melt of the Greenland ice sheet.

When ice on land melts, global sea level rises because water flows into the ocean. Global sea level rose by 10 to 20 cm during the 1900s. Scientists project that sea level may rise 60 cm by 2100. Higher sea level is expected to increase flooding in coastal areas, some of which are highly populated. New York City; Shanghai, China; and Mumbai, India; are some cities that could be affected.

15 Infer How do melting ice caps and glaciers affect sea level?

Mt. Kilimanjaro has lost much of its glacier in recent years due to rising temperatures.

Mt. Kilimanjaro
February 1993

Mt. Kilimanjaro
February 2000

A warmer climate may force some species northward, including sugar maples.

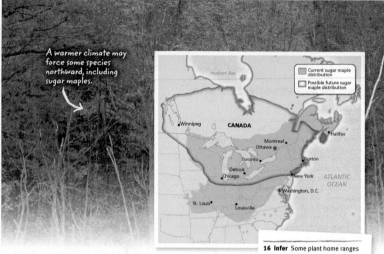

Current sugar maple distribution
Possible future sugar maple distribution

Hudson Bay
Winnipeg
CANADA
Montreal
Ottawa
Toronto
Detroit
Chicago
St. Louis
Louisville
Halifax
Boston
New York
Washington, D.C.
ATLANTIC OCEAN

16 Infer Some plant home ranges are shifting northward due to regional warming. What might happen to plant populations that are unable to spread northward?

Effects on the Biosphere

Active Reading **17 Summarize** Underline some of the effects of predicted climate change on the biosphere.

Scientists predict that global warming will change ecosystems. These changes may threaten the survival of many plant and animal species. Some species may move to cooler areas or even go extinct. Some butterflies, foxes, and alpine plants have already moved north to cooler climates. In Antarctica, emperor penguin populations could be reduced by as much as 95 percent by the end of this century if sea ice loss continues at its current rate. On the other hand, some species may benefit from expanded habitats in a warmer world.

Changes in temperature and precipitation will affect crops and livestock. If Earth warms more than a few degrees Celsius, many of the world's farms could suffer. Higher temperatures, reduced rainfall, and severe flooding can reduce crop production. Changes in weather will especially affect developing countries with large rural areas, such as countries in South Asia. A less severe warming would actually help agriculture in some regions by lengthening the growing season.

Warmer temperatures could increase the number of heat-related deaths and deaths from certain diseases, such as malaria. However, deaths associated with extreme cold could decrease.

Answers

15. As ice caps melt, sea level rises globally.

16. Populations that are unable to move or adapt to a changing climate can go extinct.

17. *See students' pages for annotations.*

Interpreting Visuals

Ask students to look closely at the photos of the melting glacier at the bottom of the page. Ask them to imagine what might happen if glaciers and polar icecaps continue to melt so dramatically. Discuss how this might affect global ecosystems.

Using Annotations

Text Structure: Summarize Actively reading a text helps students gain more from its content. Underlining key points or steps in a process reminds students that the information is important when they go back to study. Additionally, by underlining, they are kinesthetically learning. By making the task of reading active and procedural, students are increasing the likelihood that their brain will retain the information.

Probing Questions DIRECTED (Inquiry)

Application What do scientists predict will happen as a result of climate change? How do you think that climate change will affect species and their ecosystems? Sample answers: Scientists think that some species will not adapt well to the changes, and they may move to geographically different areas where conditions are closer to optimal. I think that this is likely because several species of butterfly have already begun to move.

How are climate predictions made?

Instruments have been placed in the atmosphere, in the oceans, on land, and in space to collect climate data. NASA now has more than a dozen spacecraft in orbit that are providing continuous data on Earth's climate. These data are added to historical climate data that are made available to researchers at centers worldwide. The data are used to create climate models. *Climate models* use mathematical formulas to describe how different variables affect Earth's climate. Today, there are about a dozen climate models that can be used to simulate different parts of the Earth system and the interactions that take place between them.

When designing a model to predict future climate change, scientists first model Earth's current climate system. If the model does a good job describing current conditions, then the variables are changed to reflect future conditions. Scientists usually run the model multiple times using different variables.

Climate models are the means by which scientists predict the effects of an increase in greenhouse gases on future global climate. These models use the best data available about the ways in which Earth's systems interact. No climate model can perfectly reproduce the system that is being modeled. However, as our understanding of Earth's systems improves, models of climate change are becoming more accurate.

Visualize It!

18 Predict As Earth is warming, the oceans are rising. This is due to both melting ice and the expansion of water as it warms. Predict what the change in sea level will be by the year 2020 if the current trend continues. You may draw on the graph to extend the current trend.

Sea level has been rising steadily since the late 1800s. By the year 2000, global average sea level had risen 50 mm above mean sea level, represented by 0 on the graph.

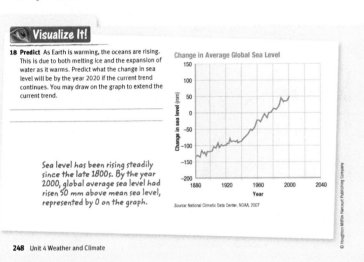

Change in Average Global Sea Level

Source: National Climatic Data Center, NOAA, 2007

Think Clean and Green

How can people reduce their impact on climate change?

People can take action to reduce climate change and its effects. Countries are working together to reduce their impact on Earth's climate. Communities and individuals are also doing their part to reduce greenhouse gas emissions.

Reduce Greenhouse Gas Emissions

The Kyoto Protocol, an international environmental agreement to reduce greenhouse gas emissions, was adopted in 1997. The Kyoto Protocol is the only existing international treaty in which nations have agreed to reduce CO_2 emissions. As of 2010, 191 countries had signed the protocol. At present, the Kyoto Protocol faces many complex challenges. One of the greatest challenges is that developing nations, which will be the largest future sources of CO_2 emissions, did not sign the protocol.

Individuals can reduce their impact on climate by conserving energy, increasing energy efficiency, and reducing the use of fossil fuels. Greenhouse gas emissions can be reduced by driving less and by switching to nonpolluting energy sources. Simple energy conservation solutions include turning off lights and replacing light bulbs. Recycling and reusing products also reduce energy use.

For most materials, recycling uses less energy than making products from scratch. That means less greenhouse gases are emitted.

Do the Math You Try It

19 Calculate How much energy is saved by using recycled aluminum to make new aluminum cans instead of making aluminum cans from raw materials?

20 Calculate By what percentage does recycling aluminum reduce energy use?

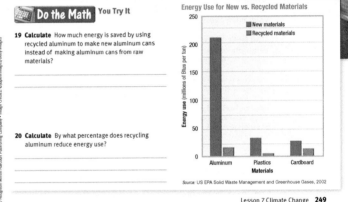

Energy Use for New vs. Recycled Materials

Source: US EPA Solid Waste Management and Greenhouse Gases, 2002

Answers

18. about 100 mm above average

19. Energy used to make raw aluminum: about 208 Btu/ton. Energy used to make recycled aluminum: about 17 Btu/ton. Savings is 191 Btu/ton.

20. about 92%

Building Reading Skills

Combination Notes This lesson contains information about different causes of climate change. Help students keep all of it straight by teaching them to create combination notes about the text as they read. Use the description and instructions in the online toolkit. Students could create diagrams that are labeled with the ways in which each natural and human activity can cause a change in Earth's climate. This activity provides a good study tool to help students remember causes of climate change.

Formative Assessment

Ask: What is the difference between natural and human causes of climate change? Natural causes of climate change are activities such as volcanic eruptions and meteorite or asteroid strikes—things that can cause change but that humans have no control over. Changes caused by human activity are things that human behavior directly influences. For example, when humans release large amounts of greenhouse gases into the atmosphere, they can raise the average global surface temperature. **For greater depth,** ask students to create Venn diagrams of the causes of climate change they've learned about. Ask them to share their Venn diagrams with a partner and add any details they missed.

- Reduce use of automobile.
- Use new, cleaner technologies.
- Plant a tree.

Reduce the Rate of Deforestation

Deforestation contributes up to 20 percent of greenhouse gases globally. Planting trees and supporting reforestation programs are ways that carbon sources can be balanced by carbon sinks. Another solution is to educate people about the importance of the carbon that is stored in forests for stabilizing climate. In 2008, the United Nations began a program called REDD, or *Reducing Emissions from Deforestation and Forest Degradation*. REDD offers incentives to developing countries to reduce deforestation. The program also teaches conservation methods, which include forestry management.

Use New Technologies

Energy-efficient practices for homes, businesses, industry, and transportation reduce greenhouse gas emissions. These practices not only reduce the amount of greenhouse gases in the atmosphere, they also save money.

Clean-energy technologies are being researched and used in different parts of the world. New biofuels, solar power, wind power, and water power reduce the need to burn fossil fuels. In the United States, water power is the leading source of renewable energy, and the use of wind power is increasing rapidly. However, many new technologies are currently more expensive than fossil fuels.

250 Unit 4 Weather and Climate

21 Summarize Use the table to summarize ways in which sources of greenhouse gases in the atmosphere can be reduced.

Sources of greenhouse gases	Ways to reduce greenhouse gases
cars	Walk or use bikes more often.

What are some economic and political issues related to climate change?

Active Reading 22 Identify Underline some of the economic and political issues that are related to climate change.

Climate change affects the entire Earth, no matter where greenhouse gases are produced. This makes climate change a global issue. The scientific concerns that climate change poses are not the only issues that have to be taken into account. There are economic and political issues involving climate change that are equally important.

Climate change is an economic issue. The cost of climate change includes the costs of crop failure, storm damage, and human disease. However, developing countries may not be able to afford technologies needed to reduce human impact on climate.

Climate change is also a political issue. Political action can lead to regulations that reduce greenhouse gas emissions. However, these laws may be challenged by groups who disagree with the need for change or disagree about what needs to change. No matter what choices are made to handle the challenges of climate change, it will take groups of people working together to make a difference.

Think Outside the Book Inquiry

23 Apply Research a recent extreme weather event from anywhere in the world. How might this event be related to climate change? Present your findings to the class as a news report or poster.

Climate change may make unusual weather the new norm. Rome, Italy, was brought to a standstill by unusually cold and snowy weather in 2010.

In Australia, years of unusually dry and hot weather led to devastating forest fires in 2009. Australia also suffered damaging floods in 2010.

24 Predict What are the possible economic and social consequences of unusually warm weather in a cold climate or unusually cool weather in a warm climate?

Lesson 7 Climate Change **251**

Answers

21. Sample answer: left column: cars; throwing away paper, plastic, and aluminum products; deforestation; right column: walk or use bikes more often; recycle; plant trees

22. *See students' pages for annotations.*

23. Sample answer: costs of failed crops, low water supply, forest fires, flood damage, snow removal, travel delays, health effects

24. Students answers will vary. Climate change may contribute to record-setting temperatures, more powerful and frequent storms, more severe droughts, and more intense El Niño and La Niña events.

Interpreting Visuals

Look at the photographs showing unusual weather events. Why are these events happening? Unusual weather patterns are happening as a result of climate change. Why do these changes contribute to making climate change a "global issue"? The effects of climate change affect everyone, whether they are contributing to its acceleration or not. You may wish to have students research other unusual weather events that have been reported in the last 50 years. Ask them to research whether scientists think these events are a result of natural or human activity and to think about how these changes can be reversed or stopped.

Using Annotations

Text Structure: Inference Have students share their answers to the Think Outside the Book interactivity with a partner. Ask them to discuss the details of their answer.

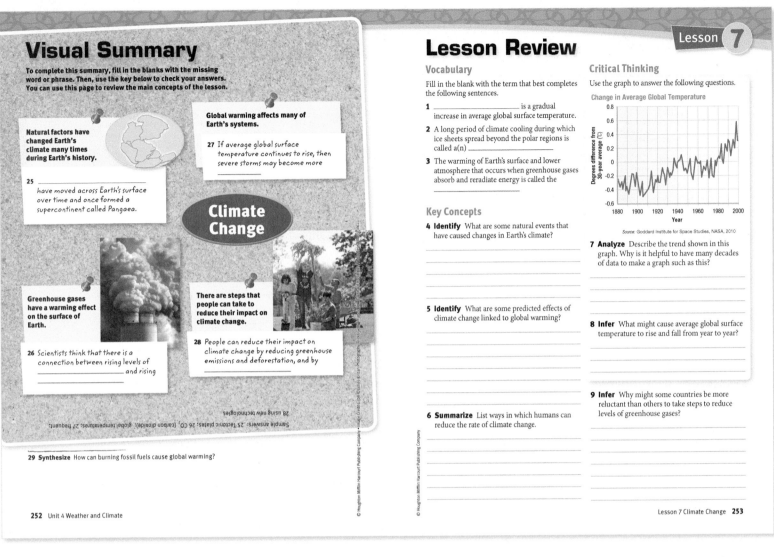

Visual Summary

To complete this summary, fill in the blanks with the missing word or phrase. Then, use the key below to check your answers. You can use this page to review the main concepts of the lesson.

Natural factors have changed Earth's climate many times during Earth's history.

25 _____ have moved across Earth's surface over time and once formed a supercontinent called Pangaea.

Global warming affects many of Earth's systems.

27 If average global surface temperature continues to rise, then severe storms may become more _____

Climate Change

Greenhouse gases have a warming effect on the surface of Earth.

26 Scientists think that there is a connection between rising levels of _____ and rising

There are steps that people can take to reduce their impact on climate change.

28 People can reduce their impact on climate change by reducing greenhouse emissions and deforestation, and by _____

28 using new technologies

Sample answers: 25 tectonic plates; 26 CO₂ (carbon dioxide); global temperatures; 27 frequent;

29 **Synthesize** How can burning fossil fuels cause global warming?

252 Unit 4 Weather and Climate

Lesson Review

Lesson 7

Vocabulary

Fill in the blank with the term that best completes the following sentences.

1 _____ is a gradual increase in average global surface temperature.

2 A long period of climate cooling during which ice sheets spread beyond the polar regions is called a(n) _____

3 The warming of Earth's surface and lower atmosphere that occurs when greenhouse gases absorb and reradiate energy is called the _____

Key Concepts

4 **Identify** What are some natural events that have caused changes in Earth's climate?

5 **Identify** What are some predicted effects of climate change linked to global warming?

6 **Summarize** List ways in which humans can reduce the rate of climate change.

Critical Thinking

Use the graph to answer the following questions.

Change in Average Global Temperature

Source: Goddard Institute for Space Studies, NASA, 2010

7 **Analyze** Describe the trend shown in this graph. Why is it helpful to have many decades of data to make a graph such as this?

8 **Infer** What might cause average global surface temperature to rise and fall from year to year?

9 **Infer** Why might some countries be more reluctant than others to take steps to reduce levels of greenhouse gases?

Lesson 7 Climate Change 253

Visual Summary Answers

25. Tectonic plates

26. CO₂ (carbon dioxide); global temperatures

27. frequent

28. using new technologies

29. Sample answer: Burning fossil fuels releases CO₂, a greenhouse gas. Greenhouse gases warm Earth's surface and lower atmosphere by absorbing some of the energy that would escape into space and reradiating that energy back to Earth.

Lesson Review Answers

1. Global warming

2. ice age

3. greenhouse effect

4. Natural events include movement of Earth's tectonic plates, particulates released into the atmosphere by volcanic eruptions and asteroid impacts, and natural cycles such El Niño, La Niña, and ice ages.

5. Some predicted effects of climate change linked to global warming include more powerful and frequent storms, rising global sea level, changing ecosystems, human health problems, and reduced crop production.

6. People can conserve energy, recycle, reduce waste, bike to school, use public transportation, and protect and plant forests.

7. The graph moves up and down each year but increases over time. With many years of data, long-term trends are easier to see.

8. Sample answer: Natural factors such as solar output and ocean temperature could cause yearly global temperature fluctuations.

9. Sample answer: Climate change issues have economic, political, and social consequences that make them difficult to solve. For example, some countries that are emitting greenhouse gases may not be financially capable of changing to a cleaner-burning energy source.

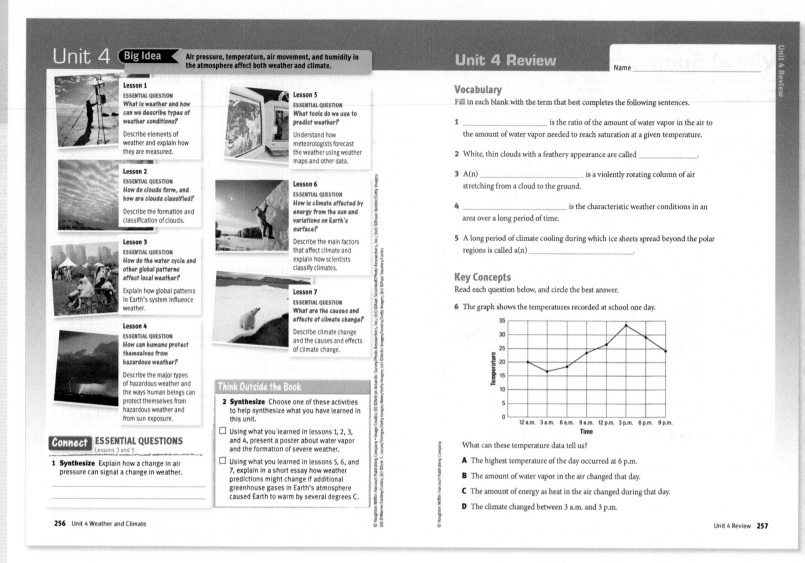

Unit Summary Answers

1. Different pressure systems have unique weather patterns. In a high-pressure system, air sinks, warms, and absorbs moisture, bringing clear skies and calm air. In a low-pressure system, air rises, cools, and forms clouds that bring precipitation.

2. Option 1: Posters should show how water vapor affects the formation of thunderstorms and hurricanes. Thunderstorms form when moist air near the ground rises and cools. Vapor condenses to form clouds. The air grows warmer, clouds grow, and a storm forms. Hurricanes can form when ocean water evaporates. As the vapor rises and condenses to form clouds, energy is released and the air grows warmer. Winds spiral into the center of low pressure, around which a hurricane can form.

   Option 2: Temperatures, especially in the polar zone, might be forecast higher than the current average. Precipitation rates might be higher in some areas; severe droughts might be forecast for other areas. In some areas, increasing temperatures might lead to more heat advisories being issued.

Unit Review   Response to Intervention

A Quick Grading Chart follows the Answers. See the Assessment Guide for more detail about correct and incorrect answer choices. Refer back to the Lesson Planning pages for activities and assignments that can be used as remediation for students who answer questions incorrectly.

Answers

1. Relative humidity The answer is relative humidity because that is the ratio used; at 100% relative humidity as much moisture condenses out of the air as evaporates into the air. (Lesson 1)

2. cirrus clouds Cirrus clouds are made up of ice crystals, and are thin and white in appearance. (Lesson 2)

3. tornado A tornado is a violently rotating column of air that forms when a thunderstorm meets high-altitude winds that cause the rising air in the storm to rotate. (Lesson 4)

Unit 4 Review continued

7 Which of these types of weather data is measured using a barometer?

A air pressure **C** relative humidity

B precipitation **D** wind speed

8 The picture below shows the four parts of the water cycle labeled A, B, C, and D.

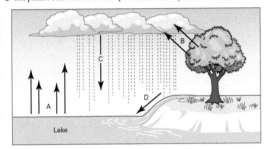

Lake

If rain (C) is falling as part of a thunderstorm, which type of clouds are shown?

A altostratus clouds **C** cumulonimbus clouds

B cirrus clouds **D** stratus clouds

9 If it rained all day but stopped and then cooled down considerably at night, what weather phenomenon would you likely see that night?

A fog **C** sleet

B hail **D** thunder

10 What results when air surrounding a bolt of lightning experiences a rapid increase in temperature and pressure?

A A tornado forms. **C** Thunder sounds.

B Hail forms. **D** Rain condenses.

11 Refer to the regions A, B, C, and D shown on the U.S. map below.

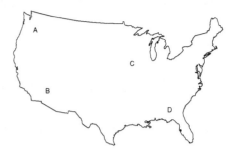

In which of these directions is the jet stream most likely to flow?

A from D to C **C** from C to A

B from A to C **D** from C to B

12 Which of the following should you do to escape a flood?

A Seek a high, safe point above the floodwaters and wait for assistance.

B Walk carefully into the floodwaters to get to safety.

C Swim through the floodwaters until you find a safer place.

D Use a lifejacket or flotation device to help you wade through the floodwaters.

13 What are the two main factors that determine climate?

A temperature and wind

B temperature and precipitation

C air pressure and humidity

D wind and precipitation

Answers *(continued)*

4. Climate Climate refers to the long-term weather typical of a given area. (Lesson 6)

5. ice age An ice age is a period of cold climate change on Earth that occurs over thousands of years. (Lesson 7)

6. Answer C is correct because energy as heat (temperature) changes according to the graph. (Lesson 1)

7. Answer A is correct because a barometer measures air pressure. (Lesson 1)

8. Answer C is correct because cumulonimbus clouds are rain clouds that can produce thunderstorms. (Lesson 2)

9. Answer A is correct because fog can occur when the surface of Earth cools off at night, lowering the air temperature until water vapor condenses out of the air to form a cloud near the ground. (Lesson 2)

10. Answer C is correct because thunder is the sound wave created by the vibration of this rapidly expanding, super-hot air. (Lesson 4)

11. Answer B is correct because the jet stream flows from west to east; the polar jet stream over the U.S. often flows from the northwest slightly south and east across the country, though it can vary considerably. (Lesson 3)

12. Answer A is correct because you should never enter floodwaters; you should look for a high area and wait for assistance. (Lesson 4)

13. Answer B is correct because the two main factors are the temperature and the precipitation. (Lesson 6)

14. Answer D is correct because the lines, called *isobars*, connect points of equal air pressure. (Lesson 5)

15. Answer D is correct because region W is in the "rain shadow" of the mountain where the air has lost its moisture and heats up rapidly. (Lesson 6)

Unit 4 Review continued

Name _____

14 What do the curved concentric lines on weather forecast maps show?

A The lines show the direction in which the wind will blow.

B The lines show where rain will fall.

C The lines connect points of equal temperature.

D The lines connect points of equal air pressure.

15 The picture below shows an exaggerated side view of an ocean on the left and a mountain range on the right. The arrows indicate the movement of air and moisture from the ocean.

Which region is most likely to have a dry, desert-like climate?

A region R **C** region T

B region S **D** region W

16 Which of these is not a currently predicted effect of global climate change?

A rising sea levels

B increased precipitation everywhere on the globe

C reduction in Arctic sea ice

D more severe storms

17 The graph below shows the amount of carbon dioxide measured in the atmosphere between about 1960 and 2005.

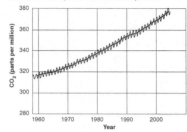

Amount of Atmospheric Carbon Dioxide per Year

What conclusion can you make from the data displayed in the graph?

A The amount of carbon dioxide in the atmosphere more than doubled between 1960 and 2000.

B An increasing number of cars on the road between 1960 and 2000 caused an increase in carbon dioxide levels in the atmosphere.

C There was an overall increase in the level of carbon dioxide in the atmosphere between 1960 and 2000.

D Average global temperatures increased between 1960 and 2000 as a result of the increase in carbon dioxide in the atmosphere.

Critical Thinking

Answer the following questions in the space provided.

18 Explain generally what makes a cloud form.

_____

_____

Describe one specific situation in which a cloud can form.

_____

_____

19 Explain two ways in which forecasters collect weather data.

_____

_____

260 Unit 4 Weather and Climate

Unit 4 Review **261**

Answers *(continued)*

16. Answer B is correct because predictions are for drought in some regions and increased precipitation in others. (Lesson 7)

17. Answer C is correct because the line graph shows a steady increase in the average carbon dioxide level over those years. (Lesson 7)

18. Key Elements:

- explains that clouds form when air is cooled to the dew-point temperature and condensation occurs (e.g., *A cloud forms when the air is cooled to the dew point, causing water vapor to condense out of the air.*)

- gives a situation in which clouds form (e.g., *A cloud can form when warm, moist air is forced upward by a cooler air mass; or A cloud can form when air is forced upward by a mountain range; or A cloud can form when two air masses at different temperatures mix together; or A cloud can form when air moves over a cold surface.*) (Lesson 2)

19. Key Elements:

- explains one method of data collection (e.g., *Data for weather forecasts are obtained from surface observations [land stations, ships, and buoys], from upper-air observations [balloons and airplanes], from remotely sensed observations [satellites, radar], and output from Numerical Weather Prediction models.*)

- explains another method of data collection (Lesson 5)

20. Key Elements:

- correctly labels two polar zones, one above 60° N and one above 60° S; two temperate zones, one between 30° N and 60° N, and one between 30° S and 60° S; and one tropical zone between 30° S and 30° N

- correctly describes the typical climate in each zone (e.g., *The polar climate zone is very cold with little precipitation. The temperate zone has moderate temperatures and some precipitation. The tropical zone is very warm with heavy precipitation.*)

Unit 4 Review continued

20 The map below shows the three different climate zones on Earth.

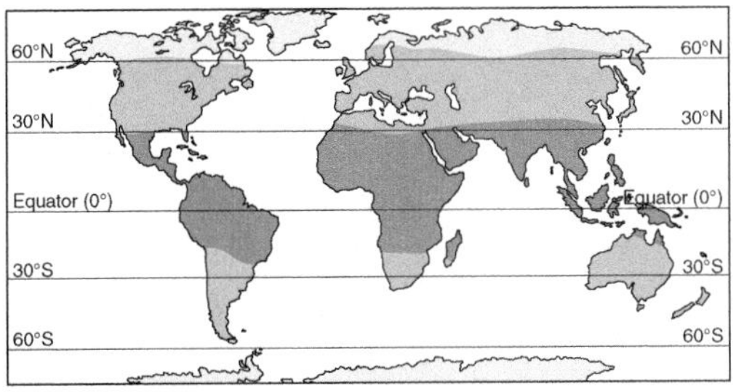

Label each climate zone on the map. Then describe the temperature and precipitation typical of each zone.

_____

_____

Explain how latitude affects the climate of each zone.

_____

_____

Connect **ESSENTIAL QUESTIONS**
Lessons 1, 2, 3, 4, and 6

Answer the following question in the space provided.

21 Even if you do not live on a coast, the movement of water in the oceans and water vapor in the atmosphere over the oceans does affect your weather. Using what you learned in lessons 1, 2, 3, 4, and 6, describe how the water cycle and the global movement of water through ocean currents and winds affect the climate of your local region.

_____

_____

_____

_____

_____

262 Unit 4 Weather and Climate

Quick Grading Chart

Use the chart below for quick test grading. The lesson correlations can help you target reteaching for missed items.

Item	Answer	Cognitive Complexity	Lesson
1.	—	Low	1
2.	—	Low	2
3.	—	Low	4
4.	—	Low	6
5.	—	Low	7
6.	C	Moderate	1
7.	A	Low	1
8.	C	Moderate	2
9.	A	Low	2
10.	C	Moderate	4
11.	B	Moderate	3
12.	A	Moderate	4
13.	B	Moderate	6
14	D	Moderate	5
15.	D	Moderate	6
16.	B	Moderate	7
17.	C	Moderate	7
18.	—	Moderate	2
19.	—	Moderate	5
20.	—	Moderate	6
21.	—	High	1–4, 6

Cognitive Complexity refers to the demand on thinking associated with an item, and may vary with the answer choices, the number of steps required to arrive at an answer, and other factors, but not the ability level of the student.

Answers (continued)

- explains how latitude determines the angle of the sun's rays (e.g., *Near the equator, the sun's rays hit Earth at a 90-degree angle, so more solar energy is transferred as heat. Near the poles, the sun's rays hit Earth at a smaller angle, so less solar energy is transferred as heat.*) (Lesson 6)

21. Key Elements:

- explains that ocean currents move warm water to cooler climates and cooler water to warmer climates (e.g., *Currents bring warm water from the Gulf of Mexico up the east coast of the U.S., helping your climate to stay mild.*)

- explains that evaporation of water over the oceans puts moisture into the air that causes precipitation in your area

- explains that uneven heating of Earth's surface causes air pressure differences that drive winds and carries water vapor into your area

- correctly describes your local climate (Lesson 1–4, 6)

Teacher Notes

Resources

Student Edition Resources

Teacher Edition Resources

Handbook

References

Mineral Properties

Here are five steps to take in mineral identification:

1 Determine the color of the mineral. Is it light-colored, dark-colored, or a specific color?

2 Determine the luster of the mineral. Is it metallic or non-metallic?

3 Determine the color of any powder left by its streak.

4 Determine the hardness of your mineral. Is it soft, hard, or very hard? Using a glass plate, see if the mineral scratches it.

5 Determine whether your sample has cleavage or any special properties.

TERMS TO KNOW	DEFINITION
adamantine	a non-metallic luster like that of a diamond
cleavage	how a mineral breaks when subject to stress on a particular plane
luster	the state or quality of shining by reflecting light
streak	the color of a mineral when it is powdered
submetallic	between metallic and nonmetallic in luster
vitreous	glass-like type of luster

Silicate Minerals					
Mineral	**Color**	**Luster**	**Streak**	**Hardness**	**Cleavage and Special Properties**
Beryl	deep green, pink, white, bluish green, or yellow	vitreous	white	7.5–8	1 cleavage direction; some varieties fluoresce in ultraviolet light
Chlorite	green	vitreous to pearly	pale green	2–2.5	1 cleavage direction
Garnet	green, red, brown, black	vitreous	white	6.5–7.5	no cleavage
Hornblende	dark green, brown, or black	vitreous	none	5–6	2 cleavage directions
Muscovite	colorless, silvery white, or brown	vitreous or pearly	white	2–2.5	1 cleavage direction
Olivine	olive green, yellow	vitreous	white or none	6.5–7	no cleavage
Orthoclase	colorless, white, pink, or other colors	vitreous	white or none	6	2 cleavage directions
Plagioclase	colorless, white, yellow, pink, green	vitreous	white	6	2 cleavage directions
Quartz	colorless or white; any color when not pure	vitreous or waxy	white or none	7	no cleavage

Nonsilicate Minerals					
Mineral	**Color**	**Luster**	**Streak**	**Hardness**	**Cleavage and Special Properties**
Native Elements					
Copper	copper-red	metallic	copper-red	2.5–3	no cleavage
Diamond	pale yellow or colorless	adamantine	none	10	4 cleavage directions
Graphite	black to gray	submetallic	black	1–2	1 cleavage direction
Carbonates					
Aragonite	colorless, white, or pale yellow	vitreous	white	3.5–4	2 cleavage directions; reacts with hydrochloric acid
Calcite	colorless or white to tan	vitreous	white	3	3 cleavage directions; reacts with weak acid; double refraction
Halides					
Fluorite	light green, yellow, purple, bluish green, or other colors	vitreous	none	4	4 cleavage directions; some varieties fluoresce
Halite	white	vitreous	white	2.0–2.5	3 cleavage directions
Oxides					
Hematite	reddish brown to black	metallic to earthy	dark red to red-brown	5.6–6.5	no cleavage; magnetic when heated
Magnetite	iron-black	metallic	black	5.5–6.5	no cleavage; magnetic
Sulfates					
Anhydrite	colorless, bluish, or violet	vitreous to pearly	white	3–3.5	3 cleavage directions
Gypsum	white, pink, gray, or colorless	vitreous, pearly, or silky	white	2.0	3 cleavage directions
Sulfides					
Galena	lead-gray	metallic	lead-gray to black	2.5–2.8	3 cleavage directions
Pyrite	brassy yellow	metallic	greenish, brownish, or black	6–6.5	no cleavage

References

Geologic Time Scale

Geologists developed the geologic time scale to represent the 4.6 billion years of Earth's history that have passed since Earth formed. This scale divides Earth's history into blocks of time. The boundaries between these time intervals (shown in millions of years ago or mya in the table below), represent major changes in Earth's history. Some boundaries are defined by mass extinctions, major changes in Earth's surface, and/or major changes in Earth's climate.

Divisions of Time

The divisions of time shown here represent major changes in Earth's surface and when life developed and changed significantly on Earth. As new evidence is found, the boundaries of these divisions may shift. The Phanerozoic eon is divided into three eras. The beginning of each of these eras represents a change in the types of organisms that dominated Earth. And, each era is commonly characterized by the types of organisms that dominated the era. These eras are divided into periods, and periods are divided into epochs.

The four major divisions that encompass the history of life on Earth are Precambrian time, the Paleozoic era, the Mesozoic era, and the Cenozoic era. The largest divisions are eons. **Precambrian time** is made up of the first three eons, over 4 billion years of Earth's history.

The **Paleozoic era** lasted from 542 mya to 251 mya. All major plant groups, except flowering plants, appeared during this era. By the end of the era, reptiles, winged insects, and fishes had also appeared. The largest known mass extinction occurred at the end of this era.

The **Phanerozoic eon** began 542 mya. We live in this eon.

The **Mesozoic era** lasted from 251 mya to 65.5 mya. During this era, many kinds of dinosaurs dominated land, and giant lizards swam in the ocean. The first birds, mammals, and flowering plants also appeared during this time. About two-thirds of all land species went extinct at the end of this era.

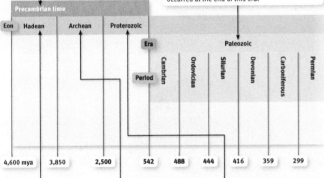

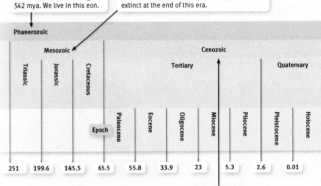

The **Hadean eon** lasted from about 4.6 billion years ago (bya) to 3.85 bya. It is described based on evidence from meteorites and rocks from the moon.

The **Archean eon** lasted from 3.85 bya to 2.5 bya. The earliest rocks from Earth that have been found and dated formed at the start of this eon.

The **Proterozoic eon** lasted from 2.5 bya to 542 mya. The first organisms, which were single-celled organisms, appeared during this eon. These organisms produced so much oxygen that they changed Earth's oceans and Earth's atmosphere.

The **Cenozoic era** began 65.5 mya and continues today. Mammals dominate this era. During the Mesozoic era, mammals were small in size but grew much larger during the Cenozoic era. Primates, including humans, appeared during this era.

Star Charts for the Northern Hemisphere

A star chart is a map of the stars in the night sky. It shows the names and positions of constellations and major stars. Star charts can be used to identify constellations and even to orient yourself using Polaris, the North Star.

Because Earth moves through space, different constellations are visible at different times of the year. The star charts on these pages show the constellations visible during each season in the Northern Hemisphere.

Spring

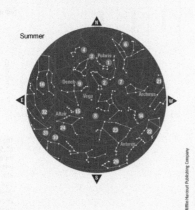

Summer

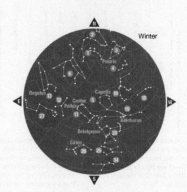

Autumn

Winter

Constellations

1. Ursa Minor
2. Draco
3. Cepheus
4. Cassiopeia
5. Auriga
6. Ursa Major
7. Boötes
8. Hercules
9. Cygnus
10. Perseus
11. Gemini
12. Cancer
13. Leo
14. Serpens
15. Sagitta
16. Pegasus
17. Pisces

Constellations

18. Aries
19. Taurus
20. Orion
21. Virgo
22. Libra
23. Ophiuchus
24. Aquila
25. Lepus
26. Canis Major
27. Hydra
28. Corvus
29. Scorpius
30. Sagittarius
31. Capricornus
32. Aquarius
33. Cetus
34. Columba

References

World Map

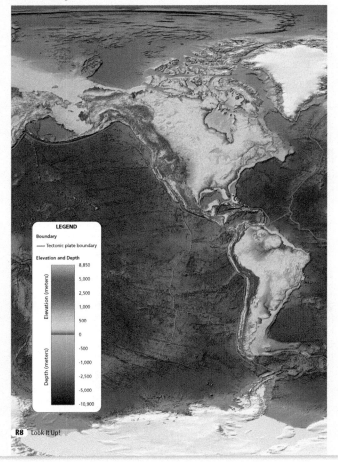

LEGEND

Boundary

— Tectonic plate boundary

Elevation and Depth

Elevation (meters)
- 8,850
- 5,000
- 2,500
- 1,000
- 500
- 0

Depth (meters)
- -500
- -1,000
- -2,500
- -5,000
- -10,900

Classification of Living Things

Domains and Kingdoms

All organisms belong to one of three domains: Domain Archaea, Domain Bacteria, or Domain Eukarya. Some of the groups within these domains are shown below. (Remember that genus names are italicized.)

Domain Archaea

The organisms in this domain are single-celled prokaryotes, many of which live in extreme environments.

Archaea		
Group	**Example**	**Characteristics**
Methanogens	*Methanococcus*	produce methane gas; can't live in oxygen
Thermophiles	*Sulpholobus*	require sulphur; can't live in oxygen
Halophiles	*Halococcus*	live in very salty environments; most can live in oxygen

Domain Bacteria

Organisms in this domain are single-celled prokaryotes and are found in almost every environment on Earth.

Bacteria		
Group	**Example**	**Characteristics**
Bacilli	*Escherichia*	rod shaped; some bacilli fix nitrogen; some cause disease
Cocci	*Streptococcus*	spherical shaped; some cause disease; can form spores
Spirilla	*Treponema*	spiral shaped; cause diseases such as syphilis and Lyme disease

Domain Eukarya

Organisms in this domain are single-celled or multicellular eukaryotes.

Kingdom Protista Many protists resemble fungi, plants, or animals, but are smaller and simpler in structure. Most are single celled.

Protists		
Group	**Example**	**Characteristics**
Sarcodines	*Amoeba*	radiolarians; single-celled consumers
Ciliates	*Paramecium*	single-celled consumers
Flagellates	*Trypanosoma*	single-celled parasites
Sporozoans	*Plasmodium*	single-celled parasites
Euglenas	*Euglena*	single celled; photosynthesize
Diatoms	*Pinnularia*	most are single celled; photosynthesize
Dinoflagellates	*Gymnodinium*	single celled; some photosynthesize
Algae	*Volvox*	single celled or multicellular; photosynthesize
Slime molds	*Physarum*	single celled or multicellular; consumers or decomposers
Water molds	powdery mildew	single celled or multicellular; parasites or decomposers

Kingdom Fungi Most fungi are multicellular. Their cells have thick cell walls. Fungi absorb food from their environment.

Fungi		
Group	**Examples**	**Characteristics**
Threadlike fungi	bread mold	spherical; decomposers
Sac fungi	yeast; morels	saclike; parasites and decomposers
Club fungi	mushrooms; rusts; smuts	club shaped; parasites and decomposers
Lichens	British soldier	a partnership between a fungus and an alga

Kingdom Plantae Plants are multicellular and have cell walls made of cellulose. Plants make their own food through photosynthesis. Plants are classified into divisions instead of phyla.

Plants		
Group	**Examples**	**Characteristics**
Bryophytes	mosses; liverworts	no vascular tissue; reproduce by spores
Club mosses	*Lycopodium*; ground pine	grow in wooded areas; reproduce by spores
Horsetails	rushes	grow in wetland areas; reproduce by spores
Ferns	spleenworts; sensitive fern	large leaves called fronds; reproduce by spores
Conifers	pines; spruces; firs	needlelike leaves; reproduce by seeds made in cones
Cycads	*Zamia*	slow growing; reproduce by seeds made in large cones
Gnetophytes	*Welwitschia*	only three living families; reproduce by seeds
Ginkgoes	*Ginkgo*	only one living species; reproduce by seeds
Angiosperms	all flowering plants	reproduce by seeds made in flowers; fruit

Kingdom Animalia Animals are multicellular. Their cells do not have cell walls. Most animals have specialized tissues and complex organ systems. Animals get food by eating other organisms.

Animals		
Group	**Examples**	**Characteristics**
Sponges	glass sponges	no symmetry or specialized tissues; aquatic
Cnidarians	jellyfish; coral	radial symmetry; aquatic
Flatworms	planaria; tapeworms; flukes	bilateral symmetry; organ systems
Roundworms	*Trichina*; hookworms	bilateral symmetry; organ systems
Annelids	earthworms; leeches	bilateral symmetry; organ systems
Mollusks	snails; octopuses	bilateral symmetry; organ systems
Echinoderms	sea stars; sand dollars	radial symmetry; organ systems
Arthropods	insects; spiders; lobsters	bilateral symmetry; organ systems
Chordates	fish; amphibians; reptiles; birds; mammals	bilateral symmetry; complex organ systems

References

Periodic Table of the Elements

The International Union of Pure and Applied Chemistry (IUPAC) has determined that, because of isotopic variance, the average atomic mass is best represented by a range of values for each of the following elements: hydrogen, lithium, boron, carbon, nitrogen, oxygen, silicon, sulfur, chlorine, and thallium. However, the values in this table are appropriate for everyday calculations.

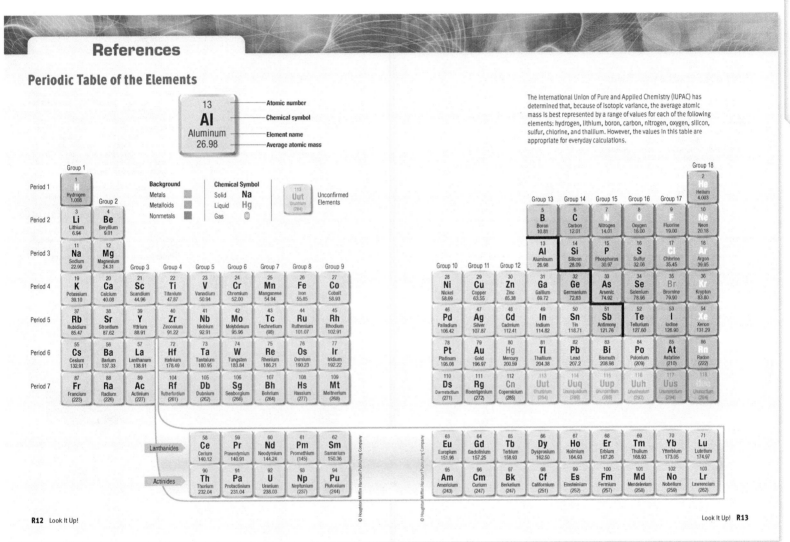

© Houghton Mifflin Harcourt Publishing Company

References

Physical Science Refresher

Atoms and Elements

Every object in the universe is made of matter. **Matter** is anything that takes up space and has mass. All matter is made of atoms. An **atom** is the smallest particle into which an element can be divided and still be the same element. An **element**, in turn, is a substance that cannot be broken down into simpler substances by chemical means. Each element consists of only one kind of atom. An element may be made of many atoms, but they are all the same kind of atom.

Atomic Structure

Atoms are made of smaller particles called **electrons**, **protons**, and **neutrons**. Electrons have a negative electric charge, protons have a positive charge, and neutrons have no electric charge. Together, protons and neutrons form the **nucleus**, or small dense center, of an atom. Because protons are positively charged and neutrons are neutral, the nucleus has a positive charge. Electrons move within an area around the nucleus called the **electron cloud.** Electrons move so quickly that scientists cannot determine their exact speeds and positions at the same time.

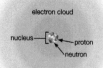

electron cloud

nucleus

proton

neutron

Atomic Number

To help distinguish one element from another, scientists use the atomic numbers of atoms. The **atomic number** is the number of protons in the nucleus of an atom. The atoms of a certain element always have the same number of protons.

When atoms have an equal number of protons and electrons, they are uncharged, or electrically neutral. The atomic number equals the number of electrons in an uncharged atom. The number of neutrons, however, can vary for a given element. Atoms of the same element that have different numbers of neutrons are called **isotopes**.

Periodic Table of the Elements

In the periodic table, each element in the table is in a separate box. And the elements are arranged from left to right in order of increasing atomic number. That is, an uncharged atom of each element has one more electron and one more proton than an uncharged atom of the element to its left. Each horizontal row of the table is called a **period.** Changes in chemical properties of elements across a period correspond to changes in the electron arrangements of their atoms.

Each vertical column of the table is known as a **group.** A group lists elements with similar physical and chemical properties. For this reason, a group is also sometimes called a family. The elements in a group have similar properties because their atoms have the same number of electrons in their outer energy level. For example, the elements helium, neon, argon, krypton, xenon, and radon all have similar properties and are known as the noble gases.

Molecules and Compounds

When two or more elements join chemically, they form a **compound.** A compound is a new substance with properties different from those of the elements that compose it. For example, water, H_2O, is a compound formed when hydrogen (H) and oxygen (O) combine. The smallest complete unit of a compound that has the properties of that compound is called a **molecule.** A chemical formula indicates the elements in a compound. It also indicates the relative number of atoms of each element in the compound. The chemical formula for water is H_2O. So, each water molecule consists of two atoms of hydrogen and one atom of oxygen. The subscript number after the symbol for an element shows how many atoms of that element are in a single molecule of the compound.

Chemical Equations

A chemical reaction occurs when a chemical change takes place. A chemical equation describes a chemical reaction using chemical formulas. The equation indicates the substances that react and the substances that are produced. For example, when carbon and oxygen combine, they can form carbon dioxide, shown in the equation below: $C + O_2 \longrightarrow CO_2$

Acids, Bases, and pH

An **ion** is an atom or group of chemically bonded atoms that has an electric charge because it has lost or gained one or more electrons. When an acid, such as hydrochloric acid, HCl, is mixed with water, it separates into ions. An **acid** is a compound that produces hydrogen ions, H^+, in water. The hydrogen ions then combine with a water molecule to form a hydronium ion, H_3O^+. A **base**, on the other hand, is a substance that produces hydroxide ions, OH^-, in water.

To determine whether a solution is acidic or basic, scientists use pH. The **pH** of a solution is a measure of the hydronium ion concentration in a solution. The pH scale ranges from 0 to 14. Acids have a pH that is less than 7. The lower the number, the more acidic the solution. The middle point, pH = 7, is neutral, neither acidic nor basic. Bases have a pH that is greater than 7. The higher the number is, the more basic the solution.

The pH of Some Common Materials

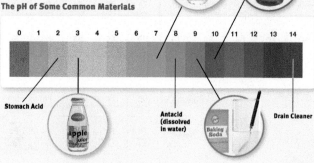

Stomach Acid

Antacid (dissolved in water)

Drain Cleaner

References

Physical Laws and Useful Equations

Law of Conservation of Mass

Mass cannot be created or destroyed during ordinary chemical or physical changes.

The total mass in a closed system is always the same no matter how many physical changes or chemical reactions occur.

Law of Conservation of Energy

Energy can be neither created nor destroyed.

The total amount of energy in a closed system is always the same. Energy can be changed from one form to another, but all of the different forms of energy in a system always add up to the same total amount of energy, no matter how many energy conversions occur.

Law of Universal Gravitation

All objects in the universe attract each other by a force called gravity. The size of the force depends on the masses of the objects and the distance between the objects.

The first part of the law explains why lifting a bowling ball is much harder than lifting a marble. Because the bowling ball has a much larger mass than the marble does, the amount of gravity between Earth and the bowling ball is greater than the amount of gravity between Earth and the marble.

The second part of the law explains why a satellite can remain in orbit around Earth. The satellite is placed at a carefully calculated distance from Earth. This distance is great enough to keep Earth's gravity from pulling the satellite down, yet small enough to keep the satellite from escaping Earth's gravity and wandering off into space.

Newton's Laws of Motion

Newton's first law of motion states that an object at rest remains at rest, and an object in motion remains in motion at constant speed and in a straight line unless acted on by an unbalanced force.

The first part of the law explains why a football will remain on a tee until it is kicked off or until a gust of wind blows it off. The second part of the law explains why a bike rider will continue moving forward after the bike comes to an abrupt stop. Gravity and the friction of the sidewalk will eventually stop the rider.

Newton's second law of motion states that the acceleration of an object depends on the mass of the object and the amount of force applied.

The first part of the law explains why the acceleration of a 4 kg bowling ball will be greater than the acceleration of a 6 kg bowling ball if the same force is applied to both balls. The second part of the law explains why the acceleration of a bowling ball will be greater if a larger force is applied to the bowling ball. The relationship of acceleration (a) to mass (m) and force (F) can be expressed mathematically by the following equation:

$$acceleration = \frac{force}{mass}, \text{ or } a = \frac{F}{m}$$

This equation is often rearranged to read *force = mass × acceleration*, or $F = m \times a$

Newton's third law of motion states that whenever one object exerts a force on a second object, the second object exerts an equal and opposite force on the first.

This law explains that a runner is able to move forward because the ground exerts an equal and opposite force on the runner's foot after each step.

Average speed

$$average\ speed = \frac{total\ distance}{total\ time}$$

Example:
A bicycle messenger traveled a distance of 136 km in 8 h. What was the messenger's average speed?

$$\frac{136\ km}{8\ h} = 17\ km/h$$

The messenger's average speed was **17 km/h.**

Average acceleration

$$average\ acceleration = \frac{final\ velocity - starting\ velocity}{time\ it\ takes\ to\ change\ velocity}$$

Example:
Calculate the average acceleration of an Olympic 100 m dash sprinter who reached a velocity of 20 m/s south at the finish line. The race was in a straight line and lasted 10 s.

$$\frac{20\ m/s - 0\ m/s}{10\ s} = 2\ m/s/s$$

The sprinter's average acceleration was **2 m/s/s south.**

Pressure

Pressure is the force exerted over a given area. The SI unit for pressure is the pascal. Its symbol is Pa.

$$pressure = \frac{force}{area}$$

Net force
Forces in the Same Direction

When forces are in the same direction, add the forces together to determine the net force.

Example:
Calculate the net force on a stalled car that is being pushed by two people. One person is pushing with a force of 13 N northwest, and the other person is pushing with a force of 8 N in the same direction.

$$13\ N + 8\ N = 21\ N$$

The net force is **21 N northwest.**

Forces in Opposite Directions

When forces are in opposite directions, subtract the smaller force from the larger force to determine the net force. The net force will be in the direction of the larger force.

Example:
Calculate the net force on a rope that is being pulled on each end. One person is pulling on one end of the rope with a force of 12 N south. Another person is pulling on the opposite end of the rope with a force of 7 N north.

$$12\ N - 7\ N = 5\ N$$

The net force is **5 N south.**

Example:
Calculate the pressure of the air in a soccer ball if the air exerts a force of 10 N over an area of 0.5 m².

$$pressure = \frac{10N}{0.5\ m^2} = \frac{20N}{m^2} = 20\ Pa$$

The pressure of the air inside the soccer ball is **20 Pa.**

Reading and Study Skills

A How-To Manual for Active Reading

This book belongs to you, and you are invited to write in it. In fact, the book won't be complete until you do. Sometimes you'll answer a question or follow directions to mark up the text. Other times you'll write down your own thoughts. And when you're done reading and writing in the book, the book will be ready to help you review what you learned and prepare for tests.

Active Reading Annotations

Before you read, you'll often come upon an Active Reading prompt that asks you to underline certain words or number the steps in a process. Here's an example.

> ### Active Reading
>
> **12 Identify** In this paragraph, number the sequence of sentences that describe replication.

Marking the text this way is called **annotating,** and your marks are called **annotations.** Annotating the text can help you identify important concepts while you read.

There are other ways that you can annotate the text. You can draw an asterisk (*) by vocabulary terms, mark unfamiliar or confusing terms and information with a question mark (?), and mark main ideas with a double underline. And you can even invent your own marks to annotate the text!

Other Annotating Opportunities

Keep your pencil, pen, or highlighter nearby as you read, so you can make a note or highlight an important point at any time. Here are a few ideas to get you started.

- Notice the headings in red and blue. The blue headings are questions that point to the main idea of what you're reading. The red headings are answers to the questions in the blue ones. Together these headings outline the content of the lesson. After reading a lesson, you could write your own answers to the questions.

- Notice the bold-faced words that are highlighted in yellow. They are highlighted so that you can easily find them again on the page where they are defined. As you read or as you review, challenge yourself to write your own sentence using the bold-faced term.

- Make a note in the margin at any time. You might
  - Ask a "What if" question
  - Comment on what you read
  - Make a connection to something you read elsewhere
  - Make a logical conclusion from the text

Use your own language and abbreviations. Invent a code, such as using circles and boxes around words to remind you of their importance or relation to each other. Your annotations will help you remember your questions for class discussions, and when you go back to the lesson later, you may be able to fill in what you didn't understand the first time you read it. Like a scientist in the field or in a lab, you will be recording your questions and observations for analysis later.

Active Reading Questions

After you read, you'll often come upon Active Reading questions that ask you to think about what you've just read. You'll write your answer underneath the question. Here's an example.

> ### Active Reading
>
> **8 Describe** Where are phosphate groups found in a DNA molecule?
> _____
> _____

This type of question helps you sum up what you've just read and pull out the most important ideas from the passage. In this case the question asks you to **describe** the structure of a DNA molecule that you have just read about. Other times you may be asked to do such things as **apply** a concept, **compare** two concepts, **summarize** a process, or **identify a cause-and-effect** relationship. You'll be strengthening those critical thinking skills that you'll use often in learning about science.

Reading and Study Skills

Using Graphic Organizers to Take Notes

Graphic organizers help you remember information as you read it for the first time and as you study it later. There are dozens of graphic organizers to choose from, so the first trick is to choose the one that's best suited to your purpose. Following are some graphic organizers to use for different purposes.

To remember lots of information	To relate a central idea to subordinate details	To describe a process	To make a comparison
• Arrange data in a Content Frame • Use Combination Notes to describe a concept in words and pictures	• Show relationships with a Mind Map or a Main Idea Web • Sum up relationships among many things with a Concept Map	• Use a Process Diagram to explain a procedure • Show a chain of events and results in a Cause-and-Effect Chart	• Compare two or more closely related things in a Venn Diagram

Content Frame

1 Make a four-column chart.

2 Fill the first column with categories (e.g., snail, ant, earthworm) and the first row with descriptive information (e.g., group, characteristic, appearance).

3 Fill the chart with details that belong in each row and column.

4 When you finish, you'll have a study aid that helps you compare one category to another.

Invertebrates

NAME	GROUP	CHARACTERISTICS	DRAWING
snail	mollusks	mangle	
ant	arthropods	six legs, exoskeleton	
earthworm	segmented worms	segmented body, circulatory and digestive systems	
heartworm	roundworms	digestive system	
sea star	echinoderms	spiny skin, tube feet	
jellyfish	cnidarians	stinging cells	

R20 Look It Up!

© Houghton Mifflin Harcourt Publishing Company

Combination Notes

1 Make a two-column chart.

2 Write descriptive words and definitions in the first column.

3 Draw a simple sketch that helps you remember the meaning of the term in the second column.

Mind Map

1 Draw an oval, and inside it write a topic to analyze.

2 Draw two or more arms extending from the oval. Each arm represents a main idea about the topic.

3 Draw lines from the arms on which to write details about each of the main ideas.

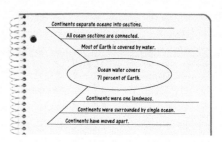

Main Idea Web

1 Make a box and write a concept you want to remember inside it.

2 Draw boxes around the central box, and label each one with a category of information about the concept (e.g., definition, formula, descriptive details).

3 Fill in the boxes with relevant details as you read.

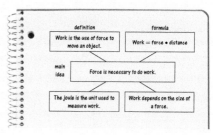

Look It Up! R21

Reading and Study Skills

Concept Map

1 Draw a large oval, and inside it write a major concept.

2 Draw an arrow from the concept to a smaller oval, in which you write a related concept.

3 On the arrow, write a verb that connects the two concepts.

4 Continue in this way, adding ovals and arrows in a branching structure, until you have explained as much as you can about the main concept.

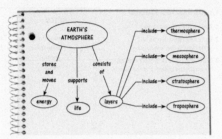

Venn Diagram

1 Draw two overlapping circles or ovals—one for each topic you are comparing—and label each one.

2 In the part of each circle that does not overlap with the other, list the characteristics that are unique to each topic.

3 In the space where the two circles overlap, list the characteristics that the two topics have in common.

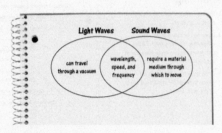

Cause-and-Effect Chart

1 Draw two boxes and connect them with an arrow.

2 In the first box, write the first event in a series (a cause).

3 In the second box, write a result of the cause (the effect).

4 Add more boxes when one event has many effects, or vice versa.

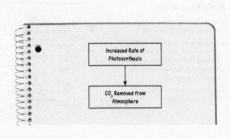

Process Diagram

A process can be a never-ending cycle. As you can see in this technology design process, engineers may backtrack and repeat steps, they may skip steps entirely, or they may repeat the entire process before a useable design is achieved.

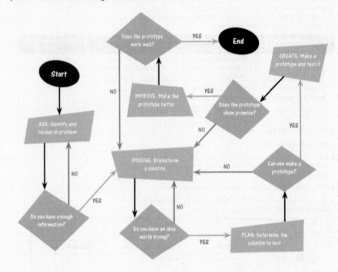

Reading and Study Skills

Using Vocabulary Strategies

Important science terms are highlighted where they are first defined in this book. One way to remember these terms is to take notes and make sketches when you come to them. Use the strategies on this page and the next for this purpose. You will also find a formal definition of each science term in the Glossary at the end of the book.

Description Wheel

1 Draw a small circle.

2 Write a vocabulary term inside the circle.

3 Draw several arms extending from the circle.

4 On the arms, write words and phrases that describe the term.

5 If you choose, add sketches that help you visualize the descriptive details or the concept as a whole.

Four Square

1 Draw a small oval and write a vocabulary term inside it.

2 Draw a large rectangle around the oval, and divide the rectangle into four smaller squares.

3 Label the smaller squares with categories of information about the term, such as: definition, characteristics, examples, non-examples, appearance, and root words.

4 Fill the squares with descriptive words and drawings that will help you remember the overall meaning of the term and its essential details.

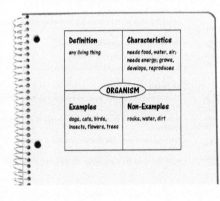

Frame Game

1 Draw a small rectangle, and write a vocabulary term inside it.

2 Draw a larger rectangle around the smaller one. Connect the corners of the larger rectangle to the corners of the smaller one, creating four spaces that frame the word.

3 In each of the four parts of the frame, draw or write details that help define the term. Consider including a definition, essential characteristics, an equation, examples, and a sentence using the term.

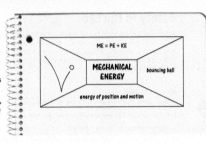

Magnet Word

1 Draw horseshoe magnet, and write a vocabulary term inside it.

2 Add lines that extend from the sides of the magnet.

3 Brainstorm words and phrases that come to mind when you think about the term.

4 On the lines, write the words and phrases that describe something essential about the term.

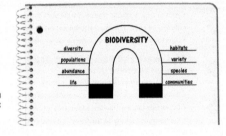

Word Triangle

1 Draw a triangle, and add lines to divide it into three parts.

2 Write a term and its definition in the bottom section of the triangle.

3 In the middle section, write a sentence in which the term is used correctly.

4 In the top section, draw a small picture to illustrate the term.

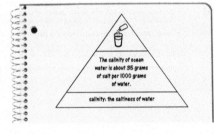

Science Skills

Safety in the Lab

Before you begin work in the laboratory, read these safety rules twice. Before starting a lab activity, read all directions and make sure that you understand them. Do not begin until your teacher has told you to start. If you or another student are injured in any way, tell your teacher immediately.

Dress Code

Eye Protection

Hand Protection

Clothing Protection

- Wear safety goggles at all times in the lab as directed.
- If chemicals get into your eyes, flush your eyes immediately.
- Do not wear contact lenses in the lab.
- Do not look directly at the sun or any intense light source or laser.
- Do not cut an object while holding the object in your hand.
- Wear appropriate protective gloves as directed.
- Wear an apron or lab coat at all times in the lab as directed.
- Tie back long hair, secure loose clothing, and remove loose jewelry.
- Do not wear open-toed shoes, sandals, or canvas shoes in the lab.

Glassware and Sharp Object Safety

Glassware Safety

Sharp Objects Safety

- Do not use chipped or cracked glassware.
- Use heat-resistant glassware for heating or storing hot materials.
- Notify your teacher immediately if a piece of glass breaks.
- Use extreme care when handling all sharp and pointed instruments.
- Cut objects on a suitable surface, always in a direction away from your body.

Chemical Safety

Chemical Safety

- If a chemical gets on your skin, on your clothing, or in your eyes, rinse it immediately (shower, faucet or eyewash fountain) and alert your teacher.
- Do not clean up spilled chemicals unless your teacher directs you to do so.
- Do not inhale any gas or vapor unless directed to do so by your teacher.
- Handle materials that emit vapors or gases in a well-ventilated area.

Electrical Safety

Electrical Safety

- Do not use equipment with frayed electrical cords or loose plugs.
- Do not use electrical equipment near water or when clothing or hands are wet.
- Hold the plug housing when you plug in or unplug equipment.

Heating and Fire Safety

Heating Safety

- Be aware of any source of flames, sparks, or heat (such as flames, heating coils, or hot plates) before working with any flammable substances.
- Know the location of lab fire extinguishers and fire-safety blankets.
- Know your school's fire-evacuation routes.
- If your clothing catches on fire, walk to the lab shower to put out the fire.
- Never leave a hot plate unattended while it is turned on or while it is cooling.
- Use tongs or appropriate insulated holders when handling heated objects.
- Allow all equipment to cool before storing it.

Wafting

Plant and Animal Safety

Plant Safety

Animal Safety

- Do not eat any part of a plant.
- Do not pick any wild plants unless your teacher instructs you to do so.
- Handle animals only as your teacher directs.
- Treat animals carefully and respectfully.
- Wash your hands thoroughly after handling any plant or animal.

Cleanup

Proper Waste Disposal

Hygienic Care

- Clean all work surfaces and protective equipment as directed by your teacher.
- Dispose of hazardous materials or sharp objects only as directed by your teacher.
- Keep your hands away from your face while you are working on any activity.
- Wash your hands thoroughly before you leave the lab or after any activity.

Science Skills

Designing, Conducting, and Reporting an Experiment

An experiment is an organized procedure to study something under specific conditions. Use the following steps of the scientific method when designing or conducting a controlled experiment.

1 Identify a Research Problem

Every day, you make observations by using your senses to gather information. Careful observations lead to good questions, and good questions can lead you to an experiment. Imagine, for example, that you pass a pond every day on your way to school, and you notice green scum beginning to form on top of it. You wonder what it is and why it seems to be growing. You list your questions, and then you do a little research to find out what is already known. A good place to start a research project is at the library. A library catalog lists all of the resources available to you at that library and often those found elsewhere. Begin your search by using:

* keywords or main topics.
* similar words, or synonyms, of your keyword.

The types of resources that will be helpful to you will depend on the kind of information you are interested in. And, some resources are more reliable for a given topic than others. Some different kinds of useful resources are:

* magazines and journals (or periodicals)—articles on a topic.
* encyclopedias—a good overview of a topic.
* books on specific subjects—details about a topic.
* newspapers—useful for current events.

The Internet can also be a great place to find information. Some of your library's reference materials may even be online. When using the Internet, however, it is especially important to make sure you are using appropriate and reliable sources. Websites of universities and government agencies are usually more accurate and reliable than websites created by individuals or businesses. Decide which sources are relevant and reliable for your topic. If in doubt, check with your teacher.

Take notes as you read through the information in these resources. You will probably come up with many questions and ideas for which you can do more research as needed. Once you feel you have enough information, think about the questions you have on the topic. Then, write down the problem that you want to investigate. Your notes might look like these.

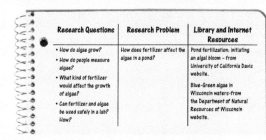

Research Questions	Research Problem	Library and Internet Resources
• How do algae grow? • How do people measure algae? • What kind of fertilizer would affect the growth of algae? • Can fertilizer and algae be used safely in a lab? How?	How does fertilizer affect the algae in a pond?	Pond fertilization: initiating an algal bloom – from University of California Davis website. Blue-Green algae in Wisconsin waters–from the Department of Natural Resources of Wisconsin website.

As you gather information from reliable sources, record details about each source, including author name(s), title, date of publication, and/or web address. Make sure to also note the specific information that you use from each source. Staying organized in this way will be important when you write your report and create a bibliography or works cited list. Recording this information and staying organized will help you credit the appropriate author(s) for the information that you have gathered.

Representing someone else's ideas or work as your own, (without giving the original author credit), is known as plagiarism. Plagiarism can be intentional or unintentional. The best way to make sure that you do not commit plagiarism is to always do your own work and to always give credit to others when you use their words or ideas.

Current scientific research is built on scientific research and discoveries that have happened in the past. This means that scientists are constantly learning from each other and combining ideas to learn more about the natural world through investigation. But, a good scientist always credits the ideas and research that they have gathered from other people to those people. There are more details about crediting sources and creating a bibliography under step 9.

2 Make a Prediction

A prediction is a statement of what you expect will happen in your experiment. Before making a prediction, you need to decide in a general way what you will do in your procedure. You may state your prediction in an if-then format.

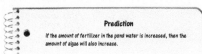

Prediction

If the amount of fertilizer in the pond water is increased, then the amount of algae will also increase.

Science Skills

3 Form a Hypothesis

Many experiments are designed to test a hypothesis. A hypothesis is a tentative explanation for an expected result. You have predicted that additional fertilizer will cause additional algae growth in pond water; your hypothesis should state the connection between fertilizer and algal growth.

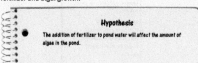

Hypothesis

The addition of fertilizer to pond water will affect the amount of algae in the pond.

4 Identify Variables to Test the Hypothesis

The next step is to design an experiment to test the hypothesis. The experimental results may or may not support the hypothesis. Either way, the information that results from the experiment may be useful for future investigations.

Experimental Group and Control Group

An experiment to determine how two factors are related has a control group and an experimental group. The two groups are the same, except that the investigator changes a single factor in the experimental group and does not change it in the control group.

Experimental Group: two containers of pond water with one drop of fertilizer solution added to each

Control Group: two containers of the same pond water sampled at the same time but with no fertilizer solution added

Variables and Constants

In a controlled experiment, a variable is any factor that can change. Constants are all of the variables that are kept the same in both the experimental group and the control group.

The independent variable is the factor that is manipulated or changed in order to test the effect of the change on another variable. The dependent variable is the factor the investigator measures to gather data about the effect.

Independent Variable	Dependent Variable	Constants
Amount of fertilizer in pond water	Growth of algae in the pond water	• Where and when the pond water is obtained
		• The type of container used
		• Light and temperature conditions where the water is stored

5 Write a Procedure

Write each step of your procedure. Start each step with a verb, or action word, and keep the steps short. Your procedure should be clear enough for someone else to use as instructions for repeating your experiment.

Procedure

1. Use the masking tape and the marker to label the containers with your initials, the date, and the identifiers "Jar 1 with Fertilizer," "Jar 2 with Fertilizer," "Jar 1 without Fertilizer," and "Jar 2 without Fertilizer."

2. Put on your gloves. Use the large container to obtain a sample of pond water.

3. Divide the water sample equally among the four smaller containers.

4. Use the eyedropper to add one drop of fertilizer solution to the two containers labeled, "Jar 1 with Fertilizer," and "Jar 2 with Fertilizer".

5. Cover the containers with clear plastic wrap. Use the scissors to punch ten holes in each of the covers.

6. Place all four containers on a window ledge. Make sure that they all receive the same amount of light.

7. Observe the containers every day for one week.

8. Use the ruler to measure the diameter of the largest clump of algae in each container, and record your measurements daily.

Science Skills

6 Experiment and Collect Data

Once you have all of your materials and your procedure has been approved, you can begin to experiment and collect data. Record both quantitative data (measurements) and qualitative data (observations), as shown below.

Algal Growth and Fertilizer

Date and Time	Experimental Group		Control Group		Observations
	Jar 1 with Fertilizer (diameter of algal clump in mm)	Jar 2 with Fertilizer (diameter of algal clump in mm)	Jar 1 without Fertilizer (diameter of algal clump in mm)	Jar 2 without Fertilizer (diameter of algal clump in mm)	
5/3 4:00 p.m.	0	0	0	0	condensation in all containers
5/4 4:00 p.m.	0	3	0	0	tiny green blobs in Jar 2 with fertilizer
5/5 4:15 p.m.	4	5	0	3	green blobs in Jars 1 and 2 with fertilizer and Jar 2 without fertilizer
5/6 4:00 p.m.	5	6	0	4	water light green in Jar 2 with fertilizer
5/7 4:00 p.m.	8	10	0	6	water light green in Jars 1 and 2 with fertilizer and Jar 2 without fertilizer
5/8 3:30 p.m.	10	18	0	6	cover off of Jar 2 with fertilizer
5/9 3:30 p.m.	14	23	0	8	drew sketches of each container

Drawings of Samples Viewed Under Microscope on 5/9 at 100x

Jar 1 with Fertilizer

Jar 2 with Fertilizer

Jar 1 without Fertilizer

Jar 2 without Fertilizer

7 Analyze Data

After you complete your experiment, you must analyze all of the data you have gathered. Tables, statistics, and graphs are often used in this step to organize and analyze both the qualitative and quantitative data. Sometimes, your qualitative data are best used to help explain the relationships you see in your quantitative data.

Computer graphing software is useful for creating a graph from data that you have collected. Most graphing software can make line graphs, pie charts, or bar graphs from data that has been organized in a spreadsheet. Graphs are useful for understanding relationships in the data and for communicating the results of your experiment.

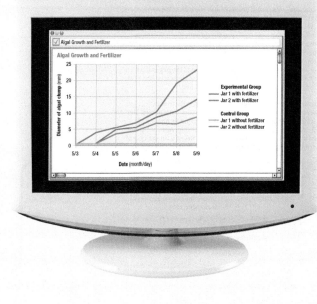

Science Skills

8 Make Conclusions

To draw conclusions from your experiment, first, write your results. Then, compare your results with your hypothesis. Do your results support your hypothesis? What have you learned?

Conclusion

More algae grew in the pond water to which fertilizer had been added than in the pond water to which fertilizer had not been added. My hypothesis was supported. I conclude that it is possible that the growth of algae in ponds can be influenced by the input of fertilizer.

9 Create a Bibliography or Works Cited List

To complete your report, you must also show all of the newspapers, magazines, journals, books, and online sources that you used at every stage of your investigation. Whenever you find useful information about your topic, you should write down the source of that information. Writing down as much information as you can about the subject can help you or someone else find the source again. You should at least record the author's name, the title, the date and where the source was published, and the pages in which the information was found. Then, organize your sources into a list, which you can title Bibliography or Works Cited.

Usually, at least three sources are included in these lists. Sources are listed alphabetically, by the authors' last names. The exact format of a bibliography can vary, depending on the style preferences of your teacher, school, or publisher. Also, books are cited differently than journals or websites. Below is an example of how different kinds of sources may be formatted in a bibliography.

BOOK: Hauschultz, Sara. *Freshwater Algae.* Brainard, Minnesota: Northwoods Publishing, 2011.

ENCYCLOPEDIA: Lasure, Sedona. "Algae is not all just pond scum." *Encyclopedia of Algae.* 2009.

JOURNAL: Johnson, Keagan. "Algae as we know it." *Sci Journal,* vol 64. (September 2010): 201-211.

WEBSITE: Dout, Bill. "Keeping algae scum out of birdbaths." *Help Keep Earth Clean. News.* January 26, 2011. <www.SaveEarth.org>.

© Houghton Mifflin Harcourt Publishing Company

Using a Microscope

Scientists use microscopes to see very small objects that cannot easily be seen with the eye alone. A microscope magnifies the image of an object so that small details may be observed. A microscope that you may use can magnify an object 400 times—the object will appear 400 times larger than its actual size.

Body The body separates the lens in the eyepiece from the objective lenses below.

Nosepiece The nosepiece holds the objective lenses above the stage and rotates so that all lenses may be used.

High-Power Objective Lens This is the largest lens on the nosepiece. It magnifies an image approximately 40 times.

Stage The stage supports the object being viewed.

Diaphragm The diaphragm is used to adjust the amount of light passing through the slide and into an objective lens.

Mirror or Light Source Some microscopes use light that is reflected through the stage by a mirror. Other microscopes have their own light sources.

Eyepiece Objects are viewed through the eyepiece. The eyepiece contains a lens that commonly magnifies an image ten times.

Coarse Adjustment This knob is used to focus the image of an object when it is viewed through the low-power lens.

Fine Adjustment This knob is used to focus the image of an object when it is viewed through the high-power lens.

Low-Power Objective Lens This is the smallest lens on the nosepiece. It magnifies images about 10 times.

Arm The arm supports the body above the stage. Always carry a microscope by the arm and base.

Stage Clip The stage clip holds a slide in place on the stage.

Base The base supports the microscope.

© Houghton Mifflin Harcourt Publishing Company

Science Skills

Measuring Accurately

Precision and Accuracy

When you do a scientific investigation, it is important that your methods, observations, and data be both precise and accurate.

Low precision: The darts did not land in a consistent place on the dartboard.

Precision, but not accuracy: The darts landed in a consistent place, but did not hit the bull's eye.

Prescision and accuracy: The darts landed consistently on the bull's eye.

Precision

In science, *precision* is the exactness and consistency of measurements. For example, measurements made with a ruler that has both centimeter and millimeter markings would be more precise than measurements made with a ruler that has only centimeter markings. Another indicator of precision is the care taken to make sure that methods and observations are as exact and consistent as possible. Every time a particular experiment is done, the same procedure should be used. Precision is necessary because experiments are repeated several times and if the procedure changes, the results might change.

Example

Suppose you are measuring temperatures over a two-week period. Your precision will be greater if you measure each temperature at the same place, at the same time of day, and with the same thermometer than if you change any of these factors from one day to the next.

Accuracy

In science, it is possible to be precise but not accurate. *Accuracy* depends on the difference between a measurement and an actual value. The smaller the difference, the more accurate the measurement.

Example

Suppose you look at a stream and estimate that it is about 1 meter wide at a particular place. You decide to check your estimate by measuring the stream with a meter stick, and you determine that the stream is 1.32 meters wide. However, because it is difficult to measure the width of a stream with a meter stick, it turns out that your measurement was not very accurate. The stream is actually 1.14 meters wide. Therefore, even though your estimate of about 1 meter was less precise than your measurement, your estimate was actually more accurate.

Graduated Cylinders

How to Measure the Volume of a Liquid with a Graduated Cylinder

- Be sure that the graduated cylinder is on a flat surface so that your measurement will be accurate.

- When reading the scale on a graduated cylinder, be sure to have your eyes at the level of the surface of the liquid.

- The surface of the liquid will be curved in the graduated cylinder. Read the volume of the liquid at the bottom of the curve, or meniscus (muh-NIHS-kuhs).

- You can use a graduated cylinder to find the volume of a solid object by measuring the increase in a liquid's level after you add the object to the cylinder.

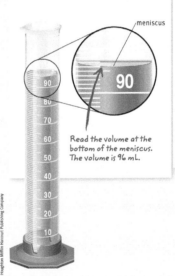

meniscus

Read the volume at the bottom of the meniscus. The volume is 96 mL.

Metric Rulers

How to Measure the Length of a Leaf with a Metric Ruler

1 Lay a ruler flat on top of the leaf so that the 1-centimeter mark lines up with one end. Make sure the ruler and the leaf do not move between the time you line them up and the time you take the measurement.

2 Look straight down on the ruler so that you can see exactly how the marks line up with the other end of the leaf.

3 Estimate the length by which the leaf extends beyond a marking. For example, the leaf below extends about halfway between the 4.2-centimeter and 4.3-centimeter marks, so the apparent measurement is about 4.25 centimeters.

4 Remember to subtract 1 centimeter from your apparent measurement, since you started at the 1-centimeter mark on the ruler and not at the end. The leaf is about 3.25 centimeters long (4.25 cm − 1 cm = 3.25 cm).

Science Skills

Triple Beam Balance

This balance has a pan and three beams with sliding masses, called riders. At one end of the beams is a pointer that indicates whether the mass on the pan is equal to the masses shown on the beams.

How to Measure the Mass of an Object

1 Make sure the balance is zeroed before measuring the mass of an object. The balance is zeroed if the pointer is at zero when nothing is on the pan and the riders are at their zero points. Use the adjustment knob at the base of the balance to zero it.

2 Place the object to be measured on the pan.

3 Move the riders one notch at a time away from the pan. Begin with the largest rider. If moving the largest rider one notch brings the pointer below zero, begin measuring the mass of the object with the next smaller rider.

4 Change the positions of the riders until they balance the mass on the pan and the pointer is at zero. Then add the readings from the three beams to determine the mass of the object.

300 g	position of largest rider
90 g	position of middle rider
+ 3 g	position of smallest rider
393 g	mass of beaker and water

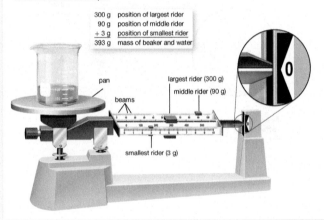

pan

beams

largest rider (300 g)

middle rider (90 g)

smallest rider (3 g)

Using the Metric System and SI Units

Scientists use International System (SI) units for measurements of distance, volume, mass, and temperature. The International System is based on powers of ten and the metric system of measurement.

Basic SI Units		
Quantity	Name	Symbol
length	meter	m
volume	liter	L
mass	gram	g
temperature	kelvin	K

SI Prefixes		
Prefix	Symbol	Power of 10
kilo-	k	1000
hecto-	h	100
deca-	da	10
deci-	d	0.1 or $\frac{1}{10}$
centi-	c	0.01 or $\frac{1}{100}$
milli-	m	0.001 or $\frac{1}{1000}$

Changing Metric Units

You can change from one unit to another in the metric system by multiplying or dividing by a power of 10.

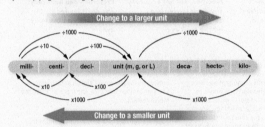

Change to a larger unit

milli- centi- deci- unit (m, g, or L) deca- hecto- kilo-

Change to a smaller unit

Example

Change 0.64 liters to milliliters.
1 Decide whether to multiply or divide.
2 Select the power of 10.

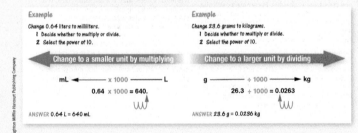

Change to a smaller unit by multiplying

mL ◄——— x 1000 ——— L

0.64 x 1000 = 640.

ANSWER 0.64 L = 640 mL

Example

Change 23.6 grams to kilograms.
1 Decide whether to multiply or divide.
2 Select the power of 10.

Change to a larger unit by dividing ►

g ——— ÷ 1000 ——► kg

26.3 ÷ 1000 = 0.0263

ANSWER 23.6 g = 0.0236 kg

Science Skills

Converting Between SI and U.S. Customary Units

Use the chart below when you need to convert between SI units and U.S. customary units.

SI Unit	From SI to U.S. Customary			From U.S. Customary to SI		
Length	**When you know**	**multiply by**	**to find**	**When you know**	**multiply by**	**to find**
kilometer (km) = 1000 m	kilometers	0.62	miles	miles	1.61	kilometers
meter (m) = 100 cm	meters	3.28	feet	feet	0.3048	meters
centimeter (cm) = 10 mm	centimeters	0.39	inches	inches	2.54	centimeters
millimeter (mm) = 0.1 cm	millimeters	0.04	inches	inches	25.4	millimeters
Area	**When you know**	**multiply by**	**to find**	**When you know**	**multiply by**	**to find**
square kilometer (km²)	square kilometers	0.39	square miles	square miles	2.59	square kilometers
square meter (m²)	square meters	1.2	square yards	square yards	0.84	square meters
square centimeter (cm²)	square centimeters	0.155	square inches	square inches	6.45	square centimeters
Volume	**When you know**	**multiply by**	**to find**	**When you know**	**multiply by**	**to find**
liter (L) = 1000 mL	liters	1.06	quarts	quarts	0.95	liters
	liters	0.26	gallons	gallons	3.79	liters
	liters	4.23	cups	cups	0.24	liters
	liters	2.12	pints	pints	0.47	liters
milliliter (mL) = 0.001 L	milliliters	0.20	teaspoons	teaspoons	4.93	milliliters
	milliliters	0.07	tablespoons	tablespoons	14.79	milliliters
	milliliters	0.03	fluid ounces	fluid ounces	29.57	milliliters
Mass	**When you know**	**multiply by**	**to find**	**When you know**	**multiply by**	**to find**
kilogram (kg) = 1000 g	kilograms	2.2	pounds	pounds	0.45	kilograms
gram (g) = 1000 mg	grams	0.035	ounces	ounces	28.35	grams

Temperature Conversions

Even though the kelvin is the SI base unit of temperature, the degree Celsius will be the unit you use most often in your science studies. The formulas below show the relationships between temperatures in degrees Fahrenheit (°F), degrees Celsius (°C), and kelvins (K).

$$°C = \frac{5}{9} \, (°F - 32) \qquad °F = \frac{9}{5} \, °C + 32 \qquad K = °C + 273$$

Examples of Temperature Conversions		
Condition	**Degrees Celsius**	**Degrees Fahrenheit**
Freezing point of water	0	32
Cool day	10	50
Mild day	20	68
Warm day	30	86
Normal body temperature	37	98.6
Very hot day	40	104
Boiling point of water	100	212

Math Refresher

Performing Calculations

Science requires an understanding of many math concepts. The following pages will help you review some important math skills.

Mean

The mean is the sum of all values in a data set divided by the total number of values in the data set. The mean is also called the *average*.

Example

Find the mean of the following set of numbers: 5, 4, 7, and 8.

Step 1 Find the sum.

$$5 + 4 + 7 + 8 = 24$$

Step 2 Divide the sum by the number of numbers in your set. Because there are four numbers in this example, divide the sum by 4.

$$24 ÷ 4 = 6$$

Answer The average, or mean, is 6.

Median

The median of a data set is the middle value when the values are written in numerical order. If a data set has an even number of values, the median is the mean of the two middle values.

Example

To find the median of a set of measurements, arrange the values in order from least to greatest. The median is the middle value.

13 mm 14 mm 16 mm 21 mm 23 mm

Answer The median is 16 mm.

Mode

The mode of a data set is the value that occurs most often.

Example

To find the mode of a set of measurements, arrange the values in order from least to greatest and determine the value that occurs most often.

13 mm, 14 mm, 14 mm, 16 mm, 21 mm, 23 mm, 25 mm

Answer The mode is 14 mm.

A data set can have more than one mode or no mode. For example, the following data set has modes of 2 mm and 4 mm:

2 mm 2 mm 3 mm 4 mm 4 mm

The data set below has no mode, because no value occurs more often than any other.

2 mm 3 mm 4 mm 5 mm

Math Refresher

Ratios

A **ratio** is a comparison between numbers, and it is usually written as a fraction.

Example
Find the ratio of thermometers to students if you have 36 thermometers and 48 students in your class.

Step 1   Write the ratio.

$$\frac{36 \text{ thermometers}}{48 \text{ students}}$$

Step 2   Simplify the fraction to its simplest form.

$$\frac{36}{48} = \frac{36 \div 12}{48 \div 12} = \frac{3}{4}$$

The ratio of thermometers to students is 3 to 4 or 3:4.

Proportions

A **proportion** is an equation that states that two ratios are equal.

$$\frac{3}{1} = \frac{12}{4}$$

To solve a proportion, you can use cross-multiplication. If you know three of the quantities in a proportion, you can use cross-multiplication to find the fourth.

Example
Imagine that you are making a scale model of the solar system for your science project. The diameter of Jupiter is 11.2 times the diameter of the Earth. If you are using a plastic-foam ball that has a diameter of 2 cm to represent the Earth, what must the diameter of the ball representing Jupiter be?

$$\frac{11.2}{1} = \frac{x}{2 \text{ cm}}$$

Step 1   Cross-multiply.

$$\frac{11.2}{1} = \frac{x}{2}$$

$$11.2 \times 2 = x \times 1$$

Step 2   Multiply.

$$22.4 = x \times 1$$

$$x = 22.4 \text{ cm}$$

You will need to use a ball that has a diameter of 22.4 cm to represent Jupiter.

Rates

A **rate** is a ratio of two values expressed in different units. A unit rate is a rate with a denominator of 1 unit.

Example
A plant grew 6 centimeters in 2 days. The plant's rate of growth was $\frac{6 \text{ cm}}{2 \text{ days}}$. To describe the plant's growth in centimeters per day, write a unit rate.

Divide numerator and denominator by 2:

$$\frac{6 \text{ cm}}{2 \text{ days}} = \frac{6 \text{ cm} \div 2}{2 \text{ days} \div 2}$$

Simplify: $= \frac{3 \text{ cm}}{1 \text{ day}}$

Answer The plant's rate of growth is 3 centimeters per day.

Percent

A **percent** is a ratio of a given number to 100. For example, 85% = 85/100. You can use percent to find part of a whole.

Example
What is 85% of 40?

Step 1   Rewrite the percent as a decimal by moving the decimal point two places to the left.

0.85

Step 2   Multiply the decimal by the number that you are calculating the percentage of.

$$0.85 \times 40 = 34$$

85% of 40 is 34.

Decimals

To **add** or **subtract decimals**, line up the digits vertically so that the decimal points line up. Then, add or subtract the columns from right to left. Carry or borrow numbers as necessary.

Example
Add the following numbers: 3.1415 and 2.96.

Step 1   Line up the digits vertically so that the decimal points line up.

$$\begin{array}{r} 3.1415 \\ + 2.96 \\ \hline \end{array}$$

Step 2   Add the columns from right to left, and carry when necessary.

$$\begin{array}{r} 3.1415 \\ + 2.96 \\ \hline 6.1015 \end{array}$$

The sum is 6.1015.

Fractions

A **fraction** is a ratio of two nonzero whole numbers.

Example
Your class has 24 plants. Your teacher instructs you to put 5 plants in a shady spot. What fraction of the plants in your class will you put in a shady spot?

Step 1   In the denominator, write the total number of parts in the whole.

$$\frac{?}{24}$$

Step 2   In the numerator, write the number of parts of the whole that are being considered.

$$\frac{5}{24}$$

So, $\frac{5}{24}$ of the plants will be in the shade.

Math Refresher

Simplifying Fractions

It is usually best to express a fraction in its simplest form. Expressing a fraction in its simplest form is called **simplifying a fraction.**

Example

Simplify the fraction $\frac{30}{45}$ to its simplest form.

Step 1 Find the largest whole number that will divide evenly into both the numerator and denominator. This number is called the greatest common factor (GCF).

Factors of the numerator 30:
1, 2, 3, 5, 6, 10, 15, 30

Factors of the denominator 45:
1, 3, 5, 9, 15, 45

Step 2 Divide both the numerator and the denominator by the GCF, which in this case is 15.

$$\frac{30}{45} = \frac{30 \div 15}{45 \div 15} = \frac{2}{3}$$

Thus, $\frac{30}{45}$ written in its simplest form is $\frac{2}{3}$.

Adding and Subtracting Fractions

To **add** or **subtract fractions** that have the same denominator, simply add or subtract the numerators.

Examples

$\frac{3}{5} + \frac{1}{5} = ?$ and $\frac{3}{4} - \frac{1}{4} = ?$

Step 1 Add or subtract the numerators.

$\frac{3}{5} + \frac{1}{5} = \frac{4}{5}$ and $\frac{3}{4} - \frac{1}{4} = \frac{2}{4}$

Step 2 Write in the common denominator, which remains the same.

$\frac{3}{5} + \frac{1}{5} = \frac{4}{5}$ and $\frac{3}{4} - \frac{1}{4} = \frac{2}{4}$

Step 3 If necessary, write the fraction in its simplest form.

$\frac{4}{5}$ cannot be simplified, and $\frac{2}{4} = \frac{1}{2}$.

To **add** or **subtract** fractions that have **different denominators**, first find the least common denominator (LCD).

Examples

$\frac{1}{2} + \frac{1}{6} = ?$ and $\frac{3}{4} - \frac{2}{3} = ?$

Step 1 Write the equivalent fractions that have a common denominator.

$\frac{3}{6} + \frac{1}{6} = ?$ and $\frac{9}{12} - \frac{8}{12} = ?$

Step 2 Add or subtract the fractions.

$\frac{3}{6} + \frac{1}{6} = \frac{4}{6}$ and $\frac{9}{12} - \frac{8}{12} = \frac{1}{12}$

Step 3 If necessary, write the fraction in its simplest form.

$\frac{4}{6} = \frac{2}{3}$, and $\frac{1}{12}$ cannot be simplified.

Multiplying Fractions

To **multiply fractions**, multiply the numerators and the denominators together, and then simplify the fraction to its simplest form.

Example

$\frac{5}{9} \times \frac{7}{10} = ?$

Step 1 Multiply the numerators and denominators.

$\frac{5}{9} \times \frac{7}{10} = \frac{5 \times 7}{9 \times 10} = \frac{35}{90}$

Step 2 Simplify the fraction.

$\frac{35}{90} = \frac{35 \div 5}{90 \div 5} = \frac{7}{18}$

Dividing Fractions

To **divide fractions**, first rewrite the divisor (the number you divide by) upside down. This number is called the reciprocal of the divisor. Then multiply and simplify if necessary.

Example

$\frac{5}{8} \div \frac{3}{2} = ?$

Step 1 Rewrite the divisor as its reciprocal.

$$\frac{3}{2} \rightarrow \frac{2}{3}$$

Step 2 Multiply the fractions.

$$\frac{5}{8} \times \frac{2}{3} = \frac{5 \times 2}{8 \times 3} = \frac{10}{24}$$

Step 3 Simplify the fraction.

$$\frac{10}{24} = \frac{10 \div 2}{24 \div 2} = \frac{5}{12}$$

Using Significant Figures

The **significant figures** in a decimal are the digits that are warranted by the accuracy of a measuring device.

When you perform a calculation with measurements, the number of significant figures to include in the result depends in part on the number of significant figures in the measurements. When you multiply or divide measurements, your answer should have only as many significant figures as the measurement with the fewest significant figures.

Examples

Using a balance and a graduated cylinder filled with water, you determined that a marble has a mass of 8.0 grams and a volume of 3.5 cubic centimeters. To calculate the density of the marble, divide the mass by the volume.

Write the formula for density: $\text{Density} = \frac{\text{mass}}{\text{volume}}$

Substitute measurements: $= \frac{8.0\,g}{3.5\,cm^3}$

Use a calculator to divide: $\approx 2.285714286\ g/cm^3$

Answer Because the mass and the volume have two significant figures each, give the density to two significant figures. The marble has a density of 2.3 grams per cubic centimeter.

Using Scientific Notation

Scientific notation is a shorthand way to write very large or very small numbers. For example, 73,500,000,000,000,000,000,000 kg is the mass of the moon. In scientific notation, it is 7.35×10^{22} kg. A value written as a number between 1 and 10, times a power of 10, is in scientific notation.

Examples

You can convert from standard form to scientific notation.

Standard Form	Scientific Notation
720,000	7.2×10^5
5 decimal places left	Exponent is 5.
0.000291	2.91×10^{-4}
4 decimal places right	Exponent is -4.

You can convert from scientific notation to standard form.

Scientific Notation	Standard Form
4.63×10^7	46,300,000
Exponent is 7.	7 decimal places right
1.08×10^{-6}	0.00000108
Exponent is -6.	6 decimal places left

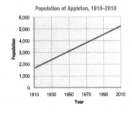

Math Refresher

Making and Interpreting Graphs

Circle Graph

A circle graph, or pie chart, shows how each group of data relates to all of the data. Each part of the circle represents a category of the data. The entire circle represents all of the data. For example, a biologist studying a hardwood forest in Wisconsin found that there were five different types of trees. The data table at right summarizes the biologist's findings.

Wisconsin Hardwood Trees	
Type of tree	Number found
Oak	600
Maple	750
Beech	300
Birch	1,200
Hickory	150
Total	3,000

How to Make a Circle Graph

1 To make a circle graph of these data, first find the percentage of each type of tree. Divide the number of trees of each type by the total number of trees, and multiply by 100%.

$$\frac{600 \text{ oak}}{3,000 \text{ trees}} \times 100\% = 20\%$$

$$\frac{750 \text{ maple}}{3,000 \text{ trees}} \times 100\% = 25\%$$

$$\frac{300 \text{ beech}}{3,000 \text{ trees}} \times 100\% = 10\%$$

$$\frac{1,200 \text{ birch}}{3,000 \text{ trees}} \times 100\% = 40\%$$

$$\frac{150 \text{ hickory}}{3,000 \text{ trees}} \times 100\% = 5\%$$

2 Now, determine the size of the wedges that make up the graph. Multiply each percentage by 360°. Remember that a circle contains 360°.

$20\% \times 360° = 72°$ $25\% \times 360° = 90°$

$10\% \times 360° = 36°$ $40\% \times 360° = 144°$

$5\% \times 360° = 18°$

3 Check that the sum of the percentages is 100 and the sum of the degrees is 360.

$20\% + 25\% + 10\% + 40\% + 5\% = 100\%$

$72° + 90° + 36° + 144° + 18° = 360°$

4 Use a compass to draw a circle and mark the center of the circle.

5 Then, use a protractor to draw angles of 72°, 90°, 36°, 144°, and 18° in the circle.

6 Finally, label each part of the graph, and choose an appropriate title.

A Community of Wisconsin Hardwood Trees

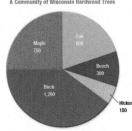

Line Graphs

Line graphs are most often used to demonstrate continuous change. For example, Mr. Smith's students analyzed the population records for their hometown, Appleton, between 1910 and 2010. Examine the data at right.

Because the year and the population change, they are the variables. The population is determined by, or dependent on, the year. Therefore, the population is called the **dependent variable,** and the year is called the **independent variable.** Each year and its population make a **data pair.** To prepare a line graph, you must first organize data pairs into a table like the one at right.

Population of Appleton, 1910–2010	
Year	Population
1910	1,800
1930	2,500
1950	3,200
1970	3,900
1990	4,600
2010	5,300

How to Make a Line Graph

1 Place the independent variable along the horizontal (x) axis. Place the dependent variable along the vertical (y) axis.

2 Label the x-axis "Year" and the y-axis "Population." Look at your greatest and least values for the population. For the y-axis, determine a scale that will provide enough space to show these values. You must use the same scale for the entire length of the axis. Next, find an appropriate scale for the x-axis.

3 Choose reasonable starting points for each axis.

4 Plot the data pairs as accurately as possible.

5 Choose a title that accurately represents the data.

Population of Appleton, 1910–2010

How to Determine Slope

Slope is the ratio of the change in the y-value to the change in the x-value, or "rise over run."

1 Choose two points on the line graph. For example, the population of Appleton in 2010 was 5,300 people. Therefore, you can define point A as (2010, 5,300). In 1910, the population was 1,800 people. You can define point B as (1910, 1,800).

2 Find the change in the y-value.
(y at point A) − (y at point B) =
5,300 people − 1,800 people =
3,500 people

3 Find the change in the x-value.
(x at point A) − (x at point B) =
2010 − 1910 = 100 years

4 Calculate the slope of the graph by dividing the change in y by the change in x.

$$slope = \frac{change \ in \ y}{change \ in \ x}$$

$$slope = \frac{3,500 \text{ people}}{100 \text{ years}}$$

$$slope = 35 \text{ people per year}$$

In this example, the population in Appleton increased by a fixed amount each year. The graph of these data is a straight line. Therefore, the relationship is **linear.** When the graph of a set of data is not a straight line, the relationship is **nonlinear.**

Math Refresher

Bar Graphs

Bar graphs can be used to demonstrate change that is not continuous. These graphs can be used to indicate trends when the data cover a long period of time. A meteorologist gathered the precipitation data shown here for Summerville for April 1–15 and used a bar graph to represent the data.

Precipitation in Summerville, April 1–15			
Date	Precipitation (cm)	Date	Precipitation (cm)
April 1	0.5	April 9	0.25
April 2	1.25	April 10	0.0
April 3	0.0	April 11	1.0
April 4	0.0	April 12	0.0
April 5	0.0	April 13	0.25
April 6	0.0	April 14	0.0
April 7	0.0	April 15	6.50
April 8	1.75		

How to Make a Bar Graph

1 Use an appropriate scale and a reasonable starting point for each axis.

2 Label the axes, and plot the data.

3 Choose a title that accurately represents the data.

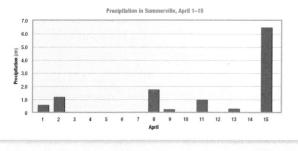

Precipitation in Summerville, April 1–15

Glossary

Pronunciation Key							
Sound	Symbol	Example	Respelling	Sound	Symbol	Example	Respelling
ă	a	pat	PAT	ŏ	ah	bottle	BAHT'l
ā	ay	pay	PAY	ō	oh	toe	TOH
âr	air	care	KAIR	ô	aw	caught	KAWT
ä	ah	father	FAH•ther	ôr	ohr	roar	ROHR
är	ar	argue	AR•gyoo	oi	oy	noisy	NOYZ•ee
ch	ch	chase	CHAYS	oŏ	u	book	BUK
ĕ	e	pet	PET	oō	oo	boot	BOOT
ē (at end of a syllable)	eh	settee lessee	seh•TEE leh•SEE	ou	ow	pound	POWND
ĕr	ehr	merry	MEHR•ee	s	s	center	SEN•ter
ē	ee	beach	BEECH	sh	sh	cache	CASH
g	g	gas	GAS	ŭ	uh	flood	FLUHD
ĭ	i	pit	PIT	ûr	er	bird	BERD
ĭ (at end of a syllable)	ih	guitar	gih•TAR	z	z	xylophone	ZY•luh•fohn
				z	z	bags	BAGZ
ī	y eye (only for a complete syllable)	pie island	PY EYE•luhnd	zh	zh	decision	dih•SIZH•uhn
				ə	uh	around broken focus	uh•ROWND BROH•kuhn FOH•kuhs
îr	ir	hear	HIR	ər	er	winner	WIN•er
j	j	germ	JERM	th	th	thin they	THIN THAY
k	k	kick	KIK				
ng	ng	thing	THING	w	w	one	WUHN
ngk	ngk	bank	BANGK	wh	hw	whether	HWETH•er

Glossary

A–B

adhesion (ad·HEE·zhuhn) the attractive force between two bodies of different substances that are in contact with each other (10)
adhesión la fuerza de atracción entre dos cuerpos de diferentes sustancias que están en contacto

air mass (AIR MAS) a large body of air throughout which temperature and moisture content are similar (184)
masa de aire un gran volumen de aire, cuya temperatura y cuyo contenido de humedad son similares en toda su extensión

air pressure (AIR PRESH·er) the measure of the force with which air molecules push on a surface (107, 160)
presión del aire la medida de la fuerza con la que las moléculas del aire empujan contra una superficie

aquifer (AH·kwuh·fer) a body of rock or sediment that stores groundwater and allows the flow of groundwater (36)
acuífero un cuerpo rocoso o sedimento que almacena agua subterránea y permite que fluya

atmosphere (AT·muh·sfir) a mixture of gases that surrounds a planet, moon, or other celestial body (106)
atmósfera una mezcla de gases que rodea un planeta, una luna, u otras cuerpos celestes

C

channel (CHAN·uhl) the path that a stream follows (34)
canal el camino que sigue un arroyo

cirrus cloud (SIR·uhs KLOWD) a feathery cloud that is composed of ice crystals and that has the highest altitude of any cloud in the sky (169)
nube cirro una nube liviana formada por cristales de hielo, la cual tiene la mayor altitud de todas las nubes en el cielo

climate (KLY·mit) the weather conditions in an area over a long period of time (226)
clima las condiciones del tiempo en un área durante un largo período de tiempo

cloud (KLOWD) a collection of small water droplets or ice crystals suspended in the air, which forms when the air is cooled and condensation occurs (166)
nube un conjunto de pequeñas gotitas de agua o cristales de hielo suspendidos en el aire, que se forma cuando el aire se enfría y ocurre condensación

cohesion (koh·HEE·zhuhn) the force that holds molecules of a single material together (10)
cohesión la fuerza que mantiene unidas a las moléculas de un solo material

condensation (kahn·den·SAY·shuhn) the change of state from a gas to a liquid (19)
condensación el cambio de estado de gas a líquido

conduction (kuhn·DUHK·shuhn) the transfer of energy as heat through a material (124)
conducción la transferencia de energía en forma de calor a través de un material

continental margin (column 2)

continental margin (kahn·tuh·NEN·ti MAR·jin) the shallow sea floor that is located between the shoreline and the deep-ocean bottom (59)
margen continental el suelo marino poco profundo que se ubica entre la costa y el fondo profundo del océano

convection (kuhn·VEK·shuhn) the movement of matter due to differences in density; the transfer of energy due to the movement of matter (122)
convección el movimiento de la materia debido a diferencias en la densidad; la transferencia de energía debido al movimiento de la materia

convection current (kuhn·VEK·shuhn KER·uhnt) any movement of matter that results from differences in density; may be vertical, circular, or cyclical (87)
corriente de convección cualquier movimiento de la materia que se produce como resultado de diferencias en la densidad; puede ser vertical, circular o cíclico

Coriolis effect (kohr·ee·OH·lis ih·FEKT) the curving of the path of a moving object from an otherwise straight path due to Earth's rotation (83, 135)
efecto de Coriolis la desviación de la trayectoria recta que experimentan los objetos en movimiento debido a la rotación de la Tierra

crest (KREST) the highest point of a wave (68)
cresta el punto más alto de una onda

cumulus cloud (KYOOM·yuh·luhs KLOWD) a low-level, billowy cloud that commonly has a top that resembles cotton balls and a dark bottom (169)
nube cúmulo una nube esponjada ubicada en un nivel bajo, cuya parte superior normalmente parece una bola de algodón y es obscura en la parte inferior

D

deep current (DEEP KER·uhnt) a streamlike movement of ocean water far below the surface (86)
corriente profunda un movimiento del agua del océano que es similar a una corriente y ocurre debajo de la superficie

deep-ocean basin (DEEP·oh·shuhn BAY·sin) the ocean floor under the deep-ocean water (59)
cuenca oceánica profunda el fondo del océano, que se encuentra bajo aguas profundas

dew point (DOO POYNT) at constant pressure and water vapor content, the temperature at which the rate of condensation equals the rate of evaporation (157, 167)
punto de rocío a presión y contenido de vapor de agua constantes, la temperatura a la que la tasa de condensación es igual a la tasa de evaporación

divide (dih·VYD) the boundary between drainage areas that have streams that flow in opposite directions (35)
división el límite entre áreas de drenaje que tienen corrientes que fluyen en direcciones opuestas

E

elevation (el·uh·VAY·shuhn) the height of an object above sea level (230)
elevación la altura de un objeto sobre el nivel del mar

evaporation (ee vap uh RAY shuhn) the change of state from a liquid to a gas that usually occurs at the surface of a liquid over a wide range of temperatures (18)
evaporación el cambio de estado de líquido a gaseoso que ocurre generalmente en la superficie de un líquido en un amplio rango de temperaturas

F

fog (FAWG) a cloud that forms near the ground and results in a reduction in visibility (172)
niebla una nube que se forma cerca del suelo y causa una reducción de la visibilidad

front (FRUHNT) the boundary between air masses of different densities and usually different temperatures (184)
frente el límite entre masas de aire de diferentes densidades y, normalmente, diferentes temperaturas

G

global warming (GLOH·buhl WOHR·ming) a gradual increase in average global temperature (246)
calentamiento global un aumento gradual de la temperatura global promedio

global wind (GLOH·buhl WIND) the movement of air over Earth's surface in patterns that are worldwide (136)
viento global el movimiento del aire sobre la superficie terrestre según patrones globales

greenhouse effect (GREEN·hows ih·FEKT) the warming of the surface and lower atmosphere of Earth that occurs when water vapor, carbon dioxide, and other gases absorb and reradiate thermal energy (110, 244)
efecto invernadero el calentamiento de la superficie y de la parte más baja de la atmósfera, el cual se produce cuando el vapor de agua, el dióxido de carbono y otros gases absorben y vuelven a irradiar la energía térmica

groundwater (GROWND·waw·ter) the water that is beneath Earth's surface (32)
agua subterránea el agua que está debajo de la superficie de la Tierra

H

heat (HEET) the energy transferred between objects that are at different temperatures (118)
calor la transferencia de energía entre objetos que están a temperaturas diferentes

humidity (hyoo·MID·ih·tee) the amount of water vapor in the air (157)
humedad la cantidad de vapor de agua que hay en el aire

hurricane (HER·ih·kayn) a severe storm that develops over tropical oceans and whose strong winds of more than 119 km/h spiral in toward the intensely low-pressure storm center (198)
huracán una tormenta severa que se desarrolla sobre océanos tropicales, con vientos fuertes que soplan a más de 119 km/h y que se mueven en espiral hacia el centro de presión extremadamente baja de la tormenta

I

ice age (EYES AYJ) a long period of climatic cooling during which the continents are glaciated repeatedly (243)
edad de hielo un largo período de enfriamiento del clima, durante el cual los continentes se ven repetidamente sometidos a la glaciación

J–K

jet stream (JET STREEM) a narrow band of strong winds that blow in the upper troposphere (138, 189)
corriente en chorro un cinturón delgado de vientos fuertes que soplan en la parte superior de la troposfera

L

latitude (LAT·ih·tood) the distance north or south from the equator; expressed in degrees (228)
latitud la distancia hacia el norte o hacia el sur del ecuador; se expresa en grados

lightning (LYT·ning) an electric discharge that takes place between two oppositely charged surfaces, such as between a cloud and the ground, between two clouds, or between two parts of the same cloud (197)
relámpago una descarga eléctrica que ocurre entre dos superficies que tienen carga opuesta, como por ejemplo, entre una nube y el suelo, entre dos nubes o entres dos partes de la misma nube

local wind (LOH·kuhl WIND) the movement of air over short distances; occurs in specific areas as a result of certain geographical features (140)
viento local el movimiento del aire a través de distancias cortas; se produce en áreas específicas como resultado de ciertas características geográficas

M-N

mechanical wave (mih-KAN-ih-kuhl WAYV) a wave that requires a medium through which to travel (70)
onda mecánica una onda que requiere un medio para desplazarse

mesosphere (MEZ-uh-sfir) the layer of the atmosphere between the stratosphere and the thermosphere and in which temperature decreases as altitude increases (108)
mesosfera la capa de la atmósfera que se encuentra entre la estratosfera y la termosfera, en la cual la temperatura disminuye al aumentar la altitud

meteorology (mee-tee-uh-RAHL-uh-jee) the scientific study of Earth's atmosphere, especially in relation to weather and climate (210)
meteorología el estudio científico de la atmósfera de la Tierra, sobre todo en lo que se relaciona al tiempo y al clima

mid-ocean ridge (MID-oh-shuhn RIJ) a long, undersea mountain chain that forms along the floor of the major oceans (60)
dorsal oceánica una larga cadena submarina de montañas que se forma en el suelo de los principales océanos

O

ocean current (OH-shuhn KER-uhnt) a movement of ocean water that follows a regular pattern (82)
corriente oceánica un movimiento del agua del océano que sigue un patrón regular

ocean trench (OH-shuhn TRENCH) a long, narrow, and steep depression on the ocean floor that forms when one tectonic plate subducts beneath another plate; trenches run parallel to volcanic island chains or to the coastlines of continents; also called a trench or a deep-ocean trench (61)
fosa oceánica una depresión larga, angosta y empinada que se encuentra en el fondo del océano y se forma cuando una placa tectónica se subduce bajo otra; las fosas submarinas corren en forma paralela a cadenas de islas volcánicas o a las costas continentales; también denominada fosa o fosa oceánica profunda

ocean wave (OH-shuhn WAYV) a disturbance on the ocean that transmits energy and takes the shape of a swell or ridge (68)
ola de mar una alteración del océano que transmite energía y adopta la forma de onda o cresta

ozone layer (OH-zohn LAY-er) the layer of the atmosphere at an altitude of 15 to 40 km in which ozone absorbs ultraviolet solar radiation (110)
capa de ozono la capa de la atmósfera ubicada a una altitud de 15 a 40 km, en la cual el ozono absorbe la radiación solar

P-Q

polarity (poh-LAIR-ih-tee) a property of a system in which two points have opposite characteristics, such as charges or magnetic poles (8)
polaridad la propiedad de un sistema en la que dos puntos tienen características opuestas, tales como las cargas o polos magnéticos

precipitation (prih-sip-ih-TAY-shuhn) any form of water that falls to Earth's surface from the clouds (19, 158)
precipitación cualquier forma de agua que cae de las nubes a la superficie de la Tierra

R

radiation (ray-dee-AY-shuhn) the transfer of energy as electromagnetic waves (120)
radiación la transferencia de energía en forma de ondas electromagnéticas

relative humidity (REL-uh-tiv hyoo-MID-ih-tee) the ratio of the amount of water vapor in the air to the amount of water vapor needed to reach saturation at a given temperature (157)
humedad relativa la proporción de la cantidad de vapor de agua que hay en el aire respecto a la cantidad de vapor de agua que se necesita para alcanzar la saturación a una temperatura dada

S

salinity (suh-LIN-ih-tee) a measure of the amount of dissolved salts in a given amount of liquid (54)
salinidad una medida de la cantidad de sales disueltas en una cantidad determinada de líquido

solvent (SAHL-vuhnt) in a solution, the substance in which the solute dissolves (11)
solvente en una solución, la sustancia en la que se disuelve el soluto

specific heat (spih-SIF-ik HEET) the quantity of heat required to raise a unit mass of homogeneous material 1 K or 1 °C in a specified way, given constant pressure and volume (11)
calor específico la cantidad de calor que se requiere para aumentar una unidad de masa de un material homogéneo 1 K ó 1 °C de una manera especificada, dados un volumen y una presión constantes

station model (STAY-shuhn MAHD-l) a pattern of meteorological symbols that represents the weather at a particular observing station and that is recorded on a weather map (214)
estación modelo el modelo de símbolos meteorológicos que representan el tiempo en una estación de observación determinada y que se registra en un mapa meteorológico

storm surge (STOHRM SERJ) a local rise in sea level near the shore that is caused by strong winds from a storm, such as those from a hurricane (199)
marea de tempestad un levantamiento local del nivel del mar cerca de la costa, el cual es resultado de los fuertes vientos de una tormenta, como por ejemplo, los vientos de un huracán

stratosphere (STRAT-uh-sfir) the layer of the atmosphere that is above the troposphere and in which temperature increases as altitude increases (108)
estratosfera la capa de la atmósfera que se encuentra encima de la troposfera y en la que la temperatura aumenta al aumentar la altitud

stratus cloud (STRAY-tuhs KLOWD) a gray cloud that has a flat, uniform base and that commonly forms at very low altitudes (169)
nube estrato una nube gris que tiene una base plana y uniforme y que comúnmente se forma a altitudes muy bajas

sublimation (suhb-luh-MAY-shuhn) the change of state from a solid directly to a gas (18)
sublimación cambio de estado por el cual un sólido se convierte directamente en un gas

surface current (SER-fuhs KER-uhnt) a horizontal movement of ocean water that is caused by wind and that occurs at or near the ocean's surface (82, 233)
corriente superficial un movimiento horizontal del agua del océano que es producido por el viento y que ocurre en la superficie del océano o cerca de ella

surface water (SER-fuhs WAW-ter) all the bodies of fresh water, salt water, ice, and snow that are found above the ground (32)
agua superficial todas las masas de agua dulce, agua salada, hielo y nieve que se encuentran arriba del suelo

T

temperature (TEM-per-uh-chur) a measure of how hot (or cold) something is; specifically, a measure of the average kinetic energy of the particles in an object (116)
temperatura una medida de qué tan caliente (o frío) está algo; específicamente, una medida de la energía cinética promedio de las partículas de un objeto

thermal energy (THER-muhl EN-er-jee) the kinetic energy of a substance's atoms (116)
energía térmica la energía cinética de los átomos de una sustancia

thermal expansion (THER-muhl ek-SPAN-shuhn) an increase in the size of a substance in response to an increase in the temperature of the substance (117)
expansión térmica un aumento en el tamaño de una sustancia en respuesta a un aumento en la temperatura de la sustancia

thermocline (THER-muh-klyn) a layer in a body of water in which water temperature drops with increased depth faster than it does in other layers (55)
termoclina una capa en una masa de agua en la que, al aumentar la profundidad, la temperatura del agua disminuye más rápido de lo que lo hace en otras capas

thermosphere (THER-muh-sfir) the uppermost layer of the atmosphere, in which temperature increases as altitude increases (108)
termosfera la capa más alta de la atmósfera, en la cual la temperatura aumenta a medida que la altitud aumenta

thunder (THUHN-der) the sound caused by the rapid expansion of air along an electrical strike (197)
trueno el sonido producido por la expansión rápida del aire a lo largo de una descarga eléctrica

thunderstorm (THUHN-der-stohrm) a usually brief, heavy storm that consists of rain, strong winds, lightning, and thunder (196)
tormenta eléctrica una tormenta fuerte y normalmente breve que consiste en lluvia, vientos fuertes, relámpagos y truenos

topography (tuh-PAHG-ruh-fee) the size and shape of the land surface features of a region, including its relief (230)
topografía el tamaño y la forma de las características de una superficie de terreno, incluyendo su relieve

tornado (tohr-NAY-doh) a destructive, rotating column of air that has very high wind speeds and that may be visible as a funnel-shaped cloud (200)
tornado una columna destructiva de aire en rotación cuyos vientos se mueven a velocidades muy altas y que puede verse como una nube con forma de embudo

transpiration (tran-spuh-RAY-shuhn) the process by which plants release water vapor into the air through stomata; also the release of water vapor into the air by other organisms (18)
transpiración el proceso por medio del cual las plantas liberan vapor de agua al aire por medio de los estomas; también, la liberación de vapor de agua al aire por otros organismos

tributary (TRIB-yuh-tehr-ee) a stream that flows into a lake or into a larger stream (34)
afluente un arroyo que fluye a un lago o a otro arroyo más grande

troposphere (TROH-puh-sfir) the lowest layer of the atmosphere, in which temperature decreases at a constant rate as altitude increases (108)
troposfera la capa inferior de la atmósfera, en la que la temperatura disminuye a una tasa constante a medida que la altitud aumenta

trough (TRAWF) the lowest point of a wave (68)
seno el punto más bajo de una onda

tsunami (tsoo-NAH-mee) a giant ocean wave that forms after a volcanic eruption, submarine earthquake, or landslide (75)
tsunami una ola gigante del océano que se forma después de una erupción volcánica, terremoto submarino o desprendimiento de tierras

U

upwelling (UHP·well·ing) the movement of deep, cold, and nutrient-rich water to the surface (88)
surgencia el movimiento de las aguas profundas, frías y ricas en nutrientes hacia la superficie

V

visibility (viz·uh·BIL·ih·tee) the distance at which a given standard object can be seen and identified with the unaided eye (161)
visibilidad la distancia a la que un objeto dado es perceptible e identificable para el ojo humano

W–Z

water cycle (WAW·ter SY·kuhl) the continuous movement of water between the atmosphere, the land, the oceans, and living things (16)
ciclo del agua el movimiento continuo del agua entre la atmósfera, la tierra, los océanos y los seres vivos

water table (WAW·ter TAY·buhl) the upper surface of underground water; the upper boundary of the zone of saturation (32)
capa freática el nivel más alto del agua subterránea; el límite superior de la zona de saturación

watershed (WAW·ter·shed) the area of land that is drained by a river system (35)
cuenca hidrográfica el área del terreno que es drenada por un sistema de ríos

wave (WAYV) a disturbance that transfers energy from one place to another; a wave can be a single cycle, or it can be a repeating pattern (68)
onda una alteración que transfiere energía de un lugar a otro; una onda puede ser un ciclo único o un patrón repetido

wave period (WAYV PIR·ee·uhd) the time required for corresponding points on consecutive waves to pass a given point (69)
período de onda el tiempo que se requiere para que los puntos correspondientes de ondas consecutivas pasen por un punto dado

wavelength (WAYV·lengkth) the distance from any point on a wave to the corresponding point on the next wave (68)
longitud de onda la distancia entre cualquier punto de una onda y el punto correspondiente de la siguiente onda

weather (WETH·er) the short-term state of the atmosphere, including temperature, humidity, precipitation, wind, and visibility (156, 226)
tiempo el estado de la atmósfera a corto plazo que incluye la temperatura, la humedad, la precipitación, el viento y la visibilidad

weather forecasting (WETH·er FOHR·kast·ing) the process of predicting atmospheric conditions by collecting and analyzing atmospheric data (210)
pronóstico del tiempo el proceso de predecir las condiciones atmosféricas reuniendo y analizando datos atmosféricos

wind (WIND) the movement of air caused by differences in air pressure (134, 160)
viento el movimiento de aire producido por diferencias en la presión barométrica

State STANDARDS FOR ENGLISH LANGUAGE ARTS
Correlations

This table shows correlations to the *Reading Standards for Literacy in Science and Technical Subjects* for grades 6–8.

Go online at **thinkcentral.com** for correlations of all *ScienceFusion* Modules to Common Core State Standards for Mathematics and to the rest of the *Common Core State Standards for English Language Arts*.

Grade 6–8 Standard Code	Citations for Module K "Introduction to Science and Technology"
READING STANDARDS FOR LITERACY IN SCIENCE AND TECHNICAL SUBJECTS	
Key Ideas and Details	
RST.6–8.1 Cite specific textual evidence to support analysis of science and technical texts.	*Student Edition* pp. 25, 75, 113 *Teacher Edition* pp. 98, 117
RST.6–8.2 Determine the central ideas or conclusions of a text; provide an accurate summary of the text distinct from prior knowledge or opinions.	*Student Edition* pp. 25, 32, 60, 75, 113, 132, 137, 149, 157, 163, 171, 189 *Teacher Edition* pp. 17, 21, 22, 35, 51, 61, 62, 98, 106, 117, 128, 130, 161, 178, 179, 206, 213, 237, 240. Also use "Synthesizing Key Topics" items in the Extend Science Concepts sections of the Teacher Edition.
RST.6–8.3 Follow precisely a multistep procedure when carrying out experiments, taking measurements, or performing technical tasks.	*Student Edition* pp. 83, 90–91 *Teacher Edition* p. 94 *Other* Use the Lab Manual, Project-Based Assessments, Video-Based Projects, and the Virtual Labs.
Craft and Structure	
RST.6–8.4 Determine the meaning of symbols, key terms, and other domain-specific words and phrases as they are used in a specific scientific or technical context relevant to *grades 6–8 texts and topics*.	*Student Edition* pp. 5, 17, 31, 43, 63, 64, 77, 93, 115, 131, 141, 153, 169, 181 *Teacher Edition* p. 111. Also use "Previewing Vocabulary" and "Reinforcing Vocabulary" items in the Explain Science Concepts sections of the Teacher Edition.

Grade 6–8 Standard Code (continued)	Citations for Module K "Introduction to Science and Technology"
RST.6–8.5 Analyze the structure an author uses to organize a text, including how the major sections contribute to the whole and to an understanding of the topic.	*Student Edition* p. 75 *Teacher Edition* pp. 51, 128, 213, 237, 240
RST.6–8.6 Analyze the author's purpose in providing an explanation, describing a procedure, or discussing an experiment in a text.	*Student Edition* pp. 25, 75 *Teacher Edition* pp. 14, 47, 98

Integration of Knowledge and Ideas

RST.6–8.7 Integrate quantitative or technical information expressed in words in a text with a version of that information expressed visually (e.g., in a flowchart, diagram, model, graph, or table).	*Student Edition* pp. 3, 35, 54, 66–67, 81, 122–123, 144, 147, 158, 159 *Teacher Edition* pp. 21, 40, 53, 54, 123, 194, 201, 206, 208, 224, 237, 240. Also use the "Graphic Organizer" items in the Teacher Edition. *Other* Use the lessons in the Digital Path.
RST.6–8.8 Distinguish among facts, reasoned judgment based on research findings, and speculation in a text.	*Student Edition* pp. 13, 25, 74–75, 113 *Teacher Edition* pp. 14, 17, 98
RST.6–8.9 Compare and contrast the information gained from experiments, simulations, video, or multimedia sources with that gained from reading a text on the same topic.	*Student Edition* pp. 113, 137, 163 *Teacher Edition* pp. 40, 79, 117 *Other* Use the Lab Manual, Project-Based Assessments, Video-Based Projects, and the lessons in the Digital Path.

Range of Reading and Level of Text Complexity

RST.6–8.10 By the end of grade 8, read and comprehend science/technical texts in the grades 6–8 text complexity band independently and proficiently.	*Student Edition* pp. 3, 22, 75, 90, 113, 132, 137, 149, 157, 163, 171, 189. Also use all lessons in the Student Edition. *Teacher Edition* pp. 47, 48, 61, 62, 117

Bibliography

This bibliography is a compilation of trade books that can supplement the materials covered in *ScienceFusion* Grades 6–8. Many of the books are recommendations of the National Science Teachers Association (NSTA) and the Children's Book Council (CBC) as outstanding science trade books for children. These books were selected because they meet the following rigorous criteria: they are of literary quality and contain substantial science content; the theories and facts are clearly distinguished; they are free of gender, ethnic, and socioeconomic bias; and they contain clear, accurate, up-to-date information. Several selections are award-winning titles, or their authors have received awards.

As with all materials you share with your class, we suggest you review the books first to ensure their appropriateness. While titles are current at time of publication, they may go out of print without notice.

Grades 6–8

Acids and Bases (Material Matters/ Express Edition) by Carol Baldwin (Heinemann-Raintree, 2005) focuses on the properties of acids and bases with photographs and facts.

Acids and Bases by Eurona Earl Tilley (Chelsea House, 2008) provides a thorough, basic understanding of acid and base chemistry, including such topics as naming compounds, writing formulas, and physical and chemical properties.

Across the Wide Ocean: The Why, How, and Where of Navigation for Humans and Animals at Sea by Karen Romano Young (Greenwillow, 2007) focuses on navigational tools, maps, and charts that researchers and explorers use to learn more about oceanography. AWARD-WINNING AUTHOR

Adventures in Sound with Max Axiom, Super Scientist (Graphic Science Series) by Emily Sohn (Capstone, 2007) provides information about sound through a fun graphic novel.

Air: A Resource Our World Depends on (Managing Our Resources) by Ian Graham (Heinemann-Raintree, 2005) examines this valuable natural resource and answers questions such as "How much does Earth's air weigh?" and "Why do plants need wind?"

The Alkaline Earth Metals: Beryllium, Magnesium, Calcium, Strontium, Barium, Radium (Understanding the Elements of the Periodic Table) by Bridget Heos (Rosen Central, 2009) describes the characteristics of these metals, including their similar physical and molecular properties.

All About Light and Sound (Mission: Science) by Connie Jankowski (Compass Point, 2010) focuses on the importance of light and sound and how without them we could not survive.

Alternative Energy: Beyond Fossil Fuels by Dana Meachen Rau (Compass Point, 2010) discusses the ways that water, wind, and sun provide a promising solution to our energy crisis and encourages readers to help the planet by conserving energy. AWARD-WINNING AUTHOR

Amazing Biome Projects You Can Build Yourself (Build it Yourself Series) by Donna Latham (Nomad, 2009) provides an overview of eight terrestrial biomes, including characteristics about climate, soil, animals, and plants.

Archaea: Salt-Lovers, Methane-Makers, Thermophiles, and Other Archaeans (A Class of Their Own) by David M. Barker (Crabtree, 2010) provides interesting facts about different types of archaeans.

The Art of Construction: Projects and Principles for Beginning Engineers and Architects by Mario Salvadori (Chicago Review, 2000) explains how tents, houses, stadiums, and bridges are built, and how to build models of such structures using materials found around the house. AWARD-WINNING AUTHOR

Astronomy: Out of This World! by Simon Basher and Dan Green (Kingfisher, 2009) takes readers on a journey of the universe and provides information about the planets, stars, galaxies, telescopes, space missions, and discoveries.

At the Sea Floor Café: Odd Ocean Critter Poems by Leslie Bulion (Peachtree, 2011) provides poetry to educate students about how ocean creatures search for food, capture prey, protect their young, and trick their predators.

Battery Science: Make Widgets That Work and Gadgets That Go by Doug Stillinger (Klutz, 2003) offers an array of activities and gadgets to get students excited about electricity.

The Biggest Explosions in the Universe by Sara Howard (BookSurge, 2009) tells the story of stars in our universe through fun text and captivating photographs.

Biology: Life as We Know It! by Simon Basher and Dan Green (Kingfisher, 2008) offers information about all aspects of life from the animals and plants to the minuscule cells, proteins, and DNA that bring them to life.

Birds of a Feather by Jane Yolen (Boyds Mills Press, 2011) offers facts and information about birds through fun poetry and beautiful photographs. AWARD-WINNING AUTHOR

Blackout!: Electricity and Circuits (Fusion) by Anna Claybourne (Heinemann-Raintree, 2005) provides an array of facts about electricity and how we rely on it for so many things in everyday life. AWARD-WINNING AUTHOR

Cell Division and Genetics by Robert Snedden (Heinemann, 2007) explains various aspects of cells and the living world, including what happens when cells divide and how characteristics are passed on from one generation to another. AWARD-WINNING AUTHOR

Chemistry: Getting a Big Reaction by Dan Green and Simon Basher (Kingfisher, 2010) acts as a guide about the chemical "characters" that fizz, react, and combine to make up everything around us.

Cool Stuff Exploded by Chris Woodford (Dorling Kindersley, 2008) focuses on today's technological marvels and tomorrow's jaw-dropping devices. OUTSTANDING SCIENCE TRADE BOOK

Disaster Deferred: How New Science Is Changing Our View of Earthquake Hazards in the Midwest by Seth Stein (Columbia University, 2010) discusses technological innovations that make earthquake prediction possible.

The Diversity of Species (Timeline: Life on Earth) by Michael Bright (Heinemann, 2008) explains how and why things on Earth have genetic and physical differences and how they have had and continue to have an impact on Earth.

Drip! Drop!: How Water Gets to Your Tap by Barbara Seuling (Holiday House, 2000) introduces students to JoJo and her dog, Willy, who explain the water cycle and introduce fun experiments about filtration, evaporation, and condensation. AWARD-WINNING AUTHOR

Eat Fresh Food: Awesome Recipes for Teen Chefs by Rozanne Gold (Bloomsbury, 2009) includes more than 80 recipes and places a strong emphasis on fresh foods throughout the book.

Eco-Tracking: On the Trail of Habitat Change (Worlds of Wonder) by Daniel Shaw (University of New Mexico, 2010) recounts success stories of young people involved in citizen science efforts and encourages others to join in to preserve nature's ecosystems.

Electric Mischief: Battery-Powered Gadgets Kids Can Build by Alan Bartholomew (Kids Can Press, 2002) offers a variety of fun projects that include making battery connections and switches and building gadgets such as electric dice and a bumper car.

Electricity (Why It Works) by Anna Claybourne (QED Publishing, 2008) provides information about electricity in an easy-to-follow manner. AWARD-WINNING AUTHOR

Electricity and Magnetism (Usborne Understand Science) by Peter Adamczyk (Usborne, 2008) explains the basics about electricity and magnetism, including information about static electricity, electric circuits, and electromagnetism.

Energy Transfers (Energy Essentials) by Nigel Saunders and Steven Chapman (Raintree, 2005) explains the different types of energy, how they can change, and how different forms of energy help us in our everyday lives.

The Everything Machine by Matt Novak (Roaring Brook, 2009) tells the silly story of a machine that does everything for a group of people until they wake up one day and discover that the machine has stopped working. AWARD-WINNING AUTHOR

Experiments with Plants and Other Living Things by Trevor Cook (PowerKids, 2009) provides fun, hands-on experiments to teach students about flowers, plants, and biology.

Exploring the Oceans: Seafloor by John Woodward (Heinemann, 2004) takes readers on a virtual tour through the bottom part of the ocean, highlighting the plants and animals that thrive in this environment.

Extreme Structures: Mega Constructions of the 21st Century (Science Frontiers) by David Jefferis (Crabtree, 2006) takes a look at how some of the coolest buildings in the world were built and what other kinds of structures are being planned for the future. AWARD-WINNING AUTHOR

Fascinating Science Projects: Electricity and Magnetism by Bobbi Searle (Aladdin, 2002) teaches the concepts of electricity and magnetism through dozens of projects and experiments and color illustrations.

Fizz, Bubble and Flash!: Element Explorations and Atom Adventures for Hands-on Science Fun! by Anita Brandolini, Ph.D. (Williamson, 2003) introduces chemistry to students in a nonintimidating way and focuses on the elements and the periodic table. PARENTS' CHOICE

Floods: Hazards of Surface and Groundwater Systems (The Hazardous Earth) by Timothy M. Kusky (Facts on File, 2008) explores the processes that control the development and flow in river and stream systems and when these processes become dangerous.

Fossils (Geology Rocks!) by Rebecca Faulkner (Raintree, 2008) educates students about rock formation and the processes and characteristics of rocks and fossils.

Friends: True Stories of Extraordinary Animal Friendships by Catherine Thimmesh (Houghton Mifflin Harcourt, 2011) depicts true stories of unlikely animal friendships, including a wild polar bear and a sled dog as well as a camel and a Vietnamese pig. AWARD-WINNING AUTHOR

The Frog Scientist (Scientists in the Field) by Pamela S. Turner (Houghton Mifflin Harcourt, 2009) follows a scientist and his protégés as they research the effects of atrazine-contaminated water on vulnerable amphibians. BOOKLIST EDITORS' CHOICE

From Steam Engines to Nuclear Fusion: Discovering Energy (Chain Reactions) by Carol Ballard (Heinemann-Raintree, 2007) tells the fascinating story of energy, from the heat produced by a simple fire to the extraordinary power contained in an atom.

Fully Charged (Everyday Science) by Steve Parker (Heinemann-Raintree, 2005) explains how electricity is generated, harnessed, and used and also the difference between electricity, including static electricity, and electronics. AWARD-WINNING AUTHOR

Galileo for Kids: His Life and Ideas by Richard Panchyk (Chicago Review, 2005) includes experiments that demonstrate scientific principles developed by the astronomer Galileo.

Genes and DNA by Richard Walker (Kingfisher, 2003) offers an abundance of information about characteristics of genes, gene function, DNA technology, and genetic engineering, as well as other fascinating topics. NSTA TRADE BOOK; OUTSTANDING SCIENCE TRADE BOOK

Hands-on Science Series: Simple Machines by Steven Souza and Joseph Shortell (Walch, 2001) investigates the concepts of work, force, power, efficiency, and mechanical advantage.

How Animals Work by David Burnie (Dorling Kindersley, 2010) provides vivid photographs and intriguing text to describe various animals and their characteristics, diets, and families. AWARD-WINNING AUTHOR

How Does an Earthquake Become a Tsunami? (How Does it Happen?) by Linda Tagliaferro (Heinemann-Raintree, 2009) describes the changes in water, waves, and tides that occur between an earthquake and a tsunami. AWARD-WINNING AUTHOR

How the Future Began: Machines by Clive Gifford (Kingfisher, 1999) acts as a guide to historical and current developments in the field of machinery, including mass production, computers, robots, microengineering, and communications technology. AWARD-WINNING AUTHOR

How Scientists Work (Simply Science) by Natalie M. Rosinsky (Compass Point, 2003) discusses the scientific method, equipment, and procedures and also describes how scientists compile information and answer questions.

How to Clean a Hippopotamus: A Look at Unusual Animal Partnerships by Steve Jenkins and Robin Page (Houghton Mifflin Harcourt, 2010) explores animal symbiosis with fun illustrations and a close-up, step-by-step view of some of nature's most fascinating animal partnerships. ALA NOTABLE BOOK

Human Spaceflight (Frontiers in Space) by Joseph A. Angelo (Facts on File, 2007) examines the history of space exploration and the evolution of space technology from the dawn of the space age to the present time.

The Hydrosphere: Agent of Change by Gregory L. Vogt, Ed.D. (Twenty-First Century, 2006) discusses the impact this 20-mile-thick sphere has had on the surface of the planet and the processes that go on there, including the ability of Earth to sustain life. AWARD-WINNING AUTHOR

In Rivers, Lakes, and Ponds (Under the Microscope) by Sabrina Crewe (Chelsea Clubhouse, 2010) educates readers about the microscopic critters that live in these various bodies of water.

A Kid's Guide to Climate Change and Global Warming: How to Take Action! by Cathryn Berger Kaye, M.A. (Free Spirit, 2009) encourages students to learn about the climate changes happening around the world and to get involved to help save our planet.

Lasers (Lucent Library of Science and Technology) by Don Nardo (Lucent, 2003) discusses the scientific discovery and development of lasers—high-intensity light—and their use in our daily lives. AWARD-WINNING AUTHOR

Leonardo's Horse by Jean Fritz (Putnam, 2001) tells the story of Leonardo da Vinci—the curious and inquisitive artist, engineer, and astronomer—who created a detailed horse sculpture for the city of Milan. ALA NOTABLE BOOK; NOTABLE SOCIAL STUDIES TRADE BOOK; NOTABLE CHILDREN'S BOOK IN THE LANGUAGE ARTS

Light: From Sun to Bulbs by Christopher Cooper (Heinemann, 2003) invites students to investigate the dazzling world of physical science and light through fun experiments. AWARD-WINNING AUTHOR

Magnetism and Electromagnets (Sci-Hi: Physical Science) by Eve Hartman (Raintree, 2008) offers colorful illustrations, photographs, quizzes, charts, graphs, and text to teach students about magnetism.

Making Good Choices About Nonrenewable Resources (Green Matters) by Paula Johanson (Rosen Central, 2009) focuses on the different types of nonrenewable natural resources, alternative resources, conservation, and making positive consumer choices.

Making Waves: Sound (Everyday Science) by Steve Parker (Heinemann-Raintree, 2005) describes what sound is, how it is formed and used, and properties associated with sound, such as pitch, speed, and volume. AWARD-WINNING AUTHOR

The Manatee Scientists: Saving Vulnerable Species (Scientists in the Field Series) by Peter Lourie (Houghton Mifflin Harcourt, 2011) discusses three species of manatees and the importance of preserving these mammals. AWARD-WINNING AUTHOR

The Man Who Named the Clouds by Julie Hannah and Joan Holub (Albert Whitman, 2006) tells the story of 18th-century English meteorologist Luke Howard and also discusses the ten classifications of clouds.

Medicine in the News (Science News Flash) by Brian R. Shmaefsky, Ph.D. (Chelsea House, 2007) focuses on medical advancements that are in the news today and the innovative tools that are used for diagnosis and treatment.

Metals and Metalloids (Periodic Table of the Elements) by Monica Halka, Ph.D., and Brian Nordstrom, Ed.D. (Facts on File, 2010), offers information about the physics, chemistry, geology, and biology of metals and metalloids.

Meteorology: Ferguson's Careers in Focus by Ferguson (Ferguson, 2011) profiles 18 different careers pertaining to the science of the atmosphere and its phenomena.

The Microscope (Great Medical Discoveries) by Adam Woog (Lucent, 2003) recounts how the microscope has had an impact on the history of medicine.

Microscopes and Telescopes: Great Inventions by Rebecca Stefoff (Marshall Cavendish Benchmark, 2007) describes the origin, history, development, and societal impact of the telescope and microscope. OUTSTANDING SCIENCE TRADE BOOK

Mighty Animal Cells by Rebecca L. Johnson (Millbrook, 2007) takes readers on a journey to discover how people and animals grow from just one single cell. AWARD-WINNING AUTHOR

Moon (Eyewitness Books) by Jacqueline Mitton (Dorling Kindersley, 2009) offers information about our planet's mysterious nearest neighbor, from the moon's waterless seas and massive craters to its effect on Earth's ocean tides and its role in solar eclipses. AWARD-WINNING AUTHOR

MP3 Players (Let's Explore Technology Communications) by Jeanne Sturm (Rourke, 2010) discusses the technological advances in music in our society.

Nanotechnologist (Cool Science Careers) by Ann Heinrichs (Cherry Lake, 2009) provides information about nanotechnologists—scientists who work with materials on a subatomic or atomic level.

Ocean: An Illustrated Atlas by Sylvia A. Earle (National Geographic, 2008) provides an overview on the ocean as a whole, each of the major ocean basins, and the future of the oceans. AWARD-WINNING AUTHOR

Oceans (Insiders) by Beverly McMillan and John A. Musick (Simon & Schuster, 2007) takes readers on a 3-D journey of the aquatic universe—exploring the formation of waves and tsunamis as well as the plant and animal species that live beneath the ocean's surface.

Organic Chemistry and Biochemistry (Facts at Your Fingertips) by Graham Bateman (Brown Bear, 2011) provides diagrams, experiments, and testing aids to teach students the basics about organic chemistry and biochemistry.

An Overcrowded World?: Our Impact on the Planet (21st Century Debates) by Rob Bowden (Heinemann, 2002) investigates how and why the world's population is growing so fast, the effects of this growth on wildlife and habitats, and the pressure on resources, and suggests ways of controlling growth.

The Pebble in My Pocket: A History of Our Earth by Meredith Hooper (Viking, 1996) follows the course of a pebble, beginning 480 million years ago, through a fiery volcano and primordial forest and along the icy bottom of a glacier and how it looks today as the result of its journey. AWARD-WINNING AUTHOR

The Periodic Table: Elements with Style! by Simon Basher and Adrian Dingle (Kingfisher, 2007) offers information about the different elements that make up the periodic table and their features and characteristics.

Phenomena: Secrets of the Senses by Donna M. Jackson (Little, Brown, 2008) focuses on the senses and how to interpret them and discusses ways that technology is changing how we experience the world around us. AWARD-WINNING AUTHOR

Pioneers of Light and Sound (Mission: Science) by Connie Jankowski (Compass Point, 2010) focuses on various scientists and their accomplishments and achievements.

Planet Animal: Saving Earth's Disappearing Animals by B. Taylor (Barron's, 2009) focuses on the planet's most endangered animals, their relationships to the environment, and steps that are being taken to try to save these animals from extinction.

Plant and Animal Science Fair Projects (Biology Science Projects Using the Scientific Method) by Yael Calhoun (Enslow, 2010) provides an array of experiments about plants and animals and describes the importance of the scientific method, forming a hypothesis, and recording data for any given project.

Plant Secrets: Plant Life Processes by Anna Claybourne (Heinemann-Raintree, 2005) includes informative text, vivid photographs, and detailed charts about characteristics of various plants. AWARD-WINNING AUTHOR

Polar Regions: Human Impacts (Our Fragile Planet) by Dana Desonie (Chelsea House, 2008) focuses on pollutants and global warming in the Arctic and Antarctic and future dangers that will occur if our planet continues on its current path.

Potato Clocks and Solar Cars: Renewable and Non-renewable Energy by Elizabeth Raum (Raintree, 2007) explores various topics, including alternative energy sources, fossil fuels, and sustainable energy.

The Power of Pressure (How Things Work) by Andrew Dunn (Thomson Learning, 1993) explains how water pressure and air work and how they are used in machines.

Protists and Fungi (Discovery Channel School Science) by Katie King and Jacqueline A. Ball (Gareth Stevens, 2003) focuses on the appearance, behavior, and characteristics of various protists and fungi, using examples of algae, mold, and mushrooms.

Protozoans, Algae and Other Protists by Steve Parker (Compass Point, 2010) introduces readers to the parts, life cycles, and reproduction of various types of protists, from microscopic protozoans to seaweedlike algae, and some of the harmful effects protists have on humans. AWARD-WINNING AUTHOR

Sally Ride: The First American Woman in Space by Tom Riddolls (Crabtree, 2010) focuses on the growth and impact of Sally Ride Science—an educational program founded by the astronaut to encourage girls to pursue hobbies and careers in science.

Science and Technology in 20th Century American Life by Christopher Cumo (Greenwood, 2008) takes readers on a history of technology from agricultural implements through modern computers, telecommunications, and skateboards.

Sedimentary Rock (Geology Rocks!) by Rebecca Faulkner (Raintree, 2008) educates students about rock formation and the processes and characteristics of sedimentary rock.

Shaping the Earth by Dorothy Hinshaw Patent (Clarion/Houghton Mifflin, 2000) combines vivid photographs with informative text to explain the forces that have created the geological features on Earth's surface. AWARD-WINNING AUTHOR

Silent Spring by Rachel Carson (Houghton Mifflin, 2002) celebrates marine biologist and environmental activist Rachel Carson's contribution to Earth through an array of essays.

Skywalkers: Mohawk Ironworkers Build the City by David Weitzman (Flash Point, 2010) focuses on the ironworkers who constructed bridges and skyscrapers in New York and Canada. AWARD-WINNING AUTHOR

Sustaining Earth's Energy Resources (Environment at Risk) by Ann Heinrichs (Marshall Cavendish, 2010) offers information on Earth's sources of nonrenewable and renewable energy, how they are used, and their disadvantages and benefits.

Team Moon: How 400,000 People Landed Apollo 11 on the Moon by Catherine Thimmesh (Houghton Mifflin, 2006) tells the story of the first moon landing and celebrates the dedication, ingenuity, and perseverance of the people who made this event happen. ALA NOTABLE BOOK; ORBIS PICTUS HONOR; NOTABLE CHILDREN'S BOOK IN THE LANGUAGE ARTS; ALA BEST BOOK FOR YOUNG ADULTS; GOLDEN KITE HONOR

The Top of the World: Climbing Mount Everest by Steve Jenkins (Houghton Mifflin, 1999) describes the conditions and terrain of Mount Everest, attempts that have been made to scale this peak, and information about the equipment and techniques of mountain climbing. ALA NOTABLE BOOK; SLJ BEST BOOK; BOSTON GLOBE–HORN BOOK AWARD; ORBIS PICTUS HONOR

Transmission of Power by Fluid Pressure: Air and Water by William Donaldson (Nabu, 2010) describes the transmission of fluid pressure as it pertains to the elements of air and water in the world of motion, forces, and energy.

Tsunami: The True Story of an April Fools' Day Disaster by Gail Langer Karwoski (Darby Creek, 2006) offers a variety of viewpoints about the wave that struck Hawaii in 1946. NOTABLE SOCIAL STUDIES TRADE BOOK

Vapor, Rain, and Snow: The Science of Clouds and Precipitation (Weatherwise) by Paul Fleisher (Lerner, 2010) answers an array of questions about water, such as "How does a cloud form?" and "Why do ice cubes shrink in the freezer?" AWARD-WINNING AUTHOR

Water Supplies in Crisis (Planet in Crisis) by Russ Parker (Rosen Central, 2009) describes a world where safe drinking water is not readily available, polluted water brings disease, and lakes are disappearing.

Weird Meat-Eating Plants (Bizarre Science) by Nathan Aaseng (Enslow, 2011) provides information about a variety of carnivorous plants, reversing the food chain's usual order. AWARD-WINNING AUTHOR

What Are Igneous Rocks? (Let's Rock!) by Molly Aloian (Crabtree, 2010) explains how granite, basalt, lava, silica, and quartz are formed after hot molten rock cools.

What's Living Inside Your Body? by Andrew Solway (Heinemann, 2004) offers information about an array of viruses, germs, and parasites that thrive inside the human body.

Why Should I Bother to Keep Fit? (What's Happening?) by Kate Knighton and Susan Meredith (Usborne, 2009) motivates students to get fit and stay fit.

The World of Microbes: Bacteria, Viruses, and Other Microorganisms (Understanding Genetics) by Janey Levy (Rosen Classroom, 2010) describes the world of microbes, a history of microbiology, and the characteristics of both harmful and beneficial bacteria.

Written in Bone: Buried Lives of Jamestown and Colonial Maryland by Sally M. Walker (Carolrhoda, 2009) describes the way that scientists used forensic anthropology to investigate colonial-era graves near Jamestown, Virginia. ALA NOTABLE BOOK; OUTSTANDING SCIENCE TRADE BOOK; NOTABLE SOCIAL STUDIES TRADE BOOK

You Blink Twelve Times a Minute and Other Freaky Facts About the Human Body by Barbara Seuling (Picture Window, 2009) provides fun and unusual facts about various ailments, medical marvels, and body parts and their functions. AWARD-WINNING AUTHOR

Correlation to
ScienceSaurus

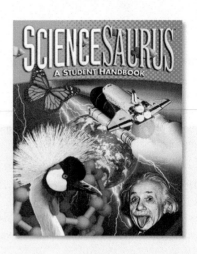

*ScienceSaurus, **A Student Handbook,*** is a "mini-encyclopedia" that students can use to find out more about unit topics. It contains numerous resources including concise content summaries, an almanac, many tables, charts, and graphs, history of science, and a glossary. ***ScienceSaurus*** is available from Houghton Mifflin Harcourt..

ScienceFusion Page References	Topics	*ScienceFusion* Grades 6-8
Scientific Investigation, pp. 1–19		
	Scientific Inquiry	Mod K, Unit 1, Lessons 1-3
		Mod K, Unit 2, Lessons 1, 3
	Designing Your Own Investigations	Mod K, Unit 1, Lessons 2, 4
Working in the Lab, pp. 20–72		
	Laboratory Safety	Mod K, Unit 2, Lesson 2
	Glassware and Microscopes	Mod K, Unit 2, Lesson 2
	Measurement	Mod K, Unit 2, Lesson 2
Life Science, pp. 73–164		
	Structure of Life	Mod A, Unit 1, Lessons 1-3
		Mod A, Unit 2, Lessons 1, 3
	Human Biology	Mod C, Unit 1, Lessons 1-6
		Mod C, Unit 2, Lesson 1
	Physiology and Behavior	Mod A, Unit 1, Lesson 5
		Mod B, Unit 2, Lessons 3-6
	Genes and Heredity	Mod A, Unit 2, Lessons 2-6
	Change and Diversity of Life	Mod B, Unit 1, Lessons 2-4

ScienceFusion Page References	Topics	*ScienceFusion* Grades 6-8
Life Science, pp. 73–164 (continued)		
	Ecosystems	Mod D, Unit 1, Lessons 1-4
		Mod D, Unit 2, Lessons 1-4
		Mod D, Unit 2, Lesson 5
	Classification	Mod B, Unit 1, Lesson 5
		Mod B, Unit 2, Lessons 3, 5
Earth Science, pp. 165–248		
	Geology	Mod E, Unit 4, Lesson 1
		Mod E, Unit 3, Lessons 1-3
		Mod E, Unit 4, Lessons 2-5
		Mod E, Unit 1, Lessons 2-4
		Mod E, Unit 2, Lessons 1-4
		Mod E, Unit 1, Lessons 3, 5
	Oceanography	Mod F, Unit 1, Lesson 1
		Mod F, Unit 2, Lessons 1, 3
	Meteorology	Mod F, Unit 3, Lesson 1
		Mod F, Unit 1, Lesson 2
		Mod F, Unit 4, Lesson 1, 2, 3, 6
	Astronomy	Mod G, Unit 3, Lessons 1-3
		Mod G, Unit 2, Lessons 2-6
		Mod G, Unit 1, Lessons 1-3
Physical Science, pp. 249–321		
	Matter	Mod H, Unit 1, Lessons 1-6
		Mod H, Unit 3, Lessons 1-4
		Mod H Unit 4, Lessons 1-3
		Mod H, Unit 5, Lessons 1-3

ScienceFusion Page References	Topics	ScienceFusion Grades 6-8
Physical Science, pp. 249–321 (continued)		
	Forces and Motion	Mod I, Unit 1, Lessons 1-5
		Mod I, Unit 2, Lessons 1-3
	Energy	Mod H, Unit 2, Lessons 1-4
		Mod I, Unit 3, Lessons 1-5
		Mod J, Unit 1, Lessons 1, 2
		Mod J, Unit 2, Lessons 1, 2
		Mod J, Unit 3, Lessons 1-4
Natural Resources and the Environment, pp. 322–353		
	Earth's Natural Resources	Mod D, Unit 3, Lessons 2-5
	Resource Conservation	Mod D, Unit 3, Lesson 5
	Solid Waste and Pollution	Mod D, Unit 4, Lessons 1-4 Mod F, Unit 4, Lesson 7
Science, Technology, and Society, pp. 354–373		
	Science and Technology	Mod A, Unit 2, Lesson 7
		Mod G, Unit 4, Lesson 2
		Mod I, Unit 3, Lesson 6
		Mod J, Unit 2, Lesson 3
		Mod J, Unit 3, Lesson 5
	Science and Society	Mod K, Unit 1, Lesson 4
		Mod K, Unit 3, Lesson 6

ScienceFusion Page References	Topics	*ScienceFusion* Grades 6-8
Almanac, pp. 374–438		
	Scientific Numbers	May be used with all units.
	Using Data Tables and Graphs	Mod K, Unit 2, Lesson 1
	Solving Math Problems in Science	May be used with all units.
	Classroom and Research Skills	May be used with all units.
	Test-Taking Skills	May be used with all units.
	References	May be used with all units.
Yellow Pages, pp. 439–524		
	History of Science Timeline	See People in Science features.
	Famous Scientists	See People in Science features.
	Greek and Latin Word Roots	Glossary
	Glossary of Scientific Terms	Glossary

Index

Key:

Teacher Edition page numbers follow the Student Edition page numbers and are printed in blue type.
Student Edition page numbers for highlighted definitions are printed in **boldface** type.
Student Edition page numbers for illustrations, maps, and charts are printed in *italics*.

Key:

Teacher Edition page numbers follow the Student Edition page numbers and are printed in blue type.
Student Edition pages numbers for highlighted definitions are printed in **boldface** type.
Student Edition page numbers for illustrations, maps, and charts are printed in *italics*.